WHEN THE MONARCHS REIGNED
KANSAS CITY'S 1942 NEGRO LEAGUE CHAMPIONS

EDITED BY FREDERICK C. BUSH AND BILL NOWLIN
ASSOCIATE EDITORS: LEN LEVIN AND CARL RIECHERS

Society for American Baseball Research, Inc.
Phoenix, AZ

When the Monarchs Reigned:
Kansas City's 1942 Negro League Champions
Edited by Frederick C. Bush and Bill Nowlin
Associate editors Len Levin and Carl Riechers

Copyright © 2021 Society for American Baseball Research, Inc.
All rights reserved. Reproduction in whole or in part without permission is prohibited.
Paperback ISBN: 978-1-970159-53-0 KC
Ebook ISBN: 978-1-970159-52-3 KC
Library of Congress Control Number: 2021912453

Book design: Jennifer Bahl Hron
Chapter fonts: Optima & Times New Roman,
Cover design: Gilly Rosenthol
Original design 1942 Kansas City Monarchs jersey courtesy of Ebbets Field Flannels
Back cover: Monarchs v Harlem Stars poster (from the collection of Frederick C. Bush)

Society for American Baseball Research
Cronkite School at ASU
555 N. Central Ave. #416
Phoenix, AZ 85004
Phone: (602) 496-1460
Web: www.sabr.org
Facebook: Society for American Baseball Research
Twitter: @SABR

CONTENTS

Preface and Acknowledgements 4

1 - **Newt Allen** by Frederick C. Bush 6
2 – **Frank "Dick" Bradley** by Kirk Jenkins 14
3 – **Willard Brown** by Rory Costello.. 20
4 – **Johnnie Dawson** by Margaret M. Gripshover 27
5 – **Frank Duncan** (player-manager) by Dave Wilkie 37
6 – **Joe Greene** by Steven Greenes 49
7 – **Paul Hardy** by Jeb Stewart 54
8 – **Connie Johnson** by Alan Cohen 62
9 – **James "Lefty" LaMarque** by Tim Tassler 70
10 – **Jack Matchett** by Bill Nowlin 78
11 – **Booker McDaniel** by Leslie Heaphy 85
12 – **Gread McKinnis** by Richard Bogovich 89
13 – **Buck O'Neil** by Bob LeMoine 104
14 – **Satchel Paige** by Larry Tye 114
15 – **Norris Phillips** by Frederick C. Bush... 119
16 – **Henry Frazier Robinson** by Bob Webster 123
17 – **Bonnie Serrell** by Mark S. Sternman 128
18 – **Willie Simms** by Jay Hurd 132
19 – **Hilton Smith** by Thomas Kern 136
20 – **Herb Souell** by Chris Hicks 146
21 – **Ted Strong Jr.** by Glen Sparks 152
22 – **Jesse Williams** by Tim Hagerty 158
23 – **J. L. Wilkinson** (co-owner) by Charles F. Faber and William A. Young 162
24 – **Tom Baird** (co-owner) by Bob LeMoine 168
25 – **Tom Baird and the KKK** by Bob LeMoine 175
26 – **William "Dizzy" Dismukes** (personnel director) by William H. Johnson 177
27 – **1942 Kansas City Monarchs Timeline** by Bill Nowlin 182
28 – **May 24, 1942: Monarchs v. Dizzy Dean All-Stars** by Tony S. Oliver 211
29 – **July 26, 1942: Paige Garners Victory on Day in his Honor** by Frederick C. Bush 214
30 – **August 16 & 18, 1942: East Team Sweeps Comiskey Classic and Cleveland Benefit Games**
     by Frederick C. Bush 217
31 – **The 1942 Negro League World Series: Kansas City Monarchs v. Homestead Grays**
     by Rich Puerzer 221
32 – **Ruppert Stadium, Kansas City** by Bill Lamberty 227
33 – **Willa Bea Harmon, *Kansas City Call* Sportswriter** by Donna L. Halper 234
34 – **The *Kansas City Call* and the Kansas City Monarchs** by William A. Young .. 237
35 – **J. L. Wilkinson and the Rebirth of Satchel Paige** by William A. Young 244
36 – **World War II and the Kansas City Monarchs** by Dr. Milbert O. Brown, Jr. ... 256
37 – **Contributors** 261

Preface and Acknowledgments

The current volume about the 1942 Kansas City Monarchs championship team had its genesis in a book project initially conceived as a solo endeavor: *Bittersweet Goodbye: The Black Barons, the Grays, and the 1948 Negro League World Series* (SABR, 2017). Subsequently, an earlier project about the 1946 Newark Eagles that had lain dormant was revived and published as *The Newark Eagles Take Flight* in 2019. Upon completion of these two volumes, a core team of SABR Negro League and Biography Project members were interested in pursuing further study of Negro League history, and new members stepped up to add their research and writing as well. Thanks to such dedicated researchers and the SABR Board's commitment to publishing new books about the Negro Leagues, *Bittersweet Goodbye* has become the first in a series about great teams of the Negro Leagues. The 1935 Pittsburgh Crawfords were featured in *Pride of Smoketown* (2020), the Monarchs receive their due here, and the next volume, which will highlight the 1920 Chicago American Giants, is already in progress.

The Kansas City Monarchs franchise is arguably the best-known of all the former Negro League squads, thanks in large part to the inimitable Satchel Paige's association with the team and longtime Monarch Buck O'Neil's role as an ambassador of Black baseball history via PBS documentarian Ken Burns's 1994 television series about the national pastime. Additionally, the Monarchs were charter members of the first Negro National League, founded at the Paseo YMCA in Kansas City, Missouri, in February 1920; this event also resulted in the city becoming home to the Negro Leagues Baseball Museum, which was founded in 1990. Add to all of this the fact that the NNL1-member Monarchs won the first-ever Negro League World Series, against the East-West League's Hilldale Club of Darby, Pennsylvania, in 1924, and it is no wonder that the Monarchs are foremost in the consciousness of many Negro League fans.

After spending the height of the Great Depression as a barnstorming squad from 1931 to 1936, the Monarchs became charter members of the new Negro American League in 1937 and proceeded to dominate that circuit in the same manner that the Homestead Grays ruled over the second incarnation of the Negro National League. Thus, when the time came for the first Negro League World Series since 1927 to be played, it was only fitting that the Monarchs and the Grays should emerge as the two teams to participate in that landmark event in 1942.

The Grays, based in the more densely populated East and using both Pittsburgh's Forbes Field and Washington's Griffith Stadium as home fields, played an extensive league schedule and, according to Seamheads.com, finished 47-19-3 (.712) in the NNL2 and 64-23-3 (.736) against all Negro major-league competition. Due to wartime travel restrictions and the availability of fewer competitors in the West, the Monarchs were unable to play as many games as normal in the NAL and completed the league season with a 27-12 (.692) record and an overall mark of 35-17 (.673) against fellow Black major-league teams. The Grays appeared to be the more battle-tested and successful of the two squads; however, as the cliché goes, "the games are not played on paper," and the Kansas Citians made mincemeat of the mighty Grays as they turned 1942 into the year *When the Monarchs Reigned*.

This book features biographies of Hall of Famers Satchel Paige, Hilton Smith, and Willard Brown; stalwarts such as Newt Allen and Buck O'Neil; and as many of the players on the team as could be identified. Also included are biographies of principal owner and Hall of Famer J.L. Wilkinson and other front-office personnel, Ruppert Stadium (which was renamed several times over the course of its existence), and groundbreaking *Kansas City Call* reporter Willa Bea Harmon. Feature articles focus on topics such as the *Call*'s coverage of the Monarchs, Wilkinson's role in helping to resuscitate Paige's career, and the fate of the Monarchs during the World War II years. In addition to an extensive season timeline, game articles highlight a contest against Dizzy Dean's All-Stars, Satchel Paige Day at Wrigley Field, the two East-West All-Star Games, and the grand finale to the season – the World Series against the Grays.

The careful reader may have noted by the wording that perhaps not all 1942 Monarchs players are included in this book. Throughout this series of Negro League books, it has been inevitable that we find one or more players who cannot be identified or about whom we can find no evidence of their participation in the year on which the book is focused. The following individuals have been omitted from this book for such reasons:

1) Ted Alexander. In his *Complete Book of Baseball's Negro Leagues*, historian John Holway lists a pitcher by only the name "Alexander" with an 0-1 record for the 1942 Monarchs. Author William A. Young presumed this to be Ted Alexander, who pitched for the Monarchs from 1943 to 1947, in his history of J.L. Wilkinson and the Kansas City franchise. However, we uncovered no press confirmation of Ted Alexander pitching for the 1942 squad.

• Preface and Acknowledgments •

2) ? Evans. This player was named as a third baseman for the Monarchs in a July 26, 1942, article in the *Munster* (Indiana) *Times*. No positive identification of the player has been made, and no other mention of his participation on the team has been found.

3) ? Henry. This player was named as a relief pitcher for the Monarchs in a May 1, 1942, article in the *Arkansas State Press*. As is the case with Evans, no identification has been made and no further mention of him has been found.

4) I. Smith. A single source identifies this player as a pitcher (perhaps for one game only), but none of our researchers was able to find mention of him in any articles about the 1942 team.

5) George Walker. A pitcher for the Monarchs from 1939 to '41 and in 1943, he was sometimes named in preview articles as a member of the 1942 team. However, it appears that – if Walker was a member of the 1942 team at all – he was released early in the season before NAL play began and no mention of his name was found in any box score, line score, or article from the 1942 season. Thus, Walker, who posted an 8-1 record and 1.99 ERA in league play for Kansas City's 1939 NAL championship squad, was not a member of the Monarchs' first NAL World Series team in 1942.

The fact that *When the Monarchs Reigned* is as comprehensive as possible is due to the efforts of all the participants in this project. Our thanks go out to fact-checker Carl Riechers, final copy editor Len Levin, and all the SABR researchers/authors who contributed their work to this book. As always, there were other individuals who contributed vital information as well, most of whom are acknowledged by the individual authors at the conclusion of their respective articles. For the majority of the photos included in this volume, we owe gratitude to SABR Negro League Committee Chair Larry Lester and his company, Noir-Tech Research, Inc. As usual, if we have neglected to mention anyone who deserves credit for any involvement in this book project, we offer our sincere apologies here and now.

Enjoy this tour of Kansas City in 1942 and join us again next year when we will travel back in time to Chicago in the year 1920. If our DeLorean holds out, we may yet take trips to Philadelphia, Baltimore, New York, Cleveland, and elsewhere. We look forward to the ride.

Frederick C. Bush
Bill Nowlin
May 2021

Although George Walker pitched for Kansas City in 1941 and 1943, no evidence of his participation in any games with the 1942 Monarchs has been uncovered to this point. (Courtesy Noir-Tech Research, Inc.)

NEWT ALLEN

By Frederick C. Bush

Second baseman Newt Allen's Kansas City Monarchs teammates gave him the nickname "Colt" in 1922 because he was the youngest member of the team.1 Over the course of a 23-plus-year career in the Negro Leagues that also included stints in other countries, Allen proved to be one of the best players ever to man the keystone sack. During his tenure with the Monarchs, Allen contributed sterling defense and a potent bat to 11 championship squads.2 At the conclusion of his second full season with Kansas City, he played in the first Negro League World Series, in which the Monarchs defeated the Hilldale Club of the Eastern Colored League. Eighteen years later, now a seasoned veteran, he helped the Monarchs triumph over the Negro National League's Homestead Grays in the first Negro League World Series between those two circuits. During the intervening years, Colt Allen had galloped over all competition so soundly that in 2006 he was on the final ballot of the Special Committee on the Negro Leagues for induction into the Hall of Fame, though he ultimately fell short of enshrinement.

Newton Henry Allen was born on May 19, 1901, in Austin, Texas, to Newton H. and Rose (Baker) Allen. The elder Newton and Rose had married in 1897 and led a hardscrabble existence as they raised a family in Texas's capital city. Newton Allen was a laborer who worked whatever odd jobs he could find while Rose worked as a laundress. Young Newt had an older sister, Dora, and was joined later by another sister, Eva Mae, and a brother, Lawrence; two other siblings, including a sister named Mary who was born in 1903, died in childhood prior to 1910.

Newt's father succumbed to tuberculosis on July 21, 1910, forcing Rose and the four children to fend for themselves. This new circumstance contributed, in a roundabout way, to Newt's arrival in Kansas City, Missouri. Rose briefly took the children to Cincinnati – presumably she had family there – and, shortly thereafter, Newt accompanied her to Missouri to visit an aunt whose young son had recently died. As Allen later recalled:

"I went to live with my auntie, Ophelia Henderson, in Kansas City. She had a boy and he and I were the same age. And he passed. And when she lost him, then she took me.

I lived at 17th Street, about 17th and Woodland. Just across the street from where I lived was a ballpark by one of them playgrounds. I was out there all the time. That was Parade Park."3

Such were the unusual circumstances by which Newt grew up in Kansas City while his siblings were raised by their mother, first in Austin and later in Cincinnati.4

Allen attended Bruce Elementary School and Lincoln High School and became close friends with Frank Duncan, a future Monarchs teammate and manager. According to Allen, another future Monarchs star, pitcher Rube Currie, was also part of their circle of friends who played sandlot ball together.5 As Allen and his friends advanced from sandlot to semipro ball, he started to chase after balls from the minor-league Kansas City Blues' games, saying, "[I would] come back with the ball and sell it or keep it. That's the way our ballteam [sic], which was a semipro team, always had balls to play with when we would go out to play."6 Allen also started to work at the Monarchs' ballpark at 20th Street and Prospect where, he said, "I pulled the canvas and filled the water jug for them, things like that."7 Allen and Duncan played for the semipro Kansas City Tigers, but Newt spent a lot of time on the bench and soon joined the Paseo Rats as well as playing for Swift's in a packinghouse league.8

Duncan began his professional career with the Chicago Giants in 1920 – the same year that Currie debuted with the Monarchs – and joined Kansas City early in the 1921 season, but Allen had to take a longer road to join his longtime friends on their hometown team. First, he ventured to Nebraska, where he honed his skills playing for the Omaha Federals in 1921. Monarchs co-owner J.L. Wilkinson had resurrected his barnstorming All-Nations team – so called because it was integrated and employed players of different races and ethnicities – and based it in Omaha. He soon took notice of Allen and gave him a tryout in 1922, after which he assigned Allen to the All-Nations team, placing him under the tutelage of the diverse squad's manager, already-legendary pitcher John Donaldson.

Allen toiled for the All-Nations team, which also served as a farm club for the Monarchs, for most of the season before being called up to the Monarchs in October for a six-game "City Championship" series against the Double-A Kansas City Blues.[9] The Monarchs won five of the six games against their White counterparts to claim the title as champions of Kansas City. Allen fared poorly at the plate, going 1-for-14 for an .071 batting average in five games, but he nonetheless had learned well in 1922 and was able to break spring training with the Monarchs the next season.

Perhaps the reason for Allen's poor performance in the City Championship series was that he was distracted by his early-October marriage to 17-year-old Mary Edwards and the impending arrival of their first child, Newton Henry Allen Jr., who was born on November 27, 1922. Newt Jr. eventually graduated from Western Baptist Bible College, the same institution his father had attended for two years before pursuing his baseball career, and he founded Kansas City's Mount Joy Missionary Baptist Church.[10] Newt Sr. and Mary had a second son and a daughter, but their marriage did not endure. Allen recalled, "After my wife and I separated, [teammate Newt Joseph] and I lived together here in Kansas City for about five years. The two Newts."[11]

The difficulty in Allen's marriage was representative of the problems that have shaken many ballplayers' marriages in all eras. According to one historian, "[M]arried players always spoke of the 'understanding' a man and his wife had to have."[12] Allen said, "It's a hard life. There has to be an understanding between you and your wife – a good understanding."[13] Whether that understanding entailed the expectation of marital fidelity or the acceptance of infidelity may have varied from marriage to marriage. Allen was known to revel in his celebrity as a ballplayer and confessed, "The women, they were lovely everywhere we went. If they didn't recognize me in my regular clothes, then I'd go up to them and tell them who I was. But sometimes they could be a worrisome deal."[14]

One concern that Allen hoped would no longer be worrisome was his status with the Monarchs, a member team of the Rube Foster-founded Negro National League. He began the 1923 season at third base with Kansas City and batted .304 in 33 league games but was returned to the All-Nations team in June and spent the summer barnstorming throughout the Midwest again.[15] The Monarchs finished with a 54-32 league record (61-37 overall) and wrested the NNL championship away from Foster's Chicago American Giants, the team that had claimed the first three league pennants. Although Allen had not spent the entire season with Kansas City, he still had been a major contributor to the first of the 11 Monarchs championship squads on which he played.

Finally, in 1924, Allen took over at second base for Kansas City for the long term. He gained his older teammates' acceptance through hard play and by taking their pranks in a good-natured way. Allen noted, "The players would ride you to see if you can take it," and recalled that one time some of the Monarchs veterans "told the hotel where we ate not to give me no meat because I'd have fits. I ate breakfast without meat and lunch without meat. So I asked them what was going on and they told me the players told them if they gave me meat, I'd have fits."[16] His first full season with the Monarchs involved a learning curve on the baseball diamond as his batting average fell to .258 and he committed 33 errors in the field in 73 league games; his .918 fielding percentage was slightly below the league average of .925.

In time, Allen remedied all shortcomings. He was not a big man – standing 5-feet-9 and weighing 165 pounds – so he learned how to become an ideal number-two hitter in the Monarchs' lineup. Later in life, when asked what he considered to be his outstanding achievement in baseball, Allen answered that he "learned how to play second base, bunt and hit behind the runner, and think while playing."[17] That Allen was a fast learner was evidenced by the improvements in his performance at the plate and in the field as the Monarchs faced the Hilldale Club in the first Negro League World Series that October.

That first World Series provided as much excitement as any fan could desire. The Monarchs prevailed 5-4-1 over Hilldale. The tie occurred in Game Three, which had to be called due to darkness with the scored knotted, 6-6, after 13 innings. Allen improved his batting average to .282 with 11 hits (seven doubles) and 8 runs scored and his fielding percentage rose to .968. However, one of the two errors he committed proved costly.

• When the Monarchs Reigned •

In Game Four, which was played on October 6 at Maryland Baseball Park in Baltimore, the teams were tied, 3-3, when Hilldale loaded the bases in the bottom of the ninth. Hilldale catcher Louis Santop hit "a routine grounder to Newt Allen at second and Allen [threw] wildly to catcher Duncan, allowing Judy Johnson to score the ugly, but winning run."[18] Hilldale's winning pitcher was Allen's childhood friend Rube Currie, and the Philadelphia-area club took a 2-to-1 Series lead.

Allen was able to redeem himself in Game 10, which took place on October 20 at Schorling Park in Chicago. Hilldale's Script Lee and Jose "The Black Diamond" Mendez, the Monarchs' Cuban hurler, engaged in an epic pitchers' duel that remained scoreless until the bottom of the eighth inning. In that fateful frame, the Monarchs offense exploded for five runs. Allen drove in the second and third runs with a single to right field and put the exclamation point on Kansas City's rally by scoring the fifth and final run on Dink Mothell's double. Mendez finished the shutout, and the Monarchs were the champions of Black baseball.

On the heels of Kansas City's championship, Allen and Monarchs teammate Wilbur "Bullet" Rogan traveled to Cuba to play for the Almendares Alacranes (Scorpions) during the 1924-25 Winter League season. Almendares fielded four future Hall of Famers in Rogan, Raleigh "Biz" Mackey, John Henry "Pop" Lloyd, and Oscar Charleston and was the dominant squad on the island. In fact, "Almendares reclaimed the title by such ample margin that the league, as was customary in those days, stopped the activities to prevent financial harm to the different clubs."[19] Allen contributed a .313 batting average in 48 at-bats while splitting the third-base duties with

Newt Allen was a member of two Monarchs World Series champions, manning the keystone sack against Hilldale in 1924 and the hot corner against Homestead in 1942.
(Courtesy Noir-Tech Research, Inc.)

Cuban Jose Gutierrez.[20] With the regular season cut short, it was decided that a special eight-game series would be held between "All Cubans" and "All Yankees" teams. The All Yankees, composed exclusively of Negro League players, finished with a 5-2-1 record in the series, and Allen went 8-for-30 for a .267 average while playing third base in all eight games.[21] He returned to Cuba only once, in 1938-39, and split the season between Almendares and Habana. He hit .269 combined between the two squads but fell short of a championship as the Santa Clara team won the title that season.[22]

In April 1925 the *Chicago Defender* noted that the Monarchs would field an all-veteran starting lineup to begin the season.[23] Kansas City's talent and experience led them to the NNL's first-half title, but the St. Louis Stars captured the second-half flag, and it took a hard-fought seven-game series for the Monarchs to retain the NNL championship. Allen once again handled the second-base chores, batted .289 in 80 regular-season games, and raised his level of play and batting average to .370 in the NNL championship series against the Stars. The Monarchs' reward was a rematch against Hilldale in the 1925 World Series. Between their exhausting series against St. Louis and an injury to pitching ace Bullet Rogan, who "was hurt in a freak accident at home and spent the entire series on the bench," the Monarchs were no competition for Hilldale this second time around.[24] Hilldale's pitchers quieted Kansas City's bats and captured the championship in six games. The Monarchs likely wished that Rube Currie had still been on their side, as their former righty, who had gone 1-1 with a 0.55 ERA in the 1924 World Series, posted two victories in the rematch. Currie threw a 12-inning complete-game victory in Game One and hurled another complete game in Hilldale's 2-1 triumph in Game Five. Meanwhile, Allen slumped to .259 and only one Monarchs hitter – Dobie Moore – managed to bat over .300 for the Series.

Rogan recovered in time to play in the California Winter League's 1925-26 season and Allen accompanied him west. The two played for the Philadelphia Royal Giants in what was at that time the only integrated professional baseball league in the United States. Allen scuffled to a .254 batting average in 29 games, but Rogan posted a 14-2 record to help the Royal Giants run away with the league title. Allen returned to California for the next five Winter League seasons, playing for the Philadelphia Royal Giants in 1926-27, 1929-30, and 1930-31 and for the Cleveland Giants in 1927-28 and 1928-29. During his six winters in the Golden State, Allen compiled a career .324 batting average, and his teams captured the league title every year except in 1927-28.

Allen's career settled into a winning pattern in both California winters and Kansas City summers. However, as successful as the Monarchs were, they were unable to return to the World Series in 1926, losing a nine-game playoff series to the archrival Chicago American Giants. There had long been bad blood between the Monarchs and the Giants, and it brought out one of Allen's less desirable traits: his temper. Chicago's Dave Malarcher had once spiked Allen as he slid into second, opening a gash that required 18 stitches. Allen held a long grudge, recollecting, "It took me three years to repay him, but they say vengeance is sweet. One day we were leading by two runs, he was on first, and I took the throw at second for a double play. Well, instead of throwing to first, I threw straight at Malarcher charging into second. I hit him right in the forehead. ... Hurt him pretty bad. He was out of the ball game for three days."[25]

Malarcher was one of many players with whom Allen had run-ins during his long career in the rough-and-tumble Negro Leagues. In looking back, Allen admitted:

> "A lot of times I had a nasty feeling within myself, not against a ballplayer. I was pretty bad playing ball, yes, I was pretty bad – run over a man, throw at him. I did a lot of wrong things. But I got results out of it, because they were leery of what I was going to do, and I'd get by with it. ...
>
> We used every trick in the book to win a ball game. All kinds of good tricks and nasty ones. In fact, there were more nasty ones than there were good. Caused many a ballplayer to get hurt."[26]

Although Allen put fear into some opponents via the use of his "tricks," he also gained the respect of his peers as one of the best second sackers to play the game. Pitcher Chet Brewer, who joined the Monarchs in 1925 and was a longtime teammate, raved, "Newt was a real slick second baseman, he could catch the ball and throw it without looking. Newt used to catch the ball, throw it up under his left arm; it was just a strike to first base. He was something! Got that ball out of his glove quicker than anybody you ever saw."[27] Buck O'Neil, who came to Kansas City in 1938 and who had an eye for talent as good as (or better than) Wilkinson's observed, "When I got there, Newt was in his mid-thirties, but even after sixteen years he was an excellent second baseman, and he had six more good years left in him. He could make all the plays around the bag, and I've never seen a second baseman with as good an arm."[28] Even White baseball took notice, as New York Giants manager John McGraw asserted, "Allen is one of the finest infielders, white or colored, in organized baseball."[29]

While their second baseman made a name for himself, the Monarchs franchise was about to embark on a new phase of its existence. Allen batted .332 for the 1929 squad as Kansas City won its final NNL championship by virtue of capturing the league title in both halves of the season, finishing with a 63-17 record in league play (66-17 overall). The Great Depression was taking its toll on NNL teams, and the league folded after the 1931 season. Wilkinson had seen the handwriting on the wall and withdrew the Monarchs from the league after the 1930 season, turning the franchise into a barnstorming team. Wilkinson figured that he could turn a profit via his innovative portable lighting system that had introduced night baseball to America in 1930. Thus, the Monarchs became an independent barnstorming team from 1931 to 1936. Although Allen spent the entirety of his career with the Monarchs, circumstances now forced him to seek employment with other teams for brief periods of time. Prior to the Monarchs beginning their barnstorming season, he played for the St. Louis Stars in 1931 and the Homestead Grays in 1932.

Additionally, while Allen had already been to Cuba, he soon got to see other parts of the world as well. On December 12, 1931, the *Chicago Defender* reported, "The Kansas City Monarchs left Tuesday morning for Mexico City to play a series of games. This trip is being made under the supervision of the Mexican government. The club will travel in a special Pullman and will be quartered in one of the best hotels in the southern republic."[30] The Mexico City Aztecas provided the primary opponent over the course of the 30-day tour, and newspaper accounts showed the Monarchs to have a 19-2 record.[31]

Two years later, during the winter of 1933-34, Allen and five Monarchs teammates – including his winter traveling companion Bullet Rogan – were members of a 12-player all-star team that toured China, Japan, and the Philippines. The three-month exhibition tour was organized by Lonnie Goodwin, the manager of the California Winter League's Philadelphia Royal Giants, and the all-stars competed against Army teams and clubs from sugar plantations.[32] On the return trip, the team played additional games in Hawaii. According to Allen:

> "A man named Yamashiro, a superintendent down at Dole Pineapple Company, offered Rogan and me a salary and the only thing we'd have to do was check crates of pineapples and play ball two days a week, Saturdays and Sundays. At the end of the ball season, the team split all the money. The factory just furnished us the suits and the name. But we decided to come on back home and play."[33]

Having returned stateside, Allen and Rogan, as members of the Monarchs, integrated the prestigious Denver Post Tournament in 1934 as they vied for the $5,000 purse that was to be awarded to the winners. The House of David team responded to the powerful Monarchs entry by hiring Satchel Paige (who later became more closely associated with the Monarchs than any other team he had played for) and catcher Cy Perkins of the Pittsburgh Crawfords as mercenaries to play for their otherwise all-White squad. Paige outdueled Chet Brewer, 2-1, in a semifinal game. The Monarchs made it to the championship game but again succumbed to the House of David, 2-0, as Brewer lost another duel, this time against Spike Hunter. Allen ended up being the tournament's leading basestealer, but that was of no consolation to him or the rest of the Monarchs.

The Monarchs, along with Paige and Perkins, as the first Black players to participate in the tournament, had to deal with a great deal of discrimination in the press. The *Post* ran numerous insulting articles; in one item, "[a]cting as if Paige's nickname of 'Satchel' wasn't good enough, the newspaper invented a new one – 'The Chocolate Whizbang.'"[34] Like most Black players, the members of the Monarchs had long ago become inured to the prejudice they encountered in the age of Jim Crow, but sometimes they could be pushed over the limit. Allen recalled one incident when, after a Michigan restaurant owner told them they could not eat inside his establishment, "We just all walked out – we left them with fifty some hamburgers on the grill. It was one of those times when you even the score."[35]

Although some White players also lacked racial tolerance, it was much rarer for the Monarchs to experience discrimination from the White players on local teams or major-league all-star teams that they played against. Allen explained, "Ball players – white and black – have a lot of respect for each other. They know they can play ball, and they know they're going to play with them or against them. You hear a lot of harsh words from the grandstand, but very seldom find prejudiced ball players."[36]

The Monarchs were also the only Negro League team under White ownership, and Wilkinson and his players gave mutual respect. Wilkinson was so proud of his players' success in exhibition games against major-league teams that he once boasted "his team could compete with the New York Giants or Yankees, the two teams in the 1937 white major leagues' World Series."[37] However, pride in their abilities alone would have meant little to the Monarchs players. They respected Wilkinson because of the way he treated them. Allen stated, "He was a considerate man; he understood; he knew people. Your face could be as black as tar; he treated everyone alike. He traveled right along with us."[38]

In 1937 Wilkinson decided that the Monarchs would rejoin a league. The franchise became one of the charter members of the Negro American League rather than enlisting with the second iteration of the Negro National League that had been established in 1933. The Monarchs dominated their new competitors, claiming the NAL championship in five of the league's first six seasons. They defeated two former NNL rivals now in the NAL, the Chicago American Giants and St. Louis Stars, in 1937 and 1939 respectively to win the pennant in those two seasons. From 1940 to 1942, Kansas City was declared the NAL champion by virtue of finishing with the league's best record. Even when the title eluded the Monarchs in 1938, the team still owned the NAL's best overall record; however, it failed to win either the first- or second-half league title.³⁹

Allen batted .314 in 51 league games and continued to man second base for Kansas City as the franchise embarked upon its first NAL title run in 1937. However, over the next three seasons his batting acumen and defensive range began an inevitable decline. In 1941 the now 40-year-old Allen was moved to third base; he also took the managerial reins and guided the Monarchs to a 25-11 league record (34-13 overall) in his lone season as the team's skipper. Despite the falloff in Allen's overall play, he was a well-established, popular star and was elected to play in four East-West All-Star Games (1936-38, 1941).⁴⁰ The fact that Allen went 0-for-15 with the bat in the four all-star contests, however, was one indicator that his best playing days were behind him.

Nevertheless, in 1942, Allen managed one last hurrah as he manned third base in 24 of the Monarchs' 39 league games and batted .304. Kansas City won the NAL with a 27-12 record in league play (35-17) overall and earned the right to face the NNL's Homestead Grays in the first World Series between the two rival leagues. Thus, almost two full decades after participating in the first-ever Negro League World Series, Allen now took part in another landmark event. The Grays ruled the NNL in the same manner as the Monarchs reigned over the NAL, so it was expected that this Series might be every bit as dramatic as its predecessor had been in 1924. The Monarchs had other ideas, however, and swept the Grays in four games. As a 23-year-old youngster, Allen had batted .282 against Hilldale in 1924. Now, at the venerable age of 41, he played in three of the four games and hit .286 against Homestead as he won the final championship of his long career.

After two subpar seasons, in which he batted .239 and .236, Allen voluntarily retired after the 1944 season. However, in March 1945 he was around in spring training to evaluate a new player for Wilkinson, a former college athlete fresh out of the Army by the name of Jackie Robinson. Allen's assessment was, "He's a very smart ball player, but he can't play shortstop – he can't throw from the hole. Try him at second base."⁴¹ Although Allen identified the position with which Robinson would become most associated after breaking the White major leagues' color barrier with the Brooklyn Dodgers in 1947, Robinson won the Monarchs' shortstop job by default in 1945 when

Legendary New York Giants manager John McGraw named second baseman Newt Allen "one of the finest infielders, white or colored, in organized baseball." (Courtesy Noir-Tech Research, Inc.)

starter Jesse Williams suffered an arm injury. Later in life, Allen continued to extol Robinson's baseball acumen, saying, "Jackie was smart, he was an awful smart ballplayer. He didn't have the ability at first, but he had the brains. ... Jackie had one-third ability and two-thirds brains, and that made him a great ballplayer."⁴²

Allen had been a great ballplayer for a long time as well, and as is often the case with such individuals, he could not resist one final attempt at playing the game he loved. In April 1947 the *Chicago Defender* listed Allen on the roster of the NAL's Cincinnati-Indianapolis Clowns, who now had future Hall of Fame shortstop Willie Wells Sr. as manager.⁴³ Allen and Wells had formed the keystone combo for the St. Louis Stars in the first half of the 1931 season, prior to

Allen's rejoining the Monarchs for their barnstorming schedule. In his limited playing time with the Clowns, Allen turned back the clock at the plate, batting .314 in 13 league games, before hanging up his spikes for good. Wells did not have the same success as manager that he had enjoyed as a player and was replaced by Jesse "Hoss" Walker after the Clowns started the season 14-29. The Clowns finished fifth in the NAL with a 31-52-1 record, while Allen's hometown franchise, the Monarchs, finished second at 52-32.

Once Allen's baseball career was at an end, he settled in Kansas City, where he became involved in Democratic Party politics and worked as a foreman in the county courthouse. In the mid-1960s, Allen enjoyed attending yearly player reunions that were usually held in nearby Kansas City, Kansas. In 1971 he stated, "[T]he last five years we've had a reunion every year, all the ballplayers, white and colored [from the area's former semipro and professional teams]."[44] He also kidded, "You talk about hearing some baseball – everybody's talking, and among the habitual drinkers, that's when the truth comes out and there are some tall tales told. One guy says that's the only time he ever hits .300, when he remembers the old days at those parties."[45]

Eventually, Allen moved back to Cincinnati to be closer to family members who lived in the area. By the time the *Kansas City Star* interviewed him for a profile article in 1985, he was already residing in an assisted-care facility. In January 1986 Allen's eldest son, Newt Jr., died. The Rev. Allen's obituary listed as survivors his wife, Bertha; his father, Mr. Newton H. Allen Sr., of Cincinnati; as well as his mother, Mrs. Mary E. Allen, and a sister, Mrs. Myrtle Vanoy, both of Kansas City.[46] No mention was made of Allen's other son, who had made a career out of the Army and may also have preceded his father in death.[47]

Newt Allen Sr. died of a heart attack on June 9, 1988, at Cincinnati's Golden Age Nursing Home. No obituaries were published in Cincinnati or Kansas City newspapers; only the *Kansas City Times* ran a short blurb about Allen's death. In the *Times's* brief write-up, Buck O'Neil was quoted as saying, "He was one of the best I've ever seen. I'd compare him with [longtime Kansas City Royal] Frank White, except Newt's arm might have been a little stronger. He had soft hands and great range. The three best players I saw at the position were Newt, Frank and Bill Mazeroski."[48] Considering such accolades, it is even more distressing that Allen lies buried in an unmarked grave in Cincinnati's Union Baptist Cemetery, a historical Black graveyard. In 2020 Negro League researcher/author Paul Debono and Cincinnati-area historian Chris Hanlin were able to identify Allen's final resting place among other members of his family. Efforts began to enlist the aid of the Negro Leagues Baseball Grave Marker Project and other entities to place a headstone at the site to commemorate the life of Newt Allen, one of the stars of the old Negro Leagues.

Sources

Ancestry.com was consulted for public records including census information; birth, marriage, and death records; military draft registration cards; and ships' passenger logs.

California Winter League statistics and records were taken from: McNeil, William F., *The California Winter League: America's First Integrated Professional Baseball League* (Jefferson, North Carolina: McFarland & Company, Inc., 2002).

Negro League player statistics and manager/team records were taken from Seamheads.com, unless otherwise indicated.

Sanford, Jay. *The Denver Post Tournament* (Cleveland: Society for American Baseball Research, 2003).

Notes

1   "Teammates' Tests Put Allen on Way to Long Career," *Kansas City Star*, July 23, 1985.

2   This number includes first-half and second-half league titles, composite-standing league titles, and World Series championships. It is not to be understood as an assertion that the Monarchs won 11 World Series titles.

3   "Teammates' Tests Put Allen on Way to Long Career." Although Allen was raised in Kansas City from about the age of 9 years, the identity of his aunt is a mystery. Allen gave her name as Ophelia Henderson in the 1985 interview with the *Star*, but the only person by that name that this author could identify was younger than Allen; therefore, this Ophelia Henderson could not have been the woman who raised him. Allen may have mixed up names, especially as this interview was given late in his life. It also would not have been the first time he had told part of his life story inaccurately: In a 1971 interview with historian John Holway, Allen claimed to have been born in Kansas City, Missouri, in 1902 (see John Holway, *Voices from the Great Black Baseball Leagues*, Mineola, New York: Dover Publications, Inc., 91). Regarding Parade Park, it may be of interest to note that it is now the home of the Kansas City MLB Urban Youth Academy (see https://kcparks.org/places/the-parade-park/).

4   The 1920 US census shows that Rose Allen was still living in Austin; however, by the time of the 1930 census she had moved her family to Cincinnati permanently. Although Newton H. Allen had died in 1910, four children – two daughters and two sons – were added to the immediate family after his death; as there is no evidence that Rose ever remarried and all four had the surname Allen, it is possible that she adopted the children, perhaps from one or more relatives (as she had allowed her own son, Newt, to be taken in by a relative). Rose Allen died in Cincinnati in 1957 at the age of 81 or 82. (She was born in 1875, but her exact date of birth is unknown.)

5 Holway, 91. Rube Currie's last name was also spelled "Currry" at times; see http://www.seamheads.com/NegroLgs/player.php?playerID=curry01reu.

6 "Teammates' Tests Put Allen on Way to Long Career."

7 "Teammates' Tests Put Allen on Way to Long Career."

8 Phil S. Dixon, *Wilber "Bullet" Rogan and the Kansas City Monarchs* (Jefferson, North Carolina: McFarland & Company, Inc., 2010), 75.

9 Dr. Layton Revel and Luis Munoz, "Forgotten Heroes: Newton 'Newt' Allen," http://www.cnlbr.org/Portals/0/Hero/Newton-Newt-Allen.pdf, accessed December 29, 2020.

10 "The Rev. Newton H. Allen Jr." (obituary), *Kansas City Times*, January 8, 1986, 39.

11 Holway, 93. Although Newt and Mary separated, this author uncovered no divorce records; thus, the couple may have remained married even though they ceased to live together.

12 Janet Bruce, *The Kansas City Monarchs: Champions of Black Baseball* (Lawrence: University of Kansas Press, 1985), 43.

13 Bruce, 43.

14 Dixon, 76.

15 Revel and Munoz, 3.

16 "Teammates' Tests Put Allen on Way to Long Career."

17 "Newt Allen Questionnaire for Normal 'Tweed' Webb's Record Book." Thanks go out to SABR Negro League Research Committee Chair Larry Lester for providing a copy of Allen's questionnaire.

18 Larry Lester, *Baseball's First Colored World Series: The 1924 Meeting of the Hilldale Giants and Kansas City Monarchs* (Jefferson, North Carolina: McFarland & Company, Inc., 2006), 134.

19 Jorge S. Figueredo, *Cuban Baseball: A Statistical History, 1878-1961* (Jefferson, North Carolina: McFarland & Company, Inc., 2003), 157.

20 Figueredo, 159.

21 Severo Nieto, *Early U.S. Blackball Teams in Cuba: Box Scores, Rosters and Statistics from the Files of Cuba's Foremost Baseball Researcher* (Jefferson, North Carolina: McFarland & Company, Inc., 2008), 161.

22 Figueredo, 222.

23 "World Champion Monarchs Start Spring Training with All Veterans in the Lineup," *Chicago Defender*, April 4, 1925: 10.

24 Kyle McNary, *Black Baseball: A History of African Americans & the National Game* (New York: PRC Publishing Ltd., 2003), 110.

25 Holway, 94.

26 Holway, 95.

27 Lester, 48.

28 Buck O'Neil with Steve Wulf and David Conrads, *I Was Right on Time: My Journey from the Negro Leagues to the Majors* (New York: Simon & Schuster, 1996), 79-80.

29 Lester, 49.

30 "Monarchs to Play Series with Mexico," *Chicago Defender*, December 12, 1931: 8.

31 Revel and Munoz, 10.

32 Bruce, 86-87.

33 Holway, 102.

34 Dixon, 144.

35 Bruce, 61.

36 Bruce, 80.

37 William A. Young, *J.L. Wilkinson and the Kansas City Monarchs: Trailblazers in Black Baseball* (Jefferson, North Carolina: McFarland & Company, Inc., 2016), 101.

38 Bruce, 19.

39 The Memphis Red Sox won the first-half championship, and the Atlanta Black Crackers clinched the second-half title in the 1938 NAL season.

40 The inaugural East-West game was played in 1933 while the Monarchs were an independent barnstorming team. Although Kansas City was still an independent team in 1936, the franchise's players were eligible to be voted onto the West team for that season's all-star game.

41 Bruce, 106.

42 Holway, 103.

43 "Red Sox to Play Three with Clowns" *Chicago Defender*, April 12, 1947: 23.

44 Holway, 104-5.

45 Holway, 105.

46 "The Rev. Newton H. Allen Jr." (obituary).

47 Holway, 104. In this 1971 interview, Allen mentioned that his younger son was making a career out of the Army and was stationed in Europe at that time.

48 "Ex-Monarch Second Baseman Dies," *Kansas City Times*, June 14, 1988: 30.

FRANK "DICK" BRADLEY

By Kirk Jenkins

Frank E. Bradley, a fireballing right-handed pitcher who played in six seasons for the Kansas City Monarchs before suffering a career-ending wound in World War II, was born on February 3, 1918, in Benton, Bossier Parish, Louisiana. He was the son of June and Adline (Gates) Bradley. If Frank had any siblings, no mention of them has survived in census records.[1] Frank appears to have been the first generation of his family to be able to write; his father's World War II draft record, dated 1942, is signed by June Bradley with his mark, and Frank's record contains his signature.[2] According to their draft records, both father and son worked at the Rough and Ready Plantation in Bossier Parish, which was owned then (and still was in 2021) by the Stinson family.[3]

Although a profile of Bradley published late in his life says Bradley's baseball career began in 1935,[4] the first newspaper mention of him is in 1936 with the Benton Eagles. "Most of us went to school together when we were kids," he told a reporter years later. "We just got together after work. We played in the park. Sometimes we played in oil fields."[5]

By the next year, Bradley had joined the Shreveport Giants. He was an immediate standout with the team, striking out 14 in a 9-1 win over the Clintonville Merchants in the summer of 1937.[6] Only two days later, he was described as the "speed ball king par excellence" and the "no. 1 man in the invaders' hurling corps" before a game with the Studebaker Athletics.[7]

But Bradley was not long for Louisiana baseball. He told the story of his discovery by scout Winfield Welch: "I was chopping cotton. The man said he was looking for Dick Bradley to play baseball. I dropped that hoe 50 feet and started running."[8] Welch was a scout for the Kansas City Monarchs. Bradley was going to the big time.

Bradley made his Monarchs debut that summer against South Bend. He was nervous early in the game and was having trouble getting his fastball over the plate.[9] Satchel Paige walked out to the mound and explained to Bradley that if he would just settle down and throw his fastball over the plate, nobody was going to get near it. "I struck out the next nine batters," Bradley recalled.[10] Bradley ultimately finished up with 17 strikeouts in the game.[11] A few days later, Bradley and Floyd Kranson threw a combined five-hitter against Indianapolis.[12] Bradley's next start did not go as well, as the Beatrice Blues beat Kansas City 13-10. Bradley started the game but was yanked during Beatrice's six-run second and took the loss.[13]

A few days later, Bradley started the second game of a doubleheader at Kansas City's Muehlebach Field against the Cincinnati Tigers. The Monarchs won the game, 7-1, "behind the brilliant mound work of Rookie Bradley, 20 years old [sic]. It was the youngster's first appearance at Muehlebach Field, and he celebrated by holding the Tigers to five hits. More than 3,200 fans attended the games."[14]

By the beginning of the 1938 season, the newspapers were touting Bradley as one of the major stars of the Monarchs pitching staff. Before an April 1938 game against the Hutchinson Larks, the *Hutchinson News* wrote that "Frank Bradley, a big right-hander who is expected to be another Satchel Paige, has already uncovered one of the fastest balls of any pitcher to ever wear a Monarch uniform."[15] The Springfield papers joined in the hype the following day: "The Kansas City Monarchs, who play our Cardinals here Saturday, have a pitcher they claim is faster than Bob Feller. He's 18-year-old Frank Bradley. The Monarchs have battled Feller four times in exhibition games, so they should know how fast he is."[16]

Bradley pitched a gem five weeks later against the Chicago American Giants, holding the Giants to only two hits. Only two months into his first full season, "Kid Bradley" was already drawing comparisons to two future Hall of Famers: "[T]he youngster is rated as the best rookie hurler the Monarchs have ever had. He has a great fast ball and is rated as speedy as 'Satchel' Paige or 'Bullet' Rogan, speed ball pitchers deluxe."[17]

Bradley continued to pile up the strikeouts as the Monarchs' year continued. The Monarchs had a laugher at the end of June, whipping the Studebaker Athletics, 15-1. Bradley threw three innings, struck out six, and surrendered two hits and one run.[18] A week later, Bradley showed off his stamina, pitching the final three innings of the first game of a doubleheader against the Memphis Red Sox and then starting the second.[19]

Bradley was clearly a gate draw in the Negro League fan community by midsummer of that year. The press raved: "Bradley, a fireball pitcher who has become the newest sensation of Negro baseball with his amazing victory record, is only 19 years old. ... [H]e is expected to start tomorrow night's game for the Monarchs."[20] Perhaps the highlight of Bradley's summer was when he pitched a six-inning no-hitter against the Birmingham Black Barons on July 14 in Oklahoma City; the game was called after 5½ innings because of rain, but Bradley had pitched the Monarchs to a 3-0 victory.[21]

Shortly thereafter, the Monarchs were in Saskatchewan and, in a promotional article headlined "The Monarchs Are Coming!" a local paper called Bradley "the 'Bob Feller of the Negro league.'"[22] Bradley relieved Floyd Kranson in the sixth inning of the next day's game, ultimately losing on a two-run rally in the bottom of the ninth that was capped off by a double by the opposing pitcher.[23]

Two weeks later, the Monarchs were in Davenport, Iowa, playing the Illinois-Iowa League All-Stars. Thanks to a four-run first, the Monarchs defeated the All-Stars, 6-1. According to the local paper, Kansas City pitchers Big Train Jackson, Johnny Marcum, and Bradley "displayed plenty of class, keeping the All-Stars under control the entire contest."[24]

The Monarchs staged a festive doubleheader against the Memphis Red Sox to open their 1939 season. Pregame ceremonies included a flag-raising and a stadium parade with the Elks band and drill team, the Negro American Legion drum and bugle corps, the Junior Negro Scouts drum and bugle corps and the Kansas City Negro jazz and swing orchestra. The Monarchs came into the season hot, having won 10 of 15 preseason games.[25] According to the *Kansas City Star*, "Manager [Andy] Cooper will pitch 'Kid' Bradley, 20-year-old speedball star, and Hilton Smith, who led the Monarch staff, with twenty-six victories and six losses, against the Memphis invaders."[26] Cooper expected Bradley to "have a big year," wrote a reporter.[27]

Bradley seemed to heat up as summer began. He beat Decatur, 7-2, on the last day of June, striking out six in six innings and adding a double from the plate. While other reporters emphasized Bradley's fastball, the Decatur paper praised his "fast breaking curve ball" as well.[28]

A few days later Bradley came in from the bullpen, relieving Monel "Lefty" Moses after he gave up four hits to the Chicago American Giants in the first inning. Bradley shut Chicago down, scattering five hits in the last eight innings.[29] One week later, Bradley was back on the mound for an important league game against the Chicago American Giants in which he tossed a five-hitter to beat the Giants, 14-1.[30]

Bradley made several relief appearances in the second half of July 1939. He got what would today be called a save in a game against Winnipeg, entering the game during a ninth-inning rally and ending the threat.[31] At the end of the month, he starred from both the mound and the plate in a league game against the American Giants. Bradley relieved Willie Jackson in the second and pitched into the sixth, when an 11-run outburst from the Monarchs decided the game. Bradley allowed only one run in his stint and hit a double while notching the win.[32]

Bradley had a hard-luck start in late August against the Muncie Citizens. Despite giving up only six hits in 8⅓ innings (with eight strikeouts), he did not get his accustomed run support and wound up losing 3-2.[33]

A week later, Bradley got a chance to take on the legendary barnstorming team, the House of David. Satchel Paige started, working the first three innings, and Bradley went the rest of the way as the Monarchs triumphed, 10-5.[34]

In late September after the Monarchs had wrapped up another championship, Bradley got a chance to wear a different uniform, joining the barnstorming Satchel Paige's All-Stars – an indication of just how high Paige's respect for the young pitcher was. The All-Stars played a doubleheader against the Monarchs, but Paige's start in game one was a disaster. The Monarchs beat the All-Stars 11-0, with most of the runs coming off their moonlighting teammate's pitching. The second game was a different story, but ultimately the same result, as the Monarchs completed the doubleheader sweep, 1-0. Johnny Marcum started for the All-Stars, giving up the only run in the fifth on Ted Strong's home run, and Bradley shut out his Monarchs teammates the rest of the way.[35]

As the 1940 season opened, Bradley was still a frequent starter for the Monarchs who also came out of the bullpen. He lost an early April game as the starter against the Tyler Black Trojans,[36] but only a week later, he was the Monarchs' third pitcher of a game with the Toledo Crawfords that had gotten away early on the Crawfords' five-run first. Bradley managed to tame the Crawfords' bats, coming in for the late innings, but it was far too late to salvage a win.[37]

On a chilly night in early June, "Frank (Fireball) Bradley" was the starter for the Monarchs in an important Negro American League game against the Chicago American Giants. According to the press account of the game, Bradley had everything working that day: "Fogging the third strike past the waving bats of 10 rivals, the Kansas City star blanked his foes in six innings, while his mates mauled Wadel Miller, losing pitcher, for 12 hits, two of them for homers and a pair of doubles."[38] In fact, one of those home runs was by Bradley himself; for the game, he was 2-for-4 from the plate.[39]

Later that month, Bradley was coming out of the bullpen again, replacing Allen Bryant on the mound in a game against the Belmar Braves. Bradley managed to hold the line, striking out six and scattering five hits over the last five innings of the game. The Monarchs game became exciting at the end as "Kansas City staged a two-run rally in the ninth, and Bradley himself started it with one out. After fouling off five straight pitches and flopping all over the plate on every swing, he caught hold of one of Sahlin's good pitches and belted it over the right field fence for a double."[40] Although the Monarchs lost the game, 5-4, "Bradley ... stole the show. He went thru more antics than were necessary, both at the plate and on the mound, but the crowd loved it."[41]

A couple of weeks later, against the Stillwater Boomers, Bradley took a no-hitter into the bottom of the eighth, ultimately striking out 13 in eight innings of work. The Boomers closed the margin in the bottom of the ninth, scoring four off the Monarchs' bullpen, but the Monarchs won the game, 12-6.[42]

Bradley was nearly as good later that month against an all-star team from the Worthington Cardinal and Sioux Falls Canaries of the Western League. On this occasion, "So effective was Bradley's 'swift' that through the first eight stanzas the All-Stars could boast of but two hits – both of which were over second base but did not reach the outfield. ... During this time Bradley had whiffed ten of the leaguers. ... In one stretch during the fourth, fifth and sixth cantos seven of the honor team were strikeout victims in succession. Bradley ended the game with 12 strikeouts."[43] A few days later, Bradley and Hilton Smith combined on

Frank Bradley played a minor role on the 1942 Monarchs. He had pitched for the team since 1937 and had his finest season in 1939 when was 7-4 with a 2.75 ERA in NAL play. (Courtesy Noir-Tech Research, Inc.)

a three-hitter as the Monarchs whipped Richland Center, 10-0.[44]

In late August, Bradley pitched twice against the Ethiopian Clowns within a few days. In the first game, a 4-3 Kansas City victory, Bradley and Hilton Smith handled the pitching duties and "showed speed and jug-handle curveballs in abundance."[45] Bradley struck out the side in the first and second and ended with 10 strikeouts in five innings of work.[46] "Speed Bradley" threw a gem against the Clowns in the second game but wound up being let down by his bullpen. Bradley gave up only a single scratch hit across the first seven innings and struck out 18 in his nine-inning stint. The Monarchs eventually lost the game in the 11th.[47]

Bradley's final recorded start for 1940 was in mid-September against the Local 210 Oilers. He entered the game in the second and pitched the final seven innings, limiting the Oilers to five hits and striking out 12.[48]

• FRANK "DICK" BRADLEY •

By the beginning of the 1941 season, Frank Bradley was routinely being called one of the veterans of the Monarchs' pitching staff.[49] He dominated in a 9-1 triumph over the La Crosse Blackhawks in June, striking out nine while going 3-for-5 from the plate.[50] A week later, he lost a heartbreaker against the New York Black Yankees, a league opponent, for which he had only himself to blame. Bradley had pitched well, holding New York to only two hits and striking out six while going 2-for-4 from the plate, but he ended up losing, 3-2, when he balked in the winning run for New York in the top of the eighth.[51]

In mid-July Bradley was the Monarchs' third pitcher in a three-way 3-0 shutout of the Belmar Braves, giving up three hits in the final three innings and striking out two.[52] The shutout lengthened Belmar's scoreless drought against the Monarchs to 29 consecutive innings.[53] Bradley threw a complete game in his next start but lost to the Brooklyn Bushwicks, 3-1, though he struck out seven, walked only two, and managed a 1-for-3 day from the plate.[54] Bradley pitched well again in an early August start against the Studebaker Athletics, but it must be conceded that the Athletics gave him a lot of help. The Monarchs won the game, 11-0, but the 11 errors the Athletics rang up probably had something to do with that. Five of those 11 errors were recorded by a single player, Athletics shortstop Stanley Wrobel, who also got the only extra-base hit among the Athletics' five hits for the day.[55]

As the 1941 season wound down, the Monarchs lost to the Birmingham Black Barons, 5-0. Bradley wasn't sharp, giving up nine hits and four runs in his seven innings of work, with only four strikeouts.[56] His final two appearances for the season were both in exhibition games. In early October the Monarchs took on Bob Feller's All-Stars, one of the series of games Negro League teams played against barnstorming White major leaguers over the years. Bradley did not pitch, but he did pinch-hit for fellow pitcher Hilton Smith in a 4-1 loss.[57] The next day the Monarchs defeated Frigidaire, 5-2. Satchel Paige started and hurled the first three frames. Bradley took the mound in the fourth and pitched five strong innings, striking out nine, walking only one, and scattering four hits. He was 2-for-2 at the plate.[58]

Bradley was eager to get started as the 1942 season approached, arriving early at the Monarchs' spring-training camp in Monroe, Louisiana.[59] The Monarchs started Bradley in the opening game of an early-season doubleheader against the Birmingham Black Barons, which the team lost by a 2-1 score. The Monarchs took the second game, 8-6, thanks to Barney "Bonnie" Serrell's circus catch of what would have been a three-run homer for the future Harlem Globetrotter Reece "Goose" Tatum.[60]

Although reports of Bradley starts are scarce for 1942, he was routinely referred to as part of the Monarchs' sterling pitching staff.[61] The *Harrisburg Evening News* was effusive in August: "Two other hurlers on the Monarchs who have exceptionally fine records and who have the throwing arms to back up arguments in their favor are Hilton Smith and Frank Bradley."[62] Although he was not used during the World Series, the newspapers took notice of Bradley as an important part of the Monarchs' pitching staff before Game One against the Homestead Grays.[63]

In 1943 several newspapers continued to list Bradley as a member of the Monarchs' pitching staff.[64] However, by this time he was in the Army and played for the 915th Squadron at Dover Air Force Base. One game account noted, "PFC Frank Bradley, formerly with the Kansas City Monarchs, drove in four runs. His homer in the third with a mate aboard accounted for two and his fifth-inning single drove in two more."[65] Bradley remained in the Army for the remainder of World War II, with the duration of his service spanning October 5, 1942 to December 8, 1945.

Tragically, due to a wound in the bend of his arm, Bradley's career ended with his Army service. He returned to his hometown of Benton and bagged groceries for a living. On the positive side, with his baseball barnstorming days and military service both at an end, he married his longtime love, Maurine Moore, on June 22, 1946.[66]

Decades later, Bradley's friends remembered his talent and what might have been. His childhood friend Riley Stewart, who knew both Bradley and Satchel Paige well, said, "Satchel said the hardest thrower, without a doubt, was Dick Bradley. Dick was a strong power pitcher with a curveball. Dick was in that class with (Nolan) Ryan."[67] "[Satchel] said [Bradley] could throw that ball and make it look like an aspirin tablet," Stewart remarked, and then added, "Dick Bradley could throw the ball as hard as any human being could in those days."[68]

Bradley attended a Monarchs reunion in 1995. "It's a really good feeling," he said. "I'm glad to go. Imagine I'll see some old friends I haven't seen in more than 50 years because I saw a lot of old teammates in Cooperstown. I'm really looking forward to seeing that old ballpark again."[69]

Several of the best stories about Bradley's career appeared after his playing time was over. Among these were the facts that "[h]e pitched a no-hitter against the Memphis Red Sox and came out on the short end of a 1-0 pitching duel with Bossier City's Riley Stewart before a four-year stint in the army beginning in 1943."[70] Like Satchel Paige, "When he had his good stuff, Bradley would call in the outfielders and infielders and strike out the side."[71]

Bradley recalled late in his life that he would frequently finish up for Paige – Satchel for the first six innings and Bradley finishing up the game. "I'd say the toughest hitter I ever faced was Josh Gibson," he said. "I think I probably faced him about 20 times."[72] Bradley admitted to having added one homer to Gibson's prodigious career total.[73]

Fifty years after he retired from the game, Bradley still remembered those days: "He [said] traveling and playing the game [were] his best memories. 'I miss the game, I miss the friendships. ... I dream about baseball all the time.'"[74]

In his later years, Bradley became known for his career with the Monarchs throughout his home parish in Louisiana. On August 11, 2001, the Shreveport Swamp Dragons honored the 83-year-old hurler, and he threw out the ceremonial first pitch before the team's game against the Wichita Wranglers.[75]

After his death on December 2, 2002, in Benton, hometown newspaper columnist Bradley Hudson wrote an elegiac tribute to the deceased Negro League star. The writer remembered Bradley walking past his house every morning and evening going back and forth to work at the local creosote plant, "carrying his lunch in a greasy brown paper bag. He was friendly, polite and a very nice man who took time occasionally to tell us to do our best in school. He would even take our baseballs and show us how to throw a curveball or a fastball. ... Little did we know that this same man once had a fastball that even Satchel Paige envied." The columnist wrote, "Bradley never seemed bitter about his fate. I never once detected a trace of anger in him. He realized that it was just the times in which he grew up. ... Major League baseball has attempted to make amends by honoring Negro League stars. They earned it. ... I'll always treasure having known him."[76]

Frank Bradley is buried in the Benton Community Cemetery, on Highway 162 just east of the hometown where he lived most of his life.

Source

Ancestry.com was consulted for public records, including census information, marriage and death records, and Frank and June Bradley's World War II draft registration cards.

Notes

1 Census records for the family for the years 1920, 1930, and 1940 have been reviewed via Ancestry.com, with no additional children listed.

2 See World War II draft registration cards for June Bradley and Frank Bradley, Ancestry.com.

3 For a brief history of the Rough and Ready Plantation, see the Bossier Parish Libraries History Center, http://bossier.pastperfectonline.com/photo/67D885DF-1394-4E78-9C89-473991522949.

4 "Negro Leagues Saw Great Baseball," *The Times* (Shreveport, Louisiana), July 24, 1991: 83.

5 Victoria L. Coman, "'I Miss the Game; I miss the friendships,'" *The Times*, November 20, 1996: 41.

6 "Colored Team Wins Against Merchants," *Green Bay Press-Gazette*, August 20, 1937: 14.

7 "Colored Nines Are Booked by Manager," *South Bend Tribune*, August 22, 1937: 11.

8 "Negro Leagues Saw Great Baseball."

9 Late in Bradley's life, a newspaper retrospective of his baseball career reported that his fastball was "99 miles-per-hour." Jerry Byrd, "Former Pitcher Is Grand Marshall [*sic*] in Benton Parade," *Bossier* (Louisiana) *Press Tribune*, December 11, 1997: 16. It is unclear whether Bradley himself made this claim, or one of his former teammates did. Since Bradley's career was before the era of even the most primitive speed guns, we will never know how seriously to take the claim.

10 "Former Pitcher Is Grand Marshall."

11 Clint Land, "Baseball Pitching Legend Honored," *Bossier Press Tribune*, August 13, 2001: 7.

12 "Monarchs Have Easy Victory," *Manhattan* (Kansas) *Mercury*, August 28, 1937: 6.

13 "Pociask Lets Barnstormers Down Rudely," *Beatrice* (Nebraska) *Daily Sun*, September 2, 1937: 6.

14 "The Monarchs Take Two," *Kansas City Times*, September 7, 1937: 13.

15 "New Players with Monarchs," *Hutchinson* (Kansas) *News*, April 28, 1938: 2.

16 John Snow, "Press Box Gossip," *Springfield* (Missouri) *Leader and Press*, April 29, 1938: 2.

17 Hank Casserly, "Invaders Have Great Record in Past Week," *Capital Times* (Madison, Wisconsin), June 1, 1938: 13.

18 Bob Overaker, "Monarchs Rout Studebakers," *South Bend Tribune*, June 28, 1938: 10.

19 "Hold Monarchs Even," *Kansas City Times*, July 4, 1938: 6.

20 "Negro Bob Feller," *Minneapolis Star*, July 11, 1938: 11.

21 Christopher Hauser, *The Negro Leagues Chronology: Events in Organized Black Baseball, 1920-1948* (Jefferson, North Carolina: McFarland & Company, Inc., 2006), 104.

22 "The Monarchs Are Coming!" *Leader-Post* (Regina, Saskatchewan), July 21, 1938: 13.

23 "Pitcher Wins for Giants," *Leader-Post* (Regina, Saskatchewan), July 23, 1938, 12.

24 "Colored Nine Gets 4 Runs in First Frame," *Daily Times* (Davenport, Iowa), August 2, 1938: 12.

• FRANK "DICK" BRADLEY •

25 "Monarchs Play Today," *Kansas City Star*, May 14, 1939: 9.

26 "Monarchs Play Today."

27 "Al Krueger Will Oppose K.C. Ball Club," *Capital Times* (Madison, Wisconsin), May 23, 1939: 21.

28 Howard V. Millard, "Bloomers Open Here Tonight; Ladies Guests," *Decatur* (Illinois) *Daily Review*, July 1, 1939: 5.

29 Hank Casserly, "Former Red Hurler Will Aid Locals," *Capital Times*, July 5, 1939: 13.

30 "K.C. Monarchs Defeat Giants," *Minneapolis Star*, July 12, 1939: 18.

31 "Monarchs Capture Twin Bill," *Winnipeg Tribune*, July 18, 1939: 13.

32 "Kansas City's Negro Team Beats Chicago," *Des Moines Register*, July 29, 1939: 9.

33 Evan Owens, "Citizens Play at Lafayette," *Muncie* (Indiana) *Evening Press*, August 25, 1939: 16.

34 "Colts Defeat Davids at Storm Lake, 10-5," *Sioux City* (Iowa) *Journal*, September 6, 1939: 12.

35 "No Run for All-Stars," *Kansas City Times*, October 2, 1939: 11; "Paige to Face Monarchs," *Kansas City Star*, October 1, 1939: 20.

36 "Black Trojans Outhit K.C. Nine but Lose, 2 to 7," *Tyler* (Texas) *Morning Telegraph*, April 8, 1940: 2.

37 "Toledo Negro Team Wins; Owens Sprints," *Fort Worth Star-Telegram*, April 17, 1940: 19.

38 Brad Wilson, "Monarchs Beat Giants, 7 to 3," *Des Moines Register*, June 11, 1940: 14.

39 Wilson.

40 "Belmar Nine Conquers Kansas City Monarchs," *Asbury Park Press*, June 22, 1940: 8.

41 "Belmar Nine Conquers Kansas City Monarchs."

42 "Kansas City Monarchs Trounce Boomers, 12-6," *Daily Oklahoman* (Oklahoma City), July 9, 1940: 11.

43 "Monarchs Win Here 7-4; Cards Beat Canaries 5-4," *Argus-Leader* (Sioux Falls, South Dakota), July 22, 1940: 8.

44 "Monarchs Whitewash Richland Center, 10-0," *Wisconsin State Journal*, July 26, 1940: 10; "K.C. Monarchs Wallop Richland Center, 10-0," *Capital Times*, July 26, 1940: 16.

45 "Negro Nines Shine," *Winnipeg Tribune*, August 23, 1940: 12.

46 "Negro Nines Shine."

47 "Winners Pair Single, Double in 11th Frame," *Daily Times*, August 28, 1940: 11.

48 "Paige Works 2 Heats; Gets 6 on Strikes," *The Times* (Shreveport, Louisiana), September 18, 1940: 22.

49 "Negro Baseball Champs to Play," *Monroe* (Louisiana) *Morning World*, May 4, 1941: 11; "Kansas City Outfit Meets Black Barons Sunday in Twin Bill," *Birmingham News*, May 9, 1941: 17.

50 Earl H. Voss, "Third Place Club Only Single Game Behind La Crosse," *La Crosse* (Wisconsin) *Tribune*, June 24, 1941: 8.

51 "Monarchs Lose on a Balk," *Kansas City Times*, July 1, 1941: 12.

52 "Monarchs Trip Braves, 3 to 0," *Daily Record* (Morris County, New Jersey), July 19, 1941: 4.

53 "Brave String of Scoreless Innings Is 29," *Asbury Park* (New Jersey) *Press*, July 19, 1941: 9.

54 "Bushwick Club Downs Monarchs," *Brooklyn Daily Eagle*, July 24, 1941: 15; "Bushwicks Win, 3-1," *New York Daily News*, July 24, 1941: 540.

55 "Monarchs Win 11-0," *South Bend Tribune*, August 7, 1941: 11-12.

56 "Black Barons Win by 5 to 0 Score from Monarchs," *Oshkosh Northwestern*, September 12, 1941: 17.

57 "Feller and Paige Good, but Others Look Better," *St. Louis Globe Democrat*, October 6, 1941: 13.

58 "Monarchs in 5-2 Win Over Frigidaire," *Journal Herald* (Dayton, Ohio), October 7, 1941: 9.

59 "K.C. Monarchs Head South for Spring Training Siege," *Pittsburgh Courier*, March 28, 1942: 16.

60 R.S. Simmons, "Speaking in General," *Weekly Review* (Birmingham, Alabama), April 24, 1942: 7.

61 "Black Barons Play Jacksonville in Opener, Sunday," *Weekly Review*, May 8, 1942: 7; "League Twin Bill Here," *Kansas City Times*, May 30, 1942: 7; "E.C. Giants Tangle with Kansas City," *The Times*, June 26, 1942: 47; "Monarchs Play Here Thursday," *St. Joseph* (Missouri) *Gazette*, July 15, 1942: 5; "'Satchel' Paige and Kansas City Monarchs in Yankee Stadium's Biggest Attraction Sunday, Aug. 2," *New York Age*, August 1, 1942: 11.

62 "Stars of Negro Loop Play Here," *Evening News* (Harrisburg, Pennsylvania), August 11, 1942: 6.

63 "Satchel Paige Faces Grays Here Tonight," *Philadelphia Inquirer*, September 29, 1942: 26.

64 "Monarchs Here Sunday," *Kansas City Star*, May 9, 1943: 24; "Kansas City Monarchs Believe They'll Win Fifth Championship," *New York Age*, July 24, 1943: 11.

65 "915th Squadron Blanks Fort Miles Hilltoppers," *News Journal* (Wilmington, Delaware), July 15, 1943: 25.

66 Her name was sometimes spelled alternately as "Maurine" or "Maureen" in various sources.

67 "Negro Leagues Saw Great Baseball," *The Times*, July 24, 1991: 83.

68 "'I Miss the Game; I Miss the Friendships,'" *The Times*, November 20, 1996: 41.

69 "Ex-Players Set for Historical Fete," *The Times*, October 24, 1995: 17.

70 "Former Pitcher Is Grand Marshall in Benton Parade," *Bossier Press Tribune*, December 11, 1997: 16.

71 "Former Pitcher Is Grand Marshall in Benton Parade."

72 "Former Pitcher Is Grand Marshall in Benton Parade."

73 "Former Pitcher Is Grand Marshall in Benton Parade."

74 "'I Miss the Game; I Miss the Friendships,'" *The Times*, November 20, 1996: 41.

75 Charlie Cavell, "Swamp Dragons Blow Three-Run Lead in Loss," *The Times*, August 11, 2001: 17.

76 Bradley Hudson, "Bradley a Silent Hero," *The Times*, December 15, 2002: 100.

WILLARD BROWN

By Rory Costello

Ese Hombre – That Man – was Willard Brown's nickname in Puerto Rico. The outfielder was one of the most feared hitters in the Negro Leagues, but he was an absolute wrecking ball in the Puerto Rican Winter League. He won the Triple Crown twice there, in 1947-48 and 1949-50. Unfortunately, he played just 21 games in what was known as the major leagues, all during the span of a month in 1947. He had problems with racism and the poor quality of his club, the St. Louis Browns. In 2006, however, Brown's greatness was recognized as a special committee selected him to enter the National Baseball Hall of Fame in Cooperstown.

Willard Jessie Brown was born on June 26, 1915, in Shreveport, Louisiana. Some sources have cited 1911 as his year of birth, but Brown's birth certificate, Social Security application, and census research have confirmed the 1915 date. It's interesting to note that when he came up to the majors, some stories billed Brown as being born in 1921.[1] In later decades, though, he took to saying that he was too old when he got his chance, and so dates such as 1911 and 1913 entered circulation.

Willard's father, Manuel Brown, was born in Texas. Manuel's wife, Allie (who died at age 100 in 1986) came from Marthaville, Louisiana.[2] As of the 1920 census, the Brown family was living in Natchitoches, about 75 miles southeast of Shreveport. Manuel's occupation was listed as mill laborer; Willard's name was recorded as "Bud." No other siblings are visible, though two cousins were in the house, including a girl named Cleo whom Willard viewed as a sister.[3] By 1930, the family had returned to Shreveport, and Manuel had his own cabinetmaking shop. The only other member of the household listed then was Allie's father, Louis Phillips.

Young Willard grew up around baseball. Among other things, he served as a batboy in spring training for his future team, the Kansas City Monarchs. In the 1920s, Shreveport was one of the places they liked to use to prepare for the long season.[4] In 1934, Brown turned pro, since he had left school and thought baseball offered his best earning potential. He joined the Monroe Monarchs of the Negro Southern League. This club, based in another northern Louisiana city about 100 miles east of Shreveport, was owned by a wealthy local businessman named Fred Stovall. Brown signed for just $8 a week as a shortstop and pitcher, but as Louisiana sportswriter Paul Letlow observed on his blog in June 2009, the players also got room and board on Stovall's plantation.[5] "I thought that was big money," said Brown with a chuckle in a 1983 interview.[6]

After one season with Monroe, Brown joined the Kansas City Monarchs, one of the premier franchises in the Negro Leagues. Owner J.L. Wilkinson spotted Buck O'Neil and Brown while Kansas City was barnstorming against the Shreveport Acme Giants in spring training.[7] Wilkinson gave his recruit a $250 bonus, a salary of $125 per month, and $1 per diem meal money.[8] Brown made the East-West All-Star game in 1936. It was the first of eight times for him in Black baseball's showcase. In 1937, though, he shifted from short to the outfield, which remained his primary position for the rest of his career. He played a good deal of center field but was also a corner outfielder much of the time.

During the winter of 1937-38, Brown got his first experience of baseball in a Spanish-speaking land as he played in Cuba for Marianao. The player-manager was the great Martín Dihigo. Brown got just eight hits in 55 at-bats over the 53-game season. He did not return to Cuba after that.

The Kansas City Monarchs were highly successful in the decade from 1937 to 1946, winning six Negro American League championships. They also won the Colored World Series (as it was known at the time) in 1942. There was a tremendous amount of talent on the team, including the brilliant pitchers Satchel Paige and Hilton Smith, plus slick second baseman Newt Allen, steady first baseman Buck O'Neil, and 6'6" outfielder Ted Strong. Their leading offensive weapon, though, was Brown. No less a figure than Josh Gibson called him "Home Run" Brown.

• WILLARD BROWN •

Hall of Famer Willard Brown manned center field for the 1942 Kansas City Monarchs while also batting .338 during the NAL season and .467 in the World Series. (Courtesy Noir-Tech Research, Inc.)

Negro League historians Larry Lester and Sammy Miller recorded the story of another of Brown's nicknames, one that was less flattering. "Brown is what we called a Sunday player," claimed former teammate Sammie Haynes. "Willard liked to play on Sundays when we had a full house. If the stands were full you couldn't get him out. He could play baseball as good as he wanted to. If the stands were half empty, you might find Brown loafing that day. In fact, he didn't play on rainy or cloudy days. That's why we called him Sonny. He loved to play on sunny days and before big crowds. And he was a real crowd pleaser."[9]

In his 1999 book about his life in the Negro Leagues, another old teammate, catcher Frazier "Slow" Robinson, echoed Haynes. "The only thing about Brown was that he never did get serious about baseball. . .he could have let the fans know he was hustling at all times." Robinson acknowledged Brown's power and speed, and that he was at his best in big games. Still, he rated Brown a cut below Josh Gibson in terms of consistency and all-around play. He also questioned his throwing arm, which is at odds with other descriptions.[10]

In this vein, many stories describe how Brown often had his nose in a copy of *Reader's Digest* while stationed in the outfield. Plenty of days, he would also seemingly be in a rush to get the game over with, and would swing at anything in sight. Once he homered on a pitch that came in on a bounce. Catcher Quincy Troupe said, "Who knows? Brown may have been as great, or greater, than Gibson, if he had been a little more patient and waited for strikes."[11] Yet there was still something endearing about Brown, as author Joe Posnanski pointed when he skillfully retold these anecdotes. Mainly, it was how good he was when he was on.[12] As various people have observed, including Buck O'Neil, Brown also made things look easy.

Brown's career with the Monarchs was interrupted in 1940, when he went to play in Mexico. Author John Virtue described how it came about. That year, "two competing six-team leagues were formed [in Mexico], creating the need for twice as many players, so the Negro Leagues were raided as never before. During the season, 63 African American ballplayers played in Mexico, four times the number that had played in 1939. They represented about 20 percent of the rosters of the Negro American League and Negro National League teams – and they were among the best players." The new league was formed by magnate Jorge Pasquel, who six years later tried to raid the major leagues.[13] The money was good: Brown got $1,000 per month. He also developed his grasp of Spanish.

Business acquaintances of Pasquel in Nuevo Laredo formed the team that Brown joined. In 294 at-bats with the Tecolotes (Owls), Brown hit .354 with 8 homers and 61 RBIs. To underscore the type of hitter he was, he drew just 10 walks but struck out only 15 times. According to Virtue, Brown decided to stay in Mexico at the beginning of 1941, declining an olive branch that the Negro Leagues owners extended to jumpers.[14] Other sources indicate that Brown did not play south of the border that year, and that 1941 Mexican batting statistics with his name are actually those of pitcher Barney Brown.

In the winter of 1941-42, with numerous other Negro Leaguers on the scene, Brown's Puerto Rican career began with Humacao. He played second base and batted .409 (50 for 122) with four homers and 26 RBIs. Despite this auspicious season, though, he would not return to the island for another five years.

For at least one stretch, in 1943-44, he played in the California Winter League for the Kansas City Royals, a team that featured Satchel Paige among others.[15]

Brown entered the U.S. Army in 1944, serving in Europe at the height of World War II. "In the Army, Brown was among those in the five thousand ships that crossed the English Channel during the Normandy invasion. A member of the Quartermaster Corps, he was not in combat but was engaged in hauling ammunition and guarding prisoners."[16] He then transferred to Special Services. In France, former Phillies pitcher Sam Nahem got him to play for the OISE All-Stars, who represented Com-Z (Communications Zone) in the 1945 ETO World Series. This integrated team boasted another Negro League star and future Hall of Famer in Leon Day. They beat the 71st Division Red Circlers, which featured several major leaguers, including Harry Walker and Ewell "The Whip" Blackwell.[17]

Returning to Kansas City in 1946, Brown had what some observers believe was his best season with the Monarchs. Although the patchy data make it difficult to underpin this idea, newspaper accounts give the impression that he was the top home run hitter in the NAL that year. He added three more homers in six games during the Colored World Series (yet the Newark Eagles won after Satchel Paige and Ted Strong jumped the team with two games remaining). Brown followed up with the first of his three Puerto Rican batting titles in 1946-47, joining the club where he would play his best, the Santurce Cangrejeros (Crabbers).

In July 1947, Brown got his shot at the majors, as the St. Louis Browns signed him and infielder Hank Thompson from the Monarchs for a reported $5,000 apiece.[18] The Associated Press reported, "Owner Richard Muckerman of the Browns said the two players were signed 'to help lift the Browns out of the American League cellar.'" The Brownies also had an option on another fine Negro Leaguer, Lorenzo "Piper" Davis. The AP article added that of all the African-American players signed in the year of integration, including Jackie Robinson, "Outfielder Brown was considered to be the prize package of the lot, with only his age against him."[19]

Janet Bruce's book on the Monarchs noted that Brown was unhappy. "The first time they told me I was going to the Browns – I didn't want to go to the Browns in the first place! I said, 'No! I wasn't going. But [the other players] just kept on, 'Why don't you go on, show them what you can do.'"[20]

Without any time at all to acclimate in the minors, however, Brown never really got on track in St. Louis (despite displaying his enormous power in batting practice). As has often been chronicled, the atmosphere around him was charged with racism. Alabaman outfielder Paul Lehner was the unfriendliest teammate; Philadelphia A's coach Al Simmons reportedly was one of those riding Brown hard.[21]

Brown's best game in the majors was his fifth, at Yankee Stadium on July 23. He went 4-for-5 and drove in three runs as the Browns won 8-2.

On August 13, Brown hit his only homer in the majors, and the first in the American League by a Black player. It was an inside-the-parker in the eighth inning off Detroit's Hal Newhouser; the pinch-hit blow helped the Browns rally after losing a lead in the top of the inning. The aftermath of that homer has become more memorable. Brown had used a bat belonging to outfielder Jeff Heath, but upon Brown's return to the dugout, Heath smashed the bat against the wall rather than allow Brown to use it again.

This has often been cited as a prime example of the racial animus that Brown (and Thompson) faced in St. Louis. No doubt the perception was awful, but it is notable that in 1965, Hank Thompson mentioned Heath as one of five Browns who "went out of their way to make life easier for me and Brown."[22] In addition, Heath had given a positive report on Brown's ability because he had faced him as Bob Feller's All-Stars faced Satchel Paige's barnstorming squad in the fall of 1946.[23] There is also an alternate explanation for Heath's behavior. In his biography of Heath for the SABR BioProject, C. Paul Rogers III noted that Heath was a quirky, superstitious player who "was very particular about his bats and would not allow teammates to borrow them." Further support for the absence of a racial motive came from Browns road secretary Charlie DeWitt after that season. DeWitt said, "He said he would not have minded if Brown got a single, but he had used up one of the bat's home runs."[24] The oddity here was that Heath had discarded the bat because it had lost its knob. Brown liked it because it was the heaviest he could find – he favored 40-ounce clubs.

On August 23, Browns manager Muddy Ruel released both Brown and Hank Thompson (they rejoined the Monarchs, where the money was actually better). Ruel had told *Baltimore Afro-American* sportswriter Sam Lacy on August 6 that "a fair trial" – which even Ruel admitted he couldn't truly define – was still in progress.[25] According to owner Muckerman, he, general manager Bill DeWitt, and Ruel had held several conferences and concluded that Brown and Thompson lacked major-league talent.[26]

In Brown's 1983 account, he said that he and Thompson, although they were dissatisfied, had a choice about whether to stay or go. He said he might have stayed if the club had given him what he asked for, such as bats he could swing with. Overall, he took a dim view of the club he had left. "The Browns couldn't beat the Monarchs no kind of way, only if we was all asleep. That's the truth. They didn't have nothing. I said, 'Major league team?' They got to be kidding."[27]

St. Louis had also harbored a vain hope that the Black players might spur attendance.[28] Kansas City teammate Buck O'Neil further alleged in his book, "Another real problem was that the Browns were going to have to pay the Monarchs some more money if those two guys lasted out the season, so they just released them before the season ended. Willard was bitter, you can believe that. He knew that at twenty-eight [sic] he'd never get another crack at the big leagues."[29]

During the winter of 1947-48, Brown felt that he had something to prove, and had a simply monstrous Triple Crown season. It may have been at this time that sportswriter Rafael Pont Flores coined the nickname *Ese Hombre*. Brown hit .432, the fourth-highest single-season mark in Puerto Rican Winter League history. His 27 homers remain far and away the most in one PRWL season; the runner-up is Reggie Jackson, who hit 20 in 1970-71. Finally, his 86 RBIs rank third on the single-season list – the best total being his own 97, set two winters later. Bear in mind that the PRWL schedule was just 60 games long and the caliber of competition was high.

Author Thomas Van Hyning, who chronicled the league and the Crabbers in two books, said that pitcher Rubén Gómez called Brown "the most dominant player he had ever played with, except for Willie Mays." Van Hyning added the view of Poto Paniagua, who took over ownership of the Santurce club in the 1970s. Paniagua "affirmed that Willard Brown was the most productive import the Puerto Rico Winter League ever had. [He] told me that Brown would have been a big league superstar had he (Brown) been given a chance at a much younger age."[30]

Brown returned to the Monarchs in 1948, pulling down a monthly salary of $600.[31] About the following summer in Kansas City, Buck O'Neil later said, "The best club I ever managed was the 1949 team." The team photo showed little Willard Jr. – the only child *Ese Hombre* had with his wife, Dorothy – posing in front of his father.[32] Unfortunately, further details about this woman are presently unavailable. As Willard Jr.'s wife Mary recalled in 2010, Dorothy was some years older than Willard Sr. The marriage broke up when the boy was about nine years old.

The winter of 1949-50 saw Brown win his second Triple Crown in Puerto Rico, earning $200 in bonus money ($100 for the batting title and $50 apiece for the other two legs). He edged his teammate Bob Thurman, another powerful Negro Leaguer, for the batting title, .354 to .353. Brown and Thurman (known as *El Múcaro,* or The Owl, in Puerto Rico) formed "the most feared tandem in league history."[33]

In February 1950, Brown batted .348 in the second Caribbean Series as a reinforcement for the PRWL champs, the Caguas Criollos. He then returned to the Monarchs, who also featured 21-year-old Elston Howard.[34] That July, Yankees scout Tom Greenwade came to check out Brown. Instead, Buck O'Neil said, "Willard's a fine player. . .but Elston Howard is the player you're looking for."[35] Brown's reaction is not known.

The following month, the Ottawa Nationals of the Border League (Class C) persuaded Brown to join them, although reportedly he was reluctant to travel that far north.[36] The *Montreal Gazette* praised his play, saying, "Willard Brown. . .whom the Nationals secured from the Kansas City Monarchs last month, proved a big factor in Ottawa's drive to the pennant. He hit at a .400 clip and saved several games through sensational fielding."[37] Including playoff action (the Nats lost the final in six games), Brown wound up hitting .352 in 128 at-bats across 30 games.

In February 1951, Santurce won the PRWL title and then went on to take the third annual Caribbean Series in Venezuela. Right around that time, a newspaper in Guadalajara, Mexico, *El Informador*, had a big headline announcing that Brown had accepted a contract with the local team, the Jalisco Charros. The manager was Quincy Trouppe.[38] As late as April, a photo with fellow Negro Leaguers Max Manning, Bill Greason, and Trouppe indicated that Willard would be a Charro.[39] Instead, after 11 years away, he returned briefly to Nuevo Laredo that month.[40] He soon came back to Kansas City, however, winning the Negro

American League batting title in 1951 with a .417 average, though by that point the level of play had dropped off sharply.

Ese Hombre also spent some time in the Dominican Republic in the summers of 1951 and 1952. Pro baseball had resumed there in 1951, but the league would not switch to the winter until 1955. With the Escogido Leones, Brown hit .253 with 17 RBIs in 1951, lifting those numbers to .301 and 28 the following year. One source says that Willard played for Cervecería Caracas in Venezuela in the winter of 1951-52.[41] This does not appear to be the case, though, because *The Sporting News* showed him in Santurce at the beginning and end of the season, noting that he had been sidelined for a month with an ailing knee.[42]

The Crabbers won the PRWL title again in 1952-53 and thus went on to another Caribbean Series. They won their second double winter championship, going 6-0 thanks to MVP Brown's four home runs and 13 RBIs. In three Caribbean Series overall, he hit .343 with five homers and 19 RBIs.[43]

Brown returned to the U.S. for the summers of 1953 through 1956, playing for various teams in the Texas League, plus a little bit in the Western League. Although the Texas League was only Double-A ball, he was still a potent hitter. His best output during this period came in 1954, when he had 35 homers and 120 RBIs while batting .314. In both 1953 (Dallas) and 1954 (Houston, where he played 36 games after 108 with Dallas), Brown's clubs won the league championship.

Turning back to winter ball in Santurce, Brown's last full season there was 1953-54, but he made a brief return in 1956-57, going 6 for 23. *Ese Hombre* finished his Puerto Rican career with a .350 batting average, the best in league history. His 101 home runs rank fourth all time behind Bob Thurman, José Cruz, and Elrod Hendricks; his 473 RBIs rank seventh. When the Puerto Rican Baseball Hall of Fame inducted its first class in October 1991, Brown was among the elite group of ten players.

In the twilight of his career, Brown played in 1957 with the Minot Mallards of the Manitoba-Dakota (ManDak) League, which featured many old Negro Leaguers: He hit .307 with 9 homers and 29 RBIs in 150 at-bats. Brown's plaque in Cooperstown indicates that he played in the Negro Leagues in 1958. Indeed, an article in the *Schenectady Gazette* from July 1958 billed him as "the star of the Monarchs" once more as the "Kansas City" club (by then based in Grand

Willard Brown was inducted into the National Baseball Hall of Fame in 2006, 10 years after he had been inducted into the Caribbean Baseball Hall of Fame as a member of its inaugural class. (Courtesy Noir-Tech Research, Inc.)

Rapids, Michigan) visited Hawkins Stadium in Albany, New York.[44] By this stage, though, the Negro American League was a lower-echelon barnstorming attraction.

After he finally retired from baseball, Brown made his home in Houston. Little information is available about his last three-plus decades. Although James Riley's *Biographical Encyclopedia of the Negro Baseball Leagues* notes briefly that Brown worked in the steel industry, there is not much more to go on. Interviews with and about him during this period focused on the past rather than the present.

In mid-December 1979, Brown returned to Puerto Rico for an Old-Timer's Day. He told local baseball man Luis Rodríguez Mayoral that the island "was where I was treated best."[45] Said Pedrín Zorrilla, who owned the Santurce Crabbers in Brown's greatest days, "it was the man. . .the artist. . .it was those things [about him] that they cheered. He didn't have to be Puerto Rican. The Puerto Ricans love baseball, and Willie Brown could play it, and by that very fact he became a brother to us."[46] Thomas Van Hyning offered still more detail about the deep affection that Brown and the *boricua* people shared.[47]

Willard Brown passed away on August 4, 1996, in Houston. He was 81, had been suffering from Alzheimer's disease since 1989, and had entered a Veteran's Administration hospital in the early '90s. A sketch about Brown in Volume 36 of *Contemporary Black Biography* said that he had previously slipped into poverty. His son Willard Jr. had died two years previously.

In his *New Historical Baseball Abstract* (2001), analyst Bill James likened Brown to one Hall of Famer, one who would go in later, and two other very potent sluggers. He said, "Maybe comparable to José Canseco, Juan González, André Dawson or Frank Robinson." [48] In February 2006, a voting committee of 12 historians specializing in Negro League and pre-Negro League baseball convened under former Commissioner Fay Vincent. They elected 17 candidates to Cooperstown, including 12 players and five executives. Among them was Willard Brown.

In 2007, Louisiana sportswriter Ted Lewis offered two quotes that summed up the choice well. "'I don't think he would have been surprised by being elected,' said Mary Brown, who represented her late father-in-law in Cooperstown last summer." Lewis also spoke to Dick Clark, co-chairman of SABR's Negro Leagues Committee and a member of the Hall of Fame selection committee. "Brown's credentials made his election an easy one. . . 'Willard Brown was the preeminent right-handed slugger for the Negro American League throughout the '40s,' Clark said."[49]

Continued thanks to Eric Costello for his additional research. Thanks also to Mrs. Mary Brown and SABR member Dwayne Isgrig.

Sources

In addition to the sources cited in the Notes, the author also consulted:

1920 and 1930 census records, courtesy of www.ancestry.com

Interview with Willard Brown for the University of Kentucky Libraries A.B. Chandler Oral History Project. Conducted by William J. Marshall in South Point, Ohio, on June 22, 1983.

Negro Leagues Baseball e-Museum profile of Willard Brown (http://coe.ksu.edu/nlbemuseum/history/players/brownw.html)

Crescioni Benítez, José A. *El Béisbol Profesional Boricua*. San Juan, Puerto Rico: Aurora Comunicación Integral, Inc., 1997.

Bjarkman, Peter C. *Diamonds Around the Globe: The Encyclopedia of International Baseball*. Westport, Connecticut: Greenwood Press, 2005.

Treto Cisneros, Pedro, editor, *Enciclopedia del Béisbol Mexicano*. Revistas Deportivas, S.A. de C.V., 1998.

Figueredo, Jorge. *Cuban Baseball: A Statistical History, 1878-1961*. Jefferson, North Carolina: McFarland & Co., 2003.

Cruz, Héctor J. *El Béisbol Dominicano*. Accessible online at http://www.scribd.com/doc/25085233/EL-BEISBOL-DOMINICANO-2

Sketch on Willard Brown with compilation of statistics from across his career, Western Canada Baseball website (http://www.attheplate.com/wcbl/majorleaguers.html)

Willard Brown discussion on Baseball Think Factory website (http://www.baseballthinkfactory.org/files/hall_of_merit/discussion/willard_brown)

Swanton, Barry. *The ManDak League*. Jefferson, North Carolina: McFarland & Co., 2006.

Henderson, Ashyia, editor. *Contemporary Black Biography, Volume 36*. Farmington Hills, Michigan: Gale Group: 2002.

Notes

1   Frederick G. Lieb, "Gates Rusting, Browns Rush in 2 Negro Players," *The Sporting News*, July 23, 1947: 8.

2   Allie Brown obituary, *Orlando Sentinel*, July 14, 1986.

3   William J. Marshall interview with Willard Brown. Allie Brown's obituary (she passed away at the age of 100) also refers to Cleo as a daughter. *Orlando Sentinel*, July 14, 1986.

4   Janet Bruce, *The Kansas City Monarchs: Champions of Black Baseball* (Lawrence, Kansas: University Press of Kansas, 1985), 27.

5   James A. Riley, *The Biographical Encyclopedia of the Negro Baseball Leagues* (New York: Carroll & Graf Publishers, 1994). Paul Letlow, "The Monroe Monarchs." Paul Letlow's Louisiana Sports Shorts (http://louisianasportsshorts.blogspot.com/2009/06/monroe-monarchs.html), June 29, 2009.

6   Interview with Willard Brown for the University of Kentucky Libraries A.B. Chandler Oral History Project. The interview was conducted by William J. Marshall in South Point, Ohio, on June 22, 1983.

7   Bruce, 26.

8   Riley.

9   Larry Lester and Sammy Miller, *Black Baseball in Kansas City* (Charleston, South Carolina: Arcadia Publishing, 2000), 65.

10   Frazier Robinson with Paul Bauer *Catching Dreams* (Syracuse, New York: Syracuse University Press, 1999), 54-55.

11   Bill James, *The New Bill James Historical Baseball Abstract* (New York: Simon & Schuster, 2001), 191.

12   Joe Posnanski, *The Soul of Baseball* (New York: HarperCollins Publishers, 2007), 107-108.

13 John Virtue, *South of the Color Barrier* (Jefferson, North Carolina: McFarland & Co., 2008), 74, 76.

14 Virtue, 94.

15 William McNeil, *The California Winter League* (Jefferson, North Carolina: McFarland & Co., 2002), 213-214.

16 Riley.

17 Profile of Willard Brown on *Baseball in Wartime* website (http://www.baseballinwartime.com/player_biographies/brown_willard.htm)

18 Lieb.

19 "Browns Sign Two Negroes; Buy Option on Another," Associated Press, July 18, 1947.

20 Bruce, 115.

21 "Lehner Kills AWOL Rumor, Was Only Visiting Doctor," *The Sporting News*, July 30, 1947: 11. Rick Swaine, *The Integration of Major League Baseball* (Jefferson, North Carolina: McFarland & Co., 2009), 122.

22 Hank Thompson with Arnold Hano, "How I Wrecked My Life -- How I Hope to Save It," *Sport*, December 1965.

23 "Prospectus Q&A: Chris Wertz." *Baseball Prospectus* website (http://www.baseballprospectus.com/article.php?articleid=11462), July 14, 2010. "Feller's All-Stars Attract 148,200 in 15 Exhibitions," *The Sporting News*, October 16, 1946: 23.

24 Gordon Cobbledick, "Premature Shower in Final Game of '47 Proved Washout for Heath as a Brownie," *The Sporting News*, December 17, 1947: 7.

25 Sam Lacy, "Looking 'em Over," *Baltimore Afro-American*, August 6, 1947. Reprinted in *Black Writers/Black Baseball* (Jefferson, North Carolina: McFarland & Company, 2007), 22.

26 Ray Nelson, "More Negroes May Be Signed in Future," Says Muckerman," *St. Louis Star & Times*, August 25, 1947, 17.

27 Originally published in the *Kansas City Star*, unknown date, 1985.

28 Lieb.

29 Buck O'Neil with Steve Wulf and David Conrads. *I Was Right on Time* (New York: Simon & Schuster, 1996), 183.

30 Thomas Van Hyning, *The Santurce Crabbers* (Jefferson, North Carolina: McFarland & Company, 1999), 28.

31 Neil Lanctot, *Negro League Baseball: The Rise and Ruin of a Black Institution* (Philadelphia, Pennsylvania: University of Pennsylvania, Press 2004), 463.

32 Lester and Miller, 52.

33 Van Hyning, 25, 32, 144. The "Owl" nickname referred to Thurman's pitching performance in night games in 1947-48.

34 "Kaysee Monarchs to Launch Training Drills on April 1," *Washington Afro-American*, March 21, 1950: 19.

35 Arlene Howard with Ralph Wimbish, *Elston and Me* (Columbia, Missouri: University of Missouri Press, 2001), 22.

36 "Nats Using New Pitcher; Brown Due?" *Ottawa Citizen*, August 11, 1950: 14.

37 "Ottawa nationals Win Border Title." *Montreal Gazette*, September 9, 1950: 8.

38 "Willard 'Home Run' Brown Ha Sido Contratado por Jalisco," *El Informador* (Guadalajara, Mexico), February 21, 1951: 1.

39 *El Informador*, April 11, 1951: 1.

40 *El Informador*, April 20, 1951: 6. Jorge Alarcón, "Crespo Wins 4 Straight in Mexican Loop," *The Sporting News*, April 25, 1951: 32.

41 William F. McNeil, *Black Baseball Out of Season* (Jefferson, North Carolina: McFarland & Co., 2007), 179. Note also that Brown is not listed in Venezuelan statistics (http://planeta-beisbol.com/lvbp/index.php?Ir=M)

42 Santiago Llorens, "Brown Goes on Hit Streak for Santurce," *The Sporting News*, February 20, 1952: 27.

43 Van Hyning, *Puerto Rico's Winter League*, 142.

44 "Negro Teams in Hawkins Over Weekend," *Schenectady Gazette*, July 5, 1958.

45 Van Hyning, *The Santurce Crabbers*: 134.

46 Samuel Regalado, *Viva Baseball!* (Urbana, Illinois: University of Illinois Press, 1998), 70.

47 Thomas Van Hyning, Thomas E. *Puerto Rico's Winter League* (Jefferson, North Carolina: McFarland & Co., 1995), 142.

48 James.

49 Ted Lewis, "Willard Brown's Legacy Remains As Prominent Slugger." Original publication may have been in the *New Orleans Times-Picayune*, where Lewis was employed as sportswriter. Reposted on the W.E.A.L.L.B.E. blog, June 15, 2007. (http://weallbe.blogspot.com/2007/06/legend-of-willard-brown-forgotten.html)

JOHNNIE DAWSON

By Margaret M. Gripshover

Johnnie Dawson's life was bookended by unknowns. His early life was full of uncertainties and the end of his life passed without mention. Even his date of birth is up for debate. Most sources agree that Dawson was born on November 8, but the year varies from 1914 to 1915 to 1916. The birth year most frequently provided in official documents is 1915. Dawson's name has appeared in newspapers and various records as John Dawson, Johnny Dawson, and Johnnie Dawson, so it seems best to let the man himself decide which is correct. Since Dawson signed his World War II draft card and a marriage license as Johnnie Dawson, that is how his name appears in this chapter.

Johnnie Dawson was born on November 8, 1915, to John and Lucy (Carter) Dawson in Flournoy, Louisiana, a small farming community in Caddo Parish, about 12 miles west of downtown Shreveport. Today, Flournoy is little more than a forlorn interchange on Interstate 20, but it was once part of the sprawling 950-acre Flournoy Plantation, established in 1836 by Tennessee-born Dr. Alfred Flournoy.[1] Dawson's paternal grandfather, Ned Dawson, a mulatto born into slavery in Georgia in 1856, was living in Flournoy as early as 1870, if not before. Ned Dawson was a farmer and landowner. He and his wife, Kitty (Jones) Dawson, had at least 13 children, one of whom was John Dawson, born in Flournoy in 1878. In 1899 John Dawson married Johnnie's mother, Lucy Carter. During the 1920s, the Dawson and Carter families of Caddo Parrish were active in local and state-level agricultural activities including winning prizes for their crops (Bermuda grass hay, cowpea hay, peanut hay, and squash) and farm products (hams) at the Louisiana State Fair.[2] When the oil boom hit northwestern Louisiana in the early 1900s, some of Ned Dawson's land was leased to drillers.[3]

None of these accomplishments, however, translated into a stable home life for young Johnnie Dawson. From the start, his family was fractured and scattered. After his parents married in 1899, the family nearly vanished from the record: It was missing from the 1900, 1910, and 1920 Censuses. The only evidence that the family still existed lies in the records of three of their children, all born in Flournoy: Tom Edward Dawson, 1905; Kemp Dawson, 1914; and Johnnie Dawson, born in 1915; these identities have been extracted from marriage and military records. There are no US Census records to indicate that all three siblings ever lived together in the same household.

What happened to Johnnie Dawson's parents between 1899 and his birth in 1915 is a mystery. The difficulty in researching Dawson's early years is due to the lack of reliable records and newspaper articles. The overt racial bias of Shreveport-area newspapers resulted in a paucity of items related to African American life. For example, the *Caucasian*, a Shreveport newspaper founded after the Civil War, had an editorial policy that supported disenfranchisement of Blacks and promoted White supremacy.[4] When an article about Caddo Parish's Black population did appear in print, it usually related to criminal or other unsavory allegations. The *Caucasian* set the tone for journalism in Caddo Parish for decades to come. During Johnnie Dawson's years in baseball, Shreveport newspapers largely ignored his accomplishments, as well as those of other African Americans, on and off the playing field.

Shortly after Johnnie Dawson's birth in 1915, his parents parted company. In 1917 his mother married Franklin "Frank" Niles, a widower with at least two children. Frank and Lucy Niles expanded the household with three children (Johnnie Dawson's half-siblings): Benjamin "Bennie" Niles, Andrew Niles, and Mattie M. Niles. Frank Niles died on June 10, 1922, at age 38, leaving the widowed Lucy Carter Dawson Niles to raise many dependents on her own. The complexities and uncertainties in his mother's life and household may explain why Johnnie Dawson and his two brothers spent their childhoods living on farms with various uncles, aunts, and cousins in rural Caddo Parish. By the early 1930s, however, Johnnie and Kemp Dawson were spending more time in Shreveport. The brothers had a little too much time on their hands as evidenced by their arrests as alleged "dangerous and suspicious character[s]," for which they were fined $5 apiece.[5]

Dawson's move from rural Caddo Parish to the city of Shreveport set the stage for the start of his baseball career. When Dawson took up the game, African American baseball teams had been playing in Shreveport for nearly 40 years. The first mention of such contests appeared in an article about a tilt between "two colored teams" from Shreveport in 1898, but it is likely that other games took place prior to that date.[6] Probably the first Negro organized baseball team in Shreveport was the 1923 Black Gassers of the Negro Texas League, whose games were played at Gasser Park.[7]

Between 1934 and 1938, Dawson played on at least four teams including the Shreveport All-Stars, Shreveport Tigers (also known as the West End Tigers and Colored Tigers), Shreveport Colored Giants (also known as the Negro Giants), and the Shreveport Black Sports. Based on newspaper accounts of his early career in Shreveport, Dawson was a catcher from day one of his career.

The earliest record of Dawson's baseball career came at the end of the 1934 season when he played for the Shreveport All-Stars in a series with the Monroe Monarchs for the "state championship."[8] The outcome of the series did not appear in either the Shreveport or Monroe newspapers. It is worth noting that Winfield "Gus" Welch, a mediocre player who hit his stride as a manager, skippered the All-Stars.[9] Between 1941 and 1948, he managed the Birmingham Black Barons, the West All Stars, and the New York Cubans. Dawson started and ended his career as a professional baseball player with Welch in Shreveport and ended his career with Welch in Birmingham. Welch had an eye for talent and recruited future Kansas City Monarch Frank "Dick" Bradley out of a Bossier Parish cotton patch in 1935.[10] At least one of Dawson's teammates on the 1934 Shreveport All-Stars also had a professional baseball career: John Matthew "Johnny" Markham, who pitched nine seasons in the Negro Leagues between 1930 and 1945, including hitches with the Kansas City Monarchs, Monroe Monarchs, and the Black Barons.

Dawson's career began in earnest in 1935 when he took the field as a catcher for the Shreveport Tigers.[11] He spent three seasons with the Tigers, also known as the Queensboro Tigers and West End Tigers.[12] Dawson's Tigers had a successful season and the reputation as the champion Negro team in Shreveport and of "the

Catcher Johnnie Dawson played briefly for both the Monarchs and Birmingham Black Barons in 1942. (Reno Gazette-Journal, July 25, 1941)

Ark-La-Tex."[13] As the season ended in September, the Tigers' record was 35 wins against five losses.[14] In their last series of the year, they faced a familiar opponent, the barnstorming Shreveport Acme Giants, with manager Winfield Welch and Johnny Markham on the mound. The 1935 series ended in a tie and the rivalry continued into the spring of 1936 when the

Giants claimed the city crown by nipping Dawson and his Shreveport Tigers, 7-6.[15] One of Dawson's future Monarchs teammates played for the Acme Giants when they did battle against the Shreveport Tigers in 1935 and 1936 – Hall of Famer Buck O'Neil.

The 1936 season ended for Dawson and the Shreveport Tigers as it did in 1935, with a game against Welch's Acme Giants. The only difference was that in 1936 the final tilt was rained out rather than ending in a tie. Dawson had a good year in 1936, hitting game-winning home runs in games against the Black Mule Riders of Magnolia, Louisiana, in June, generating pivotal RBIs, and catching a no-hitter for the Tigers.[16] His "heavy hitting pulled the locals out of a tight spot" against the Little Rock Black Tigers in August.[17] The Tigers claimed the 1936 "Ark-La-Tex crown for colored teams" and the gate receipts with a win over the Black Tigers at Dixie Park in Shreveport.[18]

Dawson's best year in baseball was 1937. He started the season with the Shreveport Tigers of the Negro Texas League, but finished with the barnstorming Shreveport Colored Giants (formerly the Acme Giants), a "farm team" for the Kansas City Monarchs.[19] Coming off a 51-win 1936 season, the Tigers opened the 1937 season in April with an exhibition game at Dixie Park against the Kansas City Monarchs. The Monarchs were no strangers to Shreveport fans. They had played exhibition games against the Black Sports, a Shreveport nine, as early as 1929.[20] The Monarchs, who used Shreveport as a pit stop before heading to Texas and Mexico, defeated the Tigers by a 12-4 score.[21]

While Dawson was enjoying his best year in baseball, his family life was less settled. His two brothers, Tom and Kemp, left Shreveport for the West Coast and settled in Los Angeles. They were just two of the thousands of African Americans who left Louisiana during the 1930s and 1940s as part of the Great Migration that bypassed industrial cities of the North for sunnier climes in California.[22] In fact, Dawson's mother and nearly all of his extended family left Shreveport for Los Angeles before 1945. Kemp Dawson, like his younger brother, was also an athlete, but he chose boxing over baseball. That may have been a practical matter of form following function. Unlike Johnnie, Kemp Dawson's massive physique was more suited for combat than catching; according to his World War II draft card from 1940, he was 6-feet tall and weighed 281 pounds. Kemp Dawson's portly profile earned him the nickname The Blimp in Los Angeles-area amateur boxing circles, and his pugilistic career was not one for the record books.[23] In one of his early bouts in 1937, "it wasn't 30 seconds before tubby Dawson had been deposited on the canvas."[24] One of Kemp's final appearances in the ring was a cruelly "laughable heavyweight bout" during which his boxing trunks "split in the fore" and "Dawson was led from the ring with a towel draped midship."[25]

Meanwhile, back in Shreveport, Johnnie Dawson was enjoying more success behind the plate than his brother experienced between the ropes. All that Johnnie needed now was a change of uniform. In March the Tigers announced that Dawson would return to his backstopping duties for the 1937 season.[26] Dawson's tenure with the Tigers was brief. It ended with an exhibition game against the Kansas City Monarchs at Dixie Park in Shreveport on April 11, 1937.[27] As of May 1937, the Shreveport Tigers became the Shreveport Negro Giants or Colored Giants, a traveling team managed by Sam Crawford that played most of its games on the road in the Midwest and the West.[28] For one such game, the Colored Giants crossed bats with the Giant Collegians of Piney Woods, Mississippi, on a diamond in Wisconsin Rapids, Wisconsin, that was billed as an exhibition by "two darkie ball clubs."[29] Shreveport was touted as a "farm team of the Kansas City Monarchs," with a lineup that included Johnnie Dawson "behind the plate … hitting well over .300."[30]

Dawson continued to display his power at the plate as the Shreveport Colored Giants traveled westward to Montana, Washington, and British Columbia. In British Columbia he hammered a homer while going 3-for-5 in a losing effort against the Chilliwack Cherries.[31] In Lewiston, Washington, one young fan who came to see the Colored Giants play was so enthused by the experience that he "insisted on blacking his face when he went in the box to pitch for his sandlot team."[32] The press remarked, "But the weather in Lewiston has been a bit hot, he perspired freely, and before the game had gone far it was difficult to determine whether he was Johnson of the Colored Giants or Walter Johnson the Great."[33] If Dawson and his teammates expected less racism in the North, they were mistaken. The following week when they played a game in Laurel, Montana, a local newspaper referred to the Colored Giants as "big [n-word] … mowing everything before them."[34] In Billings, the locals invited Dawson and his Shreveport teammates to a "Dutch lunch" but with the expectation that they would perform for their meal including "entertainment with song and dance novelties."[35]

It is likely that Dawson did not enjoy his "Dutch lunch." By the time he left Montana in late July, he was on the disabled list. When the Shreveport Colored Giants arrived in Wisconsin for a tilt with New London's Knapstein Brews, the local newspaper touted Dawson as "a hustler," but the injured Dawson was not in the lineup.[36] His next appearance came on August 21, when he played left field during a Shreveport's 4-2 victory over the Cambridge Danes in Cambridge, Wisconsin.[37] Although the nature of Dawson's injury is unknown, whatever was ailing him took a toll on his power. During the game against the Danes, Dawson went hitless in four at-bats.[38] He returned to his catching duties by early September when Shreveport played in a series of games in Iowa to cap off the 1937 season. With Dawson behind the plate, the Colored Giants defeated local nines in Storm Lake and Cedar Rapids. Shreveport's final road game of the year resulted in a win over the Muscatine Indees "on a diamond in Conesville, Iowa, by a score of 5 to 3."[39] The Muscatine newspaper erroneously referred to the Shreveport squad as the Acme Colored Giants.[40] The contest in Conesville was the featured event for the community's annual Watermelon Day.[41]

Although 1937 started with a bang and was Dawson's most productive year, it ended with a whimper. The injury he suffered in Montana in July neutralized his prowess at the plate and, for a time, sidelined him defensively as well Although the precise nature of his injury is unknown, it hindered his effectiveness. Dawson's 1940 US Army draft card provides some possible insights. According to the document, Dawson's distinguishing physical characteristics included a "scar on the left side of the forehead," and a broken "right forefinger." In any event, the cumulative effects from his injuries contributed to his decline. James A. Riley's assessment of Dawson as having "an average arm but below average in other phases of the game" was true as far as Dawson's Negro League career was concerned.[42] His best days on the diamond were already mostly behind him by the time he signed with the Kansas City Monarchs in 1938.

Dawson returned to the Shreveport Colored Giants in the spring of 1938 and was off to a good start. In the first game of the year, he banged out a double as Shreveport defeated the reigning Negro National League champions, the Homestead Grays, 6-2.[43] The victory was bittersweet as it was the swan song for the Shreveport Colored Giants. Within a week, they disbanded and reconstituted themselves as the Shreveport Black Sports, members of the Negro Texas League.[44] The "Sports" moniker was a clever play on a common abbreviation for Shreveport – "S'port." The Black Sports dubbed Dawson as their starting receiver.[45] However, just as he was set to take up his mitt with the Sports, the Monarchs came calling.

Dawson made his debut in the major Negro Leagues with the Monarchs as he joined the Monarchs' cadre of catchers that included starters Harry Else and Frank Duncan. Dawson's first game with the Monarchs took place in Chicago on July 31, 1938, when he replaced Else in the lineup during a 7-2 loss to the Chicago American Giants.[46] The next day the Monarchs traveled to Davenport, Iowa, for an exhibition tilt against the Illinois and Iowa All Stars before a crowd of about 800.[47] The Monarchs dethroned the All Stars, 6-1, giving Dawson his first taste of victory in a Monarchs uniform, albeit in a nonleague game.[48] It was not a sterling debut for Dawson given that he went 1-for-4 at the plate and was charged with two passed balls behind it.[49] Dawson had two more appearances as a Monarch in 1938, but neither effort did much to merit promotion to starting catcher. He replaced Else in the top of the ninth during the second game of a doubleheader against the Indianapolis ABCs.[50] The Monarchs won both games and Dawson's only "contribution" was one passed ball in one half-inning of work.[51] His final appearance was a rare starting role with the Monarchs in a 12-9 victory over the Birmingham Black Barons.[52] For this, the final league game of the Monarchs' season, Dawson reunited with his former batterymate from the Shreveport All Stars, Johnny Markham, who relieved starter John "Big Train" Jackson.[53] After the game, the Monarchs left Alabama without Dawson as they headed out on a barnstorming tour.[54]

Out of a job with the Monarchs and back home in Shreveport, Dawson landed right back where he had started the year – catching for the Shreveport Black Sports. Returning with him were three fellow former Monarchs and Louisiana natives: pitcher Frank Bradley, outfielder Willie "Bill" Simms, and second baseman Willie Horne.[55] The reunion lasted just one game, a season-ending contest against the Galveston Bucs, the outcome of which did not appear in the Shreveport newspapers.

• JOHNNIE DAWSON •

Dawson did not play for a Negro League team in 1939. He spent the bulk of the baseball season with the traveling edition of the New Orleans Crescent Stars, former members of the defunct first edition of the Negro Southern League. Once more Dawson found himself managed by Winfield Welch. In late April, the Crescent Stars kicked off their 1939 campaign by barnstorming with Satchel Paige's All-Stars through towns in east Texas, all within a hundred miles of Shreveport.[56] The Crescent Stars' Texas campaign concluded in the city of Tyler, hometown of Negro League catcher and 2006 Baseball Hall of Fame inductee Louis Santop.[57]

After parting company with Paige's All-Stars in June, Welch, Dawson, and the Crescent Stars headed to Canada for a tour with "Ham Olive's Bearded House of Davidites."[58] The two teams spent most of the summer of 1939 in Canada and the Northern US. For Dawson, the higher latitudes did much to improve his baseball attitudes, and he was lauded as "one of the smartest catchers seen here in many a day."[59] In the Crescent Stars' 7-3 victory over the Davidites in Calgary, Dawson "made several almost impossible catches and time and again drew the applause of fans."[60] He rediscovered his batting prowess of early 1937 and produced a .315 batting average with 10 home runs.[61] Perhaps Dawson's return to form was inspired by the company of two very different individuals with whom he shared the summer of 1939. The first was the Crescent Stars' pitcher, Johnny Blackwell, a student-athlete at Fisk University and likely the first collegian Dawson encountered as a teammate.[62] The second was Helen Stephens, who toured with the Davidites as the "famous Missouri girl athlete" and the holder of 14 "world, Olympic and Canadian records."[63] Stephens was more than just a sideshow act; during her remarkable life, she broke sporting records and societal barriers for women. Among her many accomplishments were earning a Gold Medal in the 1936 Olympics in Berlin, playing professional women's basketball, joining the US Marine Corps just after World War II, and charting a career for herself with the Defense Mapping Agency in St. Louis.[64] That summer, Stephens, who was White, also performed track event exhibitions with Jesse Owens and the House of David aggregation as well as other Negro League teams such as the Pittsburgh Crawfords.[65]

Dawson capped off his 1939 season as a member of the South All-Stars in the Negro North-South game, held in early October at Pelican Stadium in New Orleans, though he did not play in the game.[66] The South's skipper, Winfield Welch, chose Larry "Iron Man" Brown of the Memphis Red Sox over Dawson to work behind the plate.[67] Welch's choice of catcher for the all-star tilt was of little significance, however, as the North All-Stars demolished the South All-Stars, 10-1.[68] The following year, Dawson revisited this also-ran relationship when he crouched in Brown's shadow for nearly the entire 1940 season with Memphis.

Although Dawson saw no action in the major Negro Leagues in 1939, he made up for it in 1940 when he played for two teams, the Chicago American Giants and the Memphis Red Sox. Something else that Dawson did twice in 1940 was to appear in census enumerations in two different cities. In April, a census taker counted Dawson as part of his mother's household on Abbie Street in Shreveport. Two months later he was counted again, this time in Memphis, where he roomed with manager Ruben Jones and six of his Red Sox teammates, in a boarding house on Florida Street, just about a mile from Martin Park, the club's home field. Dawson stated his occupation as a professional ball player on both occasions.

Dawson made his first appearance as a catcher for the Chicago American Giants during an exhibition junket through Arkansas and Tennessee.[69] He jumped from the American Giants to the Memphis Red Sox by mid-May and remained with Memphis for the balance of the season. Dawson played in four league games for the Red Sox in place of starter Larry Brown, but he generated only a paltry .125 batting average. Conversely, Brown had a stellar year in 1940, with Cum Posey dubbing him as an "All American" catcher in the *Pittsburgh Courier*.[70] Dawson did accomplish something of note that year; he earned his first nickname. In August, during a swing through the East Coast, a Red Bank, New Jersey, sportswriter tagged Dawson with the moniker Pepper Pot Dawson.[71] The reporter gave no justification for naming Dawson after a type of an African-style soup that was popular in the Philadelphia area.[72] Although baseball scribes assigned the nickname to describe the "peppery" play and banter of St. Louis Cardinal Johnny "Pepper" Martin, the name did not stick to Dawson.[73] He finished the rest of his career without a catchy nickname, an unusual occurrence, especially in the Negro Leagues. One other thing that did not stick around was Dawson himself. Pepper Pot Dawson found himself in the soup about a week later when Memphis dropped him from its roster just before the team headed to Harrisburg, Pennsylvania, in September to face the Homestead Grays for the deceptively billed "Negro World Series."[74]

In October 1940, Dawson registered for the US Army with his local draft board. He was unemployed, living with his mother, and described as standing 6-feet-1 and weighing 176 pounds, with a scar on his forehead and a broken finger. Sometime later, Dawson's home address on his Army document was edited to read "920 E. Ninth Street Kansas City," Missouri.

Despite Dawson's inclusion in a photograph of the 1941 Memphis Red Sox, he did not play for Memphis in 1941.[75] When he first donned his catcher's mask that year, it was as a member of Satchel Paige's traveling all-stars. In June, Dawson caught both games of a doubleheader for Paige's amalgamation in Cincinnati against the Ethiopian Clowns, reported to have been Paige's first-ever appearance in the Queen City.[76] After splitting the twin bill with the Clowns at Crosley Field, Dawson and Paige's All-Stars headed to South Bend, Indiana, where they edged the local Studebaker Athletics, 1-0.[77] Paige tossed his usual three innings of work and Dawson went hitless in three plate appearances.[78] Dawson and Paige's nine returned to Cincinnati for another go at the Clowns with similar results – another split decision.[79]

After his stint with Paige's traveling show, Dawson was signed by the Monarchs once again, though he did not appear in any official league games that season. Joe Greene was crowned as the Monarchs' starting catcher and Dawson was shunted off to the Monarchs' B-team barnstorming franchise. He spent most of the summer of 1941 bouncing around the backroads of Oregon and Montana with the House of David nine, under the tutelage of player-manager Walter "Newt" Joseph.[80] It was a long and grueling slog. After a 14-0 massacre of the Eugene Athletics in July, a local sportswriter noted, "The tiring [Monarchs], who traveled over 400 miles by car in Oregon's worst heat wave in years," still managed to pound out 18 hits, one of which was an RBI contributed by Johnnie Dawson.[81] By the end of July, his road trip was over. Dawson had managed a few bright moments at bat – a double here, and a homer there – but it was becoming clear that the sun was setting on his career as a professional baseball player.

In the spring of 1942, the Unites States was at war when Dawson left his mother's house in Shreveport to return to Kansas City for his final season in Negro League baseball. Dawson wore number 14 on his uniform that year and was one of four catchers on the Monarchs roster. He was the third-string catcher behind starters Joe Greene and Frank Duncan.[82] Dawson appeared in nine league games with the Monarchs in 1942, and his abysmal .100 batting average kept him in a supporting role. A rare highlight for Dawson occurred in April, during an extra-inning game against the Homestead Grays at Pelican Stadium in New Orleans, when he hit a walk-off single that sent Monarchs center fielder Willard Brown across the plate in the bottom of the 10th to clinch the game for Kansas City, 5-4.[83] Such moments were rare for Dawson, and overall it was a season to forget. In a battle against the Birmingham Black Barons in June, his frustrations boiled over and resulted in his ejection from the game for cursing the umpire.[84] As the summer of 1942 progressed, Dawson wearily barnstormed across the Eastern US – including tilts against the Green Sox of Fremont, Ohio, and the Quakers of Scranton, Pennsylvania – the former described as a "listless battle" with the locals highly critical of his batterymate Satchel Paige's "lackluster play."[85]

Dawson's final appearance in a league game for the Monarchs came on July 26, 1942, "Satchel Paige Day," when he donned his mitt in relief of Duncan in a losing effort in the first half of a doubleheader against the Memphis Red Sox at Wrigley Field.[86] Paige won the nightcap against Memphis, but Dawson was not in the lineup.[87] His backstop work with Paige in Scranton a few days later was likely Dawson's final appearance wearing number 14 for the Monarchs. He was listed as a possible starter for a Monarchs exhibition game against the Philadelphia Stars at Island Park Field in Harrisburg on August 12, but the weather intervened.[88] In mid-August Monarchs manager Frank Duncan released Dawson from the Monarchs, thus denying him an opportunity to appear with the team in the 1942 Negro League World Series.[89] Duncan made the move to make room for a new catcher, Frazier "Pep" Robinson, previously with the Baltimore Elite Giants, to replace Dawson as the backup to injured starting catcher, Joe Greene.[90] Pep Robinson's nickname had more to do with sarcasm than with the spiciness of a pepper pot. Robinson generally lacked pep and was also known as "Slow," a nickname given to him by Paige.[91] This was the "only lineup change that Duncan deemed necessary to get the Monarchs to another league and negro [sic] world championship."[92] As it turned out, Robinson did not add any more pep to the

Monarchs than Dawson, and he saw little action after Greene returned to the lineup.[93]

After his mid-August release from the Monarchs, Dawson signed with the Black Barons. It is possible that Birmingham made the move because they were without the services of their regular catcher, Paul James Hardy, who was in Chicago to play in the East West All Star Game.[94] Dawson's old friend and mentor, Black Barons manager Winfield Welch, may have also facilitated Dawson's merger after Birmingham lost eight players to military service.[95] Dawson debuted with his new team on August 15, 1942, as the starting catcher in the first game of a doubleheader against the Cincinnati Buckeyes, which featured a "Jitterbug Contest."[96] Perhaps it was Dawson who was doing the jittering as another backup backstop for the Black Barons, Harry Barnes, relieved him of his duties.[97] For Dawson, his stint with the Black Barons was like *déjà vu* all over again; once more, he found himself as the understudy to Paul Hardy.

Dawson's tenure with the Black Barons was brief and unremarkable. Out of World Series contention, Birmingham spent the bulk of August and September barnstorming in the Midwest to capture as many gate receipts as possible. Box scores for such games were rare, making it difficult to determine Dawson's contributions. In the waning days of the summer of 1942, Dawson was the starting catcher in a just a handful of games and saw some action in right field and at third base.[98]

In mid-September the Black Barons toured through Missouri and Indiana with the Ethiopian Clowns. Dawson was the starting catcher when the Clowns swept a doubleheader at Victory Field in Indianapolis, 3-1 and 7-4.[99] His name last appeared in a line score as part of the battery for the Barons in an embarrassing 6-5 loss to the Clowns in Springfield, Illinois.[100] The Barons and Clowns shared 10 errors and a meager payday from the gate receipts from the 300 fans who braved the bitterly cold weather.[101] On September 22, 1942, they played the two final games of their road trip at City Stadium in St. Joseph, Missouri.[102] It was a bizarre doubleheader in which the winner of the opener earned the right to play the nightcap against the Monarchs, who the night before had engaged in a controversial World Series game in which the Homestead Grays used ineligible players to defeat Kansas City, 4-1.[103] The Black Barons earned the right to play the Monarchs after dispatching the Clowns, 7-2, and then vanquished Kansas City, the soon-to-be Negro League world champions, by a score of 5-0.[104] With no box score to rely on, it is unclear if Dawson took the field for the Black Barons' victory that night. The line score indicates that he was not the catcher for either contest, but, given the team's bare-bones roster, it is possible that he took the field in some capacity. For Dawson, there may have been some element of satisfaction in defeating the Monarchs since they had released him right before their World Series run. However, there was little pride to be felt given that 10 errors were racked up and both teams' lineups were so threadbare that the Black Barons' 42-year old skipper, Winfield Welch, pitched the first game while the Monarchs manager, Frank Duncan, stepped in as Kansas City's catcher for the nightcap.[105] One local sportswriter was so appalled by the lack of effort that he claimed that the "Clowns were quite frank about not wanting to play the second game," and that the "Barons were not carrying their advertised stars."[106] He accused the Clowns and Black Barons of being "interested only in grabbing their share of the gate and getting out of town."[107]

By late September it was clear that Dawson and his Black Barons were running on fumes, due to players leaving the team to serve in the military. Even Birmingham's bus went missing after an accident on an Indiana highway that totaled the vehicle and left the players no choice but to take a train back to Birmingham for their final homestand.[108] Dawson and his teammates escaped the calamity uninjured.

The last game of the Black Barons' 1942 season was against the Negro American League All-Stars. It was also the swan song for Dawson's career in Negro League baseball. The game took place at Rickwood Field on Sunday, October 4, 1942, and the Black Barons defeated the All-Stars by a 6-3 score.[109] Black Barons owner Tom Hayes promised the players a "generous portion of the gate receipts" that would serve as a year-end bonus.[110] For some Birmingham baseball fans, however, the victory brought no joy to the Magic City. The criticisms voiced in St. Joseph, Missouri, regarding lackluster play followed the Black Barons to Birmingham. The event at Rickwood was dismissed by one columnist who reported that fans complained that the "teams were badly jumbled as far as the lineups were concerned, and it seemed as though it was just something thrown together to get the fans' money."[111]

After this final debacle, Dawson and his Birmingham teammates "packed their respective grips and departed for their respective homes."[112] For Dawson, that meant using his bonus money for bus fare to return to his mother's house on Abbie Street in Shreveport. Dawson had little downtime after arriving home. On January 24, 1943, he reported to his local Caddo Parish draft board. On February 3, 1943, Dawson enlisted as a private in the Army, and, according to his enlistment documents, he was 6-feet tall, weighed 173 pounds, and possessed a ninth-grade education. His occupation category was "Athletes, sports instructors, and sports officials"; however, after he joined the Army in 1943, Dawson would never again claim the title of "professional baseball player."

During World War II, Dawson was stationed in Southern California, where he reunited with his brothers Tom and Kemp, who were living in Los Angeles. Tom and Kemp Dawson boarded in the household of another family from Shreveport. In fact, during the 1930s and 1940s, Los Angeles was such a popular destination for migrants from Caddo Parish that one neighborhood earned the name "Little Shreveport."[113] Dawson's family contributed to this migration pattern. His mother, two brothers, and other close relatives left Shreveport during this era and settled mainly in South Central Los Angeles, in Little Shreveport. After his discharge from the Army on March 28, 1946, Dawson returned to civilian life, earning a living as a barber and, once again, playing baseball.[114]

Within 10 days of his discharge, Dawson was the new catcher and occasional outfielder for the Pacific Pipe Lines, also known as the Pacific Pipe Line Colored Stars.[115] The team boasted a lineup consisting of players with "professional experience with strong Negro teams."[116] One of his new teammates was a familiar face – center fielder and fellow Shreveport native Willie "Bill" Simms, who played with Dawson and the Monarchs in 1942.[117] The Pipes were not exactly smoking up the semipro leagues. In his debut with his new team in early April, Dawson went 2-for-4 at the plate, but his efforts were for naught as the Rosabell Plumbers drained the Pipes, 11-2.[118] Dawson continued to play for the Pipes through June, when they lost to the San Pedro Merchants in a twin bill described as being "of the nightmarish type with errors, wild pitches, bases on balls and mental lapses occurring as frequently as clowns at a three ring circus."[119] Despite the Pipes' poor performance, Dawson enjoyed a bit of a personal revival. He was a regular in the lineup and swatted a respectable .286.[120]

By the end of June, however, the Pipes disbanded. A few months later, Dawson joined the Al-Leaverenz All Stars, a semipro team in the newly formed Orange Belt Winter Baseball League.[121] The A.L. Leaverenz Paving Company of Monrovia, California, sponsored the team; its name also appeared as Leverenz or Al-Leverenz.[122]

Dawson was a catcher and occasional outfielder for the Al-Leaverenz All Stars for two seasons. Many of his teammates were Negro League veterans including his manager, Nathaniel "Nate" Moreland, a former pitcher for the Monarchs and the Baltimore Elite Giants.[123] But the sun was setting on Dawson's baseball days. After the 1947 season ended for the All Stars, he married Lottie Mae Abner, a waitress, in Los Angeles, on October 15, 1947. The union did not last, and the couple had no children together.

Dawson's career in semipro baseball effectively ended with his marriage. The Al-Leaverenz team folded before the 1948 season started and Dawson did not appear on the roster for other teams in the Orange Belt League. The only "Johnnie Dawson" who continued to appear in the sports pages after 1947 was another Californian, Johnny Dawson, a notable amateur golf champion and professional golf-course designer.[124]

Little is known about Dawson's personal life after this point, other than that he continued to live in the Los Angeles area until his death at the age of 69 on August 6, 1984. No death notices or obituaries appeared in any Los Angeles or Shreveport newspapers to mark his passing or the deaths of any of his immediate family members. Dawson died almost a year to the day after his brother Kemp Dawson died in San Francisco. His brother Tom died in 1976, one year after the death of their mother, Lucy Carter Dawson Niles. Johnnie Dawson is buried in Inglewood Park Cemetery in Inglewood, California, in a section devoted to military veterans. He is not the only member of the 1942 Kansas City Monarchs interred there. Monarchs third baseman Herb Souell, who died on July 12, 1978, rests with Dawson in the cemetery.

Sources

All Negro League statistics and records were taken from Seamheads.com unless otherwise indicated. Ancestry.com was consulted for census, birth, death, marriage, military, and other public records.

• JOHNNIE DAWSON •

Notes

1 "Old Homes of Greenwood Tell Story of Caddo Pioneers," *Times* (Shreveport, Louisiana), December 13, 1925: 27.

2 "North and South Louisiana Share Awards to Negroes," *Shreveport Journal*, October 25, 1923: 12; "Award Prizes to Negro Boys, *Shreveport Times*, November 7, 1926: 3; "Caddo Negroes Given Agricultural Awards," *Shreveport Journal*, November 16, 1926: 16.

3 "Leasing Near Gulf Test Recorded," *Shreveport Times*, September 24, 1936: 16; Henry Wiencek, "Bloody Caddo: Economic Change and Racial Continuity During Louisiana's Oil Boom: 1896-1922," *Louisiana History: The Journal of the Louisiana Historical Association*," 60 (2019): 199-224.

4 Library of Congress, "About *The Caucasian*," https://chroniclingamerica.loc.gov/lccn/sn88064469/.

5 "3 Negroes Fined $100 for Having Untaxed Whiskey," *Shreveport Journal*, January 15, 1935: 1.

6 *Shreveport Journal*, April 18, 1898: 4.

7 "Beaumont Blacks Open Season with Local Negro Club," *Shreveport Times*, May 10, 1923: 8.

8 "Negro Teams in Baseball Game This Afternoon," *Shreveport Times*, October 7, 1934: 16.

9 James A. Riley, *The Biographical Encyclopedia of the Negro Baseball Leagues* (New York: Carroll & Graf, 1994), 825.

10 "Hall of Fame to Honor Two Local Negro League Stars," *Shreveport Times*, July 24, 1991: 3B.

11 "Shreveport Negro Baseball Team in 22d Straight Win," *Shreveport Journal*, July 22, 1935: 10.

12 "Negro Girl May Pitch in Contest Against Tigers," *Shreveport Times*, July 10, 1935: 11; "Tigers to Play Indians of Hope, Arkansas Sunday," *Shreveport Times*, July 18, 1935: 10.

13 "Acme Giants Won 107 Contests on Tour This Season," *Shreveport Times*, September 28, 1935: 14.

14 "Acme Giants Won 107 Contests on Tour This Season."

15 "One Bad Inning Costs Tigers Game with Acme Giants," *Shreveport Times*, April 6, 1936: 9.

16 "Monroe Monarchs Play Tigers Twin Bill Here Sunday," *Shreveport Times*, June 20, 1936: 15; "No-Hit Contest Features Twin Win by Tigers," *Shreveport Times*, July 13, 1936: 12.

17 "Shreveport Negro Team Wins Two," *Shreveport Journal*, August 17, 1936: 8.

18 "Local Negro Nine Wins Ark-La-Tex Baseball Laurels," *Shreveport Times*, September 21, 1936: 9.

19 "Colored Teams to Clash Here Tonight," *Daily Tribune* (Wisconsin Rapids, Wisconsin), June 5, 1937: 5.

20 "Black Sports Will Play Kansas City," *Shreveport Journal*, March 29, 1929: 21.

21 "Monarchs Defeat Shreveport Nine Before Big Crowd," *Shreveport Times*, April 12, 1937: 9.

22 Douglas Flamming, *Bound for Freedom: Black Los Angeles in Jim Crow America* (Berkeley: University of California Press, 2005), 48.

23 "Ralph Ring, Farrell Rematched [sic]," *Progress Bulletin* (Pomona, California), May 15, 1940: 10.

24 Eddie West, "Rattled Referee Gives Nod to Mendez, Wrong Fighter," *Santa Ana* (California) *Register*, April 17, 1937: 6.

25 "Rematches Top Amateur Card," *Los Angeles Times*, August 29, 1937: 28.

26 "Tigers to Usher in Season Today Against Houston," *Shreveport Times*, March 28, 1937: 19.

27 "Leading Negro Teams to Meet at Dixie Park," *Shreveport Times*, April 11, 1937: 24.

28 "A's Defeated in Opener, 2-1," *South Bend* (Indiana) *Tribune*, May 26, 1937: 21; "Albion Tigers Win in 10th on Squeeze Play," *Wisconsin State Journal* (Madison), June 1, 1937: 14.

29 "Colored Teams to Clash Here Tonight," *Wisconsin Rapids Daily Tribune*, June 5, 1937: 5.

30 "Colored Teams to Clash Here Tonight."

31 "Dark Boys Win and Lose to Cherries," *Chilliwack* (British Columbia) *Progress*, July 7, 1937: 10.

32 "Sport Shots," *Chilliwack Progress*, July 14, 1937: 10.

33 "Sport Shots."

34 "Colored Giants to Play Laurel Team Thursday Evening," *Laurel* (Montana) *Lookout*, July 28, 1937: 4.

35 "Gun Club Has Party," *Billings* (Montana) *Gazette*, July 31, 1937: 10.

36 "Brews Will Meet Shreveport Team," *Post-Crescent* (Appleton, Wisconsin), August 16, 1937: 16.

37 "Shreveport Tips Cambridge, 4-2," *Wisconsin State Journal*, August 22, 1937: 9.

38 "Shreveport Tips Cambridge, 4-2."

39 "Indies Win Two, Lose One Game Over Weekend," *Muscatine* (Iowa) *Journal*, September 13, 1937: 6.

40 "Indies Win Two, Lose One Game Over Weekend."

41 "Baseball," *Muscatine Journal*, September 10, 1937: 10.

42 Riley, 222.

43 "Local Negro Nine Defeats Colored Big Loop Champs," *Shreveport Times*, April 6, 1938: 12.

44 "Negroes to Open Season at League Park Here Sunday," *Shreveport Times*, April 14, 1938: 13.

45 "Local Negro Club Will Put Spring Team in League," *Shreveport Times*, April 15, 1938: 19.

46 "Giants Monarchs Split," *Chicago Tribune*, August 1, 1938: 23.

47 "Colored Nine Gets 4 Runs in 1st Frame," *Daily Times* (Davenport, Iowa), August 2, 1938: 12.

48 "Colored Nine Gets 4 Runs in 1st Frame."

49 "Monarchs Win 6 to 1 Battle from All-Stars," *Quad City Times* (Davenport, Iowa), August 2, 1938: 11.

50 "Two for the Monarchs," *Kansas City* (Missouri) *Times*, August 15, 1938: 10

51 "Two for the Monarchs."

52 "Second Half of League Race Ends in Dispute," *Chicago Defender*, September 10, 1938: 8.

53 "Second Half of League Race Ends in Dispute."

54 "Provide Fitting Setting for End of Ball Season in Lincoln, Nebr.," *Omaha Guide*, September 24, 1938: 7; Riley, 255.

55 "Negro Teams Play for Southwest Baseball Title," *Shreveport Times*, September 9, 1938: 14; "Galveston Negro Team Will Play Here Sunday," *Shreveport Times*, September 16, 1938: 16.

56 "Famous Negro Baseball Team Be Here Soon," *Kilgore* (Texas) *News*, April 30, 1939: 5; "Satchel Paige Brings All-Star Negro Nine Here," *Courier-Times* (Tyler, Texas), April 30, 1939: 13; "Second Big-Time Negro Baseball Game Tuesday, *News Messenger* (Marshall, Texas), April 30, 1939: 5.

57 "Santop Honored in Cooperstown," *Morning Telegraph* (Tyler, Texas), July 31, 2006: 23.

58 "Road Clubs in Action," *Star-Phoenix* (Saskatoon, Saskatchewan), June 23, 1939: 15.

59 "Davidites Take Beating from Orleans Stars," *Calgary Herald*, July 8, 1939: 7.

60 "Davidites Take Beating from Orleans Stars."

61 "South Team for All-Star Negro Game Announced," *New Orleans Times-Picayune*, September 28, 1939: 14.

62 "Road Clubs in Action," *Star-Phoenix*, June 23, 1939: 15.

63 "Road Clubs in Action."

64 Harry Levins, "Helen Stephens Dies at 75," *St. Louis Post-Dispatch*, January 18, 1994: 11-12.

65 "Jesse Owens to Compete Against Helen Stephens," *Cedar Rapids* (Iowa) *Gazette*, August 17, 1939: 11: "Famous Girl Sprinter Billed at Parkway," *Louisville Courier-Journal*, August 31, 1939: 16.

66 "South Team for All-Star Negro Game Announced," *Times-Picayune*, September 28, 1939: 14.

67 "South Team for All-Star Negro Game Announced."

68 "North Swamps South in Negro Ball Game," *New Orleans States*, October 2, 1939: 10.

69 "Chicago Has Big Inning," *Chicago Defender*, May 11, 1940: 22; "Chicago, Memphis Divide," *Chicago Defender*, May 11, 1940.

70 Cum Posey, "National Leaguers Dominate All-American," *Pittsburgh Courier*, November 2, 1940: 17.

71 "Pirates Meet '39 Negro Champs Tonight," *Red Bank* (New Jersey) *Daily Standard*, August 6, 1940: 15.

72 Ron Avery, "A Soup Salutes Innard [sic] City," *Philadelphia Daily News*, November 18, 1991: 6

73 "Pepper Martin May Be Traded, Hot Stovers Say," *Journal Times* (Racine, Wisconsin), January 7, 1940: 7.

74 "Negro World Series Here," *Harrisburg* (Pennsylvania) *Telegraph*, September 11, 1940: 17.

75 "1941 Edition of the Memphis Red Sox," *Chicago Defender*, June 7, 1941: 23.

76 "Negro Nines Divide Double Bill," *Cincinnati Enquirer*, June 9, 1941: 18.

77 Bob Overtaker, "Stars Defeat Studebakers by 1-0 Score," *South Bend Tribune*, June 13, 1941: 1, 2.

78 Overtaker.

79 "Satch's Team Splits with Clown Nine," *Pittsburgh Courier*, June 21, 1941: 16.

80 "Ray T. Rocene, "Sports Jabs," *Missoulan* (Missoula, Montana), June 22, 1941: 7; "Davids Annex First Game," *Billings Gazette*, June 27, 1941: 10; "Davids Rally by Monarchs for Great Crowd," *Montana Standard* (Butte), June 27, 1941: 10.

81 "Kansas City Monarchs Whitewash Eugene Athletics, 14-0," *Eugene* (Oregon) *Guard*, July 15, 1941: 6.

82 Frank A. Young, "Bob Feller Joins Dean Game Against Paige," *Chicago Defender*, May 23, 1942: 19.

83 "Kansas City Splits Even with Grays," *Chicago Defender*, May 9, 1942: 21.

84 "Black Barons Split Double-Header with Kansas City Monarchs 12-2 and 5-4," *Weekly Review* (Birmingham, Alabama), June 13, 1942: 7.

85 "Eighth Inning Miscue Gives Monarchs Unearned 7 to 5 Win," *Fremont* (Ohio) *News-Messenger*, July 24, 1942: 9; "Monarchs Down Quaker Squad in Listless Battle," *Scranton Times-Tribune*, August 1, 1942: 10.

86 "A Day for Satchel Paige," *Kansas City Star*, July 27, 1942: 8.

87 "A Day for Satchel Paige."

88 "Negro Tossers Play Here Tonight," *Harrisburg Evening News*, August 12, 1942: 18; "Games Held Up," *Evening News*, August 13, 1942: 18.

89 "New Catcher Will Show for Monarchs Tomorrow," *News-Press* (St. Joseph, Missouri), August 23, 1942: 11; "Monarchs to Tangle with Loop Rivals Here Tonight," *St. Joseph* (Missouri) *Gazette*, August 24, 1942: 7.

90 "New Catcher Will Show for Monarchs Tomorrow"; Riley, 671.

91 Riley, 671, 672; "Paige's Catcher Robinson Is Full of Stories of his Place in History," *Asheville* (North Carolina) *Citizen-Times*, July 5, 1996: 38.

92 "New Catcher Will Show for Monarchs Tomorrow."

93 Riley, 671.

94 "Black Barons Clash with Cincinnati Club in Sunday Twin Bill," *Birmingham News*, August 14, 1942: 20.

95 "Black Barons Ready for Season's Final Tilt with All-Stars," *Birmingham News*, October 4, 1942: 45.

96 "Black Barons vs. Cincinnati Buckeyes," *Weekly Review* (Birmingham, Alabama), August 15, 1942: 7.

97 "Birmingham Black Barons Trip Cincinnati 5-2, 3-0," *Jackson* (Mississippi) *Advocate*, August 22, 1942: 8.

98 "Autos Humble Birmingham Black Barons by 8-2 Last Night," *News-Palladium* (Benton Harbor, Michigan), August 27, 1942: 12.

99 "Ethiopian Clowns Trim Black Barons Twice," *Indianapolis Star*, September 21, 1942: 18.

100 "Clowns Nose Out Back Barons, 6-5," *Illinois State Journal and Register* (Springfield, Illinois), September 22, 1942: 10.

101 "Clowns Nose Out Back Barons, 6-5."

102 Monarchs Lose," *St. Joseph Gazette*, September 21, 1942: 5.

103 "Monarchs Lose."

104 "Barons Defeat Two Opponents," *St. Joseph Gazette*, September 23, 1942: 5.

105 Barons Defeat Two Opponents."

106 Gene Sullivan, "Wise Owl," *St. Joseph News-Press*, September 24, 1942: 15.

107 Sullivan.

108 "Barons Now Travel by Train as Bus Is Wrecked," *Birmingham News*, September 26: 9.

109 "Black Barons Beat Major Leaguers, 6-3," *Birmingham News*, October 5, 1942: 14.

110 "Negro American Loop All-Stars to Battle Black Barons Sunday," *Birmingham News*, October 2, 1942: 28.

111 Jay Sims, "Round the Blocks," *Weekly Review* (Birmingham), October 10, 1942: 7.

112 "Black Barons Beat Major Leaguers, 6-3."

113 Douglas Flamming, *Bound for Freedom: Black Los Angeles in Jim Crow America* (Berkeley: University of California Press, 2005), 48.

114 State of California, Department of Public Health, Certificate of Registry of Marriage, October 16, 1947.

115 "Merchants Down Pacific Pipe 21-1," *News-Pilot* (San Pedro, California), April 29, 1946: 10.

116 "Merchants to Face Strong Negro Nine," *News-Pilot*, March 23, 1946: 8.

117 "Merchants Down Pacific Pipe 21-1."

118 "Rosabell Wallops Pacific Pipe Line," *News-Star* (Pasadena, California), April 7, 1946: 16.

119 "Merchants Triumph Twice, 11-10, 17-7," *News-Pilot*, June 17, 1946: 5.

120 "Merchants to Face Soldiers, Negroes," *News-Pilot*, May 29, 1946: 4.

121 "Merchants Enter Organ Belt Loop," *News-Pilot*, October 11, 1946: 6.

122 "Monrovia Semipros Outhit Foe but Lose 4th Loop Tilt," *News-Post* (Monrovia, California), December 23, 1946: 2.

123 Riley, 567.

124 Shav Glick, "Golfer and Course Builder Johnny Dawson Dies," *Los Angeles Times*, January 22, 1986: 38.

FRANK DUNCAN

By Dave Wilkie

"When I lost Frank I lost one of my best friends. Baseball lost one of its best managers. He was one of the best catchers we ever saw." – Buck O'Neil[1]

Frank Duncan's legendary Negro League career lasted 27 years and his unquenchable zest for life was etched across each and every one of them. A consummate winner, Duncan captured titles all over the world as a dominant defensive force behind the plate and later as a well-respected manager. Monarchs star pitcher William Bell said of his well-traveled teammate: "Dunk was an excellent catcher. Every owner wanted him. He played in nearly as many places as Hamlet: The Philippines, Japan, Hawaii, Cuba, South America and North America."[2] It's true Frank Duncan never shied away from a challenge, but wherever his travels took him, all roads eventually led back to his hometown, Kansas City, and his beloved Monarchs.

Frank Lee Duncan Jr. was born on February 14, 1901, in Kansas City, Missouri. He was the only child of Frank Duncan Sr. and Elizabeth Hansberg.[3] Duncan Sr. was born on June 3, 1872, in Warrensburg, Missouri, seven years after the end of the Civil War.[4] He was well known as a coal and block-ice salesman and the 1940 census lists his occupation as peddler.[5] Elizabeth was born in Virginia in 1865 and referred to herself as a homemaker in the 1930 census. They were married until 1941, when Elizabeth, sometimes referred to as Lizzie, died. Duncan Sr. died on May 26, 1954, at the age of 81.

Duncan grew up in Kansas City playing sandlot baseball with childhood friends and fellow future Negro League standouts, Newt Allen and Rube Curry. Newt talked about their early days together: "Frank Duncan and I were boys together on the Paseo at 17th St. We were in the same school together, lived in the same neighborhood for years, and we were friends throughout our childhood days. Another fellow with us was Rube Curry. He and Frank Duncan lived almost next door to one another. We used to play sandlot ball in school. We'd put in 20 cents apiece and the winner take the pot."[6]

Duncan and his buddies went to Lincoln High School, an exemplary African American school that fought hard to give its students an education that produced more than just trade laborers. Roy Wilkins, a reporter for the *Kansas City Call,* explained, "The black schools in Kansas City were much better than they had any right to be, partly because they were full of talented teachers who would have been teaching in college had they been white, and partly because Negro parents and children simply refused to be licked by segregation."[7]

It was at Lincoln High School that Duncan met his first wife, Julia Lee.[8] Julia's older brother, George E. Lee, fronted one of the most popular jazz bands in Kansas City in the 1920s and early '30s, George E. Lee's Novelty Singing Orchestra. Duncan occasionally drove the bus for a rival Kansas City jazz band, the Bennie Moten Orchestra.[9] Julia soon followed in her brother's footsteps by becoming one of the most popular jazz and blues vocalists of the time. She was a true pioneer and the first Kansas City jazz artist to record. She was known as the "Princess of the Boogie Woogie" and her hits included "Come On Over to My House Baby," "Snatch and Grab It," and, "Gotta Gimme Whatcha Got."[10] Frank carried an empty instrument case, sat in the orchestra pit, and pretended to be a musician in order to watch her perform at the all-White music halls.[11] Seventeen-year-old Julia and 18-year-old Frank were married on September 27, 1919.[12] Less than a year later, on June 1, 1920, Frank III, their only son, was born.

It was about this time that Duncan hooked up with a local team known as Floyd "Baby" Webb's teenage Kansas City Tigers.[13] The Tigers traveled around Kansas City and the Midwest and featured five players besides Duncan who made it to the Negro Leagues: Henry "Dimp" Miller, Herlen Bagland, Eddie "Pee Wee" Dwight, Roosevelt "Chappie" Gray, and Duncan's childhood pal, Rube Curry.[14]

When the Monarchs Reigned

Duncan was playing for the Swift Packing House in St. Joseph, Missouri, when he received his big break. As he recalled, "[It was] Easter Sunday 1920, the snow was that deep. Joe Greene's Chicago Giants sent me $20 for a ticket to Chicago, so I jumped on the freight train and came on to Chicago, and I felt just like I was going to the New York Yankees."[15] Duncan had the chance to catch thanks to slugger John Beckwith's move to shortstop.[16] He appeared in 20 games but started off slowly, hitting just .161 in 62 at-bats.

At some point after his arrival in Chicago, Duncan ran into the father of the Negro National League, Rube Foster. Duncan recalled their conversation. "He said, 'You a ball player?' I said, Yeah, I think so. I can catch. He said, 'You think you can catch like Petway?' I said, Not now, but one of these days I will. Later on I reminded him of what I said. He said, 'You stuck to your word.'"[17]

After another slow start for the 1921 Giants, Duncan was traded to his hometown Kansas City Monarchs. Owner J.L. Wilkinson was looking for a catcher, and although Duncan wasn't hitting much, he was gaining a reputation for his abilities behind the plate. Wilkinson sent first baseman Lemuel "Hawk" Hawkins, catcher Jay Bird Ray, and $1,000 to the Chicago Giants for Duncan.[18] By June, Duncan was being hailed as the find of the 1921 season by the *Kansas City Star*.[19] Duncan was home, and he spent the bulk of his lengthy career with the mighty Kansas City Monarchs.

Duncan settled in nicely with his new team to close out the 1921 season, hitting .281 and solidifying the catcher position for the steadily improving Monarchs. The team finished second to Rube Foster's Chicago American Giants and featured future Hall of Famers Bullet Joe Rogan and José Mendéz. This was the beginning of one of the most successful batteries in baseball history as Duncan and Rogan worked together for more than 200 wins.[20] Duncan often spoke of Rogan's fastball: "I'll tell you how fast Rogan was. I used to buy two steaks before the game when he was going to pitch. You could buy a steak in those days for 10 cents. I'd start the game catching Joe in the first inning with that steak next to my gloved hand. After five innings the steak would be beaten to shreds. So I'd replace it with a second steak."[21] New York Giants manager John McGraw is said to have made this remark about the duo: "I would have given almost any sum if it were possible for the battery of Rogan and Duncan to perform in the major leagues and it's likely they have gone down in baseball history as one of the finest."[22]

The 1922 season brought the Monarchs even closer to their top rival and the class of the league, the Chicago American Giants. The Giants won the first three titles in the newly formed Negro National League, but Kansas City was closing ground, edged out by percentage points, .607 to .603. The Monarchs shared a ballpark with the local White minor-league team, the Kansas City Blues, in those days and played their games there when the Blues were on the road. The Blues were led by star shortstop Glenn Wright and had one of the best teams in the American Association, winning the league championship the very next year in 1923. The battle for Kansas City took place in early October of 1922 and the Monarchs thoroughly dismantled their White rivals, five games to one. The *Kansas City Star* crowned the Monarchs "The New City Champions."[23] Duncan caught all six games and hit a robust .346 in 26 at-bats. The Monarchs certainly proved they belonged on the field with their White counterparts, so much so that the commissioner of the American Association banned its teams from playing against Negro League squads after this thrashing.[24] Wright later became a scout for the Boston Red Sox and must have recalled Duncan's exploits when he on one occasion proclaimed, "I wish I could find a catcher like Frank Duncan."[25]

In February of 1923 the Monarchs traveled to Hot Springs, Arkansas, a popular spring-training destination for ballclubs, to train with White major leaguers. Quincy Gilmore, secretary for the Monarchs, told the *Kansas City Call*, "Oh boy, what a time there will be in that burg when Babe Ruth, Frank Duncan, Carl Mays, Bob Meusel, Bullet Rogan, Waite Hoyt, Bill Gisentaner, Heinie Groh, Tris Speaker, Dobie Moore, Grover Alexander, Hurley McNair, and a few more of the countries' great stars meet and talk over the great pastime."[26] This was just the beginning of a very eventful year for Duncan.

It is not known exactly when Duncan and Julia Lee were divorced, but it was probably around this time. Duncan had a daughter named Armeda who was born in 1923 in Illinois and the mother was listed as being from Texas, which ruled out Julia. Duncan was listed as single and living in Kansas City with his parents and Armeda, then 7, in the 1930 census, and Julia had remarried in 1927.[27] Duncan and Julia remained friends until her death in 1958.[28]

Newt Allen was now a full-time member of the Monarchs, joining Rube Curry and Duncan in a reunion that would have been hard for them to imagine as children playing on the sandlots of Kansas City. At the end of Duncan's career, he reminisced about sharing a field with his friend: "I have watched Newt play for over 20 years and I still get a thrill when I know he's going to put on that uniform."[29] In addition to the hometown trio, the team featured a who's who of Negro League greats including Hurley McNair, Heavy Johnson, Bullet Rogan, José Mendéz, and William Bell. It was no surprise that they finally outplayed the Chicago American Giants and captured the Negro National League championship by 3½ games in 1923.

After a train ride to Key West, Florida, and a 90-mile boat trip to Havana, Duncan found himself in Cuba for the first time, playing for the Santa Clara Leopardos during the 1923-24 winter season.[30] Many Cubans consider this Santa Clara squad to be the greatest team in the island's history and they won the pennant by 11½ games. Duncan was joined by Monarchs teammates Curry and Mendéz, and the team was bolstered by superstars Oscar Charleston and Oliver "Ghost" Marcelle.[31] Duncan hit .331 in 133 at-bats while the team as a whole hit .329 in winning 36 out of 47 games. After the regular winter season, the Leopardos entered the highly competitive Grand Winter Championship in Cuba and barely edged out the team from Habana by a half-game to win a second title.

The Monarchs kept rolling in 1924 with an imposing 57-22 record that enabled them to finish five games clear of the always competitive Chicago American Giants. Duncan was now a star; the *Chicago Defender* noted: "A tall, thin kid full of pep, [he is] the greatest catcher in the game."[32] The accolades did not stop there as teammates and opponents chimed in. Chicago American Giant Saul Davis proclaimed Duncan "a hard worker behind the plate, the best catcher I ever seen. A sweetheart of a catcher. He had better catching skills than the great Josh Gibson."[33] Cool Papa Bell said, "To this day Frank was one of the greatest catchers ever. He could throw. You had to get a better lead on the pitcher with Frank behind the plate. If you didn't, you might as well turn right around and go back to first. Nobody could hardly beat him at throwing."[34] Duncan had this to say about his own defensive prowess. "I didn't let them other fellows catch. They could outhit me, but they couldn't outcatch me, none of them. I'm not bragging, it's just facts. I don't remember dropping five popups in 20 years."[35]

The first Negro League World Series was organized and played in 1924, and the Monarchs earned a spot with their first-place finish in the Negro National League. Their opponent was the Hilldale Club, champion of the Eastern Colored League. These were two evenly matched teams at the height of their powers and it took 10 games to decide a champion.

Things looked bleak for the Monarchs when they were down three games to one after five games (Game Three was called because of darkness after 13 innings with the score tied.) Kansas City roared back to win Games Six and Seven, evening the series at three games apiece. This set up a pivotal Game Eight and set the stage for one of Duncan's early career highlights. He was having a disappointing series so far, with three hits in 29 at-bats, and he came up in the bottom of the ninth with his team trailing, 2-1, with two outs and the bases loaded. Manager José Mendéz considered pinch-hitting for the struggling catcher but decided to leave him in to face his childhood pal, Rube Curry. Curry had jumped ship the previous season and was having a fine series for Hilldale.[36] Duncan described what happened next: "I swung and the ball went straight up in the air over catcher Santop's head. It was an easy out. I was disgusted as I watched him maneuver around rather steadily as the high foul started earthward. He dropped it! I had another chance. Fully confident, I got set up again and up came one to my liking and out went a sharp single to left center scoring the tying and winning run."[37] The crowd poured onto the field and hoisted Duncan onto their shoulders in celebration.[38] The 35-year-old Louis Santop faded dramatically after this miscue, playing two more seasons as a backup for Hilldale before closing the book on his illustrious career.

The Monarchs cut their celebration short since they still had to win one more contest. Game Nine was won by Hilldale with a masterful pitching performance turned in by ace lefty Nip Winters; it was his third win of the series. After all the previous drama, the 10th and final game was a bit anticlimatic. Manager Mendéz took the ball himself and shut out Hilldale, 5-0, for the series win.[39] Frank Duncan and the Kansas City Monarchs had won the first Negro League World Series.

In what was almost a carbon copy of the previous regular season, the Monarchs and Hilldale finished the

1925 regular season atop their respective divisions. Before the two clubs could meet in the second World Series, the Monarchs had to get past Cool Papa Bell and the St. Louis Stars. It was a tight seven-game series, and thanks to three complete-game victories by Bullet Joe Rogan, the Monarchs came out on top to set up a World Series rematch. This matchup lacked the suspense of the previous years, as Kansas City was steamrolled by the Hilldale Club, five games to one. Duncan toiled, going 3-for-21 at the plate, and the team hit only .216 in the six contests. Duncan's old buddy, Rube Curry, came back to bite them, going 2-0 with two complete games and a 1.29 ERA for the champions.

Duncan's competitive nature occasionally got him into scraps, and none was bigger than the infamous brawl that took place in Chicago on May 10, 1925, against their bitter rivals, the Chicago American Giants. Duncan's teammate Dink Mothell described the melee:

> "We had a big fight in Chicago. Frank Duncan slid into John Hines, and I think he tore his chest protector off. Bingo DeMoss was manager of Chicago. Bingo grabbed Duncan, and Duncan grabbed Bingo. Bingo says, 'You turn me loose!' Dunk said, 'You turn me loose!' Well they kept rasslin' around there, and four or five policemen came out on the field. Naturally each ball club was trying to give its player protection. I believe they were colored police, some in uniform, some with plain clothes. This policeman walked up behind Duncan and hit him in the head with the butt of his pistol or a black jack, and knocked him out. Then Jelly Gardner kicked him in the mouth with his spikes. Well, that started everybody swinging at one another."[40]

> "Duncan would do anything to win and Buck O'Neil probably described it best when he said that Duncan was: 'Mean on the field and sweet off it.'"[41]

Winning had become commonplace for the Monarchs and 1926 was no different as they finished the year with a 60-22 record. Although they had the better overall record, the Monarchs were forced to play the Chicago American Giants in the Negro National League Championship Series to determine which team would advance to the World Series. The Monarchs had won the first half of the season, but the American Giants edged them out in the second half to set up this playoff. Duncan managed only three hits in 18 at-bats, but he walked seven times for a respectable .400 on-base-percentage. It was not enough, however, as Kansas City dropped the series, five games to four. The Chicago American Giants went on to capture their first World Series title with a five games to four victory over the Eastern Colored League champion Atlantic City Bacharach Giants.

In October of 1926 Duncan joined an all-star squad of players calling themselves the Philadelphia Royal Giants and competed in the California Winter League. His teammates included Turkey Stearnes, Willie Wells, Joe Rogan, Rap Dixon, Newt Allen, and Willie Foster. They made quick work of the league and took the title with a 26-11-1 record. Duncan played well, hitting .276 in 24 games.[42] It marked a triumphant winter, but the next move that the team made jeopardized their careers as Negro League players.

In Duncan's own words:

> "In the spring of 1927, I joined the Japan tour team and went to Japan, and we boarded the big Japanese steamship from San Pedro, California, and headed to Yokohama. It took us 19 days. The people were the most wonderful people I ever came in contact with. I loved them, I hated to see them go to war. We played all over, Osaka, Kobe, on into Nagasaki. They had some pretty nice teams, they weren't strong hitters but pretty good fielders and base runners, and they had some pretty nice looking pitchers. But we didn't lose any games."[43]

The Giants quickly gained the respect of the Japanese players and fans and were referred to as the gentle black giants. Their skills were far superior to those of their opponents, but they never showboated or ran up scores. Duncan and fellow catcher Biz Mackey happily coached the Japanese players on the finer points of the game.[44] Duncan played first base and led off; as a 26-year-old, before years of catching took his knees, he was timed circling the bases in 15 seconds flat.[45]

This goodwill tour was perhaps the inspiration for the inception of professional baseball in Japan, not the 1934 major-league tour as is often given credit. Unlike the Giants, the White major leaguers often disrespected and insulted their Japanese opponents. Babe Ruth took to the field holding an umbrella in a game played in the

• FRANK DUNCAN •

rain while Lou Gehrig played left field in rubber boots as Al Simmons sprawled on the field during play.[46] An article about the Royal Giants in the June 1927 issue of *Baseball World* said: "The voices they use with each other are calm, and hardly audible. You would hardly know of their existence. When there is no game, they enjoy billiards, or walking in the neighborhood. They show a great love for children and play with them happily."[47] They were greeted by dignitaries and given an escort to the palace of the emperor and generally given the respect and dignity often missing back in the United States.[48]

Duncan, Lefty Cooper, Biz Mackey, and Rap Dixon were all suspended for 30 days and fined $200 upon their return for not reporting to their respective squads for the start of the 1927 Negro League season. A five-year ban had originally been threatened by the league.[49] J.L. Wilkinson of the Monarchs was the only owner to follow through with the league's punishment, and Duncan missed a large portion of the 1927 season.[50] He didn't see action until early August, and in his first game back he showed the Monarchs what they had been missing by going 3-for-4 with a triple and a double in a 10-3 victory over the Memphis Red Sox.[51] It was too little and too late, and Duncan's absence may have been a factor in the Monarchs finishing behind both the St. Louis Stars and the Chicago American Giants.

At some point in 1927, Duncan's third child, Sidney Duncan, was born. In the 1940 census, Sidney and another son, Clarence, who was born in 1935, are listed as living with Duncan's parents, Frank and Lizzie. Sidney certainly tried to emulate his father; he is mentioned as managing the Junior Monarchs, a 17-and-under team in Kansas City's Jackie Robinson Baseball League, and playing catcher for the Minneapolis Clowns in 1950 with aspirations to play in the major leagues.[52] Very little is known about Sidney's life or fate and even less is known about Clarence. Duncan also had a second wife, Bertha Lewis, but the exact date of their marriage is unknown. Bertha remained with Duncan until his death; she died in 1985 after having lived in Kansas City for 75 years.[53]

The 1928 Monarchs were no match for Candy Jim Taylor's St. Louis Stars and they finished eight games behind the champions of the NNL. For the 1929 season, Duncan platooned at catcher with pull-hitting T.J. Young, and the occasional rest must have done wonders for the hard-working catcher: He batted .350 in 45 games. The Monarchs had a tremendous season,

Longtime Monarchs catcher Frank Duncan managed his team to the 1942 Negro League World Series championship over the perennial NNL-champion Homestead Grays. (Courtesy Noir-Tech Research, Inc.)

tearing up the league with a 63-17 record, winning both the first and second halves of the season. The Monarchs were declared the champions of the NNL, but no World Series was played in 1929; in fact, there would not be another Negro League World Series until 1942, when the Monarchs faced the Homestead Grays.

At the conclusion of the season, Duncan made the journey back to Cuba, where he had enjoyed so much success in the winter of 1923-24. He suited up for Cienfuegos, hitting .265 and getting what was possibly his first taste of managing as the team struggled to a fourth-place finish.[54] The following winter proved much more fruitful for Cienfuegos as the team took the Cuban Winter League championship.[55] Duncan recalled his experience at leading the team: "Molina was managing the team, used to bring the Cuban Stars here. He got in a little something over there with the people in his hometown and gave me the ball club. We won the championship by 10-11 games, ran away from Rube Foster and all of them."[56] It took more than a decade before Duncan got his chance to manage in the Negro Leagues.

The year 1930 turned out to be the final season for the Kansas City Monarchs in the NNL. The league itself survived only one more year and disbanded after 1931 under the financial strains of the Great Depression, though a second incarnation of the league came into being in 1933. Duncan was moved to right field for the 1930 campaign and once again tore the cover off the ball to the tune of a .360 average. The team failed to follow his lead and fell to 42-38, a distant second to the champion St. Louis Stars.

Duncan's defensive abilities were so spectacular that his hitting was often overlooked. He could not compete with the likes of Josh Gibson and Biz Mackey with the lumber, but he certainly was no slouch. Monarchs teammate and future Hall of Famer Willard "Home Run" Brown put it this way: "You couldn't fool around with him none with men on base, because he'd choke up and be right on that plate. He was a good clutch hitter. He was a line-drive hitter, and when he went up there with men on bases, he hit a whole lot of doubles."[57]

Between 1931 and 1936 the Monarchs were an independent team that barnstormed against a combination of league, independent, pro, and semipro teams.[58] One of their top competitors was the bearded House of David team, made up of an Israelite community that stressed physical and spiritual discipline. Ringers like Satchel Paige, Mordecai "Three Finger" Brown, and Grover Cleveland Alexander were known to have played for the team, sometimes even sporting fake beards.[59] Monarchs owner J.L. Wilkinson had just introduced his new system of lights enabling him to play more games and attract more fans with the novelty of a night game.[60] This was the most nomadic portion of Duncan's Negro League career as he began the 1931 season with the New York Harlem Stars but later jumped back to the independent Monarchs to finish out the season.

Duncan began 1932 with another independent club, the Pittsburgh Crawfords. The team was overloaded with catchers with Duncan, Bill Perkins, Ted "Double Duty" Radcliffe, and budding superstar Josh Gibson on the team. Perkins and Duncan left the Crawfords in midseason.[61] Duncan also played six games for the Homestead Grays in the East-West League, a league that was created by Grays owner Cum Posey but that did not even last one entire season. Duncan, along with Grays Cool Papa Bell, Newt Allen, Willie Wells, and others, left the team after not having been paid by Posey in over a month.[62] Duncan once again finished out the year with the Monarchs.

At season's end, on October 20, the Monarchs met for a series of games in Mexico City against the Mexico City Aztecs, Mexico's top baseball team.[63] Duncan, Cool Papa Bell, Newt Allen, Willie Wells, George Giles, Turkey Stearnes, Chet Brewer, and Bullet Joe Rogan all made the trip, and the Monarchs team left with a 14-2 record. Longtime traveling secretary and promotional wizard, Quincy Gilmore reported to the *Kansas City Call*: "Just as soon as we crossed the border, we were treated as real men." Gilmore also wrote: "We have been told that the Monarchs are the best behaved baseball club that has ever visited the Republic of Mexico."[64] It's no wonder that star players like Bell and Josh Gibson were so often lured by the respect offered them to play south of the border.

Very few statistics exist for Duncan and the Monarchs for the 1933 and 1934 seasons. In an effort to keep turning a profit, Wilkinson continued his brutal barnstorming tours. From Texas to Seattle to Denver and Winnipeg, the Monarchs traveled to all points north, south, east, and west in search of a game.[65] In 1933 Pittsburgh Crawfords owner Gus Greenlee resurrected the Negro National League. However, when the Monarchs were asked to join, Wilkinson turned the new league down. The 1933 season also witnessed the first Negro League East-West All-Star Game; the independent Monarchs were not represented.

• FRANK DUNCAN •

Perhaps the greatest barnstorming tour of all time took place at the conclusion of the 1934 season. Fresh off a World Series victory against the Detroit Tigers, Dizzy Dean and his brother Paul of the St. Louis Cardinals agreed to a series of games against Negro League teams. Duncan, Newt Allen, George Giles, Dink Mothell, John Donaldson, and Steel Arm Davis all suited up for manager Bullet Joe Rogan's Kansas City Monarchs to play the first six games of the schedule.[66] The Monarchs got off to a slow start as they lost the first two games in Oklahoma City and Wichita, Kansas. They came back to shut out the Deans in games three and four in Kansas City and Des Moines respectively. The Monarchs were blown out in game five in Chicago, setting up a sixth and final game in Milwaukee. Duncan had his best showing in this final contest, blasting a three-run triple in the top of the ninth and giving his team a 7-5 lead. The Monarchs could not hold the lead and the game was called because of darkness with the score tied, 8-8.[67] The tour continued with the Deans facing the Philadelphia Stars, New York Black Yankees, and the Pittsburgh Crawfords. The Negro League teams finished with an 8-5-1 record that included a three-game sweep by Satchel Paige and the Crawfords to close out the tour.[68]

Dizzy Dean and Frank Duncan had an obvious fondness for each other as evidenced by a story Duncan told to Negro League historian John Holway:

"I caught Dizzy in 1934, right after he beat the Detroit Tigers in that World Series. They took a plane, we got on a bus, we went to Oklahoma City to meet Dizzy Dean and all his stars, him and Pepper Martin, Paul Dean, Curt Davis from the Brooklyn Dodgers, Walker Cooper was catching, and they used quite a few of those boys out of the Texas League in Tulsa and Oklahoma. They didn't want me to catch him on account of that time they didn't allow the white and the colored players like they are now on the same team in the south. But Dizzy went down town to the Chamber of Commerce, got me out of the pool hall, said, "Now if you want me to play, if I'm good enough to pitch, he's good enough to catch me." He said, "Now that's the way it's going to be." I just kept my Monarch uniform on and I caught Dizzy."[69]

Dizzy had this to say about his batterymate:

"I can't say enough about him. I sure got a kick out of Duncan. One time when Duncan catches me, he has a glove that makes the ball pop, and it makes my pitch sound like a rifle shot and Duncan keeps telling them hitters, 'boy, don't get near that plate. Don't let that ball hit you or it'll kill you.'"[70]

Dizzy's fondness and respect for Duncan didn't stop there. "That fellow Duncan which catches for Kansas City is almost as good a catcher as Gabby Hartnett, and I can't say no more than that about a catcher."[71]

The 34-year-old Duncan jumped to the New York Cubans for the 1935 season and once again found himself fighting for a championship. The Cubans won the second half of the Negro National League season and faced the legendary first-half champion Pittsburgh Crawfords in the championship series. The Crawfords were a juggernaut and featured four future Hall of Famers on their squad. They had finished the league season with a 51-27-3 record that far surpassed the 31-25-5 mark of the Cubans. The Crawfords were a heavy favorite, but the Cubans fought hard and took them to a deciding seventh game. At one point the Cubans led the series three games to two, but the potent Crawfords, led by manager Oscar Charleston, took the next two games to take the series and the championship.[72]

In the autumn of 1935, Duncan formed an all-star team that played visiting teams from Mexico and Cuba in the Puerto Rican Winter League.[73] In early March of the following year, the All-Stars trounced the Cincinnati Reds, who were training in Puerto Rico, three games to one. Duncan and Buck Leonard, Ray Dandridge, Leon Day, Vic Harris, and Ray Brown all played for the victorious All-Stars.[74] Duncan said, "The Cincinnati Reds came down there training. Chuck Dressen was managing, Chuck and I used to play ball in Cuba against each other. They had Bucky Walters, Ival Goodman playing right, McQuinn first base, a Greek playing second, I forgot his name,[75] Ernie Lombardi catching. We hung Cincinnati. Shoot, we hung 'em. Couldn't win a game. Nope."[76]

Duncan remained with the New York Cubans for the 1936 campaign, but the team struggled, plummeting to the bottom of the standings. He rejoined the Monarchs in 1937, and the team went 52-19-1 to capture the Negro American League title. Duncan didn't see the finish as he was traded to the Chicago American Giants before the season ended.[77]

• When the Monarchs Reigned •

Duncan backed up catcher Subby Byas for the 1938 American Giants and turned in one of his best seasons, hitting .368 and appearing in his only East-West All-Star Game. Duncan received 72,122 votes, more than any other player for the 1938 contest, hitting seventh and going 0-for-1 with a walk for the victorious West team.[78]

Although Duncan participated in only one East-West game as a player, he was no stranger to the annual jewel of the Negro Leagues. It is a bit of a mystery as to why he did not appear in more all-star games as a player. He was third in the voting at catcher in 1934 and fourth in 1937, when he was listed as a member of the West team.[79] Duncan did manage or coach in the game from 1943 through 1947, and he listed this five-year stretch as his most outstanding achievement in baseball in a 1972 questionnaire filled out for the National Baseball Hall of Fame. Duncan was on the winning side in all five of these games.[80]

Duncan did not play in the Negro Leagues in 1939, instead opting to play for the Palmer House Hotel Team, a semipro team playing out of Chicago that featured a lineup made up almost exclusively of former Chicago American Giants.[81] Teammate Maurice Wiggins described a beaning that Duncan took while playing for Palmer House: "Duncan dropped like a rock and had to spend three days in the hospital."[82]

It was back to Mexico in 1940, where Duncan played for what was undeniably the worst team of his career. The Gallos de Santa Rosa finished 14-67 and in last place, 42 games out of first. Duncan fared no better than most of his teammates; he batted .238 (10-for-42) in 12 games.[83] He also played in at least one game for the Chicago American Giants, but otherwise seems to have had a rather uneventful year.

One of Duncan's proudest moments took place in 1941 when he caught his son, Frank III, in a game for the Monarchs, becoming the first and only father-son battery in professional baseball history. Duncan's son was a promising pitcher who spent some time with the Baltimore Elite Giants and played for the San Angelo team in the Texas League. Frank III injured his arm and his career never came to fulfillment.[84]

As Duncan's own playing career began to wind down, he again latched on to his hometown team, the Kansas City Monarchs, and never played or managed for another Negro League franchise. In a prelude to the great teams to come, the 1941 Monarchs finished atop the NAL with a 25-11 record. A 40-year-old Duncan backed up Joe Greene and got into 11 games, hitting .212. No World Series was played, but in an interview with John Holway, Duncan mentioned a matchup with the NNL champion Homestead Grays at season's end. "The Monarchs won the pennant in our league in '41 and played the Washington Homestead Grays a series of games. It wasn't exactly a world series, more like a series of games." Duncan did not mention the outcome of these contests.[85]

Submariner Dizzy Dismukes took over the reins as manager of the Monarchs to begin the 1942 season after star second baseman Newt Allen stepped down.[86] In the June 5 issue of the *Kansas City Call*, Duncan is mentioned as taking over managerial duties as Dismukes switched to being the team's business manager. The 41-year-old Duncan rarely penciled himself into the lineup, though he occasionally spelled Joe Greene at catcher, and he began a very successful run as the Monarchs' skipper.

Buck O'Neil often exclaimed, "The '42 Monarchs club was one of blackball's most luminous."[87] He called them the best team he ever played for and the equal of the New York Yankees of the time.[88] In Duncan's first season at the helm, he led the Monarchs to a 27-12 record and a four-game sweep over Josh Gibson, Buck Leonard, and the heavily favored Homestead Grays. In 1924, the young receiver had played a vital role in helping the Monarchs to win the very first Negro League World Series and now, 18 years later, Duncan was back on top as the leader of the 1942 World Series champion Kansas City Monarchs.

Soon after the 1942 season, Duncan was drafted into the US Army, which was a bit of a surprise for the 41-year-old player-manager. J.L. Wilkinson explained Duncan's circumstance in the March 3, 1943, edition of the *Kansas City Star*: "Duncan is past 41 but that early draft caught him before the 38-year-old ruling became effective." As it turned out, Duncan was honorably discharged five months and 16 days later. He explained, "I was just getting ready to go off to Officer Candidate School for second lieutenant, I was top sergeant, see when they let me out. I was over 38, over the age limit. I came out in '43."[89] Duncan set a marksmanship record during his short stint in the Army when he hit 31 out of 32 bull's eyes from 200 yards."[90]

Duncan led Kansas City's 1943 squad to a respectable 43-27 record, but the Monarchs fell short, losing out to the first- and second-half winners Birmingham Black Barons and Chicago American Giants respectively, despite having a better overall record than both teams. The following season, decimated by player losses due to the war, the team fell to fourth place with a 30-38 mark; amazingly, it was the only losing season in Duncan's 23 years with the Kansas City club.

Duncan's managerial duties went well beyond the scope of field manager, and he often drove the team bus. As Buck O'Neil explained, "Most of your bus conversation would be with the person that sat beside you. I did a lot of talking with Frank Duncan. I set right up in front of the bus and Frank would drive a lot."[91] O'Neil also had this to say about his friend and manager: "In our baseball, our manager had to be the one to go in and see if we could eat. He also went in to see if we could sleep. Frank could talk-that-talk and he had to be able to. Because if Frank didn't, we were not going to get in and out of some of the spots we were in."[92] Duncan was considered an authority on navigating highways and finding hotels and places to eat.[93] Teammate George Giles recognized his manager's special abilities: "He knew the white farmers on the back roads."[94] Duncan was also known for his show-stopping skills with a fungo bat and his ability as a gymnastics instructor during spring training.[95]

Manager Frank Duncan was feeling optimistic heading into the 1945 season, especially with a new addition to the team. Duncan pronounced, "With Jackie Robinson, the crack Pacific Coast athlete, now playing short, that he has a championship team."[96] Duncan was so impressed with his trailblazing shortstop that he recommended him for the annual East-West All-Star Game.[97] Robinson pounded the ball at a .375 clip that season, but it was not enough as the Monarchs finished in third place with a 43-32-3 record. Although the season was not the success for which he had hoped, Duncan could take pride in the fact that he was Jackie Robinson's first professional manager.

A 45-year-old Duncan finally put away his shinguards in 1946 and concentrated exclusively on managing the club. This was to be the iconic Monarchs' last hurrah. They ran away with both the first- and second-half titles with a blistering 50-16-2 record and lined up to face Larry Doby, Monte Irvin, and the Negro National League champion Newark Eagles in the Negro League World Series. The back-and-forth series took the full seven games to decide. Eventually, due in part to a Satchel Paige no-show in the pivotal seventh game, the Monarchs dropped Game Seven, 3-2, and Newark claimed the championship of Black baseball.[98]

The 1947 season was Duncan's last as the skipper of the fabled Monarchs, and the team finished second with a respectable 52-32 record. In his six years (1942-47) at the helm, he led the team to a 288-216-7 record, including two NAL titles and one World Series title with the storied 1942 team. Sportswriter Wendell Smith of the *Pittsburgh Courier* wrote of Duncan's managerial skills: "Although he is regarded as a taskmaster and a tough hombre by ball players, his record establishes him as one of the game's shrewdest managers."[99] Dick Wilkinson, owner J.L. Wilkinson's son, frustrated after a late-season loss to the lowly Indianapolis Clowns, tried to fire Duncan by taking his bus keys away and giving them to Buck O'Neil. O'Neil refused them and the proud manager was able to finish out the season.[100] O'Neil took the reins the next season and Duncan called it quits on his remarkable 27-year career, 23 of which had been spent with the Monarchs.

Duncan did not stay out of baseball for long. Beginning in 1948 he hooked up with former batterymate Bullet Joe Rogan to umpire in the Negro American League. Duncan quickly rose to the rank of chief umpire of the NAL and was responsible for giving pioneering umpire Bob Motley his first job.[101] Motley loved to talk about his outgoing mentor, saying, "Duncan was without a doubt the most personable of the crew. A very gregarious person, he always had something to say, which meant there was barely a quiet moment in the dressing room. Sometimes when he started to ramble on too much, Rogan would call him 'motor mouth.' But that wouldn't stop Duncan. He'd chuckle and keep right on blabbing."[102] Motley likened them to a Black version of Laurel and Hardy and thoroughly enjoyed the laughter and banter that came with these two baseball legends. Motley recalled, "Their faces would light up as they reminisced about their playing days."[103]

Duncan's knees finally let him down at the end of the 1949 season and he was unable to crouch any longer. Motley sadly witnessed the end of Duncan's distinguished career and declared, "I would have gladly carried Duncan on my back if necessary just for the joy of sharing the diamond with him."[104] Duncan and Rogan hung on until the midpoint of the 1950 season before finally retiring. The old friends frequently visited the park as spectators and Duncan often had a kind word for his protégé, Bob Motley.[105]

Duncan also had planned for his post-baseball future, as his many side businesses attest. In 1946 he owned some tiny kitchenette apartments on Prospect

Avenue in Kansas City. Newlyweds Buck and Ora O'Neil spent their first year of marriage in one.[106] After retiring from baseball, Duncan owned a taxi stand called the Paseo Taxi Company, with former teammate Newt Joseph at the popular Kansas City crossroads of 18th and Vine, a place where jazz and baseball came together.[107] He also owned a popular tavern, the Lone Star Tavern, and placed an ad in the December 25, 1957, issue of the *Kansas City Star* that wished everyone "joy on Christmas, happiness throughout the year."[108] Later, the always-busy Duncan worked as a bail bondsman for the Passantio Bonding Company.[109]

Duncan never received the attention he deserved, during or after his playing days, but his contemporaries recognized his greatness. A player with his résumé between the lines, and as a manager and umpire, should have a plaque reserved for him in Cooperstown. Satchel Paige certainly thought so. After being inducted into the Baseball Hall of Fame, Satch had this to say about his friend and teammate: "Frank was one we were kickin' on to get in the Hall of Fame. Campanella got a break, I got a break, but nobody was a better catcher than Frank outside of Josh. It was like clockwork pitchin' to that man. I guess I could throw harder than anybody. I musta thrown hard because no one ever hit me hard. But Frank was the man who kept me going when I wanted to quit in 1938 (bad arm), Frank kept tellin' me, keep at it, keep at it, keep at it. If it hadn't been for him, I never would have gone to Cleveland."[110]

In 1950 Monarchs owners, J.L. Wilkinson and Tom Baird, along with a group of fans, chose Duncan as the catcher for the all-time Kansas City Monarchs team.[111] He also received strong support in the 1952 *Pittsburgh Courier* poll that selected the greatest Negro League players to ever put on a uniform.[112]

In retirement, Duncan still enjoyed taking in the occasional ballgame, and he listed Stan Musial as the greatest hitter in baseball after attending the 1950 All-Star Game in Chicago.[113] He also spoke about Willie Mays and expressed displeasure about his being traded from the San Francisco Giants to the New York Mets. According to Duncan, "Mays is the greatest ballplayer that ever lived and he deserved better than to be traded."[114]

Buck O'Neil remained close to Duncan and his family and often spoke about his teammate and close friend. As O'Neil remembered, "Frank could catch and throw, a shotgun arm and a great memory. Before Frank died he would talk about a ball game, he would tell you the inning, the pitch the guy hit and how the score ended. He had a wonderful memory."[115]

In 1965 Duncan was one of the few Negro Leaguers to pay his respects to Branch Rickey when he attended Rickey's funeral. Cool Papa Bell expressed disappointment when speaking of the turnout, noting, "Besides Jackie and myself, Frank Duncan, the old Kansas City Monarchs catcher, was the only other black player there. We should have given Mr. Rickey more respect, but I guess some of our people just didn't want to make the effort."[116] On a lighter note, Duncan made an appearance with his old batterymate, Satchel Paige on the TV show *This Is Your Life,* on January 26, 1972.[117]

In his final years, Duncan did not speak much about his playing days. Instead, he was often overcome with tears of joy while watching his grandchildren, Julian and Frank IV, play.[118] Frank Duncan died on December 4, 1973, at the age of 72 after a bout with colon cancer. He was survived by his wife, Bertha, his son, Frank III, his daughter, Armeda Walker, stepson George Solomon, stepdaughter Bertha Thatcher, and two grandsons, Julian and Frank IV.[119] Sidney and Clarence were not mentioned in the obituary, adding to the mystery of their relationship with their father. Duncan – who was an Army veteran, a Mason, and a Shriner – was buried next to his mother at Highland Cemetery in Kansas City.

Duncan was an entrepreneur, a devoted family man, and he obviously had a love for his hometown of Kansas City. He was also one of the giants of baseball history, whose accomplishments were wide and varied. Once, when talking about the game he loved, he asserted, "We went into every town with two ideas. We would give the people our very best and we wanted to be their friends. We played in all the great cities of the Orient: Tokyo, Yokohama, Manila. We played in Rio, New York, everywhere. But we liked playing in our own little American towns best. We loved the kids and we liked the folks. Those were great and wonderful days."[120]

Duncan summed up his life and career in baseball by saying, "I have a good reputation, a good name. I'm proud of that, to be one of them. So I have nothing to regret. Lived a great life, thankful still to be living. Now you see the boys getting the breaks, holding on and playing good ball up there. We were among the pioneers that paved the way for them."[121]

• FRANK DUNCAN •

Source

Special thanks to Julian Duncan, Frank Duncan's grandson, for our many conversations about his grandfather, grandmother, and father. His openness and dedication to keeping their legacies alive is truly inspiring.

All statistics, unless otherwise noted, are from seamheads.com.

Notes

1   Larry Lester, *Baseball's First Colored World Series: The 1924 Meeting of the Hilldale Giants and Kansas City Monarchs* (Jefferson, North Carolina: McFarland & Company, Inc., 2006), 62.

2   Lester, *Baseball's First Colored World Series*, 63.

3   Conversations with grandson, Julian Duncan, October 23, 2020.

4   1940 US census.

5   Phil S. Dixon, *John "Buck" O'Neil: The Rookie, the Man, the Legacy 1938 (*Bloomington, Indiana: AuthorHouse, 2009), 118.

6   John Holway, *Voices From the Great Black Baseball Leagues* (New York: Da Capo Press, Inc., 1992), 91.

7   Megan Dennis, "'The Castle on the Hill': Lincoln High, Racial Uplift, and Community Development During Segregation," Kansas City Public Library,

https://pendergastkc.org/article/castle-hill-lincoln-high-racial-uplift-and-community-development-during-segregation.

8   Larry Lester and Sammy J. Miller, *Black Baseball in Kansas City* (Charleston, South Carolina: Arcadia Publishing, 2000), 120.

9   Janet Bruce, *The Kansas City Monarchs: Champions of Black Baseball* (Lawrence, Kansas: University Press of Kansas, 1985), 86.

10   Lester and Miller, *Black Baseball in Kansas City,* 120.

11   Phil Dixon and Patrick J. Hannigan, *The Negro Baseball Leagues: A Photographic History* (Mattituck, New York: Amereon Ltd., 1992), 105.

12   Lester and Miller, *Black Baseball in Kansas City*, 120.

13   Phil S. Dixon, *The Dizzy and Daffy Dean Barnstorming Tour: Race, Media, and America's National Pastime* (Lanham, Maryland: Rowman & Littlefield, 2019), 73.

14   Phil S. Dixon, *The Monarchs 1920-1938: Featuring Wilber "Bullet" Rogan the Greatest Ballplayer in Cooperstown* (Sioux Falls, South Dakota: Mariah Press, 2002), 41.

15   Dixon, *The Dizzy and Daffy Dean Barnstorming Tour,* 75.

16   John Holway interview of Frank Duncan, National Baseball Hall of Fame archives, 4.

17   Holway interview of Duncan, 3.

18   William A. Young, *J.L. Wilkinson and the Kansas City Monarchs: Trailblazers in Black Baseball* (Jefferson, North Carolina: McFarland & Company Inc., 2016), 34.

19   *Kansas City Star*, June 11, 1921: 12.

20   Dixon, *The Monarchs 1920-1938*, 133.

21   Lester, *Baseball's First Colored World Series*, 91.

22   *Kansas City Star,* May 28, 1946: 14.

23   Jason Roe, "Monarchs Defeat the Blues," https://pendergastkc.org/article/events/monarchs-defeat-blues.

24   https://pendergastkc.org/article/events/monarchs-defeat-blues.

25   *Kansas City Star*, September 27, 1971: 14.

26   Young, *J.L. Wilkinson and the Kansas City Monarchs*, 41.

27   Marv Goldberg, "Julia Lee," uncamarvy.com, 2020. http://www.uncamarvy.com/JuliaLee/julialee.html.

28   Conversations with Julian Duncan.

29   Dixon and Hannigan, 226.

30   John B. Holway, *Black Diamonds: Life in the Negro Leagues from the Men Who Lived It* (New York: Stadium Books, 1991), 64.

31   https://cubanbeisbol.com/post/18640671597/santa-clara-leopardos-1923-24.

32   Holway, *Black Ball Tales: Rollicking, All New, True Adventures of the Negro Leagues by the Men Who Lived and Loved Them* (Springfield, Virginia: Scorpio Books, 2008), 69.

33   Lester, *Baseball's First Colored World Series*, 62.

34   Lester, *Baseball's First Colored World Series*, 62.

35   Holway, *Black Ball Tales,* 71.

36   Lester, *Baseball's First Colored World Series*, 185.

37   *Pittsburgh Courier*, July 17, 1943: 19.

38   Young, 52.

39   Lester, *Baseball's First Colored World Series*, 178.

40   Holway, *Black Ball Tales*, 63.

41   Young, 103.

42   William F. McNeil, *The California Winter League: America's First Integrated Professional Baseball* League (Jefferson, North Carolina: McFarland & Company Inc., 2002), 120-121.

43   Kazuo Sayama and Bill Staples Jr., *Gentle Black Giants: A History of Negro League Baseball in Japan* (Fresno, California: Nisei Baseball Research Project Press, 2019), 94.

44   Rich Westcott, *Biz Mackey: A Giant Behind the Plate* (Philadelphia: Temple University Press, 2018), 107.

45   Sayama and Staples, 17.

46   Sayama and Staples, 16-17.

47   Sayama and Staples, 14.

48   Sayama and Staples, 201.

49   Neil Lanctot, *Fair Dealing & Clean Playing: The Hilldale Club and the Development of Black Professional Baseball, 1910-1932* (Syracuse: Syracuse University Press, 1994), 155.

50   Sayama and Staples, 258.

51   *Kansas City Times*, August 9, 1927: 10.

52   Janet Bruce, 120; *Alliance* (Nebraska) *Times-Herald*, July 4, 1950: 13.

53   *Kansas City Times,* March 19, 1985: 16.

54   Jorge S. Figueredo, *Who's Who in Cuban Baseball: 1878-1961* (Jefferson, North Carolina: McFarland & Company Inc., 2003), 351.

55   Dixon and Hannigan, 150.

56   Holway interview of Frank Duncan.

57   Lester, *Baseball's First Colored World Series*, 61.

58   Young, 69.

59   https://baseballhall.org/house-of-david-donation.

60   Young, 68-69.

61   Kyle P. McNary, *Ted "Double Duty" Radcliffe: 36 Years of Pitching & Catching in Baseball's Negro Leagues* (St. Louis Park, Minnesota: McNary Publishing, 1994), 69.

62   Phil S. Dixon, *The Monarchs 1920-1938*, 161.

63   http://www.cnlbr.org/Portals/0/Hero/Chet-Brewer.pdf, 13.

64   Young, 86.

65   Young, 88.

66 Dixon, *The Dizzy and Daffy Dean Barnstorming Tour*, 33.

67 *The Dizzy and Daffy Dean Barnstorming Tour*, 102.

68 Dixon, *The Dizzy and Daffy Dean Barnstorming Tour*, 23, 208.

69 Holway interview of Frank Duncan.

70 Lester, *Baseball's First Colored World Series*, 61.

71 Dixon and Hannigan, 246.

72 Mark Whitaker, *The Untold Story of Smoketown: The Other Great Black Renaissance* (New York: Simon & Schuster, 2018), 294.

73 Larry Lester, *Black Baseball's National Showcase: The East-West All-Star Game 1933-1962, Expanded Version* (Kansas City, Missouri: NoirTech Research Inc., 2020), 64.

74 William F. McNeil, *Black Baseball Out of Season: Pay for Play Outside of the Negro Leagues* (Jefferson, North Carolina: McFarland & Company Inc., 2007), 115-117.

75 It was Alex Kampouris.

76 Holway interview of Frank Duncan, 14.

77 Paul Debono, *The Chicago American Giants* (Jefferson, North Carolina: McFarland & Company Inc., 2007), 146.

78 Lester, *Black Baseball's National Showcase*, 110, 113.

79 Lester, *Black Baseball's National Showcase*, 60, 97; Young, 100.

80 Frank Duncan questionnaire returned to the National Baseball Hall of Fame, May 1972.

81 Debono, 151.

82 Dixon and Hannigan, 124.

83 Pedro Treto Cisneros, *The Mexican League: Comprehensive Player Statistics, 1937-2001* (Jefferson, North Carolina: McFarland & Company, Inc., 2002), 289.

84 Brent Kelley, *Voices from the Negro Leagues: Conversations with 52 Baseball Standouts* (Jefferson, North Carolina: McFarland & Company Inc., 1998), 99, 101.

85 Holway interview of Frank Duncan, 14.

86 *Chicago Defender*, April 4, 1942: 19.

87 Timothy M. Gay, *Satch, Dizzy & Rapid Robert* (New York: Simon & Schuster, 2010), 4.

88 Young, 125.

89 *Pittsburgh Courier*, July 17, 1943; Holway interview of Frank Duncan, 17.

90 https://www.baseball-reference.com/bullpen/Frank_Duncan.

91 Dixon, *John "Buck" O'Neil*, 159.

92 Lester, *Baseball's First Colored World Series*, 62.

93 *Kansas City Star*, August 14, 1950: 12.

94 Dixon, *The Dizzy and Daffy Dean Barnstorming Tour*, 44.

95 Holway, *Voices From the Great Black Baseball Leagues*, 340; *Kansas City Star*, May 28, 1946: 14.

96 Leslie A. Heaphy, 158.

97 Dixon and Hannigan, 255.

98 https://www.baseball-reference.com/bullpen/1946_Negro_World_Series.

99 *Pittsburgh Courier*, July 26, 1947: 14.

100 Young, 169.

101 Bob Motley and Byron Motley, *Ruling Over Monarchs, Giants & Stars: True Tales of Breaking Barriers, Umpiring Baseball Legends, and Wild Adventures in the Negro Leagues* (New York: Sports Publishing, 2012), 67.

102 Motley and Motley, 68, 69.

103 Motley and Motley, 71.

104 Motley and Motley, 72

105 Motley and Motley, 74.

106 Buck O'Neil, with Steve Wulf, and David Conrads, *I Was Right on Time: My Journey from the Negro Leagues to the Majors* (New York: Simon & Schuster, 1996), 172-173.

107 Motley and Motley, B159.

108 *Kansas City Star*, December 25, 1957: 17.

109 *Kansas City Star*, December 6, 1973: 29.

110 Lester, *Baseball's First Colored World Series*, 62.

111 William H. Young and Nathan B. Young Jr., *Your Kansas City and Mine* (Kansas City, Missouri: Midwest Afro-American Genealogy Interest Coalition, 1997), 127.

112 Steven R. Greenes, *Negro Leaguers and the Hall of Fame: The Case for Inducting 24 Overlooked Ballplayers* (Jefferson, North Carolina: McFarland & Company Inc., 2020), 235.

113 *Kansas City Star*. August 14, 1950: 12.

114 *Kansas City Star*, July 16, 1972: 192.

115 Dixon, *The Monarchs 1920-1938*, 40.

116 Jim Bankes, *The Pittsburgh Crawfords* (Jefferson, North Carolina: McFarland & Company Inc., 2001), 123-124.

117 Heaphy, 11.

118 Conversation with Julian Duncan.

119 *Kansas City Star*, December 6, 1973: 29.

120 *Kansas City Times*, March 10, 1967: 21.

121 Holway interview of Frank Duncan, 19.

JOE GREENE

By Steven R. Greenes

James Elbert Greene, who went by the first name Joe, was one of the iconic catchers of the Negro Leagues. Greene was born on October 17, 1911, in Stone Mountain, Georgia, an Atlanta suburb. The 5-foot-11, 190-pound Greene was a durable and solid receiver who caught Satchel Paige and the balance of the elite pitching staff of the Kansas City Monarchs in the 1940s. Behind the plate, he had a strong throwing arm and a quick release that he utilized effectively to cut down runners attempting to steal. At bat, he was a right-handed pull hitter with excellent power who hit for high average in his prime. His principal drawback as a player was his lack of speed on the basepaths.[1]

While little is known about Greene's early life, his mother, Emma Green, appears to have been working as a washerwoman at the time of his birth. By 1920, Emma Green was the head of her household and was employed as a cook for a private family.[2] Greene also had a brother, Henry, who was two years his senior. Joe attended school only through the fifth grade, and then likely already began to work to help his mother and brother pay for their family's expenses.

Historian Phil Dixon asserts that Greene broke into semipro ball with the Macon Georgia Peaches.[3] In 1932, at 21 years old, he made his debut in professional baseball, with the Atlanta Black Crackers of the Negro Southern League; it was the only year the Southern League was regarded as a Negro major league. The young and solid Greene was quickly nicknamed "Pig" for the quantity of food he consumed.[4] He began as a first baseman, but manager Nish Williams suggested, "You're big, got good weight on you, but you throw like a catcher. Can you catch?" As Greene told the story, "I said, 'I'm not scared to get back there, but I don't know how to catch. If you teach me how to catch, I'll catch.' ... I figured right quick if he was managing the ball club and if he was an ex-catcher, I'd have a better chance than anybody on that team of getting all the information I wanted. ... And I went up as a catcher because I always studied."[5]

Although like most Negro Leaguers he occasionally filled in at other positions,[6] it was as a catcher that Greene spent the bulk of his career and made his mark. He was with the Atlanta Black Crackers from 1932 through 1938. The Black Crackers sometimes played after 1932 as a member of the Negro National League, often as an independent barnstorming unit, and later as a member of the Negro American League. Because of the scanty offensive records available for this era, statistics have been uncovered for only 49 league games played by Greene with the Black Crackers, in which he hit .236 with 14 RBIs. Among the pitchers he caught early in his career was Roy Welmaker, who went on to star for the Homestead Grays.[7] Black Crackers shortstop Pee Wee Butts regarded Greene as one of the outstanding defensive stalwarts on the team: "Big [Joe] Greene ... had a good arm, could throw, could get the ball to you on time so the runner wouldn't have a chance to go through his act and spike you or something like that."[8]

In 1938 Atlanta joined the NAL and Greene's batting provided the charge needed to win the second-half title.[9] Greene batted .280 with a .782 OPS. Negro League historian James Riley has deemed Greene the NAL Rookie of the Year for his 1938 campaign.[10] Greene also played in the 1938 NAL Championship Series against the Memphis Red Sox. Over the course of the two-game series, which was swept by Memphis, Greene went 0-for-6 at the plate but maintained a perfect fielding percentage.

In 1939 the Black Crackers disbanded, and Greene was picked up by the Homestead Grays, where he roomed with future Hall of Famer Buck Leonard, who became his mentor. According to Leonard, "Greene was big, strong, had a great arm. He couldn't hit a curve ball, but he could hit a fast ball for miles. So we bought him an extra-long bat, a thirty-seven-inch bat. Then he could just get a piece of that curve ball."[11] When Josh Gibson joined the Grays as a catcher later in 1939, Greene got his big break as he was traded to the Kansas City Monarchs, where he remained through 1947.

In the early 1940s the Monarchs were the top squad for backstops to be on. They featured a stellar starting pitching lineup that included future Hall of Famers Satchel Paige and Hilton Smith, and Connie Johnson. When Johnson pitched to Greene, they were called the Stone Mountain Battery since Johnson was also from Stone Mountain.[12] According to Hilton Smith, Greene, who had turned himself into a strong curveball hitter, was an important catalyst for the Monarchs dynasty of that era: "We picked Joe Greene up as catcher in '39 and about the middle of the season he was really hitting that ball. In '40 he really *whipped* that ball."[13] Greene became the principal catcher for the great Monarchs franchise, which won league titles every year Greene was on the team between 1939 and 1946.[14] He also was part of a self-described "syndicate" of Monarchs players who demanded disciplined behavior and winning ways. They weeded out players who did not share those values.[15]

Hilton Smith once recalled: "I was telling a fellow today about Greene when he used play Cleveland when Sam Jethroe was there. [Jethroe was reputedly the fastest man in black ball at that time.] They told Greene, 'Well we're going to steal on you today. We're going to beat you, we're going to bunt and get on, then we're going to steal second, we're going to steal third, we're going to bunt in runs. … I was pitching and only six men got on [base] that day. … [S]ix of them tried to steal and he threw out five of six. … They'd get on, they'd try to go down, that's as far as they'd get. That guy could sure throw."[16] According to Greene, he carefully studied runners on the bases and coordinated closely with pitchers to catch players attempting to steal. He was so obsessed that he even dreamed at night about players trying to steal on him.[17]

Once he had become an established veteran, Greene's nickname morphed into "Pea" in tribute to the fact that he threw "peas" to second base.[18] Hilton Smith continued, "In '41, that's when Greene really came into his own. That year and the next year, '41 and '42, you can believe it or not, that guy in my opinion was the best catcher in baseball. In '42. … [T]hat man hit that ball that year. And threw out everybody. He was a *great* catcher those two years."[19]

Records bear out Smith's words. Usually batting fifth for the Monarchs behind Hall of Famer Willard Brown,[20] Greene led the Negro American League against all levels of competition in 1940 with 33 home runs.[21] In 1941 Greene's batting average against all competition was .313 as the Monarchs took the NAL pennant.[22]

Historian John Holway credits Greene with a .366 batting average in 1942, a year for which Holway has awarded Greene his Fleet Walker Award as the MVP of the NAL. In 1942 he again led the league with 38 home runs against all competition.[23] Dixon states that Greene joined an elite club in 1942 by hitting four home runs in one game, and that he drove in 15 runs in six consecutive games.[24] Buck Leonard later acknowledged that the Homestead Grays made a big mistake by giving up on Greene too early because "he turned out to be a great ballplayer."[25]

The power-hitting Greene always claimed that the Ted Williams shift was developed for him in the Negro Leagues by manager Candy Jim Taylor and then adopted by the major leagues after they saw it used against him.[26] Like Ted Williams, Greene was an extreme pull hitter who ignored the shift and just hit over it: "I hit the ball too hard for them. … In Kansas City, center field was 400-something feet. Oh, my God, you've got to drive a ball almost 500 feet to get it out of center field over that wall. I hit over the scoreboard in left-center field. I've hit lots of long home runs in Chicago's Comiskey Park way up in the stands. I hit a couple long ones in Yankee Stadium. … Josh Gibson and I were the two most powerful hitters as catchers." [27]

In the 1942 Negro League World Series, Greene's Kansas City Monarchs opposed Josh Gibson's Homestead Grays. Greene regarded himself as Gibson's equal and asserted, "Well, you've been talking 'bout the great Josh. I'm gonna let you know who's the great one."[28] Greene hit .500 with a home run to lead his team's offense to a four-game sweep of the Series. Gibson batted .077 with no home runs. Greene was Satchel Paige's catcher in the Series' classic confrontation between Paige on the mound and Gibson at the plate. In one at-bat, Paige, always the showman, announced to the crowd in advance the type of each pitch he would throw Gibson, and then struck Gibson out on three straight pitches, marking one of the legendary moments in Negro League history.[29]

Greene was named to three East-West All-Star Classics between 1940 and 1942, by which time he had become regarded as the best catcher in the Negro American League.[30] Seamheads.com, which has designated the single best catcher for each Negro League season based upon WAR,[31] has named Greene the NAL All-Star catcher in 1940, 1941, and 1942.

Greene capped 1942 by going 2-for-4, including a game-winning double, to lead his team to a 2-1 win over a team of Dizzy Dean-led White big leaguers in the armed forces before 29,000 fans in Wrigley Field.[32] Greene claimed his trick for hitting white major-league pitchers was that they often pitched low and he was a good low-ball hitter. According to Greene himself, "Sometimes they'd say, 'Joe Greene, you were on your knees when you hit that.' Sometimes I would go almost down on my right knee. But I'd hit it in the stands."[33]

In 1943, when he was at his peak ability as a player, Greene was inducted into the US Army and served three years during World War II. He was assigned to the all-black 92nd Infantry Division, the "Buffalo Soldiers," whose motto was "Deeds Not Words." As a member of the only African American division that saw combat action in Europe or North Africa during World War II, Greene fought in Oran, Algiers, and Italy. He was on the front lines for eight months. Greene was in a 57mm antitank company that opened up the third front in Italy. His harrowing job consisted of close-range combat against German tanks. Wounded by a shrapnel blast in Italy, he returned to combat after three weeks in the hospital and was awarded two battle stars. As his division drove into Milan, it was his military unit that discovered and cut down the bodies of Italian dictator Benito Mussolini and his mistress following their deaths at the hands of partisans.[34]

Yet his war experience left time for baseball after hostilities ended. Greene headed the 92nd Division team as it won the baseball championship of the Mediterranean Theater of Operations. Greene's team then played in the G.I. World Series in Marseilles where, combined with another African American division containing Willard Brown and Leon Day, the team, sparked by home runs by Greene and Brown, crushed Third Army squad, 8-0.[35]

In 1946 Greene went back to catching for the Monarchs as they again won the pennant. Holway has deemed him the 1946 All-Star catcher for the NAL.[36] According to James Riley, Greene was able to record batting averages of .300, .324, and .257 against all competition from 1946 to 1948.[37] In 1947 he blasted 16 home runs in 49 games.[38] The New York Yankees scouted Greene in the 1940s but nothing came of it.[39] The Yankees' first African American player was Elston Howard in 1955. Buck O'Neil, who discovered Howard, once observed that Greene, when he first came up in 1938, was a superior catcher to the young Howard.[40]

Joe Greene was the first-string catcher for the 1942 Monarchs and had the duty of receiving the pitches of future Hall of Famers Satchel Paige and Hilton Smith.
(Courtesy Noir-Tech Research, Inc.)

The following year featured one of Greene's career highlights when, at the age of 35, he hit a long home run off Bob Feller in an exhibition game in Los Angeles on November 2, 1947 (a nine-inning duel in which Satchel Paige bested Feller with a shutout).[41] The *Los Angeles Times* called Greene's blow a "resounding homer."[42]

But the hard truth is that Greene never really regained his prewar form.[43] In 1948 he was traded to the Cleveland Buckeyes, where he ended his Negro League career with only a .143 batting average in NAL games. He accumulated no WAR in official league games from 1946 through 1948 and his lifetime batting average fell to .242. All that was left was his power as his 1948 home-run percentage in limited plate appearances was a remarkably high 7.1 percent.

As the Negro Leagues went into a death spin after Jackie Robinson entered the major leagues, Greene followed other players to Canada. He finished his playing days at the age of 39 with one season in the independent ManDak League, hitting .301 with 16 RBIs in 1951 for the Elmwood Giants.[44]

After he retired as a player, Greene and his wife settled in Stone Mountain, where he worked for years at Sears Roebuck.[45] He was active in his community as a member of the local African American men's club.[46] Greene died in Stone Mountain on July 19, 1989, at the age of 77. He was survived by his wife, Emma

S. Greene; the couple had no children. The funeral service was held at the Bethsaida Baptist Church in Stone Mountain and Greene was buried in Stone Mountain City Cemetery.[47]

As a player, Joe Greene's importance should not be understated. He was an MVP, two-time home-run champion, Negro League World Series champion, and repeated All-Star who was responsible for handling Satchel Paige and the remarkable Kansas City Monarchs pitching staff during their multiple pennant runs in the 1940s. Even though he lost three years of his prime career to World War II, his OPS+ of 120 (many statisticians believe OPS+, which combines on-base-percentage plus slugging adjusted by ballpark and era, is the best overall measure of offensive performance)[48] stands as the fifth highest among catchers in American Negro League history. Greene's OPS+ rating for catchers in Negro League play is exceeded only by the four Negro League catchers inducted into the Hall of Fame (Josh Gibson, Louis Santop, Roy Campanella, and Biz Mackey).

Greene's WAR per 162 games of 3.3, established over the 12 years he played league ball, is the seventh highest established by any catcher in Negro League history. Bill James ranks Greene as the eighth best catcher of the Negro leagues.[49] Pitcher Jim "Fireball" Cohen, a Negro League All-Star who played at the tail end of the Josh Gibson era, chose Joe Greene as the number-one catcher on his all-time team.[50]

Ultimately, Greene's legacy is far larger than his on-field performance. He was a decorated war hero in a segregated army who fought alongside white soldiers. Since he also played against white major leaguers, he had a solid perspective from which to assess the overall quality of baseball at the highest levels. Greene become an advocate for Black ball and an outspoken spokesman for the quality of the Negro League game. In the 1940s Greene convinced leading sportswriter Fay Young of the *Chicago Defender* that the tryouts given to African American players prior to Jackie Robinson were a sham.[51] He forcefully declared that he and his African American brethren, not just Jackie Robinson, were the true pioneers who had paved the way for integration. He noted in a matter-of-fact manner that Robinson was not the best player the Negro Leagues produced, but simply representative of the excellence of Black ball.[52] According to Joe Greene, who played against them all, the Negro Leagues were "the real Major Leagues."[53]

Sources

Ancestry.com was consulted for census, military service, and death information.

Seamheads.com is the leading source for official Negro League game statistics. Other major historians, such as John Holway and James Riley, include all statistics against all opposition, including exhibition games, games against semipro teams and teams from other Negro Leagues, etc. John Holway believes that, as the majority of games played in Black ball were outside of the official league games, his approach is more indicative of the full Black baseball world. While there can be major discrepancies between the data gathered using these different approaches, both methods have value. In this article, completed early in 2021, Seamheads is the basis for player and team statistics cited in this article, except where otherwise indicated.

Notes

1 James A. Riley, *The Biographical Encyclopedia of the Negro Leagues* (New York: Carroll & Graf Publishers, Inc., 1994), 337.

2 His father may have been a Charlie Green, who is listed in the 1910 census has having been married to an Emma Green in Thomasville, Georgia; the name and birth year for Emma fit with Joe's mother, but that alone is not enough to positively state that this Charlie and Emma Green were his parents. In the 1940 census, Emma Green was listed as a widow. If Charlie Green was Joe's father, he may have died or abandoned the family at some point since he was not listed as part of the family unit in the 1920 census. It should also be noted that census takers consistently misspelled Joe Greene's family name as "Green."

3 Phil S. Dixon with Patrick J. Hannigan. *The Negro Baseball Leagues: A Photographic History* (Mattituck, New York: Amereon, 1992), 225.

4 Riley, 337.

5 John Holway, *Voices from the Great Black Baseball Leagues*, Rev Ed., (Mineola, New York: Dover Publications, 2010), 302-303.

6 In the seventh game of the 1946 Negro League World Series, Greene was pressed into serviced as a right fielder when outfielders Willard Brown and Ted Strong failed to show up until the game was almost over because they were busy negotiating winter contracts. Satchel Paige, who was scheduled to start the game, did not bother to show up at all. See Buck O'Neil, with Steve Wulf and David Conrads, *I Was Right on Time* (New York: Simon & Schuster, 1996), 177.

7 Dixon with Hannigan, 225.

8 Holway, *Voices*, 331.

9 Riley, 337-338.

10 Gary Gillette and Pete Palmer, eds., *The 2006 ESPN Baseball Encyclopedia* (New York: Sterling Publishing, 2006), 1649.

11 Holway, *Voices*, 299.

12 Frazier Robinson, *Catching Dreams: My Life in the Negro Baseball Leagues* (Syracuse, New York: Syracuse University Press, 2000), 59.

13 Holway, *Voices*, 300.

14 Aside from 1943 when Greene played in only two league games before he was called into the military. The team, denuded of much of its talent by the war, did not win the pennant that year.

15 Holway, Voices, 304-305.

16 Holway, *Voices*, 300.

17 Holway, *Voices*, 303-304.

18 Buck O'Neil, 119-120.

19 Holway, *Voices*, 300.

20 Riley, 337.

21 Riley, 337.

22 John B. Holway, *The Complete Book of Baseball's Negro Leagues: The Other Half of Baseball History* (Fern Park, Florida: Hastings House, 2001), 383.

23 Riley, 337.

24 Phil S. Dixon, *1987 Negro League Baseball Card Set*, card #8.

25 Holway, *Voices*, 299.

26 Holway, *Voices*, 301.

27 Holway, *Voices*, 301.

28 Holway, *Voices*, 300.

29 O'Neil, 133-135.

30 Riley, 337.

31 WAR (Wins Above Replacement) is a measure of a player's value based upon all facets of his performance and measures how many wins the player is worth versus an average replacement.

32 Holway, *Complete Book*, 401.

33 Holway, *Voices*, 304.

34 Timothy M. Gay, *Satch, Dizzy & Rapid Robert, The Wild Sage of Interracial Baseball Before Jackie Robinson* (New York: Simon & Schuster, 2010), 192-193.

35 Gay, 191-192.

36 Holway, *Complete Book*, 434.

37 Riley, 337;

38 Holway, *Voices*, Appendix.

39 Holway, *Voices*, 307; Gay, 252.

40 O'Neil, 189.

41 Gay, 258; Holway, *Complete Book*, 452.

42 Holway, *Voices*, 300.

43 Holway, *Voices*, 300.

44 Barry Swanton, *The Mandak League* (Jefferson, North Carolina: McFarland & Co, 2006), 108.

45 Holway, *Voices*, 309-10.

46 Dixon and Hannigan, 179.

47 *Atlanta Constitution*, July 23, 1989: 40.

48 OPS+ (On-Base Plus Slugging Plus) is a version of On-Base Percentage Plus Slugging, normalized by accounting for external factors such as ballpark and era. See Anthony Castrovince, *A Fan's Guide to Baseball Analytics* (New York: Skyhorse Publishing, Inc., 2020), 56-60, 76-81.

49 Bill James, *The New Bill James Historical Baseball Abstract*. (New York: The Free Press, 2001), 181.

50 Larry Lester. *Black Baseball's National Showcase: The East-West All-Star Game, 1933-1953* (Lincoln: University of Nebraska Press, 2001), 481.

51 Holway, *Voices*, 307.

52 Holway, *Voices*, 312.

53 Holway, *Voices*, 310.

PAUL HARDY

By Jeb Stewart

Paul Hardy was a defensive-minded catcher who played in the Negro leagues for nearly three decades, from 1931 to 1959. He stood 5-feet-10 and weighed just 162 pounds – a slight build for a backstop – but he developed a reputation for durability and regularly caught both ends of doubleheaders during his career. Nicknamed "Piccolo," "Pickemup,"[1] and "Greyhound,"[2] the right-hander was a smart player and a leader who frequently served as a player-manager.

Paul James Hardy was born on September 17, 1910, in Meridian, Mississippi. A 1920 Census record from that city notes that his mother was a single woman named Abbie Hardy, who laundered clothes in their home for work. Paul had seven siblings: Jennie, Della, Tom, Helena, Ellen, Beatrice, and Danella.[3] Little is known about Hardy's upbringing and education. However, by 1930 he was employed as a waiter in a boarding house in Meridian, Mississippi,[4] and he reportedly attended Alcorn Agricultural and Mechanical College in Lorman, Mississippi.[5]

In 1931 Hardy signed with the Montgomery Grey Sox of the newly reorganized Negro Southern League.[6] The 20-year-old made his professional debut on May 9 as the Grey Sox defeated the Chattanooga Black Lookouts, 6-1.[7] Later that month, his offensive skills powered the Grey Sox as he had three hits in an 8-7 loss to the Nashville Elite Giants.[8] He suffered an undisclosed injury during a game against the Birmingham Black Barons in June and had to be taken out of the game.[9] The injury had no lasting effect as his name again appeared in line scores within a week.[10] Hardy's rookie campaign launched his reputation as a durable receiver: He caught both games in doubleheaders on at least 11 occasions, according to the available box and line scores.[11] Even with rosters capped at 13, this was an achievement in endurance.[12]

Montgomery finished the first half of the NSL in fifth place with a 14-22 record.[13] According to NSL historian William J. Plott, the Grey Sox won the second-half title and faced the Memphis Red Sox in the playoffs. The series was tied after six games and was canceled for no apparent reason.[14]

Hardy returned to the Grey Sox in 1932 and had six straight hits in two games against Atlanta in early May.[15] The NSL was elevated to "Negro major league status by baseball historians because it survived while all others fell by the wayside during the worst of the Great Depression."[16] Montgomery had a winning record in the first half at 22-17 but finished in fourth place.[17] The results of the second half were clouded in uncertainty as the Grey Sox had a record of 1-6 in the last published standings.[18] Hardy was again the catcher of record in most of Montgomery's twin bills, which exposed his talents to owners in faraway cities.[19]

Hardy's play got the attention of Candy Jim Taylor and he joined the Indianapolis ABCs although details of his signing are lost to history.[20] The club soon moved to Detroit and was rebranded as the Stars in the reorganized Negro National League.[21] Taylor occasionally rested Hardy by penciling him into the lineup as a first baseman after he caught the first game of a doubleheader.[22] In August Hardy returned to Montgomery to face his old team; the Grey Sox took two of three games in the series.[23] The Stars finished in sixth place in the NNL with a record of 19-30.[24]

Over the next four years, Hardy continued to switch leagues and teams. In 1934 he returned to Alabama and played for the Birmingham Giants of the NSL, who newspapers sometimes called the Black Barons.[25] As usual, he rarely got a day off from behind the plate; in August, while catching both games of a doubleheader against the Brooklyn Bushwicks, he went 3-for-7 and stole a base.[26] In 1935 he played for the Columbus/Nashville Elite Giants.[27] The following year he may have returned to the Montgomery Grey Sox as a player-manager.[28] With Hardy at the helm and behind the plate, the Grey Sox dedicated a new ballpark, Brown's Park,[29] but had an otherwise disastrous season, finishing in last place in the NSL.[30] Finally, in 1937, Hardy joined Candy Jim Taylor's Chicago American Giants of the Negro American League for the next two years.[31] However, life in the Negro leagues was always hard, even if a player found stability in one city, as Hardy recalled years later to Wendell Smith:

• PAUL HARDY •

"Paul Hardy, a catcher for the old American Giants ... remembers the time his team arrived in Odessa, Tex., after a drive by car from Chicago.

"We arrived in the middle of the night," Hardy recalled. "We couldn't find a place to sleep, so we drove directly to the ball park. About an hour later the promoter of the game showed up. He was tall, white and spoke with a heavy Texas drawl. He said: 'Don't you all worry about a place to stay – because we ain't got no place for you to stay.'"

"So we slept in two cars," said Paul Hardy." [32]

With Chicago, Hardy enjoyed personal success and attention as newspapers "rated [him as] a fine hitter and an excellent receiver."[33] According to the Center for Negro League Baseball Research, "[T]he Kansas City Monarchs won both halves of the [1937] season ... [and] [t]hen beat the Chicago American Giants in a special post-season Play-Off Series when the American Giants disputed the Monarchs being awarded the Negro American League title."[34] Complete statistics for Hardy are unavailable for 1937, but he played well enough to be selected to represent the North in the NAL's All-Star game, which was played at Rickwood Field in Birmingham, Alabama, on August 22, 1937.[35] Hardy went 1-for-4, also reached base when he was hit by a pitch, and made an error behind the plate. He scored a run in the North's 13-5 win over the South.[36]

The next season, 1938, the American Giants finished 40-39, which was good for third place in the NAL.[37] Hardy remained with Chicago, and his name regularly appeared in box scores[38] as he reportedly hit .332.[39] However, he was demoted to a reserve role behind starter Richard "Subby" Byas.[40]

Whether it was due to reduced playing time in Chicago, or some other reason, Hardy joined the rival Kansas City Monarchs in 1939. The Monarchs had posted the best NAL record the previous two seasons and did so again in 1939 with a record of 42-22.[41] Kansas City won the first half of the NAL and then defeated the second-half champion, the St. Louis Stars, four games to one in a playoff series.[42] Hardy hit .324 with an on-base percentage of .410.[43] In May, he homered in a 15-8 victory over Memphis and followed that up with a key pinch hit in a win over the Paris Tigers.[44] Nevertheless, Hardy spent his second year as a backup catcher, this time behind Joe "Pea" Greene.

Birmingham had not fielded a Negro league team in 1939.[45] In 1940 the Black Barons returned to the NAL and hired Candy Jim Taylor as their manager. To improve Birmingham's catching and leadership, Taylor purchased Hardy's contract from Kansas City.[46] The *Birmingham News* applauded the acquisition, writing:

"Hardy is recognized as one of the best handlers of pitchers in Negro baseball, and he will arrive in town in time to catch the Sunday double-header. Hardy is known as such a good field general that he may be appointed captain of the Black Barons for the season of 1940." [47]

With the Black Barons, Hardy returned to the starting lineup, although he suffered a split finger in the spring, which sidelined him briefly.[48] Not only was Hardy a starter behind the plate, once again he caught both ends of doubleheaders with regularity.[49] But Birmingham finished a lackluster campaign in sixth place, with a record of 11-21.[50]

That fall, Hardy appeared for Taylor's NAL All-Stars and faced Birmingham's Industrial League All-Stars at Rickwood Field. Future Black Barons Piper Davis, Artie Wilson, Bill Powell, and Ed Steele of the American Cast Iron Pipe Company (ACIPCO) played for the Industrial Leaguers.[51]

Winfield Welch became manager of the Black Barons in 1941 and retained Hardy as his catcher.[52] In a feature article about the club, Hardy was credited as being "a hard worker, [who] handles pitchers well, and is a good director behind the bat."[53] In late April he caught both halves of a twin bill and socked a bases-clearing triple in the second game as the Black Barons earned a split with the New York Black Yankees.[54] He caught both ends of doubleheaders at least 10 times.[55] His sturdy presence behind the plate did not escape the notice of fans or sportswriters:

"Paul Hardy, selected by a vote of the fans as the most valuable Baron for the '41 season, and presented with a U.S. defense bond by President Tom Hayes, Jr., at last Sunday's double-header, will catch both Sunday games. Hardy, with a hitting average of .302, has caught most of the double-headers."[56]

The Black Barons improved to an overall record of 28-20 and finished in second place in the NAL behind Kansas City.[57] In a five-game exhibition series against local all-stars, Hardy went 3-for-4 in the deciding fifth game as the Black Barons won, 5-4.[58]

• When the Monarchs Reigned •

In the spring of 1942, newspapers hailed Hardy, now 31, as "one of the craftiest catchers in all of Negro baseball," "a steadying influence with pitchers," "the veteran catcher who meant so much to the Black Barons last season," and "one of the hardest workers in the league."[59] Hardy played well in 1942 and was voted onto the West roster for the annual East-West All-Star Game in Chicago.[60] All available box and line scores and game accounts indicate Hardy played the entire 1942 campaign for the Black Barons, who finished in third place in the NAL with a record of 27-22.[61] However, he may also have appeared in at least one game for the Kansas City Monarchs in 1942.

In *The Kansas City Monarchs: Champions of Black Baseball*, historian Janet Bruce cites Hardy as a catcher on the roster of the Monarchs in 1942.[62] Concerning the rosters from 1920 to 1955, Bruce noted, "Because players frequently jumped their contracts in midseason, rosters changed over the course of the summer … all players who were on the payroll for some part of the season are included."[63] Other sources, including William A. Young's *J.L. Wilkinson and the Kansas City Monarchs*, James A. Riley's *Biographical Encyclopedia of the Negro Baseball Leagues,* and *The Negro Leagues Book*, edited by Dick Clark and Larry Lester, list Hardy on the roster of the Monarchs in 1942, the latter identifying him as both a catcher and right fielder.[64]

Johnnie Dawson and Gread McKinnis were also members of the Black Barons in 1942.[65] According to Seamheads.com, both appeared in games with the Monarchs that season: McKinnis played in one game, while Dawson appeared in nine.[66] However, Seamheads.com does not include Hardy on the Monarchs roster.[67] Hardy himself later recalled playing "several seasons" for the Monarchs,[68] though most sources identify him on the roster only in 1939.

Hardy may have been loaned to the Monarchs for a single game, either when the Black Barons were not playing, or when the teams played one another and Kansas City could not field a full squad. Such an occurrence was not uncommon in the Negro leagues and may have been exacerbated because of the outbreak of World War II, which depleted rosters. The Black Barons lost seven players to military service during 1942 alone.[69] Loaning players was sometimes necessary to avoid losing gate revenue if a game had to be canceled. Such a practice was not without its critics, however. In 1944 the Monarchs objected when the Chicago American Giants allegedly used borrowed players to defeat Satchel Paige.[70] Columnist Wendall Smith loathed the practice, writing:

"Chicago contended that both players were originally members of its squad, but had been loaned out early in the season, subject to recall. Now we all know, of course, that such "deals" are in direct opposition to the rules and regulations of organized baseball.

If such "deals" were permissible, it would enable any team in the league to "stack up" with the star players of a club that lacked a mathematical chance of winning a pennant. It would enable one club to build up for one particular series, or mean that all the players in one league could be switched around at the will of the owners.

. . .

There is no such thing in baseball as a loaned player. A player is traded or sold to another club. He cannot be put on wheels and shoved back and forth, from one club to another, as has been the case of [Willie] Wells and [Alex] Radcliffe. And even then, there is a time limit on the trading and selling of players. Certainly such deals cannot be made in the middle of the season without the approval of the other clubs in the league."[71]

Whether Hardy appeared in a game for the Monarchs in 1942 will remain a mystery unless a box score or additional evidence is located.

The following year, 1943, marked the rise of the Birmingham Black Barons as one of the best franchises in the Negro leagues. Birmingham finished 46-35 and won the first-half title in the NAL.[72] For most of the summer, Hardy was the starting catcher, but his name last appeared in a box score on September 3.[73]

As the Black Barons prepared to face the second-half champion Chicago American Giants in the playoffs, newspapers listed Hardy on Birmingham's roster.[74] However, the US Army had already drafted him,[75] and Herman Bell replaced Hardy on the Black Barons.[76] Bell himself was then injured against Chicago and could not play in the Negro League World Series.[77] The Homestead Grays agreed to allow the Black Barons to use Ted "Double Duty" Radcliffe, player-manager of the American Giants, as their catcher.[78] The Grays won an exciting seven-game series over the Black Barons. Wendell Smith complained that Radcliffe's addition to

• PAUL HARDY •

Catcher Paul Hardy was a member of the 1942 Birmingham Black Barons but may have briefly been on loan – along with two teammates – to the Monarchs. (Courtesy Noir-Tech Research, Inc.)

Birmingham's roster, notwithstanding Homestead's approval, made the series appear "slip-shod" and called for a league commissioner.[79]

Hardy was assigned to the Army's 868th Company at Camp Knight in Oakland, California. He played baseball at Camp Knight and captained the football team while stationed at Camp Plauche, near New Orleans. During his hitch, Hardy achieved the rank of sergeant and was discharged on September 28, 1945.[80] He rejoined the Black Barons, who were on a barnstorming tour of the West Coast.[81] However, Hardy's time with Birmingham was soon over and he remained in the West the following year.

Abe Saperstein had been the business manager of the Black Barons for several years in the 1940s. In 1946 Saperstein owned a barnstorming team, the Cincinnati Crescents. He merged the Crescents with the roster of his Harlem Globetrotters baseball club to form the Seattle Steelheads; the Steelheads joined the newly formed West Coast Negro Baseball League.[82] He hired Paul Hardy, now 35, as his player-manager and rented Sick's Stadium in Seattle for most home games.[83] The new league collapsed after just two months.[84] Hardy and his players then went back to barnstorming. Later that fall, Saperstein organized a 14-game all-star trip to Hawaii where Hardy was joined by former Black Barons Piper Davis, Artie Wilson, and Ed Steele, as well as Luke Easter and Cool Papa Bell.[85]

In February 1947 the *Pittsburgh Courier* reported that Hardy was expected to join the Memphis Red Sox for spring training.[86] However, Saperstein had other plans. He hired Hardy to manage and catch for the Harlem Globetrotters, whom Saperstein reorganized through a merger of the rosters of the Crescents and Steelheads.[87] Like their basketball cousins, the Globetrotters traveled the country playing local teams, Negro league teams, all-star squads, or other barnstorming outfits, such as the House of David.[88] Globetrotters games featured shadowball performances along with appearances by baseball clown Eddie Hamman to entertain fans.[89] Hardy remained as the player-manager of the Globetrotters from 1947 to 1950.

Before arriving in a particular city, the Globetrotters would issue advertisements disguised as news stories to drum up interest in their coming appearance. Hardy was often described as being "rated as one of the greatest catchers in Negro League baseball" and "one of the best-liked fellows in Negro baseball and certain to go far as a manager."[90] One such example of the effusive praise for Hardy appeared in a 1949 article:

"If Paul Hardy wasn't happily situated as manager of the crack Harlem Globetrotters – which is scheduled at Affleck park against the House of David July 8 – he'd certainly be among the first Negro stars summoned into the major league.

Hardy, a youthful veteran, is equipped with everything to make the grade – ability, hustle, brains, a great competitive spirit and a deep love for the game. He long has rated among the greatest sepia catching stars, and he has been back of the plate and managing the Globetrotter nine since its inception."[91]

Under Hardy's leadership, the Globetrotters reportedly had a record of 500-125 (.800),[92] though newspapers seldom published game accounts or line scores. In a rare report on a contest between the Globetrotters and the House of David, Hardy's pickoff throw to first nailed a runner to end the game.[93]

Besides his baseball duties, Hardy often drove the bus for the basketball Globetrotters during the winter.[94]

However, by 1951, the Globetrotters ceased baseball operations.[95]

Winfield Welch had taken over the struggling Chicago American Giants. Thanks to Saperstein, many of the Globetrotters ended up on his roster, including Hardy.[96] Hardy was the starting catcher and shared managing duties with Welch.[97] His defensive prowess was on display in a barnstorming victory over the South Bend Indians in May as "Hardy won a round of applause after a long run, climaxed by a one-hand catch of Scott's foul in the seventh."[98] Buoyed by former Globetrotters, the American Giants improved on their 1950 record (15-31 and last place in their division) to finish 34-24 and claim second place in the NAL West in 1951.[99] Later that fall, Hardy played catcher and shortstop on Roy Campanella's All-Stars, along with Piper Davis, Larry Doby, Luke Easter, Monte Irvin, Willie Mays, Verdell Mathis, Hank Thompson, Joe Black, Don Newcombe, and Jimmie Newberry, among others.[100]

In 1952 the Chicago American Giants finished 32-31 for a third-place finish in the team's coda in the NAL. The reliable Hardy returned as player-manager until the end amid dubious reports that the 41-year-old catcher had "refused numerous major league offers to remain as manager of the Giants on a year-round basis."[101] Hardy again barnstormed with the Roy Campanella All-Stars after the season. In one of his final games, the All-Stars faced the Birmingham Black Barons before a crowd of 2,227 at Rickwood Field. Hardy singled to drive in Willie Mays for the final run in the All-Stars' 5-3 win.[102]

After his apparent retirement from baseball, Hardy continued driving the bus for the Globetrotters basketball squad for several years.[103] However, in 1959 he may have returned to the NAL to play for the Birmingham Black Barons. From June 19 to July 20, the name "Hardy" appeared in the line score as a catcher four times during the Black Barons' NAL championship season.[104] The question is whether it was Paul Hardy.

In Appendix B to *Black Baseball's Last Team Standing: The Birmingham Black Barons, 1919-1962*, William J. Plott concluded that the catcher was indeed Paul Hardy."[105] His inclusion, even as a 48-year-old catcher on the Black Barons, would have made some sense. Piper Davis was the manager and considered the team to be an "exhibition outfit by then."[106] He and Hardy had been teammates on the Black Barons in 1943 and 1945. Also, both had regularly driven the Globetrotters' bus during offseasons; Davis had done so during the winters of 1958 and 1959.[107]

The Globetrotters employed Hardy for 37 years.[108] By 1964, he estimated he had already "driven more than 1.7 million miles in the United States and other parts of the world minus a single accident," a distance he figured as second only to Abe Saperstein.[109] In the same feature story, he described his greatest baseball moment for columnist Al Warden: "This happened in Merrill, Wisconsin. Our rivals had the bases loaded and the batter put on the squeeze play and I was the starter of a sensational triple play. This was my biggest baseball thrill."

Hardy died on August 28, 1979, at the Lakeside Veterans Hospital in Chicago.[110] He left behind his wife, Ruthe Hardy, and three daughters, Vivona Summers, Peggy Love, and Emily Norris.[111]

Acknowledgments

The author wishes to thank fellow SABR researchers Bill Young, Chris Hicks, Alan Cohen, Donna Halper, Tim Tassler, and Bill Plott, who took time to answer emails about whether Paul Hardy played for the Kansas City Monarchs in 1942. In addition, Janet Bruce Vaughn, Gary Ashwill, and Larry Lester were generous with their time and helpful in responding to questions about Hardy. Finally, the author is grateful to Cassidy Lent, reference librarian at the National Baseball Hall of Fame and Museum, who provided him with Paul Hardy's obituary.

Notes

1. https://www.seamheads.com/NegroLgs/player.php?playerID=hardy01pau.
2. William J. Plott, *Black Baseball's Last Team Standing: The Birmingham Black Barons, 1919-1962* (Jefferson, North Carolina: McFarland Publishing, 2015), 248.
3. Mississippi. Lauderdale County. 1920 US Census.
4. Mississippi. Lauderdale County. 1930 US Census.
5. "Grey Sox Divide Tilts With 'Nooga; Hit Road Till June," *Montgomery Advertiser*, May 12, 1931: 10. It is possible, the reference to Paul Hardy attending Alcorn may have been mistaken as Grey Sox pitcher Wheeler Hardy also attended the school. William J. Plott, *The Negro Southern League: A Baseball History, 1920-1951* (Jefferson, North Carolina: McFarland Publishing, 2014), 83. The author was unable to confirm whether Paul Hardy played baseball at Alcorn because the school does not have records from the 1930s. Robbie Kleinmuntz, assistant athletic director for sports information at Alcorn State University, email correspondence with author, September 23, 2020. Assuming Hardy attended Alcorn, he apparently did not mention this to Al Warden when he was featured in his column in 1964. Al Warden, "The Sports Highway," *Odgen* (Utah) *Standard-Examiner*, February 10, 1964: 6. Also, Hardy's obituary made no mention of his education. "Obituaries: Paul Hardy," *Chicago Tribune*, August 30, 1979: 49.

• PAUL HARDY •

6 "Negro Southern League Organized," *Nashville Banner*, March 15, 1931: 28; "Grey Sox Divide Tilts With 'Nooga; Hit Road Till June."

7 "Grey Trounce Chattanooga," *Montgomery Advertiser*, May 10, 1931: 9.

8 "Elites Subdue Grey Sox, 8-7," *Nashville Banner*, May 24, 1931: 28.

9 "Black Barons Bow to Grey Sox, 7 to 5," *Montgomery Advertiser*, June 7, 1931: 7.

10 "Grey Sox Beaten By Atlanta, 11-1," *Montgomery Advertiser*, June 12, 1931: 10.

11 "Grey Sox Divide Tilts With 'Nooga; Hit Road Till June"; "Barons Lose Night Games to Grey Sox," *Birmingham Reporter*, June 27, 1931: 7; "Grey Sox Split With Memphis," *Montgomery Advertiser*, June 29, 1931: 7; "Grey Sox Beat Knoxville Nine," *Montgomery Advertiser*, July 6, 1931: 10; "Grey Sox Capture Double Bill, 6-1 – 3-0," *Montgomery Advertiser*, July 20, 1931: 6; "Mobile Loses Three Straights to Sox," *Montgomery Advertiser*, July 25, 1931: 7; "Grey Sox Split With Giant Foe," *Montgomery Advertiser*, August 3, 1931: 12; "Grey Sox Romp on Jacksonville 'Stingerees,'" *Birmingham Reporter*, August 8, 1931: 7; "Sox Defeat Giants in a Twin Bill," *Birmingham Reporter*, August 22, 1931: 3; "Sox and Barons Split Twin Bill," *Birmingham Reporter*, August 29, 1931: 3; "White Sox Win, Lose," *Louisville Courier-Journal*, August 31, 1931: 7.

12 Plott, *The Negro Southern League*, 82.

13 "Elites Lead Dixie League," *Pittsburgh Courier*, July 18, 1931: 14.

14 Plott, *The Negro Southern League*, 88. Adding to the confusion, newspapers cited the Nashville Elite Giants as being champions of the Negro Southern League in advertisements for the Negro Dixie Series against the Negro Texas-Louisiana League champions, the Monroe Monarchs. "Negro Dixie Series," *Times* (Shreveport, Louisiana), September 5, 1931: 11.

15 "Grey Sox Open Season With Atlanta Team Here Today," *Montgomery Advertiser*, July 20, 1931: 6; Plott, *The Negro Southern League*, 95.

16 Plott, *The Negro Southern League*: 91.

17 "Monarchs Triumph in Colored League," *Monroe* (Louisiana) *News-Star*, July 6, 1932: 6.

18 Plott, *The Negro Southern League*, 100.

19 "Grey Sox Take Two from Crax," *Montgomery Advertiser*, April 25, 1932: 5; "Barons Win Four, Lose One," *Montgomery Advertiser*, May 21, 1932: 4; "Grey Sox Lose to Louisianans," *Montgomery Advertiser*, May 30, 1932: 6; "Little Rock Loses Twice to Grey Sox," *Montgomery Advertiser*, June 6, 1932: 6; "Black Caps Take Two from Montgomery Sox," *Louisville Courier-Journal*, July 11, 1932: 5; "Grey Sox Grab Two Games from Louisville In 2nd Place Fight," *Montgomery Advertiser*, July 25, 1932: 6.

20 "Lincoln Giants Defeat Indianapolis Team, 9-7," *Town Talk* (Alexandria, Louisiana), April 7, 1933: 12.

21 https://www.blackpast.org/african-american-history/the-indianapolis-abcs-1907-1942/.

22 "Nashville Takes Lead from Giants in Negro National," *Birmingham News*, August 7, 1933: 7.

23 "Detroit Team Plays Here Against Locals Tonight," *Montgomery Advertiser*, August 11, 1933: 3; "Grey Sox Capture Abbreviated Game," *Montgomery Advertiser*, August 12, 1933: 6; "Grey Sox, Detroit Divide Twin Bill," *Montgomery Advertiser*, August 14, 1933: 6.

24 http://www.cnlbr.org/Portals/0/Standings/Negro%20National%20League%20(1920-1948)-2020.pdf.

25 "Negro Teams Play Sunday at 'Wood,'" *Birmingham News*, May 13, 1934: 16; "Cincy Takes Double Bill From Barons," *Pittsburgh Courier*, June 16, 1934: 15. According to Plott, "The Birmingham News referred to the ball club as 'Birmingham Giants, alias the Black Barons.'" Plott, *The Negro Southern League*, 117.

26 "Chambers and Grampp Defeat Black Barons; Farmers Win Twin Bill," *Brooklyn Daily Eagle*, August 20, 1934: 8.

27 "Elite Giants Make Debut Here Sunday," *Tennessean* (Nashville), April 4, 1935: 15; "Black Eagles Gain Split With Elites," *Times Union* (Brooklyn), June 24, 1935: 11; "Grays Divide with Columbus," *Pittsburgh Sun-Telegraph*, June 30, 1935: 42; "Eagles Defeated by Strong Rivals," *Times Union*, July 22, 1935: 11; "Dukes Beaten by Elite Nine in Thrillers," *Times Union*, September 16, 1935: 13.

28 No other "Paul Hardy" has been identified as playing in the Negro Leagues in 1936. Newspapers referred to the Grey Sox player-manager only as "Hardy." Adding to the confusion, a 1937 article stated, "Hardy worked for Manager Taylor at Washington." Hank Casserly, "Chicago Club Faces Locals Wednesday and Thursday," *Capital Times* (Madison, Wisconsin), May 25, 1937: 17. This reference was likely to the 1936 season when the Elite Giants played in Washington. However, given Hardy's prior connection with the Montgomery club and his position as a catcher (which was the same as Montgomery's player-manager named "Hardy"), the author assumes the Montgomery references to "Hardy" were to Paul Hardy. His association with Candy Jim Taylor was probably during the 1935 season when Hardy played with the Columbus/Nashville Elite Giants before the club played in Washington. "Columbus Giants to Play Grey Sox in New Ball Park," *Montgomery Advertiser*, April 12, 1936: 23; "Grey Sox to Play Chicago Negro Ball Club Today," *Montgomery Advertiser*, April 26, 1936: 6; "Tigers Stage Rally," *Cincinnati Enquirer*, May 18, 1936: 18.

29 "Grey Sox Host In Twin Bill Today to Atlanta All-Star," *Montgomery Advertiser*, July 19, 1936: 22.

30 Plott, *The Negro Southern League*, 140; http://www.cnlbr.org/Portals/0/Standings/Negro%20Southern%20League%20%20(1920-1951)-2020.pdf.

31 "Black Barons and Chicago Club to Open 1937 Season," *Birmingham News*, April 24, 1937: 8; Hank Casserly, "Chicago Club Faces Locals Wednesday and Thursday," *Capital Times*, May 25, 1937: 17.

32 Wendell Smith, "Baseball Pays Bill to Satchel," *Boston Globe*, February 10, 1971: 39.

33 Casserly, "Chicago Club Faces Locals Wednesday and Thursday."

34 http://www.cnlbr.org/Portals/0/Standings/Negro%20American%20League%20(1937-1962)-2020.pdf.

35 "Negro Teams Set for Battle Here," *Birmingham News*, August 22, 1937: 20.

36 "Northern Negro All-Stars Down Southern Team," *Birmingham News*, August 23, 1937: 8.

37 https://www.seamheads.com/NegroLgs/team.php?yearID=1938&teamID=CAG&LGOrd=2.

38 "Black Barons Go Down in Defeat in Pair of Battles," *Birmingham News*, May 2, 1938: 13; "Locals Error in Fifth to Help Visitors," *South Bend* (Indiana) *Tribune*, May 28, 1938: 8; "Colored Team Boasts Great Hurling Staff," *Sheboygan* (Wisconsin) *Press*, August 9, 1938: 10.

39 Ray T. Rocene, "Sports Jabs," *Missoulian* (Missoula, Montana), June 22, 1939: 6.

40 Hank Casserly, "Great Negro Club Here Wednesday and Thursday," *Capital Times*, June 7, 1938: 13.

41 https://www.seamheads.com/NegroLgs/year.php?yearID=1939&lgID=All&tab=standings.

42 "Kansas City Monarchs Win American League Pennant by Beating St. Louis Three Straight," *Pittsburgh Courier*, September 9, 1939: 16.

43 https://www.seamheads.com/NegroLgs/player.php?playerID=hardy01pau.

44 "Monarchs Win," *St. Joseph* (Missouri) *Gazette*, May 19, 1939: 6; "Monarchs Rally to Beat Paris," *Paris* (Texas) *News*, May 21, 1939: 9.

45 Plott, *Black Baseball's Last Team Standing*, 121.

46 "Black Barons Clash with Baltimore Club in Twin Bill Sunday," *Birmingham News*, April 20, 1940: 8.

47 "Black Barons Clash with Baltimore Club in Twin Bill Sunday."

48 "Black Barons to Have Their Full Forces for St. Louis Sunday," *Birmingham News*, May 8, 1940: 8.

49 "American Giants Win Twice from Birmingham Nine," *Chicago Tribune*, May 31, 1940: 20; "First Game Goes 14 Innings," *Pittsburgh Courier*, June 8, 1940: 17; "Black Barons Divide Double-Header Here With Cleveland Team," *Birmingham News*, June 24, 1940: 11; "Black Barons Defeat Chicago Team Twice by Scores of 4-2, 3-2," *Birmingham News*, August 19, 1940: 13; "Bushwicks Cash In Twice Behind Effective Hurling," *Brooklyn Daily Eagle*, August 26, 1940: 15; "Black Barons to Play Baltimore Team Here in Twin Bill Sunday," *Birmingham News*, September 21, 1940: 10.

50 https://www.seamheads.com/NegroLgs/year.php?yearID=1940&lgID=NAL.

51 "Jim Taylor to Send His All-Star Squad Against Local Team," *Birmingham News*, October 6, 1940: 29.

52 "Black Barons Open Season Here April 20 Against New Yorkers," *Birmingham News*, April 13, 1941: 21.

53 "Black Barons Headed for Home; 'Welch Day' Here to Be Season's Big Attraction," *Weekly Review* (Birmingham, Alabama), August 15, 1941: 7.

54 "Black Barons Divide Pair With Yankees; Gone for Two Weeks," *Birmingham News*, April 21, 1941: 12.

55 "Black Barons Divide Pair With Yankees; Gone for Two Weeks"; "Black Barons Defeat Eagles in Nightcap After Losing Opener," *Birmingham News*, May 5, 1941: 14; "Black Barons Split Memphis Twin Bill," *Birmingham News*, June 2, 1941: 14; "Black Barons Victors in Opener, but Lose Nightcap To Memphis," *Birmingham News*, June 9, 1941: 14; "Black Barons Capture First Game, 4 to 3, but Lose Second, 4-0," *Birmingham News*, June 30, 1941: 16; "Black Barons Defeat Red Caps in First Game but Lose Second," *Birmingham News*, July 5, 1941: 10; "Black Barons Divide Twin Bill With Caps; Both Are Close Tilts," *Birmingham News*, July 7, 1941: 13; "Black Barons, Red Sox Split Two in Memphis; Welch Day Here Aug. 27th," *Weekly Review* (Birmingham, Alabama), August 8, 1941; H.J. Williams, "Barons Win Double Bill," *Weekly Review*, August 29, 1941: 7; "Black Barons Close Out Successful Year Against New Yorkers," *Birmingham News*, September 28, 1941: 20.

56 "Diamond Strategist of Negro Champions to Play With Team," *Birmingham News*, September 14, 1941: 14.

57 https://www.seamheads.com/NegroLgs/year.php?yearID=1941&lgID=NAL&tab=standings.

58 "Black Barons Victors Over All-Stars," *Birmingham News*, October 5, 1941: 22.

59 "Black Barons Will Open Season Against Kansas City Outfit," *Birmingham News*, April 17, 1942: 31; "Black Barons, Monarchs Will Initiate Season," *Birmingham News*, April 19, 1942: 23; "Black Barons to Show Classy Outfit Here Monday Night," *Montgomery Advertiser*, May 16, 1942: 7.

60 "Ethiopian Clowns Bring Pranks for Black Baron Frays," *Birmingham News*, August 23, 1942: 11D.

61 http://www.seamheads.com/NegroLgs/year.php?yearID=1942&lgID=NAL.

62 Janet Bruce, *The Kansas City Monarchs: Champions of Black Baseball* (Lawrence: University Press of Kansas, 1985), 139. Ms. Bruce, who is now Janet Vaughan, no longer has her research on the rosters. Email from Janet Vaughan, October 25, 2020.

63 Bruce, 133.

64 William A. Young, *J.L. Wilkinson and the Kansas City Monarchs* (Jefferson, North Carolina: McFarland & Company, Inc., 2016), 202; James A. Riley, *The Biographical Encyclopedia of the Negro Baseball Leagues* (New York: Carroll & Graf Publishers, Inc., 1994), 355; Dick Clark and Larry Lester, eds., *The Negro Leagues Book*, (Cleveland: SABR, 1994), 131. Bill Young was kind enough to check his notes from the 1942 *Kansas City Call* but found no references to Hardy on the Monarchs roster. Email from Bill Young, December 5, 2020. Likewise, Larry Lester confirmed that Paul Hardy was not included in any of Kansas City's team photographs in 1942; and the sources listing him on the Monarchs' roster are wrong. Email from Larry Lester, April 24, 2020.

65 http://www.seamheads.com/NegroLgs/team.php?yearID=1942&teamID=BBB&LGOrd=2.

66 https://seamheads.com/NegroLgs/team.php?yearID=1942&teamID=KCM.

67 Seamheads.com's Gary Ashwill has not located any box scores with Hardy included on the club. Nevertheless, he has not ruled out the possibility that Hardy played for the club briefly. Facebook message from Gary Ashwill, October 12, 2020.

68 Al Warden, "The Sports Highway," *Ogden Standard-Examiner*, February 10, 1964: 6. Hardy may have played for the Monarchs on June 7. The Black Barons and Monarchs played a doubleheader before 7,000 fans at Rickwood Field. Double Duty Radcliffe caught both games for the Black Barons "during the absence of Captain Hardy," which the article did not explain. Monarchs catcher Johnnie Dawson was thrown out of the second game for cursing at an umpire, which created the need for a replacement. However, the article did not mention who took over behind the plate and the line scores did not list the batteries. "Barons Put On Hitting Spree to Win 12-2, but Lose Heart Breaker 5-4," *Weekly Review*, June 13, 1942: 7. However, a box score in another newspaper lists both Frank Duncan and Joe Greene as appearing at catcher after Dawson's ejection. "Black Barons Divide Couple With Monarchs," *Birmingham News*, June 8, 1942: 17.

69 "Black Barons Meet New York Cubans in Double Bill Sunday," *Birmingham News*, September 14, 1942.

70 "'Loaned' Players Beat Paige, Kansas City Protest," *Pittsburgh Courier*, July 15, 1944: 12.

71 "'Smitty's' Sports Spurts," *Pittsburgh Courier*, July 15, 1944: 12.

72 http://www.seamheads.com/NegroLgs/year.php?yearID=1943&lgID=NAL&tab=standings.

73 "Fore River Battles Barons to 2-2 Tie," *Boston Globe*, September 3, 1943: 26.

74 "Negro Giants, Barons Start Series Today," *Chicago Tribune*, September 12, 1943: 38.

75 "Sox Park Is Site of Negro Game Today," *Chicago Tribune*, September 26, 1943: 34.

76 "Black Barons Drop Opener to Giants," *Birmingham News*, September 14, 1943: 17; "Black Barons Trip Chicago in Bowl, 4-1," *Montgomery Advertiser*, September 18, 1943; "Black Barons Clinch Negro American League Flag; Whip Giants, 1-0," *Birmingham News*, September 20, 1943: 17.

77 "Black Meet Homestead Grays at Rickwood Sunday," *Birmingham News*, September 29, 1943: 19.

78 "Sox Park Is Site of Negro Game Today," *Chicago Tribune*, September 26, 1943: 34.

79 "'Smitty's' Sports Spurts," *Pittsburgh Courier*, October 2, 1943: 16.

80 "Harlem Baseball Team to Play at East Helena," *Independent-Record* (Helena, Montana), June 19, 1947: 9; "Hardy Leads Globetrotters," *Salt Lake Tribune*, July 20, 1948: 17.

81 "First Loss for Barons," *San Francisco Examiner*, October 22, 1945: 17; "Meusel All Stars Defeated by Barons," *San Bernardino County* (California) *Sun*, October 27, 1945: 8.

82 Norm King, "Abe Saperstein," accessed at https://sabr.org/bioproj/person/abe-saperstein/; http://sportspressnw.com/2145947/2013/wayback-machine-seattle-steelheads-short-life.

83 Lee Dunbar, "On the Level," *Oakland Tribune*, May 3, 1946: 20; "Negro Teams in League Contest," *San Bernardino County Sun*, May 17, 1946: 19; David Eskenazi, "Wayback Machine: A legacy of black baseball," May 5, 2015: accessed at http://sportspressnw.com/2203231/2015/wayback-machine-a-legacy-of-black-baseball.

84 Eskenazi.

85 Don Watson, "Speaking of Sports," *Honolulu Star-Bulletin*, July 27, 1946: 17; Al Warden, "Patrolling the Sport Highway," *Ogden Standard-Examiner*, September 26, 1946: 8.

86 "Memphis Reds Bolster Team," *Pittsburgh Courier*, February 22, 1947: 17.

87 "Harlem Team to Train In South," *Weekly Review*, April 5, 1947: 7; "Globetrotters Doing well," *Weekly Review,* April 12, 1947: 7.

88 "'Trotters Will Play Detroit," *Pittsburgh Courier*, April 12, 1947: 15; "Harlem Baseball Team to Play at East Helena"; "Davids Lose 2 to 0 as Ball Season Ends," *Herald-Press* (Saint Joseph, Michigan), September 13, 1947: 5.

89 "Trotters in Game Here," *Kansas City Times*, August 23, 1948: 12; "City League All-Stars Play Harlem Globetrotters June 17," *La Crosse* (Wisconsin) *Tribune*, June 11, 1950: 29.

90 "Globetrotters Boast Best Negro Catcher; Test Hawaii Stars Here Today," *Ogden Standard-Examiner,* July 22, 1948: 23; "Hardy Leads Globetrotters," *Salt Lake Tribune*, July 20, 1948: 17.

91 "Trotters Have Great Star in Paul Hardy," *Ogden Standard-Examiner*, July 30, 1949: 21.

92 "Everett to Be Scene of Negro League Contest," *Cumberland* (Maryland) *Evening Times,* August 13, 1951: 7; "League Game Set at Everett by Negro Loop," *Bedford* (Pennsylvania) *Gazette,* August 10, 1951: 3.

93 "Davids Lose 2 to 0 As Ball Season Ends."

94 "Trotter Boss Dies at 47," *St. Joseph News-Press*, January 15, 1951: 8.

95 "Indians and Giants Play at Lippincott," *South Bend Tribune*, May 29, 1951: 13.

96 "Indians and Giants Play at Lippincott."

97 "Black Barons Open Spring Training Drills Sunday at State College," *Montgomery Advertiser*, April 8, 1951: 22 (Hardy identified as manager); "Sea Gulls Meet Chicago Giants," *Pensacola News Journal,* April 15, 1951: 17 (Welch identified as manager); "Chicago Giants Invade City Monday to Face Black Barons," *Montgomery Advertiser*, April 22, 1951: 23 (Hardy identified as manager); "Negro Big League Clubs Play Here," *Monroe Morning World*, May 13, 1951: 10 (Welch identified as manager); "League Game Set at Everett by Negro Loop," *Cumberland Evening Times*, August 13, 1951: 7 (Welch identified as manager).

98 "Bob Towner, Indians Lose Home Opener by 4-2 Score," *South Bend Tribune*, May 30, 1951: 16.

99 http://www.cnlbr.org/Portals/0/Standings/Negro%20American%20League%20(1937-1962)-2020.pdf.

100 http://www.cnlbr.org/Portals/0/Rosters/Rosters%20-%20Barnstorming%20Teams%20(1946-1988).pdf.

101 "Takes Charge," *Kokomo* (Indiana) *Tribune*, August 5, 1952: 9.

102 "Joe Black Pitched His Team to 5 To 3 Victory Over Barons," *Alabama Tribune* (Montgomery), October 24, 1952: 7.

103 Al Warden, "The Sports Highway," *Ogden Standard-Examiner*, February 10, 1964: 6.

104 "Memphis Clips Barons in 10th," *Shawnee* (Oklahoma) *News-Star,* June 19, 1959: 11; "Raleigh Tigers Split Twinbill," *Raleigh News and Observer,* June 29, 1959: 14; "Tigers Win, 7-2," *News and Observer*, June 30, 1959: 14; "Black Barons' Lead Still Intact," *Birmingham News*, July 20, 1959: 23.

105 Plott, *Black Baseball's Last Team Standing*, 284. On page 125, Plott concluded that Hardy's "career with Birmingham spanned three decades."

106 Prentice Mills, "The Baron of Birmingham, an Interview with Lorenzo 'Piper' Davis," *Black Ball News*, Vol 1. No. 5, 1993: 12.

107 Mills.

108 "Obituaries," Paul Hardy, *Chicago Tribune*, August 30, 1979: 49.

109 Warden, "The Sports Highway": 6.

110 "Obituaries": 49.

111 "Obituaries": 49.

CONNIE JOHNSON

By Alan Cohen

"He would come in and relieve Satchel, and when they put Johnson out there, we thought we'd have it easy then. And he would come in and throw harder than Satchel did! Just like jumpin' from the frying pan into the fire." – Warren Peace, Newark Eagles[1]

Connie Johnson made his White major-league debut with the Chicago White Sox on April 17, 1953, pitching the final two innings against the St. Louis Browns. He entered the game with his team behind 6-4 and pitched two scoreless innings. Only the remnants of the 972 spectators who had braved the cold of a Chicago afternoon in April were in the stands as Johnson became the first Black man to pitch for the White Sox. In the top of the ninth, with one out, Satchel Paige came to bat for the Browns. The ageless one had entered the game in the seventh inning. When Johnson took the mound in the eighth inning, it was the first time two Black pitchers had opposed each other in an American League game.

Clifford Johnson Jr. was born on December 27, 1922, in Stone Mountain, Georgia, a town about 15 miles east of Atlanta. He was the second of three sons born to Clifford and Rosa Allen Johnson. His older brother, Jack, was born in 1911, and his younger brother, Victor, was two years younger than Clifford. His father was a paving cutter at a granite quarry. The senior Johnson lived almost his whole life in Stone Mountain and died in 1961.

The Johnson family moved to Atlanta when Clifford was about 5 years old, and he attended school there until the family moved back to Stone Mountain a few years later. He attended Stone Mountain Elementary School and completed one year of high school, his formal education ending in 1938 when he went to work with his father at the granite quarry. He saw his first professional game, between the Toledo Crawfords and Kansas City Monarchs, at Ponce de Leon (Poncey) Park in Atlanta in June 1940.

The next day, as Johnson told the *Baltimore Afro-American* in 1956, "I went to work with my dad up in the mountains. A big limousine (it was a LaSalle) came by." Jesse Owens and a Stone Mountain neighbor, James "Joe" Greene, were in the car. Greene was a catcher with the Kansas City Monarchs, and Owens was a part-owner of the Crawfords. "Greene had told Owens that I could throw hard. So Owens asked me to pitch for (the Crawfords). I told him I couldn't, but he told me to try and my dad said to go ahead. So I got my spikes and glove and went along."[2] In the second game in Atlanta between the Crawfords and the Monarchs, Johnson, in a uniform two sizes too large, excelled.[3] After the game, he was asked to travel with the Crawfords; team manager Oscar Charleston assured his mother that he would watch out for the young pitcher.

Johnson first played with the Crawfords (formerly of Pittsburgh but by then splitting their time between Toledo and Indianapolis) in 1940, joining them shortly after being recruited by Owens. He made his debut in Indianapolis on June 28, 1940, appearing in place of John Wright against the Kansas City Monarchs. He pitched all nine innings as the Crawfords came from behind to win, 5-4. In the winning eighth-inning rally, the key hits were a run-scoring double by Willie Spencer and a single by Jimmy Johnson.[4] In his very first season, at the tender age of 17, Cliff Johnson was selected to play for the West All-Stars in the annual East-West Game. He entered the game with one out in the sixth inning and his team trailing 8-0. He had come on in relief of Walter "Lefty" Calhoun, who had been ineffective. There were runners on first and second. Johnson was quickly faced with a bases-loaded situation when he failed to cover first base on a groundball to the right side of the infield. He then settled down and pitched the final two outs of the sixth inning, striking out Marvin Barker and retiring Bill Perkins on a foul popup to the catcher. No runs scored on his watch. After he left the game, the East padded its lead with another three runs and won the game 11-0.[5]

"The night no one would warm me up. They say I was throwing too hard. I had a week rest. I walk the first three men – three

• CONNIE JOHNSON •

balls on the other one. They got one hit and I struck out 22." – Connie Johnson, remembering a game against the Chicago American Giants in 1941.[6]

The Crawfords folded after the 1940 season, and Johnson spent the next two seasons with the Kansas City Monarchs. The Monarchs played in towns big and small and Johnson, like most of his teammates, played in the shadow of Satchel Paige. Johnson got his chances, though, and one of his impressive early outings with the Monarchs was a 2-0, four-hit win over the Chicago American Giants on August 19, 1941, at Perry Stadium in Indianapolis.[7]

During a spring-training game on April 16, 1942, in Port Arthur, Texas, Johnson pitched two scoreless innings in a 19-9 win over the Cleveland Buckeyes.[8] Over the course of the season, he had more opportunities to shine.

On June 21, 1942, at Ruppert Stadium in Kansas City, it was Elks Day with about 3,500 members of Black Elks lodges attending from an eight-state Midwest Association region meeting. The total attendance was around 5,000. Findley Wilson of Washington, the Elks grand exalted ruler, threw out the first pitch for the 3:00 P.M. start. With the score tied at 4-4, Johnson was brought in to pitch with two outs in the fifth inning and surrendered the lead. He then pitched scoreless ball through the ninth inning. The score was 5-4 after 8½ innings. In the bottom of the ninth, Monarchs catcher Joe Greene hit a home run over the center-field scoreboard to tie the game. Buck O'Neil singled over second base, then advanced to second and third on back-to-back infield outs. Johnson was due up, but manager Frank Duncan had another pitcher – Hilton Smith – pinch-hit for him. On a 2-and-2 count, Smith singled to right field. Johnson was credited with the win and Memphis Red Sox lefty Verdell Mathis bore the complete-game loss.[9]

Paige was the drawing card for the June 24 game in Rochester, New York, against the semipro Eber-Seagrams team. The Monarchs won, 6-1, as 4,500 fans saw Paige throw one-hit ball and walk two in his five innings. Veteran White major-league right-hander Ted Kleinhans was "imported from Syracuse for the occasion" to pitch for Eber-Seagram.[10] The team was the three-time Western New York semipro champion.[11] Kleinhans struck out 11 Monarchs, two more than Paige, though Paige got to him for a double and a run batted in. Three errors (one committed by Kleinhans) and a wild pitch helped the Monarchs add two runs in the fifth and three runs in the sixth. In the three-run sixth, O'Neil tripled, Paige singled him in, and Bonnie Serrell singled. Kleinhans threw away the ball on a bunt he fielded, and a fly ball scored the last of the Monarchs' runs. Johnson pitched the last four innings, allowing just one hit, a ninth-inning homer.

On July 2 the Monarchs faced the Chicago American Giants in a doubleheader at Ruppert Stadium. Johnson entered the second game with two out in the sixth inning. The Giants had rallied to tie the game at 6-6 and Johnson was able to stop the damage. In the bottom of the inning, the Monarchs retook the lead, 7-6, and Johnson pitched a scoreless seventh inning for the win.[12]

Two days later, after a bus trip of 450 miles on back roads, the Monarchs were in Memphis to play the Red Sox in a July 4 doubleheader. Memphis had been on a tear, winning 15 straight games, and they won the first game of the doubleheader to make it 16 in a row. Johnson pitched the seven-inning second game and was able to win the game for the Monarchs, scattering eight hits.[13]

In St. Joseph, Missouri, on July 16, 1942, the Monarchs played Memphis in front of 1,900 fans, the largest turnout of the season in St. Joseph. Johnson came on in relief with one out in the eighth inning and the game tied, 3-3, pitched flawlessly, and drove in the winning run with a triple. He tried to stretch the triple into an inside-the-park homer but was out at the plate on a perfect relay throw.[14] In Scranton, Pennsylvania, on July 31, 1942, Johnson took the mound against the Philadelphia Stars and won, 7-4. The crowd of 2,361 was disappointed that Paige made only a token appearance, relieving Johnson in the eighth inning, and pitching the last two innings.[15]

Johnson was back in St. Joseph on August 24 and got the start against the Chicago American Giants. He struck out 11 batters and scattered nine hits in winning the game, 10-4, in front of a record crowd of 2,400. The Monarchs had 14 hits in the game, including a home run by Serrell and a pair of doubles by Ted Strong.[16]

It was in 1942, by Johnson's own account, that he was first called Connie. Johnson's favorite song was "Basin Street Blues," sung by Connie Boswell with Bing Crosby. Johnson would sing it himself and took to calling other folks Connie (including fellow pitchers Satchel Paige and Hilton Smith), or so the story goes.

Eventually, his teammates started to call him Connie.[17]

The fact that Negro League statistics are incomplete is well-known, but according to several articles, one of which appeared in the *Capital Times* (Madison, Wisconsin), Johnson led the Negro American League in strikeouts in 1942.[18] In the 1942 Negro League World Series, the Monarchs swept the Homestead Grays, but Johnson saw no action as manager Frank Duncan used only three pitchers – Paige, Smith, and Jack Matchett – in the four games.

Johnson entered the Army on January 26, 1943, and spent the next three seasons away from the Monarchs. He was honorably discharged on February 5, 1946.

He returned to the Monarchs in 1946 and was undefeated through June. On Opening Day he relieved Hilton Smith in the eighth inning and pitched the final two innings as the Monarchs defeated Memphis, 3-0. In his two innings, he struck out four batters and allowed only one hit. His first win of the season came against the House of David on May 27. Smith had started and was ineffective. Johnson came on in the fourth inning with his team trailing and struck out seven batters in three innings. The Monarchs came from behind and took the lead in the fifth inning, making him the pitcher of record.

Johnson excelled in a game at Dexter Park in Queens, New York, on July 12, throwing a two-hitter as the Monarchs defeated the Brooklyn Bushwicks, 3-0; he struck out the side in each of the first two innings.[19] Johnson won eight of 10 decisions, had 95 strikeouts in 86 innings, and was scheduled to appear in the East-West Game in Washington on August 15.[20] However, he appeared in neither the game in Washington nor the East-West Game in Chicago on August 24. He did receive the George Stovey Award, given to the top pitcher in the Negro Leagues.

Nineteen-year-old pitcher Clifford "Connie" Johnson, pictured here in the uniform of Canada's St. Hyacinthe Saints in 1951, posted a perfect 4-0 record for the 1942 Monarchs. (Courtesy Noir-Tech Research, Inc.)

Johnson was absent from the East-West games because he had injured his arm. During the offseason he went to a chiropractor in Laredo, Texas, and, upon the recommendation of manager Buck O'Neil, began a running regimen. When he returned to the Monarchs in 1947, his blazing speed was gone, but he had better control of his pitches.

Johnson's last year with the Kansas City Monarchs was 1950. On June 11, 1950, in a doubleheader at Blues Stadium in Kansas City between the Monarchs and the Indianapolis Clowns, the crowd of 9,165 had an opportunity to see that the future of Black baseball would be not in the Negro Leagues but in White Organized Baseball. Johnson won his sixth game of the season in the nightcap, 3-1, as he limited the Clowns to five hits, only three after the first inning. In the fourth inning, O'Neil singled and the team's young left fielder, Elston Howard, homered for the decisive runs. In the opener that day, also won by the Monarchs, 5-1, the Clowns scored their only run of the game on a throwing error by Monarchs shortstop Ernie Banks. Both Howard and Banks had RBI singles during a five-run eighth inning in the opener.[21] Each went on to White major-league stardom and All-Star recognition and was named his league's Most Valuable Player.

For his part, Johnson was named to the West All-Star team for the annual East-West Game on August

20, 1950. He entered the game in the fourth inning with the West leading, 2-1. After giving up a game-tying run in his first inning, he settled down and was the beneficiary of three fifth-inning runs. He came out of the game after the sixth inning with his team leading 5-2. The East managed only one run in the seventh inning off Bill Powell, and Johnson was credited with the 5-3 win.

After finishing the 1950 Negro American League season with an 11-1 record,[22] Johnson barnstormed with Satchel Paige. One of the stops was at Wrigley Field in Los Angeles, and Johnson pitched in relief of Paige on October 15. He gave up four runs, three on a homer by Del Crandall, in four innings.[23]

Before the 1951 season, the Monarchs sold Johnson's contract to St. Hyacinthe in the Class-C Quebec Provincial League. The team finished in fifth place with a 55-67 record. Johnson led his team's pitchers with 15 wins (against 14 losses), and his 172 strikeouts paced the league.

In 1952, on the recommendation of scout John Donaldson, Johnson's contract was purchased by the Chicago White Sox and he was assigned to Colorado Springs in the Class-A Western League. At the time there were still relatively few Black players in the minor leagues and one display of verbal abuse was particularly disturbing. The offenders were the Omaha Cardinals and their manager, George Kissell. After a game on July 18, Colorado Springs club officials in a telegram to league officials, said, "This club does not feel there is a place in the Western League or in baseball for discriminatory remarks directed against our players nor for profanity directed toward our fans, not for general poor sportsmanship."[24] Kissell denied the allegations.

Johnson's pitching in 1952 was noteworthy. The 6-foot-4, 200-pound right-hander set the Western League season strikeout record with 233 in 248 innings, surpassing the 212 strikeouts by Bobby Shantz in 1948. Johnson finished the season with an 18-9 record.

The blazing fastball that had keyed his success in his early days in the Negro Leagues was a bit slower by then due to the arm problems that dated back to 1946. In 1952 he said, "I found out later that I'd been pitching too often and not warming up enough. I relied mostly on curves at first, but lately I'm getting more confidence back in my fast ball. I'll throw either one in the clutch now."[25] On June 11 he tied the Western League record for strikeouts in a game when he fanned 17 in a 13-inning, 8-5 win over the Pueblo Dodgers.[26]

Johnson joined the White Sox in 1953, becoming the 31st player of color to join the White major leagues, although he was only the seventh Black pitcher. Among his teammates was Orestes "Minnie" Miñoso, against whom he had pitched in the Negro Leagues.

Although the big leagues had initiated integration in 1947, acceptance of that fact was not universal as Johnson discovered during spring training in 1953. When the White Sox headed north, neither he nor Miñoso was allowed to play when the team traveled to Memphis to face the Philadelphia Athletics.[27]

Johnson's first start for the White Sox came on April 28 against the Washington Senators. He came out of the game with one out and two on in the fourth inning. Although he had a 5-1 lead, he had walked four and got the early hook.

When the time came to cut the rosters to 25 players, Johnson was optioned to Charleston, West Virginia, in the Triple-A American Association. His record was 0-1 when he was sent down and he had a 6-6 record in 15 appearances (14 starts) with Charleston.

Johnson was recalled by the White Sox on July 29. He earned his first big-league win on August 1 when he shut out the Senators, 4-0, striking out 10 batters. The win brought the White Sox to within 4½ games of the league-leading New York Yankees. On August 7 Johnson started the opener of a four-game series at Yankee Stadium against New York's Eddie Lopat. The Yankees, with an inside-the-park homer by Mickey Mantle followed by a homer by Yogi Berra, took a 4-1 lead in the third inning. Johnson lost the game, and his record fell to 1-2. For the season, he was 4-4 for the White Sox, posting an ERA of 3.56.

During his time with the White Sox, Johnson recommended one of his Monarchs teammates to manager Paul Richards. The White Sox front office did not follow up on the tip, and Ernie Banks wound up signing with the Cubs.

After the season, Johnson barnstormed with the Roy Campanella All-Stars and defeated a team made up of Pacific Coast League players, 8-5, at Seals Stadium in San Francisco.[28]

He pitched the entire 1954 season with the Toronto Maple Leafs of the International League, going 17-8 with 145 strikeouts. His batterymate that season was former Monarchs teammate Elston Howard. Johnson began 1955 with Toronto and, in early July, after posting a 12-2 record with a 3.05 ERA in Triple A, was called up to the White Sox once more.

Johnson's deliberate style confounded batters as he went 7-4 with a 3.45 ERA in 1955. In his first game back with the White Sox, on July 4 in the first game of a doubleheader, he defeated the Kansas City Athletics, 8-3, at Kansas City, pitching a complete game. The occasion marked his first game back in Kansas City since his days in the Negro Leagues. His second win was a 6-0 whitewashing of the Cleveland Indians in which he struck out 12 batters.

The White Sox were in an exciting pennant race with five teams within 5½ games of one another. On July 28 Johnson edged New York, 3-2, to put the White Sox into a first-place tie with the Yankees. His next start, at Boston, attracted a monster crowd of 35,455 to Fenway Park for the matchup between the first-place White Sox (62-39) and the third-place Red Sox (60-43). Johnson prevailed over Tom Brewer of the Red Sox, 2-1, to bring his record to 4-1 and he lowered his ERA to 2.25. After August 21 Johnson tailed off, going 1-3 in his last five starts. The White Sox were in first place as late as September 3, but they lost 12 of their last 23 games to finish in third place, five games behind New York.

After the season, Johnson barnstormed with the Willie Mays-Don Newcombe All-Stars. On October 15 he pitched a one-hitter as the All-Stars defeated a group of American League players 2-0 at Columbus, Mississippi, in front of 1,617 spectators.[29]

Johnson's pitching woes at the end of the 1955 season continued in the early part of 1956. In his first five appearances, he was 0-1 with a 3.65 ERA. He had control problems in each of his two starts, walking seven batters in seven innings. In the second start, on May 10 at Boston, he was pulled from the game in the first inning after loading the bases and allowing the Red Sox to tie the game at 1-1. The 33-year-old pitcher was put on the trading block.

On May 21, 1956, in a six-player deal, Johnson, George Kell, Bob Nieman, and Mike Fornieles were sent to Baltimore for Jim Wilson and Dave Philley. Not long after the trade, Johnson faced his old mates and won a 3-2 verdict on June 1, allowing five hits.

Johnson brought his family with him to Baltimore. He had met his wife, Harion Orita Caver, in Kansas City in 1947 and they were married on September 28, 1953. By 1956, there were two children: Daughter Denise was born in 1954 and son Clifford was born a year later. They later welcomed another son, Kevin. The family's home base remained Kansas City.

Harion, who worked at the Betty Rose Coats and Suit Company, died on December 21, 1971, at the youthful age of 47.[30]

In Baltimore, Johnson was reunited with Paul Richards, who, through the proverbial grapevine, had heard that Johnson had been tipping off his curveball while with the White Sox. Richards worked with Johnson to make the necessary change in his motion. Although his 9-11 record in 1956 hardly placed him among the league leaders, his manager had great praise for Johnson. After Johnson defeated the Indians, 4-1, in Cleveland on September 13, Richards proclaimed, "He's the best right-hander in the league."[31]

Johnson's losing record reflected the fact that he pitched in bad luck in 1956. On June 21 he was matched up against Chicago's Jack Harshman. The only run of the game was scored by the White Sox in the first inning. Jim Rivera walked, stole second, and scored on a double by Nellie Fox. Johnson then hurled hitless ball until he was pulled for a pinch-hitter in the top of the eighth inning. Harshman, like Johnson, yielded only one hit, a seventh-inning double by Gus Triandos, as the White Sox won, 1-0.

On August 14 Johnson recorded his first shutout with Baltimore, a six-hit, 11-strikeout gem. He followed it with a 3-2 complete-game win against the Yankees. The back-to-back wins brought his season's record to 6-7 and set the stage for a night in his honor held at Memorial Stadium on August 28.[32]

On September 23 in Baltimore, Johnson shut out Washington, 6-0, on three hits. The win assured the Orioles of a sixth-place finish, their best result since moving to Baltimore from St. Louis in 1954, and the best season record for the franchise since 1945.

Of his success in 1956 as opposed to his problems at the end of the 1955 season with the White Sox, Johnson said, "They don't read me the way they used to. I didn't hide my grip of the ball very well in previous years and coaches on opposing teams were reading me like a book. Now I cover the right hand up with my glove. I'm also throwing the slider better than I used to."[33]

For the season he went 9-10 with the Orioles (9-11 overall). He had two shutouts and his ERA was 3.44. In five of his losses, he allowed three or fewer runs. He led the Orioles staff in ERA (3.43), shutouts (2), and strikeouts (130), and tied for the team lead with nine complete games.

In 1957 Johnson won 14 games against 11 losses for the Orioles. He tied with Bob Turley for the most wins by an Orioles pitcher since the team moved to Baltimore. Three of Johnson's wins were shutouts. The first was a 2-0 two-hitter against Kansas City on May 20. He struck out four batters, walked one, and set down the A's one-two-three in seven of nine innings.

Johnson's 1-0 blanking of the Kansas City Athletics on June 26 was the third of four consecutive shutouts by Orioles pitchers, tying an American League record. The others were thrown by Hal "Skinny" Brown, Billy Loes, and Ray Moore. Johnson in his shutout allowed only three hits, struck out four, walked none, threw 86 pitches, and finished the game in a tidy 1:45. Jim Busby provided all the offense needed with a fifth-inning home run.[34]

Johnson struck out 10 or more batters five times in 1957. He tied the Orioles team record of 14, initially set by Turley on April 21, 1954, in a 6-1 win over the Yankees on September 2 in the second game of a doubleheader at Memorial Stadium. The 14 strikeouts were the most in a game by an American League pitcher in 1957. Speaking of this performance, the ever-understated Johnson said, "It was awful close and hot out there, and I was sweating a powerful lot. I felt strong, but kind of mushy-like." The room erupted in laughter.[35] Johnson was not much into discussing his pitching ability. As writer Lou Hatter said, "Getting Johnson, a baseball disciple of Satchel Paige, to talk about his mound skills is like trying to extract a wisdom tooth from a full-grown Georgia alligator. Not really hazardous; it simply isn't done."[36]

Johnson's 14 wins set the American League record at the time for wins by a Black pitcher. Satchel Paige had gone 12-10 for the St. Louis Browns in 1952. Jim "Mudcat" Grant raised the bar with 15 wins in 1961. Johnson was third in the league in strikeouts (177), and he had the best strikeout-to-walk ratio (2.68) of the league's starters.

Despite Johnson's pitching acumen and the team's record shutout streak, the 1957 Orioles were not contenders. After the four shutouts, their record stood at 32-34, and they wound up the season in fifth place with a 76-76 record, 21 games behind the pennant-winning Yankees.

Johnson slipped to 6-9 with a 3.88 ERA in 1958. The season did not start at well, but eventually he found his rhythm and won three consecutive starts from August 11 through August 22 that brought his record up to 6-7 and his ERA down to 3.19. However, his 35-year-old arm betrayed him, and he went 0-2 with a 10.64 ERA in the last three appearances of his big-league career.

Johnson began the 1959 season at spring training with the Orioles. His best outing of the spring came on April 1 against the Pittsburgh Pirates in Miami. He entered the game in the top of the ninth inning with the score tied, 3-3, and pitched four hitless innings. Johnson received credit for the win when the Orioles scored the decisive run on a single by Al Pilarcik in the bottom of the 12th.[37] In his final outing of the spring, he allowed three runs and six hits to the Cardinals on April 5.[38]

Although Johnson's career was nearing its end, there was still time for a bit of levity. At that point, the Orioles had a pitching phenom by the name of Steve Dalkowski whose wildness was the stuff of legend. Wrote David Condon in the *Chicago Tribune*, "The day the 21-year-old southpaw was scheduled to pitch bunting practice for pitchers, Connie Johnson stepped up to the plate attired in shin guards, a chest protector, and a mask, clutching a bat in one hand and a list of his next of kin in the other."[39]

Johnson did not break training camp with the Orioles, who were in the midst of a youth movement. On April 9, 1959, after boarding the team bus for the presidential opener in Washington, Johnson was informed that he was being was sent to Vancouver of the Pacific Coast League.[40] "The Tall Statuesque Great Stone Face from Stone Mountain, Georgia," as Lou Hatter of the *Baltimore Sun* depicted Connie Johnson, finished his time in the majors with a record of 40-39 with an ERA of 3.44. The blazing fastball that had so impressed Jesse Owens 19 years earlier was no longer in evidence and Johnson's flirtation with greatness in 1957 could not be replicated.

Although he went 8-4 with a 3.16 ERA at Vancouver in 1959, there was no late-season call-up. Johnson did not return to the major leagues. In a relief effort on August 8, 1959, he had been credited with his last win in White Organized Baseball. The Mounties finished second to Salt Lake City in the PCL.

In 1960 Johnson was back with Vancouver, but it was apparent early on that he would not be there long. In his only appearance, on April 16, he gave up three runs and six hits in 2⅔ innings and was charged with the loss as Sacramento defeated Vancouver, 5-1.[41] A week later, he was released.

The following season Johnson was still pitching, but his career had come full circle. He was barnstorming with the Philadelphia Stars of the Negro American League, back in the league where he started his career as a teenager.[42]

Johnson's time in the major leagues lasted less than four full seasons. Based on the rules in place when he finished his big-league career in 1958, he was not entitled to a pension. However, in 1997, Major League Baseball awarded annual pensions of $10,000 to a group of about 90 Black ballplayers, including Johnson, whose combined service in the Negro Leagues and the White Majors totaled four or more years.[43]

After baseball, Johnson went to work as an inspector for the Ford Motor Company in Claycomo, Missouri, staying with them until he reached retirement age in 1985.

Johnson served as an honorary pallbearer at the funeral of Satchel Paige on June 12, 1982.

He was an active supporter of the Negro League Baseball Museum in Kansas City, Missouri, and was among a number of Negro League ballplayers who shared their experiences with students in the Kansas City public schools.

In 1994, on the eve of the airing of Ken Burns' series, *Baseball*, Johnson was among several veterans of the Negro Leagues who appeared at a picnic at the White House.[44]

Clifford "Connie" Johnson died on November 28, 2004, in Kansas City and was buried at Leavenworth National Cemetery.

> *"Connie was a good pitcher in the major leagues, but he was a great pitcher in the Negro Leagues. No comparison. He threw hard for the Monarchs. Hard. He had good control. Could have won 20 games in the big leagues. Oh yeah. Could have won 20 games every year. That's Connie Johnson."* – Connie Johnson's Kansas City Monarchs teammate and manager Buck O'Neil.[45]

Acknowledgments

In addition to fact-checker Carl Riechers and copy editor Len Levin, the author is highly indebted to Cassidy Lent at the National Baseball Hall of Fame's Giamatti Research Center for her assistance in gaining access to Connie Johnson's file and Hall of Fame questionnaire.

Sources

In addition to the sources shown in the Notes, the author used Baseball-Reference.com, the *Encyclopedia of Minor League Baseball*, Seamheads.com, Ancestry.com (1930 Federal Census), Johnson's page on the Negro League Baseball Museum website, and the following:

Bready, James H. *Baseball in Baltimore: The First 100 Years* (Baltimore: Johns Hopkins University Press, 1998)

Hoffman, John C. "Hats Off: Connie Johnson," *The Sporting News*, August 31, 1955: 19.

Kelley, Brent. "Connie Johnson Remembers His Pitching Days," *Sports Collector's Digest*, June 15, 1990: 260-263 (Recorded interview is available at SABR.org)

Luke, Bob. *Integrating the Orioles: Baseball and Race in Baltimore* (Jefferson, North Carolina: McFarland Publishers, 2016)

Vanderberg, Bob. "Sox Footnote Provides Rich Anecdote," *Chicago Tribune*, September 23, 1990: 2.

Notes

1. Brent Kelley, *Voices from the Negro Leagues: Conversations with 52 Baseball Standouts of the Period 1924-1960*, (Jefferson, North Carolina: McFarland Publishers, 1998), 174.

2. Sam Yette, "'Happy to Pitch for Orioles, Says Connie," *Baltimore Afro-American*, August 28, 1956: 13.

3. Tom Hawthorn, "Connie Johnson: 1922-2004: Ace Pitcher Was Too Old to Fully Benefit from Desegregation and Instead Became the Strikeout King on Three Canadian Teams," *Globe and Mail* (Toronto), January 25, 2005: S7.

4. "Crawfords Defeat Loop Leaders, 5-4," *Indianapolis Star*, June 29, 1940: 19.

5. William G. Nunn, "23,000 See East Maul West, 11-0," *Pittsburgh Courier*, August 24, 1940: 16; Art Carter, "East Blanks West 11-0 in Baseball's Big Classic," *Baltimore Afro-American*, August 24, 1940: 19.

6. California League questionnaire completed by Connie Johnson, April 26, 1952.

7. "Kansas City Monarchs Win at Perry Stadium," *Indianapolis Star*, August 20, 1941: 19.

8. "Monarchs in 19-9 Victory," *Port Arthur* (Texas) *News*, April 17, 1942: 5.

9. "Game to Monarchs in 9th," *Kansas City Times*, June 22, 1942: 12.

10. Paul Pinckney, "Paige Yields 1 Hit in 5 Frames as Monarchs Trip Ebers, 6-1," *Democrat and Chronicle* (Rochester, New York), June 25, 1942: 25, 30.

11. "Satchel 'Born with Control,': Paige Explains Hurling Feats," *Democrat and Chronicle* (Rochester, New York), June 21, 1942: 3C. An advertisement for the game on page 17 of the June 20 *Democrat and Chronicle* declared of Satchel Paige that "Countless expert(s) and big league players rate him the greatest pitcher of all time."

12. "Twin Monarch Triumph," *Kansas City Times*, July 3, 1942: 13.

13. Sam Brown, "Kansas City and Red Sox Divide Pair," *Chicago Defender*, July 11, 1942: 19.

14. "A Close One to Monarchs," *Kansas City Times*, July 17, 1942: 13; Biggest Crowd of Year Sees Monarchs Defeat Memphis, "*St. Joseph* (Missouri) *Gazette*, July 17, 1942: 13.

15. Chic Feldman, "Indifferent Paige Hooted by 2,361 Irked Stadium Guests for Brief, Late Appearance," *Scranton Tribune*, August 1, 1942: 11.

16. "Record Stadium Crowd Watches Monarchs Win," *St. Joseph Gazette*, August 25, 1942: 5.

17 Yette.

18 "Cliff Johnson Leads Monarch Pitching Staff this Season," *Capital Times* (Madison, Wisconsin), July 19, 1946: 13.

19 "Monarchs Top Bushwicks, 3-0," *New York Times*, July 13, 1946: 19.

20 "West Favored Over East in Dream Game," *Philadelphia Tribune*, August 13, 1946: 11.

21 "Monarchs Take Two," *Kansas City Times*, June 12, 1950: 13.

22 "League Highlights," *Alabama Citizen* (Tuscaloosa, Alabama), September 16, 1950: 7.

23 "Lemon's All-Stars Nip Paige's Royals, 7-6," *Los Angeles Times*, October 16, 1950: C-4.

24 "Sky Sox Protest Cards' Conduct: Accuse Kissell, Team, of Abusing Negroes," *Council Bluffs* (Iowa) *Nonpareil*, July 20, 1952: 23.

25 Maury White, "Bruin Bats, Vocal Efforts Fail to Bother Sky Sox Ace," *Des Moines Tribune*, June 26, 1952: 36.

26 "Cliff Johnson Ties Western League's Strikeout Record," *Atlanta Daily World*, June 12, 1952: 7.

27 Wendell Smith, "Memphis Bars Minoso as Chisox Play," *Pittsburgh Courier*, April 11, 1953: 1, 4.

28 "Campanella Shows Way," *New York Times*, October 24, 1953: 20.

29 "Mays-Newk Gates in Dixie Dropping with Temperature," *The Sporting News*, October 26, 1955: 23.

30 "Mrs. Clifford Johnson, Jr. Obituary," *Kansas City Times*, December 27, 1971: 48.

31 Jim Ellis, "Con Johnson Best in A.L., Chirps Boss," *The Sporting News*, September 26, 1956: 17.

32 "Connie Johnson Gets $500, Gifts at the Stadium Tonight," *Baltimore Afro-American*, August 28, 1956: 22.

33 Ellis, *The Sporting News*, September 26, 1956: 17

34 Ellis, "Nieman Ready to Return to Oriole Lineup," *Baltimore Evening Sun*, June 27, 1957: 55.

35 Lou Hatter, "Johnson Feeling 'Mushy' While Tying S.O. Record," *Baltimore Sun*, September 3, 1957: 17, 19.

36 Hatter, September 3, 1957: 17.

37 Jack Hernon, "Orioles Edge Pirates in 12 Innings, 4-3," *Pittsburgh Post-Gazette*, April 2, 1959: 26.

38 Eddie Storin, "Orioles Defeat Cards Win Grapefruit Title," *Miami Herald*, April 6, 1959: C1.

39 David Condon, "In the Wake of the News," *Chicago Tribune*, June 30, 1960: F-2.

40 Lou Hatter, "C. Johnson Cut, Hale Retained by Orioles," *Baltimore Sun*, April 10, 1959: 23, 26.

41 Merv Peters, "Goss (Plus Pills) Puts Pep in Mounties' Bats," *Vancouver Sun*, April 18, 1960: 10.

42 "Birds Test Philly Stars," *Daily Sentinel* (Grand Junction, Colorado), August 4, 1961: 8.

43 Murray Chass, "Pioneer Black Players to be Granted Pensions," *New York Times*, January 20, 1997: C9.

44 Donnie Radcliffe, "The White House Pitches In; At Picnic for Ken Burns' 'Baseball,' Hopes Are High for Extra Innings," *Washington Post*, September 12, 1994: D-01.

45 Frank Russo, "Clifford "Connie" Johnson, Jr. in "Find a Grave Memorial," December 1, 2004.

JAMES "LEFTY" LaMARQUE

By Tim Tassler

"LaMarque was probably the most unassuming of all the Monarch players. ... He didn't stand out. And he liked it like that. Lefty quietly went about his business." – Ray Doswell, curator, Negro Leagues Baseball Museum[1]

Jim LaMarque, who like so many southpaws was nicknamed Lefty, said he almost quit in 1942, his first year in professional baseball. He was 21 years old when the season began, and said he became homesick and tired of being the youngest player on the team. Some taunted him by calling him Dizzy's Boy, in reference to Dizzy Dismukes, who scouted him and recruited him to the Monarchs. One time, while playing in St. Louis that season, LaMarque was only 72 miles from home. He related how his "escape plan" was foiled: "So I stashed my bag under the bed and hid until the team bus was gone. Just as I was getting the bag out, Satchel Paige walked in. He was our top pitcher, and I had been living with him since I joined the team. He drove his own automobile to the games, and he told me just to throw that bag in his car and to get in and hurry up about it. So I did. And I'm awfully glad."[2]

James Hardin LaMarque Jr. was born on July 29, 1920, in Potosi, Missouri, a farming town about 75 miles southwest of St. Louis, to James and Martha (Casey) LaMarque. The third of six siblings who grew up on the family farm, he had two older sisters and three younger brothers.

His first marriage was at age 19 just before joining the Monarchs. LaMarque was 6-feet-2 and weighed 182 pounds.[3] The 1940 census lists LaMarque as a laborer with an eighth-grade education, working odd jobs. He married Theresa Stanley, the first of his two wives, on August 9, 1939. Their first child, Joyce, was born in December 1940.[4]

Before LaMarque signed with the Monarchs, he said, he had played "just sandlot ball and baseball with a team that was from where I was from. It was a white team."[5] When the Potosi Lions, a White team, needed help, they wanted to add him as their primary pitcher. As LaMarque recalled, "We had a black club and a white club. The white club's pitcher hurt his arm some kind of way, so they asked me – a black boy – if I would pitch for the white club. We only played a few games a season, but I played two seasons with them and we won most of our games. The Kansas City Monarchs heard of me and they wondered why a black boy would be pitching on an all-white team, so they got in touch with me and I came to the Monarchs in 1942, and I guess, I left them in 1950."[6]

LaMarque saw limited action, especially in official Negro American League games, during much of his 1942 debut season, because the team's pitching staff included two future Hall of Famers, Satchel Paige and Hilton Smith, as well as Jack Matchett and Booker McDaniel. He pitched in some preseason games, throwing five shutout innings against the Cincinnati-Cleveland Buckeyes on April 14 before turning the game over to Paige.

LaMarque appeared primarily in exhibition games, but he did pitch to a 2-0 record and 3.46 ERA in NAL play. He pitched a couple of exhibition games in May in Council Bluffs and Sioux City, Iowa, before shutting out the Birmingham Black Barons, 1-0, at Ruppert Stadium on the last day of the month.

He pitched against the Memphis Red Sox on July 10 in Wichita Falls, Texas, and on July 16, in front of the largest gross gate at City Stadium in St. Joseph, Missouri, LaMarque went seven strong innings, getting the 4-3 win over the Memphis Red Sox. He was beginning to make a name for himself; in an article previewing the Monarchs coming to Yankee Stadium to play the New York Cubans in early August, the *New York Age* referred to him as "the Southpaw strikeout kid, 'Jimmie' LaMarque."[7] In the St. Joseph game, he contributed with the bat. Leading off the seventh inning he drew a walk, stole second, moved to third on a passed ball, and scored on a triple by Newt Allen.[8] In between occasional starts, LaMarque worked in relief, one such standout effort coming against the Ethiopian Giants in Toledo on August 27. Paige threw two hitless innings and LaMarque pitched seven scoreless innings in a game the Monarchs won, 1-0.

• JAMES "LEFTY" LaMARQUE •

Exhibition games were crucial to the financial success of teams like the Monarchs, and LaMarque was building a solid reputation as an integral part of a standout pitching staff.

During the 1942 Negro World Series, the Monarchs and Homestead Grays took a six-day break between weekend Games Three and Four. The Grays filled the time with games against the Newark Eagles, Philadelphia Stars, and Baltimore Elite Giants. The Monarchs played one, in Louisville on September 18, against the Cincinnati Clowns. The game ran 13 innings, and LaMarque went the distance for a 1-0 victory.[9]

LaMarque spent most offseasons working in Pacific, Missouri, at the Pioneer Silica Products factory.[10] He missed the 1943 season after breaking his pitching arm in a workplace accident, but he rejoined the Monarchs in 1944.[11] He was with the team from spring training in Houston through the season, but the statistical record does not reflect as much action. He is shown with a 1-0 record in 1944 (the Howe News Bureau statistics show him as 2-3). He sometimes played other positions; playing first base on July 20, he hit a two-run homer in the bottom of the sixth to get the Monarchs on the scoreboard.[12] He worked in both games of a June 25 doubleheader against the Homestead Grays at Washington's Griffith Stadium.[13]

LaMarque got more and more key assignments as the Monarchs continued to be one of the best teams in the league, always drawing good-sized crowds during league and exhibition games. Even during World War II, the Monarchs often "sold out or came close to selling out most of their home games at 17,000-seat Ruppert Stadium (which eventually was renamed Municipal Stadium)." They also continued to be a popular draw on the road. LaMarque said, "Everywhere we went, people came to see us. ... Everyone wanted to see the Monarchs."[14]

The 1945 Monarchs, for whom Jackie Robinson played, went 43-32 and finished second to the 59-15 Cleveland Buckeyes. LaMarque's 59 strikeouts were second on the team to Bookie McDaniel's 113.

The June 22 *Brooklyn Eagle* noted LaMarque in a headline, reporting him as undefeated to that point.[15] Satchel Paige had thrown five shutout innings against the Philadelphia Stars in front of 14,000 fans at Yankee Stadium on June 18; LaMarque worked the last four innings without allowing a hit.[16] The July 8, 1945, *Kansas City Star* said he was "undefeated in the loop."[17] In late July, LaMarque was reported to have won eight consecutive games.[18] Josh Gibson's two-run homer into the upper deck of Shibe Park's center-field stands beat him, 3-2, in Philadelphia against the Homestead Grays on August 7.[19] In NAL play, however, he was still reported as "undefeated in league competition" as late as August 22.[20] He is listed as finishing the season 5-2 in 73⅔ innings of pitching in league games. He pitched in after-season games as well, beating the Cincinnati Clowns, 6-0, with a six-hitter on September 18.[21]

The 1946 season was a big year for both the Monarchs and LaMarque. He had begun to see increased action in league games in 1945 and now was counted on as a more regular contributor. When he was discovered by the Monarchs on the amateur fields in Potosi, LaMarque averaged 12 strikeouts per game; in early 1946, he was averaging seven per game. NAL competition was obviously tougher than semipro squads and LaMarque had suffered the broken-arm setback, but he was holding his own against opponents.[22] He threw a complete game on July 21, going nine innings against the Cincinnati-Indianapolis Clowns and surrendering five hits and two runs, giving those up in the top of the ninth to lose a heartbreaker.[23] One noteworthy win was against the Memphis Red Sox, 3-1, in the six-inning second game of a Sunday doubleheader on August 25, holding Memphis to three hits.[24]

The 1946 Monarchs captured the NAL pennant with a 50-16-2 league record (55-26-2 overall), claiming both the first- and second-half league titles. They faced the Newark Eagles in one of the best Negro League World Series ever played. The Series was tied when LaMarque started Game Three in Kansas City on September 22. He struck out eight while walking three in a complete-game effort. Although he allowed Newark to score five runs, he was more than adequate to the task on this day as his teammates clobbered the Eagles' pitching in a 15-5 triumph. The Monarchs had a three-games-to-two lead when LaMarque again took the hill in Game Six. This time, he never got out of the first inning. After the Monarchs roared out to a 5-0 lead in the top of the first, LaMarque walked three consecutive batters and then allowed two singles that resulted in four runs for the Eagles. LaMarque did not see the mound again in the World Series as the Eagles won Game Six by a 9-7 score and took the Series with a 3-2 victory in Game Seven.[25]

After the World Series, LaMarque joined the barnstorming Satchel Paige's All Stars for a tour.

Paige and LaMarque combined efforts but still came up short, 3-2, against Bob Feller's All-Stars in an October 12 game at Council Bluffs, Iowa, in front of a "shivering crowd" of 4,000.[26]

LaMarque then headed to a warmer land – Cuba, where he pitched for the Habana Leones. Habana finished 40-26, which was only good enough for second place, two games behind Almendares. LaMarque compiled a 7-6 record, pitching two complete games, with 44 strikeouts in 89 innings pitched; he walked 59.[27]

By 1947, the year that Jackie Robinson broke the White major leagues' color barrier, LaMarque was playing year-round. Now that Blacks were being signed for the White leagues, LaMarque was bound to gain the notice of some scouts. Indeed, at one time he reportedly had an opportunity to sign with the Yankees, but negotiations fell through. LaMarque explained the situation:

"There was a time. I used to belong to the Monarchs which was owned by a man named Wilkinson at first, and his partner was named Tom Baird. I talked to the chief scout of the Yankees at that time. He was named Tom Greenwade. After Tom Baird found out that they might want me, he hiked the price on me, so Greenwade told me 'At your age, I can't pay this kind of money.' So, I didn't go with him."[28]

Even without a shot at making the White majors, LaMarque continued to thrive on constant work. He had come a long way since his broken arm, noting, "I've played several seasons of winter ball and my arm feels great."[29] He had a strong season in 1949. One notable early game was on May 25 when the Monarchs swept a doubleheader from Memphis at Kansas City's Blues Stadium; LaMarque won the first game, 4-2, while going 3-for-4 at the plate with two doubles.[30] One win that must have been especially satisfying for the native of nearby Potosi was playing in St. Louis's Sportsman's Park and throwing a three-hitter to beat the Memphis Red Sox, 6-0, on August 28.[31]

The 52-32 Monarchs finished second in the league in 1947, behind the 42-12 Cleveland Buckeyes, who played far fewer games.[32] Seamheads shows his record for the season as 8-3 with 80 strikeouts, more than twice as many as any other Monarchs pitcher.[33]

After the season, LaMarque rejoined the Habana Leones. Habana won the league title with a 39-33 record, finishing one game ahead of Almendares. LaMarque was one of three Habana pitchers who finished with double-digit win totals as he went 11-7 with 62 strikeouts and a 3.93 ERA in 128 innings pitched.[34]

After returning from Cuba, LaMarque found additional success with Kansas City in 1948. The Monarchs finished 60-30-2 and won the NAL's first-half championship. Connie Johnson recalled, "Sometimes it was hot here in Kansas City. Lefty was the only one who could go nine innings. The rest of us could only go three innings. During the games," Johnson said, "Lefty would be drenched in sweat. Between innings, he placed his feet in a bucket of ice water. It was so hot, by the time he pulled his feet out, his feet were dry."[35]

That season, LaMarque made his first appearance in the annual East-West All-Star Games. He pitched in both games, a total of five innings, giving up five hits. On August 22 at Comiskey Park in Chicago, he combined with Birmingham's Bill Powell and Chicago's Gentry Jessup to shut out the East All-Stars, 3-0. LaMarque pitched innings three through six and gave up two hits while walking none.[36] The second All-Star Game in 1948 was played at Yankee Stadium two days later. This time, LaMarque entered the game in the top of the seventh inning with his West team trailing, 4-1. He pitched two innings in which he surrendered three hits and the West's final two runs, both of which were unearned, as the East lost, 6-1.[37]

On September 11, 1948, the Monarchs met the Birmingham Black Barons in the American East playoffs. LaMarque got the ball in Game One. He held the Barons hitless until the fifth but the Monarchs lost the opener, 5-4. LaMarque returned to the hill in Game Three, relieving starter Connie Johnson. He held the Barons close but could not gain a win for the Monarchs. With thr Monarchs down three games to none, Buck O'Neil turned to his ace to take the mound in Game Four. Tying up the Barons hitters, LaMarque also delivered at the plate, hitting a sacrifice fly in the eighth inning and adding a run to give the Monarchs a 3-1 lead. In doing so LaMarque gained his first victory in the Series. Game Six saw LaMarque score the winning run, as a pinch-runner. The Monarchs won, 5-4. Game Seven saw him work the fourth time in eight games. He gave up runs in the fourth, fifth, and eighth innings before being lifted but the damage had been done. The Barons moved on to a showdown with the Homestead Grays.

After the season, LaMarque pitched with Paige's All-Stars once more. On October 25 he came into the game in relief and shut down Gene Bearden's All-

• JAMES "LEFTY" LaMARQUE •

Stars, 4-3, at Los Angeles' Wrigley Field. With the bases loaded and one out, he got Al Zarilla to hit the ball back to him and threw home to start a 1-2-5 game-ending double play.[38]

After the 1948 season, LaMarque joined the Santurce Crabbers in Puerto Rico, where he spent the next two offseasons (1948-49 and 1949-50). On February 15, 1949, LaMarque hurled a six-hit shutout in Game Four of the league finals at Mayagüez. He blanked a powerful lineup featuring Luke Easter, Alonzo Perry, Artie Wilson, Wilmer Fields, and Johnny Davis.[39] Over those two seasons, he went 13-10 with a 2.59 ERA, pitching 219 innings.[40] His catcher with the Monarchs in 1946-48 and in Santurce was Earl Taborn, a fellow resident of Potosi.

By the 1949 season, LaMarque was seen as one of the best pitchers in the Negro Leagues and was consistently at the top in most pitching categories. He finished his final full season with the Monarchs with a 13-7 record, 96 strikeouts, and a 3.08 ERA over 196 innings.[41] His numbers garnered him another selection to the West team for the All-Star Game at Comiskey Park on August 14. LaMarque pitched the ninth inning, giving up one hit, as the East won, 4-0.[42] During the season Monarchs co-owner Tom Baird interviewed LaMarque about his biggest thrill in baseball. "I struck out Josh Gibson 3 times in one game," he responded, "But next time up Gibson hits the ball out of the park with plenty to spare."[43]

The 1950 season was LaMarque's last campaign with the Monarchs. In addition to pitching, he was often used as a pinch-hitter or outfielder. In his Opening Day start in Kansas City, LaMarque fired a five-hit gem against the Cleveland Buckeyes, going the distance and getting the win, 3-0.[44] It was a solid pitching staff with LaMarque, George Walker, Cliff Johnson, Frank Barnes, and Mel Duncan. The first 11 games they pitched were all complete games.[45] By early summer LaMarque also was leading the NAL with a .433 batting average.[46]

Pitcher Jim LaMarque, who carved out a six-year career with the Monarchs, went 2-0 in limited duty as a 21-year-old rookie in 1942. (Courtesy Noir-Tech Research, Inc.)

The Indianapolis Clowns won the Eastern Division and the Monarchs won the Western Division, but there were no playoffs between the division champs in 1950. LaMarque finished 6-7 with 53 strikeouts and a 3.25 ERA in 119 innings during his final season with Kansas City.[47]

As the integration of the White minor and major leagues, caused the Negro Leagues to diminish in stature and quality of play, another team became interested in LaMarque, and it had money and a strong team to create great appeal. The Fort Wayne Capehearts were preparing for another trip to Wichita for the semipro National Baseball Congress tournament. Lester Lockett was on the team but was unable to make the trip for the tournament. Most players were working full-time and sometimes could not get time off for the trip. Fort Wayne manager Red Braden always looked to add pitching around tournament time because teams played a lot of games in a short period of time. Braden added Pat Scantlebury but needed another durable starting lefty. The Monarchs had been to Fort Wayne a few times and Braden had seen LaMarque play, so he made him an offer to join the club. LaMarque was "wooed away from the Monarchs" and it "paid off handsomely" for Fort Wayne.[48] On July 25 LaMarque made his Fort Wayne debut as a pinch-hitting left fielder. He then began to be used primarily as a pitcher. Prior to the tournament, LaMarque traveled back and forth between Fort Wayne and Kansas City and played for both the Capeharts and the Monarchs.

Fort Wayne headed to Wichita in late August to defend its national semipro championship. LaMarque's first pitching assignment came in the team's second game, on August 26, He pitched a complete game, scattering three hits against the Huntsville (Alabama) Boosters.[49] His first loss came when he walked in the winning run after relieving Pat Scantlebury in the ninth inning. The Capeharts needed to win two more games in order to hold the national championship. Scantlebury got the ball in the first game, going 12 innings and winning 1-0. LaMarque got the ball for the deciding game and notched his third win in the tourney as he fanned 11 Elk City (Oklahoma) batters en route to a 5-2 championship win.[50]

The winners of the tournament were invited to play baseball in Japan and the Fort Wayne team headed for Tokyo for what was dubbed "the first inter-hemispheric series."[51] The Capeharts opened their tour of Japan with a win. LaMarque got the ball for game two against Kanebo and gave up eight hits in a 13-inning complete game that ended in a tough 1-0 loss in front of 30,000 at Osaka.[52] At season's end, LaMarque joined Scantlebury on the National Baseball Congress All-American team.[53]

LaMarque ventured to Mexico for the 1951 season. Joining a number of former Negro American Leaguers, he pitched for the Mexico City Red Devils, for whom he went 19-6 with a 4.17 ERA in 233⅓ innings pitched.[54]

There were reports that LaMarque was coming back to Fort Wayne for the 1952 season. However, the Vans, as the Fort Wayne team was now called, wondered about reports that he had signed with the Milwaukee Brewers of the American Association.[55] Monarchs owner Tom Baird told Vans skipper Red Braden that he had first claim on LaMarque but would waive the claim in favor of the Vans. A call was also made to Milwaukee to clear the air on the issue.[56]

The holdup could have been the Chihuahua Dorados in the Class-C Arizona-Texas League. LaMarque was listed as a pitcher for the team and was being counted on as its ace. By this time he was living in Fort Wayne and working for General Electric. He appeared in at least some games for the Vans.[57] The following season, 1953, LaMarque looked to be the ace in Fort Wayne. He beat both the Clowns and Havana Cuban Giants in exhibition games in town, even pinch-hitting against his old team, the Monarchs, in one game. LaMarque returned to Fort Wayne in 1953 and continued to 1955 but the talent for the team was just not up to standard. The 1953 Vans did not qualify for the semipro tournament.

LaMarque was back in 1954 as Fort Wayne tried to get back to Wichita. LaMarque was primarily playing outfield as manager Braden liked his bat in the lineup. The Vans won the Indiana state title but were beaten in Wichita.

By 1955 Fort Wayne had lost a few of its better players. LaMarque went from playing outfield to some relief pitching but the team was just not as good as in years past.

The year 1956 brought renewed hope that Fort Wayne – now named the Allen Dairymen after a new sponsor – had assembled a team that could once more compete for the semipro world title. The schedule for the Fort Wayne team was to play all home games, and the Wichita tournament was the goal. LaMarque pitched regularly during the season but did not take the mound often during tournament time, though he did contribute at the plate and in the outfield. The team added three other former Negro League players: Jim Mason, speedster *John Kennedy*, and Wilmer Fields. The team finished the home schedule 18-1 and qualified for the Wichita tourney. The Dairymen won the playoffs there and went on to Milwaukee, winning the Semipro Global World Series, by a 2-0 score over Hawaii.[58]

In 1957 LaMarque and Fields played again for Fort Wayne. The Dairymen went to the NBC tournament finals but lost to Sinton, Oklahoma.[59]

By 1958 LaMarque was winding down his career. He left Fort Wayne about midseason and moved to Kansas City, Missouri, where he began assembly-line work for the Ford Motor Company in nearby Claycomo. "He was a final repairman on the assembly line at Ford Motor Company. He worked there 31 years, before retiring in 1997," his wife, Antoinette, said in 2021.[60]

• JAMES "LEFTY" LaMARQUE •

He and Antoinette had met in 1969. She recalled, "I had worked at a clothing company and managed a clothing store. I took a part-time job as a bartender because I had children of my own to take care of. The Ford Motor Company was on strike and he came in to have a drink. The bar was on the corner. In fact, we lived down the street from each other and we didn't know each other. We did eventually marry. We married in '74.[61]

LaMarque received sad news on June 13, 1982. Satchel Paige had died, and LaMarque was asked to be one of the 13 honorary pallbearers for the Hall of Fame hurler. As the outside world learned more about the Negro Leagues, LaMarque was invited to make several appearances at events in the Kansas City area, including one with former Monarchs, Blues, A's, and Royals players. He was also invited to a number of baseball card shows and became something of a Negro League ambassador.

A few months after the death of Cool Papa Bell, LaMarque said in an interview, "When you watch Rickey Henderson, you are watching Cool Papa. He was good a baserunner as I've ever seen. Compared with Rickey, I would take Bell because I think Cool was quicker than him. And Cool Papa wouldn't take a big lead when he was on base; he'd only be one to three feet off the bag when he tried to steal."[62]

At the opening ceremony of the Satchel Paige School in Kansas City, LaMarque asserted, "I think it's one of the greatest things that ever happened. I hope these children will learn and grow and remember the man their school was named after." The school was closed in 2018.[63]

During the opening ceremonies for the Negro League Museum in Kansas City in July 1994, LaMarque said, "To me, it's about the greatest thing that's ever happened to me."[64] In an earlier interview he said, "It's good for the younger generations: they need to know their history. Now it's only fathers and grandfathers who remember us."[65] In 1995 he was one of the Negro Leagues players pictured on a series of cellphone cards issued by the PhoneLynx company.

Asked in 1997 about playing with Jackie Robinson in 1945, LaMarque said, "Jackie Robinson was tough enough to take the abuse he'd get in the major leagues." He added, "We helped him learn how to steal bases. But he learned other things too, and that's what made him the right choice, in my opinion. He was really intelligent. We had guys who were better on the field, but he was a great person. And the first black player in the major leagues had to be flawless." Having been able to play with Robinson still brought a smile to LaMarque's face. "It was a special time, when I was playing with him, he was just another ballplayer to me, maybe to everyone else. But now you think of it as history, and we were there with him."[66]

Antoinette LaMarque said Jim maintained contact with other Negro Leagues veterans:

"They enjoyed being together. They kept on with each other over the years. They were each there for the other ones. They were quite a group. A lot of people thought they made millions of dollars. But they didn't. They made maybe $600 or $700 a month.

"He was involved quite a bit, even after he retired from baseball. He did a lot of community work. He especially loved children. He wasn't too concerned about the adults. They were just out to get his autographs and put it on eBay so they could sell it. But he was always interested in the children. Whenever they would write and they would be doing Black history or whatever, and they would send him cards, he would always sign cards and send them back to them. He did that up until the day he died."[67]

Major League Baseball's recognition of the Negro Leagues to have been major leagues means LaMarque is now defined as a former major-league ballplayer. That probably feels good, it was suggested to her. "Yes, it does. It does. It's quite exciting."[68]

James Hardin LaMarque died on January 15, 2000, with his wife, Antoinette, and youngest daughter, Kimberly, by his side. He had two daughters from an earlier marriage (Joyce LaMarque Smith and Gloria Jean LaMarque Clay) and a son James Jr., who died in 1975. "He died from COPD, because of smoking," Antoinette said. "I tried for years to get him to stop smoking, but he would hide cigarettes. It became a family joke. He would hide them around, in places. I would find them and throw them out. He'd just go get some more. That's what he died from."[69] His headstone gives his birth year as 1921, though most documents show 1920.[70] He was buried at Forest Hills Cemetery in Kansas City, Missouri.

After LaMarque's death, Bob Kendrick, a Negro League Museum spokesman who is now the institution's president, said, "He had some impressive numbers with the Kansas City Monarchs. He was part of an impressive pitching staff. He was one of the aces of the staff. He should have gotten a strong look by the majors." Although LaMarque had been one of the premier lefties in the Negro Leagues during the 1940s,

"He wasn't like Satchel Paige or Josh Gibson with a household name. He was an example of the kind of player that just loved playing the game of baseball. And the Negro Leagues gave Lefty the opportunity to do just that."[71]

Sources

Seamheads.com was used for most Negro League season statistics. Negro League statistics vary from source to source; thus, the author also used the website of the Center for Negro League Baseball Research, if a newspaper story corroborated the numbers supplied. These statistics were posted by the Howe News Bureau, which was the official statistician for the Negro Leagues.

Notes

1 Steve Penn, "Lefty's Baseball Legend Lives On," *Kansas City Star*, February 9, 2000: City 3.

2 Shelley Smith, "Remembering Their Game," *Sports Illustrated*, July 6, 1992, https://vault.si.com/vault/1992/07/06/remembering-their-game.

3 Ancestry.com United States Federal Census 1930; United States WW II Draft cards young men 1940-47.

4 Laura Miserez, "Family Remembers Kansas City Monarchs' All-Star Pitcher 'Lefty' LaMarque," Missoulian.com, March 4, 2021. https://www.emissourian.com/features_people/family-remembers-kansas-city-monarchs-all-star-pitcher-lefty-lamarque/article_a4ada812-7c7f-11eb-b089-ffc6d1ab4464.html. Accessed March 5, 2021.

5 Brent P. Kelley, *The Negro Leagues Revisited* (Jefferson, North Carolina; McFarland, 1998), 164.

6 *The Negro Leagues Revisited*, 164.

7 "'Satchel' Paige and Kansas City Monarchs in Yankee Stadium's Biggest Attraction Sunday August 2," *New York Age*, August 1, 1942: 11.

8 "Johnson Bangs Long Wallop to Decide Contest," *St. Joseph (Missouri) Gazette*, July 17, 1942: 13.

9 "Clowns in Midst of Long Playing Tour," *Jackson* (Mississippi) *Advocate*, October 3, 1942: 6.

10 Miserez.

11 James A. Riley, *The Biographical Encyclopedia of the Negro Baseball Leagues* (New York: Carroll & Graf Publishers, Inc., 1994), 469.

12 It was a game in which the visiting Birmingham Black Barons had already run up a 20-0 lead by the time LaMarque homered; the final score was 20-6. LaMarque was not among the four Kansas City pitchers in this game. See "Monarchs in 20-6 Loss," *Kansas City Times*, July 21, 1944: 13. Three days later, he was one of two pitchers victimized by the Buckeyes in a 16-9 loss at Ruppert. LaMarque played other positions as well, when needed, for instance as center fielder in a July 14, 1948, game in Benton Harbor, Michigan, against the local Buds. See "Buds Defeat Kansas City Monarchs, 7-6," *News-Palladium* (Benton Harbor), July 15, 1948: 16. He played left field against the Atchison (Kansas) Colts on August 6. See "Colts Bow to Monarchs," *Atchison Daily Globe*, August 7, 1948: 5.

13 Ric Roberts, "Paige on Mound in First Tilt," *Pittsburgh Courier*, July 1, 1944: 12.

14 Jeffrey Flanagan, "A Stop in KC," *Kansas City Star*, April 15, 1997: 8.

15 "LaMarque to Hurl Against Dexters for K.C. Monarchs," *Brooklyn Daily Eagle*, June 22, 1945: 13.

16 "14,000 Witness Paige Score 4 Hits at Yankee Stadium, Sun.," *New York Age*, June 23, 1945: 11. The final score was 4-1, the Stars getting their one run on two walks and two infield outs.

17 "Monarchs to Play Barons," *Kansas City Star*, July 8, 1945: 18.

18 "Monarchs Beat Barons," *Dayton Daily News*, July 27, 1945: 21.

19 "A Homer Beats Monarchs," *Kansas City Times*, August 8, 1945: 7.

20 "Monarchs to Play Here," *Kansas City Star*, August 22, 1945: 14.

21 "Shut Out the Clowns," *Kansas City Times*, September 19, 1945: 7.

22 "Beers to Face Monarchs Here," *South Bend Tribune*, June 23, 1946: 32.

23 "Clowns Top Kansas City Twice, 10-3 and 2-0," *Pittsburgh Courier*, July 27, 1946: 17.

24 "Memphis, Monarchs Split Two," *Pittsburgh Courier*, August 31, 1946: 17.

25 Rich Puerzer, "September 17-29, 1946: Newark Eagles Get the Best of Kansas City Monarchs in Negro League World Series," SABR Games Project,

https://sabr.org/gamesproj/game/september-17-29-1946-newark-eagles-get-the-best-of-kansas-city-monarchs-in-negro-league-world-series/.

26 LaMarque gave up the three runs and was the losing pitcher. See "Feller, Satchel in Scoreless Three Inning Mound Stints," *Council Bluffs Nonpareil*, October 13, 1946: 17.

27 Jorge S. Figueredo, *Cuban Baseball: A Statistical History, 1878-1961* (Jefferson, North Carolina: McFarland & Company, Inc., 2003), 278, 281.

28 Kelley, 166.

29 "4 Monarchs Play Baseball All Year Long," *St Joseph Gazette*, June 4, 1949: 9.

30 "Kansas City Trips Memphis, 8-2, 9-3," *Pittsburgh Courier*, May 31, 1947: 14.

31 "9000 See Monarchs Beat Memphis, 6-0," *St. Louis Globe-Democrat*, August 29, 1947: 15.

32 https://www.seamheads.com/NegroLgs/year.php?yearID=1947&lgID=NAL.

33 As always, there are discrepancies in reporting statistics, typically due to a lack of definition between league and nonleague games. The August 8 *Alabama Tribune* of Montgomery, for instance, reported that LaMarque's 9-2 record was at that point the best in the NAL. "Art Wilson Sets Pace in Negro American League," *Alabama Tribune*, August 8, 1947: 6. The August 27 *St, Louis Globe-Democrat* reported him as 11-2.

34 Figueredo, 293-94.

35 Penn.

36 Larry Lester, *Black Baseball's National Showcase: The East-West All-Star Game, 1933-1953* (Lincoln: University of Nebraska Press, 2001), 313.

37 Lester, 321.

38 It was Satchel Paige Day at Wrigley. "Satch Paige's Day Success; Defeats Bearden Team, 4-2," *Los Angeles Mirror-News*, October 25, 1948: 56.

39 Thomas Van Hyning, *Santurce Crabbers: Sixty Seasons of Puerto Rican Winter League Baseball* (Jefferson, North Carolina: McFarland & Company, Inc., 1999). Mayaguez won the series.

40 LaMarque's nickname in Puerto Rico was Libertad after the Argentine singer, Libertad Lamarque. Thomas Van Hyning, *Santurce Crabbers*, 30.

• JAMES "LEFTY" LaMARQUE •

41 "Negro American League 1949 Statistics," http://www.cnlbr.org/Portals/0/Stats/NAL%201949/NAL1949.pdf, accessed February 22, 2021.

42 Lester, 335-36.

43 C.E. McBride, "Sporting Comment," *Kansas City Star,* April 14, 1949: 18.

44 Elston Howard, left fielder for the Monarchs, doubled and scored the first run of the game in the second inning. "Shut Out Bucs," *Kansas City Times,* May 8, 1950: 15.

45 "Two Stars with Memphis," *Kansas City Times,* June 1, 1950: 20.

46 "Black Barons Striving to Overtake Monarchs in Series; Clubs Play Here Tonight," *Montgomery Advertiser,* July 3, 1950: 7.

47 "Negro American League 1950 Statistics," http://www.cnlbr.org/Portals/0/Stats/NAL%201950/NAL1950.pdf, accessed February 22, 2021.

48 Ed Shuoe, "Now Hear This," *Emporia* (Kansas) *Gazette,* September 5, 1950: 3.

49 Bill Hodge, "Fort Wayne Cashes In on Errors to Ease by Boosters, 4-3," *Huntsville Times,* August 27, 1950: 12.

50 Associated Press, "TU Hurler Named 'Most Popular'; Elk City Loses," *Tulsa World,* September 7, 1950: 31. See also United Press, "Elks Lose but Break Ump's Nose," *Clinton* (Oklahoma) *Daily News,* September 7, 1950: 5.

51 "Win Fourth Straight Non-Pro Title," *The Sporting News,* September 13, 1950: 13. A photograph of the team accompanied the article.

52 "Kanebo Club Beats Capes in 13th^h, 1-0," *Fort Wayne Journal Gazette,* September 14, 1950: 23. The September 14 issue of *Pacific Stars and Stripes* offers good coverage of this game. LaMarque was 3-for-5 at the plate in the 13-inning game, according to the September 17 *Pacific Stars and Stripes.*

53 International News Service, "Lafayette's DeWitt on All-Star Nine," *Journal and Courier* (Lafayette, Indiana), September 12, 1950: 20.

54 Pedro Treto Cisneros, *The Mexican League Player Statistics 1937-2001* (Jefferson, North Carolina: McFarland, 2011), 474.

55 The signing was reported in, among other publications, the *Pittsburgh Courier.* "Brewers Ink Lamarque," *Pittsburgh Courier,* May 24, 1952: 15.

56 "Vans' LaMarque Hasn't Signed with Milwaukee," *Fort Wayne Journal Gazette,* May 7, 1952: 18. Five days later, the *Gazette* said that LaMarque had been giving Vans officials "insomnia with his wanderings about the country." See "LaMarque Due In Today," *Fort Wayne Journal Gazette,* May 12, 1952.

57 See "Auscos Tip Sutherland in 3-1 Tilt," *News-Palladium* (Benton Harbor, Michigan), August 13, 1952: 18.

58 Bob Pinkowski, "US Beats Hawaii, 2-0, for Global Baseball Title," *Milwaukee Journal,* September 14, 1956: 15. Pete Olsen threw a three-hitter for Fort Wayne.

59 "Texas Club Wins NBC," *Grand Rapids* (Michigan) *Press,* September 3, 1957: 30.

60 Interview with Antoinette LaMarque by Bill Nowlin on February 20, 2021.

61 LaMarque interview.

62 "Negro League Nostalgia; Memories as Great as Players," *Democrat and Chronicle* (Rochester, New York), August 19, 1991: 8.

63 Tim O'Connor, "Players, Family Help Dedicate Paige School," *Kansas City Star,* October 10, 1991: 31.

64 "Negro League Museum Makes Debut in Kansas City," *St Louis Post-Dispatch,* July 17, 1994: 63.

65 David Conrads, "Rescuing the Rich History of Black Baseball," *Christian Science Monitor,* February 8, 1991: 14.

66 Flanagan, 8, 9.

67 LaMarque interview.

68 LaMarque interview.

69 LaMarque interview.

70 Two such documents are his listing on the Social Security Death Index and his World War II draft registration card, which he completed himself, At the time, he was 21 and working for the Sanitary Barber Shop in Potosi.

71 Penn.

JACK MATCHETT

By Bill Nowlin

Jack Matchett made his debut with the Kansas City Monarchs in Memphis on May 12, 1940; he shut out the Birmingham Black Barons.[1] In 1942, when the Monarchs swept the Homestead Grays in the best-of-seven Negro Leagues World Series, Matchett won Games One and Three. The first game was a two-hit shutout.

He was one of the "big four" – along with Satchel Paige, Hilton Smith, and Booker McDaniel – a pitching rotation that might well have rivaled any throughout baseball. The Monarchs won Negro American League pennants for five of six years, from 1937 through 1942, save for 1938.

Piecing together the career of most players from the Negro Leagues is a difficult task. So, in some cases, is pinning down the players' dates of birth and death. All documentation indicates that Clarence "Jack" Matchett was born in Palestine, Texas, as was his father before him. Charlie Matchett (October 10, 1884-August 6, 1968) was a farm laborer, the son of Jane and Sam Matchett, himself a general farm laborer. At the time of the 1910 census, the family unit consisted of four people: Sam Matchett, age 56, his son Charlie, Charlie's wife, Minnie, and their son, Clarence, age 2. Minnie herself was also listed as a farm laborer. All were natives of Texas. Charlie Matchett served in the United States armed forces during the First World War and was stationed at Camp MacArthur in Texas. He died in Houston.

Unlike his father, Jack Matchett's actual birthdate is unclear. When he registered for Selective Service in October 1940, he provided his birthdate as February 4, 1907. That date would have made him age 3 at the time of the 1910 census. At the time of registration, he was described as 6-feet-2 and listed at 193 pounds, with black eyes, black hair, and black complexion, and a scar over his right eye.

But when he died, on March 19, 1979, in Los Angeles, two different birthdates were indicated. The California Death Index shows that he was born on January 3, 1905, while the United States Social Security Death Index gives a date of January 3, 1908. A "5" can sometimes look like an "8," and the 1908 date would conform with the 1910 census.

James A. Riley described Matchett the pitcher: "[T]he right-hander had a free, easy motion and good control of a variety of pitches, including a fastball, screwball, quick-breaking curve, and a very good change of pace. When on the mound nothing seemed to bother him, and his even temperament, hearty determination, and bountiful stamina enabled him to fashion some well-pitched games for the Monarchs."[2] One thing Riley didn't mention was what Buck Leonard said: "Jack Matchett was an underhand pitcher."[3] Though he pitched right-handed, he batted from the left side.

As to what Jack Matchett did before he joined the Monarchs, aside from a few brief mentions of his playing baseball, there are very few clues. He seems to have moved around 300 miles to the west, to Sweetwater, Texas, and to have been employed baling cotton with compress companies in both Lubbock (another 150 miles farther northwest) and Sweetwater. A May 1938 newspaper article reported him filing a claim for a January arm injury in a door of a press at Lubbock Compress.[4] He is named as Jack Matchett of Nolan County; Sweetwater is the county seat of Nolan County. When Matchett registered for the draft in October 1940, he provided an address in Sweetwater and the name of his employer as Western Compress of Sweetwater.

The arm injury may not have been to Matchett's pitching arm, and/or may not have been serious enough to prevent him from playing baseball. He had apparently begun playing professionally in the early 1930s in the Texas-Oklahoma-Louisiana League, an all-Black league with teams in San Antonio, Dallas, Fort Worth, Tulsa, Waco, Odessa, and Abilene, all in Texas, and one in Louisiana. Catcher Frazier "Slow" Robinson reported playing with the Abilene Eagles in 1930 or 1931 and said, "Our best pitcher was a boy called Jack Matchett."[5]

Robinson said, "Matchett was always a cutup," then added information regarding Matchett's lack of formal education. "He was a guy who never did go to school. He didn't have no education. I learned him how to read and write his name." Robinson also offered a bit about Matchett's personality: "He was that type of person who figured that whatever he did, he would be right doing it on his own. You know how these people are. If you kind of talk to him or scold him about it, he'd get angry. You'd best serve him with kid gloves. He was that type but he was a good pitcher."[6]

Robinson said that he caught for Abilene until the league folded, and then he and Matchett both caught on with a team in Odessa, Texas, in 1936. He recounted a story of playing against a local team in Hobbs, New Mexico, that year. Before the game, the umpire announced over the park's loudspeaker system, "For the white boys, it's Ted Blankenship pitching and Beans Minor catching. And for the niggers, it's a big nigger pitching [Matchett] and a little nigger catching [Robinson.]"[7] It wasn't surprising that the umpire gave Matchett a very small strike zone.

Charlie Matchett had moved to Lubbock and Robinson wrote, "I was on the road most of the time but kept a room in Lubbock, Texas, at Jack Matchett's father's house."[8]

Matchett may have lived in Lubbock for much of the 1930s. A 1931 city directory shows a Jack and Lula Matchett both at 1711 Av C, with Jack working as a bootblack and Lula as a maid. No marriage record has yet been located, and this may or may not be Jack Matchett the future Monarch. On October 31, 1932, a Jack Matchett married Alberta Brady in Lubbock. The 1937 city directory has him as a laborer at Lubbock Compress Co. Neither a street address nor spouse is mentioned.

In July 1938 Matchett is found in an Odessa newspaper pitching for the Odessa Oilers team. Indeed, "Big Black Jack" threw a 4-0 no-hitter against the Austin Black Senators in a July 7 night game in Midland, striking out 13.[9] The catcher in the game was Oilers manager Slow Robinson. Matchett was described as a "combination outfielder and pitcher" and "the new Oiler sensation." He was 5-for-5 in the game.[10]

Matchett was with the Black Oilers again in 1939, apparently a popular player and dubbed "The Iron Man" in the April 30 *Odessa American*. The Oilers were due to play the Mt. Pleasant Black Cubs on May 24, with Matchett on the mound. The article announcing the game said the Cubs had defeated such teams as the Kansas City Monarchs. Matchett beat the Cubs, 3-2.[11] The game account introduced another element to Matchett's story. It asserted that Mt. Pleasant's starting pitcher, Joe Davis, was Matchett's half-brother. It said he had been an Oiler and was considering remaining in Odessa and becoming an Oiler once more.

The May 31 *American* reported that the Kansas City Monarchs were trying to get Matchett for their club.[12] He seems to have spent some portion of 1930 playing for Satchel Paige's All-Stars, a traveling team that was the "B" team of the Monarchs.[13] Robinson suggests that it was he who helped bring Matchett and some others to the Monarchs.[14]

In March 1940 Matchett was still with the Black Oilers, though he spent some time pitching in at least a couple of exhibition games.[15]

Matchett first shows up in Negro Leagues records in 1940. He was 32 years old at the time. Historian Leslie Heaphy, however, turned up three articles from 1939 that show him pitching for the Monarchs in a couple of exhibition games. In a July 11 game, he worked in relief of Johnny Donaldson in a game in Vancouver, British Columbia, against the local Lowney All-Stars. He walked the first batter he faced, then struck out three in a row to preserve a 6-5 victory.[16] Four days later, Satchel Paige pitched the first four innings of a game against the House of David team and Matchett pitched the last five. Each pitcher gave up two hits, and the Monarchs won, 3-0.[17] The same two pitchers were slated to pitch in Reno against the House of David.[18]

Matchett also turned up in a 1940 newspaper, when a dispatch from Marshall, Texas, in the *Plaindealer* of Kansas City included "Jack Matchett, P, Odessa, Texas" on the 1940 Monarchs roster.[19]

It was in 1940 that he had his league debut. As noted above, he pitched a shutout against Birmingham in his first game, on May 12. It was a three-hitter, a 6-0 win.[20] On the 19th he beat the Memphis Red Sox, 5-3. In several 1940 games reported in the *Kansas City Star*, Matchett relieved. He sometimes started in doubleheaders, and sometimes he did both on the same day – for instance, quelling a rally in the ninth inning of the first game on August 18 at Ruppert Stadium in Kansas City to beat the Toledo Crawfords, 4-2, and then pitching a complete seven-inning second game to beat Toledo again, 4-3. The score had been tied, 3-3, after 6½. Matchett led off the bottom of the inning with a triple to right-center. After a base on balls, Jesse Warren singled in Matchett with the winning run. James Riley writes that Matchett's record in 1940 was 6-0 in league play.[21]

• When the Monarchs Reigned •

Coverage of the 1941 season is spotty, but Matchett turns up with the team in a few newspaper stories. In June he outpitched Peanuts Nyasses of the Ethiopian Clowns, 1-0, in a four-hitter at Crosley Field.[22] The team made its way to the West Coast in July, and Matchett, a "big black boy with a hard one that sizzled," beat the Medford (Oregon) Craters, 5-4. He struck out 10. His single in the ninth inning won the game for the Monarchs."[23]

Portland's *Oregonian* lists Matchett as one of the pitchers who might take on the House of David team at Portland's Vaughn Street ballpark in a July 22 night game, a contest featuring two of the top barnstorming teams of the day.[24] The game drew 8,000 fans and resulted in an 8-4 Monarchs win featuring the "superb chucking of Jack Matchett, husky colored ace of the Monarch squad." He allowed seven hits and struck out 10.[25] He appears to have spent most of the year as part of Satchel Paige's All-Stars.[26]

As to what Matchett did throughout 1941, information has so far proved elusive.

As the April 25 *Detroit Tribune* story indicates, the "top-notch" Matchett seemed to have started 1942 with the Cincinnati Clowns. The March 28 *Chicago Defender* announced that he had indeed signed with the national semipro champion Clowns.[27] By the time of the Monarchs' home opener, however, he was with Kansas City. Norris Phillips was released and Matchett added, the announcement made on Opening Day.[28]

In the home opener, Matchett kicked off the season with a five-hit, 7-0 shutout against Memphis on May 17. He was 2-for-4 at the plate with a single and a double and scored one of the Monarchs' runs. Satchel Paige pitched the second game, losing to Memphis, 4-1.[29]

Jack Matchett was one of only three pitchers used by the Monarchs in the 1942 World Series; he was 1-0 with a 2.45 ERA in 14 2/3 innings over three appearances that included one start.
(Courtesy Noir-Tech Research, Inc.)

At the end of May, Matchett worked the second game of a May 30 doubleheader against the Chicago American Giants and then was called on to get the final three outs of the first game against Birmingham on May 31.

On July 5 he started both games of a doubleheader in Birmingham, throwing the first 2⅓ innings in a 10-5 first-game win (relieved by Booker McDaniel), and then pitching all six innings of a complete-game seven-inning 2-1 loss.

Matchett was known to speak up at times and had been ejected from the June 17 game against the Baltimore Elite Giants. He "waved to the dugout after a prolonged argument with Umpire Frank McCrary over a called strike."[30]

At the end of July, Monarchs owner J.L. Wilkinson declared that there were at least 25 Negro League players who were of major-league caliber. He didn't name them all, but the Associated Press story mentioned "Jack Matchett, 28-year-old Kansas City pitcher, who sometimes operates from the mound accoutered in full dress ensemble topped by a plug hat."[31] That he sometimes enjoyed dressing up during games is reflected in a *Plaindealer* story saying he was "popular for his antics on the mound in full dress regalia."[32]

There were at least a few games in which Matchett played outfield. In a game against the East Chicago Giants on July 25, he played left field. On August 16 and 17 he played right field in back-to-back games.

On August 3 Matchett threw a three-hit shutout against the Baltimore Elite Giants, winning 3-0 at Baltimore's Bugle Field.[33] On the 25th, he threw a three-hitter against the Chicago American Giants, winning that one, 6-1.

• JACK MATCHETT •

The 1942 Negro World Series between the Homestead Grays of the Negro National League and the Kansas City Monarchs of the Negro American League was the first postseason championship between the pennant winners of two Negro leagues teams since 1927. The series pitted two top teams against each other. The Monarchs, as mentioned, had won five NAL titles and the Homestead Grays had won three consecutive NNL pennants.

Had there been an award for the MVP of the Series, Matchett might well have received it. Game One was held at Griffith Stadium in Washington on September 8. Satchel Paige started and worked the first five innings, allowing just two harmless hits in the fourth. Matchett came in and pitched the final four innings, facing 12 batters and setting every one of them down in order. He struck out two. At the plate, he was 1-for-2 and stole a base. The Monarchs won, 8-0, accumulating a number of runs thanks to six Grays errors. Different scoring conventions applied at the time, and Matchett was awarded the win.

The Monarchs won Game Two in Pittsburgh, 8-4, Hilton Smith the winning pitcher.

Game Three was held at Yankee Stadium on September 13. Once again Paige started. He gave up two runs in the first inning. Willie Simms hit a grand slam in the top of the third for the Monarchs, and Matchett was brought in. Wendell Smith of the *Pittsburgh Courier* wrote that Paige had suffered a stomach ailment.[34] Matchett pitched the rest of the game – seven innings, allowing just four hits and one unearned run. The final score was Monarchs 9, Grays 3. The Monarchs were 3-0 in the best-of-seven series and Jack Matchett was 2-0, with 11 innings pitched and no earned runs.

Game Four was played in Kansas City, under protest, because the Grays had brought in players from the Newark Eagles and Philadelphia Stars. With their lineup thus bolstered, the Grays outscored the Monarchs, 4-1, but the next day the game was disallowed. Matchett had left the team to return to Kansas City and rest up for the game, while the Monarchs played a few non-Series games against the Cincinnati Clowns during the week. But Matchett apparently had a bit of a drinking problem at times and was not in condition to start the game.[35]

Matchett, however, started the next game, the legitimate Game Four, on September 29 at Shibe Park in Philadelphia. Satchel Paige had been due to start, but simply wasn't there at game time. Not expecting to have to start, Matchett was pressed into action. He was tagged for three runs in the first inning and two more in the third. The Monarchs got one run in each of the same two innings. Paige then arrived, saying he'd been detained and given a traffic ticket in Lancaster, Pennsylvania (some 80 miles away), on his way to the game. With two on and two out in the fourth inning, Matchett was relieved by Paige and the Grays failed to score again while the Monarchs came back with seven unanswered runs to win the game and the World Series.

Perhaps Matchett's growing reputation had prompted a promotion of sorts in stature, as in 1943 he was often referred to as "Big Jack Matchett" and seen as one of the "big four" in the Monarchs rotation, with Satchel Paige, Hilton Smith, and Booker McDaniel.[36] The Monarchs had another very good season, but the Cleveland Buckeyes – playing 10 fewer league games – wound up with a slightly higher winning percentage (38-22 for a .633 winning percentage, while the Monarchs were .614 (43-27).[37]

Matchett pitched a 1-0 (seven-inning) shutout in the second game of the May 16 Opening Day doubleheader at Ruppert Stadium.[38] On May 24 he lost a heartbreaker, pitching all 12 innings of a game lost to the Cleveland Buckeyes in part due to a Monarchs error, 2-1.[39] As in every year, he both started and relieved in games. On June 3 he worked the first eight innings of a game against the Chicago American Giants at Comiskey Park and, with his third hit of the game, struck a one-out, bases-loaded single in the ninth inning to drive in two runs and win the game, 4-3.[40]

Precisely how Matchett fared in the 1943 regular season is difficult to pin down, but when the "Royal Giants" arrived in Long Beach to play a game against Red Ruffing's All-Stars on October 17, a Long Beach newspaper said he had been 23-5 during the season.[41] The *San Diego Union* wrote five days later that he had been a "27-game winner during the recently completed Negro National League season."[42] That would represent a pretty spectacular season.

World War II was in progress and coverage of Negro League ballgames was perhaps sparser than usual. The NAL opened on May 30, 1943, and Matchett and 18,000 fans flocked to Comiskey Park to see the Monarchs play the Chicago American Giants. Matchett worked eight innings but was facing a 3-2 deficit. In the top of the ninth, the Monarchs hit three singles in succession, a batter struck out, and then

Matchett (he was 3-for-4 in the game) singled into center field for two runs, to give Kansas City a 4-3 lead. Paige relieved in the bottom of the ninth and secured the win.[43] Matchett pitched a three-hit shutout of Nashville on June 17 in Louisville.

After the 1943 season was complete, Matchett and many of his Monarchs teammates played as Chet Brewer's Kansas City Royals through the winter in Southern California, playing games in San Diego and Los Angeles in November, December, and January. He appears to have picked up another nickname: Big Train Matchett.[44]

Matchett also seems to have become a name to be reckoned with: When an advertisement was placed in the *San Antonio Light* for a May 10, 1944, game against the Memphis Red Sox, the ad read: "Featuring Jack Matchett."[45]

He had a successful regular season with the Monarchs in 1944. On September 3 he beat the visiting Memphis Red Sox, 3-1, the one run unearned.[46]

Matchett apparently was a good hitter. In early June 1944, he was reported as leading the Negro American League with a .471 batting average, four points ahead of Cleveland's Sam Jethroe.[47] A column in the *Pittsburgh Courier* called him "one of the best hitters on the club."[48] According to the *New Orleans Times-Picayune*, he had won 10 games before being prepared to pitch for the South team of Negro League All-Stars in an October 1 North-South All-Star game.[49]

It is worth parenthetically noting that not only did Slow Robinson write "Matchett could hit" but he added, "There were several pitchers that could field their position. Jack Matchett was one of the best."[50]

A number of the Monarchs entered military service during the course of the Second World War, but Matchett's age may have proved an advantage that kept him out of the service. The same "big four" rotation remained through the 1945 season and Frank Duncan continued as manager through the war years. During the 1945 season, the Monarchs added a new infielder during spring training in Houston – Jackie Robinson. Paige, Matchett, and Double Duty Radcliffe were bombed for 12 runs on June 24, and the Monarchs lost both games of a doubleheader against the Grays at Griffith Stadium, as Robinson hit safely seven times in succession.[51]

Seamheads shows Matchett pitching in only one game, for two innings, though scattered stories throughout the season list him as one of the possible pitchers for given games.

In 1946 the *Chicago Sun* listed Matchett among the Monarchs pitchers returning for the season, as did the *Chicago Tribune* on the morning of Opening Day.[52] He does not appear in such game accounts as could be found. A pair of stories in June have him pitching for the Abilene Black Eagles against the Fort Worth Black Giants on June 19 and against Waco on July 1. Abilene lost to Waco, 7-4, but Matchett "with triples and a single, paced the Abilene attack."[53]

A month later, Matchett pitched for the San Antonio Giants in a July 26 road game against the Council Bluffs Browns, losing 8-0, with all eight runs scoring in the home fifth inning. Matchett had pitched to the minimum 12 batters through the first four, but then everything fell apart.[54] Perhaps it was a one-off. Two days later, he was mentioned as possible starting pitcher for Abilene.

In the next two or three years, Matchett appears to have played baseball in Saskatchewan, perhaps arriving later in 1946. He was reportedly the playing manager of the Saskatoon Legion in the Saskatoon Senior Baseball League.[55] In August 1947 a story in the *Saskatoon Star-Phoenix* reported that he had pitched at Cairns Field in Saskatoon for the Canadian Legion ballclub, battling the Colonsay club to a 3-3, 10-inning tie game called due to darkness. "Matchett, colored, pitched, went all the way for Legion and held the visitors to seven hits, four of which Colonsay bunched in the first three frames to score their three counters." He struck out three.[56]

In 1948, the start of the season was on May 20, and a newspaper story featured Matchett's photograph. He was one of three holdovers for the Legion team, described as "Jack Matchett, the popular colored player from Kansas City who broke in with the Legion last year. Matchett, by the way, has taken over the coaching duties. He will do a turn on the mound as well as fill in as an outfielder."[57]

A June 22, 1949, report previewed a game "at the senior baseball enclosure" between the Delisle club and the Cubs. The "boss" of the Cubs, Al Verner, wrote the paper, "was also seen eyeing big Jack Matchett. Could it be Matchett is headed for a Cub uniform?"[58] Whether he played in 1949 is yet undetermined.

After this, Jack Matchett seems to nearly drop off the map. Perhaps he liked life in California. In 1977, he was listed as one of 14 former Negro Leagues players at an event at the Hollywood Palladium to honor Sammie Haynes. Matchett was identified as with the Kansas City Monarchs; former batterymate

Joe Greene and pitcher Chet Brewer were the two other Monarchs.[59]

There was one nice moment to remember Matchett near the end of his life. As part of Black History Month, he was among more than two dozen former players presented awards at an Old Negro Leagues night held at Sportsman's Park Auditorium on February 24, 1978.[60] Among them was his old batterymate Slow Robinson, who wrote in his book that he had caught two one-hitters thrown by Matchett.[61]

Jack Matchett died in Los Angeles in March 1979, Seamheads showing a date of March 19.

Without an obituary or other clues, such as relatives who could perhaps be tracked down, the story of Matchett's later years remains a mystery.

Sources

Thanks to Seamheads.org, Gary Ashwill, Rick Bush, Larry Lester, Andy McCue, Bill Mortell, and Jim Overmyer.

Notes

1   "Open with Memphis Here," *Kansas City Star*, May 19, 1940: 19.

2   James A. Riley, *The Biographical Encyclopedia of the Negro Baseball Leagues* (New York: Carroll & Graf, 1994), 520.

3   Buck Leonard, with James A. Riley, *Buck Leonard – The Black Lou Gehrig* (New York: Carroll & Graf, 1995), 138.

4   *Lubbock Morning Avalanche*, May 6, 1938: 2.

5   Frazier "Slow" Robinson with Paul Bauer, *Catching Dreams: My Life in the Negro Baseball Leagues* (Syracuse, New York: Syracuse University Press, 1999), 13.

6   *Catching Dreams*, 13.

7   *Catching Dreams*, 17.

8   *Catching Dreams*, 18.

9   "Big Black Jack's a Pitcher, Too – Hurls No Hitter, No Runner Against Austin Senators at Midland Park," *Odessa American*, July 8, 1938: 7.

10   "Altus Negroes to See Big Black Jack Sunday at Local Ball Park at 3:30," *Odessa American*, July 10, 1938: 7.

11   "Oilers Win, 3 to 2, In Brother Duel," *Odessa American*, May 25, 1949: 4.

12   "San Angelo Beats Big Jack Matchett," *Odessa American*, May 31, 1939: 2.

13   William A. Young, *J.L. Wilkinson and the Kansas City Monarchs* (Jefferson, North Carolina: McFarland, 2016), 111. A photograph of Matchett with Satchel Paige's All-Stars appears in Slow Robinson's *Catching Dreams* on page 23.

14   *Catching Dreams*, 25.

15   Jada Davis, "Waal, It's Like This," *Odessa American*, March 17, 1940: 7.

16   "Catcher's Hand Was Too Sore, So 'Satchel' Just Couldn't Pitch Here Last Night, Nohow," *Daily Province* (Vancouver, British Columbia), July 12, 1939: 23.

17   "Kansas Monarch Aces Paige and Matchett Tie Whiskers in Knot," *Vancouver Sun*, July 17, 1939: 10.

18   Prof. Heaphy's book indicated that Matchett had been with the Monarchs in 1939, something none of the other standard sources had mentioned. On request, she supplied the articles noted here. See Leslie A. Heaphy, ed., *Satchel Paige and Company* (Jefferson, North Carolina: McFarland, 2007), 228.

19   "Monarchs Prepare for 1940 Season in Texas," *Plaindealer* (Kansas City, Kansas), April 5, 1940: 3.

20   "Monarchs Win and Lose at Birmingham," *Plaindealer*, May 17, 1940: 3.

21   Riley, 520.

22   "Paige to Hurl Here," *Winnipeg Tribune*, June 21, 1941: 26.

23   "Monarchs Nip Craters, 5 to 4, on 3-Run Explosion in 9th," *Medford (Oregon) Mail Tribune*, July 17, 1941: 4.

24   "Monarchs to Battle Davis in Vaughn Street Game," *Oregonian* (Portland), July 22, 1941: 23.

25   "Monarchs Win by 8-4 Score," *Oregonian*, July 23, 1941: 29.

26   "Clowns Loom as Strongest in New League," *Detroit Tribune*, April 25, 1942: 8. That Matchett spent 1941 with Paige's touring team is also supported by "'Pepper' Bassett Signed by Clowns," *Columbus (Ohio) Dispatch*, June 3, 1942: 17.

27   "Clowns Will Open Season on April 1," *Chicago Defender*, March 28, 1942: 21.

28   "Monarchs Take Doubleheader from Chicago in The American League Opener Sunday, 7-4; 6-0," *Kansas City Call*, May 15, 1942.

29   "Only 2 Monarch Hits," *Kansas City Star*, May 18, 1942: 9.

30   "Elites Lose Night Game to Monarchs," *Afro-American* (Baltimore), June 20, 1942: 27.

31   Associated Press, "Claims 25 Negro Stars Good Enough for Majors," *Chicago Daily Times*, July 30, 1942: 78. If the 1908 birthdate is correct, Matchett was 34 years old at the time.

32   ANP, "Owner of Monarchs Okeys Big League Tryout," *Plaindealer*, August 7, 1942: 34.

33   "Shutouts for Monarchs," *Kansas City Times*, August 6, 1942: 13.

34   Wendell Smith, "Third Straight Loss Dooms Grays Hopes," *Pittsburgh Courier*, September 19, 1942: 17.

35   *Catching Dreams*, 62, 94, 95.

36   For the "big four" comment, see, for instance, "Monarchs to Show Powerful Outfit," *Daily Illinois State Journal* (Springfield), September 12, 1943: 17. A "Big Jack Matchett" reference is found in "Parker, Royal Nines Battle at Lane Field," *San Diego Union*, October 31, 1943: 39.

37   Statistics come from Seamheads, at seamheads.com/NegroLgs/year.php?yearID=1943.

38   Paige and McDaniel combined on a 2-0 shutout in the first game, whitewashing the Chicago American Giants twice. "No Run for the Giants," *Kansas City Times*, May 17, 1943: 8.

39   "Monarchs Lose in 12th," *Kansas City Times*, May 25, 1943: 14.

40   "Matchett's Single in 9th Beats Chi Before 18,000," *Pittsburgh Courier*, June 5, 1943: 18.

41   "Three Top Ballclubs in Doubleheader at Local Park Today," *Long Beach Independent*, October 17, 1943: 24.

42   "Parker's Nine to Boast Real Power Lineup," *San Diego Union*, October 22, 1943: 22. That the article placed Matchett in the wrong league doesn't inspire confidence in the accuracy of the total.

43   "Monarchs Score in 9th Inning, Beat Giants 4-3," *Chicago Sun*, May 31, 1943: 24.

44   "Lindell Hurls Tonight as Majors, Negroes Vie," *Los Angeles Times*, November 10, 1943: A10; "Black, Matchett in Mound Duel," *Los Angeles Times*, November 14, 1943: 23.

45   Advertisement, *San Antonio Light*, May 7, 1944: 21.

46 "Kansas City Splits with Memphis Red Sox," *Pittsburgh Courier*, September 9, 1944: 12.

47 "Bell's .515 Tops Hitters," *Pittsburgh Courier*, June 3, 1944: 12. Bell was in the Negro National League.

48 Ric Roberts, "Grays and Kansas City Split Before 15,000," *Pittsburgh Courier*, July 1, 1944: 12.

49 "North, South Battle Today," *New Orleans Times-Picayune*, October 1, 1944: 24. Paige and McDaniel handled the pitching chores in the game, a 6-1 win.

50 *Catching Dreams*, 154, 155.

51 "Grays Defeat Kansas City," *Chicago Defender*, June 30, 1945: 7. Matchett had previously pitched in the June 2 game against the Barons, a 4-3 win. See "Barons Lose to Kansas City," *Chicago Defender*, June 9, 1945: 7. Stories as late as August include him as a member of the Monarchs pitching staff. See, for instance, "Black Barons Clash with Philadelphia; Yanks With Kay See," *New York Amsterdam News*, August 11, 1945: B8.

52 "Negro Baseball Season Opens," *Chicago Sun*, May 5, 1946: 38. See also "Negro Nines Open Today in Sox Park," *Chicago Tribune*, May 5, 1946: A2.

53 See "Black Eagles Vie with Fort Worth, *Abilene Reporter-News*, June 19, 1946: 7; "Black Eagles Vie with Waco Today," *Abilene Reporter-News*, June 30, 1946: 26; and "Black Eagles Lose to Waco '9,' 7-4," *Abilene Reporter-News*, June 30, 1946: 8.

54 "All Scoring in Fifth as Browns Win," *Daily Nonpareil* (Council Bluffs, Iowa), July 27, 1946: 5.

55 Barry Swanton and Jay-Dell Mah, *Black Baseball Players in Canada* (Jefferson, North Carolina: McFarland, 2009), 110. Their book says he started in Saskatoon in 1946.

56 "Colonsay, Legion in Tie Game," *Star-Phoenix* (Saskatoon, Saskatchewan), August 6, 1947: 11.

57 "Senior Ball Starts Tomorrow," *Star-Phoenix*, May 19, 1948: 19.

58 *Star-Phoenix*, June 22, 1949: 17.

59 "Chico Renfroe, "Los Angeles Honors Former Atlantan," *Atlanta Daily World*, October 6, 1977: 14.

60 Brad Pye Jr., "Prying Pye," *Los Angeles Sentinel*, March 2, 1978: B1. The venue is now known as Jesse Owens Community Regional Park. The others honored included Chet Brewer, Don Newcombe, Effa Manley and her late husband Abe Manley, Fran Matthews, Frazier Robinson, Herb Souell, and Quincy Trouppe.

61 *Catching Dreams*, 207, 208.

BOOKER McDANIEL

By Leslie Heaphy

Over the course of seven seasons, from 1940 through 1946, Booker McDaniel both pitched and played in the outfield for the Kansas City Monarchs. During four of those seven seasons the Monarchs were Negro American League champions and twice competed in the Negro League World Series. McDaniel joined the club in 1940 as a 26-year-old, playing left field and hitting only .190 in 63 at-bats. The 1941 season saw McDaniel settle in as a mainstay on the pitching staff for the remainder of his career. He ended his career with a 24-11 record for the Monarchs in NAL play, with his best seasons coming in 1943 and 1945.[1]

Booker Taliaferro McDaniel was born on September 28, 1913, in Blackwell (Conway County), Arkansas, not far from the town of Atkins, where his family lived. He was the second of four sons born to Henry and Lottie (Lewis) McDaniel, all of whom worked as local farm laborers to help the family after their father died in 1919 while Booker was still a young boy. On November 29, 1931, 18-year-old Booker McDaniel married 17-year-old Lavada Myers, but little else is known about his early life. McDaniel first gained notice as a ballplayer around 1938 while playing for teams in his home state, and he joined the Monarchs in 1940.[2]

McDaniel was a local hero as he pitched for the Morrilton Sluggers in 1938 and the Fort Smith Grays in 1939. He earned his nickname, "Cannonball," due to his blazing fastball. In one 1938 game local papers credited him with 17 strikeouts against the Dubisson Tigers.[3] One thing that plagued McDaniel his whole career was the misspelling of his name from the start. Newspapers called him McDaniels, McDaniel, McDonald, and McDonel as just a few examples. As a result, finding his records and ascertaining that game reports and statistics truly are about McDaniel has always been a difficult endeavor.

With the Monarchs from 1940 to 1946, McDaniel soon was listed as one of the big four of the pitching staff with Satchel Paige, Hilton Smith, and Jack Matchett. He and Smith often came in to relieve Paige.

A late-September contest in 1941 saw McDaniel on the winning end of a 7-2 score against the Chicago Spencer Coals as he pitched seven innings of shutout ball and struck out 10 en route to the win. In 1942 one reporter stated that, while the focus on the Monarchs staff was on Paige and Smith, other pitchers – like McDaniel – should not be overlooked. After receiving such accolades, McDaniel pitched 14 straight scoreless innings in June against Cleveland and Dayton.[4] In his first full season, 1942, McDaniel had a 5-1 record in 59 innings. By 1943 he had established himself as a pitcher to be reckoned with as he was 8-2 in 83 innings, placing him third on the Monarchs staff behind Paige and Smith.[5]

After the NAL season ended in 1943, McDaniel headed west to play alongside Satchel Paige for the Baltimore Colored Giants of the California Winter League.[6] Paige, engaging in a bit of typical hyperbole, told a reporter, "He is a better pitcher than I ever was or ever will be."[7] In a game against San Diego, Paige and McDaniel combined for a 10-inning, 2-1 win. As if pitching to justify Paige's compliment, McDaniel continued to build impressive strikeout numbers as his career progressed.

McDaniel was a key pitcher in 1945 for a Monarchs roster that included Jackie Robinson. In a 1945 exhibition game against the Chicago American Giants, McDaniel pitched five innings and struck out 10 as Kansas City won 3-1. Additional highlights that season included a 7-0 shutout over Birmingham in early April in which Robinson drove in the first two runs, and a 9-3 win over the Bushwicks in which he struck out eight while allowing only five hits.[8]

Like many strikeout artists, McDaniel struggled with his control, which was a problem that plagued him periodically throughout his career. In a 1944 game against Memphis, he pitched four brilliant innings and then gave up two hits, two walks, and a wild pitch in one inning that led to a 6-5 loss. In a June game against Cincinnati, Paige started and held his opponent scoreless, but McDaniel came on in relief and walked four, resulting in a 4-1 loss.[9]

Nonetheless, McDaniel had a good time and performed well far more often than not during his time with the Monarchs. He showed off his speed and decent control as he compiled a record of 24-11 with a 2.96 ERA. He has been credited with 236 strikeouts in 338 innings pitched. These numbers are as complete as the newspaper box scores allow but it must be remembered that strikeouts and walks were not always reported; thus, his numbers were likely higher on both counts.

McDaniel played in two All-Star games during his Negro League career – in 1943 for the South All-Stars and in 1945 for the West All-Stars. In 1943 he pitched three innings of shutout ball. The result was not so positive in 1945. Though the West held on to win, 9-6, all six runs were charged to McDaniel in 2⅔ innings pitched.[10]

At the conclusion of the 1945 NAL season, McDaniel journeyed to Cuba, where he played for Marianao during the 1945-46 winter season. Although Marianao finished in last place, McDaniel compiled a 9-7 record – with his nine victories accounting for 39 percent of his team's 23 wins – and made the all-star squad.

In 1946 McDaniel joined a group of Negro Leaguers who jumped to the Mexican League for better pay and a less segregated life. McDaniel signed with the San Luis Potosi Tuneros for a supposed $9,000 for the season, according to fellow player Art Pennington.[11] McDaniel pitched in 234⅓ innings, compiling a 14-18 record and a 3.26 ERA, which earned him a spot on the all-star team. Local Mexican papers also made note of his pitching speed, referring to him as "Balazo," which translates to "gunshot." In Mexico's North-South All-Star game McDaniel got the start and gave up two hits and two runs in the first inning as his North teammates went on to lose 11-8.[12]

During the winter season, McDaniel rejoined the Marianao team in Cuba and went 0-2. Due to a dispute with US Organized Baseball, a new Cuban league known as the National Federation was founded, and McDaniel ended up pitching for Oriente, for whom he put up a 3-0 record before returning to Mexico for the 1947 season.

This time around McDaniel pitched for the Veracruz Azules, who fell to last place even though McDaniel was credited with a 14-14 record and pitched to a 3.41 ERA in 242⅔ innings. He again led the league in both strikeouts (127) and walks (161). Cuba beckoned again for the 1947-48 winter season and McDaniel

Pitching in a rotation that included two future Hall of Famers, Booker McDaniel held his own with a 5-1 record and 2.44 ERA in NAL games in 1942. (Courtesy Noir-Tech Research, Inc.)

participated in the Players Federation, pitching both for Santiago (3-2) and Alacranes (0-3). Afterward, he headed back to Mexico and rejoined San Luis Potosi, the club for which he had pitched in 1946. He finished the 1948 season with the Diablos Rojos in Mexico City and compiled a combined 12-12 record between the two teams.[13] McDaniel stayed in Mexico for the winter season, pitching for Los Mochis Caneros. In the February 1949 all-star game between the National team and one composed of foreign players, McDaniel pitched two innings to help the foreign team win a shutout.[14]

After the 1948 season, the NAL owners voted to lift the five-year ban they had placed on players who had jumped to the Mexican Leagues. This allowed McDaniel to return to the Monarchs for the 1949 season. According to records published in the papers, he pitched in nine games and compiled a 4-4 record including one shutout. Commissioner Happy Chandler also had informally banned players who had jumped to the Mexican League and nothing was done to change that until the summer of 1949. A writer for the *Indianapolis Recorder* suggested that this circumstance accounted for McDaniel never having the opportunity to play in the White majors.[15]

After Chandler said that players who had jumped to Mexico could be re-signed, McDaniel was signed by the Chicago Cubs and assigned to the Los Angeles Angels of the Pacific Coast League. He integrated the Angels in June and was the first Black pitcher in the PCL.[16] Before joining the Angels, McDaniel had pitched a couple of early games for the Monarchs. In an April game against the Clowns, he pitched three superb innings to help his team win, 5-1. His new team, the Angels, struggled, finishing far out of first place, but McDaniel managed to put up a respectable 8-9 record. His first start was a huge success as he pitched the Angels to an 8-3 win over Portland in spite of having to battle his nerves as the trailblazing pitcher integrated the PCL. McDaniel held the opposition to five hits while striking out six, but he also kept to his career pattern and walked eight. In his second straight victory after joining the Angels, McDaniel threw a six-hitter to beat the Seattle Rainiers, 17-0.[17] In early July McDaniel had won four straight games, with the fourth being a 5-3 complete-game victory over the San Francisco Seals. He gave up all three runs in the first two innings and then held the Seals scoreless, working out of a bases-loaded jam in the ninth inning to preserve the victory. Another win for McDaniel was a three-hit 6-1 victory over Oakland, where the reporter referred to him simply as "Cannonball." His winning streak eventually came to an end with an 8-6 loss to Portland in which he was knocked out in the first inning, giving up four runs.[18]

McDaniel came back for a second season in 1950, but now he was used primarily as a relief pitcher and put together a 3-4 record with an ERA over 6.00. He did show signs of his old speed in a relief appearance against Portland. McDaniel blanked the Beavers over the final three innings of a 4-1 loss, striking out three of the 10 batters he faced. As his age seemed to be catching up to him and slowing his speed, the Angels let him go before the 1951 season. Instead of taking another minor-league contract, McDaniel returned to the Monarchs for the 1951 and 1952 seasons. Proving he could still pitch, he put together an 8-9 season in 1951. In a complete game against the Indianapolis Clowns, McDaniel went the distance in a 5-4 loss to Willie Collins. One reporter compared McDaniel to Dazzy Vance and said he served up "aspirin tablets."[19]

Over the winter, McDaniel pitched 45 innings for Mexico City Diablos Rojos. His final record was 1-2 with a 5.16 ERA.[20] He pitched in 11 games for the Monarchs in 1952, completing six games with a 3-5 record. He struggled but still showed flashes of his old speed. In a 7-5 May loss to the Clowns, McDaniel gave up nine hits and seven runs but still struck out six. McDaniel continued to play locally through much of the 1950s while taking a job with the Wyandotte Grain Elevator Company. He retired in 1969 and died of throat cancer on December 12, 1974, in a Kansas City, Missouri, hospital.[21]

McDaniel pitched for several excellent Monarchs teams in the 1940s as part of the supporting cast for Hall of Famers Satchel Paige and Hilton Smith. One reporter called McDaniel Satchel's policeman, coming in to hold the fort.[22] Even so, he made a name for himself in the United States, Cuba, and Mexico. Although he had a short minor-league career, he played a key role in the integration of the PCL. Although a lack of control over his pitches troubled McDaniel throughout his career, he still compiled impressive strikeout statistics with his blazing fastball and deserves to be remembered for the fine player he was during his decade-plus career.

Sources

Ancestry.com was consulted for census, birth, death, marriage, and other public records.

Cuban League records and statistics were taken from the following (unless otherwise indicated):

Figueredo, Jorge S. *Cuban Baseball, A Statistical History, 1878-1961* (Jefferson, North Carolina: McFarland & Company, Inc., 2003).

Figueredo, Jorge S. *Who's Who in Cuban Baseball, 1878-1961* (Jefferson, North Carolina: McFarland & Company, Inc., 2003).

Mexican League statistics were taken from the following (unless otherwise indicated):

Treto Cisneros, Pedro. *The Mexican League: Comprehensive Player Statistics, 1937-2001* (Jefferson, North Carolina: McFarland & Company, Inc., 2002).

Seamheads.com was consulted for Negro League records and statistics, except where otherwise indicated.

• When the Monarchs Reigned •

Notes

1 http://www.seamheads.com/NegroLgs/player.php?playerID=mcdan01boo.

2 Arkansas County Marriage Index, https://www.familysearch.org/ark:/61903/1:1:NMKF-DBH; Social Security Death Index, https://www.familysearch.org/ark:/61903/1:1:JG86-S3F.

3 "Booker McDaniels," *Arkansas Baseball Encyclopedia*, http://arkbaseball.com/tiki-index.php?page=Booker+McDaniels; Larry Lester and Sammy Miller, *Black Baseball in Kansas City* (Charleston, South Carolina: Arcadia Publishing, 2000), 56.

4 "Monarchs Trim Spencers 3-2," *Times* (Munster, Indiana), September 11, 1941: 35; "Negro Elks to Game Here," *Kansas City Times*, June 17, 1942: 10.

5 Booker McDaniel Stats, http://www.seamheads.com/NegroLgs/player.php?playerID=mcdan01boo.

6 *Indianapolis Recorder*, May 22, 1943; "Stars of Negro Loop Play Here," *Evening News* (Harrisburg), August 11, 1942: 6; "Paige and other Negro Stars Will Play at Stadium," *Times-Tribune* (Scranton), July 29, 1942: 27.

7 "Andy Pafko to Test Paige's Slants Sunday," *California Eagle* (Los Angeles), October 21, 1943: 13.

8 'Exhibition to Monarchs," *Kansas City Star*, April 3, 1945: 8; "Satchel Paige Wins," *Montana Standard* (Butte, Montana), December 6, 1943: 8; "Birmingham, Monarchs Split Two Sunday Tilts," *Pittsburgh Courier*, April 14, 1945: 12; "Monarchs Show Bushwicks Some Stylish Tricks," *Brooklyn Daily Eagle*, August 16, 1945: 14.

9 "Monarchs to 13,000," *Kansas City Times*, 22 May 1944, 9; "Monarchs Defeated 4-1," *Kansas City Star*, June 19, 1944: 9.

10 Larry Lester, *Black Baseball's National Showcase: The East-West All-Star Game, 1933-1953* (Lincoln: University of Nebraska Press, 2001), 255.

11 *Arkansas Baseball Encyclopedia*; "Weather Hot; Food Bad; Pay Less Than Whites in Mexico, Player Tells Afro," *Afro-American*, July 13, 1946: 16; "Gardella Is Mexico Ace," *Honolulu Advertiser*, July 10, 1946: 10.

12 *Arkansas Baseball Encyclopedia*; "Weather Hot; Food Bad; Pay Less Than Whites in Mexico, Player Tells Afro"; "Gardella Is Mexico Ace."

13 *Arkansas Baseball Encyclopedia*.

14 *Arkansas Baseball Encyclopedia*; "Stars Game, Nationals vs Foreigners, February 24, 1949," http://www.historiadehermosillo.com/htdocs/BASEBALLCOSTA/costa/1948-1949/juegodeestrellas.htm.

15 "High Hopes for a Young Star," *Kansas City Star*, April 14, 1949: 18; "Monarchs' Player-Manager, Popular Hurler Sign for '49," *Indianapolis Recorder*, February 26, 1949: 11; "Official 1949 NAL Pitching Records," http://www.cnlbr.org/Portals/0/Stats/NAL%201949/NAL1949.pdf; "Old Monarchs to Return," *Kansas City Times*, December 2, 1948: 26.

16 "Dasso and Raimond," *Press Democrat* (Santa Rosa, California), June 22, 1949: 6.

17 "McDaniel Bows In for Angels with Five-Hitter," *Los Angeles Times*, June 16, 1949: 61; Dick Walton, "Angels Try Power on Suds' Fletcher," *Los Angeles Evening Citizen News*, June 22, 1949: 14.

18 "LA Angels Sign Booker McDaniel," *Journal Herald* (Dayton, Ohio), June 11, 1949: 9; "Kansas City 9 Takes Battle from Clowns," *Charlotte Observer*, April 29, 1949: 15; "McDaniels Keeps Victory String Intact, Wins Fourth Straight," *Pittsburgh Courier*, July 9, 1949: 22; "Padres Thump Portland 12-2," *Statesman Journal* (Salem, Oregon), July 10, 1949: 14; "Austin Homer Clinches First," *Statesman Journal*, July 18, 1949: 9.

19 "Clowns Show Class in Win," *Knoxville News-Sentinel*, September 13, 1951: 35; "Angels' McLish attempts to Even Beaver Series Tonight," *Los Angeles Mirror-News*, June 9, 1950: 55.

20 *Arkansas Baseball Encyclopedia*.

21 Official NAL stats as compiled by Howe News Bureau at CNLBR, http://www.cnlbr.org/Portals/0/Stats/NAL%201952/NAL1952.pdf; *Arkansas Baseball Encyclopedia*; PCL statistics, https://www.baseball-reference.com/register/player.fcgi?id=mcdani001boo; "Booker McDaniels Back with the Monarchs," *Chicago Defender*, February 26, 1949; "McDaniel Bows in for Angels with Five-Hitter"; Amy Essington, *The Integration of the Pacific Coast League* (Lincoln: University of Nebraska Press, 2018), 84-85; "Clowns Beat Monarchs by Score of 7-5," *Asheville* (North Carolina) *Citizen-Times*, May 8, 1952: 27.

22 "Royals to Open Season with Coast League Team on Sept. 25," *California Eagle*, September 13, 1945: 16.

GREAD McKINNIS

by Richard Bogovich

"That McKinnis is one of the best pitchers I have ever seen," said future Hall of Famer Alex Pompez, owner of the New York Cubans, in mid-1943. Pompez had experience dating back to 1916, and the Hall of Fame describes him as an "adroit talent evaluator."[1] Therefore, his was high praise indeed for 29-year-old lefty Gread McKinnis, who was in his third Negro American League season. And the best was yet to come, including three consecutive East-West All-Star teams plus a no-hitter and a one-hitter in the NAL, both against the Kansas City Monarchs. But his ban for entering the outlaw Mexican League in 1946 undercut his prominence.

McKinnis was born in Bullock County, Alabama, on August 11, 1913. He may have been born in the county seat, Union Springs, though the 1900 and 1910 censuses identify his parents, William and Emma Jane McKinnis, as farmers near the (Old) Union Church, close to the Montgomery County border. Conversely, in the 1920 census they farmed in Montgomery County, though close to Bullock.[2] The 1910 census indicated that one of Gread's siblings had passed away before he was born. Gread was 12th of 13. His sister Hattie died in 1928 around the age of 20.

African Americans were a large majority of Bullock County's population,[3] even after many began migrating to Northern cities around the time of Gread's birth, but White politicians dominated. "Bullock County's elected officials' failure to uphold basic civil liberties played a great part in the exodus," according to its Tourism Council. "Bullock County had seven documented lynchings from 1889-1921 with the 1911 public lynching of Aberdeen Johnson resulting in the National Guard being called out by Governor O'Neal."[4] Alabama's Supreme Court later upheld the sheriff's termination for dereliction of duty, and Chief Justice R.T. Simpson was furious in his written opinion.[5]

One of Gread's sisters moved to Montgomery before 1920, and by 1930 the entire family joined her. Gread appeared twice in that census, first with his parents, and later as "Graydy" in a separate household with five siblings. On the latter page he was marked as illiterate, but in both the 1930 entry with his parents and in 1920 Gread had recent schooling. The first school for African Americans in Bullock County predated Gread by about 40 years.[6] However, in early 1911, at least one of those schools was open only two months a year.[7]

McKinnis's whereabouts from 1932 to 1939 are unknown. His mother was widowed by 1940 but still resided in Montgomery. He lived in Birmingham, according to a city directory, and worked for the American Cast Iron Pipe Company. ACIPCO had an African American baseball team in the semipro Birmingham Industrial League. McKinnis was a newcomer in 1940 but became the pitching ace. His 1940 military registration showed his height as 6-feet-1 and his weight as 170 pounds. It also identified a wife, Lillian.[8]

McKinnis joined the Birmingham Black Barons of the NAL in 1941. Opening Day was May 11,[9] but his debut was apparently on May 25, starting the first game of a doubleheader against the visiting Jacksonville Red Caps in front of 4,200 fans at Rickwood Field. He pitched a complete-game 7-2 victory, offsetting five walks and a hit batsman with seven strikeouts while surrendering only five singles. He also overcame errors by his four infielders.[10] On June 10 he beat the same team 3-1.[11] Late that month he had a complete-game win over the Chicago American Giants, 4-3.[12]

A high point for McKinnis in his first pro season occurred on August 24 against the St. Louis Stars in front of 6,000 Birmingham fans. In the seven-inning second game of a doubleheader, he hurled a 4-0 four-hitter.[13] He matched that low number of hits at the end of the regular season, on September 11, against the Kansas City Monarchs in Oshkosh, Wisconsin. That game ended as a 5-0 triumph.[14]

The Barons held their spring training for 1942 in Algiers, Louisiana. McKinnis reported late.[15] On May 10 he started the second game of the Opening Day doubleheader against Jacksonville at home, but he did not last half the game.[16] He ended the month with a tougher loss. "McKinnis pitched masterful ball for the Barons, holding the Monarchs scoreless until the sixth," noted a Kansas City newspaper, but the home team won, 3-1.[17] The Monarchs tormented him again on June 7 in the seven-inning second game of a doubleheader at home. The Barons led 4-0 after five innings but McKinnis was unable to finish the sixth as the Monarchs tied the score. The visitors scored the decisive run in the next and final inning.[18]

A brighter moment took place on June 28 at home, in a 2-1 win against the Memphis Red Sox in which he held the opposition to four singles.[19] He won by the same score in the seven-inning second game of a doubleheader hosting the Monarchs on July 5, which was redemption for the fact that in the first game's first inning, he had not retired a single batter and had been the losing pitcher.[20]

McKinnis subsequently bounced around between no fewer than five teams. On July 12 he pitched for the Minneapolis-St. Paul Gophers. However, "baseball historians don't even bother to call it a franchise," according to SABR members Peter Gorton and Steven Hoffbeck. "The league they joined, the Negro Major Baseball League of America, was a flimsy patchwork that existed merely to provide opponents for the Cincinnati Clowns, which had been denied entry into the Negro American League."[21] One of the league's co-founders was Abe Saperstein of Harlem Globetrotters fame, who also co-owned the Black Barons.[22] The Gophers' opponents, the Chicago Brown Bombers, also belonged to that upstart league. Before 1,500 fans, McKinnis struck out 12 Bombers in a 3-0 two-hitter in which he also homered and doubled.[23]

From July 19 into the first week of August he was a Black Baron again. On July 22 he led them to a 4-1 win against the Cubans in Nashville, "before 3,000 white and colored spectators, the largest crowd of the year," according to one paper there.[24] Then on August

Gread McKinnis spent most of 1942 with the Birmingham Black Barons, but he helped Kansas City to the NAL pennant by winning a game while "on loan" to the Monarchs. (Courtesy William Valencia.)

19 McKinnis was reportedly with the New York Lincoln Giants.[25]

On September 6, he relieved for the Clowns against the Monarchs in the second game of a four-team doubleheader before 8,000 fans at Chicago's Wrigley Field. The Black Barons played Memphis in the first game.[26]

On September 13, McKinnis pitched in a doubleheader at Yankee Stadium before a crowd of 20,000 to 30,000. The day began with the third game of the Negro World Series between the Monarchs and the Homestead Grays of the Negro National League. McKinnis pitched the seven-inning second game for the Monarchs, but it was merely an exhibition. Nevertheless, the lineups differed little. One newspaper called McKinnis's performance "masterful" as he hurled a 5-0 three-hitter.[27] By the following Sunday, he was again with the Black Barons in a rough outing against the New York Cubans.[28]

The Black Barons' 1943 spring training began at home on March 29, though they spent time in New Orleans starting on April 21. They played the Monarchs on April 25, and McKinnis started a game against Satchel Paige before 14,000 fans at Pelican Stadium. McKinnis pitched a complete game in a 3-0 loss (though Paige exited after four innings).[29] On May 2 McKinnis won a rematch in Birmingham, 4-2, on "Satchel Paige Day" as he again went the distance.[30]

Birmingham did not play its home Opening Day doubleheader until May 30, when the team squared off against Memphis before about 12,000 fans. McKinnis pitched another complete game in the first contest as the Black Barons won, 6-2.[31] One week later, a home crowd of comparable size saw McKinnis shut out the Clowns – newly admitted to the NAL – a game in which he struck out 11 batters, four consecutively.[32]

McKinnis's win against the New York Cubans on June 23 may have been the motivation for the compliment given him by Alex Pompez. It was a seven-inning night game before 3,700 fans in Columbus, Ohio, and McKinnis scattered six hits as the Black Barons prevailed, 2-1.[33]

On Independence Day, McKinnis hurled a 5-1 complete game that clinched first place for the NAL's first half and home-field advantage in the postseason playoff.[34] On August 1 McKinnis played in his first East-West All-Star Game, at Chicago's Comiskey Park, which was attended by 51,723 fans, a staggering number for a baseball game. McKinnis pitched the middle three innings and allowed just one single as his West squad earned a tense 2-1 triumph.[35]

No more than three days later, McKinnis became a Monarch for the second time, and pitched at least twice for the team. On August 4, he started against the Philadelphia Stars at Shibe Park, where 11,786 watched. McKinnis used 13 pitches to strike out the first three Stars, and he used 12 more to retire the next four hitters. He exited with a 2-1 lead after only four innings but was credited with the win. Paige finished the game. Six days later, McKinnis relieved for Paige in an easy win against the Homestead Grays in Washington, before more than 20,000 fans in Griffith Stadium.[36]

By August 18, McKinnis was back with the Black Barons, and he won a 5-0, five-inning game against Memphis, the second of a doubleheader at Cincinnati's Crosley Field. He also won late in the month against the Cleveland Buckeyes on the road, 3-1.[37]

On September 13 McKinnis lost the first game of the NAL championship series against the American Giants, 3-2, in Toledo.[38] He apparently didn't pitch in the remainder of the series, but Birmingham advanced to the Negro World Series against the Homestead Grays. McKinnis suffered losses on September 26 and 29, though both were shutouts by the Grays' Johnny Wright, who later joined the Montreal Royals alongside Jackie Robinson in the spring of 1946. In his first loss, McKinnis yielded three runs in four innings.[39] In his second loss, by a score of 8-0, it's unclear how many runs were earned.[40] The Grays won the decisive eighth game on October 5, in Montgomery, 8-4. McKinnis relieved at the end.[41]

The spring of 1944 began uneventfully for McKinnis, but on May 8 he was assigned to the American Giants to complete the trade for Ted "Double Duty" Radcliffe more than a month earlier. Surprisingly, this swap between Negro League franchises was even reported in *The Sporting News*.[42] McKinnis's debut with the American Giants may have been in a loss to Memphis before 10,000 fans at Comiskey Park on May 14.[43]

On the night of June 7, the Giants played a White team near Columbus, Ohio, with famous guests pitching the first three innings. Satchel Paige hurled opposite Dizzy Dean. Dean later played first base and his side won, 10-2. McKinnis's one inning was bad, and he was charged with the loss.[44] On June 18 McKinnis suffered a complete-game loss, 3-1, in the seven-inning second game of a doubleheader against the Cleveland Buckeyes in front of 10,000 to 13,000 fans at Comiskey Park. The outing was noteworthy for the fact that he retired the first three batters on one pitch each.[45]

Beginning on Independence Day, McKinnis had a better stretch. The Giants hosted Memphis and 15,000 fans for a doubleheader at Comiskey Park. In the seven-inning second game, McKinnis hurled a 7-0 three-hitter. Five days later, he hurled his second consecutive seven-inning shutout at Comiskey as he outdueled Paige, 2-0.[46] Through July 29, McKinnis's record in NAL games was 4-5, and two days later he added a complete-game win against the Black Barons. By early August he was named to his second East-West All-Star Game, on August 13.[47]

• When the Monarchs Reigned •

On August 6 McKinnis and Paige faced off again for 26,689 fans at Detroit's Briggs Stadium. The Monarchs scored twice in the ninth to win it, 2-0.[48] On August 10, the day before his 31st birthday, McKinnis crafted a seven-inning no-hitter before 4,000 fans in Indianapolis to outduel Paige, 4-0. McKinnis struck out seven Monarchs.[49]

Attendance for that year's East-West classic was 46,247. McKinnis allowed two runs in 1⅓ innings, but his West team won, 7-4.[50] Afterward McKinnis was among several players whom Gus Greenlee signed to his independent Pittsburgh Crawfords.[51] McKinnis reportedly received $200 to jump. Details are minimal, but he apparently won his first (and possibly only) game for the Craws on August 16, by a score of 13-2. McKinnis may have been spotted back with the Giants at Comiskey Park on August 20, though not in uniform.[52] He was thought to be with both the Giants and the Craws more than a week later.[53] Instead, on September 14 he pitched for the Black Barons against the Cubans in Knoxville, in a 3-1 loss.[54] On October 1 a reliever named McKinnis pitched for the Black Crackers against the Clowns in Birmingham.[55]

The Crawfords were reportedly McKinnis's first team of 1945. They had joined the upstart United States League, which continued play into 1946. McKinnis may have taken part in three weeks of workouts.[56]

However, on April 22, a paper in Knoxville reported that McKinnis had recently joined that city's Grays, of the Negro Southern League. He pitched in a preseason game that day.[57] Still, during the first half of May he was also said to be with the American Giants.[58] He was simultaneously reported to be on the Craws as late as June 2.[59]

Wherever McKinnis may have roamed, early in the season he certainly pitched for Knoxville. On April 29, before 15,000 fans in Washington's Griffith Stadium, McKinnis was the losing pitcher in the first game of a doubleheader against the Homestead Grays, 2-1, and then Knoxville was no-hit by two hurlers in the nightcap, 5-0.[60] He was also the losing pitcher in the first game of Knoxville's Opening Day doubleheader on May 6 in which the team hosted the Atlanta Black Crackers,[61] but he soon fared much better.

Just two days later, McKinnis contained the Crackers at home, 6-0. "McKinnis, as you no doubt knew, is one of the greatest pitchers in baseball," sportswriter J.C. Chunn asserted.[62] A day later, Albert G. Barnett of the *Chicago Defender* happened to list a few top players, and specified "Satchel Paige and Lefty McKinnis, pitchers; Archie Ware, Buck Leonard and other ace first basemen and Josh Gibson, catcher," and that spoke volumes about Knoxville's new ace.[63]

Knoxville was scheduled to visit the New Orleans Black Pelicans for a doubleheader on Sunday, May 13, but rain delayed it for two days. Newspaper coverage of that series was surprisingly minimal, but McKinnis reportedly no-hit the Pelicans that week by an unstated score. Chunn was a primary contemporaneous source, though well over a week afterward.[64] In the absence of details, William J. Plott, author of a thorough history of the NSL, called this no-hitter "unconfirmed," but if it did happen, he put the date as May 15.[65] However, one paper that printed Chunn's report also included scores of three games between the Pelicans and the Grays, without dates but none was played later than May 19. The first two could not conceivably have been no-hitters because of the Pelicans' high run totals: Knoxville 11, New Orleans 10, and New Orleans 9, Knoxville 3. If the sequence was correct, those were the scores of the doubleheader on May 15. The third score was Knoxville 9, New Orleans 1. That was likely McKinnis's no-hitter, and May 16 seems more probable than May 15.[66]

Through games of May 26, McKinnis had a record of 4-1. On May 27 he added a four-hitter against the Mobile Black Bears in an easy 8-2 win.[67] McKinnis was reacquired by the American Giants around May 31, and on June 3 he gave them two scoreless innings of relief.[68] On June 11, he hurled a 6-1 three-hitter in Milwaukee against Birmingham in which he struck out 11 Black Barons. On July 2 he went the distance in a 12-inning, 7-3 triumph over the Clowns in Dayton, Ohio, and struck out 15 batters.[69]

Beginning on July 13, McKinnis began to see a heavier workload. That day he pitched into the eighth inning of a game against Memphis that the Giants won in the 10th, and two days later he defeated the same team with a seven-inning complete game, 4-1.[70] On July 18 McKinnis tossed a 5-0 five-hitter against Memphis in Racine, Wisconsin. A local reporter noted that the Red Sox had only 28 plate appearances, one above the minimum possible for a nine-inning game. One runner was out at second trying to steal, and McKinnis picked off three more.[71] Two days later, he hurled the final eight innings of a 13-inning tie against Memphis in Dayton, and just two more days after that he won a seven-inning game against Birmingham back at Comiskey Park, 3-2.[72] In his first five NAL games that counted in the standings, he had a record of 2-3.[73]

• GREAD McKINNIS •

By that time, Gread McKinnis had been named to the East-West All-Star Game for the third straight year. It was held on July 29. That recent workload may have caused the forearm injury that kept him from pitching in it, but players received $100 just for being on the rosters.[74]

Two weeks later McKinnis lost the seven-inning second game of a doubleheader at Griffith Stadium opposite a perfect game by future Hall of Famer Ray Brown of the Homestead Grays.[75] Another two weeks later, before 4,000 fans at Comiskey Park on August 26, McKinnis approximated Brown's feat: McKinnis hurled a nine-inning, one-hitter against the Monarchs, and Chicago romped, 15-0. The only hit was by the very first Monarch, Jesse Williams. McKinnis retired the Monarchs in order from the second through the eighth innings, except for a walk in the sixth. He walked one more Monarch in the ninth in his otherwise superlative game.[76]

On September 16 Birmingham ended the American Giants' 14-game home winning streak by defeating McKinnis in the first game of a doubleheader, 4-2. That was Chicago's final home date of the regular season, and they finished in second place in the second half of the season. All told, McKinnis reportedly compiled a record of 16-4.[77]

Around that time, Winfield Welch, who had been McKinnis's manager in Birmingham, announced that he would take an all-star team to the Pacific Coast in October, and McKinnis was included on the roster. Reporting of the games was minimal, but on October 24 McKinnis helped another hurler or two shut out the Saltillo Pericos of Mexico at Los Angeles' Wrigley Field.

In the spring of 1946, McKinnis's preseason began with the American Giants.[78] However, on April 17 he joined teammates Art Pennington and Jesse Douglas on a drive to Mexico, to play for the Monterrey Industriales in the outlaw Mexican League. McKinnis and Pennington played in a 5-1 loss to La Junta on May 2, and likely had participated in earlier games already.[79]

Monterrey had a good team,[80] but toward the end of May the trio wanted to return home and phoned the American Giants "at their own expense," said the sports editor of the *Chicago Daily Times*. They requested reinstatement but the NAL had banned them indefinitely.[81] Although the three players had gone to Mexico as a "package deal," Pennington said they had no assurance the three would remain together.[82] About three months after they jumped, Pennington was still with Monterrey, but Douglas was on the Mexico City Reds and McKinnis was not on any roster.[83]

On June 5 a Lefty "McGinnis" pitched a complete-game loss for the Chicago Brown Bombers, an "associate" member of the aforementioned United States League.[84] Three days later, McKinnis won a game for the Chicago Monarchs, a strong semipro team over more than two decades.[85] Additional games for either team may have gone unreported.

In pursuit of other baseball options, in June or July he took Abe Saperstein's advice and visited a boxing promoter in Rochester, Minnesota, named Ben Sternberg. Sternberg got McKinnis onto a team in nearby Zumbrota; he debuted on July 28 under the name Al Saylor. The real Saylor, a right-hander and thus not Zumbrota's "Lefty Saylor," played for Birmingham from 1943 to 1945.[86] Four weeks later "Saylor" helped Zumbrota to win the playoffs of the eight-team Southeastern Minnesota Baseball League and to qualify for the state tournament.[87]

Saylor was then ruled ineligible, but tourney officials insisted race was not involved. However, almost 20 years earlier, the Association of Minnesota Amateur Baseball Leagues had advised members to adopt a bylaw that "all colored players are barred." After that, none played in the state tournament until 1947. By rule, Saylor had to play in more than two of Zumbrota's regular-season games, but he played only once after July 28. Without its ace, Zumbrota was pulverized in its tournament game, 23-2.[88]

In mid-September, McKinnis joined Saperstein's Cincinnati Crescents to play in Hawaii, and Jesse Owens accompanied them.[89] They flew from San Francisco on September 20. In the trip's opener he was the winning pitcher against a team called the Braves as he struck out 10 batters in seven innings.[90] The Crescents went 12-0, and McKinnis appeared in six games.

The Crescents also played in California after flying back. On October 17 McKinnis started before 2,500 fans in Emeryville, a city near Oakland. In the decisive sixth inning, New York Giants rookie Bill Rigney – an All-Star two years later – ignited a rally for his team with a homer.[91]

In 1947 Sternberg signed McKinnis to his Rochester (Minnesota) Queens, in the league that had included Zumbrota. McKinnis's salary was so low that he also shined shoes at Rochester's Boston Shoe Shine and Hat Shop to earn more money.[92] On June

10 and 11, the NAL and NNL held meetings during which McKinnis and Ray Brown had their five-year suspensions relating to the Mexican League lifted.[93] McKinnis eventually rejoined the American Giants for a brief time. He was mentioned in previews of games into early August, and he did pitch on July 24 against the Kansas City Monarchs. The score was 1-1 after two innings when McKinnis exited the game for an unspecified reason.[94]

McKinnis helped Rochester play its way into the Minnesota state tournament again. On September 7, his 3-0 one hitter won them the regional championship.[95] A week later he hurled a two-hit shutout against Nashwauk from northeastern Minnesota. McKinnis and Nashwauk shortstop Charlie Moore "reopened the door to black players in the state tournament," noted Frank M. White, RBI Consultant for the Minnesota Twins.[96] On September 20 McKinnis's homer was the only run as his second two-hitter put the Queens in the next day's finale. He started against Chaska in front of 7,715 fans but tired in the third inning as Rochester lost, 10-6. Nevertheless, he was named the tournament's most valuable player.[97] McKinnis averaged an astonishing 16 strikeouts per game as he compiled a record of 26-4.[98]

In 1948 Sternberg signed McKinnis by mid-February.[99] Before rejoining the Queens, he reunited with an old Black Barons teammate, Tommy Sampson, on the Sampson Stars. On April 11 they played the Atlanta Black Crackers in Birmingham.[100]

The Queens joined the Bi-State League for 1948 and, on June 6, McKinnis was the winning pitcher in their fourth regular-season game.[101] Three days later he was reported to be a member of the Twin City Colored Giants in Michigan.[102] By the end of June, he was with the South Bend (Indiana) Studebakers in the semipro Michigan-Indiana League, and he played with them into late August, past his 35th birthday.[103]

McKinnis was back with Rochester on August 30, and on September 2 he struck out 17 Winona Merchants to win Rochester's first playoff game. He struck out 19 Merchants six days later to put the Queens into the state tournament again. Rochester could not recapture its 1947 magic.[104] Almost 30 years later, Sternberg recalled a conversation with McKinnis:

> "During the 1948 season he told me he had a kid who could help the team at any position. He said his name was Willie Mays. What did I know? I said we didn't want a 16-year-old kid. Now skip a few years to 1950 or 1951, whenever it was when Willie was hitting about .500 for the [Minneapolis] Millers. Me and Lefty went up to see him play and I introduced myself. He looked at me for some time and then said, "Ben Sternberg, I was supposed to play for you, wasn't I? I think I could have helped your ball club.""[105]

McKinnis participated in spring training with the American Giants in 1949. He won the Opening Day assignment, on May 1, but rain ended the game early.[106] In his first five games, he struck out 31 hitters in 32 innings.[107]

McKinnis was the first NAL pitcher to reach 10 wins. He had 74 strikeouts in 85 innings around the time he was named to his fourth East-West All-Star team.[108] On August 14, a crowd of 30,000 to 35,000 was at Comiskey Park for the game. McKinnis's side lost, 4-0. He pitched 1⅔ innings and gave up two runs.[109]

At the end of August, McKinnis started for the Giants in Winona, Minnesota, against the Cleveland Buckeyes. He struck out four batters in the first two innings and led, 2-0, but then exited for an unstated reason.[110] It is possible that this appearance marked his last game with Chicago in 1949. McKinnis had a record of 12-7, and his 2.35 earned-run average was just behind Bob Griffith of the Philadelphia Stars at 2.31.[111]

By September 15 McKinnis had joined the New York Stars for a flight to Venezuela. Future Hall of Famer Buck Leonard explained to the *Afro-American* that the Stars scheduled nine games against teams representing Cuba, Puerto Rico, and the host country. On October 6 the Stars were to travel to Barranquilla, Colombia, for three more games over the following six days.[112]

In 1950 McKinnis started the season with the Rochester Royals of the South Minnesota League, where he played alongside a number of other former Negro League standouts.[113] The Royals' holdover from 1949 was Marlin Carter, a longtime infielder for the Memphis Red Sox and a member of the American Giants in 1948. Another was Gene Smith, a veteran pitcher who was with the American Giants in 1949.[114] Before mid-June, Sternberg signed two former Memphis pitchers, Verdell Mathis and Willie Hutchinson.[115]

On July 5 McKinnis "suffered severe lacerations of his throwing hand," as Winona's daily newspaper reported. In a freak accident, "McKinnis injured the hand when he struck a chandelier in the office of manager Ben Sternberg while demonstrating a pitching delivery." He was expected to be out two weeks.[116] At that point he had the South Minny's best record, at 8-1, and he still finished atop the league's hurlers at 11-3 while striking out 121 batters in 117 innings and walking only 48.[117]

In 1951 McKinnis rejoined the American Giants for at least part of their preseason and also pitched in at least two regular-season games.[118] On May 13 he was the losing pitcher in a 2-1 game in New Orleans, and on May 23, he relieved in a loss to the Black Barons in Chattanooga.[119] However, by the end of May, McKinnis joined the Brandon Greys, one of five franchises in the independent Manitoba-Dakota (ManDak) League. On May 30 he helped Brandon defeat Winnipeg, 5-2. He experienced a tough loss at home to Carman on July 18 in which both pitchers lasted all 14 innings. A high point was on August 6, when he hurled a five-hit shutout against Minot. Three weeks later he threw a complete game as the Greys clinched the pennant.[120]

The Greys faced elimination in the subsequent playoff semifinals, but McKinnis forced a sixth game against Carman with a complete game on September 5. Two days later, he secured Brandon's comeback by recording the final out in a 1-0 nailbiter. As Brandon swept Winnipeg in the finals, he logged a win and a save. In the regular season he had pitched to a record of 11-6 in 19 games.[121]

On March 11, 1952, McKinnis reportedly signed with the Waseca Braves, about 55 miles west of Rochester. Instead, he played in a four-team league in the Dominican Republic.[122] On April 1 McKinnis flew from New York with catcher Luther "Shanty" Clifford and Bob Griffith to the island nation, where all three joined the Estrellas Orientales.[123]

Within three weeks of his mid-June return stateside, McKinnis was back in Canada. When future Hall of Famer Willie Wells was named player-manager of Brandon in early July, McKinnis was expected to rejoin them. Instead, on July 7, McKinnis lost a game with the St. Thomas Elgins of Ontario's semipro Intercounty League.[124]

August was momentous for Gread McKinnis, because he entered White Organized Baseball, shortly before turning 39, with the Tampa Smokers of the Class-B Florida International League.[125] He debuted on August 1 by recording the final two outs of a 9-2 loss in St. Petersburg. He was the second reliever behind starter Camilo Pascual, whose 18-year major-league career began the following season.[126]

McKinnis's 10 other games were all starts. His first appearance at home, on August 9 against the Lakeland Pilots, was astonishing. In the seven-inning first game of a doubleheader, he impressed 912 fans by working speedily and retiring the first 13 batters. That streak ended when an error gave Lakeland its first baserunner. McKinnis then walked a batter, and another in the sixth inning, but without further incident. With a 4-0 lead, McKinnis retired the first two hitters in the seventh and final inning. A curveball to Lakeland's 24th batter resulted in a grounder that Tampa's first baseman fielded without difficulty, but no Smoker got to the base in time for a putout. A fielder's choice then ended it, and McKinnis had a one-hitter. What's more, he started the doubleheader's second game, following "a quick shower and rubdown," as one local paper reported, and he hurled four more scoreless innings. He exited after giving up two runs in the top of the fifth, but Tampa eventually won, 3-2.[127]

On August 21 McKinnis went the distance to earn his second win, at home against Key West, 7-2. Both runs resulted from miscues.[128] McKinnis was the losing pitcher in a 4-1 contest on September 6 that concluded the Smokers' regular season. He did not pitch in Tampa's five playoff games after having compiled a 3-5 record with a 3.21 ERA for the season.[129]

Before the 1953 season, the Crawfords had hopes McKinnis would join them,[130] but he remained with Tampa. On March 23 he reported for the opening of the Smokers' training camp.[131] On April 7 he started against Charleston of the Triple-A American Association. He yielded just one hit in five scoreless innings, and was the winning pitcher.[132]

McKinnis got his first start of the regular season in St. Petersburg on April 17. He hurled the Smokers to a 3-1 win, and that lone run was unearned.[133] His next four decisions were losses, including one by a score of 2-0 on May 16.[134] Shortly afterward, he simply quit due to an argument with his new manager, Ben Chapman, who managed the Phillies when Jackie Robinson was a rookie and infamously taunted him with racial slurs.[135]

On May 17 Chapman fined McKinnis $25 for missing that day's game and other uncommunicated absenteeism. "I've tried to be fair and square with every man on the club and intend to continue with that practice," Chapman said. "I expect every man to do his part and when he doesn't or won't then he is going to be fined or may even be traded. There is no room for prima donnas on the club."[136] A *Tampa Daily Times* reporter felt McKinnis got off "lightly," to which an unnamed Smoker official replied, "McKinnis is the only lefthander on the club and the club has to have a lefthander."[137]

On May 27 Tampa business manager Milton Karr asked the Florida International League to declare McKinnis ineligible. "We have tried everywhere to locate McKinnis," Karr said. "We have tried to call him at his address in St. Petersburg, sent a representative to look for him and can't find him." According to stats in the *Tampa Daily Times*, McKinnis pitched 45 innings in 12 games and gave up 26 runs. If those were all earned, then his earned run average was 5.20. He gave up 52 hits and 22 walks, with 18 strikeouts.[138]

By May 21, Brandon manager Willie Wells resecured McKinnis, and he arrived three days later. He pitched well in a start on May 27 but ended up with no decision.[139] On his 40th birthday, he came within one out of a shutout but still won, 5-2, while also contributing a single and a double.[140] He compiled a record of 7-5 for Brandon and won two playoff games.[141]

On August 29 McKinnis started against Minot in a game that decided the regular season's championship. Tensions increased in the top half of the eighth inning after Brandon's first-base coach was ejected, but the Greys led, 4-2, going into Minot's half. Minot had a runner on first base when the home-plate umpire called three straight balls on McKinnis. As McKinnis bolted toward the plate to argue, he misplayed his catcher's return throw, and the runner advanced a base. McKinnis then threatened that ump, flung the ball over the grandstand, and was ejected, as was Wells moments later. McKinnis grabbed a bat and turned toward home, but teammates pushed him into the dressing room. Minot scored seven runs that inning and won, 9-4.[142]

McKinnis's next start was in the playoffs, against Carman on September 7. He pitched a complete-game 6-1 victory, and the Greys advanced to the finals against Minot.[143] McKinnis started the third game, which Brandon won after he was no longer the pitcher of record. He helped force a seventh game with a win in relief on September 15 before more than 3,500 Brandon fans, the season's largest crowd. He entered the next day's finale in the third inning, though after Minot was well on its way to victory and the championship.[144]

Not quite a month later, McKinnis applied for a marriage license in St. Petersburg. He married Naomi Doris Fluitt, who had attended J.R.E. Lee High School in Wildwood, about 100 miles northeast of St. Petersburg. Early the next year she joined an organization for new wives at Bethel Metropolitan Baptist Church and, in May, she was named young mother of the year.[145]

The newlyweds received hopeful news to start 1954 when the Tampa Smokers reinstated McKinnis around January 18. He was not among the 13 pitchers signed when spring training began on March 15, but he was in camp within a week. Still, the *Times* said he would "leave as soon as the club can make a deal for his sale." In fact, his *Sporting News* index card indicates he was released on March 24.[146]

In early April, McKinnis struck out 17 Lacoochee Pirates for the St. Petersburg Tigers of Florida's semipro West Coast Negro League to win a four-hitter, 4-2. Later that month, the Rochester Royals announced his return for a tryout.[147] He reached Rochester on May 7 and played his first preseason game four days later.[148] He added a complete-game win shortly before the regular season, but he was released toward the end of June with a record of 1-2 and an earned-run average of 6.72.[149]

Around Independence Day, McKinnis rejoined the Tigers. On July 18 he pitched very well in long relief for a West Coast all-star team. His record was 6-1 when he was selected to start a contest in mid-August between his league's all-stars and counterparts from the Florida State Negro League. Coverage afterward was minimal.[150]

Gread McKinnis began his second and final stint in White Organized Baseball around April 22, 1955, when he joined the St. Petersburg Saints, a new franchise in the Class-D Florida State League. His signing may have resulted from a journalist's criticism after the regular season began.[151] "It is my impression that the Saints have already passed up a couple of fine prospects because they were Negroes," wrote *St. Petersburg Times* sports editor Bill Beck on April 20. "The inclination here would be to pass up no prospects for any reason. Baseball fans are interested in players, not colors."[152]

On April 23 McKinnis pitched a complete-game loss for the Saints in Gainesville. The score was 7-6, though three Gainesville runs were unearned.[153] Three days later, he doubled twice to help defeat Lakeland, 7-4, and won the next day in relief. He was 2-2 within his first week.[154]

• GREAD McKINNIS •

McKinnis started May with an impressive complete-game loss. At Daytona Beach, he allowed a run on two hits in the first inning, and the home team's only other run resulted from two errors. He allowed just two more hits, but the Saints were shut out.[155]

On May 16 McKinnis won a starting assignment for the final time in his professional career, and he hurled a complete game. On May 20 he entered a game in the eighth inning with two outs, the bases loaded, and the tying run on first. His strikeout extinguished the threat, and he then pitched a scoreless ninth.[156] McKinnis's final two victories of his professional career were in relief on June 6 and 7, at home. In the first of those, the Saints scored the tying and game-ending runs on the same play.[157]

McKinnis's final success for the Saints was in a loss at home on June 24, in front of 623 fans. He entered for the sixth inning, and struck out the first six Sanford batters he faced. The only run off him was after a two-base error.[158]

On July 2, the *St. Petersburg Times* noted that McKinnis had struggled recently, and was almost out of chances. He was clobbered during a short relief outing that very day, and roughed up at home on Independence Day. He was released the next day. McKinnis started seven of his 28 games, and only two Saints had pitched more innings. He finished at 5-8 with a 4.58 earned-run average.[159] McKinnis rejoined St. Petersburg's team in the West Coast Negro League, and compiled a record of 7-3 by October 9.[160]

In early 1956, Naomi joined the Merrymakers Federated Club, and little more than two months later, the City Federation of Colored Women's Clubs named her chairwoman of its 1956 Coronation Ball.[161] Gread's professional baseball career did continue briefly in the first half of 1956, back in the ManDak League (without Manitoba teams that season). By early May he signed with the Minot Mallards. He pitched in a preseason game on May 19 and was the Opening Day starter on May 25. He faced six batters, retiring just one. His final game as a professional was in Williston on June 1. McKinnis yielded five earned runs in seven innings, though Minot was shut out.[162]

It's unknown whether McKinnis pitched later in 1956, but on March 23, 1957, he struck out 21 batters in a preseason game for the St. Petersburg Braves. A week later he struck out 16 batters and allowed just one hit in a six-inning relief outing. He relieved for the Braves in their Opening Day win on April 14, and a week later he was on the wrong end of a 2-0 game.[163] After that, coverage of the team plummeted.

In early October, the Merrymakers reported that Naomi had moved to Chicago.[164] Gread and Naomi raised children there and eventually welcomed grandchildren.[165] In early 1969, Gread and Naomi were among 27 plaintiffs with the Contract Buyers League who sued 10 developers to undo a "Black tax" in home sales. In April 1970 they suffered retaliatory evictions. Gread was among 20 residents arrested, and Naomi was pictured in the *Chicago Tribune* examining belongings removed from their home. Gread accused authorities of beating and choking him, causing him to miss work more than a week. The US Justice Department opened an investigation.[166] The League won the war, if not that battle.[167]

Gread McKinnis died in Chicago on March 4, 1991. His grave is in suburban Dolton. In 2005 the Gread "Lefty" McKinnis Memorial Foundation was established to award a $1,000 scholarship annually to a male African American high school senior in Chicago.[168]

In 2009, at the age of 76, Naomi received an award from the Illinois Department on Aging for her work at Chicago's Atlas Senior Center and volunteerism for a food pantry at St. Ailbe Catholic Church.[169] As a baseball player, Gread McKinnis did not let age slow him down much. Clearly, his wife didn't let age hinder her, either.

Sources

Unless otherwise indicated, NAL statistics through 1945 are from Seamheads.com, while all statistics after 1945 are from baseball-reference.com.

Notes

1 Wendell Smith, "'Smitty's Sports Spurts," *Pittsburgh Courier*, July 10, 1943: 18. See also https://baseballhall.org/hall-of-famers/pompez-alex.

2 Gread was presumably the second-to-last of the 12 McKinnis children listed in the 1920 census, though his name looks more like Gladys. His death record indicated his birthplace was in Bullock County and an airline passenger list in 1949 specified the county seat, Union Springs, not Union *Church*. As of this writing, some websites list his birthplace as Union in Greene County, Alabama, but that is located near Mississippi and thus not in the eastern half of Alabama. Some genealogical sources identify his mother's maiden name as Vaughn(s) but others show it as Barnes.

3 "No Garden, No Money, Says Alabama Judge," *Pittsburgh Courier*, October 14, 1933: 5.

4 Tourism Council of Bullock County, "Bullock County's African American Heritage: Their Southern Legacy," pamphlet excerpt available at http://www.unionspringsalabama.com/African-American-History-of-Bullock-County.html.

5 "Successful Impeachment," *The Freeman* (Indianapolis), June 3, 1911: 7. *The Freeman* noted that Dr. Booker T. Washington had condemned the sheriff in the *Montgomery Times* earlier that week.

6   See Note 4, and https://www.derryschapel.org/our-history.

7   Dr. Booker T. Washington, "Defending the Negro," *Washington Bee*, January 14, 1911: 1. Dr. Washington had delivered "an Emancipation address at Union Springs," the Bullock County seat, on New Year's Day.

8   Negro Southern League Museum, "American Cast Iron and Pipe (ACIPCO)," pages 11 and 12, available at http://www.negrosouthernleaguemuseumresearchcenter.org/Portals/0/Birmingham%20Industrial%20League/ACIPCO.pdf. The 1940 roster also included "future Negro League players" Lorenzo "Piper" Davis, William Powell, Ed Steele, and Artie Wilson.

9   McKinnis wasn't among rookies mentioned in these reports: "Black Baron Outfit at Shreveport Camp for Month's Practice," *Birmingham News*, April 6, 1941: 22. "Black Barons to Battle Black Yankees in First Home Tilt of Season," *Birmingham News*, April 20, 1941: 21. "Black Barons to Open '41 Season With Knasas [sic] City," *Weekly Review* (Birmingham), May 9, 1941: 7. "Negro American Loop Season Will Open at Rickwood Park Sunday," *Birmingham News*, May 11, 1941: 19.

10 "Black Barons Take Double-Header From Jax Red Caps, 7-2, 6-5," *Birmingham News*, May 26, 1941: 12. The paper referred to him as a "new Black Baron twirler," possibly implying he had in fact just been signed.

11 "Baseball," *Weekly Review*, June 13, 1941: 7.

12 "Black Barons Capture First Game, 4 to 3, But Lose Second, 4-0," *Birmingham News*, June 30, 1941: 16.

13 H.J. Williams, "Barons Win Double Bill," *Weekly Review*, August 29, 1941: 7.

14 "Black Barons Win by a 5 to 0 Score from Monarchs," *Oshkosh* (Wisconsin) *Northwestern*, September 12, 1941: 17. "Black Barons Defeat Kansas City, 5-0," *Birmingham News*, September 12, 1941: 40. Satchel Paige pitched the final two innings for the Monarchs, though "with an underarm throw," according to the *Northwestern*, which printed a detailed article and a full box score.

15 "Speaking in General about Baseball," *Atlanta Daily World*, April 21, 1942: 5. He had an 11-inning, complete-game loss, according to "Buckeyes Trim Birmingham, 3-2," *Chicago Defender*, May 6, 1942: 20.

16 "Black Barons and Red Caps Split, 9-2, 6-3," *Birmingham News*, May 11, 1942: 13.

17 "K.C. Out Muds Barons," *Arkansas State Press* (Little Rock), June 5, 1942: 7. "Monarchs Go to Top," *Kansas City Times*, June 1, 1942: 12.

18 "Black Barons Divide Couple with Monarchs," *Birmingham News*, June 8, 1942: 17.

19 "Black Barons Win Double Bill From Memphis, 2-1, 7-4," *Birmingham News*, June 29, 1942: 14.

20 "Black Barons Take Second Game, 2 to 1, in Hurling Match," *Birmingham News*, July 6, 1942: 15.

21 Peter Gorton and Steven R. Hoffbeck, "John Donaldson and Black Baseball in Minnesota," *The National Pastime*, Spring 2012: 121. See https://sabr.org/journals/baseball-in-the-north-star-state/.

22 Norm King, "Abe Saperstein," https://sabr.org/bioproj/person/abe-saperstein/.

23 "Twin City Negroes Divide Double Bill," *Minneapolis Morning Tribune*, July 13, 1942: 6. "Gophers Defeat Brown Bombers; Lose to Clowns," *Chicago Defender*, July 18, 1942: 21. While in Minnesota he reportedly also hurled a one-hitter against St. Paul's Lexington Park club (unless this bifurcated somewhat inaccurate details of the July 12 game), and on July 12 struck out *18* Chicago Brown Bombers, according to "Autos Expect Stiff Tussle with Giants," *Herald-Press* (St. Joseph, Michigan), August 18, 1942: 11.

24 "Black Barons Get Split with Memphis Red Sox Sunday," *Birmingham News*, July 20, 1942: 15. "Barons Beat Cubans on McGinnis' [sic] Hurling," *Nashville Banner*, July 23, 1943: 20.

25 "Autos Face New York's Lincoln Giants Under Arcs Tonight," *News-Palladium* (Benton Harbor, Michigan), August 19, 1942: 6. McKinnis's name wasn't in the box score the next day, nor in the *Enquirer*'s box score on July 23. On August 20 the Lincoln Giants and the Black Barons split a doubleheader at Milwaukee's Borchert Field but McKinnis didn't play for either team in either game, according to box scores under the headline "Negro Teams Split Two Games Here," *Milwaukee Journal*, August 21, 1942: 11.

26 "Trophy to Be Presented," *Cincinnati Enquirer*, August 31, 1942: 16. "Black Barons, Monarchs Win Negro Games," *Chicago Tribune*, September 7, 1942: 27. See also "Clownagrams," *Weekly Review*, September 5, 1942: 7. The latter said McKinnis "was the second pitcher called on by the West in the Negro all-star classic before 48,000 fans at Comiskey Park in Chicago, August 16," but that is incorrect.

27 "Monarchs Trounce Grays for 3-0 Edge in Series," *Afro-American* (Baltimore), September 15, 1942: 19. Fay Young, "Through the Years," *Chicago Defender*, September 19, 1942: 23. The former said the attendance was 30,000, but a total of 20,000 was reported in "Paige Ousted, but Beats Grays, 9-3," *New York Daily News*, September 14, 1942: 43. Splitting the difference with a figure of 25,000 was "Monarchs 3 Up in Negro Series," *Brooklyn Daily Eagle*, September 14, 1942: 9. The *Chicago Defender*'s summary of the game instead reported that he limited the Grays to two hits, but the *Afro-American*'s box score showed them with three, all singles.

28 "Ed Steele in Heated 8-1 Victory for Black Barons," *Atlanta Daily World*, September 22, 1942: 5. This article called Birmingham's opponents the New York Cuban Stars.

29 "Black Barons Open Sunday with Memphis," *Weekly Review*, April 3, 1943: 7. "Negro Nines Here for Three Games," *Times-Picayune* (New Orleans), April 22, 1943: 1. "Monarchs Win Double Bill from Black Barons," *New Orleans States*, April 26, 1943: 10.

30 "Black Barons Tangle with Kansas City In 'Satchel Paige Day,'" *Birmingham News*, April 25, 1943: 19. "Black Barons Take Double-Header From Kansas City Team," *Birmingham News*, May 3, 1943: 14. "Yak" Collins, "Rambling Round the Realm of Sports," *Weekly Review*, May 8, 1943: 7.

31 "Black Barons Open Season with Wins Over Sox, 6-2, 10-1," *Birmingham News*, May 31, 1943: 12.

32 "Black Barons Hand Ethiopian Clowns Pair of Losses, 13-0, 2-1," *Birmingham News*, June 7, 1943: 18. "Birmingham Black Barons Win Twinbill from Cincinnati Clowns, 13-0 and 2-1," *Atlanta Daily World*, June 8, 1943: 5.

33 "Black Barons Edge New York Cubans, 2-1," *Columbus* (Ohio) *Dispatch*, June 24, 1943: 17.

34 "Black Barons Halve Double-Header With Giants, 5-1 and 3-7," *Birmingham News*, July 5, 1943: 28. The *News* didn't mention the attendance, but it was "record-breaking," according to R.S. Simmons, "American Giants and Black Barons Split," *Atlanta Daily World*, July 5, 1943: 5. Simmons didn't offer an estimate.

35 "Pitchers Star as West Beats East in Thriller," *Pittsburgh Courier*, August 7, 1943: 19. McKinnis's strikeout was reported about a year later in "How This Year's Pitchers Performed in Past Classics," *Pittsburgh Courier*, August 12, 1944: 12.

36 "11,786 Watch Paige Pitch, Stars Lose, 5-1," *Philadelphia Inquirer*, August 5, 1943: 23. "Negro Star's No Hit, No Run Streak Ends," *Sacramento Bee*, August 5, 1943: 22. "Jolted by Monarchs, Grays Await Cubans," *Washington Evening Star*, August 11, 1943: A17. McKinnis may have won for the Monarchs against the Grays a second time, as implied in "Grays Primed for Series with Birmingham Barons," *Pittsburgh Courier*, September 4, 1943: 19.

37 "Barons Win Double," *Cincinnati Enquirer*, August 19, 1943: 18. "Buckeyes Win, 5-4, After 3-1 Loss in Opener," *Cleveland Plain Dealer*, August 30, 1943: 17.

38 "Black Barons Drop Opener to Giants," *Birmingham News*, September 14, 1943: 17. McKinnis didn't pitch a complete game, so it's unclear whether he was actually the losing pitcher. The first game of the series was supposed to be at Comiskey Park on September 12, but the weather didn't cooperate.

39 "Homestead Grays Beat Barons 9-0," *Chicago Sun*, September 27, 1943: 17. "Grays Take Series Lead as Wright Clips Barons," *Washington Evening Star*, September 27, 1943: 21. "Washington Grays Take Lead in Negro Series," *Baltimore Sun*, September 27, 1943: 14. The latter two papers both used Associated Press accounts, but they disagreed on whether McKinnis pitched four or five innings and thus also on whether the six-run inning off Huber was in the fifth or the sixth inning. Regardless, as of this writing the six runs Huber gave up appear to have been charged to McKinnis on the Seamheads website.

40 "Grays Take 3-2 Lead over Barons; Win, 8-0," *Birmingham News*, September 30, 1943: 21.

41 "Washington Trims Birmingham to Capture Negro Baseball Title," *Montgomery (Alabama) Advertiser*, October 6, 1943: 8. One of the eight games early in the series was a tie. It's unclear what the score was when McKinnis relieved late in the game, though it seems likely the Grays had already scored at least six of their eight runs.

42 "American Giants Get M'Kinnis, Turner," *Chicago Sun*, May 9, 1944: 17. "Caught on the Fly," *The Sporting News*, May 18, 1944: 30. After the trade, "McKinnis left without notice for his home in Birmingham," according to "Jim Taylor Signs as Manager of Am. Giants," *Chicago Defender*, January 13, 1945: 7. However, that doesn't appear to have been correct, at least not for very long. For an example of McKinnis's preseason work, see "Birmingham Trims Bucks," *Chicago Defender*, April 15, 1944: 9.

43 "Memphis and Chicago Split," *Chicago Defender*, May 20, 1944: 9. "Chicago Negro Giants Divide with Memphis," *Chicago Tribune*, May 15, 1944: 22. The American Giants and the Black Barons were scheduled to play on May 9 but that game was rained out. They did play the next day but McKinnis didn't pitch. He also didn't pitch in Chicago's game against the Clowns on May 12.

44 "Paige Beats Dizzy Dean on Mound," *Newark (Ohio) Advocate and American Tribune*, June 8, 1944: 14.

45 "Chicago Splits with Cleveland," *Chicago Defender*, June 24, 1944: 9. The lower attendance estimate of 10,000 was stated in "Chicago, Cleveland Divide in Negro Double Header," *Chicago Tribune*, June 19, 1944: 16.

46 "American Giants Split with Memphis," *Chicago Sun*, July 5, 1944: 13. "Giants Lose to Monarchs, 3-1, Then Beat Paige, 2-0," *Chicago Tribune*, July 10, 1944: 17. "McKinnis Seeks 3d," *Chicago Daily Times*, July 13, 1944: 29.

47 "Black Barons Play Giants Here Again Tonight," *Montgomery Advertiser*, August 1, 1944: 6. "Managers Name 50 Players for East-West Classic," *Pittsburgh Courier*, August 5, 1944: 12. McKinnis's NAL record through July 29 was reported in "How This Year's Pitchers Performed in Past Classics," *Pittsburgh Courier*, August 12, 1944: 12.

48 "26,689 See Satch Win," *Detroit Times*, August 7, 1944: 13.

49 "McKinis [sic] Hurls No-Hitter as Chicago Wins Twice," *Indianapolis Star*, August 11, 1944: 16. Based on this article's pair of line scores, each game of this doubleheader was limited to seven innings. See also "Negro American League Lead August 16th," *Weekly Review*, August 26, 1944: 7.

50 Bob Tatar, "West Whips East in Negro Classic," *Chicago Sun*, August 14, 1944: 13. Wendell Smith, "West Bombs East in 'Dream Game,' 7 to 4," *Pittsburgh Courier*, August 19, 1944: 12.

51 This was Greenlee's second Crawfords club. The original's final season in Pittsburgh was in 1938, when he sold the franchise and it relocated to Toledo for 1939 and then to Indianapolis for 1940, before folding.

52 Fay Young, "Through the Years," *Chicago Defender*, August 26, 1944: 7. "Gus Greenlee Signs Four Stars at Classic," *Philadelphia Tribune*, August 26, 1944: 13. See also Greenlee's biography by Brian McKenna at https://sabr.org/bioproj/person/gus-greenlee/.

53 "Chicago American Giants Hope to Crack Cleveland Buckeyes Here Tomorrow Night," *South Bend Tribune*, August 29, 1944: 10. "Pittsburgh Here Tonight to Meet Globetrotters," *Dayton (Ohio) Herald*, September 1, 1944: 19. Greenlee was an organizer of the first East-West game, but his revived Crawfords club wasn't being received warmly by the NAL and NNL in mid-1944.

54 "St. Louis Plays Pitt Twice Here Sunday," *Knoxville News-Sentinel*, September 15, 1944: 10.

55 "Clowns Top Crax, 9-4, Play to Scoreless Tie," *Birmingham News*, October 2, 1944: 14. However, a few days later the scheduled starting pitcher for the Black Crackers was the recently acquired Junior McFarland, according to "Black Crackers Play Negro Yanks Friday," *Atlanta Constitution*, October 5, 1944: 10. It's conceivable that someone in Birmingham confused McFarland and McKinnis.

56 "Rookies Star in Crawford Training Camp Sessions," *Pittsburgh Courier*, April 21, 1945: 17. "Crawford Sign Three Holdouts," *Chicago Defender*, April 21, 1945: 7.

57 "Large Crowd Expected to Attend Tiff Today," *Knoxville Journal*, April 22, 1945: 11. "Baltimore Giants Play Knox Grays Tomorrow," *Knoxville News-Sentinel*, April 23, 1945: 8.

58 "Cleveland Buckeyes and Chicago Giants Play Here Tonight," *Montgomery Advertiser*, May 1, 1945: 6. "Negro League Baseball Opens Season Sunday," *Dayton Herald*, May 9, 1945: 16.

59 "Negro Teams to Battle Tonight," *Daily Mail* (Hagerstown, Maryland), May 17, 1945: 14. "Cuban Hurls Crawfords to Victory Over Philadelphia," *Pittsburgh Courier*, June 2, 1945: 17. The latter attributed his absence from the Craws to "sweating it out with his draft board." The earlier article was a preview of a game between the Brooklyn Brown Dodgers and the Crawfords. "Lefty McGinnis" was identified as one of the Crawfords' pitchers.

60 "Grays Show Pennant Class in Winning Double Bill," *Washington Evening Star*, April 30, 1945: 10. "Grays Return in Good Shape for First Game," *Knoxville Journal*, May 4, 1945: 17. McKinnis gave up six hits in the game.

61 "Knox Grays Defeated by Black Crackers," *Knoxville Journal*, May 7, 1945: 9.

62 "Grays Defeat Crackers, 6-0, in 4th Game," *Knoxville Journal*, May 9, 1945: 18. J.C. Chunn, "Nashville Black Vols Will Open Southern Here Sunday," *Atlanta Daily World*, May 11, 1945: 5. Chunn said the score of the game was 3-0, not 6-0.

63 Albert G. Barnett, "Chandler Doesn't Believe in Barring Negro Players," *Chicago Defender*, May 12, 1945: 8. This was an interview with professional baseball's new commissioner, Happy Chandler. Barnett asked, "Don't you think, that in all fairness, due recognition should be given players of the caliber of Satchel Paige and Lefty McKinnis, pitchers; Archie Ware, Buck Leonard and other ace first basemen and Josh Gibson, catcher, whose hitting ability has won him the nickname, 'the Negro Babe Ruth?'" Chandler quickly and convincingly answered in the affirmative.

64 "Black Pels and Knoxville Card Two Tilts Tuesday," *Times-Picayune* (New Orleans), May 14, 1945: 12. "Southern League Getting Warmer," *New York Amsterdam News*, May 26, 1945: 8B. In other weeklies, the latter was credited to J.C. Chunn (see Note 74). Through Saturday, May 19, McKinnis had a record of 3-1, according to "Grays Return Home After Trouncing Mobile Bears," *Knoxville Journal*, May 20, 1945: 11. That record is consistent with his having won a game in New Orleans.

65 William J. Plott, *The Negro Southern League: A Baseball History, 1920–1951* (Jefferson, North Carolina: McFarland & Company, Inc., 2015), 149, 202.

66 J.C. Chunn, "Negro Southern Leagues Are Fighting," *Weekly Review*, May 26, 1945: 7. This was the same content as in the *New York Amsterdam News* on the same date (see Note 72), but added were scores of 16 NSL games (without dates or locations) and the circuit's standings through May 19, which confirmed Chunn's comment that the Pelicans were undefeated until the Grays beat them twice.

67 "Knoxville Grays Face Bears in Double Bill," *Knoxville Journal*, May 27, 1945: 13. "Knoxville Grays Beat Bears, 8-2; Tie Second, 1 to 1," *Knoxville Journal*, May 28, 1945: 7. League standings published in the *Journal* on June 3 and 10 didn't jibe. The earlier standings showed the Grays in first place, with a record of 9-5, but a week later they were 6-7. The June 10 standings were accompanied by batting and pitching stats, the latter showing McKinnis's record as just 3-2.

68 "McKinnis to Giants," *Chicago Daily Times*, June 6, 1945: 42. "Only 900 See Games in Chicago," *Pittsburgh Courier*, June 9, 1945: 16. "Memphis and Chicago Divide Doubleheader," *Chicago Defender*, June 9, 1945: 7.

69 "American Giants Beat Birmingham," *Milwaukee Journal*, June 12, 1945: 7. "Giants' Rally Bests Clowns," *Dayton* (Ohio) *Journal*, July 3, 1945: 9.

70 "Am. Giants Win Three from Memphis Red Sox," *Chicago Defender*, July 21, 1945: 7.

71 C.W. "Bub" Martin, "Mathis Handcuffs Memphis Red Sox as American Giants Win, 5 to 0," *Racine* (Wisconsin) *Journal Times*, July 19, 1945: 18. The headline was supposed to name McKinnis, not Memphis pitcher Verdell Mathis, but Martin reversed the two in each of the first two sentences. McKinnis helped his own cause by starting a three-run rally in the seventh inning with a triple.

72 "Hurlers Duel to Deadlock," *Dayton Herald*, July 21, 1945: 6. "13 Inning Tie Game," *Chicago Defender*, July 28, 1945: 7. "Chicago Giants Win Two from Barons, 8-2, 3-2," *Chicago Tribune*, July 23, 1945: 18. "Chicago Wins 2 from Barons," *Chicago Defender*, July 28, 1945: 7. The *Tribune*'s line score showed the Barons with six hits, but the *Defender*'s showed them with five.

73 "How This Year's Pitchers Performed in Past Classics," *Pittsburgh Courier*, July 28, 1945: 12.

74 "Scalpers Take Good Beating," *Chicago Defender*, August 4, 1945: 7.

75 "Brown of Grays Joins Perfect Game Clan," *Washington Evening Star*, August 13, 1945: A8. "Ray Brown Hurls Perfect Game as Grays Divide," *Afro-American* (Baltimore), August 18, 1945: 25.

76 "American Giants Win 2 over Monarchs, 15-0, 2-1," *Chicago Tribune*, August 27, 1945: 20. "Chicago Wins 2 From Kansas City to Move Into 2nd Place," *Chicago Defender*, September 1, 1945: 7. In a preview, one Chicago paper printed uniform numbers for both teams, and McKinnis's was 18. See just above the headline of "American Giants to Play Monarchs," *Chicago Times*, August 24, 1945: 25.

77 "Satchel Paige's Succession-Baronite," *Weekly Review*, September 29, 1945: 7. "American Giants Start Long Trip to Dixie Towns," *Chicago Defender*, September 22, 1945: 7. "Royals, Barons Meet Tonight," *Los Angeles Times*, October 31, 1945: 21. As of this writing, after his rookie season, Seamheads.com shows McKinnis with losing records through 1945, for a total of 9-22 across those four seasons. However, despite valiant efforts, Seamheads has been hamstrung by a lack of box scores for many games, and 1943 provides a good illustration. Seamheads shows McKinnis's Barons with winning records of 46-35-2 in NAL play and 60-49-2 overall, yet is also shows the pitching staff with a losing record of 18-24.

78 "Chicago Loses Two Games to Red Sox," *Chicago Defender*, April 13, 1946: 10.

79 "Chicago Giants Lose Three to Mexican League," *Chicago Tribune*, April 18, 1946: 31. "3 More Ex-Giants in Mexican Loop," *Reno Evening Gazette*, April 24, 1946: 14. "La Junta Beats Monterrey 5-1," *Laredo Times*, May 3, 1946: 9. McKinnis was one of four Monterrey hurlers but, as the starter, was the losing pitcher. As of this writing, both baseball-reference.com and statscrew.com don't have McKinnis on Monterrey's roster but they instead list a George McGinnis about whom they lack such basic details as birth date.

80 "Monterrey Keeps Leadership in Mexican League," *Laredo Times*, May 6, 1946: 7.

81 Gene Kessler," Lyons Goes to Work," *Chicago Daily Times*, May 25, 1946: 29.

82 Brent Kelley, *Voices from the Negro Leagues: Conversations with 52 Baseball Standouts of the Period 1924-1960* (Jefferson, North Carolina: McFarland & Company, Inc., 2005), 77.

83 "Ex-Major Leaguers, Tan Stars Teammates in Mexico," *Afro-American*, July 20, 1946: 27.

84 "Autos Defeat Bombers, 6 to 2, Play Black Barons Here Friday," *News-Palladium* (Benton Harbor, Michigan), June 6, 1946: 16. "92-Game Slate Is Adopted by USL," *Afro-American*, May 11, 1946: 14.

85 "Braves Trim Truckers in Eighth Inning Rally," *Manitowoc* (Wisconsin) *Herald Times*, June 10, 1946: 7. Leslie A. Heaphy, *Black Baseball and Chicago: Essays on the Players, Teams and Games of the Negro Leagues' Most Important City* (Jefferson, North Carolina: McFarland & Company, Inc., 2006), 37.

86 Armand Peterson and Tom Tomashek, *Town Ball: The Glory Days of Minnesota Amateur Baseball* (Minneapolis: University of Minnesota Press, 2006), 276. According to baseball-reference.com, in 1946 the real Al Saylor was with the Seattle Steelheads of the West Coast Baseball League.

87 Howard Brantz, "A Sporting Glance," *Winona* (Minnesota) *Republican-Herald*, August 27, 1946: 11. During the intervening month, a preview of a game between the American Giants and the Black Barons scheduled for August 6 in Anniston, Alabama, mentioned McKinnis, though that could have been a result of information held over from the preseason or even the prior year; in fact, in the first sentence the article mentioned "1945" instead of 1946. See "Black Barons Face Giants Here Tomorrow," *Anniston Star*, August 5, 1946: 8. There was no coverage of the game in that paper the day after the game.

88 "Sport Scraps," *Albert Lea* (Minnesota) *Evening Tribune*, August 31, 1946: 8. Frank M. White, *They Played for the Love of the Game* (St. Paul: Minnesota Historical Society Press, 2016), 57. "Saylor Not Barred Because of Color," *Albert Lea Evening Tribune*, September 3, 1946: 12. The box score for Zumbrota's painful loss to Albert Lea was printed to the left of the latter article.

89 "Paige May Forego [sic] Trip Here," *Honolulu Advertiser*, September 17, 1946: 13.

90 "Negro All-Star Nine Hits Town for Stadium Games," *Honolulu Star-Bulletin*, September 21, 1946: 11. Dick Klenhard, "Two Homers Aid Crescents in 8-3 Win Over Braves," *Honolulu Star-Bulletin*, September 23, 1946: 12. Among the Braves were catcher Charles Luis, who had a batting average of .311 in the New York Yankees' farm system in 1948, and Sal Recca, a five-year Yankees farmhand. Several other Braves had at least a year in the White minor leagues around that time.

91 "Raimondi Stars Beat Cincy 5-4," *San Francisco Chronicle*, October 18, 1946: 13. See also "Stars, Crescents Split Double Bill," *San Francisco Examiner*, October 28, 1946: 18.

92 Peterson and Tomashek, 277.

93 George Lyle Jr., "League Moguls Lift Ban on 2 Players," *Afro-American*, June 17, 1947: 19. His name appeared in this article as "Preed McGinnis." See also Doron Goldman, "1933-1962: The Business Meetings of Negro League Baseball," at https://sabr.org/journal/article/1933-1962-the-business-meetings-of-negro-league-baseball/.

94 "Chicago Giants Defeat Kansas City Nine, 2 to 1," *Chicago Tribune*, July 25, 1947: 25. An example of his being mentioned shortly thereafter is "McKinnies [sic] to Hurl for Chicago Giants," *Chicago Sun*, July 31, 1947: 15. However, he was not listed in the battery in the next day's

• GREAD McKINNIS •

Tribune. Similarly, see "Black Yanks, Giants Play 2 Games Today," *Chicago Tribune,* August 3, 1947: 37.

95 "Rochester Beats Wells, 3 to 0; McKinnis Hurls One-Hit Ball," *Albert Lea Evening Tribune,* September 8, 1947: 7. The lone single was a bunt.

96 "Hurling Is Key at State Meet," *St. Cloud* (Minnesota) *Daily Times,* September 16, 1947: 12. "Governor's Cup Goes to McKinnis, Rochester Ace," *Winona Republican-Herald,* September 24, 1947: 16. White (see Note 98), 102.

97 Ted Peterson, "Rochester, Chaska Win, March to State Baseball Meet Finals," *Minneapolis Sunday Tribune,* September 21, 1947: 33. Ted Peterson, "Record 7,715 Fans See Albert Lea, Chaska Win," *Minneapolis Morning Tribune,* September 22, 1947: 18. On the latter page, see also "McKinnis Is Most Valuable; Manderfeld Leading Hitter." His homer on September 20 was off a Stan Stevenson, quite possibly the Minnesota native by that name who had two minor-league games in 1941 with La Crosse in the Wisconsin State League.

98 Peterson and Tomashek, 277.

99 Joe Hendrickson, "Amateur, You Say?" *Minneapolis Morning Tribune,* February 13, 1948: 20. "Sports Scraps," *Albert Lea Evening Tribune,* February 14, 1948: 8. In the first article, Ben Sternberg's brother Mike said other towns tempted McKinnis with incredible amounts, an indication they were more semipro than amateur.

100 Joel W. Smith, "Black Crax Win Over All Stars, 7-5," *Atlanta Daily World,* April 13, 1948: 5.

101 "Errors Help Rollingstone Tip Merchants," *Winona Republican-Herald,* June 7, 1948: 12.

102 "Indians Play Colored Nine 4:30 Thursday," *Ironwood* (Michigan) *Daily Globe,* June 9, 1948: 6.

103 "South Bend in Sunday Clash," *Lafayette* (Indiana) *Journal and Courier,* June 25, 1948: 12. "Studebaker Locals Gunning for Ninth Exhibition Win," *South Bend Tribune,* July 15, 1948: Section 2, 3. "Red Sox Drop Two Contests; Lafayette, South Bend Cop," *Kenosha* (Wisconsin) *Evening News,* August 9, 1948: 22. Bob Towner, "Saints Bow to Automen by 11-2 Score," *South Bend Tribune,* August 27, 1948: Section 3, 1. McKinnis's desire to moonlight was understandable. He didn't pitch in Rochester's game on July 11, and a week later the team had played only its sixth Bi-State game.

104 Peterson and Tomashek, 277. "Merchants Beaten by Rochester Queens, 9 to 3," *Winona Republican-Herald,* September 3, 1948: 14. "Rochester and Belle Plaine Win Crowns," *Albert Lea Evening Tribune,* September 9, 1948: 10. Winona played the first game under protest because it believed Rochester had four outside players, two more than rules allowed. Reports of the second game credited him with 20 K's, not 19, but about a year later a sportswriter noted that among the 20 was a foul bunt after two strikes. AL rules credited that to the pitcher as a strikeout but NL rules didn't, and the state tourney used the latter. See Augie Karcher, "Behind the Eight Ball," *Winona Republican-Herald,* August 17, 1949: 13.

105 Joe Soucheray, untitled column, *Minneapolis Tribune,* June 19, 1977: 2C.

106 "Rain Halts Memphis Opener with Chicago," *Chicago Defender,* May 7, 1949: 14.

107 "Steele Top NAL Batter With .402," *Chicago Defender,* June 11, 1949: 16. For additional NAL stats of his, see "Carl Mays Regains NAL Batting Lead With .413," *Chicago Defender,* June 18, 1949: 16, and "Hot Off Baseball Griddle," *Plain Dealer* (Kansas City, Kansas), June 24, 1949: 4.

108 "Hot Off Baseball Griddle," *Plain Dealer* (Kansas City, Kansas), July 15, 1949: 4. "Monarchs Take Lead in Hitting," *Chicago Defender,* July 30, 1949: 16. "Three Giants Named to West All-Star Squad," *St. Petersburg* (Florida) *Times,* July 21, 1949: 4.

109 Edward Prell, "Eastern Negro Stars Defeat West Team, 4-0," *Chicago Tribune,* August 15, 1949: Part 3, 1, 4. Wendell Smith, "Chandler Sees East Cop Negro All-Star Game," *The Sporting News,* August 24, 1949:

21. The latter had the lower attendance estimate.

110 "Chicago Giants Edge Cleveland in 11 Innings," *Post-Bulletin* (Rochester, Minnesota), September 1, 1949: 20.

111 "Lenny Pigg Officially Designated as Champion Batter In the NAL," *Chicago Defender,* December 24, 1949: 14. By contrast, during the first week of September his record was 14-5, according to "Ware Is Pacing Buckeyes At Bat With .329 Mark," *Dayton Daily News,* September 8, 1949: 19.

112 Art Carter, "Old Satch Plagued by Stomach Trouble," *Afro-American,* October 1, 1949: 25. See also "N.Y. Stars Ahead in Latin Series," *Afro-American,* October 15, 1949: 29. The latter article reported partial won-lost records: Stars 5-2, Puerto Rico 4-2, Cuba 5-3, and Venezuela 0-6 (which add up to 14-13, so it was off by one). For the full roster of the New York Stars, see the Center for Negro Leagues Baseball Research, "Rosters of Barnstorming and Independent Black Baseball Teams (1946-1988)," page 22, at http://www.cnlbr.org/Portals/0/Rosters/Rosters%20-%20Barnstorming%20Teams%20(1946-1988).pdf. According to one of the manifests, McKinnis's passport was issued on August 8, 1949.

113 Augie Karcher, "Behind the Eight Ball," *Winona Republican-Herald,* March 2, 1950: 20.

114 Bud Burns, "Touchin' 'em All," *Albert Lea Evening Tribune,* April 6, 1950: 12. For more information about Smith, see https://nlbemuseum.com/history/players/smithe.html. Frederick C. Bush's biography of Mathis, at https://sabr.org/bioproj/person/verdell-mathis/, includes a paragraph about Rochester and McKinnis.

115 "Chiefs Open S-M Play Sunday Against Waseca," *Winona Republican-Herald,* May 12, 1950: 18. "Rain Washes Out Packer-Faribault Game in Second Inning," *Albert Lea Evening Tribune,* June 9, 1950: 7. Due to Smith's extended sore arm, the four African-American pitchers weren't necessarily all active simultaneously; see Augie Karcher, "Behind the Eight Ball," *Winona Republican-Herald,* July 1, 1950: 10.

116 "McKinnis Injured," *Winona Republican-Herald,* July 6, 1950: 15.

117 Bud Burns, "Touchin' 'em All," *Albert Lea Evening Tribune,* July 10, 1950: 10. "Bartkowski Leads Austin to Victory," *Albert Lea Evening Tribune,* July 26, 1950: 9. "Lindgren Cops S-M Bat Title with .392 Mark," *Winona Republican-Herald,* August 29, 1950: 23.

118 "Black Barons Impressive in Chicago Split," *Birmingham News,* April 23, 1951: 25. He was presumably the "McGinnis" in the battery listed beneath one of the doubleheader's line scores. It was clear by the end of March that McKinnis wouldn't continue with Rochester, according to "Player Changes Numerous as S-M Campaign Nears," *Austin* (Minnesota) *Daily Herald,* March 31, 1951: 5.

119 "New Orleans Eagles Earn Even Break Against Giants," *Times-Picayune,* May 15, 1951: 21. "Black Barons Trip Giants," *Chattanooga Daily Times,* May 24, 1951: 18. In the former he was "Gerald" McKinnis, and in the latter he was presumably the Giants' third pitcher in the box score, "McGnnis."

120 The primary source for this information is http://www.attheplate.com/wcbl/1951_20i.html, part of a website created by Jay-Dell Mah, a SABR member who is in the Saskatchewan Baseball Hall of Fame. See also "Buffs and Carman Score Mandak Wins," *Leader-Post* (Regina, Saskatchewan), July 19, 1951: 19.

121 See http://www.attheplate.com/wcbl/1951_20h.html and the statistics provided at https://www.statscrew.com/minorbaseball/stats/t-bg10617/y-1951.

122 "Dominican Season Opens," *The Sporting News,* May 7, 1952: 39. The regular season began on April 26.

123 Bienvenido Rojas, "1952, Refuerzos Ganaron los Lideratos Ofensivos," *Diario Libre* (Santo Domingo, Dominican Republic), September 1, 2015: 35.

124 "Brandon Hires New Ball Boss," *Regina Leader-Post,* July 2, 1952: 19. As of this writing, he isn't mentioned among the plentiful ManDak game reports provided at http://www.attheplate.com/wcbl/1952_20i.html.

However, there are a few games for which the pitchers remain unknown. His Intercounty League game is mentioned at http://www.attheplate.com/wcbl/1952_90i.html.

125 "Smokers Return to Plant Field to Meet Saints Tonight," *Tampa Daily Times*, August 1, 1952: 13. "Smokers Drop Murphy, Hire Quebec Lefty," *Palm Beach Post*, August 2, 1952: 7. His index card maintained by *The Sporting News* identified August 1 as his first day with Tampa. The club was not in any major-league team's farm system

126 Byron Hollingsworth, "Saints Lick Smokers by 9-2 Score," *Tampa Morning Tribune*, August 2, 1952: 11, 13.

127 Bob Hudson, "McKinnis Tops Pilots on One Hit," *Tampa Sunday Tribune*, August 10, 1952: Section B, 1.

128 "FIL Roundup," *Palm Beach Post*, August 14, 1952: 12. "Pilots Beat Smokers by 3-2 Score," *Tampa Morning Tribune*, August 18, 1952: 13, 15. "Smokers Win Second Straight from Key West, 7 to 2," *Tampa Morning Tribune*, August 22, 1952: 2-B.

129 His ERA is from baseball-reference.com. As of this writing, that site's web page for McKinnis shows him having given up 70 hits and 40 walks in 73 innings, and no figure is shown in the strikeouts column. By contrast, he pitched 77⅔ innings, had 41 walks, and 36 strikeouts, according to "Smoker Data," *Tampa Daily Times*, September 8, 1952: 10. Conversely, his total innings were 73, as shown by baseball-reference.com, but with 35 strikeouts and just 37 hits, according to "Pitching Records," *Tampa Morning Tribune*, September 14, 1952: 35.

130 "Pitt Crawford Opener with House of David," *Philadelphia Tribune*, March 31, 1953: 10. The concluding sentence: "The Crawfords have lost the services of Lefty McKinnis to the Tampa Smokers, a class A club, and have signed Ray Moore who was with the Indianapolis Clowns to replace him." This Pittsburgh Crawfords team was a revival of the name under player-manager Sy Morton, with no apparent involvement of Greenlee or connection to his second Crawfords franchise of 1944-1946.

131 "17 Players Report to Smokers," *Tampa Morning Tribune*, March 24, 1953: 15.

132 Bobby Hicks, "Smokers Post 6-3 Win Over Senators," *Tampa Morning Tribune*, April 8, 1953: 19.

133 Bobby Hicks, "Smokers Win No. 2 from Saints, 3-1," *Tampa Morning Tribune*, April 18, 1953: 13.

134 "Saints Top Smokers by 2-0 Margin," *Tampa Sunday Tribune*, May 17, 1953: B-1, 6-B.

135 Among many other places, the Robinson incident is covered at length in Bill Nowlin's SABR biography of Chapman, at https://sabr.org/bioproj/person/ben-chapman/. It's possible no journalist even hinted at McKinnis's reason for leaving around that time, but see Bill Beck, "Saints Bow 7-6 as Rally Fails; Drop 3 Players," *St. Petersburg Times*, April 23, 1955: 12.

136 "McKinnis Fined $25," *Tampa Morning Tribune*, May 18, 1953: 15.

137 Wilbur Kinley, "Sport-Rays," *Tampa Daily Times*, May 20, 1953: 13.

138 "Smoker Data," *Tampa Daily Times*, May 22, 1953: 13. The *Times* tended to print stats with a bit more detail than the *Tribune*. As of this writing, his baseball-reference entry with Tampa for 1953 only has his record of 1-4, and 13 games played, not 12. Official league stats published in December supposedly included all pitchers with at least 45 innings yet McKinnis was omitted. For example, see "Official FIL Averages Bring Few Surprises," *St. Petersburg Times*, December 13, 1953: 4-C.

139 "Greys Take over Top Place in Mandak League," *Brandon (Manitoba) Daily Sun*, May 22, 1953: 6. "Greys Continue Romp with Win over Carman," *Brandon Daily Sun*, May 25, 1953: 6. "Greys Win on Mitchell's Pinch-Hit Single," *Brandon Daily Sun*, May 27, 1953: 6. In fact, shortly before the start of the ManDak season, McKinnis was expected to pitch for the Greys, according to Jim Reid, "Sport Scripts," *Brandon Daily Sun*, May 7, 1953: 6.

140 "McKinnes [sic] Celebrates Birthday with Victory," *Brandon Daily Sun*, August 12, 1953: 6.

141 See the website of Jay-Dell Mah, at http://www.attheplate.com/wcbl/1953_20i.html.

142 "Finals Delayed as Cards-Royals Deadlocked," *Brandon Daily Sun*, August 31, 1953: 6.

143 "Greys Oust Cardinals from Mandak Playoffs," *Brandon Daily Sun*, September 8, 1953: 6.

144 "Brandon Forces Deciding Game in Series," *Brandon Daily Sun*, September 16, 1953: 6. "Minot Crowned Champs," *Winnipeg Free Press*, September 17, 1953: 26.

145 "Marriage Licenses," *St. Petersburg Times*, October 14, 1953: 27. "Local Student to Attend NHA Annual Convention," *St. Petersburg Times*, June 11, 1950: 39. "Young Matrons Add 2 Members," *St. Petersburg Times*, February 10, 1954: 29. "Special Services on Mother's Day to Honor Nine Local Churchwomen," *St. Petersburg Times*, May 7, 1954: 29. In the first of these two 1954 articles her surname was "McKenzie" but the article three months later is strong evidence that the February one referred to the same woman.

146 "Smokers to Open Practice," *Tampa Morning Tribune*, March 15, 1954: 15. "Smokers Swing into Full Work at Cuscaden Park," *Tampa Daily Times*, March 23, 1954: 9.

147 "Tigers Sweep Doubleheader with Pirates," *St. Petersburg Times*, April 5, 1954: 32. "Lefty McKinnis to Get Trial at Rochester," *Austin (Minnesota) Daily Herald*, April 29, 1954: 10.

148 "Austin at Rochester Tonight; Lawler and DeRose to Pitch," *Austin Daily Herald*, May 11, 1954: 10. Tom Koeck, "Packers Edge Rochester 2-1," *Austin Daily Herald*, May 12, 1954: 12. Just a few days later, the Royals signed former major leaguer Dale Matthewson, a pitcher with the Phillies in 1943 and 1944 who was a very successful teammate of McKinnis's at Tampa in 1952 and 1953. It's likely McKinnis was instrumental in that acquisition. Matthewson had a good year for Rochester.

149 Ralph Reeve, "Chiefs Split with Rochester in Exhibitions," *Winona Republican-Herald*, May 17, 1954: 16. "Thompson Named Laker Manager," *Albert Lea Sunday Tribune*, June 27, 1954: 10.

150 "Tigers Seek Double Win over 9 Devils," *St. Petersburg Times*, July 25, 1954: 13. Carl Wright, "St. Pete Drops Devils Twice," *Bradenton (Florida) Herald*, July 26, 1954: 6. "West Coast League Holds Edge in All-Star Contest," *St. Petersburg Times*, August 14, 1954: 12. The first of these articles called him "Red McGinnis" but specified he was a former Tampa Smoker who had most recently played for a club in Minnesota. His surname was also McGinnis in the other two articles.

151 McKinnis wasn't on their Opening Day roster nine days earlier, nor when spring training started on April 3. See Lonnie Burt, "Saints Open Spring Drills," *St. Petersburg Times*, April 4, 1955: 18, and "Saints Meet Lakeland in FSL Opener Tonight," *St. Petersburg Times*, April 13, 1955: 18. For details about some of his teammates, see "Saints Spring Roster," *St. Petersburg Times*, April 3, 1955: 1-C.

152 Bill Beck, "Saints Bow 7-6 as Rally Fails; Drop 3 Players," *St. Petersburg Times*, April 23, 1955: 12. Bill Beck, "$40,000 Lesson Costly if You Don't Learn It," *St. Petersburg Times*, April 20, 1955: 12. In his article on April 23, Beck noted that besides McKinnis, two infielders were also expected to join the Saints "and they are likely to be Negroes."

153 "Saints Blow 3-Run Lead, Lose 7-6 to G-Men in 9th," *St. Petersburg Times*, April 24, 1955: 2-C.

154 "McKinnis Pitches, Slugs Saints 7-4 Over Pilots; 3-Run Rally in 7th Wins," *St. Petersburg Times*, April 28, 1955: 20. "Saints Beat Pilots 10-8, Climb Into 3-Way Tie for 6th Place," *St. Petersburg Times*, April 29, 1955: 14. The latter article was accompanied by team stats showing McKinnis with five hits in nine at-bats and five runs batted in.

GREAD McKINNIS

155 "McKinnis Hurls Four-Hit Game but Loses 2-0," *St. Petersburg Times*, May 2, 1955: 20.

156 Lonnie Burt, "Saints Get Off Floor to Slug Daytona 13 to 7," *St. Petersburg Times*, May 17, 1955: 23. "Saints Sweep Series With 5-2 Defeat of WPB," *St. Petersburg Times*, May 21, 1955: 9.

157 Lonnie Burt, "Saints Count Pair in 9th To Shade Gainesville 7-6," *St. Petersburg Times*, June 7, 1955: 10. "Saints, 8; G-Men, 4," *Tampa Morning Tribune*, June 8, 1955: 18.

158 "3-in-a-Row Jinx Frustrates Saints Again; It's Cards 5-3," *St. Petersburg Times*, June 25, 1955: 7. "Snyder's Homer Beats St. Pete," *Daytona Beach* (Florida) *Morning Journal*, June 25, 1955: 8.

159 "Renfroe Gives Orlando Two Hits but Loses 1-0," *St. Petersburg Times*, July 2, 1955: 9. McKinnis's index card maintained by *The Sporting News* shows the date of his release as July 5. As of this writing, a few of his baseball-reference.com stats differ somewhat from those shown by the *St. Petersburg Times* on July 11 (page 12) and the *Palm Beach Post* on July 17 (page 32).

160 "Waitman Fund Game Slated Here Today," *St. Petersburg Times*, October 9, 1955: 10. St. Pete's team in the West Coast Negro League was no longer called the Tigers. This article called them the Giants, but articles in August called them the Braves.

161 "What's Doing Around Town," *St. Petersburg Times*, February 1, 1956: 32. "The Social Whirl," *St. Petersburg Times*, April 15, 1956: 6-C. "Ball Chairman," *St. Petersburg Times*, May 9, 1956: 37. "The Social Whirl," *St. Petersburg Times*, June 21, 1956: 30. Because of her leadership roles, Naomi was mentioned frequently in the *St. Petersburg Times* in 1956 and 1957, and her photo appeared more than once.

162 "Cread McKinnes [sic] Signs with Minot Mallards," *Bismarck* (North Dakota) *Tribune*, May 3, 1956: 21. "Barons Rout Minot 17-7 to Open Man-Dak Season," *Bismarck Tribune*, May 26, 1956: 8. "Elkins Cops Third Win for Oilers," *Bismarck Tribune*, June 2, 1956: 10.

163 "Florida-Georgia Diamond Battle Slated Saturday," *St. Petersburg Times*, March 29, 1957: 12-B. "Macon Tops Braves, 5-4, in Thriller," *St. Petersburg Times*, April 2, 1957: 24. "Braves Down Clearwater in Opener," *St. Petersburg Times*, April 16, 1957: 23. Ralph H. Middleton, "Devils Blank St. Pete, 2-0," *St. Petersburg Times*, April 22, 1957: 10. From the last week of April onward, the team was more likely to be mentioned in the *Bradenton Herald*.

164 "The Social Whirl," *St. Petersburg Times*, October 6, 1957: 8-C.

165 Their grandson Gread McKinnis III was quoted by Jodi S. Cohen in "2 Finalists for CSU President Denounced," *Chicago Tribune*, April 2, 2009: 8. Their granddaughters Elisabeth and Naomi Walley were quoted by Jane Gordon Julien in "How Did They Know? (The Signs Showed the Way)," *New York Times*, December 30, 2018: ST.11.

166 Sheryl Fitzgerald, "27 Hit Black Tax in Home Sales Lawsuit," *Chicago Defender*, January 21, 1969: 1. Toni Anthony, "Jail 16 in Cop, CBL Row," *Chicago Defender*, April 23, 1970: 1. Ronald Koziol and Arthur Siddon, "20 Arrested as Crowd Hurls Rocks, Bottles During Evictions," *Chicago Tribune*, April 23, 1970: 18. "U.S. Begins Rights Probe in C.B.L. Member Evictions," *Chicago Tribune*, May 3, 1970: 22.

167 Barbara Brotman, "Black Homebuyers' Battle for Justice," *Chicago Tribune*, July 26, 2015: 7.

168 For information about his Foundation and its scholarship, see https://cps.academicworks.com/opportunities/4314.

169 "Illinois Department on Aging Recognizes Workers and Employers in Observance of National Employ the Older Worker Week," September 25, 2009, news release available at https://www2.illinois.gov/aging/Resources/NewsAndPublications/PressReleases/Pages/2009-0925neoww.aspx.

BUCK O'NEIL

By Bob LeMoine

To tell the story *of* Buck O'Neil, one needs only to retell the stories *by* Buck O'Neil. He told stories of Satchel Paige, Josh Gibson, and other Negro League greats forgotten to history because of the color of their skin. He told them with a twinkle in his eye, a smile from ear to ear, and a laugh that conveyed his passion to pass his stories on to the next generation. "Sometimes I think the Lord has kept me on this earth as long as He has so I can bear witness to the Negro Leagues," he said.[1] While he became the storyteller of the Negro Leagues, Buck O'Neil himself is an amazing story.

The grandson of a slave, O'Neil couldn't attend high school in the segregated South, but the 12-year-old decided there had to be more to life than working in the celery fields. There was much more available to him but he had to go out and find it, his father told him. He would face many obstacles, including the Jim Crow South. Yet despite the ways he was treated as a person of color, he loved both the National Pastime and his country, serving the latter in World War II. He lived long enough to see dramatic changes in baseball and American society, although they came too late for Buck the ballplayer. It was utterly unfair that, had he been born later, he might have been a major leaguer. Yet when asked if he had regrets in missing such opportunities, his answer was definitive. "Waste no tears for me," he said. "I didn't come along too early—I was right on time."[2]

Buck O'Neil told his stories for decades but few people heard them until the power of television brought him celebrity status in his 80s. A new generation that never knew what he experienced now saw the sparkling, silver-haired O'Neil describe the players who paved the way for a better country and better game. Seeking to preserve the memory of the Negro Leagues for all time, he helped establish a museum so those stories would never disappear from history again. O'Neil, in the words of Jules Tygiel, "reigned as a symbol of baseball's past and the game's greatest good-will ambassador."[3]

John Jordan O'Neil Jr. was born on November 13, 1911, in Carrabelle, a fishing village on the Florida panhandle. The O'Neil family descended from the Mandingo tribe of West Africa. Buck's grandfather, Julius O'Neil, was born on the banks of the Niger River and brought to America as a boy on a slave ship. Julius worked the cotton fields in the Carolinas for an owner with the surname of O'Neil, which Julius adopted as his own, a common practice. Buck remembered Julius, in his late 90s, sitting him down on his knee to tell him of the days on the plantation. When Julius was freed he moved to southern Georgia where Buck's father, John Jordan O'Neil Sr. was born. John Sr. met Luella, also a descendent of slaves, and the two were married. John Sr. worked in a sawmill which often took him away from home to cut timber. Later he was a foreman in the celery fields. Luella took the main responsibility to raise the children, Buck with his older sister Fanny and younger brother Warren.[4]

On the weekends, John Sr. brought Buck along when he played on a local baseball team in Springdale. The team would survive by passing a hat for donations. In 1920 the O'Neil family moved to Sarasota. Luella was a cook for the Ringlings, the famous circus family, and later she opened a family restaurant. Sarasota was also the spring training home of the New York Giants. The Philadelphia Athletics and New York Yankees were also just a short distance away. Young O'Neil met legends such as Babe Ruth, Dizzy and Daffy Dean, and Lefty Grove.

Over the winter months, Buck's uncle, who worked on the railroad, would travel to Florida and take Buck and his dad to West Palm Beach to see Rube Foster, the Chicago American Giants and Indianapolis ABCs of the Negro Leagues. Many of the players worked as porters at the Royal Poinciana Hotel, and played ball on their off days.[5] O'Neil had never seen baseball like this. "It's fast, it's quick," he said. "You know how the dull moments in baseball can be. In this type of baseball, never a dull moment."[6] In his youth O'Neil was known as Jay, J.J. or Foots, due to his size-11 shoe when he was just 12. That year – 1924 – he was recruited by the Sarasota Tigers semipro team, where he played first base for two seasons.

"When I was twelve years old, I worked in the celery fields," O'Neil recalled. "I would put the boxes out so they could pack the celery in the boxes to ship it. I was sitting behind the boxes one day in the fall of the year, and it was hot in Florida, and I was sweating and itching in that muck. My father was the foreman on this job and he was on [one] side of the boxes, and I was on the other side. And I said, '*Damn*. There's got to be something better than this.' So, when we got off the truck that night my daddy said, 'I heard what you said behind the boxes.' I thought he was going to reprimand me for saying 'damn.' But he said, 'I heard what you said about there being something better than this. There is something better, but you can't get it here, you're gonna have to go someplace else.'"[7]

"Someplace else" was also where O'Neil had to go for an education. Sarasota High School was not one of the only four high schools in the state of Florida that would accept African-Americans. "When I finished elementary school in 1926," he recalled, "my grandmother sat me down and said, 'John, you can't go to Sarasota High School. Sarasota High School is not for black kids.' I shed a few tears at the time, but she said, 'Don't cry. One day all kids will go to Sarasota High School.'"[8]

O'Neil received a scholarship to Edward Waters College, a black school in Jacksonville. Baseball coach Ox Clemons nicknamed him "Country" and also made him a lineman on the football team. O'Neil attained his high school diploma and two years of college. O'Neil also briefly played for the semipro Tampa Black Smokers in 1933. In 1934 he signed to play for the Miami Giants. They were owned by a Buck O'Neal (with a different spelling).[9] The Giants were an unofficial minor league club for the Negro Leagues. O'Neil made $10 per week plus room and board on the barnstorming team.[10]

In 1935 O'Neil joined the New York Tigers. "We had nothing to do with New York," O'Neil confessed, "but we figured the name would get us some attention from the people fascinated with Harlem. Out west where we were headed, nobody was going to know the difference."[11] The Tigers barnstormed the country in two old Cadillacs, but one had to be sold to pay rent and the other broke down. The players hitched rides and hopped trains, playing in the *Denver Post* and National Baseball Congress (Wichita, Kansas) semipro tournaments. "Since hobos were a common sight in the Depression, we didn't have any trouble," O'Neil said.[12] It was in Wichita where O'Neil first met his soon-to-be lifelong friend, Satchel Paige, whose pitching dominated the tournament and brought the championship to his racially-integrated team from Bismarck, North Dakota.

The Tigers lived hand-to-mouth, sometimes depending on O'Neil's ability to win games of pool to make enough money for the guys to eat. He had learned to play pool at the pool hall next to his parent's restaurant. The players once snuck out a window of a boarding house when they couldn't afford the bill. O'Neil left the landlady a note, promising to pay her when they had the money. She never cashed the check he sent, and upon returning years later O'Neil found that the check had been framed.[13]

In 1936 O'Neil joined the Acme Giants, an unofficial minor league team for the Kansas City Monarchs in Shreveport, Louisiana. When the season concluded, some of the team joined the Texas Black Spiders from Mineola, Texas, who needed players for a trip to Mexico. The team played well and were offered a chance to join a Mexican league if they won an exhibition game. But the Spiders lost and had to return to the US. "You know it's a tough league when they *deport* you for losing," O'Neil joked.[14]

In 1937 he played for the Memphis Red Sox of the new Negro American League. O'Neil also made more money when he joined the Zulu Cannibal Giants of Louisville, Kentucky. Owner Abe Saperstein's players wore grass skirts, war paint and nose rings while "acting like a bunch of fools to draw white folks to the park," O'Neil remembered.[15] Saperstein is famous for creating the Harlem Globetrotters. "We would do anything to play ball," O'Neil admitted. "We had become conditioned to racism. Hatred will steal your heart, man. You don't have any fight left in you. You accept what's around you. That's what this country was like. We thought it would change someday. We just waited for it to change."[16] Fortunately, the racial humiliation didn't last long. One lasting significance from the Zulus, however, was the fact O'Neil was mistaken for his old team owner Buck O'Neal. "My name went up on the placards as Buck O'Neil," he said concerning his new nickname, "and it's been that way ever since, although the black papers didn't get around to calling me that for a while."[17]

The Kansas City Monarchs came to Shreveport in the spring of 1938. Kansas City's pioneering owner, J.L. Wilkinson, the only Caucasian team owner in the

• When the Monarchs Reigned •

Negro Leagues, gave O'Neil a tryout. He soon began his legendary career at first base with Monarchs, a powerhouse of Negro League baseball. The team stayed in a hotel at Kansas City's famous 18th and Vine area, where O'Neil rubbed elbows with musical greats Cab Calloway, Billie Holiday, and Bojangles Robinson, as well as boxer Joe Louis. It seemed like the center of the universe. "New Orleans might have been the birthplace of Jazz," O'Neil said, "but Kansas City is where it grew up. At 18th and Vine, you couldn't toss a baseball without hitting a musician, and you couldn't whistle a tune without having a ballplayer join in. Baseball and jazz, two of the best inventions known to man, walked hand in hand along Vine Street."[18] O'Neil's debut came in a doubleheader on May 15 before 6,000 fans at Ruppert Stadium in Kansas City as the Monarchs took on the Chicago American Giants. He played right field in the opener and went 1-for-4 in a 4-2 loss. "In the second game," he remembered nearly 60 years later, "I played first. A dozen years later, I was still there." He also had a single and an RBI in that nightcap, a 3-0 win.[19]

From 1939-1942, the Monarchs won four straight Negro American League pennants, with the 1942 team being the greatest team O'Neil believed he ever played on. "I do believe we could have given the New York Yankees a run for their money that year," he boasted.[20] That season O'Neil was also voted by the fans as the starting first baseman for the West squad at the annual East-West All-Star Game. The Monarchs swept the Homestead Grays in the Negro League World Series.

Satchel Paige joined the Monarchs in 1939 and O'Neil, in an oft-told story, earned the nickname "Nancy" from him. Paige had met a young lady named Nancy while the team was in Chicago and invited her to his hotel room. O'Neil suddenly realized Paige's fiancé Lahoma was making an unexpected visit. He did some quick thinking, moving Nancy to a room next his. In the middle of the night, Paige came knocking on Nancy's door, calling out, "Nancy! Nancy!" O'Neil heard Paige's door opening and knew Lahoma was curious to see what was going on. O'Neil bolted up and opened his door, asking, "Yeah, Satch. What do you want?" Realizing Buck had just saved his hide, Paige responded, "Why Nancy. There you are." Forever after, Paige called O'Neil "Nancy."[21]

On Easter Sunday, 1943, O'Neil hit for the cycle against Memphis. The day was memorable for him, however, for what happened that night. He met school teacher Ora Lee Owens, who became the love of his life. Her father was a freed slave and a farmer who had lost everything during the Depression. "That was my best day," O'Neil said. "I hit for the cycle and I met my Ora."[22]

Their relationship became a long-distance one as O'Neil was drafted into the Navy that year. He was assigned to the Stevedore Battalion. "Our job was to load and unload ships," the veteran remembered, "first in the Mariana Islands and then at Subic Bay in the Philippines."[23] He saw the same type of segregation in the Navy as he saw in the Jim Crow South. "Our own government, which was putting our lives on the line for freedom, was the one telling us to sit at the back of the bus," he said. "If I had captured a Japanese prisoner, I do believe the Navy would have treated him better than it did me."[24] O'Neil was a Bosun (or Boatswain) First Class officer responsible for a crew of a dozen men. He was once complimented on his leadership skills. "If you were white, you'd be an officer by now," he was told.[25]

O'Neil spent his free time writing letters home to Ora, who accepted his proposal for marriage when the war was over. Friends also sent him clippings from the black newspapers so he could stay updated on the Monarchs. "The Negro Leagues didn't exist as far as the *Stars and Stripes* (the newspaper of the armed forces) was concerned," O'Neil said.[26] In those clippings, he learned about a rising star on the 1945 Monarchs, Jackie Robinson, who tore up the league with a .384 average. Later that fall, O'Neil was summoned by his commanding officer. "I just thought you should know that the Brooklyn Dodgers have just signed Jackie Robinson," he told O'Neil. "He's going to play for their minor league team in Montreal next year." Overjoyed, O'Neil jumped on the intercom and announced the news to the crew. "We started hollering and shouting and firing our guns into the air," he remembered. "I don't know that we made that much noise on VJ Day. This was progress for the whole country. It didn't matter who was the first or which team had the courage; this was the real first step toward integration, toward equality, since maybe Reconstruction."[27]

O'Neil came home and married Ora on January 17, 1946. "Her parents didn't want her to marry a ballplayer, you know," he recalled six decades later. "But I won them over. Her father asked me what my father did. I told him: 'He's in recreation.' And he was too. He ran a pool hall. He did some bootlegging. You know…recreation."[28]

After spring training, the newlyweds moved to Kansas City and Ora secured a teaching job. Buck returned to his familiar first base position for the Monarchs, who played the Newark Eagles in the World Series. The series went back and forth and concluded with a Game Seven in Newark before 7,500 fans. O'Neil, never a power hitter, hit his second home run of the series in the sixth inning to tie the score, 1-1.[29] Newark won the tight contest, 3-2, their only Negro League championship. Wilkinson, who had created the franchise in 1920, sold out his ownership shares to long-time partner Tom Baird, who then named the 36-year-old O'Neil as player-manager.[30] Traveling secretary Dizzy Dismukes helped Buck understand his new role as "some guys need pats on the back, some guys need kicks in the butt, and some guys just plain need to be left alone," O'Neil said. "And some guys need all three."[31]

O'Neil guided the Monarchs to the Negro American League championship, winning the first half of their season while Birmingham won the second half. They played each other in a seven-game series, won by Birmingham, which went on to win the final Negro League World Series over the Homestead Grays.

The Negro National League folded that offseason. The Monarchs were still successful into the early 50s, but by then the existing Negro American League was a shell of its former greatness. To survive, clubs needed to act as minor league teams, discovering young talent they could then sell to major league teams for profit. Besides handling expenses, schedules, travel arrangements and personnel matters, O'Neil now needed to become a scout to keep the team afloat. Integration meant newspapers provided very little coverage of the Negro Leagues, which were greatly depleted.

Still, O'Neil discovered and mentored some of the greatest players in baseball history. When New York Yankees scout Tom Greenwade came looking to sign Willard Brown, Buck steered him in another direction. "The player you should be looking at is our young catcher," he told him. For $25,000 Elston Howard became the first African-American New York Yankee, enjoying a 14-

Legendary Monarchs first baseman Buck O'Neil batted .280 during the 1942 NAL season, but he took the wood to the Grays at a .375 clip in the World Series. (Courtesy Noir-Tech Research, Inc.)

year, all-star filled career.[32] In 1950, Cool Papa Bell told O'Neil that he needed to go see a 17-year-old shortstop playing for the Black Sheepherders in San Antonio, Texas. O'Neil drove to Dallas and signed the prospect without even seeing him play. "Cool's word was good enough for me," O'Neil said. "Turns out it was good enough for the Hall of Fame. The young man was Ernie Banks."[33] After a couple of years in the military, Banks returned to the Monarchs and now attracted great attention around baseball. So, in 1953, the Chicago Cubs offered the Monarchs $20,000 for the man who would become "Mr. Cub." "Buck O'Neil helped me in many ways. He installed a positive influence," Banks said.[34] "He was a delight right from the start, on the field and off," O'Neil remembered of Banks.[35]

"Toward the end," O'Neil recalled of his last years in Kansas City, "the league got so raggedy that I used myself as a pitcher." After winning his first game, he started himself again the next day. "Buck O'Neil the pitcher might still be out there if Buck O'Neil the manager hadn't taken him out after goodness knows how many runs and just a few innings."[36] In 1955, Baird sold the Monarchs to Ted Rasberry, who turned the club into a barnstorming team based out of Michigan. The Philadelphia Athletics moved to Kansas City the same year, so now local baseball fans had a major league team to cheer for. For at least a three-year period (1953-1955), O'Neil managed the West squad at the annual All-Star game of the Negro American League.[37]

At the end of the 1955 season, O'Neil's long association with the Kansas City Monarchs came to an end. His statistics, like all statistics from the Negro Leagues, are incomplete and often fail to tell the true story. There were so many games in so many places, and O'Neil believed his best games were never recorded. "I was a .300 hitter, no doubt," he said. The Seamheads Negro Leagues Database gives O'Neil a lifetime batting average of .261, while Baseball-Reference.com credits him with a .283 average and the Center for Negro League Baseball Research gives the highest projection of .303.[38] The Negro Leagues Baseball Museum credits O'Neil with a .288 career average. O'Neil also led the Negro American League in batting with a .353 average in 1946.[39] Whichever statistical source is used, it is agreed O'Neil was a solid contact hitter who played fine defense at first base.

O'Neil was signed to scout for the Chicago Cubs at the end of the 1955 season. He would focus on the South, looking for African-American players who would feel at ease with his visits. He would also work with players during spring training as well as drive around in his Plymouth Fury looking for talent wherever his hunches would lead him. Whereas today scouting is based on statistics and advanced analytics, O'Neil depended on his instincts, which led him to some excellent and even legendary players.

One day in 1968 O'Neil watched a group of unimpressive semipro players in Montgomery, Alabama. On his way out he saw a small, skinny, 18-year-old. There was something about how this kid maneuvered on the field. O'Neil raced out to him to say hello. "I'm Buck O'Neil, a scout for the Cubs," he said. "And I want to see you play." The youngster stuttered and tripped over his words trying to explain how to find a field he would be playing at the next day. O'Neil drove down the dusty back roads until he found a beautiful little park with people sitting on lawn chairs. He stayed in his car and just watched one at-bat. It didn't matter that the kid flied out—O'Neil saw his bat speed, his timing, and heard the crack of his bat. He sped off immediately to go file his report to the Cubs, describing this kid from the Alabama woods they needed to sign. "It's a great name, isn't it?" O'Neil said when recounting the story. "Oscar Gamble! That sounds like a ballplayer. And he was. He was a heck of a ballplayer." Gamble would go on to a memorable 17-year career and become a postseason hero.[40]

O'Neil also watched a freshman at Southern University who struggled at the plate but had tremendous speed. Despite his up-and-down success at the plate, O'Neil promised he would top any offer from another team. "He got me started on a journey that became a 19-year major league baseball career," said Lou Brock, a future Hall-of-Famer. "He shaped the character of young black men. He touched the heart of everyone who loved the game. He gave us all a voice that could be heard on and off the field. We who were close to him will forever seek to walk in the shade of his shadow."[41]

The Chicago Cubs promoted O'Neil to its major league coaching staff in 1962, making Buck the first African-American coach to serve on a major league roster.[42] Such an accomplishment earned him recognition in both *Sports Illustrated* and *Ebony*. "When a fellow makes a mistake," O'Neil told *Ebony*, "you don't ride him. You show him what he's supposed to do and make him believe he can do it. You have to make him believe in himself."[43]

It was difficult to believe the Cubs managerial situation. The unique setup of owner Phil Wrigley had a regular rotation among several coaches to take the stress off of one individual. "It was a ridiculous idea," O'Neil said long after the fact, "although I was quoted in the *Ebony* article as saying it was a 'wonderful innovation' that would 'be adopted by most teams.' What was I supposed to say?"[44] O'Neil was told he would become part of the rotation, which would have made him the first African-American to manage a major league game, but the promise wasn't fulfilled and it would be over a decade before a major league team would hire a minority manager.

O'Neil returned full time to scouting with the Cubs in 1964, where he remained through the 1988 season. Two future stars he signed were Hall of Fame closer Lee Smith, who finished with 478 career saves, and Joe Carter, who slammed 396 home runs and became a World Series hero.

O'Neil planned to retire after the 1988 season. Ora had retired in 1983 after 31 years of teaching in the Kansas City Public School system. But then he got a call from the Kansas City Royals and was soon scouting for the team in the city he had first moved to 50 years before, long before the days of million-dollar salaries and television broadcasts. "I've been fortunate enough to make my living at something I've loved," O'Neil said. "When I started I was making $100 a month, with $1 a day for meal money. But in those days you could get breakfast for 25 cents and dinner for 35 cents. We didn't eat more than two meals a day."[45]

While much had changed over his lifetime, the crack of the bat was the same as ever for O'Neil. He remembered distinct cracks that became milestones in his life. As a boy in St. Petersburg he clearly remembered the sound "like a small stick of dynamite going off" when Babe Ruth was batting. He heard the sound again in 1938 and ran out to the field to see Josh Gibson at the plate. Now with the Royals 50 years later, he heard the same crack from Bo Jackson's bat. "I'm going to keep going to the ballpark until I hear that sound again," was O'Neil's promise.[46]

O'Neil also worked tirelessly towards the creation of a permanent Negro Leagues museum. The original museum began in a small, one-room office in 1990. O'Neil and Kansas City Royals legend Frank White were among the original board of directors and they took turns paying the rent.[47] A better facility was needed. "If we don't do something with the museum, the memory of black baseball is going to die," he said. "All that's left is a few of us, and we're losing them every year. We're going to preserve stuff that's in attics and going to rot and guy's grandkids are going to throw out. It's kind of an exciting time around here for me right now."[48] A new expanded museum opened in 1994.[49]

A month later, millions of people discovered O'Neil for the first time thanks to film director Ken Burns' epic nine-part documentary series *Baseball*, produced for Public Television. "I think what I have talked about are the same things I have talked about for a long time, but now someone is listening," O'Neil said about the large audience which could now hear his stories. "I've been talking about this for 60 years. Now I've got an ear."[50] O'Neil became a celebrity of sorts, a living legend who traveled with Burns to promote the film. "It's kind of nice to be discovered when you're eighty-two years old," he said.[51] Burns remembered the awe surrounding O'Neil when they met for the interviews. "There's nothing you can say about Buck O'Neil that one second in his presence won't prove a hundred times over," Burns said. "It is impossible to resist the positive force that lights him from within and then spreads out and lights and warms you, too."[52]

In 1995 Buck returned to Sarasota High School to finally receive his diploma. "Sixty-nine years after I cried because I couldn't go to Sarasota High School, I was crying because I was about to graduate," O'Neil said. "I was almost too choked up to speak. But I did. I told those students that I had talked to my parents and my sister the day before. And in my conversation, I let Mamma and Papa and Fanny know that I would be going to Sarasota High School the next day to graduate. You can't see them, I told the students, but they're here today. I feel them."[53]

Kansas City began plans for an expanded facility to house both the Negro Leagues Museum and the new American Jazz Museum.[54] The project was part of Kansas City's revitalization of the historic 18th and Vine district. The new museum opened November 1, 1997.[55] For all the hard work that had gone into the museum, it was a somber time for O'Neil; Ora passed away from cancer the following day after 51 years of marriage.[56] She had battled the disease the last 15 years of her life but was committed to her dream to live long enough to see the project to its finish. "'She said I made it,'" O'Neil recalled. "And she died in my arms."[57]

• When the Monarchs Reigned •

Buck O'Neil continued scouting through the 1990s and was named the Midwest Scout of the Year in 1998.[58] In 2001, the Kansas City area celebrated Buck's 90th birthday by renaming a street "John 'Buck' O'Neil Way" and hearing best wishes read from President George W. Bush.[59]

An unlikely friendship developed in 2001 as O'Neil welcomed Japanese hitting star Ichiro Suzuki to the Negro Leagues Museum. Ichiro noticed the well-dressed man hanging around the batting cages when the Mariners visited Kauffman Stadium. They were from two totally different cultures, eras, and bank accounts: the multi-millionaire star from Japan and the poor boy from the Jim Crow south. Yet O'Neil, as he did in many situations, connected with people from all walks of life. "With Buck, I felt something big," Ichiro said. "The way he carried himself, you can see and tell and feel he loved this game. And when you see that presence, it makes you want to know more about him."[60] The two formed a close friendship.

O'Neil spent the days around his 94th birthday in 2005 traveling to Washington D.C. and speaking before Congress, asking for an official proclamation that the Negro Leagues Museum be designated as America's Negro Leagues Baseball Museum.[61]

In 2006, O'Neil was still listed in the Royals Media Guide as a part-time scout.[62] It is believed that O'Neil scouted 13 eventual major leaguers over his career.[63] Sportswriter Joe Posnanski had the priceless opportunity to travel with O'Neil across the country for speaking engagements and other events to promote the Negro Leagues. Their road trip is chronicled in Posnanski's book *The Soul of Baseball: A Road Trip Through Buck O'Neil's America*.

On one occasion, the duo were parked at 18th and Vine. Despite the attempts at revitalization, it was still just a shell of its glory days. O'Neil was now the last of the Kansas City Monarchs from the 1930s, but the images were still fresh in his mind. "One day I was walking around here with Duke Ellington," he recalled of the Jazz legend. They went into a club and "we hear this chubby Kansas City kid blowing on his saxophone. He played it fast and wild and all over the place." It was another Jazz legend: Charlie Parker. "People feel sorry for me," O'Neil said. "Man, I heard Charlie Parker."[64]

O'Neil served as a representative of the Negro Leagues on the Hall of Fame Veterans Committee from 1981-2000, and 11 Negro Leagues players were inducted through 2001 for a total of 18. Yet there was still a feeling that many more had been missed.[65] In 2000, Major League Baseball supplied a grant to the Baseball Hall of Fame to conduct extensive research on the history of the Negro Leagues. This fruitful work led to 9,500 pages of compiled data on games and over 6,000 players, information now available to the modern researcher. This work also led to the formation of a committee in 2005 to consider Negro League players and executives who deserved to be inducted into the Hall of Fame the following year.[66] Many felt O'Neil was long overdue for election because of his many contributions in representing the Negro Leagues. There was public outrage, especially in the Kansas City area, when he missed election by one vote.

"All his life," wrote Posnanski in the *Kansas City Star*, "Buck O'Neil has had doors slammed in his face. He played baseball at a time when the major leagues did not allow black players. He was a gifted manager at a time when major league owners would not even think of having an African-American lead their teams. For more than 30 years, he told stories about Negro League players and nobody wanted to listen. Now, after everything, he was being told that the life he had

Buck O'Neil on the basepaths for the Monarchs. He later co-founded the Negro Leagues Baseball Museum and was featured in Ken Burns' television documentary series on baseball. (Courtesy Noir-Tech Research, Inc.)

spent in baseball was not worthy of the Hall of Fame. It was enough to make those around him cry. But Buck laughed." O'Neil simply said, "That's the way the cookie crumbles. I'm still Buck. Look at me. I've lived a good life. I'm still living a good life. Nothing has changed for me."[67]

"You know why Buck is alive today, playing golf, driving his Caddy, traveling the globe and enjoying unprecedented popularity and support?" asked writer Jason Whitlock. "Because he never got swallowed by anger, because he never allowed other people's behavior to dictate his behavior, because he refused to view himself as a victim. He's no victim today."[68] While O'Neil exhibited no anger, the same could not be said for Ernie Banks. "All of those people whose lives he touched and played with . . . it is a travesty. It really hurt my heart. It hurt me. I wish I could surrender my election to baseball's Hall of Fame to him, because I always felt that he deserved it more than I did."[69]

While friends took swings at the seemingly neglectful committee, O'Neil took his final swings at the plate. O'Neil actually played in the All-Star game of the Northern League, an independent professional league, in Kansas City, Kansas, on July 18. The 94-year-old, batting leadoff for the West club, took a couple of pitches before drawing the planned intentional walk. He was quickly replaced, then was "traded" to the Kansas City T-Bones, allowing him to lead off the bottom of the first. He drew his second walk of the game.[70]

O'Neil took to the podium at the Hall of Fame Induction Ceremony at the end of July to speak for the 17 Negro League players and executives who never lived to see such recognition. "I've been a lot of places," he said. "I've done a lot of things I really liked doing ... but I'd rather be right here, right now, representing the people who helped build a bridge across the chasm of prejudice." He added, "I'm proud to have been a Negro Leagues ballplayer." In his last few minutes on stage, O'Neil asked the Hall-of-Famers behind him and the audience to join hands as he led them in singing, "The greatest thing in all my life…is loving you."[71]

It was a fitting conclusion to Buck O'Neil's life. He passed away on October 6, 2006, just shy of his 95th birthday. He had, as even he said, lived "a full life."[72] A funeral was held at the African Methodist Episcopal church in Kansas City which the O'Neils had attended since 1947. Thousands attended a public memorial service held later that day at Kansas City's Municipal Auditorium.[73] Many of his words were recalled, including these:

People ask me: How do you keep from being bitter? Man, bitterness will eat you up inside. Hatred will eat you up inside. Don't be bitter. Don't hate. My grandfather was a slave. He was not bitter. I learned that from him. And you know what? I wouldn't trade my life for anybody's. I've had so many blessings in my life. I don't want people to be sad for me when I go. Be sad for the kids who die young. You shouldn't feel sad for a man who lived his dream. You know what I always say? I was right on time.[74]

Awards and recognitions continued to come for O'Neil. He was posthumously awarded the Presidential Medal of Freedom, the nation's highest civilian honor, by President George W. Bush. "A beautiful human being," Bush said of O'Neil, with Warren O'Neil accepting the award on his brother's behalf. "Buck O'Neil lived long enough to see the game of baseball, and America, change for the better. He's one of the people we can thank for that."[75] In 2008, the Baseball Hall of Fame unveiled a life-sized statue of O'Neil placed inside the front entrance, and also introduced the Buck O'Neil Lifetime Achievement Award, presented every three years "to honor an individual whose extraordinary efforts enhanced baseball's positive impact on society, broadened the game's appeal, and whose character, integrity and dignity are comparable to the qualities exhibited by O'Neil."[76]

A bust of O'Neil was placed in the third-floor rotunda at the Missouri state capitol of Jefferson City and he was inducted into the Hall of Famous Missourians. "There is no doubt that he (O'Neil) belongs here among the greatest citizens in the history of our state," House Speaker Steven Tilley said.[77] In 2016, Kansas City's Broadway Bridge was renamed the Buck O'Neil Bridge.[78] O'Neil's legacy also lives on in a physical way at Kauffman Stadium. The very seat he occupied behind home plate was designated the Buck O'Neil Legacy Seat. The seat is filled for every Royals home game by "a member of the community who, on a large or small scale, embodies an aspect of Buck's spirit."[79]

The former YMCA building near 18th and Vine which served as the site of the founding of the Negro National League in 1920 became the Buck O'Neil Research and Education Center in 2017.[80] The facility provides educational programs for students. In the summer of 2018, vandals caused $500,000 damage to the facility. An outpouring of financial support, called a "Buck-like" measure of love, followed "to heal and focus on what can be done instead of what went wrong," wrote Vahe Gregorian of the *Kansas City Star*.

And the stories continue, right on time.

Sources

In addition to the sources listed in the notes, special thanks are given to Cassidy Lent, reference librarian at the A. Bartlett Giamatti Research Center at the Baseball Hall of Fame. Other sources include:

Baseball-Reference.com

Seamheads Negro Leagues Database

Wulf, Steve. "The Guiding Light: Buck O'Neil Bears Witness to the Glory and Not Just the Shame of the Negro Leagues," *Sports Illustrated*, September 19, 1994: 169-179.

Notes

1   Buck O'Neil with Steve Wulf and David Conrads, *I Was Right on Time* (New York: Simon & Schuster, 1996), 4.

2   O'Neil, Wulf, and Conrads, 3.

3   Lawrence D. Hogan, *Shades of Glory: The Negro Leagues and the Story of African-American Baseball*.

4   O'Neil, Wulf, and Conrads, 17-19.

5   O'Neil, Wulf, and Conrads, 17-24.

6   Interview with Ken Burns. pbs.org/kenburns/baseball/shadowball/oneil.html Retrieved November 25, 2018.

7   Interview with Burns.

8   O'Neil, Wulf, and Conrads, 230.

9   O'Neil, Wulf, and Conrads, 12.

10 O'Neil, Wulf, and Conrads, 36-42.

11 O'Neil, Wulf, and Conrads, 46.

12 O'Neil, Wulf, and Conrads, 55.

13 O'Neil, Wulf, and Conrads, 52-54.

14 O'Neil, Wulf, and Conrads, 66.

15 O'Neil, Wulf, and Conrads, 66.

16 Joe Posnanski, *The Soul of Baseball: A Road Trip Through Buck O'Neil's America* (New York: Harper, 2007), 21.

17 O'Neil, Wulf, and Conrads, 73.

18 O'Neil, Wulf, and Conrads, 76.

19 O'Neil, Wulf, and Conrads, 86; "No Run off Kranston," *Kansas City Times*, May 16, 1938: 12.

20 O'Neil, Wulf, and Conrads, 119.

21 O'Neil, Wulf, and Conrads, 14-15.

22 Joe Posnanski, "A KC Legend Dies—Baseball Icon 'Lived a Full Life' as he Came to Symbolize the Glory of the Negro Leagues," *Kansas City Star*, October 7, 2006: 1.

23 O'Neil, Wulf, and Conrads, 159.

24 O'Neil, Wulf, and Conrads, 159.

25 O'Neil, Wulf, and Conrads, 160.

26 O'Neil, Wulf, and Conrads, 162.

27 O'Neil, Wulf, and Conrads, 165.

28 Posnanski, *The Soul of Baseball*, 50.

29 "Newark Eagles New Diamond Champs," *Pittsburgh Courier*, October 5, 1946: 15.

30 "A Ball Club Sale," *Kansas City Star*, February 12, 1948: 20.

31 O'Neil, Wulf, and Conrads, 186.

32 O'Neil, Wulf, and Conrads, 189; Cecilia Tan, "Elston Howard." SABR BioProject. sabr.org/bioproj/person/e6884b08 Retrieved November 22, 2018.

33 O'Neil, Wulf, and Conrads, 189-190.

34 Joseph Wancho, "Ernie Banks." SABR BioProject. sabr.org/bioproj/person/b8afee6e Retrieved November 22, 2018.

35 O'Neil, Wulf, and Conrads, 190.

36 O'Neil, Wulf, and Conrads, 195-196.

37 "O'Neil Named Pilot of Negro West Squad," *Chicago Tribune*, July 10, 1955: A4.

38 Dr. Layton Revel and Luis Munoz, "Forgotten Heroes: John 'Buck' O'Neil," Center for Negro League Baseball Research, 2013. www.cnlbr.org/Portals/0/Hero/John-Buck-ONeil.pdf; Thanks to Gary Ashwill of the Seamheads database for providing context on these statistics.

39 "John 'Buck' O'Neil," nlbemuseum.com/history/players/oneil.html

40 Joe Posnanski, "Gamble Made Legendary O'Neil Proud," mlb.com/news/oscar-gamble-made-buck-oneil-proud/c-265614542 Retrieved November 23, 2018.

41 Associated Press, "Brock, Others, Remember Buck O'Neil at Funeral," October 15, 2006. espn.com/mlb/news/story?id=2625618 Retrieved November 22, 2018.

42 Richard Dozer, "Cubs Sign Negro Coach," *Chicago Tribune*, May 30, 1962: 47.

43 "First Negro Coach in Majors," *Ebony* 17, no. 10 (1962), 29; The *Sports Illustrated* blurb was in "Faces in the Crowd,"   (June 24, 1962), 75.

44 O'Neil, Wulf, and Conrads, 213.

45 Laura R. Hockaday, "Baseball Has Changed a Lot in 53 Years. Buck O'Neil, Formerly a KC Monarch, Recalls $100-a-month Salaries," *Kansas City Star*, November 24, 1991: F4.

46 O'Neil, Wulf, and Conrads, 3-4.

47 Maria Torres, "Royals Legend Frank White will be Honored with Buck O'Neil Legacy Award," kansascity.com/sports/mlb/kansas-city-royals/article181136991.html Retrieved January 19, 2019; Jack Etkin, "Negro Leagues to be Preserved. Museum Set to Unveil an Early-Day Display of Black Baseball Stars," *Kansas City Star*, February 12, 1991: C1; Jack Etkin, "Museum Looks for Support," *Kansas City Star*, June 21, 1990: D1.

48 Jack Etkin, "In More Ways Than One, O'Neil Holds Special Spot; Ex-KC Monarch has Seat, Ideas of His Own in Role as Royals Scout," *Kansas City Star*, September 8, 1991.

49 Howard Richman, "Museum Has Grand Beginning; Negro Leagues Stars Now at 18th and Vine For Everyone to See," *Kansas City Star*, August 6, 1994: D1.

50 La Velle E. Neal III, "A Star is Born…at 82. 'Baseball' Becomes O'Neil's Private Forum," *Kansas City Star*, September 22, 1994: D1.

51 O'Neil, Wulf, and Conrads, 2.

52 O'Neil, Wulf, and Conrads, xiii.

53 O'Neil, Wulf, and Conrads, 232-233.

54 "About NLBM," nlbm.com/s/about.htm Retrieved November 25, 2018.

• BUCK O'NEIL •

55 Yael T. Abouhalkah, "Baseball's Champion Buck O'Neil Stands Tall as Negro League Museum Opens," *Kansas City Star*, October 31, 1997: C6.

56 Tom Smith, "Big Weekend Turns Sad for O'Neil," *Kansas City Star*, November 3, 1997: C2.

57 Randy Covitz, "Buck and Ora Were About Love," Kansascity.com, October 8, 2006. kansascity.com/sports/article295461/Buck-and-Ora-were-about-love.html Retrieved December 1, 2018.

58 Dick Kaegel, "Pitching Coach Kison is Fired by the Royals," *Kansas City Star*, October 21, 1998: D5.

59 Joe Posnanski, "This Buck Won't Stop—This KC Legend May be 90, but the Stories Keep Coming—Like the One About…" *Kansas City Star*, November 14, 2001: D1.

60 Jeff Passan, "Ichiro Draws From Lessons Learned From Friend Buck O'Neil as He Ponders Future with Mariners," Yahoo Sports, July 19, 2012. yahoo.com/news/ichiro-draws-from-lessons-learned-from-friend-buck-o-neil-as-he-ponders-future-with-mariners.html Retrieved December 1, 2018.

61 Joe Posnanski, "Politicians Pay Attention When Mr. O'Neil Goes to Washington," *Kansas City Star*, November 16, 2005: D1.

62 Jeffrey Flanagan, "O'Neil to Royals Hall Would Be a Nice Gift," *Kansas City Star*, September 26, 2006: C2.

63 Thanks to Rod Nelson of the SABR Scouts Research Committee for this information.

64 Posnanski, *The Soul of Baseball*, 38.

65 "Past Inductions," baseballhall.org/hall-of-famers/past-inductions/past-inductions

66 "Negro League Researchers and Authors Group," baseballhall.org/hall-of-famers/rules/759 Retrieved January 19, 2019.

67 Joe Posnaski, "Injustice, and Then a Gutless Committee Clams up," *Kansas City Star*, February 28, 2006: A1.

68 Jason Whitlock, "Buck's Love Overpowers the Injustice," *Kansas City Star*, March 1, 2006: D1.

69 "Buck O'Neil, 1911-2006," *Chicago Tribune*, October 8, 2006.

70 Associated Press, "At 94, O'Neil Oldest-Ever Pro Baseball Player," *Hays Daily News* (Kansas), July 19, 2006: 11.

71 Bob Dutton, "Showstopper—Buck O'Neil Puts Personal Disappointment Aside as He Celebrates the Lives of Other Negro League Legends During Induction Ceremony," *Kansas City Star*, July 31, 2006; C1.

72 Posnanski, "A KC Legend Dies,"

73 Associated Press, "Brock, Others Remember Buck O'Neil at Funeral," October 15, 2006. espn.com/mlb/news/story?id=2625618 Retrieved November 25, 2018.

74 Joe Posnanski, "Farewell, Old Friend—The Man Who Was More Than a Baseball Great is Gone, But he Leaves a Legacy of Living, Loving," *Kansas City Star*, October 15, 2006: A1.

75 Matt Stearns, "Bush Confers Honor on Buck—He is Awarded the Presidential Medal of Freedom, the Nation's Highest Civilian Honor," *Kansas City Star*, December 16, 2006: 1; The citation reads: "Buck O'Neil represented excellence and determination both on and off the baseball field. Rising above the injustice of a segregated country and sport, he served his Nation in World War II, was a talented player and manager in the Negro Leagues, and was Major League Baseball's first African-American coach. As a co-founder of and inspiration for the Negro Leagues Baseball Museum, he served as the Museum's Chairman of the Board and worked to ensure that generations of baseball legends would not be forgotten. The United States posthumously honors John 'Buck' O Neil for his generous spirit, devotion to baseball, and unyielding commitment to equality."

76 "Buck O'Neil Award," baseballhall.org/discover-more/awards/890 Retrieved November 25, 2018.

77 Wes Duplantier, "Buck O'Neil Honored as a Famous Missourian," kansascity.com/news/local/article301253/Buck-ONeil-honored-as-a-famous-Missourian.html Retrieved November 27, 2018.

78 Andrew Lynch, "A Dream Come True: Broadway Bridge Renamed for Monarchs Legend Buck O'Neil," fox4kc.com/2016/06/24/a-dream-come-true-broadway-bridge-renamed-for-monarchs-legend-buck-oneil/ Retrieved November 25, 2018.

79 "Buck O'Neil Legacy Seat Program." mlb.com/royals/community/buck-oneil-seat Retrieved December 22, 2018.

80 Editorial Board, "Vandals Damaged Buck O'Neil Center. KC Should Rally Around a Baseball Legend's Vision," *Kansas City Star*, June 26, 2018.

SATCHEL PAIGE

By Larry Tye

Satchel Paige threw his first pitch in professional baseball in 1926 for the Chattanooga White Sox, an inappropriately-named team in the lower levels of the segregated Negro Leagues. He played his last game in organized baseball in 1966 — a full 40 years later — for a Virginia club called the Peninsula Pilots. In between, the Hall of Famer pitched more baseballs, in more ballparks, for more teams, than any player in history. It also is safe to say that no pitcher ever threw at a higher level, for longer, than the ageless right-hander with the whimsical nickname.

Satchel entered the world as Leroy Robert Page. He was delivered at home into the hands of a midwife, which was more help than most poor women could afford in 1906 in Mobile, Alabama. His mother, Lula, was a washerwoman who already spent her nights worrying how to feed and sustain the four daughters and two sons who had come before. Five more would follow. Leroy's father, John, alternated between the luxuriant lilies in the gardens he tended uptown and the corner stoops on which he liked to loiter, rarely making time to care for his expanding brood. With skin the shade of chestnut and a birthplace in the heartland of the former Confederacy, the newborn's prospects looked woeful. They were about to get worse.

For more than 200 years Mobile had welcomed outsiders — Irish Catholics fleeing the famine, Jewish merchants, along with legions of Creoles, the free offspring of French or Spanish fathers and chattel mothers — and they in turn challenged inbred thinking on everything from politics to race. The result, during the post-Civil War period of Reconstruction, was a blurring of color lines in ways unthinkable in Montgomery, Selma, and most of the rest of Alabama.[1] Unfortunately for young Leroy, that live-and-let-live mindset had begun fraying by the turn of the century and it unraveled entirely the very season of his birth, when a local ordinance mandated separate seating on streetcars. Blacks were barred from most restaurants, cemeteries, saloons, hotels, and brothels. Whites and Blacks were not allowed to attend the same school, marry one another, or play baseball on the same fields of green. Leroy Page was too young to understand those developments but they were reinforced every day he spent in his native city. Those first few years, "I was no different from any other kid," he wrote half a century on, "only in Mobile I was a nigger kid. I went around with the back of my shirt torn, a pair of dirty diapers or raggedy pieces of trousers covering me. Shoes? They was someplace else."[2]

All the Page kids knew by the age of six that they had to help to put food on the table and, in a good year, shoes on their feet. Leroy worked the alleyways like a pro, cashing in empty bottles he found there. Delivering ice also brought in small change. But he was springing up like a weed in a bog, and as he grew so did Lula's and John's expectations of his earning power. The obvious place to look for work was the nearby L&N station, where the pint-sized porter polished the boots of wealthy white travelers or carried their bags to hotels like Mobile's luxurious Battle House for as little as a dime. Realizing he could not bring home a real day's pay if he made just 10 cents at a time, he got a pole and some rope and jerry-rigged a contraption that let him sling together two, three, or four satchels and cart them all at once. His invention quadrupled his income. It also drew chuckles from the other baggage boys. "You look like a walking satchel tree," one of them yelled. The description fit him to a tee and it stuck. "LeRoy Paige," he said, "became no more and Satchel Paige took over."[3]

His last name eventually was rewritten, too, from Page to Paige. "Page looked too much like page in a book," his mother offered. Satchel had a more exotic explanation: "My folks started out by spelling their name 'Page' and later stuck in the 'i' to make themselves sound more high-tone."[4]

While he played baseball as a boy, it was in reform school that he became a player. Two weeks before his 12th birthday Satchel was sentenced to the Alabama Reform School for Juvenile Negro Law-Breakers. It was partly that he missed school so often. And at the L&N station he stopped pulling and started purloining suitcases, along with anything else that was easy to grab. Now court officials were telling him he would not see freedom again for six long years. It seemed like a bad dream until they shut the door on him. That is when he knew it was real.

The good news was that his new home gave him endless time for his favorite pastime: pitching a baseball. There was a coach, too, Edward Byrd, who for the first time taught Satchel the fundamentals, and for the first time Satchel paid attention. Byrd's young protégé had an anatomy that was all up and down. Rising more than six feet and weighing barely 140 pounds, Satchel joked that if he stood sideways you could not see him. His wiry arms and stilt-like legs were aerodynamically perfect to propel a ball from mound to plate. They gave him motion. Momentum. Strength. And he had the ideal launching pads: hands so huge they made a baseball look like a golf ball, with wrists that snapped with the fury and flash of a catapult. Byrd understood what God had given this manful boy with his outsized appetites, limbs, and talents, and the coach was determined that it not be squandered. He showed Satchel exactly how to exploit his storehouse of kinetic energy. The first thing was to kick his foot so high before unleashing the baseball that it blacked out the sky and befuddled the batter. Then the novice pitcher swung his arm far enough forward that it seemed like his hand was right in the batter's face when he let go of the ball. So was born the Paige pose, the look that over the decades made Satchel stand out from pitchers before and after: left leg held skyward, right arm stretched as far as it would go behind him, the catapult cocked to give the ball maximum power as he whirled forward to release it.[5]

His coach also showed him that physical gifts were not all it took to win. Satchel had to outwit his opponent. Watch a batter's knees, Byrd advised, the way a bullfighter studies a bull. Detect any weakness in the setup of his feet, his stance, the positioning of his bat. Then put the ball where the slugger can't hit it. Satchel was better at doing that than anyone who had ever come through the reform school. It was less his accuracy, more his velocity. He threw hard. No curveball or slider, no change of pace or special finesse. Not yet. Oftentimes he almost fell off the mound as he was letting go of the ball. He was as wild as young and untamed pitchers often are. Sometimes his pitches hit a batter, or several. However unconventional his demeanor, he delivered. A baseball weighs just five ounces — it is a mass of cork wound with woolen yarn and bound in cowhide — but flying off of Satchel's fingers it resembled a cannonball. Most who came to the plate failed to connect by what looked like a mile. And he kept getting better, the way Coach Byrd said he could. Looking back, Satchel said of his time under Byrd's tutelage, "You might say I traded five years of freedom to learn how to pitch."[6]

The young hurler quickly put those lessons to work for a series of Negro League teams, starting with Chattanooga and progressing to bigger, better clubs in Birmingham, Baltimore, Cleveland, Pittsburgh and Kansas City. The best available information suggests that he had an overall record in Black baseball of 103-61, with 1,231 strikeouts and just 253 bases on balls.[7] Those numbers, compiled for a study supported by Major League Baseball, understate his dominance because he was not used in a conventional way. Stats of Negro Leaguers continue to be reevaluated as new records are unearthed. The latest on Satchel, as of early 2021 on seamheads.com, are 115-62, with 1,524 strikeouts and just 360 bases on balls.[8]

As the best drawing card in the Negro Leagues, he started often, but might leave the game after three or four innings, which was too short an appearance to be credited with a win but long enough to be stuck with a loss. The records also don't include his games barnstorming in small towns across the country the way he did between games and seasons for more than 40 years, playing against sandlotters, semi-pros, and big leaguers from California to the Caribbean, or playing for teams like the one in Bismarck, North Dakota, where he managed a 35-2 mark over two seasons. Even the official Negro League games did not always produce records that were complete or reliable, since Blackball generally could afford neither statisticians nor record keepers.

Satchel defied that shadowy system by keeping his own records. He carried a notebook listing innings pitched, game scores, opponents, strikeouts, bases on balls, and, according to one sportswriter who said he saw it, "a very important item to [Satchel], his end of the gate."[9] The Paige almanac had him pitching in more than 2,500 games and winning 2,000 or so. He professed to have labored for 250 teams and thrown 250 shutouts. His per-game strikeout record was 22, against major-league barnstormers, which would have been an all-time record for all of baseball. Other claims that would have set marks: 50 no-hitters, 29 starts in a month, 21 straight wins, 62 consecutive scoreless innings, 153 pitching appearances in a year, and three wins the same day.[10]

• When the Monarchs Reigned •

The numbers were dizzying, but each required an asterisk explaining that Satchel kept records the way he set them: with flair, grace, and hoopla. The numbers changed as he added to his accomplishments and as yet another reporter wanted to peak at his books. Each longed for something new and daring, an exclusive to impress their editors; none asked why the numbers or stories kept shifting. His tally of no-hitters was as low as 20, as high as a hundred, and perhaps most accurately, "so many . . . I disremember the number." The picture was equally muddled for shutouts. Press accounts, and Satchel's, offered options: 250, 300, or 330. Sometimes he dished out a figure so outrageous he seemed to be testing whether his reader was paying attention, like when he wrote that "I never batted less than .300 any season." (His career Negro Leagues average was .218; in the majors he dropped to .097.)[11]

Just when any serious statistician might be tempted to dismiss it all as a ruse, closer scrutiny suggests that much of it was true. Pitching 2,500 games seems inconceivable since the major-league record-holder, Jesse Orosco, managed just 1,252. But Orosco's numbers are just for the big leagues, where he pitched 24 years starting every April and ending, when he was lucky, in October. Satchel's include games played as a semipro and professional, in the Negro Leagues, on barnstorming tours, in Latin America and Canada as well as the United States, and in the major and minor leagues. He played spring and summer, fall and winter. He often threw just three or four innings a game, but he did it every day or two for 41 years. By that schedule, pitching 2,500 games amounts to slightly more than 60 games a year, which actually does not seem high enough.

The same is true for his other assertions. One hundred no-hitters, or even 20, looks dubious considering that Nolan Ryan holds the major-league record with just seven, followed by Sandy Koufax with a mere four. But press accounts detail Satchel doing it against highly-touted opponents like the all-Black Homestead Grays, and it is easy to imagine him repeating the feat with relative ease and considerable frequency against the sandlot teams he faced in his wayfaring across the Western Hemisphere. His 2,000 wins would give him four times as many as Cy Young, whose name is attached to the award signaling pitching excellence. His calculation of career strikeouts would have bested Ryan not by a hair but by several thousand. Some pitchers were brilliant during short runs at glory; others made their names for duration as much

Hall of Fame pitcher Satchel Paige, whose name is synonymous with Negro League baseball, signs a souvenir for one of his legions of fans. (Courtesy Noir-Tech Research, Inc.)

as dominance. Satchel excelled at both, to the point where it is difficult to overstate all that he did or to dismiss even his most outrageous boasts.[12]

Satchel's stats are clearer when he finally made it to the majors, belatedly signed by owner Bill Veeck in the summer of 1948 to play for the Cleveland Indians. That milestone occurred on July 7, Satchel's 42nd birthday. His earned-run average for the remainder of that season, a measly 2.48, was second best in the American League. His performance over the half-season he played so impressed the nation's baseball writers that, when the Associated Press polled them, 12 voted for Satchel as Rookie of the Year in the American League, enough to place him fourth (he joked that if he had won the honor he would have declined since "I wasn't sure what year the gentlemen had in mind.").[13] His 6-1 record was neither a joke nor an afterthought; it was the highest winning percentage on an outstanding Indians staff and a crucial factor in the team capturing the pennant, which it did by a single game over the Red Sox. Each game he won had fans and writers marveling over what he must have been like in his prime and which other lions of Blackball had been lost to the Jim Crow system of segregation.

That was the best of his six seasons in the majors, two of which were with the Indians, parts of three with the old St. Louis Browns, along with one unforgettable game with Charles O. Finley's A's of Kansas City. Satchel's record in the big leagues was just 28-31, with a 3.29 earned run average. Mediocre — until you consider that he was 42 when he launched his major-league career, and 59 years, two months and eight days when he ended it with the Athletics in 1965. That final appearance set a major-league record that might never be broken. He was two years older than the runner-up, 33 more than his catcher that night, and Paige seemed as old as baseball itself when he shut out the hard-hitting Boston Red Sox for three innings. He needed just 28 tosses to get nine outs. He struck out one and walked none over three innings. Batters popped up his pitches and tapped meek grounders. The only base hit was a double by Carl Yastrzemski, an All-Star who led the league in doubles that season and had seen his father hit against Satchel a generation earlier in a semipro game on Long Island.[14]

The denizens of baseball were impressed enough with that and all Satchel's other achievements that they inducted him into the Hall of Fame in 1971, the first vintage Negro Leaguer to be voted into this most exclusive club.

Satchel's last years were quiet ones. Too quiet for this man who adored being on the mound, in the middle of the action. Satchel last appeared in public on June 5, 1982, in Kansas City, where he had spent most of his adult years and, with his wife Lahoma, raised seven children. The roar was gone from his voice as he wheeled closer to the microphone, an oxygen tube strapped to his face while his hand gripped a baseball. "I hope the next time you come out, I can stand up," he said hopefully as the thin crowd stood in his honor. They were dedicating in his name a baseball stadium near his home. The ballpark was as decrepit as the old ballplayer, weeds poking through fresh-cut grass and wind pouring through breaches in the grandstand roof. Friends who knew his condition had rushed to organize the naming ceremony, hoping it would lift his spirits. But it would take more than that. "I am honored with the stadium being named for me. I thought there was nothing left for me," he said. "I've been in Kansas City 46 years and I can walk down the street and people don't know me."[15]

Two days later Kansas City was battered by a rainstorm that felled trees and knocked out power. Satchel woke that night with a headache. The next morning, the 8th of June, he could not find a comfortable position to lie or sit. His shoulder was throbbing. He had the chills. Lahoma applied a hot water bottle and draped her jacket around him, then she headed to the store for ice to keep food from spoiling during the outage. While she was gone Carolyn, their second oldest, found Satchel in a daze. She fanned him, calling, "Daddy, daddy can you hear me?" All he could manage was, "Ugh." His daughters called the paramedics, but their arrival was delayed by a fallen tree. In the meantime Lahoma got home and tried to resuscitate Satchel using the CPR she had learned as a nurse's aide. He was "limp as a dish rag," she said. His heart gave out for good in the ambulance and he was pronounced dead at 1:15 p.m. at Truman Medical Center. In the days just before "he knew he was going to pass on," his wife recalled. "We would try and not talk about it."[16]

Looking back, we can see that it was more than his memorable pitching form that made Paige stand apart and earned him a cherished spot not just in the Hall of Fame, but in a Satchel statue that now graces its grounds. There was also his role as a racial pioneer, a role that got lost in his showmanship and bluster. Satchel pitched spectacularly enough during the era of segregated baseball, especially when his teams were beating the best of the white big leaguers, that white sportswriters turned out to watch Black baseball. He proved that Black fans would fill ballparks, even when those parks had concrete seats and makeshift walls, and that white fans would turn out to see Black superstars. He barnstormed here and in the Caribbean alongside Dizzy Dean, Bob Feller, and other Caucasian champions, winning them over to him and to the notion that Negro Leaguers could really play ball. He drew the spotlight first to himself, then to his Kansas City Monarchs team, and inevitably to the Monarchs' rookie second baseman Jackie Robinson.

The truth is that Satchel Paige had been hacking away at baseball's color bar decades before the world got to know Jackie Robinson. Satchel laid the groundwork for Jackie the way A. Philip Randolph, W.E.B. DuBois, and other early Civil Rights leaders did for Martin Luther King Jr. Paige was as much a poster boy for Black baseball as Louis "Satchmo" Armstrong was for Black music and Paul Robeson was for the Black stage — and much as those two became symbols of their art in addition to their race, so Satchel was known not as a great Black pitcher but a great pitcher. In the process Satchel Paige, more than anyone, opened to Blacks the national pastime and forever changed his sport and this nation.

Acknowledgement

This article draws from the author's book *Satchel: The Life and Times of an American Legend* (New York: Random House, 2008).

Notes

1   Michael V.R. Thomason, ed., *Mobile: The New History of Alabama's First City* (Tuscaloosa: University of Alabama Press, 2001), 1-2 and 155-67.

2   Satchel Paige and David Lipman, *Maybe I'll Pitch Forever: A Great Baseball Player Tells the Hilarious Story Behind the Legend* (Lincoln: University of Nebraska Press, 1993), 16 and 19.

3   *Maybe I'll Pitch Forever*, 17-18.

4   Arthur P. Glass, "How Old Is Satch?" *Sports Illustrated*, February 1949.

5   *Maybe I'll Pitch Forever*, 26; and Mark Ribowsky, *Don't Look Back: Satchel Paige in the Shadows of Baseball* (New York: Simon & Schuster, 1994), 34.

6   *Maybe I'll Pitch Forever*, 24 and 26.

7   This information was compiled by Negro Leagues researchers Larry Lester and Dick Clark for a study supported by Major League Baseball and the National Baseball Hall of Fame. It was published in Lawrence D. Hogan, *Shades of Glory: The Negro Leagues and the Story of African-American Baseball* (Washington, DC: National Geographic Society, 2006), 406-407.

8   https://www.seamheads.com/NegroLgs/player.php?playerID=paige-01sat

9   Joe Williams and Peter Williams, ed., *The Joe Williams Baseball Reader* (Chapel Hill: Algonquin Books, 1989), 199.

10   The almanac is the author's compilation of every stat Paige wrote about himself -- or reported to sports writers, authors, teammates, and others -- over his four decades in baseball.

11   Frank Finch. "Satchel Still Going Strong," *Los Angeles Times*. July 15, 1958; *Maybe I'll Pitch Forever*, 57; Satchel Paige and Hal Lebovitz, *Pitchin' Man: Satchel Paige's Own Story* (Westport, Connecticut: Meckler, 1992), 41 and 54; Baseball Hall of Fame; and Lawrence D. Hogan, *Shades of Glory: The Negro Leagues and the Story of African-American Baseball* (Washington, DC: National Geographic Society, 2006), 394-95.

12   Henry Metcalfe, *A Game for All Races: An Illustrated History of the Negro Leagues* (New York: MetroBooks, 2000), 95-96.

Satchel Paige suffered from a dead arm when Monarchs owner J. L. Wilkinson signed him in 1938. By 1942, Paige was back and went 2-0 with a 2.20 ERA in the World Series.
(Courtesy Noir-Tech Research, Inc.)

13   David Sterry and Arielle Eckstut. *Satchel Sez: The Wit, Wisdom, and World of Leroy "Satchel" Paige* (New York: Three Rivers Press, 2001), 91.

14   Author interviews with Carl Yastrzemski, Bill Monbouquette, Ed Charles, Lee Thomas, and Eddie Bressoud.

15   E.A. Torriero, "'We Lost Satchel': KC Neighbors Shed Tears as Legendary Baseball Pitcher Dies." *Kansas City Times*, June 9, 1982; and Rick E. Abel, "After Honors, 'Satchel' Paige Dies." *Kansas City Call*, June 11-17, 1982.

16   E.A. Torriero, email to author, 2007; and "'We Lost Satchel.'"

NORRIS PHILLIPS

By Frederick C. Bush

Norris Phillips may have had a short-lived career in the Negro Leagues, but he had the distinction of being a member of the powerhouse 1942 Kansas City Monarchs pitching staff during the regular season.[1] The team captured the Negro League World Series championship, but since Phillips was a back-end starter who toiled behind Hall of Famers Satchel Paige and Hilton Smith, he ended up being left off the World Series roster.[2] However, Phillips held his own when he was called on to pitch during the 1942 and 1943 seasons, and he amassed many fond memories along the way. In 1995, he recalled, "The one I will always cherish was at (Washington's) Griffith Stadium and I came in to relieve Satchel Paige. ... I struck out Josh Gibson. I got him swinging at a high fastball between the letters and the belt. We all stayed at the same hotel and we talked about it when we all got back."[3]

Norris Phillips was born on June 18, 1916, in Rosenberg, Texas, a town on the Brazos River 32 miles southwest of Houston. He was the fifth of seven children born to farmer Isiah Phillips and his wife, Della (Milligan) Phillips. Isiah Phillips may have died, or may simply have abandoned his family, while Norris was still a young boy, though the exact year of his departure is unknown.[4] At the time of the 1930 census, Della Phillips was listed as a widow and the family was being supported financially by Norris's 21-year-old brother, James, who worked in a brickyard, and his 17-year-old sister, Lillie, who worked as a nursemaid for a private family.

Little is known about Phillips's early life, but, unlike many children of poor African American families in the South, he did complete all four years of high school. In 1940, Phillips was living in the home of his uncle, Alvin Jackson, in Rosenberg and worked in a barbershop. It is uncertain why Phillips no longer lived at home; he still listed his mother, Della, as the person who would always know his address on the World War II draft registration card that he filled out in October of that year.

Also lost to time is how Phillips got his start in baseball, although it is likely that he played for a local town or business team at some point before he was discovered by the Monarchs. The Lone Star State was known for producing talented ballplayers; in addition to Phillips, fellow 1942 Monarchs Newt Allen, Jack Matchett, Hilton Smith, and Jesse Williams all hailed from different cities in Texas. Whichever way events may have transpired, Phillips's draft card shows that he moved from his hometown of Rosenberg to Kansas City, Missouri, where he lived at 420 East 9th Street upon joining the Monarchs as an almost 26-year-old rookie.

The first report of Phillips, who stood 5-feet-9 and weighed 174 pounds, pitching for Kansas City involved an April 23 game against the Memphis Red Sox at Travelers Field in Little Rock, Arkansas. Five was Norris's number for much of the day as he pitched five innings of five-hit ball during which he struck out five Memphis batters. However, after he allowed a run in the sixth inning, he was taken out of the game at the top of the seventh, and the Red Sox rallied in the ninth to win, 3-2.[5]

Phillips must have impressed the Memphis management as the Red Sox apparently enticed the hurler to jump to their team. He may have imagined that he had a better chance to pitch more often for the Red Sox than for the Monarchs. In a preview of the Chicago American Giants' upcoming tilt against Memphis on May 31, the *Chicago Defender* noted, "The Sox will present several new faces in their 1942 lineup. Fred McDaniels, the hard-hitting outfielder, along with pitchers Percy Keys, 'Kid' Lipsey and Norris Phillips and several others will greet the Giants."[6]

Whatever opportunities Phillips may have envisioned with Memphis, his stint with the Red Sox was a short one. Official statistics credit him with one relief appearance that lasted 2⅔ innings in which he struck out two batters, walked one, and allowed two hits and one earned run. Once again, circumstances remain unclear due to a lack of press coverage, but it is likely that Phillips was forced to return to the Monarchs to honor his contract obligations to Kansas

City. Negro League teams often raided other squads for players, and many disputes were settled by having the player return to his original team.

On July 14, Phillips once again took the mound for the Monarchs against the Red Sox at Oklahoma City's Holland Field. He allowed the Red Sox only four hits as he went the distance in Kansas City's 5-0 victory, a triumph that the press hailed as "revenge for a 4-2 loss suffered against the Red Sox at Houston recently."[7] Phillips's last start for the Monarchs in 1942 came against the Chicago American Giants at Kansas City's Ruppert Stadium on August 23. The Monarchs prevailed, 4-3, in 14 innings, but Booker McDaniel earned the victory in relief of Phillips.[8] It marked the end of Phillips's 1942 campaign as the Monarchs used only three pitchers – Paige, Smith, and Matchett – in their four-game sweep of the Homestead Grays in the World Series.

Phillips had acquitted himself well enough that he returned to Kansas City for the 1943 season. The game he considered to be the highlight of his career – the one in which he struck out Gibson – took place in front of 23,000 fans at Griffith Stadium on June 17. Paige had been slated to start, but "he missed train connections from Pittsburgh ... and finally arrived by plane ... around the fourth inning."[9] Phillips, who filled in for Satchel on the mound, was dealing and held the mighty Grays lineup to only two hits over seven innings in a 2-1 Monarchs victory; the game was called in the seventh inning due to a heavy rainstorm.

On July 5 Phillips once again took the mound against Memphis in the first game of a doubleheader at Ruppert Stadium. According to the news account of the game, he "lacked control in the first inning with a pair of walks followed by [catcher Herb] Barnhill's wild peg to second put the visitors off to a short-lived lead."[10] Phillips regained his composure, and the Monarchs soon took the lead in an eventual 6-3 win; the Monarchs also captured the second game, 4-0, to end the first half of the Negro American League season on an upbeat note.

The Birmingham Black Barons had won the NAL's first-half title, but the Monarchs expected to compete for the second-half crown. Kansas City manager Frank Duncan pointed out that his squad had lost players to military service, holdout, and injury, but that his roster had now rounded into shape. Among the positive items Duncan mentioned was his confidence in "Norris Phillips having developed into an able replacement for [Frank] Bradley," a pitcher who had been lost to the military.[11] The Chicago American Giants ended up as second-half champions, which left the defending World Series champion Monarchs out of the playoff picture in 1943. Phillips pitched to a 2-2 record and a 3.62 ERA, but he had serious control issues as he walked 25 batters (while striking out only 11) in 27⅓ innings pitched over six appearances. After the 1943 season, Phillips's baseball career was at an end.

Considering both his age and his control problems, Phillips moved into the next phase of his life. Once again, his draft registration card provides insight, as his employer was now listed as the Canal War Apartments, Building 69-E, in Richmond, California. The city was a center of wartime activity and employment. According to the National Park Service, "The four Richmond shipyards with their combined 27 shipways, produced 747 ships, more than any other shipyard complex in the country. Richmond was home to 56 different war industries, more than any other city of its size in the United States. The city grew nearly overnight from 24,000 people to 100,000 people."[12] Phillips was one of the many people who sought gainful employment in support of the war effort on the home front.

Before long, Phillips moved up the Pacific coast to Portland, Oregon, most likely to work in the shipyards there. While in Portland, he met divorcee Sally K. Miller, a 25-year-old waitress who became his wife. There was an obstacle to the couple's marriage, however, and it had nothing to do with the stigma that divorce carried at that time. The impediment in question was race, because Miller was white, and Oregon still had a law against interracial marriage. Phillips and his bride overcame this hurdle by getting married in Clark County, Washington, on February 3, 1947. Washington had repealed its law against interracial marriage (and cohabitation) prior to being admitted to the Union as a state, and the couple now settled in Seattle.[13] Phillips was a seaman in the US Merchant Marine and sailed back and forth between Seattle and Sasebo, Japan, numerous times in the early years after the war as America helped its enemy-turned-ally to rebuild.

Phillips lived out his life as a family man with baseball no longer in the picture until September 9, 1995. On that day, the Seattle Mariners held "Tribute to Negro Leagues Night" and recognized the Seattle Steelheads of the short-lived West Coast Negro Baseball Association and other former Negro League players who were now residing in Seattle; Phillips

• NORRIS PHILLIPS •

was among the latter group.[14] A few months later, Phillips died on February 4, 1996, at the age of 79. He was survived by his five children: Clarence, Marilyn, Teresa, Regina, and Richard.[15]

Phillips is among the many Negro League players whose career was brief, but during that short time he moved among the giants of the game, having been on the same pitching staff as Paige and Hilton Smith and having faced such luminaries as Gibson. Although he had to play baseball in a segregated league and then continued to confront discrimination based upon the color of his skin – most notably in regard to his marriage – he persevered to raise a family and contributed his efforts to the improvement of the country he called home.

Author's Note

Phillips's obituary states that he was a member of the 1946 Portland Roses (a.k.a. Rosebuds) of the West Coast Negro Baseball Association. Phillips did live in Portland in 1946, but he listed his occupation as "Seaman" on his January 1947 marriage license application, and this author was unable to find a single news article to corroborate that Phillips was a member of the team. Press coverage of the league was admittedly sparse, but even retrospective articles fail to mention Phillips. *The Negro Leagues Book, Volume 2*, also lists Phillips on the roster of the Portland team as well as the Harlem Globetrotters baseball team; the Globetrotters briefly became the Seattle Steelheads and then reverted to the Globetrotters name not long after the demise of the West Coast Negro Baseball Association. Again, this author turned up no evidence that Phillips was a member of either squad, or any indication that Phillips ever made such a claim for himself.

Norris Phillips had a brief two-year career in the Negro Leagues, but he was a contributor on the 1942 championship team's pitching staff. (Courtesy Noir-Tech Research, Inc.)

An August 8, 1946, news article stated that the Oakland Larks, champions of the West Coast Negro Baseball Association, "possess several ex-Kansas City Monarchs," and there were other ex-Monarchs in the league. Thus, it is possible that Phillips could have played for Portland; however, again, it seems unlikely since he already listed his occupation as "Seaman" for 1946.

For sources that mention Phillips as a member of the Portland team or fail to mention him as such, see:

"1946 Coast Negro Champs to Face Strengthened Hills Creek Monday," *Eugene* (Oregon) *Guard*, August 8, 1946: 20. (This is the article that stated the Oakland Larks team had several ex-Monarchs on its roster.)

Eskenazi, David. "Wayback Machine: Seattle Steelheads' Short Life," sportspressnw.com/2145947/2013/wayback-machine-seattle-steelheads-short-life. (No mention of Phillips at all in this article about Seattle and the West Coast Negro Baseball Association)

Lester, Larry, and Wayne Stivers, eds. *The Negro Leagues Book, Volume 2* (Kansas City, Missouri: NoirTech Research, Inc., 2020). (Names Phillips as a member of both the Portland Rosebuds and Harlem Globetrotters.)

"Norris Phillips, Negro Leagues Pitcher, Dies/Played with Satchel Paige, Once Struck Out Josh Gibson" (obituary), *Seattle Times*, February 8, 1996, genealogybank.com/doc/obituaries/obit/0FA3744D55657D68-0FA3744D55657D68?h=1&fname=Norris&lname=Phillips&fullname=&rgfromDate=&rgtoDate=&formDate=02/08/1996&formDateFlex=exact&dateType=date&kwinc=&kwexc=&sid=ncqwrikazwtqqtfupapczhegaaucvw bk_s072_1592248849759. (States that Phillips was a member of the Portland team.)

Sherwin, Bob. "Mariner Log/Seattle 6, Kansas City 2: M's Pay Tribute to Ex-Negro Leagues Players," *Seattle Times*, September 10, 1995, archive.seattletimes.com/archive/?date=19950910&slug=2140878. (States that Phillips was a member of the Kansas City Monarchs, but does not mention any other team.)

Whirty, Ryan. "Remembering the Steelheads, Seattle's Negro League Team," *Seattle Magazine*, May 2013, seattlemag.com/article/remembering-steelheads-seattles-negro-league-team. (No mention of Phillips at all in this article about Seattle and the West Coast Negro Baseball Association.)

Sources

Ancestry.com was consulted for census information, World War II draft registration, marriage and death records, and ships' passenger and crew lists.

Seamheads.com provided all player statistics and team records (unless otherwise indicated).

Notes

1. There is uncertainty as to whether Phillips pitched left-handed or right-handed. Historian James A. Riley states that Phillips threw and batted left-handed, but the Seamheads website states that Phillips threw right-handed but batted left-handed. News articles never referred to Phillips as either a lefty or righty; thus, they are of no help on the matter and the uncertainty remains for now.

2. James A. Riley, *The Biographical Encyclopedia of the Negro Baseball Leagues* (New York: Carroll & Graf Publishers, Inc., 1994), 626.

3. Bob Sherwin, "Mariner Log/Seattle 6, Kansas City 2: M's Pay Tribute to Ex-Negro Leagues Players," *Seattle Times*, September 10, 1995, archive.seattletimes.com/archive/?date=19950910&slug=2140878, accessed June 14, 2020. The game that Phillips remembered took place on June 17, 1943, but Phillips started in place of Paige rather than relieving him; see "Monarchs Beat Grays Minus Paige on Hill," *Washington Evening Star*, June 18, 1943: 16.

4. The 1920 census gives Norris's father's name as "Isaac" and his age as 53. On his marriage certificate, Norris spelled his father's name as "Isiah." Additionally, Della Phillips was listed as 30 years old in the 1920 census and, while there certainly could have been a 23-year age difference between husband and wife, it seems less likely in light of the death certificate for one "Isiah" Phillips. A Negro man named Isiah Phillips died in Rosenberg, Texas, on January 29, 1947; his year of birth was listed as 1890, his marital status as "married," and his father's name as Norris Phillips. It would make a lot of sense that this was the ballplayer Norris Phillips' father: 1) His father and mother would have been the same age; 2) Norris would have been named after his paternal grandfather; and 3) Della would have given her status as "widowed" to future census takers to conceal her husband's abandonment of her and the family, as many women did in those days. A preponderance of the evidence suggests that this was the true history of Norris Phillips's father.

5. "Red Sox Nose Out K.C.M.," *Arkansas State Press* (Little Rock), May 1, 1942: 7.

6. "Memphis Is Here May 31," *Chicago Defender*, May 30, 1942: 20.

7. "Monarchs' Homers Jolt Memphis, 5-0," *Daily Oklahoman* (Oklahoma City), July 15, 1942: 34.

8. "Monarchs Tip Giants, 4 to 3, in 14 Innings," *Chicago Sun*, August 24, 1942: 17. Negro League statistics are notoriously incomplete and difficult to pin down due to inconsistent press coverage. Seamheads.com lists Phillips as having made only two appearances (one start) for the Monarchs in 1942; however, this author found articles about three games in which Phillips appeared for Kansas City, and all three were starts. Additionally, Seamheads.com lists a record of 0-0 for Phillips in 1942, but his July 14 shutout of Memphis gave him a 1-0 ledger for the season.

9. "Monarchs Beat Grays Minus Paige on Hill," *Washington Evening Star*, June 18, 1943: 16.

10. "A Pair for Monarchs," *Kansas City Times*, July 6, 1943: 12.

11. "Monarchs Expect to Capture Championship 5th Time," *Weekly Review* (Birmingham, Alabama), July 17, 1943: 7.

12. "Rosie the Riveter – World War II Home Front National Historic Park," National Park Service, nps.gov/nr/travel/wwIIbayarea/ros.htm, accessed June 15, 2020.

13. The state of Oregon repealed its law against interracial marriages in 1951. In 1967, the US Supreme Court ruled, in *Loving v. Virginia*, that laws against interracial marriages were unconstitutional, leading to their repeal in all states.

14. Sherwin.

15. "Norris Phillips, Negro Leagues Pitcher, Dies/Played with Satchel Paige, Once Struck Out Josh Gibson" (obituary), *Seattle Times*, February 8, 1996, genealogybank.com/doc/obituaries/obit/0FA3744D55657D68-0FA3744D55657D68?h=1&fname=Norris&lname=Phillips&fullname=&rgfromDate=&rgtoDate=&formDate=02/08/1996&formDateFlex=exact&dateType=date&kwinc=&kwexc=&sid=ncqwrikazwtqqtfupapczhegaaucvwbk_s072_1592248849759, accessed June 15, 2020. The obituary states that Phillips died on February 7, but both the state of Washington Death Index and the US Social Security Death Index list his date of death as February 4. Additionally, the obituary made no mention of Phillips's wife; thus, she either preceded him in death or they were divorced.

HENRY FRAZIER "SLOW" ROBINSON

By Bob Webster

Henry Frazier Robinson was born on May 30, 1910, in Birmingham, Alabama, to the Rev. Henry and Corrine (Black) Robinson.[1] The Robinsons had seven children: Edward, Theophilus, Maybelle, John, Estelle, Henry Frazier, and Norman.[2]

The family moved to Oklahoma City when Frazier was less than a year old to escape the segregation of the South and to start a better life. Claudia Black, Frazier's maternal grandmother, lived with them and took care of Frazier when he was a baby.[3] Claudia was the only grandparent Frazier ever knew and he always heard that she was a freed slave. From what Frazier had been told, his mother and father were both from North Carolina and their parents also had been slaves.[4]

The family eventually moved to Okmulgee, Oklahoma.[5]

The elder Robinson, a Protestant minister, was serious about his religion and made sure his family attended church. The children were rarely, if ever, in any trouble at all, according to young Frasier's autobiography. All seven graduated from Dunbar High School in Okmulgee, and Edward, Maybelle, and Norman all went to Langston University, a historically Black university in Langston, Oklahoma.[6]

Frazier played baseball for his high school in the spring, and when school was out for the summer, he played for a team in Okmulgee coached by a Catholic priest, Father Bradley. One day the Tulsa Blackballers came to town for a game and the team's owner, Mr. Lewis, wanted Frazier to join the team. Father Bradley wanted Frazier to attend the Catholic school and play baseball for them. The two coaches argued over Frazier every time the teams played each other. Since playing baseball was his goal in life, Frazier went with the Blackballers and played the 1927 and 1928 seasons with them.[7]

At age 19, Frazier moved to Akron, Ohio, to live with his oldest brother, Edward, who worked at Goodyear Tire and Rubber Company. Edward got Frazier a job there, too. Frazier also played baseball for Goodyear's company team, the Wingfoot Tigers.[8]

The Wingfoot Tigers beat almost every team they played and caught the attention of a man named Bullock who wanted to put together a Negro League team in Pittsburgh in 1930. He signed Frazier and four other players from the Wingfoots. While waiting for Bullock's team to be accepted into the league, they played a few exhibition games. Frazier also attended as many Homestead Grays games as he could. (The Grays were playing in Akron at the time.)

Bullock's team never materialized, so he cut all the players loose. Instead of staying in Akron, Robinson returned to Oklahoma, where he hooked up with the Abilene Eagles of the Texas-Oklahoma-Louisiana League, a Black league.[9] Robinson stayed with Abilene until the league folded, and in 1936 he joined a team in Odessa, Texas. The team was on the road a lot, and Robinson kept a room in Lubbock at Jack Matchett's father's house. Matchett and Robinson had played together in Abilene, so they had known each other for a few years. After returning home from a road trip, Matchett's father handed Robinson a telegram saying that his father had died. It hit Robinson hard, because he always stayed in touch with his parents. He could not make it back in time for the burial, but he did finally get home a few months later.[10]

In 1939 the Kansas City Monarchs asked Robinson's brother, Norman, who was three years younger than Frazier, to play for them. The Monarchs needed another catcher, and Norman recommended Frazier.[11] Robinson reported to Satchel Paige's All-Stars, the Monarchs "B" team.[12]

A team from the House of David was the All-Stars' first booking of the 1939 season, and the two teams traveled west on a barnstorming tour in which they played against each other. Frazier broke his thumb early in the season and had to return to Texas.

When Frazier Robinson started catching Satchel Paige in 1939, Paige was suffering from an arm injury. After Robinson worked with Paige to get over his injury, Paige told Robinson that he had better be ready because Paige himself was ready. Robinson told him, "Man, I can catch what you've been throwing with a work glove." When the first batter came to bat, Robinson called for a fastball. Paige threw the ball so hard that it knocked the glove off Robinson's hand and the mask off his face.[13]

In the spring of 1940, Robinson returned to New Orleans to train with the All-Stars, but his brother Norman did not go with him because he did not like the fact that their manager swore all the time.[14] After training camp broke, the All-Stars and Monarchs went their separate ways until a little past midseason, when the bookings between the All-Stars and House of David ran out. Robinson, Paige, and a pitcher named Washington reported to the Monarchs and the rest of the All-Stars were sent home.[15]

That season Paige gave Robinson the nickname "Slow." "He said I talked slow and moved around slow so that's what he called me," Robinson said.[16]

After the 1940 season, Robinson went to Baltimore to spend the winter with his brother Norman, who had spent the season with the Baltimore Elite Giants as a utility player and was also a starter for a Baltimore area team, the Sparrows Point Giants. The Sparrows Point team was owned by Dr. Joseph Thomas, who wanted to get his team into the Negro National League.[17]

Robinson was still under contract with the Monarchs, but he went to the Sparrows Point Giants camp with Norman and made the team. Partway through the 1941 season, Frazier started to catch for the Elite Giants, too. He returned to both the Elites and Sparrows Points Giants for the 1942 season. While in Baltimore, Robinson became a father. His son, Luther, was born to Robinson's girlfriend, but the couple did not stay together very long.[18]

In August 1942 the Monarchs came to town to play Sparrows Point and Robinson watched from the stands again. He could not resist the temptation to say hello to his former teammates and met them at their bus after the game. Dizzy Dismukes, who used to pitch for the Monarchs and was now in the front office, asked Robinson if he could be ready to leave on this bus. Dismukes warned him that Monarchs owner J.L. Wilkinson would blackball him if he was

Catcher Frazier Robinson, pictured here during his time with the Baltimore Elite Giants, began his career in the Negro major leagues with the Monarchs in 1942. (Courtesy Noir-Tech Research, Inc.)

not on the bus when it left. The Monarchs needed Robinson because their catcher, Joe Greene, had hurt his finger and the only backup catcher was manager Frank Duncan.[19]

Robinson played for the Monarchs over the last month of the season with the Monarchs and a highlight was catching a Satchel Paige no-hitter against a semipro team in Detroit that had been undefeated up until that point. Paige followed up that performance by pitching four innings the next night against the minor-league Toledo Mud Hens.[20] In addition to playing in exhibition games, Robinson was 1-for-8 with one run batted in, on August 6 in two league games against the Philadelphia Stars.

HENRY FRAZIER "SLOW" ROBINSON

The Monarchs were the 1942 Negro American League champions and played the Homestead Grays, champions of the Negro National League in Black baseball's World Series. Robinson traveled with the team throughout the postseason but did not see any action since the Monarchs' first-string catcher, Greene, was back from his injury.[21]

The Monarchs swept the Grays, but Robinson was in no mood to celebrate. During the final game of the series, he was handed a letter from his draft board ordering him to report for induction.[22]

Although Robinson joined the Navy in 1943, Seamheads shows him as appearing in one game for the Monarchs that year. It was against the Homestead Grays in Wrigley Field on August 29.[23] James A. Riley says he made a brief appearance with the New York Black Yankees in 1943 as a reserve catcher and also briefly joined the Baltimore Elite Giants early in the season before joining the Navy.[24]

Robinson served in the South Pacific and Japan until he received his honorable discharge on October 20, 1945. He went to Baltimore to see his son and the two went to Oklahoma to visit Robinson's mother.[25] He then returned to Baltimore to stay with his brother Norman. After leaving the service, Frazier was not at full strength, so he just worked odd jobs for the winter and spent the evenings going to nightclubs. At one, he met a woman named Catherine whom he married by the end of the year (1945).[26]

In the spring of 1946, after asking J.L. Wilkinson for his release from the Monarchs, Robinson went to the Baltimore Elite Giants' training camp, a team that had plenty of catchers, including Roy Campanella. Campanella was not yet that good a catcher, but the manager of the Elite Giants was Biz Mackey, who in his day was known as the best defensive catcher in the Negro Leagues. After converting Campanella into a star backstop, Mackey began to mentor Robinson.[27]

Buck O'Neil was glad to see that Robinson had found another team. He later wrote the foreword to Robinson's autobiography in which he asserted, "'Slow' had good, quick hands and a strong, accurate arm as a catcher. A quick compact swing with average power as a hitter. Joe Greene was our starting catcher, and I felt that 'Slow' had too much to offer as second string. Therefore, I was very pleased when he went to the Elites."[28]

Robinson caught the Elites' pitchers for about half the season, but he was not feeling well. He thought it must have had something to do with being in the hot weather in the South Pacific. Tom Wilson, owner of the Elites, told manager Vernon Green to send him down to the Nashville Black Vols for the rest of the year.[29]

In 1947 Robinson was back in Baltimore and able to be near his son and play with his brother on the Elites. He caught 42 league games that season as the Elites finished slightly over .500.

Robinson was back with the Elites in 1948 at the age of 38. In 62 games, he hit .182 with 37 hits. Some of the other teams in the league started losing players to the White major leagues and the Elites easily won both halves of the Negro National League season.

The NNL folded after at the 1948 season, and the Negro American League absorbed most of the teams for the 1949 season. Robinson, still with Baltimore, said that this team was the best Elites team he had played for. The season was going well with Robinson catching most of the games until late in the 1948 season, when he slid into third base and his foot went under the bag, snapping his ankle. The injury caused him to miss the playoffs.[30]

Robinson arrived at the Elites' training camp in 1950, but his ankle was not healed yet and it took some time before he was ready to play. Once he started playing, he was able to perform well again. Late in the season, the Chicago American Giants were in Baltimore for a series. Chicago was short on catchers, so Giants manager Ted "Double Duty" Radcliffe asked Baltimore owner Wilson if they could borrow Robinson for the rest of the season. Powell agreed and Robinson was gone. After the first game, Robinson had a chat with Dr. J.B. Martin, the Giants' owner, and he found out that Martin wanted to pay him $50 less per month than Radcliffe had promised. After a week in Chicago, th Winnipeg Buffaloes of the semipro Man-Dak League offered Robinson a catching spot and he accepted.[31] The Man-Dak league was an integrated league, but Winnipeg was an all-Black team.[32]

Robinson roomed with future Hall of Fame pitcher Leon Day in Winnipeg. They watched out for each other. "Off the field, Canada was like no place I'd ever been," said Robinson. He added, "Living and eating conditions were very much nicer. Canada was like paradise."[33]

Winnipeg, which finished in second place during the regular season, advanced to the playoffs and played third-place Minot in the first round. Winnipeg came from behind in each of the first two games of the five-game series, and then trounced Minot 13-4 in

Game Three to advance. Robinson homered in Game Three.[34] In the other first-round series, the regular-season champion Brandon Greys held off the Carman Cardinals three games to two.[35]

Winnipeg took on Brandon in the best-of-seven league championship. The Buffaloes took the first three games of the series. Brandon took Game Four to set up what turned out to be one of the best pitching duels ever seen in any league. Both pitchers, Leon Day of Winnipeg and Manuel Godinez of Brandon, pitched all 17 innings of the 1-0 Winnipeg victory that crowned the Buffaloes as the 1950 league champions.[36] Robinson caught all 17 innings for Winnipeg.[37]

Robinson was back with the Buffaloes for the 1951 season and hit .318 with a homer and 37 RBIs. On July 28 he connected for three hits, including his lone home run of the season.[38]

The season did not pass without serious problems for Winnipeg. The Toronto Maple Leafs of the Triple-A International League, a St. Louis Browns farm team, sent a scout to Winnipeg to look at a couple of players. Toronto and St. Louis took five Winnipeg players. Winnipeg's owner, Stanley Zedd, was so unhappy that he disbanded the franchise at the end of the season.[39]

Winnipeg did finish the regular season with a 34-29 record, good for second place, three games behind the regular-season champion Brandon Greys. The same four teams from the 1950 playoffs returned for the 1951 postseason. Winnipeg and Brandon each won their first round series to meet for the finals. Brandon swept the four-game series. Robinson hit a home run in Game Four.

When the Winnipeg team folded, Robinson thought it marked the end of his baseball career. He liked Baltimore, but there was no reason to go back there. His apartment had burned down and his wife, Catherine, had initiated divorce proceedings.[40] In April 1952 the Brandon team offered him a job. The 42-year-old Robinson joined his brother, Norman, and longtime friend Willie Wells in Brandon for the 1952 season. Brandon finished in last place in the four-team league with a 24-30 record, eight games behind the league-leading Minot Mallards.[41] Robinson batted .253 with no homers and 13 RBIs.[42]

Robinson played the 1952 and 1953 seasons in Brandon and then, at age 43, he called it a career.

Robinson's brother Edward still lived in Akron, so Robinson settled in nearby Cleveland. He called for his son Luther to come stay with him, but after a few months Luther was homesick for his mother and friends and moved back to Baltimore. Robinson frequented nightclubs, as he had always done, and in 1954, a friend introduced Robinson to Wynolia Griggs. Robinson called her Winnie, and, after dating for a few years, they were married in 1960.[43]

After retiring from baseball, Robinson's brother Norman lived in Chicago and he often drove to Cleveland to visit Frazier. Eventually, Norman moved to Los Angeles and worked for A.R.A Services, a provider of food services and merchandise. Norman suffered from stomach pains from a bleeding ulcer, Frazier went to California to visit Norman and decided that his brother needed his help. In 1966 Frazier and Winnie moved to California to take care of Norman.

Norman got his brother a job with A.R.A, but Frazier gave it up and went to work as a Los Angeles school custodian in 1967.[44] In 1977 he opened his own business, Sweep it Right Parking Lot Maintenance.[45]

Robinson and Satchel Paige remained good friends until Paige died in 1982, and Paige visited the Robinsons in both Cleveland and California.[46] Robinson was an honorary pallbearer at Paige's funeral.[47]

Winnie's family was from Kings Mountain, North Carolina, and, after Norman died in 1984, the Robinsons moved to Kings Mountain in 1988.[48]

During All-Star week in Baltimore in 1993, the Upper Deck baseball card company and the Orioles honored members of the Baltimore Elite Giants. Robinson and 25 other Negro American League players were introduced.[49]

In 1997, in nearby Shelby, North Carolina, the Antioch Missionary Baptist Church was being built and its gymnasium was named after Frazier Robinson because of "the support he has given the church, his ties to athletics, and the grace in which he has carried himself," said the Reverend James Robinson (no relation).[50] When Frazier's health declined, construction of the gym was accelerated and it was dedicated on October 12, 1997. Among the 350 guests at the dedication was his nephew, Grammy Award-winning singer James Ingram.[51] Buck O'Neil said that Robinson had talent as well: "'Slow' was a religious person who enjoyed Negro spirituals and sang them very well. He organized a quartet on every team he played on. On the Kansas City Monarchs, it was Satchel Paige, John Markham IV, Barnes, and himself."[52] On the very next day after the gym dedication, Robinson died.[53]

• HENRY FRAZIER "SLOW" ROBINSON •

Robinson's legacy continued after his death. The Kings Mountain Historical Museum had his artifacts on exhibit in 2002.[54] Wynolia kept a special room in their home that contained memorabilia from Robinson's baseball career.[55]

Wynolia Robinson died on February 3, 2010. Her funeral was held at the church where the gymnasium was named after her late husband.[56]

Sources

The author used Baseball-Reference.com and Seamheads.com for stats and team information. In addition, the author relied on Frazier Robinson's autobiography *Catching Dreams, My Life in the Negro Baseball Leagues*.

Notes

1 Gerald Early, "Introduction: Freedom and Fate, Baseball and Race," in Frazier Robinson with Paul Bauer, *Catching Dreams: My Life in the Negro Baseball Leagues* (Syracuse, New York: Syracuse University Press, 1999), xix.

2 Robinson with Bauer, *Catching Dreams: My Life in the Negro Baseball Leagues*, 2.

3 Robinson with Bauer, 1.

4 Robinson with Bauer, 1.

5 Robinson with Bauer, 2.

6 Robinson with Bauer, 2.

7 Robinson with Bauer, 8.

8 Robinson with Bauer, 9.

9 Robinson with Bauer, 13.

10 Robinson with Bauer, 18-19.

11 Brent Kelley, *Voices from the Negro Leagues: Conversations with 52 Baseball Standouts of the Period 1924-1960* (Jefferson, North Carolina: McFarland and Company, 1998), 85.

12 Robinson with Bauer, 21.

13 Kelley, 85.

14 Robinson with Bauer, 51.

15 Robinson with Bauer, 53.

16 Richard Walker, "For the Love of the Game," *Charlotte Observer*, July 24, 1993: 100.

17 Robinson with Bauer, 77-78.

18 Robinson with Bauer, 84.

19 Robinson with Bauer, 78-83.

20 Robinson with Bauer, 84

21 Robinson with Bauer, 86.

22 Robinson with Bauer, 97.

23 Email from Gary Ashwill, May 3, 2021.

24 James A. Riley, *The Biographical Encyclopedia of the Negro Baseball Leagues* (New York: Carroll and Graf, 1994), 671.

25 Robinson with Bauer, 103.

26 Robinson with Bauer, 105. Her last name was not mentioned in Robinson's biography.

27 Robinson with Bauer, 106-108.

28 Buck O'Neil, "Foreword," in Robinson with Bauer, xi.

29 Robinson with Bauer, 115.

30 Kelley, *Voices*, 87.

31 Robinson with Bauer, 163-164.

32 Robinson with Bauer, 168.

33 Robinson with Bauer, 167.

34 Barry Swanton, *The ManDak League: Haven for Former Negro League Ballplayers, 1950–1957* (Jefferson, North Carolina: McFarland and Company, 2009), 19.

35 Swanton, *ManDak League*, 19.

36 Swanton, *ManDak League*, 20.

37 Robinson with Bauer, 170-171.

38 Barry Swanton, *Black Baseball Players in Canada* (Jefferson, North Carolina: McFarland and Company, 2009), 144.

39 Swanton, *ManDak League*, 24-25.

40 Robinson with Bauer, 183.

41 Swanton, *ManDak League*, 29.

42 Swanton, *Black Baseball Players*, 144.

43 Robinson with Bauer, 183-190.

44 Robinson with Bauer, 192-193.

45 Henry Robinson, Negro Leagues Baseball Museum eMuseum, https://nlbemuseum.com/history/players/robinsonh.html.

46 Robinson with Bauer, 202.

47 Larry Tye, *Satchel* (New York: Random House, 2009), 297.

48 Robinson with Bauer, 204.

49 Walker, "For the Love of the Game," 99.

50 Mark Terrell, "Church Names Gym for Negro Leagues Catcher," *Charlotte Observer*, October 12, 1997: 1B, 5B.

51 Associated Press, "Frazier Robinson: Catcher in Negro Leagues," *Pittsburgh Post-Gazette*, October 18, 1997: 16. See also Robinson with Bauer, 213.

52 Buck O'Neil, "Foreword."

53 Ancestry.com, "Henry Frazier Robinson in the North Carolina, US, Death Indexes, 1908-2004.

54 Michael Nixon, "Negro League Star Celebrated at Museum," *Charlotte Observer*, July 21, 2002: 167.

55 Kamie Champion, "Catching Dreams," *Kings Mountain Herald*, June 24, 1999: 15.

56 Wynolia Robinson, legacy.com/obituaries/shelbystar/obituary. https://www.legacy.com/obituaries/shelbystar/obituary.aspx?n=wynolia-robinson&pid=139663996&fhid=7723.

BONNIE SERRELL

By Mark S. Sternman

During World War II, the Kansas City Monarchs had two middle infielders who hit for average, exhibited extra-base power, and played defense with flair. Born in the winter of 1919, Jackie Robinson not only changed baseball history but altered U.S. history as well. Born in the winter of 1920, Bonnie Serrell toiled in a far dimmer spotlight but played an impactful role on one of the best teams in the storied history of the Monarchs. Although a year younger than Robinson, Serrell preceded him as a Kansas City middle infielder.

Born in Natchez, Louisiana, on March 9, 1920, Barney Clinton Serrell went by many names. Better known in baseball circles as Bonnie, Serrell also went by Barney Clinton Hoskins, taking on the surname of his maternal grandparents, Will and Mattie Hoskins.[1] Bonnie's mother, Piccola, married Frank Serrell in Upshur, Texas, on August 6, 1925. According to his World War I draft registration card, Frank, born on February 26, 1896, came from Gilmer, Texas, in Upshur County. At the time of the 1930 census, Piccola, Bonnie, and his two brothers (Leon, born in 1922, and James, born in 1924) lived with the widowed Mattie Hoskins.[2]

Like many contemporaries, Serrell sought to make himself appear younger, and many sources list his birthdate as 1922, suggesting that he took on his brother Leon's birth year as his own. The 1940 Census reported an expansion in the family that now included Bonnie's siblings Margaret (born in 1933), Thomas Jr. (1938), and Donald (1940).

Bonnie's father had gone north in search of improved employed possibilities. "In 1933," a biographical dictionary wrote, "the family was reunited in Chicago … [Bonnie] Serrell left high school before graduation and developed his baseball skills on Chicago's sandlots."[3] Having attracted the attention of the American Giants, Serrell made his professional debut with a one-game cup of coffee in left field for Chicago in 1941.

After this modest debut, Serrell went from spare part to star with Kansas City in 1942. One preview overlooked Serrell entirely, excluding him from a list of 15 Monarchs and suggesting that Newt Allen would play second base.[4] Subsequent data reveal that the underrated Serrell represented a major offensive force in the Negro American League for his first three full seasons (the chart below draws from statistics posted on Seamheds.com):

	1942	1943	1944
RUNS	T-3	T-2	T-1
HITS	3	2	2
2B		1	T-3
3B	1	1	T-2
HR	5		T-1
RBI	4	T-2	1
BA	2		5
OBP	3		7
SLG	T-2	6	5
OPS	3	9	5

Bonnie Serrel top 10 NAL offensive categories

Hardly an accumulator of empty statistics, Serrell had multiple meaningful hits during the magical run by the Monarchs in 1942. Getting revenge against his former team, the Chicago American Giants, Serrell on June 28 singled in Buck O'Neil from second base in the top of the 13th inning with the go-ahead run and then scored an insurance tally as Kansas City won 9-7. On July 5 Serrell hit two homers, likely the only multiple-homer game of his Negro League career,[5] as the Monarchs beat the Birmingham Black Barons

11-5 in the opener of a doubleheader. On July 7 Serrell tripled in the 10th off Memphis Red Sox ace Verdell Mathis in a game started by Satchel Paige that turned into a classic pitching duel at Pelican Stadium in New Orleans. Serrell did not score, and Kansas City lost 1-0.[6] On August 24 before a record crowd exceeding 2,400 at City Stadium in St. Joseph, Missouri, the Monarchs mauled the American Giants 10-4 thanks in part to Serrell, who "hit a long homer over the right field wall (and) also did some neat work at second."[7]

This debut would have appeared impressive for a one-dimensional slugger in the prime of his career, but Serrell stands out even more given that he combined these offensive outbursts as a 22-year-old rookie with a slick defensive skillset that earned him the nickname of the Vacuum Cleaner for his defensive flashiness. Kansas City teammate Connie Johnson recalled, "He played fancy, but that's the only way he could play. He wasn't clownin' but he'd get the ball and throw it over his shoulder and behind him and all like that and make the double play."[8]

While predominantly a second baseman, Serrell played at least once at every position except pitcher and catcher. On April 19, 1942, in right field, he made a game-saving catch to rob Birmingham's Goose Tatum of a walk-off homer in a game that Kansas City held on to win, 8-6.

As the youngest player to appear in the 1942 Negro League World Series, Serrell exceeded his strong regular-season numbers with a superlative slash line of .412/.412/.588 in the Monarchs' sweep of the NNL champion Homestead Grays.

Both Serrell and the Monarchs played well in 1943, but they were unable to match the success of the 1942 championship campaign. The Birmingham Black Barons were the first-half champions of the NAL, while the Chicago American Giants captured the second-half title; although the Monarchs had a better composite record than both teams, Kansas City failed to make the playoffs in 1943. Serrell, though still a strong player compared to league norms, regressed offensively in 1943 with his on-base percentage dropping from .403 to .325 and his slugging percentage falling from .565 to .421.

The fortunes of Serrell and the Monarchs diverged in 1944. While Kansas City faded to fourth, Serrell surged with a season similar to his first with the Monarchs by batting .364 (he had hit .366 in 1942) with a career-high on-base percentage of .407. The high point of Serrell's season occurred at Comiskey Park in Chicago, where he had played as an amateur and now returned to triumphantly as a professional on the most prominent stage of the Negro Leagues. There, Serrell took part in his only East-West All-Star Game. Batting sixth and playing the whole contest, he went 2-for-3 with a run and an RBI as the West rallied for a 7-4 win.

In 1945 Serrell played just four games for Kansas City before traveling to Mexico for the summer and to Cuba for the winter. As a result, Bill James later wrote, "the Monarchs signed Jackie Robinson, who was three years older than Serrell and not considered to be as good a player."[9] Serrell played in the Mexican League from 1945 to 1948, spending the first three seasons with Tampico and splitting the 1948 campaign between San Luis Potosi and Veracruz. He also plied his trade for the Marianao team of the Cuban Winter League for two consecutive seasons. During his first campaign in Cuba, the 1945-46 season, he led the league with 14 doubles.[10]

Hilton Smith, the Monarchs' Hall of Fame pitcher, believed that Serrell should have been the player to break the color barrier rather than Jackie Robinson. According to Smith, "Jackie couldn't touch that boy. He could do everything. It just killed him when they picked Jackie and not him. He left, went to Mexico and never came back."[11] Smith was not entirely correct about Serrell never coming back until after Bonnie received what he had hoped was a legitimate opportunity to make it to the major leagues. As Robinson went on to greater glory in Montreal and Brooklyn, Serrell returned to Kansas City for three more seasons, 1949 to 1951. In 1951, as the Monarchs were bleeding money, the team sold Serrell to the San Francisco Seals of the Pacific Coast League for $1,000; the Seals were the Triple-A franchise of the New York Yankees.[12]

Lefty O'Doul managed the Seals when the 31-year-old Serrell joined the team in 1951. Serrell asserted that O'Doul discriminated against Blacks, saying: "What should have been the highlight of my career became a disaster. The source of my problem was the Seals' manager Lefty O'Doul. … Lefty was a racist and didn't try to hide his feelings." After meeting Serrell for the first time and watching him practice with teammate Bob Thurman, O'Doul, according to Serrell, loudly declared to team management, "I told you to get ballplayers, not monkeys!"[13]

Playing on the same team with a National League star of the future in Lew Burdette and an American

After hitting .360 in NAL play, 22-year-old second baseman Bonnie Serrell batted .412 (7-for-17) with five RBIs in Kansas City's four-game World Series sweep of the Homestead Grays. (Courtesy Noir-Tech Research, Inc.)

League star of the past in Joe Page, Serrell, perhaps unsurprisingly given the attitude of his manager, struggled with a .243/.273/.320 slash line. The Seals likewise sputtered to a last-place record of 74-93.

After his unpleasant experiences in San Francisco, Serrell never played professional baseball for a U.S.-based team again. Returning to Mexico, he spent 1952 to 1956 with the Nuevo Laredo team and split his last season as a player south of the border between Nuevo Laredo and Monterrey. Although Serrell never had received the fair shot at making the major leagues that he had wanted so badly, he still merited occasional mentions in his home country, thanks to the back pages of *The Sporting News*, which showed that he ranked among the top five hitters in both summer and winter Mexican leagues,[14] and retained his talent for the clutch hit.[15] Serrell could still swing a sweet stick as he batted .370 in the Mexican League in 1952 and .376 for the Arizona-Mexico League in his swan song season of 1958.[16] In 10 seasons in Mexico, Serrell had a robust .311 batting average with 162-game equivalencies of 206 hits, 105 runs, and 12 triples.[17]

Serrell lived nearly 40 years after his playing career ended and had two tough stints as manager that left him with a record of 100-130 as a skipper. After managing Juarez in the Arizona-Mexican League in 1958, he "managed the San Luis Potosi Indians for part of the 1963 Mexican Center League season. Serrell married a woman from Mexico and settled there after his playing career ended."[18] He died in East Palo Alto, California, on August 15, 1996.

While Serrell never kept company with Robinson in the big leagues, he did have a longer baseball career and outlived his more famous teammate by nearly a quarter of a century. Robinson rightly deserves the everlasting gratitude of all baseball fans for permanently smashing the color line. Serrell deserves respect for both his more modest but still impressive accomplishments as a Negro League star and the choice he made to play a significant portion of his career in Mexico, which provided a much less racist environment than the United States. This latter decision clearly freed him from having to carry the enormous burdens assumed by Robinson and likely led Serrell to enjoy a more peaceful existence.

Sources

In addition to the sources cited in the Notes, the author consulted Seamheads.com.

Notes

1 Because Serrell sometimes used Hoskins as his last name, he may also have taken on William as his first name to match his grandfather.

2 Thanks to Rick Bush for his extensive genealogical research that provided much of the information for this paragraph and helped to flesh out Serrell's family background.

3 David L. Porter, ed., *Biographical Dictionary of American Sports: Baseball Revised and Expanded Edition Q-Z* (Westport, Connecticut: Greenwood Press, 2000), 1387.

4 "Baseball Notes," *The Afro American*, April 21, 1942: 12. Serrell would play 29 games at second for Kansas City in 1942. Allen had just nine appearances at that position.

5 Of the five seasons with statistics for Serrell in the Seamheads Negro Leagues database, Serrell has just two multi-homer seasons (3 in 1942 and 2 in 1944). See seamheads.com/NegroLgs/player.php?playerID=serre01bon (accessed October 8, 2020).

6 Frederick C. Bush, "Verdell Mathis," sabr.org/bioproj/person/verdell-mathis/ (accessed September 15, 2020).

7 "Record Stadium Crowd Watches Monarchs Win," *St. Joseph (Missouri) Gazette*, August 25, 1942: 5.

8 Scott Simkus, "Strat-O-Matic Negro League All-Stars Guide Book," 2009.

9 Bill James, *The New Bill James Historical Baseball Abstract* (New York: The Free Press, 2001), 184. Like others, James erroneously saw Serrell as having a birth year of 1922 rather than 1920.

10   "William (Bonnie) Serrell Record in Cuba," Ashland Collection clipping in the National Baseball Hall of Fame and Museum's file on Serrell. Thanks to Reference Librarian Cassidy Lent for scanning the Serrell file.

11   Janet Bruce, *The Kansas City Monarchs: Champions of Black Baseball* (Lawrence: University of Kansas Press, 1985), 113.

12   William A. Young, *J.L. Wilkinson and the Kansas City Monarchs* (Jefferson, North Carolina: McFarland & Company, Inc., 2016), 175.

13   Amy Essington, *The Integration of the Pacific Coast League* (Lincoln: University of Nebraska Press, 2018), 98.

14   "Toppers in Mexican Coast," *The Sporting News*, January 26, 1955: 23; "Mexican Averages," *The Sporting News*, September 5, 1956: 35.

15   "[T]he Tomateros won a 16-inning thriller, 6 to 5, when Barney Serrell singled home the clincher." See A.O. Camou, "Obregon Sweeps Four Tilts; Ramirez' Zero Skein Halted," *The Sporting News*, November 30, 1955: 34.

16   Dick Clark and Larry Lester, eds., *The Negro Leagues Book* (Cleveland: Society for American Baseball Research, 1994), 301.

17   Pedro Treto Cisneros, *The Mexican League: Comprehensive Player Statistics, 1937-2001* (Jefferson, North Carolina: McFarland & Company, 2011), 253. The author calculated the full-season averages using data from this book.

18   "Barney Serrell," baseball-reference.com/bullpen/Barney_Serrell (accessed September 15, 2020). He worked as a laborer according to Porter, 1388.

WILLIE SIMMS

By Jay Hurd

Before the lumber,[1] natural gas,[2] and oil[3] industries brought unprecedented economic growth to Louisiana in the late nineteenth and early twentieth centuries, baseball had already established itself as a favorite pastime throughout the state, centering on the cities of New Orleans and Shreveport.[4] Baseball teams, created and maintained by industrial magnates, emerged. One such team, the Monroe Monarchs, developed from the multiple business enterprises of Fred Alonzo Stovall. Stovall acquired great wealth from the oil industry, and later from numerous other business ventures. He employed Whites and Blacks, provided housing for all, and encouraged the formation of baseball teams.

By 1920, Stovall had time and money to form a Negro baseball team, the Monroe Monarchs. This team, originally part of the Texas League, became a premier attraction due to its talent level. After the Great Depression, and the demise of Rube Foster's Negro National League, the Monarchs formed the cornerstone of the Negro Southern League: after "the collapse of the first version of the Negro National League, in 1932, the NSL turned out to be the only African American baseball league operating that year, making it black baseball's de-facto 'major league,' which turned the Monroe Monarchs, for one brief, shining moment, into the center of the blackball world" Regarding Stovall as a team owner, Buck O'Neil said Stovall was just like J.L. Wilkinson in Kansas City… when things got tough in the winter and his players needed some spare change to get by, he'd give it to them."[5]

Former Monroe Monarch Marlin Carter talked about playing for Stovall: "Fred Stovall was a very wealthy man. On his plantation he built a ballpark for his team. He also built a recreation center where the players relaxed when they weren't playing. Stovall spent a lot of money on his ball team. The players lived in houses on Stovall's plantation, and our meals were prepared by a cook the Stovalls employed … [and] most importantly, we always got paid."[6] The Monarchs gave professional starts to Negro League greats – and Hall of Famers – Willard "Home Run" Brown and Hilton Smith; the Monarchs also developed lesser-known players such as Willie "Bill Simms.

Willie Simms was born on December 23, 1908, in Shreveport. While records are not particularly clear, it does appear that his father was William Simms, a farm laborer, and his mother was Elizabeth "Lizzie" Gould Simms. If indeed these were his parents, he also had six brothers and sisters. Willie said that he loved to play baseball and played as a young boy on "the sandlot" in Shreveport.[7] By the time he was 14 or 15 years old, he played more regularly with a team organized by a friend's father, who was a carpenter by trade. These teams played often; they became popular for entertainment and provided opportunities for betting.

As Simms grew older, his love for baseball grew as well. In Shreveport he attended as many games as possible played by a local team (perhaps the Shreveport Sports) that competed in the Texas League. When he could not attend games, he would listen to the radio (local stations, including KWKH and WCAQ, provided music and sports news in the Shreveport area.)[8] When he approached the age of 20, in 1928, he played with traveling teams of the Sawmill (also known as Sawdust) League. From Shreveport he traveled to the surrounding towns of Leesville, Boley, and Mansfield. A year or so later, his baseball talent earned him a spot on the roster of another traveling team which barnstormed as far north as Canada.[9] Now around 23 years old, he enjoyed traveling and playing in different cities, and thought he could get used to playing under these conditions: "Shucks, I like this. I'm gonna make a career out of this. … One day I might get a chance to play some big league baseball."[10] While records are uncertain, the Negro Southern League Museum Research Center website notes that Simms may have played with the following teams (prior to playing with the Monroe Monarchs and Negro League teams): Shreveport Black Gassers, 1923-27; Shreveport-Leesville, 1928-31; Alexandria Giants, 1932-33; Shreveport Cubs (as Sims), 1933.[11]

• WILLIE SIMMS •

Despite information supporting the fact that he played baseball into and beyond the 1930s, confusion arises around his personal life. The 1930 US Census notes that Simms lived in Shreveport, but it lists him as the adopted son of a 62-year-old "washwoman" named Lorine Harris. In this record, Simms is identified as 21 years old and a professional baseball player; interestingly, professional baseball was linked with the agriculture industry. Also, records are not clear as to when Simms met his wife-to-be, Mazie Elemease Brown. Mazie was also from Shreveport and was born on December 15, 1913, to Wylie and Helen Brown. The 1940 US Census indicates that Simms, 31 years old, was married, although Mazie's name is not recorded; Simms was identified as a "lodger" who was married and lived with his wife in Shreveport. Records indicate that Simms registered for the World War II draft on October 16, 1940, and named his next of kin as Mazie Simms. Simms's draft registration also noted that he was employed by H.G. Hall (Horace G. Hall), owner of the Chicago American Giants.

Whatever the exact circumstances of his personal life may have been, Simms's consistent play continued to draw attention and in 1934 he began a stint as an outfielder with Fred Stovall's Monroe Monarchs, managed by Frank Johnson. Early that year, Simms (also identified as Sims) was one of the players seeking a spot on the team.[12] The 5-foot-10, 160-pound Simms did make the team, and the left-handed-batting, right-hand-throwing player could be seen in left field and center field. The Monroe Monarchs played numerous teams that season, including the Pittsburgh Crawfords, the Bastrop Red Sox, the Van Dyke's House of David team, and the Birmingham Black Barons. In an exhibition game against the Crawfords, he had two hits, one a home run, off Satchel Paige.

In 1936, after his time with the Monroe Monarchs, Simms joined the Cincinnati Tigers, of an Independent Clubs organization,[13] managed by Carl Glass. Simms appeared in eight games for the Tigers, playing in right field, and had a .320 batting average. Candy Jim Taylor, then player-manager of the Chicago American Giants, signed him to play with Chicago in 1937. Simms did play with the Giants, and with two other teams that season: the Kansas City Monarchs, managed by Andy Cooper; and the Cincinnati Tigers, now managed by Ted "Double Duty" Radcliffe He played 30 games in center field with the Monarchs, had 30 hits, a .283 batting average, and 10 stolen bases. With the Tigers, he played in three games in right field and was 1-for-7; and with the Giants he appeared in two games in left field, had two hits and was 2-for-7. In a 1937 Monarchs exhibition game versus a White major-league team led by Bob Feller, Simms went 0-for-5 at the plate.

In 1938 Simms played for both the Chicago American Giants, managed by Candy Jim Taylor, and the Kansas City Monarchs, managed by Andy Cooper. For the Giants, he appeared in 16 games, all in center field, had 18 hits, a .245 batting average, and two stolen bases. He appeared in three games in center field for the Monarchs and went 3-for-12. In 1939, now 30 years old, Simms appeared in 29 games with Candy Jim Taylor's Chicago American Giants. He was the top hitter on the team with 34 hits and a .296 batting average. Defensively, he was again in center field. At this point in his career, he certainly wanted to play every day, and with more game appearances with the Giants, he remained there through the 1940 season. That season, the Giants, managed by Wilson Redus, Simms was in 17 games, playing center field, and had 14 hits, a .209 batting average, and one stolen base.

Throughout his career Simms was known as a solid defensive outfielder, and "the quintessential leadoff batter: [had] an excellent eye, patience at the plate, a good base stealer, and the speed to take an extra base if the opportunity was presented."[14] These skills brought him to the Kansas City Monarchs for three more seasons. In 1941, as the left fielder, he shared outfield duty with Willard Brown in center field and Ted Strong in right field. Also on that team were pitchers Satchel Paige and Hilton Smith. In 32 games played, Simms had 22 hits, a .183 batting average, and six stolen bases.

Simms remained with the Monarchs, managed by Frank Duncan, through the 1942 season. Now 33 years old, he played in 36 games, all but one in left field. In 152 at-bats he had 29 hits for a .191 batting average, with three stolen bases. The Monarchs won the Negro American League title with a 35-17 record. The Monarchs faced the Negro National League's Homestead Grays in the Negro League World Series. Simms (then called Bill) appeared in four of the games, playing left field. He had five hits, one a triple. Although not one of the stars of the Monarchs that year, he was still an integral part of getting the team to and winning the World Series. Also during the 1942 season, in a Monarchs game versus a White major-league aggregation, Simms went 2-for-5 at the plate off Dizzy Dean, Johnny Grodzicki, and Al Piechota.

• When the Monarchs Reigned •

In 1943 Simms was once again a member of the Monarchs. In 30 games, with 110 plate appearances, he had 15 hits and a lowly .160 average. Also, in 1943 he played left field for the South All-Stars in a North-South All Star Game; he went 2-for-4. His team included Josh Gibson, Satchel Paige, Buck Leonard, Willard Brown, and Sam Bankhead on its roster.

At the end of the 1943 season, Simms thought his time in professional baseball might be over. He moved to California in February of 1943 and got a job. Simms worked five days a week but played semipro ball on Saturdays and Sundays in the California Winter League (with the Kansas City Royals, 1943-1945).[15] Soon however, he heard his Kansas City teammates asking him, "What's the matter – you not comin' back with us. … We need you."[16] He received a call from "*Mister* Wilkinson" (J.L. Wilkinson, owner of the Monarchs) and by the end of May 1944, Simms was again in Kansas City with the Monarchs, playing center field.[17]

After playing for Kansas City again in 1944, Simms and his wife, Mazie, moved permanently to Los Angeles. He now found employment with the Sinclair Paint Company, for whom he worked until retirement. He was able to buy a home, and the 1948 California US Voter Registrations for 1948 indicate that he and Mazie, both registered Republicans, lived at 738 East 51st Street, Los Angeles.

While in California, Simms began to play golf and took great pride in his 6 handicap.[18] He was a member of the "T" Masters' Golf Club and was the handicap chairman in Los Angeles. On August 29, 1974, at the age of 61, Mazie died. The location of her burial is unclear. Soon after, Simms left Los Angeles and moved to Perris, California, about 70 miles east of Los Angeles, and lived there until his death at the age of 93 on May 10, 2002. He is buried in the Perris Valley Cemetery.

Willie Simms patrolled the outfield for the Monarchs for parts of five seasons, including the 1942 championship campaign during which he was the team's starting leftfielder. (Courtesy Noir-Tech Research, Inc.)

Willie Simms – nicknamed Bill, Simmy, and Jeep[19] – was a modest man who was not certain if he could have played in the White major leagues, but he would have welcomed the opportunity to try. He loved baseball and asked himself, "Why in the world didn't I get a job managin' before I put the game down."[20] According to Percy Reed, a semipro ballplayer and a Negro League umpire (1929-1947), Simms was an "average ballplayer. Clean cut."[21] Average or not, Willie Simms certainly was a player many professional teams would have liked to have fielded. He admitted that his speed on the bases could not match that of Cool Papa Bell, but he regarded himself as an ideal leadoff hitter who could get on base and make things happen.

Sources

In addition to the sources cited in the Notes, the author consulted Seamheads.com, Baseball-Reference.com, Ancestry.com, GenealogyBank.com, FamilySearch.org, findagrave.com, and newspapers.com.

Notes

1 Donna Fricker, "The Louisiana Lumber Boom c. 1880-1925," Historic Context, https://www.crt.state.la.us/Assets/OCD/hp/nationalregister/historic_contexts/The_Louisiana_Lumber_Boom_c1880-1925.pdf. Accessed May 8, 2021.

2 "History of the Industry," Louisiana Mid Continent Oil and Gas Association, https://www.lmoga.com/about-us/history-of-the-industry. Accessed May 8, 2021.

3 "The History: How Did This All Start?" Louisiana's Oil, https://www2.southeastern.edu/orgs/oilspill/history.html.

4 "Louisiana Club of New Orleans v. Louisiana Club of New Orleans 29 July 1859," Protoball. https://protoball.org/index.php?search=louisiana&title=Special%3ASearch&go=Go; "Pre-pro Clubs and Games in Shreveport, La." Accessed May 8, 2021.

5   Paul Letlow, "The Monroe Monarchs," Paul Letlow's Sport Shorts, http://louisianasportsshorts.blogspot.com/2009/06/monroe-monarchs.html. Accessed May 8, 2021.

6   Paul Letlow, "The Monroe Monarchs," Paul Letlow's Sport Shorts. Accessed May 8, 2021.

7   Brent Kelley, *The Negro Leagues Revisited: Conversations with 66 More Baseball Heroes* (Jefferson, North Carolina: McFarland & Company, Inc., 2000), 44.

8   Lillian Jones Hall. "A Historical Study of Programming Techniques and Practices of Radio Station Kwkh, Shreveport, Louisiana: 1922-1950." Louisiana State University Historical Dissertation and Thesis, 1959. https://digitalcommons.lsu.edu/cgi/viewcontent.cgi?article=1557&context=gradschool_disstheses. Accessed May 8, 2021.

9   Possibly the Shreveport Acme Giants.

10 Kelley, 45.

11 "Negro League Player Register," Negro Southern League Museum Research Center, http://www.negrosouthernleaguemuseumresearchcenter.org/Portals/0/Birmingham%20Player%20Profiles/R-S.pdf. Accessed May 8, 2021.

12 "Monroe Monarchs Squad Stages Daily Workouts," *Monroe (Louisiana) Star News*, March 13, 1934: 5.

13 Seamheads, https://www.seamheads.com/NegroLgs/team.php?yearID=1936&teamID=CT&LGOrd=2. Accessed May 8, 2021.

14 Kelley, 44.

15 "Negro League Player Register," Negro Southern League Museum Research Center, 352, http://www.negrosouthernleaguemuseumresearchcenter.org/Portals/0/Birmingham%20Player%20Profiles/R-S.pdf. Accessed May 8, 2021.

16 Kelley, 45.

17 Kelley, 45-46.

18 "Willie Simms," Negro Leagues Baseball Museum, eMuseum Electronic Resources for Teachers, https://nlbemuseum.com/nlbemuseum/history/players/simms.html. Accessed May 8, 2021.

19 "Bill Simms," Baseball Reference. https://www.baseball-reference.com/bullpen/Bill_Simms. Accessed May 8, 2021.

20 Kelley, 46.

21 Kelley, 34.

HILTON SMITH

By Thomas Kern

I was born in 1912 [sic] in Giddings, Texas, a little town between Austin and Houston. Rube Foster came from about twenty-five miles from my house, a little town right above me.

— Hilton Smith [1]

Something must have been in the air as the state of Texas produced eight Negro League Hall of Famers [2] including Hilton Smith, whose early local prominence as a lights-out pitcher helped to springboard him to an accomplished career in the Negro Leagues that led to his induction into Cooperstown's shrine.

Although Smith told historian John Holway that he was born in 1912, official records confirm that he was born on February 27, 1907.[3] When asked about it, Hilton's son, DeMorris Smith, said that "as the oldest of six, Hilton helped raise his siblings. He did not get out of Giddings until later and his career in baseball got delayed." Smith put his age back to enhance his career prospects, his son also said, and did so after he left Prairie View A&M College in the late 1920s.[4]

Hilton Smith's reminiscences offer important insights to his youth and his pathway to baseball:

"I patterned myself after my uncles. I had two uncles that my mother would let me play with. They were powerful good ballplayers. I guess I inherited my ability from them. They were good, but they played out in the country there, played for fun. I just loved it, and that was what started me off. I just made myself, didn't have a teacher. I kept picking up and looking and learning as I went up." [5]

He continued:

"I started out playing with my dad, who was a schoolteacher. I played for my dad's team when I was in the tenth grade. I guess I was about fifteen. During the summertime I played with older boys – they were all grown men. I pitched against the town high school team and shut them out 2-0." [6]

Smith attended Prairie View State Normal and Industrial College in 1928 and 1929.[7] According to the school's records, he received academic honors both years and was on the dean's list as well. "Smith was an Agricultural Science major ... and played in the outfield during 1928 and as pitcher in 1929." Prairie View inducted Smith into its sports hall of fame in 2011.[8]

After attending Prairie View, Smith turned full time to baseball. He told Holway:

"Austin had a team, the Austin Senators, a semipro team that played Houston and all the towns down there. They had a pitcher named Willie Owens who had played with Birmingham in the Negro League. In 1931, I was nineteen [*sic*; he was actually 24], I went down and pitched against him one Saturday and beat 'em, I just beat 'em good. He went back to Austin and said, "My goodness, there's a little kid there, he's something else." So when the Chicago American Giants came down to play Austin the next weekend, Austin came down and got me to pitch for them. I beat 'em [the American Giants] 5-4 in eleven innings." [9]

His audition won Smith a spot in the rotation of the Austin Black Senators, a Texas Negro League team considered part of the feeder system for the Negro Southern League. Fast-forward to 1932 and Smith's career clicked up a notch to the Monroe Monarchs of the Negro Southern League.

"Monroe [Louisiana] had a really good Negro team then. They were champions of the southern conference [NSL], had beaten everybody. ... They came to Austin and played us two games. They were talking about they heard of this little schoolboy up there and said, "Well, we came up here to work him over." But we had a great big ballpark and I beat 'em 2-1. They couldn't believe it. They said, "Well, this big old park, no wonder you won. When you come to Monroe" – Monroe had a small park – "we'll hit so many home runs off you. ..." So I went to Monroe the following Sunday and beat 'em 4-2." [10]

The *Monroe Morning World* described Smith's first performance in what was styled the Negro Dixie League Series this way: "A young pitcher named Hilton Smith gave up 11 hits, but only one earned run to tie the series at two games apiece."[11] Monroe won the series four games to two.

As was the norm in Negro League ball, ballplayers, managers, owners all would scout the opposition looking for talent to stock their own teams. There was no better sign of talent than an opponent who could beat you. Smith continued, "Monroe picked me up to play with them and carried me to Pittsburgh. ... I played with Monroe for the next three years. I had a great year in '32, won thirty-one games, didn't lose a ball game."[12]

Not only did Hilton Smith find momentum for his baseball career in Monroe, but he also met and then married Louise Smith, a native of Monroe, in 1934. They had two sons – Hillton (yes, that is the correct spelling), born in 1935 and DeMorris, in 1938.[13]

Smith's sojourn with Monroe lasted into 1935, when a pivotal moment in his career took place:

"I went to Bismarck, North Dakota, in 1935. The League broke up down South and Monroe went on a tour around the Midwest. We weren't making any money, just touring around, but we were playing good ball, beating just everybody we met. I didn't know what it was to lose a ballgame. I hadn't lost a ballgame. We got into Bismarck the fifth of July – I will never forget that. A guy named Churchill was mayor of the city and had a ball club. ... Satchel Paige was pitching for them. ... They were getting ready to go to this Wichita semipro tournament and they needed another pitcher. Churchill asked me about staying and I said I didn't know. ... How about $150?" I told him okay." [14]

The Bismarck Churchills were one of baseball's most iconic semipro teams. In his biography of Ted Radcliffe, a teammate of Smith's in Bismarck, Kyle McNary wrote:

"It was a common occurrence from the beginning of small-town baseball to hire "ringers" to bolster teams for important games on which big money was bet. Usually the ringers were ex-minor or major-leaguers, but as small town baseball became more competitive, teams ... moved to the last remaining pool of untapped talent ... the Negro Leagues, and towns in Minnesota and North Dakota were the first to hire black pitchers and catchers for big games, and eventually for entire seasons." [15]

Neil Churchill of Bismarck, North Dakota, epitomized this obsession to sign pro talent to enhance a local team's competitiveness. Baseball was a big deal in the American breadbasket and Churchill, a local auto dealer with a love for baseball, played for and later managed the Bismarck team. He "could not abide Bismarck playing second baseball fiddle to Jamestown [Bismarck's in-state competition]." To him, it was obvious what he needed to do to strengthen his new team: sign Black players." Churchill worked with Abe Saperstein in Chicago (a booking agent) to provide a pipeline for Negro League talent.[16]

Churchill's signing of Negro Leaguers, led by Satchel Paige, was central to achieving his purpose of winning the first National Semipro Championship tournament, defeating the Duncan (Halliburton) Cementers of Oklahoma, 5-2, in the championship game. The 1935 tournament, held in Wichita, Kansas, included 32 teams from 16 states. Bismarck ran the table, winning seven games for the championship. Satchel Paige pitched in five games, winning four and striking out 60. This fully integrated team had at its core five white and six black players. The Negro Leaguers were Satchel Paige, Hilton Smith, Ted Radcliffe, Quincy Troupe, Barney Morris, and Red Haley.[17]

Smith did not pitch much for Bismarck in 1935 – Paige was the star. Paige first played for Bismarck in 1933 and came back in 1935 after Pittsburgh Crawfords owner Gus Greenlee refused to give him a raise for the 1935 season. According to Smith himself, "I didn't lose a ball game with Bismarck the whole year, but I didn't pitch much. I played right field on that club most of the time and batted third or fourth."[18] But Smith played the outfield and in the final, he batted cleanup and went 2-for-4, driving in one run and scoring one in the victory.[19]

• When the Monarchs Reigned •

According to Smith, "The next year [1936] when I went back to Bismarck, Satchel had gone east, so I did all the pitching down there in Wichita [in the Tournament]. I won four games and all four of them were shutouts [tournament records indicate not all the games were shutouts]."[20]

And while now led by Hilton Smith, who admirably filled Paige's pitching void by winning those four games in the tournament (he was being held out of Game Six, the semifinal, to pitch the final), Bismarck lost 6-2 in the semis to the team it had defeated the year before, the Cementers.

Smith's Bismarck tenure ended up linking him to the team with which he spent his remaining career, the Kansas City Monarchs. It has been noted that the key to Monarchs owner J.L. Wilkinson's success was his keen eye for talent: "While barnstorming, Wilkinson continued to evaluate opposing players. He signed Hilton Smith after seeing him pitch for the Bismarck, North Dakota, team."[21] Smith confirmed that "Wilkinson called him during the 1936 season, while he was playing for the Bismarck semipro team and asked him if he would be willing to finish the season with the Monarchs. Smith agreed and was paid $175 a month."[22]

Hall of Famer Hilton Smith, who long had the unjust reputation as Satchel Paige's designated relief pitcher, was considered by his peers to be every bit Paige's equal on the mound. (Courtesy Noir-Tech Research, Inc.)

The Wichita tournament ended on August 28 with Bismarck's loss to the Cementers, and Smith traveled to Kansas City to begin his 13-year career with the Monarchs. He pitched in one game for the Monarchs that year at the end of the season, but he likely played in more over the course of the ambitious independent schedule that Kansas City engaged in throughout the Midwest.

Smith joined a franchise that was considered by many to be the gold standard for Negro League teams. Owner J.L. Wilkinson had formed the Monarchs in 1920 as an inaugural member of the Negro National League from players of the All Nations touring team he had previously assembled. Under his ownership (1920-1948), the Monarchs thrived in every league or independent setting. They played in the first two Negro World Series between the NNL and the Eastern Colored League, winning in 1924 against Hilldale but losing to them in 1925. Kansas City was always competitive, winning the NNL twice more before it disbanded in 1932. The Monarchs then played as an independent team for several years until Wilkinson made the franchise a member of the Negro American League in 1937.

The Monarchs had a stellar reputation throughout the country:

"For black youngsters in the Midwest and Southwest, the Monarchs were the tops. "It was the ambition of every black boy to be a

138

Monarch, just as it was for every white boy to become a Yankee," contended Monarchs shortstop Jesse Williams. "That was the tradition back then. You didn't play ball until you became a Monarch." And in segregated America, ace pitcher Hilton Smith knew that "when you got with the Monarchs, you were as high as you could go.'"[23]

Smith was glad to be with the Monarchs, but he was the first person to admit that, despite his early acclaim, he had room for growth. He recalled, "Actually, I didn't really learn how to pitch until I came to the Monarchs that fall. I just had natural stuff before that. I learned from having such guys for teachers as Frank Duncan, Bullet Rogan, and Andy Cooper."[24]

Thanks to the two future Hall of Famers Rogan and Cooper, Smith's development hastened and helped polish him into the premier talent he became. As Smith explained:

"'I'd be pitching and right after the ball game [Rogan would] come out and he'd tell me, 'You've got a lot of stuff, but why'd you do such-and-such a thing?' I'd say, 'Well, I don't know.' He'd say, 'Well, from now on, you *know*.' I'd answer, 'Okay, I'll do it.' Next time … I got in the ball game, he'd say, 'Uh-huh, I see you're picking up.'

"Andy Cooper was a smart manager, and he was a great teacher, great teacher! A student of baseball. He would take me aside and just sit there and talk to me, and I'd watch how he'd pitch. And my owner, Wilkinson, would talk to me. He was a doll, that guy. He had played a little semi-pro ball himself and he really knew baseball. He said, 'Look, you've got everything, but use your wrist a little more, see if you can't get a little more hop on your ball.' I took him at his word, and sure enough, it worked."[25]

In 1937 Smith had as good a season as the Monarchs could have asked for. He started the season with a no-hitter, went 11-4 in NAL play (starting 16 games and completing nine), was selected for his first All-Star Game, and helped the Monarchs defeat the Chicago American Giants for the pennant. Smith recalled his first full season in Kansas City fondly, saying:

"The first game I pitched in this park out here in Kansas City was a no-hitter. I beat the Chicago American Giants 4-0. Nobody got on first base –I mean a perfect game. The giants had Sug Cornelius pitching, Larry Brown catching, Alex Radcliff. They were hard to beat. I didn't lose too many games that year. I probably lost three the whole season." [26]

Hilton played in seven consecutive East-West Classics (1937, 1938, both 1939 games, 1940, 1941, and 1942) and posted an all-star game record of 1-1, an ERA of 4.26, and 16 strikeouts. His victory came in 1938, thanks to four innings of solid relief. Famously, he started the 1942 All-Star Game when Paige, who was supposed to take the first turn on the mound for the West team, was late getting to the ballpark. Smith and Dave Barnhill engaged in a pitchers' duel and, with the score tied at 2-2 after six, Paige finally showed up and was brought in to relieve Smith, only to lose the game to the East.[27]

At the end of his first full season with Kansas City, Smith journeyed to Cuba to play for Martin Dihigo's Marianao team. This was not Smith's first foray south of the border. According to author Donn Rogosin, "In 1933 the Austin Black Senators with Hilton Smith barnstormed to Mexico City and back. … American black ball players found a haven in Mexico after 1930."[28] It was Mexican fans who first gave Smith's Curve Ball the name El Diablo – the devil.[29]

The Cuban Winter League season ran from October 1937 to February 1938 and Smith served as one of three primary starters for Dihigo's squad, alongside Barney Brown and Dihigo himself. Records compiled by Jorge Figueredo in his book on Cuban baseball show Smith appearing in 14 games, starting seven, and finishing with a 6-3 record for a team that finished 35-28 in third place, behind Santa Clara and Almendares.[30] Smith played one more winter in Cuba in 1939-40, teaming up with a Santa Clara team that finished under .500.[31]

In 1938 Smith became the premier starter for the Monarchs. It has been observed that "the real strength of the 1938 Monarchs was pitching. The ace was … Hilton Smith, who had an outstanding control, a fast ball that moved, and an unrivaled curve ball."[32] The Monarchs finished 1938 with the best overall record in the NAL, but they were bested in both halves by the Memphis Red Sox and Atlanta Black Crackers respectively, keeping them out of the NAL championship series that the Red Sox won.

• When the Monarchs Reigned •

In 1939 the Monarchs were first-half champions, and they defeated the second-half winners, the St. Louis Stars, for the NAL championship. Smith looked back on those early years with the Monarchs and recalled:

"In '37, '38, and '39 I had tremendous years. I could pitch and hit, both. Andy Cooper'd pinch-hit me for his fourth-place hitters as quick. Several years I hit over .400 pinch-hitting, outfield, first base and pitching.[33]

I was pitching about four times a week, because we were playing six or seven games a week, and we only carried about four pitchers. Maybe sometimes we'd have five, that was the most. We didn't know what it was to relieve. When you went out there, you didn't look at the bull pen, you were expected to go the whole route.

They knew I wasn't wild; they knew I threw strikes. We didn't hardly walk anyone. The curve, we'd just slice it off, pfffft. And everybody threw hard. Good curve balls, and that live fast ball moved. ... We had to have two curve balls, a big one and a small one. Now they call it a slider, but those guys were throwing it years back. It kind of darted over the corner like that. Good control." [34]

It was also in 1938 that a player named Buck O'Neil came to Kansas City. O'Neill was Smith's roommate for the next 10 years. Buck believed, "[f]rom 1940 to 1946 Hilton Smith might have been the best pitcher in the world."[35]

Statistically, Hilton leveled off in 1940 but still helped lead the Monarchs to the NAL championship, besting the second-place Memphis Red Sox by 7½ games. The 1940 Monarchs blended the experience of Turkey Stearnes, Jack Matchett, and Newt Allen with the relative youth of O'Neil, Joe Greene, and Jesse Williams to lead the league.

Two years earlier, in 1939, J.L. Wilkinson had transformed the image of the Monarchs with the signing of Satchel Paige who, alongside Josh Gibson, was the face of the Negro Leagues. Paige had been playing for the Monarchs' traveling B team, but his signing was now about to pay dividends. Paige's career had been at its low point due to a sore arm, but at the beginning of 1941, he miraculously recovered. According to Negro League historian Mark Ribowsky,

"Wilkinson believed the time was right for Paige to don the Monarchs uniform."[36] Kansas City's attendance increased dramatically and Wilkinson's vision of the Monarchs as a national attraction was realized.

The implications for the team, however, were complicated. The addition of Paige and players like Willard Brown helped build a squad that won the NAL in the two seasons after Paige's arrival. It also led to the 1942 Monarchs' storied victory over the Negro National League's Homestead Grays in the Negro League World Series. However, all that winning came with a price: team chemistry.[37]

Paige biographer Larry Tye wrote that Hilton Smith "had issues with Satchel, telling one interviewer ... Satchel's miraculous recovery from arm troubles [was] 'the worst break I got.'"[38] That said, Tye still noted that "Hilton Smith was master of the curveball and, in the minds of many, the best black pitcher of his age."[39]

Smith himself reflected on that time, saying:

"I played twelve years with the Kansas City Monarchs, 1937-48, and I won twenty games or more every year. Not counting exhibitions, I won 161 league games and lost 22, but most people have never heard of me. They've only heard of Satchel Paige. That's because I was Satchel Paige's relief.

Every Sunday I'd start, then Monday night come on in relief, start Wednesday, and maybe Friday, according to how Satchel was feeling. It was my turn to relieve him on all big games. He'd go two or three innings; if there was a big crowd and we had to win it, I'd go in there and save it. I just took my baseball serious; I just went out there to do a job. But Satchel was an attraction, he could produce, and he'd clown a lot. I guess it really hurt me. I tried to get away, but there wasn't anything I could do about it." [40]

He also claimed, "I actually hit my peak, too, in '41. I was to a place then that I could do just do anything, I felt that good."[41] His 1941 statistics included a 13-6 record with nine complete games and a 2.53 ERA. The Monarchs won the NAL pennant, besting the Birmingham Black Barons.

From Buck O'Neil's perspective, Hilton just got on with it: "I was Hilton's roommate for ten years, and I can tell you he never brooded about [pitching in Paige's shadow] then. He was playing for a salary, just like everyone else, and this was his job. Satchel was pitching in a ballgame just about every night to draw a crowd, and someone had to pick him up. Hilton wasn't the only man pitching behind Satchel Paige; everybody who pitched did that."[42] Putting it another way, O'Neil said, "Hilton felt he was as good a pitcher as Satchel, but he had to understand that he wasn't the one drawing the crowds."[43]

Smith's son said that when it came down to it, his father "did not complain one way or another." In fact, "Satchel and his dad remained fishing buddies and friends."[44] Years later, Hilton Smith was an honorary pallbearer at Paige's funeral.[45]

In spite of Smith's later consternation with pitching in Paige's shadow, his connection with Satchel also had its benefits. As one of Paige's teammates, it dealt him ample opportunity to play in exhibition games against White major leaguers that Satchel's fame and reputation made possible, In a 1937 series between Satchel and Rogers Hornsby's All-Stars, Smith pitched in three games and was not scored on. One of those games was a 10-0 Monarchs win with Smith pitching a complete-game shutout.[46] In October 1941, a matchup between Paige and Bob Feller took place at Sportsman's Park in St. Louis. Paige gave up four runs and lost the game, 4-1, but Smith entered the game in the fifth inning and held the major leaguers scoreless on four hits. The *St. Louis Globe Democrat* wrote, "Smith, showing the best speed and sharpest curve of the quartet [Paige, Feller, and Ken Heintzelman, who was Feller's reliever], fanned six and walked only one."[47] Buck O'Neil played in the 1941 exhibitions and noted another game in the series in which Paige pitched the first three innings against Feller and was followed once again by Smith. According to O'Neil, "[Stan] Musial hit a home run on Satchel on the roof of that stadium. But Musial and John Mize said they'd never seen a curve ball like Hilton's curve ball."[48]

Smith continued to pitch in further Paige-Feller exhibition games, most notably in 1946 after the Monarchs lost the Negro World Series to the Newark Eagles. Smith noted, "That fall I went with Satchel to play against Bob Feller's big-league all-stars. … We played fifteen or sixteen games, and I relieved in two and pitched two complete games. I broke even with them."[49] In his two complete games, both against Bob Feller, he won one (3-2) and lost the second (6-3).[50]

Prior to those later exhibitions, however, came the 1942 season, which was one for the ages for the Monarchs. Kansas City won an epic exhibition game on Sunday, May 24, 1942, against a lineup of current and former major leaguers for the Navy Relief Fund. The game marked the first time a Black team played at Wrigley Field. The significance of the exhibition, five years before Jackie Robinson broke the color line, was not lost on Frank A. Young, the *Chicago Defender's* sports editor, who wrote, "[H]ere was Satchel Paige, Hilton Smith, and the Monarchs performing in big league style but denied the right to play in the big leagues because of their color."[51] The *Pittsburgh Courier's* headline also underscored Hilton Smith's contribution: "29,000 See Satch and Company Defeat Dizzy Dean's All-Stars: Hilton Smith Stars in Relief Role as Monarchs Win, 3-1."[52]

Smith recalled about the game:

"One of my greatest thrills was beating Dizzy Dean in Wrigley Field, Chicago, in 1942. … Satchel pitched the first five [six] innings for us and came out with the score 1-1' … [I came in in the seventh and] I struck out three, walked one, and gave up two hits and no runs." Hilton continued, "Big Joe Greene, our catcher, got a hit with two men on around the seventh, and I held 'em. In the ninth, [Cecil] Travis came up with one on. Barney Serrell, our shortstop, said, "[M]ake him hit it on the ground," and that's just what it was, a double play, and the ball game was over." [53]

Reflecting on the entire 1942 season, Smith added:

"We had a tremendous ball club that year. … We had Joe Greene catching, John [Buck] O'Neil first base, Jesse Williams short, Newt Allen second. Outfield we had Ted Strong, Willard Brown and a boy named Bill Simms. … Ted Strong was just as good a ballplayer as there was in baseball. … We also had a tremendous pitching staff in '42. We had Satchel, Jack Matchett, a boy named Connie Johnson who played in the majors. And Lefty LaMarque and a boy named Booker McDaniel. Nobody hardly beat us. That particular year, '42, I don't think I lost maybe one or two ball games the entire year." [54]

The Monarchs' season climaxed with a World Series sweep of the Homestead Grays in September. Smith pitched five innings and won Game Two, but the Series belonged to Paige. Satchel started Games One and Three and relieved and finished Games Two and Four. He famously said to Smith in Game Two, "You've been relieving me all year. Let me relieve you."[55] He did just that and earned the save while also striking out Josh Gibson with the bases loaded and two outs in the seventh.

From 1943 to 1945, the Monarchs hit a lull in NAL play. The Birmingham Black Barons won the pennant in 1943 and 1944, advancing to the Negro League World Series but losing both years to Homestead. In 1945 Kansas City finished third behind the Cleveland Buckeyes, who went on to defeat the Grays in the Series. It didn't help the Monarchs that Smith got hurt. He remembered, "My arm went dead in 1943. I hurt it, and I played first base and outfield for two years. In '44 I began working back into shape, so I went out on the Coast that fall and played baseball against Bob Lemon."[56]

This was Smith's only foray to the California Winter League, as he had opted for Mexico, Cuba, and Venezuela when it came to winter ball. In October 1944, after a disappointing fourth-place NAL finish, Smith and several teammates helped form the Kansas City Royals, one of four teams to play in the California Winter League. The standings showed the Royals with more wins than first-place Birmingham, but a lower winning percentage due to a different number of games played. Three Hall of Famers played on the Royals – Smith, Willie Wells, and Ray Dandridge – along with Chet Brewer and Sam Jethroe.[57]

The World War II years were tough on the Monarchs. Like most Negro League teams, the franchise fielded a squad that was depleted of players who were drafted into military service. Smith, too, was called up; however, due to his age, he served stateside rather than overseas.[58] Eventually, Smith noted, "My arm came back in 1945 or '46, and in '46 we played Newark for the Negro world championship."[59] The Monarchs won both halves of the NAL and were back in the World Series against the NNL champions after a three-year hiatus. The competition was tough – the Newark Eagles had numerous future Hall of Famers, including Larry Doby, Monte Irvin, Leon Day, and Biz Mackey. Newark defeated Kansas City, four games to three, but Smith pitched admirably in his last postseason. He pitched into the sixth in Game One, leading 1-0, but walked Larry Doby and was then relieved by Satchel Paige; the Monarchs won the game, 2-1. The Monarchs lost two of the next three, but Smith pitched a complete-game 5-1 victory in Game Five, giving up 10 hits and striking out eight. Game Five marked the Monarchs' high-water mark as they lost Games Six and Seven, with the final game being notable due to an AWOL Satchel Paige.[60]

With the breaking of the color barrier in 1947, Negro League attendance suffered as Black baseball fans shifted their interest to the slowly integrating White major leagues and their emerging African American stars. Box-office receipts were down, so Negro League team owners altered their financial model to the sale of contracts of promising players to the White major-league teams. It would not be enough and, in any event, the vision of one league for all was the endgame for a society struggling with its separate-but-equal legacy. In failing health, Wilkinson sold the Monarchs to his business partner, Tom Baird, in early 1948, which was Hilton's last year with the team. Player salaries were dropping due to the struggles of the Negro League franchises, and Smith, who was believed to be 37 but was actually 41, saw fit to step away from the game.[61]

Before his playing career ended after the 1948 season, Smith was one of several Negro League players who were considered for the White majors, or at least to play in the minors as a way of auditioning for the parent club. Smith acknowledged, "I got a feeler from the big leagues in 1946. But my age was against me."[62]

Smith recalled in detail:

> "[Roy] Campanella came down to the Polo Grounds one night when we were playing Newark in the World Series and asked me what did I think about playing for the Dodgers. He said the front office had told him to talk to me' ... I figured I was too old ... and we were afraid to go down to the minors [with the Dodgers] and take a pay cut. ... Had it been opened up – had there been some other team beside the Dodgers – I probably would have taken a chance. I knew the Dodgers were pretty loaded and I'd have to sit around in the minors and they'd be slow about bringing me up, and at my age, that would be too much."[63]

Like many Negro League ballplayers, Smith was often asked how felt about not playing in the White majors. In his view, "Had I been three or four years younger, I probably would have been the first Negro signed in Organized Baseball."[64] "I pitched against enough major leaguers to see if I was on the level. ... I played against them enough, and they never hit me. So I feel that had I had the chance, I could have pitched in the major leagues."[65]

Although Smith himself would never play in the White majors, he was part of the Jackie Robinson story. As the tale goes, "Hilton Smith claimed he first met Jackie Robinson in 1942 when a team of black stars – including Robinson – played an exhibition game against a service team of White major leaguers. According to one account, Smith contacted J.L. Wilkinson after the encounter and urged him to sign Robinson right away."[66] Later, after Robinson's discharge from the military in 1944, he wrote to the Monarchs for a tryout, which Wilkinson agreed to. Robinson would play for the Monarchs in 1945, only to be signed secretly by Branch Rickey to a Dodgers contract in August and then later made official in October of that year.[67] Smith reflected later regarding Robinson's elevation to the Dodgers in 1947, "Even if we were playing here in Kansas City, everybody wanted to go over to St. Louis to see Jackie. So our league really began to go down, down, down."[68]

In 1947 Kansas City finished second to the Cleveland Buckeyes, and at the age of 40, Smith carried less of the pitching load. Late that season, he was offered the chance to manage the Monarchs after Frank Duncan was fired, but he demurred. Although he was no longer at the top of his game, that year still provided him satisfaction. In early 1947, the spring of his next to last campaign with the Monarchs, Smith went to Venezuela to play winter league ball on the famous Vargas team alongside Bill Cash, Hank Thompson, Luis Aparicio Sr., Parnell Woods, and Ray Dandridge. Smith recounted his game against the Yankees, who had traveled to Venezuela as part of their spring training:

> "I guess one of my greatest thrills was pitching against the New York Yankees in 1947 – March 17 – in Caracas, Venezuela. That was the first time I pitched against a whole major league ball club. And they had quite a club, too, believe you me. ... I pitched six innings, didn't give up any runs and gave up one hit, to Rizzuto. We won 4-3." [69]

Smith went 8-5 in the 1946-1947 winter season; alongside his success against the Yankees, it made for a fitting ending to his exhibition and winter league career.[70]

In 1948 the Monarchs were first-half champions in the NAL but lost to second-half champion Birmingham for the right to play in what turned out to be the last Negro League World Series. It was also Smith's last year with Kansas City, though it would not be the end of his baseball career.

In early 1949 he was recruited to play for a semipro team in Fulda, Minnesota. The Fulda Giants sought talent to increase attendance and to help them gain membership in the First Night league in southwestern Minnesota. Smith was paid approximately $1,000 a month for his sojourn with Fulda. His presence, although he mostly played the outfield, helped to ensure a successful season and enough money for Fulda to install lights and be accepted into the league the following year.[71] Hilton's son DeMorris, who had been a batboy for the Monarchs in the 1940s and went with his father to Fulda, reflected that Hilton was so well liked by the locals that they invited him back the following year.[72]

Smith later reminisced about the state of Negro League baseball which, according to him

> "… looked like it was dead, so I played in Fulda, Minnesota, in '49 and in '50 out to Armco-Sheffield Steel here in Kansas City. They had a ball club and they wanted me to manage it. … I could have pitched a little more. But I'd seen so many ballplayers that just kept a-hanging around when they were over the hill, so I'd always made up my mind when I got to the place where I was going down, I'd just give up. I am a supervisor at Armco now. I'm lucky, I got a real job." [73]

DeMorris spoke about his father's many commitments to the Kansas City community. He was a trustee, usher, and board president at St. Stephen Baptist Church and occasionally coached semipro and amateur teams, offering guidance to young players, some of whom made it to the major leagues.[74] Frank White, a longtime star for the Kansas City Royals and one of a number of players that Smith coached who made it to the majors, epitomized what DeMorris called his father's wish: for his legacy to be one of giving back to the game and to those who came after him.

At the time of Smith's posthumous induction into the Hall of Fame, White said, "Hilton coached me … when I was 18 or 19. He not only taught me the game, he got you to love the game. He had this real soothing approach and emphasized that you had to understand baseball before you could fully appreciate it. He had a big influence on my career and on my life."[75]

In his later years, Smith talked about the game's grind as well as his ultimate satisfaction:

> "It was a rough life – ride, ride, ride, and ride. I remember many a day, ride a bus, get out and get you a little bit to eat, go to the ballpark, go out there and pitch nine innings, play a doubleheader, play outfield the second game. But I enjoyed baseball, I really did. It was spoiling me. I loved it, and it was sweet. We had some great moments. I enjoyed every bit of it."[76] … "Honestly true, if I had to live my life over, I'd live it the same. No regrets." [77]

Not only did Smith enjoy himself, he also left a great impression on his teammates. Joe Greene, his Monarchs catcher, observed, "He had a real fast curve ball. It wasn't a big one, but he had good control. The manager would call him in sometimes to make just one pitch. And he did a lot of pinch hitting, too. He was a long ball hitter. He couldn't run, but he could really hit."[78]

Fellow Monarch Connie Johnson said, "If I had to get a pitcher to put out there and say, 'Get this man out,' I'd send Hilton Smith. He was better than anybody I ever seen. … Bob Feller had a great curve ball, but Hilton's was a little better. And he could hit as good as anybody on the team. … He was a hitter! Three hits wasn't nothing for him."[79] Another teammate, Lefty Bryant, remarked, "Hilton never got the credit he deserved. We never told him, but Hilton was the best pitcher we had, including Satchel."[80]

Smith's love for the game never diminished, and even in his 70s, he remained involved in baseball by scouting players for major-league teams. Buck O'Neil remembered, "When he died in 1983, we were both scouting for the Chicago Cubs."[81]

Hilton Smith knew he was Hall of Fame-worthy, but he did not live to see his induction. The first 11 Negro Leaguers entered Cooperstown's Hall between 1971 and 1987, after which the Veterans Committee was given a mandate to elect more players. Smith was inducted in 2001 as the 18th Negro League player to enter the Hall. His widow, sister, and two sons attended the induction ceremony.

DeMorris remembered his father as being low-key; he never argued and was a silent leader. Hilton Smith's life is well defined by his membership in three halls of fame (Prairie View A&M, the Texas Black Hall of Fame, and Cooperstown). It is worth noting, also, that Hilton's hometown, Giddings, Texas, named a baseball field after him – the Hilton Lee Smith Field – and assembled a baseball memorabilia collection of Smith that is displayed at the Giddings Library and Cultural Center.[82]

Smith's wife, Louise, summed him up best when she remarked, "Hilton loved baseball and gave his life to baseball. … My husband just let his performance do the talking."[83]

Sources

Unless otherwise noted, Seamheads.com was used as the database of record for all player statistics and team records.

Notes

1 John B. Holway, *Blackball Stars: Negro League Pioneers* (Westport, Connecticut: Meckler Books, 1988), 284. Giddings is about 20 miles north of La Grange (where Foster was born), so it was "below" him rather than "above."

2 Alongside Hilton in the Hall are fellow Texan Negro Leaguers Andy Cooper, Rube Foster, Bill Foster, Biz Mackey, Louis Santop, Willie Wells, and Smoky Joe Williams.

3 Untitled document, Hilton Smith player file at the National Baseball Hall of Fame, 1.

4 Interview with DeMorris Smith, July 24, 2020.

5 Holway, *Blackball Stars*, 284.

6 Holway, *Blackball Stars*, 284. The 1930 US Federal Census identifies Hilton's father, John H. Smith; as a farmer. The 1940 Census listed him as a schoolteacher.

7 The institution is now Prairie View A&M University. It is about 29 miles west of Houston.

8 "Hilton Lee Smith Inducted into the Prairie View Sports Hall of Fame," Prairie View A&M National Alumni Association, pvualumni.org/2011/01/07/hilton-lee-smith-inducted-into-the-prairie-view-am-sports-hall-of-fame/, January 7, 2011.

9 Holway, *Blackball Stars*, 284.

10 Holway, *Blackball Stars*, 285.

11 William J. Plott, *The Negro Southern League: A Baseball History, 1920-1951* (Jefferson, North Carolina: McFarland & Company, 2015), 101.

12 Holway, *Blackball Stars*, 285. Seamheads lists Monroe with a 34-14 record in the NSL and a 42-20-1 record overall for 1932. Smith's reflection may not be accurate, or include exhibitions not otherwise captured in records that have been documented.

13 DeMorris Smith interview.

14 Holway, *Blackball Stars*, 286.

15 Kyle P. McNary, *Ted "Double Duty" Radcliffe: 36 Years of Pitching and Catching in Baseball's Negro Leagues* (Minneapolis: McNary Publishing, 1994), 78.

16 McNary, 79.

17 Tom Dunkel, *Color Blind: The Forgotten Team That Broke Baseball's Color Line* (New York: Atlantic Monthly Press, 2013), 198.

18 Holway, *Blackball Stars*, 286-7.

19 "All Hail Bismarck's First National Championship Team," *Bismarck Tribune*, August 28, 1935: 6.

20 Holway, *Blackball Stars*, 287.

21 Janet Bruce, *The Kansas City Monarchs: Champions of Black Baseball* (Lawrence: University Press of Kansas, 1985), 25.

22 William A. Young, *J.L. Wilkinson and the Kansas City Monarchs: Trailblazers in Black Baseball* (Jefferson, North Carolina: McFarland & Company, 2016), 96.

23 Bruce, 40.

24 Holway, *Blackball Stars*, 287.

25 Holway, *Blackball Stars*, 287.

26 Holway, *Blackball Stars*, 288.

27 Larry Lester, *Black Baseball's National Showcase: The East-West All-Star Game, 1933-1953* (Lincoln: University of Nebraska Press, 2001), 104.

28 Donn Rogosin, *Invisible Men: Life in Baseball's Negro Leagues* (New York: Atheneum, 1985), 47.

29 Timothy M. Gay, *Satch, Dizzy & Rapid Robert: The Wild Saga of Interracial Baseball Before Jackie Robinson* (New York: Simon & Schuster, 2010), 68.

30 Jorge S Figueredo, *Cuban Baseball: A Statistical History, 1878-1961* (Jefferson, North Carolina: McFarland & Company, 2003), 220-221.

31 Figueredo, 232.

32 Young, 103.

33 Holway, *Blackball Stars*, 289.

34 Holway, *Blackball Stars*, 289.

35 Bruce, 95.

36 Mark Ribowsky, *A Complete History of the Negro Leagues: 1884-1955* (New York: Carol Publishing Group, 1995), 237.

37 Ribowsky, 237.

38 Larry Tye, *Satchel: The Life and Times of an American Legend* (New York: Random House, 2009), 157.

39 Tye, 102.

40 Holway, *Blackball Stars*, 281-2.

41 Holway, *Blackball Stars*, 282.

42 Buck O'Neil, with David Wulf and David Conrads, *I was Right on Time* (New York: Simon & Schuster, 1996), 89.

43 Buck O'Neil, 117.

44 DeMorris Smith interview.

45 Tye, 297.

46 Young, 101.

47 Robert L. Burnes, "Feller and Paige Look Good, but Others Look Better," *St. Louis Globe Democrat*, October 6, 1941: 13.

48 John B. Holway, *Black Diamonds: Life in the Negro Leagues from the Men Who Lived It* (New York: Stadium Books, 1991), 96.

49 Holway, *Blackball Stars*, 292-3.

50 McNeil, *Black Baseball*, 105.

51 Ribowsky, 247-248

52 R.S. Simmons, "29,000 See Satch and Company Defeat Dizzy Dean's All-Stars: Hilton Smith Stars in Relief Role as Monarchs Win, 3-1," *Pittsburgh Courier*, May 30, 1942: 16.

53 Holway, *Blackball Stars*, 281.

54 Holway, *Blackball Stars*, 281

55 Brad Snyder, *Beyond the Shadow of the Senators: The Untold Story of the Homestead Grays and the Integration of Baseball* (New York: Contemporary Books, 2003), 160.

56 Holway, *Blackball Stars*, 291.

57 William F. McNeil, *The California Winter League: America's First Integrated Professional Baseball League* (Jefferson, North Carolina: McFarland & Co, Inc., 2002), 217.

58 Timothy M. Gay, *Satch, Dizzy & Rapid Robert: The Wild Saga of Interracial Baseball before Jackie Robinson* (New York: Simon and & Schuster, 2010), 16.

59 Holway, *Blackball Stars*, 291.

60 Frederick C. Bush and Bill Nowlin, eds., *The Newark Eagles Take Flight: The Story of the 1946 Negro League Champions* (Phoenix: SABR, 2019), 212-215.

61 Young, 167.

62 John Holway, Hilton Smith interview manuscript, Hilton Smith player file at the National Baseball Hall of Fame, p.29.

63 Holway, *Blackball Stars*, 292.

64 Bruce, 113.

65 Holway, *Blackball Stars*, 293.

66 Young, *Wilkinson*, 142.

67 Young, *Wilkinson*, 142-150.

68 Holway, *Blackball Stars*, 294.

69 Holway, *Blackball Stars*, 294.

70 McNeil, *Black Baseball*, 219.

71 Patrick Reusse," Fulda to Have Its Own Hall of Famer," *Minneapolis Star Tribune*, August 4, 2001.

72 DeMorris Smith interview.

73 Holway, *Blackball Stars*, 294-5.

74 Larry Lester and Sammy J. Miller, *Black Baseball in Kansas City* (Chicago: Arcadia Publishing, 2000), 127.

75 Robert Falkoff, "Humble Hilton: Negro Leagues Hurler Hilton Smith Shined in Satchel Paige's Shadow with the Great K.C. Monarchs," MLB.com, 2001.

76 Holway, *Blackball Stars*, 295.

77 Bruce, 131.

78 Thom Loverro, *The Encyclopedia of Negro League Baseball* (New York: Facts on File, 2003), 273.

79 Kelley, 120.

80 Bruce, 95.

81 McNeil, *Black Baseball*, 90.

82 Hilton Lee Smith Collection, City of Giddings, Texas, giddings.net/index.asp?SEC=7B423286-5333-4194-806C-C4D42ACAE15F&Type=B_BASIC.

83 Falkoff, MLB.com.

HERB SOUELL

By Chris Hicks

Herb "Baldy" Souell, 5-feet-9 and 150 pounds, carved out an 11-year career as an undersized third baseman for the Kansas City Monarchs from 1940 to 1950. He threw right-handed but was a switch-hitter whose valuable bat kept him in the top third of the Monarchs' lineup for most of his career. Once Souell's time with the Monarchs had passed, he played both north and south of the border and had a brief stint in the minor leagues before he hung up his spikes for good.

Herbert Souell was born on February 5, 1913, in West Monroe, Louisiana, to Fredrick Souell and Clara Davenport.[1] Fredrick Souell worked different jobs throughout his life, including as a porter and laborer, until his death in 1971.[2] Clara Davenport died at the age of 17 in 1916.[3]

Little is known about Souell's childhood until 1930, when he is listed as a laborer in a West Monroe barbershop in the US census. He lived with his maternal grandfather, Charlie Davenport, his aunt Minnie, and two cousins, Walter and Charlie Phillips. According to the census, he was still in school. No school records could be located, but the local school for African Americans was Monroe Colored High school, now Boley Elementary. Despite its being called a high school, in the 1930s Monroe Colored High School educated children in the first through 11th grades and was the only secondary school for African Americans in the area.[4]

It is unclear when and how Souell got his start in baseball, but the earliest box score that has been found has him playing third base in 1936 for the Claybrook Tigers in Crittenden County, Arkansas, which is part of the greater Memphis metropolitan area.[5] He is listed as Cyrus on the box score, but researchers believe it to be Souell since he played under the name Herb Cyrus until 1943.[6]

The Claybrook Tigers were owned by John C. Claybrook, who, despite reportedly being unable to read, was a successful African American farmer and businessman in the timber industry. The town of Claybrook, which no longer exists, was built around his 3,500 acres of land. He is also said to be one of the first African Americans in the Southern United States to be selected to be on a trial jury.[7]

Claybrook started the baseball team to coax his son John Jr. to stay in Claybrook to continue the family business. He was worried that John Jr., like many other young men, would move to the city to take advantage of the social life of Memphis. By 1933, Claybrook had a ballpark fully constructed on his land and had signed his first team. His desire to have the best players made games against his team tough ones for all competition. Within a few years, the Tigers were Negro Southern League champions in 1935, beating the Memphis Red Sox in a seven-game series.[8] In 1936, Claybrook signed Ted "Double Duty" Radcliffe as manager, Souell to be the third baseman, Bill Ball, touted as "the greatest one-armed centerfielder in the game," and others.[9] The team did not survive the midseason collapse of the Negro Southern League. Most of the players either signed with the Pittsburgh Crawfords or followed Radcliffe to play for the Cincinnati Tigers for 1937.[10]

Souell's baseball career appears to have gone on hiatus during the years 1937 and 1938 as no box scores for either Herb Souell or Herb Cyrus have been located. Neither do any other records reveal what he was doing at this time.

In 1939 Souell signed on to play for Satchel Paige's All-Star team. This barnstorming squad, formerly known as the Kansas City Travelers, was a second-tier team that also served as a feeder franchise for the Kansas City Monarchs. In 1938, while Paige had been playing in Puerto Rico, he had hurt his arm, possibly tearing his rotator cuff. Monarchs owner J.L. Wilkinson took a flyer on him and signed him to the Travelers. Wilkinson renamed the team after Paige, knowing that Paige's reputation would result in an increased draw at the gate. The plan was that Paige would pitch when his arm was feeling good enough, and when it was not, he would be in the lineup as the team's first baseman.[11]

HERB SOUELL

Souell's performance with the All-Stars earned him a contract with the Monarchs in 1940. Many newspapers touted the Monarchs rookie as a player who helped to "compose one of the cleverest infields in the game."[12] He hit .340 with five doubles and six stolen bases while the Monarchs compiled a 30-10-2 record in league play, and went 31-15-2 overall.

In 1941 Souell not only returned to the Monarchs, but also married Gladys Edna Lee. The couple did not have any children and eventually divorced in 1972. On the diamond, Souell was touted as a "homerun hitter."[13] It appears that he was used in just one at-bat for the season, getting one hit. According to one teammate, Souell started losing his hair at this time. His teammates, in jest, started referring to him as Baldy, a nickname that stuck with him throughout his career.[14]

In 1942 Souell batted .272 over the course of 23 NAL games as the Monarchs claimed the league pennant and swept the NNL's Homestead Grays in the first Negro League World Series between those two circuits and the first of any kind since 1927.

In 1943 the Monarchs were looking to repeat as the top team in the league. Herb now appeared under his given name, Souell, rather than Cyrus. (There was still no explanation as to why he went by the name of Cyrus at the beginning of his career).[15] Souell went on to produce a .256 average over 203 at-bats, now as the full-time third baseman. He also appeared in the North-South All-Star Game, going 1-for-4 with a double and run scored.[16] The game featured top players from Negro League teams in the North versus Negro League teams in the South and was played in New Orleans.[17] For the season, the Monarchs went 43-27-1 against NAL teams and 51-39-1 overall, landing in second place.

In 1944 Herb continued as the Monarchs third baseman and increased his average to .261 in 29 games. One of the more memorable moments of his career came at Yankee Stadium, when he hit a home run that traveled 400 feet in game one of a doubleheader. He did well in the second game, too, getting three RBIs to secure a Monarchs victory in front of 28,000 fans.[18] The Monarchs finished 30-38 in NAL games and 35-51 overall to end the season in fourth place.

The 1945 season continued to see players drafted into the armed forces. Rosters suffered, resulting in Souell's taking the field as one of the more seasoned veterans on the team in spite of the brevity of his career to that point.[19] His average continued to rise. He hit .312 in 40 games. Famously, the Monarchs had a newcomer this season named Jackie Robinson, who hit a team-high .375 in his 34 games at shortstop. The Monarchs finished second with a record of 43-32-3 in the NAL and 49-38-4 overall.

After the Monarchs season concluded, Souell joined the Kansas City Royals in the California Winter League. He had a .500 average in six known at-bats.[20] During this time, Jackie Robinson had two of his Kansas City Royals teammates, Souell and catcher Buster Haywood, go with him to Lane Field on October 2. He told them this was for a workout. A photographer from *Look* magazine was also invited to take photos and record the so-called workout.[21]

It turned out the Brooklyn Dodgers were having Robinson photographed for an article to appear in the magazine announcing his signing with the Dodgers. Neither Haywood nor Souell knew what was happening, according to an interview with Haywood in later years. (Souell was deceased by the time of this interview.) Most of these photos and the accompanying article were never published, and they sat in a box at the National Baseball Hall of Fame until the late 1980s. Only a few were published in a later *Look* article.[22]

With the end of World War II, players who were in the military started reuniting with their teammates and spring training got underway for the Monarchs in 1946. Souell returned from the California Winter League to take his place at third. During the season, he hit .273 and the Monarchs went 50-16-2 in the NAL and 55-26-2 overall. The Monarchs made another appearance in the 1946 Negro World Series with Souell batting .344. This time, however, the Newark Eagles were crowned the champions after a tense seven-game series.

After the season, Souell joined Jackie Robinson's All-Star team and played third base.[23] He spent the winter in San Luis Potosi, playing for the Cactus Pear Growers in the Mexican League, where he batted just .191 (9-for-47) in 12 games.[24] He left Mexico early to return to the Monarchs in time to play Opening Day of the 1947 season and avoided receiving a five-year ban from the league for jumping to Mexico. He did not enjoy his time south of the border, and was reported as saying "he would never play there again," and that he had "lost thirty-five pounds." It was also reported that he was successfully regaining his weight and rebuilding his strength.[25]

• When the Monarchs Reigned •

In 1947, after one season with the Montreal Royals, Jackie Robinson broke the color barrier of white major-league baseball. Throughout the season, major-league teams began scouting players from around the Negro leagues. Some put "feelers" out for other Monarchs players, among them Herb Souell. Inquiries were as far as it went for Souell, however, as he spent the entire season with the Monarchs.[26] He had a very successful season, and he was selected to play in his first of five career East-West All-Star games. (He played in both games in the 1947 and 1948 seasons.)[27] In the first game, at Comiskey Park in Chicago, he hit a triple, while in the second game, at the Polo Grounds in New York, he went hitless. Game one had some controversy in that the players were offered only $50 for playing. The players, feeling that was not enough, decided to strike, returning to the field when they were promised $200 each.[28]

Souell then spent the winter months of 1947-48 playing for Ponce in the Puerto Rican Winter League. The Ponce team finished in last place with a 24-36 record.[29] However, Souell acquitted himself well as he saw regular action and batted .345 (87-for-252).[30] The time in Puerto Rico also served as a vacation of sorts, as airline travel records show that he was joined by his wife for part of the season.[31]

Souell continued to build on his reputation as a top defender in 1948, with the *Detroit Tribune* referring to him as a "stellar third baseman."[32] He became the top fielder at his position.[33] His hitting prowess also was on display when he hit an inside-the-park home run in the first game of a doubleheader against the Indianapolis Clowns in July. Later that year he was named to the West team in both 1948 East-West All-Star Games.[34]

Herb Souell, also known as Herb Cyrus, split the third base duties with Newt Allen on the 1942 Monarchs' championship squad.
(Courtesy Noir-Tech Research, Inc.)

The 1949 season began with Souell being the final player to sign his Monarchs contract.[35] He was reportedly working out with some of his teammates at the Paseo YMCA in Kansas City, Missouri, before making the trek to the familiar Monroe, Louisiana, for spring training.[36] The *Quad-City Times* described Souell as "one of the best lead off men in Negro baseball, and he gets so many free trips to first that he has become a pain in the neck to rival pitchers."[37] Souell hit .269 in 88 games. The Monarchs finished the season 54-37, but lost the top spot in the Western Division to the Chicago American Giants after losing some players to the White major leagues.[38]

The Monarchs held spring training in San Antonio, Texas, in 1950.[39] Souell once again found himself penciled into the lineup as the leadoff hitter.[40] He excelled at the plate. While batting .325, he was named as a reserve to the West team for his third and final All-Star Game appearance.[41] Souell went 0-for-1 with a run scored and an error.[42] After finishing the season batting .301 for the 52-21 Western Division champion Monarchs, he spent the offseason appearing in games for both the Satchel Paige All-Stars and the Kansas City Royals.[43]

The year 1951 brought an end to Souell's Monarchs career: On April 22 the *Kansas City Star* announced that he was retiring after 10 years with the Monarchs.[44] However, he eventually signed to play with the Carman Cardinals in the Manitoba-Dakota (ManDak) League. The ManDak League was popular among former Negro League players because they did not have to deal with the Jim Crow laws since all but one team called Canada its home.[45] Willie "Curly" Williams, Souell's teammate on the Carman Cardinals in 1953, said, "[In Canada] we were treated so well. … We had so much fun there and everyone was accepted, you know, didn't have problems going any place we wanted to eat. Just wonderful people. May not have made a whole lot of money but people were excited and they enjoyed you and would invite you to their homes."[46] In 59 games, Souell hit an impressive .306 with 7 home runs and 39 RBIs.[47]

The Carman Cardinals had Souell on their roster in 1952, but he made his debut in White Organized Baseball with the Spokane Indians of the Class-A Western International League, signing with the team on March 5.[48] The team's manager, Don Osborn, touted the 39-year-old player, whose career stretched back to at least 1936, to the owner of the Indians as a 24-year-old rookie who had played for the Monarchs since 1948.[49] A later newspaper article referred to him as a 27-year-old who played for the Monarchs from 1946 to 1950.[50] Both sources also claimed that Souell had never batted below .300.

Another newspaper article profiled both Souell, listed as a 28-year-old rookie, and Herb "Briefcase" Simpson, first baseman, not to be confused with Harry "Suitcase" Simpson. The article highlighted both players' dry senses of humor, following them to a barbershop where they ran into a man whom the players knew to be the designer of their uniforms. When he asked how they liked the uniforms, the teammates played a joke, saying they did not like them. The man got upset and they both started laughing, revealing the prank. In truth, neither had seen the new uniforms at that point.[51]

Monarchs owner T.Y. Baird protested to George M. Trautman, the president of the National Association of Professional Baseball Leagues, stating that Souell was still under contract with his team and therefore could not sign a contract with the Spokane club. When pressed by the league office to provide proof of a contract, Baird was unable to do so. Without the required proof, Souell was able to continue playing with the Indians.[52]

Things were not always so good for Souell with Spokane. Despite opening the season by going 4-for-4, he was plagued by inconsistency in his performances, both in the field and at the plate.[53] One article spoke of Souell either missing or ignoring signs. It reported that he was replaced by a pinch-hitter in the middle of one at-bat because he took a swing at a pitch that the coach had signaled him to take.[54] He was benched within weeks of that game and thereafter was designated as the backup third baseman.[55] In mid-May, he was released because of a rule that teams had to have an 18-man roster before ultimately cutting it to 17.[56]

Souell was signed by the Tucson Cowboys of the Class-C Arizona-Texas League within a week of his release by Spokane.[57] He made a splash with his new team, hitting a 350-foot home run and two doubles in a 17-7 rout of the Bisbee-Douglas Copper Kings on May 26.[58] Souell, still known for his hitting prowess, was selected along with two teammates to put on a hitting demonstration at local batting cages.[59] Nevertheless, he had some difficulty breaking into the lineup consistently and also played second base and the outfield to garner more playing time.[60]

At the end of June, the Cowboys sold Souell to the league's Chihuahua Dorados, where he finished out the 1952 season.[61] During his time with Spokane, Souell had a line of .264/.354/.306. In 91 total games with Tucson and Chihuahua, his line was .297/.361/.392 with 8 triples, 18 stolen bases, and a .909 fielding percentage.[62]

In 1953 Souell returned to the Carman Cardinals of the ManDak League. He performed as well as he had in the 1951 season, batting .302 with 5 home runs, and 39 RBIs in 72 games.[63] After the season ended, he returned home to Los Angeles and made a life for himself there.

The *Pittsburgh Courier* had reported that Souell was going into business in Los Angeles when it announced his retirement from the Monarchs.[64] What the business was, though, could not be determined. Souell and his wife, Gladys, divorced in 1972. In 1973 he married Lizzie Mae Baldwin in Las Vegas.

Souell died on July 12, 1978, from an unknown cause. He was buried in Inglewood Park Cemetery in Inglewood, California. Lizzie Mae Souell was buried in the plot with him on December 27, 1991.

Sources

Ancestry.com and Familysearch.org were consulted for census information; birth, marriage, and death records; military draft registration cards; and other public records.

Negro League player statistics and manager/team records were taken from Seamheads.com, unless otherwise indicated.

Notes

1 As was the case with many individuals in early census records, Souell's name can be found spelled in various different ways, including "Sowell," "Sowells," and "Sorrells." Herb spelled his last name "Sowell" on his World War II draft registration card, and his father, Fredrick, spelled it the same way on his World War I draft registration card, suggesting that this was the original and accurate spelling of the family

name. Herb Souell also went by the name Herb Cyrus – and he is named that way in many game articles and box scores. The reason for his adoption of this name is unknown.

2   When he was 16, he worked as a laborer at a pressing club. Around the time of Herb's birth, the Monroe city directory shows him still living with his family working as a laborer at Union Oil Mill. He served briefly during World War I at age 24. By 1930 he had remarried and owned a cafe/boarding house with his wife, Delia. By 1933 he returned to live with his mother, and in 1940 ran his own auto garage.

3   Ancestry.com has incorrect information for Herb's mother, Clara Davenport. Per Herb's first cousin twice removed, C. Brandon Brewer, who posted on Ancestry.com, Herb's mother died young, and this is corroborated by the death record from familysearch.org.

4   Thomas Aiello, *The Kings of Casino Park* (Tuscaloosa: University of Alabama Press, 2011), 6.

5   "Claybrook Defeats Elmer 15-3," *Macon* (Missouri) *Chronicle-Herald,* August 19, 1936: 6.

6   "Claybrook Tigers," *Arkansas Baseball Encyclopedia*, February 2, 2020, http://arkbaseball.com/tiki-index.php?page=Claybrook+Tigers.

7   "Claybrook Tigers Baseball Team," *Encyclopedia of Arkansas*, November 12, 2008, https://encyclopediaofarkansas.net/entries/claybrook-tigers-baseball-team-2608/.

8   "Negro Southern League (1920-1951)," *Negro Southern League Research Center.*

9   For Bill Ball see: "Tigers to Play Black Barons of Birmingham," *Clarksdale* (Mississippi) *Press Register,* June 3, 1936: 6.

10   "Claybrook Tigers Baseball Team."

11   Jason Roe, "The Greatest Pitcher Ever," Kansas City Public Library, February 1, 2021, https://kchistory.org/week-kansas-city-history/greatest-pitcher-ever.

12   "Old Pals Will Fete Milton at Tuesday Clash," *Times* (Munster, Indiana), July 28, 1940: 13.

13   Ray T. Rocene, "Sport Jabs," *Missoulian* (Missoula, Montana), June 19, 1941: 9.

14   Frazier Robinson with Paul Bauer, *Catching Dreams: My Life in the Negro Baseball Leagues* (Syracuse, New York: Syracuse University Press, 1999), 54.

15   "Monarchs Return Popular Players for Clown Frolic," *Daily Oklahoman* (Oklahoma City), August 20, 1943: 14.

16   "1943 South All-Stars," Seamheads.com, February 1, 2021.

17   Ryan Whirty, "Negro Leagues All-Stars Were a Big Hit in the Big Easy in 1939," NOLA.com, October 1, 2009, https://www.nola.com/sports/article_27c3605f-583f-56db-aa5c-02ac79dddb31.html.

18   Wendell Smith, "Split Even in Tilts at Stadium," *Pittsburgh Courier*, September 2, 1944: 12.

19   "Red Sox and Monarchs at League Park," *Mississippi Enterprise* (Jackson), April 14, 1945: 1.

20   William McNeil, *The California Winter League: America's First Integrated Professional Baseball League* (Jefferson, North Carolina: McFarland & Company, 2002), 228.

21   John Thorn and Jules Tygiel, "Jackie Robinson's Signing: The Real Story," in *From Rube to Robinson* (Society for American Baseball Research, 2021), https://sabr.org/journal/article/jackie-robinsons-signing-the-real-story/.

22   Thorn and Tygiel.

23   "Jackie Robinson's Stars Play Oakland Larks at Perris Hill," *San Bernardino Sun*, October 27, 1946: 23.

24   Pedro Treto Cisneros, *The Mexican League: Comprehensive Player Statistics, 1937-2001* (Jefferson, North Carolina: McFarland & Company, Inc., 2002), 300. Souell's name is misspelled as "Hebert Sovell" in this source, but information from other sources helps to confirm that this was Herb Souell.

25   "2 Monarch Stars Now with St. Louis Club," *St. Cloud* (Minnesota) *Times,* July 22, 1947: 13.

26   "Majors Grab Monarch Stars," *Herald and Review* (Decatur, Illinois), August 20, 1947: 9.

27   Riley, 732.

28   Larry Lester, *Black Baseball's National Showcase: The East-West All-Star Game, 1933-1953* (Lincoln: University of Nebraska Press, 2001), 284, 294, 301.

29   Thomas E. Van Hyning, *Puerto Rico's Winter League: A History of Major League Baseball's Launching Pad* (Jefferson, North Carolina: McFarland & Company, Inc., 1995), 241.

30   William F. McNeil, *Black Baseball Out of Season: Pay for Play Outside of the Negro Leagues* (Jefferson, North Carolina: McFarland & Company, 2007), 215.

31   "So*ell, Gladys," (Air Passenger Manifest, Eastern Airlines, Plane No. 54365, November 12, 1947), Ancestry. Courtesy of Fredrick Bush.

32   "Monarchs Coming," *Detroit Tribune,* June 5, 1948: 6.

33   "Birmingham Shortstop Hits .402," *Pittsburgh Courier*, January 22, 1949: 12.

34   "A Monarch Is in Form," *Kansas City Times*, July 26, 1948: 11.

35   "Souell Last of Kansas City Regulars to Sign," *Pittsburgh Courier*, March 12, 1949: 12.

36   "Kan. City Monarch Begin Drills at Monroe, La. Camp," *Pittsburgh Courier,* April 2, 1949: 23.

37   "Gene Baker of Davenport Is Monarchs' Star," *Quad-City Times* (Davenport, Iowa), May 31, 1949: 15.

38   Cnlbr.org.

39   "Gene Baker of Davenport Is Monarchs' Star."

40   "Monarchs, Buckeyes Are Ready," *Kansas City* (Missouri) *Call,* May 5, 1950: 21.

41   "17th All-Star Tilt at Comiskey Park," *New Tribune* (Detroit), August 19, 1950: 23.

42   Lester, 349.

43   "Lemon, Paige Nines to Clash Here Today," *San Bernardino Sun*, October 18, 1950: 25.

44   "Two with the Clowns," *Kansas City Star*, April 22, 1951: 26.

45   Barry Swanton, *The ManDak League: Haven for Former Negro League Ballplayers, 1950-1957* (Jefferson, North Carolina: McFarland & Company, Inc., 2006), 1.

46   Jay-Dell Mah, "122. Curly Williams: A Good First Impression That Lasts and Lasts," The Infinite Baseball Set, June 22, 2012, http://infinitecardset.blogspot.com/2012/06/122-curly-williams-good-first.html?m=1.

47   Swanton, 186.

48   "Herb Souell," The Sporting News Baseball Players Contract Cards Collection, https://digital.la84.org/digital/collection/p17103coll3/id/146685/rec/1.

49   "Spokane Signs Third Baseman," *Spokane Spokesman-Review,* March 9, 1952: 33.

50   Danny May, "May-Be So," *Spokane Spokesman-Review*, March 25, 1952: 10.

51   "Meet the New Indians," *Spokane Spokesman-Review*, April 11, 1952: 12.

52   "About Herbert Souell," 1952, Box: 1, Folder: 4, T.Y. Baird

Collection, RH MS 414, Kenneth Spencer Research Library, University of Kansas.

53 "Indians Delight in Opener, Dump Salem 7-1," *Spokane Spokesman-Review*, April 23, 1952: 14; "Indians' Souell Given Release," *Spokane Spokesman-Review*, May 21, 1952: 10.

54 Danny May, "May-Be So," *Spokane Spokesman-Review*, April 30, 1952: 16.

55 "League Leading Indians Open Here with Tri-City," *Spokane Chronicle*, May 9, 1952: 13.

56 "Indians' Souell Given Release," *Spokane Spokesman-Review*, May 21, 1952: 10.

57 "Herb Souell," The Sporting News Baseball Players Contract Cards Collection, https://digital.la84.org/digital/collection/p17103coll3/id/146685/rec/1.

58 Abe Chanin, "Cowboys Thump Four Pitchers in 17-7 Victory," *Arizona Daily Star* (Tucson), May 27, 1952: 16.

59 "Three Cowboys Slate Batting Session," *Arizona Daily Star*, June 6, 1952: 23.

60 Lou Pavlovich, "Phoenix Takes Sweep of Four-Game Series," *Arizona Daily Star*, June 12, 1952: 20; Ray McNally, "Two Wins Pulls Pokes Out of Cellar," *Tucson Daily Citizen*, June 23, 1952: 21.

61 "Souell Is Sold to Dorados Club," *Arizona Daily Star*, June 29, 1952: 21.

62 Baseball-Reference.com.

63 Swanton, 192.

64 "K.C. Monarchs Near Top Form," *Pittsburgh Courier*, April 28, 1951: 14.

TED STRONG JR.

By Glen Sparks

Ted Strong Jr. thrilled baseball fans with a hard-hitting swing that he displayed over his 10 seasons in the Negro Leagues and in Mexico. The tall, muscular Strong played in seven All-Star games as a member of the Kansas City Monarchs and other teams. This two-sport superstar also toured the country as a member of the Harlem Globetrotters basketball squad.

Strong batted .321 with 40 home runs in 1,285 at-bats over his career. He posted a .406 on-base percentage and a .518 slugging percentage.[1] No less an authority than Cum Posey marveled at Strong's talents. Posey, who had played ball and managed and was the principal owner of the Homestead Grays, called Strong "the best young player of Negro baseball" in 1937.[2]

Strong never got the chance to compete against White major-league baseball teams and to take his swings against Bob Feller, Dizzy Dean, or the other top big-league pitchers from that time. In a *Chicago Tribune* article, Strong's biographer, Sherman L. Jenkins, called that a source of "frustration and disappointment" for the player.[3] Jenkins remembered Buck O'Neil praising Strong as "the best athlete he had ever seen."[4]

Theodore Relighn Strong Jr. was born on January 2, 1917, in South Bend, Indiana, an industrial/college city located on the Saint Joseph River. He was the eldest child of Theodore Strong Sr. and Vera Leona Smith. In June the young family, which eventually consisted of 13 children, moved to Chicago.

Strong Sr., a former lightweight boxer, liked to describe his first-born son as "big for his age."[5] The youngster excelled at baseball and basketball at Wendell Phillips High School in Chicago. Even as a freshman, "his muscular six-foot-two-inch frame made him standout among his peers," Jenkins wrote.[6] Soon enough, he attracted the attention of a 5-foot-3-inch basketball fanatic.

Abe Saperstein had moved with his family from London, England, to Chicago in 1907 when he was 5 years old. The so-called Windy City was "a swirl of constant motion."[7] Saperstein, who loved sports, thrived in the fast pace and founded the Trotters in 1928. (Saperstein later added "Harlem" to the Trotters brand as a salute to the largely African American section of New York City.) Almost from the start, the Globetrotters melded great basketball with a touch of comedy. One writer commented after a game, "The crowd was in an uproar during the last three quarters at the antics and clowning the Trotters mixed with their stellar playing."[8]

Strong began his Globetrotter career in 1936. He had grown a few inches over the past few years. Various sources list Strong's ultimate height at anywhere from nearly 6-foot-4 to about 6-foot-6, or even taller. He also played his rookie season in the Negro Leagues that year. Strong batted a meager .167 as a shortstop for the American Giants.

The next year, though, he earned a spot in the fifth annual East-West All-Star Game, played at Comiskey Park in Chicago. The East won, 7-2, thanks in part to fielding miscues committed by Strong and other West players. Strong singled home a run and drove another pitch that bounced off the center-field wall and eluded outfield defenders long enough for him to secure an inside-the-park home run. "Strong rounded third like a big locomotive being waved on home by (third-base coach) 'Candy Jim' Taylor,'" said the *Chicago Defender*.[9] Strong played for the American Giants, the Indianapolis Athletics, and the Kansas City Monarchs in 1937. He batted .359 with 3 home runs and 31 RBIs.

Strong returned to Indianapolis in 1938, as a member of the ABCs, and once again earned an All-Star berth. More than 30,000 fans watched the action at Comiskey Park after Chicago Mayor Edward J. Kelly threw out the first pitch. Strong went hitless in three at-bats but walked and scored a run as the West won, 5-4. The African American press corps argued that the top Negro League players were just as good as major leaguers. It was asserted that players like Buck Leonard, Willie Wells, Ray Dandridge, and Josh Gibson "would make it tough sledding for their big league opponents."[10]

• TED STRONG JR. •

Many in the White press still offered only grudging respect for the Negro Leagues. In an article titled "How Good Is Negro Baseball?" Lloyd Lewis of the *Chicago News* wrote on August 22, 1938, that although "Negro professional baseball … is faster on the bases than major league ball now played in the American and National circuits" and "is almost as swift and spectacular on the field, it lacks the batting forms of the white man's big leagues."[11] Lewis took a few shots at Strong, "the tall, magnificently proportioned first baseman[,]" as he criticized him for "showboating with his glove."[12] For the second straight year, Strong also saw action with the Monarchs and he hit for a combined .373 average with Indianapolis and Kansas City.

Strong played the entire 1939 season with the Monarchs. For the young ballplayer, Jenkins wrote, "it was probably a dream come true" as the Monarchs were "beginning to blossom as a standout team in the Negro Leagues."[13] J.L. Wilkinson, an Iowa native and a solid semipro pitcher during his playing days, had founded the club in 1920. Years earlier, he had put together a squad called the All-Nations team for which he hired Whites, Blacks, Asians, Native Americans, and Polynesians to play ball. Wilkinson and Kansas City businessman Thomas "T.Y." Baird, both White men, attended an organizational meeting of the Negro National League, held at the Paseo YMCA in Kansas City on February 13, 1920, and applied for membership. Rube Foster, owner of the Chicago American Giants, hesitated to accept a White owner into the league, "but he relented because of Wilkinson's reputation for integrity and fairness."[14] Wilkinson "built the Monarchs into the most successful NNL club of the 1920s."[15] (The Monarchs competed in the Negro National League through 1931 and as an independent club from 1932 to 1936. Kansas City joined the Negro American League in 1937.)

In 1939 the outstanding Monarchs roster included hitters such as first baseman O'Neil, second baseman Newt Allen, left fielder Willard Brown, and center fielder Turkey Stearnes while the pitching staff was led by future Hall of Famer Hilton Smith. Strong and O'Neil became good friends. O'Neil described Strong, with some exaggeration, as "near seven-feet tall" and claimed that "[t]hey put him at short because he had great hands and rifle arm."[16] Strong hit .304 with 3 homers and 30 RBIs in 53 games as the Monarchs finished 42-25 and won the franchise's sixth league title.

Strong also married during this time. Records indicate that he and Ruth Jackson took out a marriage application in Jackson County, Missouri, on September 2, 1939. Strong jumped to the Mexican League and the La Junta de Nuevo Laredo squad in 1940. He batted .332 with a team-high 11 home runs. According to at least one observer, Strong "proved to be the best third baseman in the circuit."[17]

At the conclusion of every baseball season, Strong rejoined the Globetrotters, who were easily one of the best basketball teams in the country. In their first 14 seasons, the squad won 2,022 of 2,164 games.[18] Strong was certainly an important part of that success. The *Ogden* (Utah) *Standard-Examiner* noted, "This chap Ted Strong has the largest hands in the game. He is the only man who can catch and snatch the ball in mid-air with the fingers of one hand. It's one of the miracles of the sport to see Strong catch a pass or stop a dribble in this manner."[19]

Strong also took part in some of the team's trademark comedic antics. During one game, he "drew gales of laughter with his moans of 'foul, foul.'"[20] Strong played center and was eventually named captain of the Globetrotters. In 1940 Saperstein's squad beat George Halas's Chicago Bruins to capture the World's Basketball Championship. A childhood friend of Strong's recalled, "We were so proud of them. We used to sneak up to Ted's room and get his Globetrotters jacket and wear it around the neighborhood."[21]

After his foray into Mexico in 1940, Strong returned to the Monarchs for the 1941 season. He batted .284 and helped Kansas City capture yet another league title. In 1942 Strong batted .364 and the Monarchs won the Negro League World Series. Kansas City swept the Homestead Grays in a best-of-seven series played at four different sites. (Griffith Stadium hosted Game One. The teams played Game Two at Forbes Field, Game Three at Yankee Stadium, and Game Four at Shibe Park.) Strong batted .316 in the Series and had an on-base percentage of .381. He scored a run in each of the games and hit a three-run homer in Game Three.

Strong still dreamed of playing in the major leagues. That dream took a step closer to reality when the Pittsburgh Pirates announced plans to hold tryouts for a select group of players after the 1942 season. Strong's name was listed on a group of eight alternates. Those dreams were dashed when the Pirates announced just a few months later that the tryouts were canceled. The *Chicago Defender* told its readers,

"The day will come when Negroes may get a tryout in the major leagues."[22]

With World War II raging, Strong enlisted in the Navy on April 22, 1943. He entered as an apprentice seaman and trained for Seabee duty at the Great Lakes (Illinois) Naval Training Station.[23] Strong later earned the Asiatic-Pacific Campaign Ribbon, the Seabee insignia, and the Philippine Liberation ribbon. He also took part in capturing Majuro Atoll in the Marshall Islands and was granted his honorable discharge on January 20, 1946.[24]

While in Hawaii, Strong wrote a letter that offered advice to hopeful young Negro League ballplayers. "I started this letter for a purpose," Strong began. "It's about the young kids who are trying to fill the shoes of those who have gone to war. Naturally, at first, no one would expect those kids to perform like established stars, (but) all they needed was encouragement and time for them to find themselves." Strong and some of his fellow Seabees rarely got a chance to play baseball while overseas. "Then when we did, brother, we thought we were some of the luckiest guys in the world by being able to play. And every chance we had, we did."[25]

Strong added, "This war has taught me a lot and it had made me realize somewhere there's someone who is worse off than yourself. And the sooner [American readers] understand that, the better off things will be in the future. ... In the meantime, I say, lay off the [young ballplayers] and they won't let you down. Someday, we'll be back, maybe to play more ball, but you must admit new blood will be needed and this is the chance we probably needed to give COLORED baseball a new meaning to a new generation."[26]

Once Strong returned stateside, he continued his career with both the Globetrotters and the Monarchs in 1946. He also indulged in life off the field and away from the court. He liked to hang out with his teammates and enjoy a few drinks, sometimes a few too many. "If truth be told," Jenkins wrote, "Ted Jr. had started nipping at the rim of a shot glass early in his sports career."[27]

Strong was now 29 years old. He batted .321 in his first season back with the Monarchs but failed to make the annual All-Star team. The Monarchs lost a thrilling seven-game World Series to the Newark Eagles that season. Six players from the two squads – Willard Brown, Leon Day, Larry Doby, Monte Irvin, Satchel Paige, and Hilton Smith, plus Eagles manager Biz Mackey – were later inducted into the National Baseball Hall of Fame in Cooperstown, New York.

The following season, as Strong suited up for the Monarchs, Jackie Robinson played his first game for the Brooklyn Dodgers. White baseball's shameful color barrier finally had been broken. The Monarchs had signed Robinson in early 1945. With stars like Strong, O'Neil, and Hank Thompson off to war, Wilkinson needed ballplayers. Robinson, in turn, had already completed his military service and now needed a job. A friend had told him "there's good money in black baseball,"[28] so the former UCLA Bruin signed to play with Kansas City for $400 a month.

Robinson, a Georgia native, grew up in Southern California and was, like Strong, a standout multisport athlete. He had earned letters in football, basketball, and baseball at UCLA while also running track and playing tennis.

Some had thought Strong might be the White major leagues' first Black player of the twentieth century. Baseball historian John Kovatch recalled talking to Ted "Double Duty" Radcliffe about Strong. Radcliffe, born in Mobile, Alabama, in 1902, played for 15 teams in the Negro Leagues from 1928 through 1946. "(Radcliffe) said that Ted was one of the most talented athletes" in the Negro Leagues, Kovatch said. "He sounded like a good candidate to break the major league color barrier." Kovatch lamented, "Radcliffe and a number of the older Negro League players felt that [Strong's] drinking and carousing kept him from being the choice."[29]

Strong turned 30 years old on January 2, 1947. By baseball standards, he was a grizzled veteran and "[t]hat kind of put him on the back burner."[30] Bob Kendrick, president of the Negro League Baseball Museum in Kansas City, agreed: "Ted was getting a little long in the tooth as well by the time they get to this point where they're really considering breaking the color barrier."[31]

In his biography of Strong, Jenkins added, "Ted Jr. wouldn't have taken what Jackie Robinson took when he joined the Dodgers farm system and big-league teams. Yes, Ted Jr. played with the Globetrotters in all-white, small-town America for a number of years, but 'an eye for an eye and a tooth for a tooth' had been taught to him by Ted Sr."[32]

Strong's career with the Monarchs ended after the 1947 season. He batted just .210 (21-for-100) in 37 league games during his final campaign. Younger, faster, and – surprisingly – even bigger and stronger athletes looked to take his place. In 1948 Strong joined

• TED STRONG JR. •

the Indianapolis Clowns, a squad that mixed serious action with comedy hijinks. Globetrotter Reece "Goose" Tatum also played for the Clowns. Born on May 3, 1921, in Arkansas, Tatum was the Trotters' original Clown Prince. He stood 6-feet-4 and boasted an 84-inch wingspan.

Goose had started playing professional baseball in 1937 and had seen action with the Birmingham Black Barons prior to joining the Clowns during their time in Cincinnati. "Tatum was a decent hitter, spraying the ball to all fields," according to Ben Green in his history of the Globetrotters. The ballplayer struggled in the field, however. "He played outfield, but his long arms seemed to interfere with his fielding and coordination."[33]

Like Strong, Tatum enjoyed the nightlife. Neither player lasted long in Indianapolis. Although he batted .389 and drove in 10 runs, Strong played in only 12 games. Jenkins surmised, "Chances are they overstayed their welcome when they coupled their playing time with sampling the nightlife and having a good time."[34] Strong stayed with the Trotters through the 1949 season and then retired. Divorced from Ruth, he also remarried, this time to 22-year-old Florence Faulkner of Chicago.

Outfielder Ted Strong led all Monarchs hitters with a .364 batting average in 1942. When he was not roaming the outfield on baseball diamonds, Strong played basketball for the Harlem Globetrotters. (Courtesy Noir-Tech Research, Inc.)

Strong took a brief Hollywood turn in the early 1950s when he appeared in a movie about Saperstein's basketball team. *The Harlem Globetrotters* opened in theaters on October 24, 1951. Produced by Columbia Pictures, the film stars Dorothy Dandridge and features Thomas Gomez as Saperstein. Jasper Strong recalled, "Oh, man, seeing my big brother on that big screen just made me so proud. No one else I knew in my neighborhood could say they had their brother in the movies."[35]

In January of 1952, Strong began working as a clerk at a post office in Chicago, where he earned $1.66 an hour. In March, he was let go "due to absence from duty without leave." Jenkins speculates that "marriage difficulties probably contributed to Ted Jr. only sporadically showing up for work." Instead of going to work, Strong "would handle small assignments for Abe Saperstein."[36]

Strong "slowly faded into the memory of the sports world as the years progressed."[37] He sometimes attended Globetrotter games played in the Chicago area and reminisced with old friends. His marriage to Florence ultimately ended in divorce.

Strong had developed emphysema, and his condition flared up on the afternoon of March 1, 1978, and it worsened throughout the day. He began to cough and struggled to catch his breath. Sensing trouble, a visitor to his house called for an ambulance. Strong died at 1:35 A.M. on March 2 at Provident Hospital on Chicago's south side. He was 61 years old. Strong was "virtually penniless at the time of his death."[38] He was buried in an unmarked grave at Lincoln Cemetery in Blue Island, Illinois, a Chicago suburb.

Dave Condon briefly mentioned Strong's passing in his column for the *Chicago Tribune*. The note had a few inaccuracies, including Strong's age when he died and the length of his playing career with the Trotters. "Theodore 'Ted' Strong Jr., 62, who made sports history in 20 years with the Harlem Globe Trotters [*sic*] and as an infielder-outfielder for the Kansas City Monarchs and the Indianapolis A's, died Friday."[39]

The inspiration for Jenkins' biography of Strong goes back to 1977. At that time, Jenkins wrote an article about Strong Sr.'s career in the Negro Leagues for a journalism class at Northern Illinois University. Decades later, he began to work on a book about Strong Jr. "After doing a little research, [Jenkins] realized the younger Strong had quite an extraordinary duo-sport career, and he would make an ever more fascinating subject than his father,"[40] said an article in the *Aurora Beacon-News*. In the preface to his biography of Strong, Jenkins wrote, "His full story needed to be told. ... He is like the hundreds of African American men and women who played in the Negro Baseball Leagues and are unsung heroes."[41] As to the absence of a plaque for Strong at the Hall of Fame, Jenkins said, "There was a little taint on his legacy," referring to the ballplayer's heavy drinking. "And it makes it hard to say, 'OK, he should be in the Hall of Fame.' But, heck, Ty Cobb and Babe Ruth drank. That's what (players) did at the time."[42]

No one can doubt Strong's extraordinary athletic talent. Kendrick has compared him to longtime outfielder and Hall of Famer Dave Winfield. The 6-foot-6-inch Winfield played 22 seasons in the major leagues and hit 465 home runs. He batted .283, stole 223 bases, and drove home 1,833 runs, mostly for the San Diego Padres and New York Yankees. He made 12 All-Star teams and earned a plaque in the Hall of Fame in 2001, his first year on the ballot.

Winfield, a seven-time Gold Glove winner, has the distinction being drafted by four teams in three different sports. The Padres selected him with the fourth overall pick of the June 1973 amateur draft. The NBA's Atlanta Hawks and ABA's Utah Stars also drafted him, as did the NFL's Miami Dolphins, although Winfield never played that sport at the University of Minnesota. "I tell people all the time that Ted Strong was Dave Winfield before we knew who Dave Winfield was," Kendrick said.

"To me, Ted Strong epitomized that great athlete," Kendrick wrote. "You'll hear me refer to the players as some of the greatest athletes to play baseball – Ted Strong falls into that category. Six foot, six inches, freakish athlete. Powerful, great hitter, played every position except for pitcher and catcher."[43]

Negro League stars like Satchel Paige and Josh Gibson earned far more attention than Strong on the baseball field. Globetrotters Goose Tatum and Marques Haynes did the same on the basketball court. Even so, Jenkins wrote, Strong "lived a life unlike any other."[44]

Sources

In addition to the sources cited in the Notes, the author consulted seamheads.com and baseball-reference.com.

Notes

1 Seamheads.com https://www.seamheads.com/NegroLgs/player.php?playerID=stron01ted

2 Ryan Whirty, "Shining a Light on an Ex-Star," *South Bend* (Indiana) *Tribune*, June 3, 2014: B1.

3 Denise Crosby, "Aurora Resident Authors Book about 'Untold' Baseball All-Star, Globetrotter," *Aurora* (Illinois) *Beacon-News*, October 28, 2016, https://www.chicagotribune.com/suburbs/aurora-beacon-news/opinion/ct-abn-crosby-negro-league-baseball-st-1030-20161028-column.html

4 "Biography of Ted Strong Jr. Brings Light to Two-Sport Star," Homeplatedontmove.wordpress.com https://homeplatedontmove.wordpress.com/2019/12/09/biography-of-ted-strong-jr-brings-light-to-two-sport-star/

5 Sherman L. Jenkins, *Ted Strong Jr.: The Untold Story of the Original Globetrotter and Negro League All-Star* (Lanham, Maryland: Rowman & Littlefield, 2016), 12.

6 Jenkins, 15.

7 Bob Green, *Spinning the Globe: The Rise, Fall, and Return to Greatness of the Harlem Globetrotters* (New York: Harper, 2005), 17.

8 Green, 55.

9 Jenkins, 18.

10 Jenkins, 23.

11 Jenkins, 23.

12 Lloyd Lewis, quoted in Jenkins, 23.

13 Jenkins, 26.

14 Bill Young and Charles F. Faber, "J.L. Wilkinson," SABR.org https://sabr.org/bioproj/person/j-l-wilkinson/

15 Young and Faber, "J.L. Wilkinson."

16 Jenkins, 27.

17 "Globe Trotters Work Out with Sheboygan." *Chicago Defender*, November 23, 1940: 22.

18 Jenkins, 49.

19 Jenkins, 32.

20 Green, 101.

21 Jenkins, 35.

22 Jenkins, 61.

23 Jenkins, 66.

24 Jenkins, 68.

25 Whirty, "Shining a Light on an Ex-Star."

26 "Shining a Light on an Ex-Star."

27 Jenkins, 70.

28 Jackie Robinson, *I Never Had It Made* (New York: HarperCollins, 1995), 24.

29 "Shining a Light on an Ex-Star."

30 "Shining a Light on an Ex-Star."

31 Austin Hough, "South Bend's Connection to Negro Leagues Runs Deep," *Goshen* (Indiana) *News*, June 4, 2020. Goshennews.com

32 Jenkins, 124

33 Green, 159.

34 Jenkins, 95.

35 Jenkins, 100.

36 Jenkins, 104.

37 Jenkins, 117.

38 "Shining a Light on an Ex-Star."

39 David Condon, "In the Wake of the News," *Chicago Tribune*, March 4, 1978: 70.

40 Denise Crosby, "Aurora Resident Authors Book about 'Untold' Baseball All-Star, Globetrotter."

41 Jenkins, IX.

42 "Shining a Light on an Ex-Star."

43 Hough, "South Bend's Connection to Negro Leagues Runs Deep."

44 Jenkins, 124.

Willard Brown (at left) and Ted Strong, two fleet and powerful starting outfielders on the 1942 Monarchs team that beat the Homestead Grays in the World Series. (Courtesy Noir-Tech Research, Inc.)

JESSE WILLIAMS

By Tim Hagerty

Jesse Williams was one of the premier defensive infielders in the Negro Leagues during his career. "He could field anything that came his way at short and throw batters out from deep in the hole," one writer said in describing his skills.[1] He is also known as the Kansas City Monarchs player who switched positions to make room for Jackie Robinson.

Jesse Horace Williams was born to Willie W. Williams and Carrie M. Austin on June 22, 1913, in Henderson, Texas, 130 miles east of Dallas. Little is known about his parents or his childhood other than the fact that he was living with his widowed maternal grandmother, Julia (Austin) Gipson, at the time of the 1920 census.

Williams played for the semipro barnstorming Mineola (Texas) Black Spiders in the late 1930s. "The Spiders, dressed in grey baseball jersey [*sic*], played other all-Black teams from across the country. Each baseball game drew nearly 200 people. The team became well-known, and liked, by their fast-paced, Harlem Globetrotter style."[2] The Black Spiders entertained fans before games with routines like shadow ball, a pantomime show with an imaginary ball and players making acrobatic catches. Other Black Spiders antics included their catcher receiving pitches during games while sitting in a rocking chair behind home plate.[3]

In 1939 Williams played in an exhibition game for the Chicago American Giants that ended up being an audition. The American Giants faced the Kansas City Monarchs that day in Waco, Texas, and Williams got two hits and fielded every groundball in his vicinity.[4] The Monarchs were so impressed by Williams's performance against them that they decided to sign him.

Joining the Monarchs was a dream come true for Williams. "It was every Black boy's ambition to become a Monarch," he once said. "And white guys around there would want to become a Yankee. That's the only thing that you knew."[5]

Williams, who was 5-feet-11, weighed 160 pounds, and threw and batted right-handed, hit .216 as a utilityman in 26 Monarchs games in 1939. He played more often and performed much better offensively the following year, hitting .368 with one home run and 24 RBIs in 31 games. Even in the seasons in which Williams delivered a high batting average, he never hit more than two home runs, "but he could bunt and loved being up in clutch situations. He generally batted near the bottom of the batting order."[6]

The Monarchs won the Negro American League pennant every season from 1939 through 1942 and Williams was part of all four championship teams. In 1941 he played a steady shortstop and hit .257 in 31 games. The Monarchs' barnstorming tour that fall included a high-profile matchup against the Major League All-Stars at Sportsman's Park in St. Louis on October 5. The starting pitchers were future Hall of Famers Bob Feller for the All-Stars and Satchel Paige for the Monarchs. The major leaguers won 4-1 in front of 10,124 fans.[7]

Williams's most significant contribution to a Monarchs championship came in 1942. After a decent regular season (.262 with 2 home runs and 19 RBIs in 40 games), the shortstop starred in the postseason. The Monarchs met the Homestead Grays in the Negro League World Series and Williams hit a team-leading .500 in the series. Paige was on the mound when the Monarchs clinched the championship in front of 14,029 at Philadelphia's Shibe Park.[8]

On August 1, 1943, Williams played in the first of his two career East-West Games, the Negro Leagues' annual all-star game. He started at shortstop and led off for the West team, going 2-for-4 with two putouts and two assists. The West team scored two early runs and won, 2-1, ending their stretch of five consecutive East-West Game losses. Future Hall of Famers Cool Papa Bell, Willard Brown, Leon Day, Josh Gibson, Buck Leonard, and Paige also appeared in the game, which drew 51,723 fans to Chicago's Comiskey Park.

Sportswriter Wendell Smith of the *Pittsburgh Courier* summarized that the 1943 game "was a great ball game. One packed with thrills and surprises. One cast in a setting as colorful and picturesque as any movie saga. One that will go down in history in brilliant lettering and stand out in bold relief until the pages upon which it is written wither in the dust of time."[9]

Williams returned as the Monarchs' shortstop in 1944, batting .240 in 20 games as the team went 35-51 and finished in fourth place, their first losing season since they joined the Negro American League in 1937.

While his defense continued to receive praise in the press, Williams switched to playing second base in 1945 to make room at shortstop for Robinson. Williams's slick fielding and Robinson's athleticism formed "one of the speediest doubleplay combinations in the league."[10]

Williams's superb defense continued after his transition to second base. "At second base is Jesse Williams who can go his left or right with equal ability," the *Davenport* (Iowa) *Daily Times* wrote in 1945.[11] He hit .285 in 32 games for the Monarchs in 1945 and the team returned to its winning ways, going 39-35 and finishing in third place.

On July 29 of that year, Williams returned to the East-West Game at Comiskey Park. He played second base and led off, with Robinson hitting second and playing shortstop. Williams went 2-for-5 with a triple and four RBIs in the West's 9-6 win in front of 31,174 fans.[12]

The 1945 season was Williams's last in the Negro Leagues. In 1946 he joined the Mexican League's San Luis Potosi Tuneros, a team that finished last in the eight-team circuit. Williams batted .277 with 3 homers and 44 RBIs.[13] (He was suspended by the Negro American League for his jump to Mexico.)[14]

In 1947 Williams toured with the Harlem Globetrotters baseball team, a sister squad to the flashy basketball team. Williams played shortstop for the Globetrotters when they barnstormed throughout the Midwest and West that summer to face local clubs or the traveling House of David team.

On May 30, 1948, Williams and the Globetrotters played the Cincinnati Crescents in Muncie, Indiana. The spectators also saw a sprinting and jumping demonstration by Olympic gold medalist Jesse Owens.[15] Five months later, Williams reunited with his former Monarchs teammate Paige in an exhibition game at Wrigley Field in Los Angeles. Paige was available to pitch because his season with the Cleveland Indians had ended a few weeks earlier.

With his three-year Negro American League suspension for his jump to Mexico now over, Williams returned to the NAL in 1949. The press noted that "[T]he sensational shortstop, Jesse Williams, who was a tower of strength with the Kansas City Monarchs a few seasons back, has been obtained from that club and signed to a Clowns' contract."[16] The Indianapolis Clowns, who had joined the NAL in 1943 when they were based in Cincinnati, finished the season in fourth place with a 37-67 record.

In early April of 1950, Williams's absence from the Clowns was the talk of training camp in Jacksonville, Florida. According to the *Pittsburgh Courier*, "The holdout of two veteran performers, infielder Jesse Williams and hurler Andy Porter, kept the Negro American League Indianapolis Clowns from having their complete roster as they opened their 1950 training camp here this week."[17] Williams and the Clowns were at odds over salary. He ended up leaving the team and returning to the Globetrotters.

Williams journeyed to Mexico again in 1951, playing in one game for the Nuevo Laredo Tecolotes.[18] The reason for his ever-so-brief stint with Nuevo Laredo is unknown, but he went from Mexico to Canada when he signed with the Class-A Vancouver Capilanos of the Class-A Western International League for the 1952 season. The 39-year-old Williams shifted from middle infield to third base for the Capilanos and made an immediate impression on his new fan base. It was cold on Opening Night when Williams "made his brilliant, smooth-as-cornsilk stop of Dario Lodigiani's sharp smash to third base in an early inning in Monday night's opener against Yakima," a sportswriter noted.[19] Williams batted .251 in 126 games for Vancouver.

The Capilanos released Williams before the 1953 season and a letter to the editor of the *Vancouver Province* speculated as to why Williams was let go: "Jesse Williams is much too old," a fan wrote to the newspaper.[20] Williams still felt youthful and signed with the Yakima Bears of the same league after his release.

Williams did not stick with the Bears; he was driving a bread truck in Kansas City by June.[21] He was 40 years old in April 1954, when he signed with the Beaumont Exporters of the Double-A Texas League, a Chicago Cubs affiliate. He went 1-for-6 with Beaumont in what became the final eight games of his career.

Williams saw former Monarchs teammates and opponents move on to the American League or National League, but he never had that opportunity. Although he certainly had major-league fielding abilities, he was now too old to merit serious consideration from AL or NL clubs. Williams was 33 in April 1947, when Robinson famously joined the Brooklyn Dodgers.

Williams's former Monarchs teammate and longtime major-league scout Buck O'Neil said in 1990 that Williams would have succeeded in the majors. "Jesse would be a very good player because he could do the job very well defensively," O'Neil told the *Kansas City Star*. "Jesse ran well. He was a contact, spray-type hitter. Hit behind the runner. Get the runner over. I imagine in major-league baseball Jesse should be about a .265 hitter."[22]

Whatever disappointment Williams carried from the unfortunate timing of his playing career did not change his positive disposition. Articles about him late in his life paint a portrait of a likable person with an inspirational perspective. When Williams went blind in 1985 after years of cataract issues, he reacted by saying, "I'm so thankful all of this happened in my old age. It could've happened earlier."[23]

Slick-fielding Jesse Williams was the starting shortstop for the 1942 Negro World Series champion Kansas City Monarchs. (Courtesy Noir-Tech Research, Inc.)

Blindness prohibited Williams from playing golf in the late 1980s, but it did not stop him from riding in the golf cart and laughing on the course with friends like O'Neil. "I had promised Jesse – and he wanted to do it – I was going to take him out to the driving range and let him see if he could hit that golf ball. He thought he could do it," O'Neil said.[24]

Williams died in Kansas City at age 76 on February 27, 1990. He was survived by his wife of almost 26 years, Elaine Carmelita (Lee) Williams; two sons, Rostell and Ostell; 11 grandchildren; and 25 great-grandchildren.[25] He is buried in Kansas City's Mount Moriah Cemetery. Williams's obituary noted that he was an active member of the Bethel AME church, the Pioneer Club Inc., and the Heart of America Golf Club.[26] In addition to his family and community activities, he also left behind a legacy as one of the finest fielders in Negro Leagues history.

JESSE WILLIAMS

Sources

In addition to the sources cited in the Notes, the author consulted Ancestry.com, Baseball-Reference.com, and Newspapers.com. For Williams's Negro Leagues statistics, the author used Seamheads.com.

Notes

1 Leslie A. Heaphy, ed., *Satchel Paige and Company: Essays on the Kansas City Monarchs, Their Greatest Star and the Negro Leagues* (Jefferson, North Carolina: McFarland, 2007), 255.

2 "'Mineola Black Spiders' Make Their Mark on Baseball History," KETK-TV (Lufkin/Longview, Texas), September 29, 2016.

3 "Old Alex to Appear Here," *Tyler* (Texas) *Courier-Times*, May 14, 1939: 8.

4 Jack Etkin, "Ex-Monarch Remained Strong to the End," *Kansas City Star*, March 6, 1990: C-6.

5 "Monarchs, Blues Predate Seasons in Majors," *Kansas City Star*, April 9, 1990: 2.

6 Heaphy, 255.

7 "10,124 Fans See Feller and Paige Pitch Here," *St. Louis Star and Times*, October 6, 1941: 14.

8 "Kansas City Monarchs Capture Negro Title," *Capital Times* (Madison, Wisconsin), September 30, 1942: 18.

9 Wendell Smith, "Pitchers Star as West Beats East in Thriller," *Pittsburgh Courier*, August 7, 1943: 19.

10 "Monarchs Play Barons Tonight," *Daily Oklahoman* (Oklahoma City), July 6, 1945: 15.

11 "Negro League Teams Meet Here Tonight; Hot Battle Slated," *Daily Times* (Davenport, Iowa), August 28, 1945: 9.

12 "1945 East-West Game," Baseball-Reference Bullpen, baseball-reference.com/bullpen/1945_East-West_Game.

13 Pedro Treto Cisneros, *The Mexican League: Comprehensive Player Statistics, 1937-2001* (Jefferson, North Carolina: McFarland & Company, Inc., 2002), 279.

14 "Sports Reviews & Previews," *Weekly Review* (Birmingham, Alabama), January 21, 1949: 8.

15 "Olympic Sprint Champion and Famous Diamond Clown on Sunday Baseball Bill," *Muncie* (Indiana) *Evening Press*, May 29, 1948: 8.

16 "Sports Reviews & Previews."

17 "Two Veterans Only Clowns Not Signed," *Pittsburgh Courier*, April 1, 1950: 23.

18 Cisneros, 279.

19 Don Carlson, "The Classy Caps," *Vancouver* (British Columbia) *Province*, April 29, 1952: 6.

20 Alf Cottrell, "But Listen!" *Vancouver Province*, January 24, 1953: 14.

21 Clancy Loranger, "Week's Work," *Vancouver Province*, June 6, 1953: 16.

22 Etkin.

23 Etkin.

24 Etkin.

25 "Jesse H. Williams," obituary, *Kansas City Star*, March 3, 1990: 39.

26 "Jesse H. Williams."

J.L. WILKINSON

By Charles F. Faber and William A. Young

J. Leslie Wilkinson (1878-1964) was one of the most respected and influential figures in the history of Black baseball. His trailblazing role in helping to found the Negro National League in 1920, in addition to his establishing and operating the renowned Kansas City Monarchs for many years, earned him a plaque in the National Baseball Hall of Fame in 2006.

Wilkinson was born on May 14, 1878, in Algona, Iowa. He was the oldest child of Myrta "Mertie" Harper and John J. "J.J." Wilkinson. His father was a teacher and superintendent of schools in Algona and participated in local politics. J.J. also served as president of Northern Iowa Normal School in Algona before moving his family to Omaha, Nebraska, and then to Des Moines, Iowa, where he became a manager in the Iowa National Life Insurance Company.[1]

Young J.L. learned the basics of baseball on the sandlots of Algona. He became an accomplished pitcher on an Omaha high-school team and later attended Highland Park Normal College in Des Moines, where he was one of the school's leading pitchers.

Beginning in 1895, Wilkinson played semipro baseball for more than a decade, at first using the pseudonym "Joe Green" to protect his amateur standing. In the 1900 census J.L. was listed as a clerk at Chase Brothers, a leading Des Moines grocery store, although his real job was probably pitching for the store's outstanding semipro baseball team. Des Moines newspapers hailed his skills on the mound. But in 1900 a broken wrist brought his dreams of a professional pitching career to a sudden halt.

In 1904 Wilkinson joined a new semipro team organized by Hopkins Brothers Sporting Goods in Des Moines. The club traveled throughout Iowa, beating almost all comers and, at one point, winning 17 of 18 games. Although he no longer pitched, Wilkinson played a fair game at shortstop.

The Hopkins team closed its 1904 season with a doubleheader against the all-Black Buxton Wonders. Buxton was a thriving coal-mining community in southeastern Iowa with a population of 2,700 Blacks and 2,000 whites. Wilkinson undoubtedly took note of the racial harmony in Buxton, which was evident in the large, integrated crowd at the games. Hopkins Brothers won the first contest, and the Wonders (augmented by several Black players from Chicago) took the second.

Wilkinson became the Hopkins captain and manager in 1905. The decision to go into management may have been made after a Des Moines sportswriter opined that he was a good defensive shortstop and played with his head but that he fell short as a hitter.

Wilkinson's promotional acumen was soon evident. He took his Hopkins teammates on the road throughout Iowa, Minnesota, and the Dakotas, booking games against local teams in small towns. To increase attendance, Wilkinson came up with a new gimmick in 1907. He scheduled games that coincided with fairs, carnivals, festivals, and reunions. When people came to the games, they saw a juggernaut. In one stretch in 1908, the Hopkins team won 31 of 33 games.

Wilkinson was married in 1908. According to his daughter, Gladys, the parents of his wife, Bessie, were not pleased that she had taken up with a "baseball man." They were devout Methodists who considered baseball players to be ruffians. However, Bessie grew to love the game and traveled with her husband on barnstorming tours. In addition to Gladys, J.L. and Bessie had a son, Richard.

At the end of the 1908 season, Wilkinson disbanded the Hopkins men's team and created a barnstorming club of "Bloomer Girls" named the Hopkins Brothers Champion Lady Baseball Club. He recruited the best female baseball players he could find, including a superstar from the Boston Bloomer Girls, who played under the name Carrie Nation, the famous ax-wielding temperance activist and suffragette. Wilkinson augmented the team with at least three male players, including a catcher who was also a wrestler and who was willing to take on all comers in the small towns in which they played. Beginning in June 1909, the club traveled in style when Wilkinson leased a Pullman Palace railroad car for their barnstorming tours. In addition to the players and a bulldog mascot, he took along a portable ballpark, consisting of a canvas fence 14 feet high and 1,200 feet long, and a canopy-covered grandstand that could seat 2,000 fans. The next year he added a lighting system for use in night games. It would not be the last time he experimented with lights.

Wilkinson continued to be a baseball innovator. Although ethnic teams, such as African American clubs, were popular in the early 1900s, no one had ever fielded a team made up of different nationalities and ethnic groups. Wilkinson recruited Native Americans, African Americans, Chinese, Japanese, Hawaiians, Frenchmen, Cubans, Filipinos, Scotsmen, Germans, and Caucasian American players. Fittingly, he called his new team All Nations. Beginning in May 1912, All Nations toured the country all the way to the West Coast and back to Iowa. In 1913 the team won 119 games and lost 17. After the 1915 season Wilkinson moved the All Nations operation to Kansas City. The club flourished there in 1916 but was disbanded in 1918 because some of the players had been drafted to serve in World War I.

After the war Wilkinson, who was now living with his family in Kansas City, revived the All Nations club. During its tenure All Nations featured several players of major-league caliber. Among them were African Americans John Donaldson and Frank Blattner, as well as Cubans José Méndez and Cristobal Torriente.

Donaldson was a left-handed pitcher with a good fastball and changeup, outstanding control, and a hard, sharp-breaking curve. In 1916-17 Donaldson pitched in 10 games with All Nations, striking out 64. Wilkinson told reporters that Donaldson was one of the greatest pitchers who ever lived, White or Black. Méndez, known as the "The Black Diamond," was one of the first internationally known Cuban players. He had a blazing fastball and a sharp curve. Méndez was elected to the National Baseball Hall of Fame with Wilkinson in 2006. Torriente was perhaps the most famous Cuban player of his era. He was a left-handed power hitter who was also an effective basestealer, and an outstanding center fielder with excellent range and a strong, accurate arm. He was also inducted into the National Baseball Hall of Fame in 2006. In an effort to make the All Nations team appear more diverse, Blattner played under the name "Blukoi" and often claimed he was Hawaiian. At other times Blattner was introduced as a full-blooded American Indian.

Another All Nations player of note was Goro Mikami, an outfielder, who joined the team in 1912, as the first-ever Japanese professional baseball player.

Other All Nations players who excelled were two right-handed pitchers, Bill "Plunk" Drake and Wilber "Bullet Joe" Rogan. Rogan, considered by many baseball historians to be one of the best pitchers of all time, was inducted into Cooperstown in 1998.

The All Nations team showed that Wilkinson was well ahead of his times as a baseball promoter and advocate of racial integration. In an era when the racist movie *The Birth of a Nation* was so popular that it was shown by President Woodrow Wilson in the White House, and three decades before the breaking of the color barrier in the White major leagues, Wilkinson's All Nations proved that an interracial team could not only succeed but flourish.[2]

In 1920 another opportunity presented itself to Wilkinson when Rube Foster took the lead in organizing the Negro National League. The organizational meeting was held at the Paseo YMCA in Kansas City in February 1920, and the first games were played in May. Wilkinson, joined by a Kansas City, Kansas, businessman, Thomas "T.Y." Baird (who played a largely behind-the-scenes role), formed a club called the Kansas City Monarchs and applied for membership in the new league. At first Foster was reluctant to accept White ownership of a club in his circuit, but he relented because of Wilkinson's reputation for integrity and fairness. In fact, Wilkinson earned such respect from his fellow owners that he was named the league's secretary. Together, he and Foster led the new league into a decade of success and prosperity. Wilkinson also tapped two African American leaders to represent the team in Kansas City's Black community: Quincy Gilmore (who served as the team's traveling secretary and publicist) and Dr. Howard Smith, a physician and superintendent of Kansas City's Black hospital. Serendipitously, the year before the Monarchs were founded, an African American weekly, the *Kansas City Call,* began publication. The *Call* provided coverage of the Monarchs and other Negro Leagues teams, while dailies like the *Kansas City Star* largely ignored them.

Wilkinson took some of the best players from his All Nations team to fill his new club's roster, including Donaldson, Méndez, and Blattner. (Torriente went to the rival Chicago American Giants but joined the Monarchs in 1926.) Acting on a tip from a friend, Kansas City native Casey Stengel, Wilkinson added some players from the 25th Infantry Wreckers, an all-Black US Army team. Included in this group were Rogan, power-hitting outfielder Oscar "Heavy" Johnson, talented first baseman Lemuel "Hawk" Hawkins, crafty southpaw Andy Cooper (who was inducted with Wilkinson into the National Baseball Hall of Fame in 2006), and shortstop Dobie Moore. Moore, known as The Black Cat, won the NNL batting title in 1924 with a .453 average and was considered the top shortstop in the league for six years until his career was cut short early in the 1926 season. At a celebration after a ladies day game on May 17, Moore was shot in the leg by a woman who claimed he had assaulted her. Moore then broke his leg jumping from a window to escape from her.

Wilkinson, affectionately called "Wilkie" by his players, fans, and fellow executives, built the Monarchs into the most successful NNL club of the 1920s. The team won the league pennant four times in the decade – 1923, 1924, 1925, and 1929. In 1924 the Monarchs played the Eastern Colored League champion Hilldale club in the first Colored World Series. With the hard-fought best-of-nine series tied at four games, José Méndez, told by doctors he was too ill to play, pitched a three-hit shutout and Kansas City captured the title. In 1925 the league played a split season and the Monarchs defeated the St. Louis Stars for the championship. The Monarchs lost the 1925 World Series to Hilldale, partly because ace pitcher Bullet Joe Rogan was sidelined by a freak accident. In 1926 Wilkinson purchased the first of a number of buses, touring cars, and trailers (with portable kitchens) that the Monarchs used on their barnstorming tours. With these vehicles, Wilkinson was able to schedule games in towns without rail connections. The players also slept in the buses when, often because of Jim Crow restrictions, other accommodations were not available.

Wilkinson tapped Méndez to manage the Monarchs their first two seasons. Another pitcher, Sam Crawford, was the skipper for a portion of the 1921 season and the 1922 and 1923 campaigns. Mendez resumed the helm during the 1923 season and continued as skipper through the 1925 season. Rogan was Monarchs manager for the rest of the seasons of the decade. Among the not-yet-mentioned stalwart players Wilkinson signed for the Monarchs during the 1920s were Roy "Bubba" Johnson, Carroll "Dink" Mothell, Hurley McNair, Otto "Jaybird" Ray, Zack "Hooks" Foreman, George "Tank" Carr, Clifford "Cliff" Bell, William Bell, Newton "Newt" Allen, Walter "Newt" Joseph, Bartolo Portuando, Frank Duncan, Alfred "Army" Cooper, Rube Currie, Chet Brewer, and Eddie "Pee Wee" Dwight.

As early as 1921 Wilkinson booked the first of what would become many games between the Monarchs and all-star teams of major leaguers that featured legends such as Babe Ruth, Dizzy Dean, Stan Musial, and Bob Feller. The Monarchs won the majority of these interracial contests, but the substantial sums taken in at the gates were what counted most.

The Great Depression of the 1930s wreaked havoc upon baseball in general and Black baseball in particular. The Eastern Colored League had folded in 1928. The Monarchs withdrew from the NNL after the 1930 season and the league disbanded in 1931. The Monarchs survived because of Wilkinson's vision and ingenuity. In 1929 he commissioned an Omaha company to design a portable lighting system for night games. Wilkinson had experimented with baseball under the lights before, but this system was far better. Powered by a 250-horsepower motor and a 100-kilowatt generator, the equipment illuminated lights atop telescoping poles extending 40 feet above the field. With the support of his wife, Bessie, Wilkinson mortgaged everything he owned to purchase the system, and his gamble paid off. Wilkinson believed that just as talkies saved the movies, lights would save baseball, and he was right. The Monarchs' first night game was played in Enid, Oklahoma, on April 28, 1930. Within a few months, night games proved to be a huge success and Wilkinson quickly recouped his initial investment.

From 1931 through 1936 the Monarchs were an exclusively barnstorming team. They often played in daylight and after dark on the same day and became the most popular touring team in the nation. Frequently they were accompanied by the bearded House of David, another hugely successful barnstorming club. In order to enhance revenue, the Monarchs sometimes rented the lighting equipment to their friendly rivals. Among the standout players for the Monarchs during these barnstorming seasons were Bullet Joe Rogan (who managed the team in 1931, 1933, and 1934), Dink Mothell (manager in a portion of the 1930 season and 1932), Newt Allen, Newt Joseph, John Donaldson, Norman "Turkey" Stearnes, Frank Duncan, Chet Brewer, Army Cooper, Andy Cooper (who was skipper during the 1936 and 1937 seasons), Willie Foster, George Giles, Willie Wells, James "Cool Papa" Bell, Quincy Trouppe, Rube Currie, Frank Duncan, Pee Wee Dwight, Eldridge "Ed Chill"

• J.L. WILKINSON •

Mayweather, and Willard Brown. Sam Crawford was manager in 1935. In addition to Rogan and Andy Cooper, National Baseball Hall of Fame inductees from this group were Bell (1974), Foster (1996), Wells (1997), Stearnes (2000), and Brown (2006).

In 1933 the Negro National League was revived, but it was no longer under the leadership of Wilkinson or Foster, who had died in 1930. In 1937 Wilkie helped form a new circuit, the Negro American League and served as the league's first treasurer. His Kansas City Monarchs continued to be a power in the new circuit. They won the NAL pennant in 1937, 1939, 1940, 1941, 1942, and 1946. In 1942 they swept the Homestead Grays in four games in the first Colored World Series since 1927. The 1942 Series featured an encounter between two of the legends of the game, Satchel Paige and Josh Gibson. In an example of his generosity and in one of the early instances of revenue-sharing, Wilkinson divided the Monarchs' portion of the Series gate among the players. The Monarchs lost the 1946 World Series to the Newark Eagles in seven games.

Between 1937 and 1948 (the last year Wilkinson owned the Monarchs), prominent players included Andy Cooper (also manager, 1937-40), Ed Mayweather, Newt Allen (skipper during the 1941 season), Willard Brown, Byron "Mex" Johnson, Pee Wee Dwight, Bullet Joe Rogan, Hilton Smith, John Markham, John "Buck" O'Neil (manager in 1948), T.R. "Ted" Strong, Turkey Stearnes, Frank Duncan (at the helm, 1942-47), Leroy "Satchel" Paige (inducted into the Hall of Fame in 1971), Chet Brewer, Clifford "Connie" Johnson, Jack Matchett, Booker McDaniel, William "Bonnie" Serrell, Jesse Williams, Henry "Hank" Thompson, Ted Alexander, James "Lefty" LaMarque, Jackie Robinson (the first African American inductee at Cooperstown, in 1962), Elston Howard, and Earl Taborn.

The Monarchs were so dominant in the late 1930s and early to mid-1940s that they became known approvingly as the Negro Leagues' version of the New York Yankees. The best players wanted to play on a winning team. Also helpful were Wilkinson's reputation for fairness and integrity and his efforts to secure proper accommodations for his players during the Jim Crow era. A mutual respect developed between the players and the ownership of the Monarchs. Wilkinson also expected his players to be wholesome ambassadors for the Monarchs and Black baseball. He bought suits for ballplayers and expected them to wear them in the community. In addition, he often took care

Majority owner J. L. Wilkinson, a White owner in the world of Black baseball, had the respect of his players because, according to Newt Allen, "He was a considerate man [and] he treated everyone alike." (Courtesy Noir-Tech Research, Inc.)

of their medical needs. Monarchs players were treated as celebrities, particularly in the area around 18th and Vine in Kansas City (where the Negro Leagues Baseball Museum is now located), and they could often be seen in venues such as the famed Rose Room of the Streets Hotel alongside stars like Count Basie.

Two of Wilkinson's stellar achievements during this period were the resurrection of the career of Satchel Paige and the signing of Jackie Robinson. The two players were quite different in background and temperament, but they shared one attribute: tremendous talent. Paige had been an outstanding pitcher for many years, and Wilkinson had "rented" the lanky right-handed hurler to play in exhibition games with the Monarchs on a number of occasions. Wilkie and Satchel got along well despite Paige's reputation for being hard to manage. In 1938 Paige was banned for life from the Negro National League for contract-jumping. He joined the Mexican League, where he suffered his first sore arm in 12 years. Wilkinson was the only Negro Leagues executive willing to take a chance on Paige. He signed the wounded veteran to a team that he christened Satchel Paige's All-Stars and sent them on a wildly successful barnstorming tour through the Northwest and Canada. By 1939 Paige's arm had healed and, with Hilton Smith, he became the leading pitcher for the Monarchs in the NAL. Paige and Wilkinson developed a close bond. In commenting on how Wilkinson treated him, Paige said, "[T]hat's how Mr. Wilkinson was. If you were down and needed a hand, he'd give you one."[3] Paige remained with the Monarchs until Bill Veeck signed him to a major-league contract with the Cleveland Indians in 1948.

Jackie Robinson had starred in baseball, basketball, track, and football at UCLA, earning a reputation as one of the best all-around athletes in the country. While serving in the Army and stationed at Camp Hood (now Fort Hood) in Texas, Robinson had the opportunity to play some baseball, and was spotted by Hilton Smith, who recommended him to Wilkinson. After his discharge from the Army, Robinson joined the Monarchs for the 1945 season, but he was with Wilkie's team for only a few months. As is well known, Branch Rickey signed Robinson to break Organized Baseball's color barrier on August 28, 1945. Rickey claimed that Robinson did not have a legitimate contract and paid nothing to the Monarchs for signing him to the Brooklyn Dodgers organization. Wilkinson graciously responded, saying: "Although I feel the Brooklyn club ... owes us some kind of compensation for Robinson, we will not protest to Commissioner [Happy] Chandler. I am very glad to see Jackie get this chance and I'm sure he'll make good. He's a wonderful ballplayer. If and when he gets into the major leagues he will have a wonderful career."[4]

Nearly blind and suffering from other ailments in 1948, Wilkie sold his interest in the Monarchs to his longtime business partner, Tom Baird, and retired from baseball. Wilkinson, however, had not lost his good business sense, and he arranged to receive a portion of any amount Baird received for selling a Monarchs player to the major or minor leagues if that player had been with the team while Wilkinson was still an owner. J.L. "Wilkie" Wilkinson died in a Kansas City nursing home on August 21, 1964. His remains rest in the Garden Mausoleum at the Mount Moriah Cemetery in Kansas City, Missouri. Many of the old Monarchs attended his funeral.

Years later Buck O'Neil, who had been his close friend since signing with the Monarchs in 1938, paid this tribute to Wilkinson: "[H]e "didn't have a prejudiced bone in him. ... While Wilkinson could have been lynched just for owning a Black ball baseball team, he never allowed the ugly racial prejudice of his day to keep him from doing what he loved and believed – Black baseball at its highest. J.L. Wilkinson, he looked down on no one and he brought out the best in everyone. That's J.L. Wilkinson. ... I love that man."[5]

In addition to Robinson and Paige, a number of Monarchs who had played under Wilkie's management of the team went into Organized Baseball, including Elston Howard, the first African American to play for the New York Yankees. Thirteen Monarchs players are in the National Baseball Hall of Fame: Ernie Banks, Cool Papa Bell, Willard Brown, Andy Cooper, Bill Foster, José Méndez, Satchel Paige, Jackie Robinson, Bullet Joe Rogan, Hilton Smith, Turkey Stearnes, Cristobal Torriente, and Willie Wells. Wilkinson joined them when he was inducted posthumously in 2006, His plaque at Cooperstown is inscribed as follows:[6]

J. LESLIE WILKINSON
"J.L." "WILKIE"
KANSAS CITY MONARCHS, 1920-1948

AN INNOVATIVE AND GENEROUS OWNER WHO FOUNDED AND OPERATED THE KANSAS CITY MONARCHS FROM 1920-1948. RESPECTED FOR HONESTY AND FAIRNESS WITH HIS PLAYERS. HIS MONARCHS DOMINATED BLACK BASEBALL, WINNING THE MOST LEAGUE TITLES AND TWO NEGRO LEAGUE WORLD SERIES CHAMPIONSHIPS. CREATED MULTI-RACIAL ALL-NATIONS BARNSTORMING TEAM THAT FLOURISHED FROM 1912-1918, THEN HELPED FOUND THE NEGRO NATIONAL LEAGUE IN 1920. DEVISED PORTABLE LIGHTING SYSTEM WHICH ALLOWED TEAMS TO PLAY NIGHT GAMES AND SURVIVE THE GREAT DEPRESSION. SENT MORE PLAYERS, INCLUDING JACKIE ROBINSON, TO MAJOR LEAGUES THAN ANY OTHER NEGRO LEAGUES OWNER.

Sources

In addition to the following sources listed below and cited in the Notes, the authors also consulted a number of web sites, including Ancestry.com, Baseball-Reference.com, www.baseballhall.org, www.entertainment, howstuffworks.com, www.iptv.org, and seamheads.com.

Clark, Dick and Larry Lester, eds. *The Negro Leagues Book* (Cleveland: Society for American Baseball Research, 1994).

Heaphy, Leslie A. *The Negro Leagues: 1869-1960* (Jefferson, North Carolina: McFarland & Co., 2003).

Heaphy, Leslie A. *Satchel Paige and Company: Essays on the Kansas City Monarchs, Their Greatest Star and the Negro Leagues* (Jefferson, North Carolina: McFarland & Co., 2007).

Hogan, Lawrence. *Shades of Glory: The Negro Leagues and the Story of African American Baseball* (Washington, DC: National Geographic, 2006).

Johnson, Lloyd, Steve Garlick, and Jeff Magaliff, eds. *Unions to Royals: The Story of Professional Baseball in Kansas City* (Cleveland: Society for American Baseball Research, 1996).

Peterson, Robert. *Only the Ball Was White: A History of Legendary Black Players and All-Black Professional Teams* (Englewood Cliffs, New Jersey: Prentice-Hall, 1970).

Riley, James. *The Biographical Encyclopedia of Negro Baseball Leagues* (New York: Carroll and Graf, 1994).

Tygiel, Jules. "Black Ball," in John Thorn et al., eds., *Total Baseball: The Ultimate Baseball Encyclopedia* (Wilmington, Delaware: Sport Media, 2004).

Young, William A. *J.L. Wilkinson and the Kansas City Monarchs: Trailblazers in Black Baseball* (Jefferson, North Carolina: McFarland & Co., 2016).

Notes

1 Ralph J. Christian, "Wilkie: James [sic] Leslie Wilkinson and the Iowa Years," *Iowa Heritage Illustrated* (Spring 2006). This is by far the most thorough account of Wilkinson's early life and start in baseball.

2 Timothy Gay, *Satchel, Dizzy and Rapid Robert: The Wild Saga of Interracial Baseball Before Jackie Robinson* (New York: Simon and Schuster, 2010), 25-26.

3 Leroy "Satchel" Paige, as told to David Lipman, *Maybe I'll Pitch Forever; A Great Baseball Player Tells the Hilarious Story Behind the Legend* (Lincoln: University of Nebraska Press, 1993 [1962]), 123-31.

4 Janet Bruce, *The Kansas City Monarchs: Champions of Black Baseball* (Lawrence: University of Kansas Press, 1985), 112. This is the first comprehensive survey of the Monarchs, drawing on interviews with players and their families as well as the families of J.L. Wilkinson and Tom Baird.

5 Sam Mellinger, "J.L. Wilkinson: He Was a Man Apart," *Kansas City Star,* July 30, 2006: C1, C12.

6 http://baseballhall.org/hof/wilkinson-jl

TOM BAIRD

By Bob LeMoine

Tom Baird was present at the beginning of the Negro National League in 1920 and stayed nearly to the conclusion of the Negro Leagues themselves in 1956. His long tenure was spent solely with the Kansas City Monarchs, the dominant and longest-running franchise in the history of the Negro Leagues. He was the longest-serving club owner in the history of those leagues and he and long-time co-owner J.L. Wilkinson served as the only two white executives in the league. His greatest accomplishment, beyond the storied success of the Monarchs, is likely found in the number of players he sold to major-league teams after the integration of Organized Baseball. While the Negro Leagues were in decline from the late 1940s on, Baird found ways to keep the Monarchs competitive by scouting, developing, and trading talented players, who then had new opportunities in the majors.

Thomas Younger Baird was born January 27, 1885, in Madison County, Arkansas. His father was Hampton "Noah" Baird, a plumber who ran his own business and, in 1902, moved the family to the Armourdale section of Kansas City, Kansas. Thomas's mother was Harriette "Hattie" (Duncan) Baird, and her side of the family presents an interesting backstory to his life. She was the daughter of Sally (Younger) Duncan, and Harriet's maiden name was given to Thomas for his middle name. Sally had 13 siblings in all, including brothers Bob, Jim, John, and Cole, who were members of the famous James-Younger outlaw gang, led by Frank and Jesse James. The Younger name became associated with robbing banks, trains, and stagecoaches throughout the Midwest. Their careers ended in 1876 when three of the remaining brothers were arrested. Only Jim and Cole lived to see the twentieth century when they were paroled in 1901. A year later Jim put a bullet in his head, but Cole lived a few more years doing Wild West shows. Due to the notoriety of the Younger name, Thomas never used it, and was known as "T.Y." He likely did not take kindly to anyone asking him about his uncle Cole.

Tom also had younger brothers William and Floyd and a sister, Bertha. At the 1910 census a boarder named William Arnold also lived with the family at 1213 Kansas Ave. Tom worked as a cutter for the Peet Brothers Soap company. On January 22, 1912, Baird married Frances E. Stuart, also of Kansas City, Kansas. By the 1915 Kansas state census, Tom was working for the Rock Island Railroad Company in White City, Kansas.

Baird formed T.Y. Baird's Baseball Club, which became one of the best semipro baseball teams in Kansas City, Kansas. The club leased Billion Bubble Park, an amusement park on Mill Street and Scott Avenue that was run by the Peet Brothers. The team was often nicknamed the Soapmakers. Baird also purchased a set of uniforms left from the Federal League's Kansas City Packers, and his team – hand-me-down outfits and all – was the semipro champion of the city in 1916 and 1917.[1] Around 1917 Baird also opened a pool hall at 1139 Kansas Ave. An advertisement boasted that a person could play pool and get candy, soda pop, cigars, and tobacco at the shop. Baird opened several pool halls and bowling alleys throughout the area.[2]

In May of 1918, Baird became wedged between two sets of train cars while setting a brake and suffered a broken leg. He was laid up in the hospital for months and sued the company for $30,000.[3] The news about Baird, who was well-known by the community, was devastating. "Mr. Baird has done more than any other man the last few years to give the public a decent brand of the national pastime," wrote The Press in Kansas City, Kansas.[4] Although physically unable to play again, Baird managed his own team as well as a second team organized by the Peet Brothers.[5]

By the 1920 census, the Baird family lived at 413 N. 18th St. and included daughters Harriet and Ellen with a boarder couple named Bauer. The family moved to a new five-bedroom house at 1818 Grandview Boulevard, on the corner of North 19th St. Baird's move was reported in the newspaper, showing how well-known he already was throughout the city.[6] Baird was also a member of the Kansas Billiard Men's organization.[7]

• TOM BAIRD •

Just as Baird had a history in baseball prior to the Monarchs, so did his future longtime business partner, J.L. Wilkinson. "Wilkie," also White, was one day recognized for his contributions to the Negro Leagues with a plaque at the National Baseball Hall of Fame. In 1908 he formed a traveling all-female team. Women's teams had been popular since the nineteenth century and Wilkinson established his own "Bloomer" team, as they were called after the clothing they wore. In 1912 he formed the All-Nations club, made up of players of every imaginable nationality. This team barnstormed the country over the next several years. Traveling by Pullman car, Wilkinson even dabbled in a primitive, yet effective, portable lighting system so games could be played at night. Some players Wilkinson either hired or observed would become key members of those early Monarchs teams, including African Americans John Donaldson and Bullet Joe Rogan and Cuban José Méndez.

Rube Foster's Chicago American Giants team was the best independent Black club while Wilkinson's melting-pot team toured the country. Foster sought to organize an all-Black league, something that had been unsuccessfully attempted by others in the past. In February 1920, Foster realized his dream and the Negro National League was founded at a YMCA in Kansas City, Missouri. Wilkinson was one of the original founders of the league.

What role Baird played in those earliest days and how he met Wilkinson is not entirely known. Baird is not mentioned by name in the early reports, although later accounts describe him as being there with Wilkinson from the very beginning. Both men were well-known and likely their paths had crossed. Wilkinson was always the public face of the Monarchs and Baird worked behind the scenes. Wilkinson was a player's owner, known for his friendly demeanor, while Baird was tall and lean and more standoffish. Some players interviewed decades later did not even know Baird had been a part-owner of the club. Whatever the exact role Baird played, his partnership with Wilkinson lasted nearly 30 years.

The Monarchs rented Association Park from the white Kansas City Blues of the American Association. The two clubs often played a postseason series for bragging rights in the city. Babe Ruth also appeared with his traveling all-stars on a postseason barnstorming tour.[8]

Foster's Giants dominated the Negro National League for the first three years, but the Monarchs had winning clubs. The Monarchs won the pennant in 1923, the first of many during Baird's tenure, and now established themselves as a premier club. In 1923 the Monarchs also moved into the Blues' new ballpark, Muehlebach Field.

The Monarchs won the 1924 NNL pennant behind the solid pitching of Bullet Joe Rogan and the powerful lineup of Hurley McNair, Dobie Moore, Newt Joseph, and Heavy Johnson. They played Hilldale of the new Eastern Colored League in the first Negro League World Series, which was then called the Colored World Series. It was a hard-fought best-of-nine series that went the distance in a deciding 10th game (one game finished tied) before a small and bundled crowd on a cold day in Chicago on October 20. In heroic fashion, José Méndez, recovering from surgery, took the mound against doctor's orders and shut out Hilldale, 5-0.

The Monarchs dominated the start of the 1925 season and stormed into the new NNL playoff system, in which the winners of each half-season faced each other to determine who played the Eastern Colored League champion. The Monarchs defeated St. Louis but lost the World Series to Hilldale. A new acquisition by Wilkinson and Baird in 1926 was Cuban legend Cristóbal Torriente, once an All-Nations standout, who led the team in batting. The Monarchs dropped the NNL playoffs to Chicago.

With the demise of the Eastern Colored League, no World Series was played for a decade. The Monarchs won the 1929 pennant but became an independent barnstorming club in 1931 as the Great Depression made playing in large stadiums impractical. The NNL itself folded after the 1931 season, leaving no professional Black baseball league. The Monarchs still found a way to be profitable through barnstorming small towns and capitalizing on Wilkinson's portable lights.

Baird is credited with providing the finances needed ($100,000 by some accounts) for this new lighting system.[9] With the loss of a league schedule, the main booking responsibility fell to Baird. He also booked games for the House of David, the independent barnstorming club from the religious commune in Michigan noted for men following scriptural commands by not shaving. The new lighting system helped both clubs survive during the Depression. During the first half of the summer, the Monarchs leased its lights to the House of David team, allowing it to play more contests. Once Wilkinson and Baird saved enough money through the rentals, they began the Monarchs' season. Sometimes that season did not begin until August, but they still earned enough funds to be profitable. With other teams winding down, star players left their clubs, such as legendary greats Cool Papa Bell and Willie Wells. The night games drew large crowds and huge paychecks, irritating other club owners.[10]

One example of Baird's brilliant booking was the exhibition games against barnstorming White major leaguers. In the fall of 1933, Dizzy Dean and Pepper Martin of the St. Louis Cardinals Gas House Gang brought a team to Muehlebach Field. Negro League baseball had also returned; the Negro National League had been resurrected under the leadership of Cumberland Posey and Gus Greenlee. The league that year held its first East-West Game, the equivalent to the White major leagues' inaugural All-Star Game. The Monarchs continued as an independent club and barnstormed their way to the *Denver Post* tournament in 1934; the Monarchs were the first Black team to be invited to the tournament. Chet Brewer dominated most opponents, but he ran into pitcher Satchel Paige, who won three games in leading the House of David to the championship. Later that fall, after leading St. Louis to a World Series championship, Dizzy Dean, his brother Paul, and others promoted a "Dizzy and Daffy Tour." The Deans and Monarchs played to huge crowds and profits, although Monarchs players received considerably less money than their white counterparts.[11]

The Monarchs continued as a hot attraction in 1935 as they barnstormed with the House of David and also an integrated club from Bismarck, North Dakota, which included Paige. Bismarck won the National Baseball Congress semipro tournament in August. In September, Paige pitched for the Monarchs in the stretch run and against another Dizzy Dean postseason barnstorming team.[12] A decade later, Baird showed appreciation to Paige and gifted him with a two-seater airplane.[13] Baird also had a strong relationship with Syd Pollock, the owner of the Indianapolis Clowns, and the two franchises held barnstorming tours.

In June of 1935, Babe Ruth quit the Boston Braves, ending his legendary major-league career. Sensing opportunity, Baird wired Ruth an offer for $20,000 to play for the House of David club. Baird told Ruth he would not even have to have whiskers. Ruth refused.[14] In 1940 Baird became the head booker for the Negro National League, replacing Abe Saperstein.[15]

The Monarchs returned to league play when the Negro American League was formed in 1937, and won the inaugural season's pennant. Their pitching stars were Hilton Smith and Andy Cooper, while Willard Brown was the top hitter. The Monarchs won four straight NAL pennants (1939-1942). Buck O'Neil began his long tenure with the team at first base, and a rejuvenated Paige dominated on the mound. In 1942 the Negro League World Series returned and the Monarchs swept the Homestead Grays, 4-0. "I do believe we could have given the New York Yankees a run for their money that year," O'Neil remembered.[16]

Baird operated a pool hall and recreation center at Tenth Street and Minnesota Avenue and later at 1401 Minnesota Ave. with a partner, Ollie S. Stratton. Stratton was a former semipro player and had been a boxing manager for several years. Stratton sold his shares to Baird in 1945.[17] Baird had plenty of other businesses to attend to, including his bowling alleys and rental properties. He also collected rent from a flower shop, tavern, and hotel. In addition to all of those ventures, Baird owned property in Kansas that he researched for drilling oil, but that endeavor failed.[18] As the war years of the 1940s rolled on, Baird began taking over responsibilities from Wilkinson, including promotion of the team.[19]

The 1945 season was notable for Baird and Wilkinson signing UCLA athletic star Jackie Robinson to a baseball contract. The *Kansas City Call*, the local Black newspaper, hailed Robinson as the "prize freshman" on the 1945 Monarchs.[20] Robinson destroyed Negro League pitching and batted anywhere from .345 to .414.[21] No matter the statistic, Robinson was a true baseball star, and the time for integration had arrived. While the integration of the national pastime had been a longtime dream, the sustainability of the Negro Leagues was an uncomfortable subject. Wilkinson and Baird provided an alternative perspective from those who were dependent on the Negro Leagues for survival.

Clyde Sukeforth was a career baseball man and now chief scout for President Branch Rickey of the Brooklyn Dodgers. In 1945 Sukeforth's main job was to scout the Negro Leagues for Rickey's Brooklyn Brown Dodgers Black minor-league club in the new United States League.[22] Sukeforth, however, met Robinson and informed him of Rickey's interest in putting him on the major-league Dodgers. Rickey signed Robinson and sent him to the Dodgers' minor-league affiliate in Montreal in 1946. Robinson returned

• TOM BAIRD •

(L-R) Tom Baird, Kansas City Call *editor C. A. Franklin, and J. L. Wilkinson review travel restrictions that were to impede the Monarchs' ability to continue play during World War II.* (Courtesy Noir-Tech Research, Inc.)

briefly to the Monarchs to finish the 1945 season. "I went to the management of the Kansas City club to get permission to play up until September 21 in exhibition games and then go home, as I was tired," Robinson remembered. "I was told I would have to play all the games or none. I was left with no other alternative than to leave the ball club."[23]

Robinson didn't have a contract with the Monarchs for 1946, but Baird considered it common courtesy to give the Monarchs the first chance to sign him. From Baird's perspective, Rickey's signing of Robinson with no compensation for the Monarchs was unjustifiable. Baird and Wilkinson wanted to appeal to Commissioner Happy Chandler and ask him to bar Robinson from leaving the Monarchs. There was support among other Negro League club owners who saw a grim future of major-league owners raiding their talent. But the Monarchs owners soon decided otherwise. "For many years we have urged organized baseball to accept Negro players," Wilkinson said. "Whether we get any recompense in return for Robinson may be considered beside the point – we want Jackie to have a chance."[24]

Hard feelings still festered with Baird. Rickey "stooped to unethical methods," he said. "Rickey didn't pay us one cent for Jackie Robinson. He sneaked around and signed Robinson. His actions hurt us at the box office. But Rickey never even so much as thanked us for Robinson. We wrote him several months ago. He never even had the common courtesy to answer our letter. We're glad to see any of our boys get a chance. Robinson has helped the Negro race a great deal. But we hate to have our property just taken away from us. We've sold players to other teams – they dealt with us in an honorable way."[25] Baird even wrote that Rickey's tactics were like "Hitler's march through Hungary."[26]

Robinson responded to Baird's claims that he was "stolen" from the Monarchs. "I was left with no other alternative than to leave the club," he said. "The owner's (Wilkinson) son gave me a lecture and assured me that if I left the club I was through, that I could play no place outside the Negro National League. The 'cooperation' I received that afternoon made me glad I no longer had to play with the Monarchs."[27]

The Monarchs achieved one last Negro World Series appearance in 1946, losing to the Newark Eagles in seven games. After Robinson and other players left the Negro Leagues, attendance declined. Complicating matters, Wilkinson was involved in a car accident and lost sight in one eye, and was unable to read or drive. The task of the ownership duo was now in discovering talent, developing it as a minor-league team would, then selling the player for a top price to a major-league club. Hank Thompson and Willard Brown were players involved in two such deals.

The 1948 season was the last for the Negro League World Series and Wilkinson sold his ownership shares in the team to Baird for $27,000, ending their nearly three-decade partnership. Buck O'Neil was named the new Monarchs manager.[28] Baird was involved in a more "honorable" transaction than the way Robinson had been dealt with. He sold Satchel Paige to the Cleveland Indians, who won the American League pennant. Baird received $20,000 and Paige received a $16,000 salary from the Indians.[29]

Baird thought business maneuvers like this would help the Negro Leagues survive. "Negro baseball is like any other business," he said. "[A]s times get tougher it will be the survival of the fittest." A.S. "Doc" Young of the *Chicago Defender* described the different approaches club owners in the Negro Leagues were taking to stave off extinction. The Monarchs, he wrote, were a "prize franchise." One club owner said, "The Monarchs are drawing top crowds. That's because Tom Baird is in there working hard." "Did Baird sit back and let his franchise, which he rates as Triple-A caliber, go to pot?" wrote Young. "Nope! He went out and corralled more good players with the result that fans are behind him." In addition to Paige, Thompson, and Brown, Baird sold off Booker T. McDaniels and Ford Smith.[30] In 1950, Baird made $25,000 by selling Elston Howard and Frank Barnes to the New York Yankees.[31]

The Negro American League created Eastern and Western divisions in 1949 in order to carry out a postseason series in the absence of the National League. Baird withdrew the Monarchs from a postseason series as players were injured or jumping to the majors. Baird dabbled in football in 1950 when he staged a preseason game in Kansas City between the New York Yanks and Washington Redskins of the NFL. The contest attracted a little over 13,000 patrons, but Baird lost money.[32]

In 1952 Baird was presented a plaque by Ray "Hap" Dumont of the National Baseball Congress, which hosted a semipro tournament every year in Wichita, Kansas. The plaque honored Baird for sparking interest in baseball among the small towns in America. Baird received praise for "his work in helping to improve relations between the races."[33] It was in 1923 that Baird had convinced Dumont, then a high-school student, to sponsor a Monarchs game.

Also in 1952, one of Baird's pool halls was raided by the police because of a dominoes game being conducted there. The suspicion was that illegal gambling was happening at the business, which Baird denied. "If there was no gambling going on," the head of the vice squad said, "why did those who escaped feel they had to run?"[34]

It was a better story for Baird on the field as the Monarchs won yet another pennant during his era, winning both halves of the 1953 Negro American League season. The Monarchs were powered by the young phenom Ernie Banks, who was sold to the Chicago Cubs at the end of the season. The Monarchs had winning streaks of 14 and 17 games during the season.[35] The success could not be sustained into 1954, however, despite signing female player Toni Stone. The team bus also burned during a pit stop.

The biggest threat came after the season when the Philadelphia Athletics moved to Kansas City and the Monarchs had to compete for attendance against a major-league club. Baird remained positive, at least publicly. "It will only serve to spur us on to greater achievements," he said.[36] But the Monarchs were able to play only two home games in Kansas City because of declining fan interest and the increased rent for their home ballpark, now remodeled to fit major-league standards and renamed Municipal Stadium.

In 1955 only the Monarchs, Birmingham, Detroit, and Memphis remained in the Negro American League. Baird reacquired Paige for $40,000.[37] It was Paige's last run with the Monarchs, for whom he pitched on and off from 1935 to 1955. It was also the last season for player-manager Buck O'Neil, who became a Chicago Cubs scout. The Monarchs won the pennant in the last hurrah for these legends, but by that time the league was so disorganized that no one was exactly sure who the champion was. The Monarchs won 14 pennants and two postseason titles during Baird's tenure.

"I am not an alarmist," Baird wrote to NAL President J.B. Martin, "but facts are facts and I know all owners are losing plenty. I have been in baseball long enough to see what might happen to us."[38] The writing was on the wall. In January 1956 Baird sold 12 players to major- or minor-league clubs. "It looks like I sold everybody but the bus driver," he said, still finding a sense of humor. "But I'm happy to see these players get their chance in organized baseball."[39] This all but signified the end of the Kansas City Monarchs franchise he had been with since the beginning. "I haven't made a definite decision yet," Baird said in response to whether the Monarchs would even field a team in 1956. "I've been in baseball more than thirty-six years and will not decide until later on." A report at the time stated that in the previous 10 years Baird had sold 29 players to major-league teams and another nine to the minor leagues.[40] It was a final parting gift to his players and cemented his legacy of running what was unofficially an African American minor-league development system.

Less than a month later, Baird decided it was time to go and accepted a position as a scout with the Kansas City A's. "I'm happy to be with the Athletics," Baird said, "and I hope I can be of assistance to them in their building program."[41] Baird concentrated on finding and developing African American talent. It seemed to spell the complete dissolution of the Monarchs, but Baird was determined to put the club in good hands. He sold the Monarchs to Ted Rasberry, who also owned the Detroit Stars. One meager report said Rasberry bought the entire franchise for $3,500.[42] Rasberry kept the club in operation through 1962, keeping the Kansas City Monarchs name but running the club out of Grand Rapids, Michigan. Baird became the business manager of the Harlem All-Stars in 1957, a barnstorming Black basketball team. He also opened a $400,000 16-lane bowling alley in Kansas City, Kansas.[43]

In 2007 historian Tim Rives wrote that his research revealed Baird to have been a member of the Wyandotte County, Kansas, Ku Klux Klan. (Kansas City is the dominant community in the county.) The Klan did occupy a certain space in some areas which, though exclusionary in its membership, may not always have been violent toward others. Had Tom Baird been a member of the Klan in 1922? We don't know. See the sidebar for further discussion on this subject.

We are left with many questions about Tom Baird that can only be answered through further research. What we do know is that Baird worked tirelessly for the Monarchs for over 35 years and much of his skill in the later years was found in developing and promoting players so they could move on to better opportunities in the major leagues. He was highly respected among players, other club owners in both the White and Black major leagues, and fans.

Tom Baird died in his sleep on July 2, 1962, in Kansas City, Kansas, at the age of 77.

Sources

In addition to the sources in the Notes, the author was assisted by the following:

Lent, Cassidy, A. Bartlett Giamatti Research Center, Cooperstown, New York, who provided a copy of Baird's file.

Faber, Charles F., and William A. Young. "J.L. Wilkinson," SABR BioProject.

Familyseach.org

Findagrave.com

"KC Monarchs to Travel in New Bus," *Atlanta Daily World*, May 7, 1954: 7.

"Major Duncan Answers Last Call on Memorial Day," *Kansas City Globe*, May 31, 1911: 1.

"Negro American League Standings (1937-1962)," Center for Negro League Baseball Research. cnlbr.org/Portals/0/Standings/Negro%20American%20League%20(1937-1962)%202016-08.pdf. Retrieved May 13, 2020.

"Negro National league Standings (1920-1948)," Center for Negro League Baseball Research. cnlbr.org/Portals/0/Standings/Negro%20National%20League%20(1920-1948)%202016-08.pdf. Retrieved May 13, 2020.

Dixon, Phil S. *The Dizzy and Daffy Dean Barnstorming Tour: Race, Media, and America's National Pastime* (New York: Rowman & Littlefield, 2019), 93-95.

"Semi-Pro Clubs to be United in West," *Jefferson City* (Missouri) *Post-Tribune*, February 3, 1937: 6.

"Ted Raspberry Buys Monarchs," *Chicago Defender*, February 25, 1956: 17.

"Topics in Chronicling America." Library of Congress. loc.gov/rr/news/topics/jessejames.html. Retrieved April 25, 2020.

"Younger Brothers," *Encyclopedia Britannica*. britannica.com/topic/Younger-brothers. Retrieved April 25, 2020.

• When the Monarchs Reigned •

Notes

1 "This Is a Sure Sign of Spring," *Kansas City Kansan*, March 17, 1917: 1; "Sportlets," *The Press* (Kansas City, Kansas), October 12, 1917: 8.

2 *The Press*, August 31, 1917: 7; C.E. McBride, "A Sports Cocktail," *Kansas City* (Missouri) *Times*, October 28, 1952: 17.

3 "T.Y. Baird's Leg Broken," *The Press*, May 10, 1918: 10; "T.Y. Baird Asks $30,000," *The Press*, August 23, 1918: 1.

4 "Sportlets," *The Press*, June 14, 1918: 1.

5 "Gossip of the Semi-Pros," *Kansas City* (Kansas) *Kansan*, April 30, 1919: 1.

6 *Kansas City Kansan*, April 14, 1921: 3.

7 "Billiard Men Organize," *Kansas City Kansan*, December 2, 1921: 16.

8 William A. Young, *J.L. Wilkinson and the Kansas City Monarchs: Trailblazers in Black Baseball* (Jefferson, North Carolina: McFarland, 2016), 39.

9 Young, 71; Janet Bruce, *The Kansas City Monarchs: Champions of Black Baseball* (Lawrence, Kansas: University of Kansas Press, 1985), 70.

10 Bruce, 72-73.

11 Young, 92.

12 Young, 95.

13 "The Famous Mr. Paige Becomes Air-Minded," *Chicago Defender*, July 6, 1946: 11.

14 "House of David Wires Ruth $20,000 Offer," *St. Louis Globe-Democrat*, June 6, 1935: 12.

15 "Wilson Retains NNL Post," *Afro-American*, March 2, 1940: 19.

16 Buck O'Neil with Steve Wulf and David Conrads, *I Was Right on Time* (New York: Simon & Schuster, 1996), 119.

17 "Ollie S. Stratton," *Kansas City Times*, October 13, 1952: 14.

18 Young, 169.

19 Young, 157.

20 "Monarchs Ready for Training," *Kansas City Call*, March 16, 1945.

21 Seamheads lists Robinson batting .384 with the Monarchs, while Baseball-Reference credits him at .414. The Center for Negro League Baseball Research records him batting .345 in 41 games.

22 Jules Tygiel, *Baseball's Great Experiment: Jackie Robinson and His Legacy* (New York: Oxford University Press, 1997), 57.

23 Robinson, "What's Wrong with Negro Baseball?" *Ebony* magazine, June 1948: 22.

24 "Monarch Owners Won't Block Move," *St. Louis Star & Times*, October 25, 1945: 25.

25 United Press, "Kansas City Owner Raps Dodger Prexy," *Honolulu Advertiser*, February 21, 1948: 11.

26 A.S. Young, "Tom Baird Resents Rickey's Contract Methods," *Cleveland Call and Post*, February 28, 1948: 6B.

27 "Jackie Robinson Rebukes Unruly Fans; Hits Baird," *Cleveland Call and Post*, May 8, 1948: 6B.

28 Associated Press, "Gets Monarch Control," *St. Louis Globe-Democrat*, February 13, 1948: 16; Associated Negro Press, "John O'Neil, New Manager K.C. Monarchs," *Atlanta Daily World*, January 8, 1948: 5; Young, 166-167.

29 "Indians Sign Satchel Paige," *New York Amsterdam News*, July 10, 1948: 24; "National Baseball Congress to Honor Owner of K.C. Monarchs," *Philadelphia Tribune*, June 28, 1952: 10.

30 A.S. "Doc" Young, "Sportivanting," *Chicago Defender*, July 9, 1949: 16.

31 William A. Young, 171.

32 "Negro World Series Open Friday: Baltimore to Host 2 Games," *Philadelphia Tribune*, September 13, 1949: 11; "Skins in Upset," *Kansas City Times*, September 8, 1950: 22.

33 Leslie A. Heaphy, *The Negro Leagues 1869-1960* (Jefferson, North Carolina: McFarland, 2003), 216-217; "NBA [sic] Cites Tom Baird of K.C. Monarch Club," *Atlanta Daily World*, May 2, 1952: 7.

34 "Last Domino by Police," *Kansas City Times*, March 11, 1952: 3.

35 "K.C. Has Top Season's Mark," *Pittsburgh Courier*, September 12, 1953: 14; "Good Year Coming to End for KC," *Pittsburgh Courier*, September 5, 1953: 27.

36 "Coming of Major League Baseball to Kansas City Will Help – Baird," *Chicago Defender*, January 15, 1955: 10.

37 "Satchel Paige Rejoins the Monarchs," *Chicago Defender*, June 11, 1955: 10.

38 William A. Young, 180.

39 "Tom Baird Quits Baseball," *Chicago Defender*, February 4, 1956: 18.

40 Paul O'Boynick, "Monarchs Sell 12 Players," *Kansas City Times*, January 27, 1956: 38.

41 Joe McGuff, "Baird Joins A's," *Kansas City Times*, February 10, 1956: 34.

42 William A. Young, 181.

43 William A. Young, 182.

Tom Baird and the KKK

By Bob LeMoine

Tim Rives's research is based on a roster of that particular Klan group archived at the Library of Congress. On that roster of the 1922 Klan membership was the name "T. Baird," who lived in Ward 5, Tom Y. Baird's district. City directories at the time as well as federal censuses in 1920 and 1930 show only one T. Baird living in that section of Kansas City. As noted, Baird signed his name "TY" Baird in his professional dealings. The KKK roster lists only "T" Baird, for which, Rives notes, "his signature blurs the Y to the point where it looks like a mere line linking the T with Baird."[1]

"His personal papers are full of corroborating evidence," Rives wrote. "The newspaper clippings and other items deposited in his personal archive at the University of Kansas's Research Library document a web of relationships entangling nearly every aspect of his personal, social, business, and political life with other Klan members."[2] Rives claims there is ample evidence of the Baird family mingling with other Klan members in their neighborhood, church and family. Their home on Grandview Boulevard was in the same block as those of several other Klan members, and Baird's pool hall was in a building on Central Avenue that also housed a Klan headquarters. Rives writes: "The records reveal that Baird not only broke bread with other Klansmen, he literally breathed the same air."[3]

Rives points out racial overtones in letters in the Tom Baird Collection at the Spencer Research Library at the University of Kansas. In a letter to Jack Sheehan of the Chicago Cubs in reference to former Monarchs player Yellow Horse Morris, Baird wrote that he was "above the average in intelligence for a Negro." Baird also wrote to an executive that he had Monarchs players who were Black but did not really look Black. "Lefty LeMarque," [sic] he said, "is an intelligent looking Negro, in fact he might even pass for an Indian." Bill Breda, Baird said, "looks like a white man from the stands," and with Gene Richardson you couldn't tell what color he was.[4]

Yet Rives has written elsewhere of the large numbers of citizens who embraced the ideology of the Ku Klux Klan. Many were Klan members, including future Supreme Court Justice Hugo Black and Mount Rushmore sculptor Gutzon Borglum. President Harry Truman briefly belonged to the group, and Woodrow Wilson is said to have admired them. Crowds would turn out in Kansas City for Klansmen parades, and the Klan sponsored baseball games, picnics, barbecues, dances, and other community endeavors. "The KKK's dual offer to receive the fortunes of the country's white Protestants and solve their local problems found plenty of buyers in Kansas City," Rives wrote. "The sense of loss that nurtured Klan growth in the city was emotional, but it was also real. The nation's complexion, if not its soul, had changed between 1890 and 1920, when a tidal wave of immigration crashed the nation's shores bearing twenty-five million newcomers on its crest. More than 80 percent of the newcomers were from southern or eastern Europe. The community Klan hall promised a return to a homogenous world free from the intrusions of foreigners."[5] Baird was "one of nearly a thousand Kansas City men revealed in a Ku Klux Klan membership roster," Rives wrote.[6]

Public statements by Baird, however, seem to tell a much different story. "You know, I was born in Arkansas – in the free Ozark hill country. But I early learned to look on men, white and Black, for what they individually are. I've lived over on the Kansas side where I started out in semipro baseball, and the one thing that has grown upon me as the greatest need is for simple everyday contact between people. When people really know each other there is little room for suspicion and hatred."[7] In a letter to Baird, J.B. Martin wrote, "I'll still say you have done more for Negro baseball than any man living."[8]

We are left with several questions about Tom Baird in relation to race:
- Is the "T. Baird" listed on the Klan roster actually him? There is no current evidence of another person in Kansas City at the time who fits that name.

- How accurate is that roster of 1,000 Klan members in Kansas City? In 1922 many believed there were 5,000 Klan members in Wichita.[9] Few would argue with Kansas journalist William Allen White's statement that the Klan had "introduced into Kansas the curse that comes to civilized people, the curse that rises out of unrestricted passions of men governed by religious intolerance and racial hatred."[10] This roster was compiled by federal agents who had investigated the Klan. Baird, as a well-known businessman who was White, middle-class, and Protestant (He attended a Disciples of Christ church.) would have had interactions with many Klan members. Rives even admits, "True Klan membership numbers are difficult to find. Both the Klan and its enemies had reasons to inflate the count."[11]
- Was Baird falsely listed, much like people later suffered in the era of the Red Scare and McCarthyism?[12]
- If Baird was a KKK member, did he remain so his entire life? Many men were sympathetic to the views of the Klan and even belonged for a time. Was this a younger Baird caught up in the protests of the time and then later realize it was counter to his life with the Monarchs?
- Did Baird live a secret life under the white hood while profiting from the African American community? There have been and always will be those who present one life in public but live the opposite in private.
- Did Baird use the racist jargon of his day to relate to other club owners even though he did not subscribe to their beliefs? History is full of people who disagree with the prejudices society considers the norm, whether race, gender, language, sexual orientation, or other biases, yet fail to stand up to such discrimination until others do. For every Jackie Robinson, Branch Rickey, or Martin Luther King Jr. there are thousands who fail to act but wait for change to happen. As Buck O'Neil said, "We had become conditioned to racism. Hatred will steal your heart, man. You don't have any fight left in you. You accept what's around you. That's what this country was like. We thought it would change someday. We just waited for it to change."[13]
- Was Baird a KKK member who was afraid severing ties with the group at the risk of losing his business and social contacts in the Kansas City community? Was he content that he was making strides toward desegregation behind the scenes?

These questions provide for stimulating discussion, but we come up empty in a search for definite answers. We just don't know. Perhaps it is best to reaffirm that no matter what truth may or may not be hidden in Tom Baird's personal life, his professional contributions to the Monarchs, Kansas City, and Negro League baseball are beyond reproach.

Notes

1   Tim Rives, "Tom Baird: A Challenge to the Modern Memory of the Kansas City Monarchs," in Leslie A. Heaphy, ed., *Satchel Paige and Company: Essays on the Kansas City Monarchs, Their Greatest Star and the Negro Leagues* (Jefferson, North Carolina: McFarland & Company, 2007), 148.

2   Rives, 147.

3   Rives, 147.

4   Rives, 151.

5   Tom Rives, *The Ku Klux Klan in Kansas City, Kansas* (Charleston, South Carolina: The History Press, 2019), 27.

6   Rives, *The Ku Klux Klan*, 86.

7   William H. Young and Nathan B. Young Jr., "The Story of the Kansas City Monarchs," in *Your Kansas City and Mine* (Kansas City: Midwest Afro-American Genealogy Interest Collection, 1950), 129. Quoted in William A. Young, 169.

8   Ernest Mehl, "Effort to Put Negro Team in N.L. in '30s Disclosed," article from *Kansas City Star* in Baird's Hall-of-Fame file labeled "1958."

9   "Seeking Roster of Ku Klux Members," *Wichita Eagle*, November 25, 1922: 1.

10   "Ku Klux Klan in Kansas," Kansas Historical Society. Retrieved May 20, 2020. kshs.org/kansapedia/ku-klux-klan-in-kansas/15612.

11   Rives, *The Ku Klux Klan*, 92.

12   During the Cold War era the country was gripped with hysteria during the rise of communism. Some were suspected of having Communist ties and were arrested or even deported. Senator Joseph McCarthy led the charge to purge such people and the FBI under J. Edgar Hoover kept extensive files and wiretaps on persons of interest. Martin Luther King Jr. was one such target. See "McCarthyism and the Red Scare," The Miller Center. millercenter.org/the-presidency/educational-resources/age-of-eisenhower/mccarthyism-red-scare. Retrieved May 20, 2020.

13   Joe Posnanski, *The Soul of Baseball: A Road Trip Through Buck O'Neil's America* (New York: Harper, 2007), 21.

WILLIAM "DIZZY" DISMUKES

By William H. Johnson

He was a star pitcher, one who not only threw a no-hitter – against none other than Rube Foster's 1915 Chicago American Giants[1] -- but also tossed a four-hit complete game against the 1911 Pittsburgh Pirates. He was, for parts of two decades, a manager who is credited with at least 196 career wins. He was the traveling secretary for the 1942 Kansas City Monarchs. He was a part-time baseball writer with the *Pittsburgh Courier*. He was, for a time, the secretary of the Negro National League. In the early 1950s, he became one of the first Black scouts in Organized Baseball, working for both the Chicago Cubs and the New York Yankees, and in 1952 the *Pittsburgh Courier* listed him among the best Negro League pitchers of all time.[2] Dizzy Dismukes was all of those things, making him one of the more important people in baseball history, yet one whom relatively few have ever heard of.

William Dismukes was born on March 13, 1890, in Birmingham, Alabama.[3] His father was likely Isaac Dismukes,[4] a laborer, and his mother Sally, a laundress.[5] According to the 1910 US Census, after the young pitcher had already left home, Isaac was working as a soft-drink retailer, and the children still at home were James, Vashti, and Lucille.[6]

Evidently the Dismukes family valued education, so William attended Talladega College in Alabama before taking up professional baseball.[7] It is not clear whether he graduated from that or any college, but as he demonstrated throughout his life, he developed the gift of clear, cogent prose along the way. In 1908, though, at 17 years of age, William began his baseball career as a right-handed submarine pitcher for the East St. Louis Imperials.[8]

His baseball skill and mercenary approach took him to the Kentucky Unions in 1909,[9] and briefly to the Indianapolis ABCs, for whom he pitched against C.I. Taylor's Birmingham Giants in a late July barnstorming series in Indiana. Dismukes lost his game, 17-2, but he likely caught the eye of the Giants' manager. The next year, the 20-year-old pitched briefly with the Minnesota Keystones and manager Irving Williams.[10] That team, though largely overshadowed by the nearby and much more prestigious St. Paul Gophers, still had players like Topeka Jack Johnson, and the 1910 version featured future star pitcher Hurley McNair, as well as an aging outfielder named Bill Binga. Fourteen years earlier, Binga had been a starter for the legendary Adrian Page Fence Giants.

Later that year, Dismukes joined the powerful West Baden (Indiana) Sprudels, a resort team then led by newly relocated manager Charles Isham Taylor. While he worked during the day as a resort hotel waiter, it was with the Sprudels that the pitcher tossed what proved to be one of the most notable games of his career, the four-hitter in an exhibition against the Pittsburgh Pirates on September 10, 1911.

In that game, played in West Baden, the Pirates were not at full strength. The team had arrived that morning after an all-night train ride from St. Louis, where they had lost a tough Sunday afternoon game to the Cardinals, 7-6. In West Baden the next day, Pirates manager Fred Clarke sat Honus Wagner, Chief Wilson, George Gibson, and pitcher Howie Kamnitz due to injuries, but players like Bill McKechnie and future Federal Leaguer Vin Campbell were in the losing team's lineup. Infielder Bill Keen, from Oglethorpe, Georgia, managed the Bucs that afternoon, and the *Pittsburgh Post-Gazette* noted that he failed "to see anything humorous in defeat at the hands of a colored team."[11] In other words, while the Pirates may not have been at full strength, they were highly motivated to defeat their hosts, making Dismukes' effort all the more impressive.

While Dismukes ultimately returned to Taylor's teams, he hit the road and spent parts of 1912 with the St. Louis Giants, joined the Brooklyn Royal Giants in 1913 and 1914, and played for the New York Lincoln Stars in 1914-1915.[12] It was with the latter team that Dismukes enjoyed suiting up with the likes of Louis Santop and Spottswood Poles, and toured Cuba for Dismukes' first trip out of the country.[13] In 1915 he also made four appearances with Fé of the Cuban League.[14] Some sources list a brief stint with the Philadelphia

Former star pitcher Willliam "Dizzy" Dismukes entered the 1942 season as the Monarchs' manager but ceded that position to catcher Frank Duncan and became the team's personnel director. (Courtesy Noir-Tech Research, Inc.)

Giants (1913) in Dismukes' vitae, but the statistics for his time there are not available.[15]

Dismukes returned to the C.I. Taylor-led ABCs in April 1915. In his nonbarnstorming appearances, he is credited with a 14-5 record in 188⅔ innings pitched.[16] In his second start with Indianapolis, he threw a no-hitter against Rube Foster's powerful Chicago Union Giants on May 9. In that game, Oscar Charleston homered and Bingo DeMoss singled and stole a base in Indianapolis's 7-0 win.[17] The following winter, Dismukes returned to Cuba, this time with San Francisco Park, but started only one game and made the rest of his appearances in relief.

In January 1916 Dismukes rejoined the ABCs in Palm Beach, Florida, where manager Taylor had taken them to represent the Royal Poinciana Hotel.[18] Upon return to Indianapolis, Dismukes resumed his role as staff ace, posting a 2.73 earned-run average against a competitive slate of Western independent clubs that included the Chicago American Giants, the Cuban Stars West, Kansas City All Nations, and the St. Louis Giants. Dismukes routinely faced gifted hitters of the caliber of Cristobal Torriente, Pete Hill, Pop Lloyd and Bingo DeMoss, and he acquitted himself well throughout the season.

The real fireworks began after the end of the regular season. Rube Foster had been quick to tout his American Giants as the true champions of the world to any reporter who would listen, but Taylor's ABC squad had defeated them often enough over the season that a "Colored Championship of the West" series between the two was necessary to crown the true champion.

After the ABCs dropped Game One to Chicago, C.I. Taylor started Dismukes in Game Two against Frank Wickware. It was, in short, a masterpiece. Wickware allowed only six hits and no earned runs, while Dismukes gave up only three hits and no runs at all. The ABCs won, 1-0, because of a rare error by shortstop John Henry "Pop" Lloyd. Indianapolis won Game Three, 9-0, and then Dismukes returned to the mound against Game One winner Tom Johnson. This time the ABCs prevailed, 8-2, as Dismukes scattered seven hits.[19]

After an offday for the teams, Dismukes was back on the hill and took the ball for Game Five. Fatigued after only one day of rest, he allowed two runs to cross in the first inning and gave up another run in the second, then settled in to allow only one more hit through the next seven frames. After he had left the game, Indianapolis exploded for seven runs on seven hits in the sixth and held on for a 12-8 win. The *Indianapolis Freeman* headline proclaimed: "A.B.C.'s WIN WORLD SERIES."[20]

The 1917 season marked some regression for both Indianapolis and Dismukes, the latter managing a meager 2-5 record. The team suffered several key injuries, and even lost an exhibition to the Indianapolis Indians (of the organized American Association). After the season, the ABCs played a three-game set against white touring teams and took two of three against those squads. The next year Dismukes accepted an offer from the Dayton Marcos to be their player-manager, but the team managed only a 1-6 record under their novice skipper before Dismukes' season ended early due to World War I.

• WILLIAM "DIZZY" DISMUKES •

Dismukes was assigned to the Army's 809th Pioneer Infantry, almost immediately headed off to France, and ultimately was promoted to sergeant.[21] The unit was not permitted into combat, as the Army was still feeling its collective way regarding units manned exclusively by black soldiers, but according to diaries of several participating soldiers, it was demanding duty. According to various accounts:

"The Negro Service of Supply men acquired a great reputation in the various activities to which they were assigned, especially for efficiency and celerity in unloading ships and supplies of every sort at the base ports. They were a marvel to the French and astonished not a few of the officers of our own army."[22]

"During the 14-day voyage aboard the troop ship *President Grant*, about half of the 5000 men on board fell ill with 'Spanish flu.' They were from many regiments being posted to Europe. So many men died enroute that their bodies had to be buried at sea."[23]

After surviving such a horrifying year, Dismukes returned to Dayton in a pitcher-only role for 1919. At some point in his career, Dismukes was tagged with the nickname "Dizzy." It was certainly an ironic moniker, as he was regarded as one of the more cerebral and calm players of the time: "A college man, he was a smart, studious player with a wonderful memory and was a strategist. He knew a batter's tendencies and would almost unerringly position his infielders where the batter would hit according to the pitches he was throwing. He had a variety of breaking pitches and was considered by some to be a 'trick pitcher' because of the way his breaking balls moved."[24] Dismukes was valuable enough, nickname notwithstanding, to return to Indianapolis for the 1920 season.

Turning 30 years old in 1920, Dismukes logged 187 innings in the new Negro National League, and the team enjoyed a winning record. Near the end of the 1921 season, he moved to the Pittsburgh Keystones as player-manager. The 1922 season in Pittsburgh proved important in Dismukes' career and life: He was invited to contribute the occasional baseball column to the *Pittsburgh Courier*. Teaming with Homestead Grays owner Cumberland "Cum" Posey, Dismukes would opine on the state of the game and the level of play, and generally bridge the gap between newspaper-reading fans and the players on the field. In a 1930 example of his direct prose style and candor, Dismukes wrote:

"The crop of young catchers breaking into the game in the past ten years have been so poor that I can only find three, namely: Frank Duncan of the Kansas City Monarchs, Raleigh Mackey of Hillsdale, and Larry Brown of Memphis Red Sox showing enough skill to qualify in my selection of nine best catchers. Topping the list is none other than Bruce Petway…"[25]

Dismukes continued to write his columns for many years, finally giving up the typewriter in order to work as a front-office executive for the Kansas City Monarchs in the 1940s.

He returned to the ABCs in as player-manager in 1923, following the sudden death of mentor C.I. Taylor. After leading the team to a 51-33 record in 1923, but only a 5-21 mark in 1924, Dismukes left in midseason to manage the Birmingham Black Barons. After a reported disagreement with Black Barons owner Joe Rush, Dismukes left again and finished the year with the Homestead Grays.[26]

Playing the role of a baseball nomad, Dismukes spent 1925 pitching for and managing the Memphis Red Sox, and spent 1926-27 at the helm of the St. Louis Stars. While there is no existing statistical record of Dismukes' baseball life between 1928 and 1931, it is likely that he remained with St. Louis through 1929, then took over the Chicago American Giants after Rube Foster's mental breakdown and death.[27] He may have been out of baseball in 1931, or he may have managed the American Giants, but he definitely returned to the diamond as manager of the Detroit Wolves of the East-West League in 1932. He spent 1933 and 1934 managing the Columbus Blue Birds of the new Negro National League, returned to the American Giants in 1935, and to St. Louis for 1936 and 1937.

After a brief encore as the Birmingham Black Barons' manager in 1938, the Atlanta Black Crackers in 1939, and the Homestead Grays in 1940, Dismukes was named to his final, interim managerial job with Kansas City after Newt Allen's surprise resignation in 1942. He moved into the role of traveling secretary when Frank Duncan took over as player-manager during that memorable campaign.[28] According to Monarchs legend Buck O'Neil, Dismukes was known for "his arbitration abilities with ball players and upper management, and had tremendous influence with his mannerisms on and off the field."[29] In 1944 he and Monarchs co-owner Tom Baird represented the team at a league meeting intended to name a new, joint Negro National and American League commissioner.[30]

Dismukes remained with the Monarchs' front office as traveling secretary until 1951,[31] but he had begun to work as a bird-dog scout for the New York Yankees starting in 1949.[32] In 1953 the Yankees offered him a full-time job as a scout, focusing his search on the array of untapped talent that still existed in the Negro American League.[33] Dismukes told Wendell Smith, his old friend and *Pittsburgh Courier* columnist:

> "It's a good job, but not an easy one. You are constantly on the go, riding trains, planes, and even buses. There is plenty of competition, too. Every big league club has a squad of scouts. Sometimes you think you have a kid in the bag, ready for delivery. ... Only to discover that one of the other fellows has snatched him from under your nose."[34]

The move was significant, in that the Yankees still had not fielded a black player eight years after Jackie Robinson broke the color line for the crosstown rival Brooklyn Dodgers. Every move the Yankees made drew the attention of the writers, and they were beginning to wonder aloud when the club might add a Black player to their roster. Dismukes was brought in as an experienced former player and manager and judge of talent, but also as an educated man with a communications pedigree that included his national column with the *Courier*. Dismukes defended the team:

> "The general public," he said, "feels that the Yankees are against Negro players, and that makes it tough for me. Just recently I had a good Negro prospect lined up but lost him. A scout from another team came along and signed the boy after his father told him that the Yankees didn't really want Negro players. ... The people who have been critical of the Yankees have been most unfair. Just because they didn't keep (Vic) Power and sent Howard to Toronto does not mean they are anti-Negro. I know that they are not adverse [*sic*] to Negro players. All they are looking for is the Yankee type of player, race or color does not matter."[35]

The scouting job also proved to be the most lucrative in Dismukes' career. He had never married, so the arduous road-wearying lifestyle was fine with him, and the $10,000 per year that he earned certainly made the effort worthwhile.[36] Once the Yankees introduced Elston Howard as their first Black big leaguer in 1955, and began to populate their minor-league system with talented minority players at all levels, Dismukes moved on. He did some scouting for the Chicago White Sox,[37] and returned to the field that same year,[38] replacing Jelly Taylor as manager of the Kansas City Monarchs.[39] After the 1958 season, Dizzy Dismukes hung up his spikes for good.

Over the next few years, Dismukes' health began to falter, and in 1961 he moved in with his sister, Vashti Owens, at her home in Campbell, Ohio. He died on June 30, 1961. After an autopsy, the cause of death was listed as hardening of the arteries.[40] He is buried at the Mount Hope Veterans Memorial Cemetery in Campbell, Ohio.

Sources

This biography relied on information culled from various archives of the Center for Negro League Baseball Research, Seamheads.com, and the *Pittsburgh Courier*, as well as several books on this era of the Negro Leagues (as identified in the notes). Jorge Figueredo's summary *Cuban Baseball: A Statistical History, 1878-1961* was the primary source for Dismukes' time in Cuba.

Notes

1   Center for Negro League Baseball Research: cnlbr.org/Portals/0/RL/Negro%20League%20No-Hitters%202019-10.pdf Accessed July 11, 2020.

2   From the *Pittsburgh Courier*, cited on johndonaldson.bravehost.com/a.html, accessed July 10, 2020.

3   This date differs among Internet sources, some of which list his date of birth as March 15, 1890. Both Dismukes' World War II draft registration card and his posthumous application for a veteran's headstone, however, state that he was born on March 13, 1890.

4   There is no primary-source documentation linking Isaac and William, but the latter's sister, Vashti, was the applicant for Dismukes' veteran's headstone. The only Vashti Dismukes in Birmingham, Alabama, between 1893 and 1920 was the daughter of Isaac Dismukes, so it is likely that Isaac was also Dizzy's father.

5   1920 US Federal Census, Birmingham, Alabama. Accessed July 11, 2020.

6   1910 US Federal Census, Birmingham, Alabama. Accessed July 10, 2020.

7   Russ Cowan, "Teams Went 'Pow, Pow, Pow,' Until Ku Klux Klan Invaded Diamond," *Pittsburgh Courier*, August 5, 1961: 37.

8   "Dizzy Started Back in 1908, Beat Pirates, 2-1, in 1911," *Pittsburgh Courier*, August 5, 1961: 37.

9   From the Negro Leagues Baseball Museum biography of Dizzy Dizmukes. nlbemuseum.com/nlbemuseum/history/players/dismukes.html. Accessed July 12, 2020. It is possible that the Kentucky Unions

were formed after the collapse of the more prominent Louisville Unions in 1908, but beyond the archives at the Kansas State University College of Education and James Riley's *Biographical Encyclopedia of the Negro Baseball Leagues* (New York: Carroll & Graf Publishers, Inc., 1994), there is little primary source material corroborating the team's existence or roster.

10 Todd Peterson, *Early Black Baseball in Minnesota* (Jefferson, North Carolina: McFarland and Co., 2010), 145.

11 C.B. Power, "Pirates Beaten, 2 to 1, by Colored Sprudels," *Pittsburgh Post-Gazette*, September 12, 1911: 9.

12 Unless otherwise noted, the statistical references in this essay are all drawn from Seamheads.com, seamheads.com/NegroLgs/player.php?playerID=dismu01diz. Accessed most recently July 17, 2020.

13 Eduardo Servero Nieto Misas, *Early U.S. Blackball Teams in Cuba* (Jefferson, North Carolina: McFarland, 2008), 116.

14 Jorge Figueredo, *Cuban Baseball: A Statistical History, 1878-1961* (Jefferson, North Carolina: McFarland, 2003), 114.

15 Negro Leagues Baseball Museum (NLBM) biography of Dizzy Dizmukes. nlbemuseum.com/nlbemuseum/history/players/dismukes.html. Accessed July 12, 2020.

16 seamheads.com/NegroLgs/player.php?playerID=dismu01diz.

17 "Dismukes Hurls No-Hit Shutout," *Indianapolis Freeman*, May 15, 1915.

18 According to the Center for Negro League Baseball Research, "The Florida Hotel League, or the Coconut League as it was sometimes called, was a two-team league in Florida that was comprised of all-Black baseball teams representing the Breakers Hotel and the Royal Poinciana. … During the winter Black ball players would travel to Florida and take jobs as bellmen, porters, cooks, dishwashers and wait staff personnel in the restaurants of the big resort hotels. … Management … would form baseball teams and games would be scheduled for the entertainment of the hotel guests." From Layton Revel and Luis Munoz's monograph *Forgotten Heroes: Charles Isham "C.I." Taylor*, 1916. nlbemuseum.com/nlbemuseum/history/players/taylorc.html.

19 Revel and Munoz, 17-18.

20 "A.B.C.s Win World Series," *Indianapolis Freeman*, November 4, 1916, also cited by Paul Debono in his book *The Indianapolis ABCs* (Jefferson, North Carolina: McFarland and Co., 1997), 69.

21 It is often cited that he served in the 803rd Pioneer Infantry during the war. According to his application for a federal headstone or grave marker (DD Form 1330, submitted and verified July 2, 1961, he enlisted on August 22, 1918, and was discharged on August 2, 1919. He served in Company A, 809th Pioneer Infantry.

22 W. Allison Sweeney, *History of the American Negro in the Great World War.* gutenberg.org/files/16598/16598-h/16598-h.htm. Accessed July 13, 2020.

23 Global Security archives. globalsecurity.org/military/systems/ship/ap.htm. Accessed June 12, 2020.

24 NLBM biography: Dizzy Dizmukes.

25 "Dizzy" Dismukes, "Petway Rated Greatest Thrower and Johnson Best Receiver by Dismukes," *Pittsburgh Courier*, March 1, 1930: 14.

26 "Dismukes Leaves Black Barons; May Hook Up with Grays," *Pittsburgh Courier*, August 23, 1924: 12.

27 NLBM biography: Dizzy Dizmukes.

28 "Newt Allen Quits KayCee," *Pittsburgh Courier*, April 4, 1942: 17; Dick Clark and Larry Lester *The Negro Leagues Book* (Cleveland: Society for American Baseball Research, 1994), 133; Wendell Smith, "Smitty's Sports-Spurts," *Pittsburgh Courier*, October 10, 1942: 17.

29 Larry Lester, *The Negro Leagues Book, Volume 2* (Kansas City, Missouri: Noir-Tech Research, Inc., 2020), 172.

30 William A. Young, *J.L. Wilkinson and the Kansas City Monarchs: Trailblazers in Black Baseball* (Jefferson, North Carolina: McFarland & Co., 2016), 136.

31 Buck O'Neil, *I Was Right on Time* (New York: Simon & Schuster, 1996), 181-184.

32 Young, 174.

33 Wendell Smith, "Wendell Smith's Sports Beat," *Pittsburgh Courier*, September 4, 1954: 22.

34 Smith, September 4, 1954.

35 Smith, September 4, 1954.

36 "Dismukes Was the Original 'Dizzy' of Baseball," *Pittsburgh Courier*, July 15, 1961: 56.

37 NLBM biography: Dizzy Dizmukes.

38 Young, 181.

39 *Kansas City Times*, July 25, 1957: 18.

40 "Dizzy Dismukes, ABC Pitcher, Dies," *Indianapolis Recorder*, July 1, 1961: 11; "William Dismukes," findagrave.com/memorial/96698303/william-dismukes. Accessed June 12, 2020.

1942 Kansas City Monarchs Timeline

By Bill Nowlin

"The Negro American League defending champions will present this year, in addition to a few newcomers, the same roster which captured the pennant save for the exception of two players lost to Uncle Sam's armed forces. A notable addition to the Monarchs' ranks will be Quincy Troupe, star performer acquired in a deal with the St. Louis Stars. Following their first exhibition game at Monroe, La., on Easter Sunday, the Monarchs will engage in a series of benefit games for Army camps throughout the South before opening the league season on May 10."[1]

Spring training began on March 31 in Monroe, Louisiana. In a surprise, Newt Allen resigned as manager of the team but planned to continue as second baseman "while Dizzy Dismukes moves in as the new selectee for the managerial post."[2]

R.S. Simmons, publicity director for the Negro American League, wrote a column that appeared in the *Weekly Review* of Birmingham: "Dizzy Dismukes, manager of the 1941 Champion Kansas City Monarchs, and a man of few words but plenty of action, feels satisfied with the showing his team in making in this short period. The Monarchs have with them some of the most well known players in Sepia baseball speaking of such men as: Satchel Paige, famous pitcher, Hilton Smith who always holds his own, Newt Allen, former manager, Oneal, Strong, Williams and Brown the team's home run king."[3] The column was obviously written as much as a week before publication date, since it referred to a forthcoming game against Jacksonville at the Steers' Park, Dallas, on Sunday, April 12, "followed by a three game series at Port Arthur, Texas."

Before the NAL season began, in a December 28, 1941, meeting in Chicago, the league said that clubs were not to play the Ethiopian Clowns, seeing the "paint on their faces and the circus stunts as having no place in organized baseball." Clubs likewise were not to play any club bearing the name "Cubans unless they were the actual Cuban Stars ballclub owned by Alex Pompez.[4]

The Monarchs were often a big draw. A story in advance of their visit to Lima, Ohio, in late June said they were "perhaps the most glamorous team in either colored major league." The *Lima News* continued, explaining, "The Monarchs have won the last three colored American league championships and in so doing have dominated their league as much as the New York Yankees have the American professional league. The Monarchs attracted better than one million paid customers last season and are well on their way to improve that mark this season. The Monarchs boast a number of spectacular players, who know how to put on a show."[5]

PRESEASON EXHIBITION GAMES

The Monarchs held spring training in Monroe, Louisiana, with more or less the same roster they had fielded in 1941, save for two team members who had joined the armed forces.

Satchel Paige was well-rested, not having pitched in winter ball for the first time in 10 years, but he had dental surgery in Kansas City over the offseason and was late reporting to spring training. Ted Strong had been playing with the Harlem Globetrotters; he was late as well, reporting after considering an offer from a White baseball team, the Grumman Flyers of Long Island.[6]

Newcomers were Jim "Lefty" LaMarque, signed off the sandlots, and a right-hander named Douglass, who didn't make the team.

The Monarchs were to open the season on Sunday, April 5, and then play a series of benefit games for Army camps over the weeks leading up to Opening Day, May 10.

Before the main group left Kansas City for Louisiana, Newt Allen resigned as field manager. Team owner J.L. Wilkinson named Dizzy Dismukes to be manager.[7]

• 1942 Kansas City Monarchs Timeline •

April 5, 1942: Cincinnati-Cleveland Buckeyes 12, Kansas City Monarchs 9, at Casino Park, Monroe, Louisiana

The 2:30 game was the first of the spring exhibition season. The Buckeyes started Willie Jefferson and the Monarchs started Hilton Smith, who had been playing baseball in Monroe since 1932, when he put in the first of four years with the Negro Southern League's Monroe Monarchs.

April 12, 1942: Kansas City Monarchs 13, Cleveland Bears 1, at West End Park, Houston, Texas

Some 3,500 watched the game. Paige pitched three innings of no-hit ball. Nothing else was explained in the *Houston Chronicle* story, other than to report the score as 11-1 and to tell readers that "An exhibition of ball handling and batting was given by Happy Frank McKeown, the armless ball-player."[8] The *Kansas City Call*, on the other hand, reported the score as 13-1. The lone Bears run came in the second inning when Connie Johnson walked a man and then allowed a triple and a double – which would normally lead one to think that two runs scored, but perhaps a baserunner was tagged out at the plate. The *Call* said that Paige walked one and allowed a scratch hit, but that Norris Phillips pitched three perfect innings to close out the game. Pitching for the Bears, Preacher Henry got through the first three innings without allowing a run but his game deteriorated and the score "took on the aspects of a football game."[9]

April 14, 1942: Kansas City Monarchs 9, Cincinnati-Cleveland Buckeyes 0, at Legion Park, Port Arthur, Texas

Three Monarchs pitchers combined on a shutout – LaMarque pitched the first five innings, Paige pitched the next two, and Douglass the final two. LaMarque and Douglass each gave up two hits; Paige gave up none. (He hit a double in his one at-bat.) First time up, Willard Brown hit a two-run homer – a "towering smash over the left field fence."[10] Later in the game, Brown doubled to right-center. Kansas City's big inning was a five-run seventh.

April 15, 1942: Kansas City Monarchs 10, Cincinnati-Cleveland Buckeyes 9, at Legion Park, Port Arthur, Texas

Cleveland scored three runs in the top of the first off Monarchs starter "Gurly." The Monarchs got two runs back in the bottom of the first. Frank Bradley pitched the second through fourth innings, allowing three runs in the fourth. Satchel Paige came in and gave up one run in the sixth, the second of his two innings. The Monarchs shaved the 7-2 lead by a couple of runs in the bottom of the sixth. The score was 7-4. The inning that turned the tide was the bottom of the seventh, when Kansas City scored six runs and took a 10-7 lead. Hilton Smith pitched the final three innings, and Cleveland got two runs off him in the top of the ninth, but fell short by one run. The only extra-base hit for the Monarchs was a double by Buck O'Neil.[11]

April 16, 1942: Kansas City Monarchs 19, Cincinnati-Cleveland Buckeyes 9, at Legion Park, Port Arthur, Texas

It was "ladies night" and Paige pitched again, this time working the fifth and sixth. Starting for the Monarchs was a pitcher named Grant, who gave up two runs in the first inning and five runs in the second. A pitcher named Patterson started for Cleveland. He got through the first, but was whacked for five runs in the second and another run in the third inning. Clifford "Connie" Johnson pitched a scoreless third and fourth; Paige worked the fifth and sixth (tagged for one run in the sixth); and Booker McDaniel allowed one run over the last three innings.

Third baseman Parnell Woods was the offensive star for Cleveland, with two doubles and a home run. Joe Greene's three-run second-inning homer over the left-field fence was the biggest blow for the Monarchs.[12]

As with Gurley, the first name of the pitcher named Grant is unknown.

For the three games, the Port Arthur newspaper called the Cleveland team the "Bears."

April 19, 1942: Birmingham Black Barons 2, Kansas City Monarchs 1 (first game), at Rickwood Field, Birmingham

Frank Bradley, Norris Phillips, and Hilton Smith shared pitching duties in the first game, holding the Barons to two second-inning runs (off Bradley), but scored only one, in the top of the ninth inning. The doubleheader drew 10,000.

April 19, 1942: Kansas City Monarchs 8, Birmingham Black Barons 6 (second game, 7 innings), at Rickwood Field, Birmingham

Booker McDaniel pitched the second game and was in a 6-0 hole after two innings; the Barons scored three runs in the first and three in the second. In the fourth, the Monarchs scored twice, and in the fifth they scored thrice. In the seventh and final inning, the Monarchs scored three more runs to take an 8-6 lead. The Barons got a couple of runners on in the bottom of the seventh. Bonnie Serrell was playing right field when Goose Tatum hit a ball that would have been a home run into the right-field stands, except that Serrell leapt and snared it.

April 21, 1942: An afternoon game scheduled between the Black Barons and the Monarchs at Johnston Field in Anniston, Alabama, was postponed a few days beforehand.[13]

April 23, 1942: Memphis Red Sox 3, Kansas City Monarchs 2, at Travelers Field, Little Rock, Arkansas

Researchers in Little Rock and elsewhere have yet to turn up any information regarding this game. Further mystery regarding Arkansas and these few days relates to the following day. The *New York Amsterdam News* said the Birmingham Black Barons were to play the Monarchs in Pine Bluff on April 24. We have been unable to find any details regarding this possible game.

April 26, 1942: Kansas City Monarchs 6, Homestead Grays 5 (first game, 10 innings), at Pelican Stadium, New Orleans

An overflow crowd of 14,000 turned out to see the top team from the 1941 Negro National League (the Homestead Grays had led all other teams by 8½ games) play the top team from the 1941 Negro American League (the Kansas City Monarchs had finished 2½ games ahead of the Birmingham Black Barons). There had been no World Series between the NNL and NAL in 1941. Though no one could know it at the time, these same two teams would meet in the 1942 World Series.

The first game featured Hilton Smith and Connie Johnson pitching for Kansas City. The tiebreaking run came on a slow-rolling single to second base by Brown. Brown went to third on a hit by Ted Strong, and then scored when backup catcher Johnnie Dawson singled. Dawson had taken over for Greene in the ninth. Smith pitched seven innings; Johnson worked the final three and got the win.[14]

April 26, 1942: Homestead Grays 10, Kansas City Monarchs 7 (second game, six innings), at Pelican Stadium, New Orleans

The second game saw Satchel Paige work the first five innings, yielding only one run. The Grays got a couple more runs (accounts differ as to who gave up the second and third runs), but the score was still 7-3 in the Monarchs' favor – until the Grays mounted a seven-run rally against Bradley in the seventh inning. The Monarchs went through three pitchers in the final inning – with Phillips, McDaniel, and Bradley all taking turns. The crowd played something of a part in the game. The *New Orleans Times-Picayune* reported that Paige allowed six hits, "three of which would have been easy putouts without the crowd."[15] Ted Strong homered in the fifth inning of the second game.

May 3, 1942: Kansas City Monarchs 13, Memphis Red Sox 5 (first game), at Martin's Park, Memphis

One game was lopsided, the other a one-run game, but the Monarchs won them both. The first game was close through six – in fact, tied 3-3 after the first six innings. The Monarchs busted through for seven runs in the top of the seventh and added three more in the eighth. Johnson and Bradley pitched for Kansas City. The Red Sox got 10 hits; the Monarchs got 16, including home runs by Willard Brown and catcher Joe Greene.

May 3, 1942: Kansas City Monarchs 4, Memphis Red Sox 3 (second game, 7 innings), at Martin's Park, Memphis

Paige pitched the first four innings, giving up three runs in the first on two triples sandwiched around a walk and then an infield out. He settled down, turning things over to Hilton Smith. The Monarchs had scored two runs in the top of the first, then added two more in the top of the fourth, and that fourth run provided the margin of victory. The runs in the fourth came on O'Neil's single and then Greene's double to center field. Allen singled, Greene holding up at third. He then scored on a double steal when the Red Sox shortstop misplayed the throw from the catcher.

May 6, 1942: Kansas City Monarchs 15, Memphis Red Sox 6, at Recreation Park, Greenville, Mississippi

Scoring eight runs in the top of the first inning gave the Monarchs all the runs they needed to outlast the Memphis Red Sox.

• 1942 Kansas City Monarchs Timeline •

Satchel Paige had been expected to pitch, and was at the ballpark, but "declined to take the mound."[16] He was fined $25, "which went to buy equipment for negro soldiers at the Greenville Army flying school."[17]

May 7, 1942: Memphis Red Sox 3, Kansas City Monarchs, 2, at Travelers Field, Little Rock, Arkansas

To date, we have been unable to find more information about the May 7 game.

REGULAR SEASON

As the regular season was about to get underway, the May 10 *Kansas City Star* noted that the team's first home games would be at Ruppert Stadium on May 17. The Monarchs had won eight pennants since 1924. In 1942 they would be shooting for their fourth consecutive league title. Second baseman Newt Allen had "asked to be relieved of his managerial duties to devote all of his time to active play."[18] Dizzy Dismukes would be the Monarchs manager. Satchel Paige was back to pitch.

May 10, 1942: Kansas City Monarchs 7, Chicago American Giants 4 (first game), at Comiskey Park, Chicago

As if an Opening Day doubleheader wasn't enough, 63-year-old tap dancer Bill "Bojangles" Robinson said that between games he would run backwards for 75 yards and was confident he could beat any one of the players who would run 100 meters against him.[19]

League President Dr. J.B. Martin escorted Marva Louis, the wife of heavyweight champion Joe Louis, to the mound. She threw out the first pitch.

The Monarchs scored first. With two outs in the top of the first, Willard Brown singled to center. A throwing error on Ted Strong's grounder allowed Brown to score all the way from first base. In the second, Bonnie Serrell tripled and Hilton Smith doubled. Willie Simms lined to left, scoring Smith. Cyrus (Herb Souell) singled and drove in Simms. Brown reached on an error at third base, Strong walked, and Greene singled in both of them. Six runs were two more than it turned out they needed, but they added a seventh run in the third. Smith got the win – and had himself a 3-for-5 day at the plate.

May 10, 1942: Kansas City Monarchs 6, Chicago American Giants 0 (second game), at Comiskey Park (7 innings)

Satchel Paige picked up his first win on Opening Day, too. He scattered three hits over five scoreless innings. He struck out three. The Monarchs scored three in the second inning, with "an old time batting rally" featuring six singles and a pair of stolen bases. They added three more in the fifth, with two bases on balls followed by a Dawson double and a "well-executed squeeze play on which two runners cross the plate," when Jesse Williams bunted for a single, and Radcliff's throw went wide. Connie Johnson wrapped up the game with two scoreless innings, "permitting but two measly singles."[20] Johnnie Dawson caught both pitchers. Some 7,000 attended the doubleheader.

Who made the runs in the day's second game? It was an odd feature of Negro League game coverage that often the second game got short shrift in newspaper accounts – even when an established star such as Satchel Paige was throwing a shutout. Fortunately, the *Call* provides some information. The first three Monarchs runs came in the second inning on six singles and a pair of stolen bases. The other three came in the fifth inning when two Monarchs drew bases on balls, Dawson doubled, and then a squeeze play managed to score two runners. There followed a bunt single by Williams that may have scored another run. Once again, there would appear to have been another run not accounted for unless there was a runner through out at some point unreported.[21]

May 17, 1942: Kansas City Monarchs 7, Memphis Red Sox 0 (first game), at Ruppert Stadium

After Opening Day ceremonies that included three bands, a drum and bugle corps, and 10 majorettes, Jack Matchett pitched the home opener for the Monarchs, limiting the Memphis Red Sox to five hits and no runs. He walked one and struck out four. Right-hander Porter "Ankleball" Moss pitched for Memphis but was hit for one run in the first inning and five more in the fourth. He was relieved by Verdell Mathis and then Norris Phillips. Allen, Strong, Serrell, and Matchett all doubled, and each scored a run in the 7-0 victory.

The Monarchs Boosters and other civic organizations took part in a pregame parade, joined by the Wayne Minor American Legion Post drum and bugle corps, the Lincoln High School band, and a junior high school band. An undertaker from Kansas City, Kansas, joined with one from Kansas City, Missouri, at the Elks Rest the night before, declaring they were ready to "bury them pesky Red Sox."[22]

Despite threatening weather, 10,000 turned out for the games. Soldiers in uniform were to be admitted free to all Monarchs games.[23]

William A. Young said that at the time a little more than 17 percent of Kansas City's population was African American. He quotes Sam McKibben of the *Kansas City Call* as saying that Black spectators who attended to Kansas City Blues games were "forced to sit in the bleachers, exposed to the sun and rain" but that at the Monarchs' opener "whites and Negroes sat together, cheered together, slapped each other on the back."[24]

The *Kansas City Call* noted that Frank Duncan was helping Dismukes manage the team. A few weeks later, the June 5 issue of the *Call* reported that Duncan was named playing manager and Dismukes business manager.

Plaindealer, Kansas City

May 17, 1942: Memphis Red Sox 4, Kansas City Monarchs 1 (second game), at Ruppert Stadium

Verdell Mathis outpitched Satchel Paige in the second game. Mathis had worked one inning of relief in the first game, but pitched all seven innings in the second one. The only run he surrendered was in the seventh when Willard Brown walked and then scored when Ted Strong "busted one to the scoreboard."[25] The only other Monarch to manage a hit was shortstop Jesse Williams, earlier in the game. Paige allowed three hits and one run in the first inning, then three more runs in the top of the sixth on two walks and three hits.

May 24, 1942: Kansas City Monarchs 3, Dizzy Dean's All-Stars 1, at Wrigley Field, Chicago

"Old Diz's" team was comprised of former major- and minor-league players serving in the Army. Bob Feller was supposed to have pitched but had been called back to duty with the Navy. The fee Feller would have received was donated to Navy relief. The game drew a large turnout reported as 29,775.[26]

Dean himself pitched the first inning and retired all three Monarchs. John Grodzicki (2-1 with the St. Louis Cardinals in 1941) worked the next five innings, giving up one run in the fourth inning on a single by leadoff batter Cyrus (Souell), a sacrifice, and a single by Brown. That one run tied the score; the All-Stars had gotten a run off Satchel Paige in the third inning. Paige worked six innings and gave up only two singles, both "of the scratchy variety."[27] Hilton Smith pitched the last three innings for the Monarchs, allowing only one hit and no runs. The Monarchs won the game thanks to a pair of runs in the eighth off righty Al Piechota, who had been 2-5 with the Boston Braves in 1940 and 1941. Bill Simms singled to lead off. He took second on a sacrifice by Cyrus, and third on a long fly ball by Strong. Brown was intentionally walked and then James "Pig" Greene doubled in both baserunners.[28]

Promoted by Abe Saperstein, the game was said to have been the first played by Black ballplayers at Wrigley Field. Most of the fans were Black as well. "The fans were a jovial lot," reported the *Chicago Defender*, "going into hysterics and having spasms when the Monarchs tied the score and going wild with enthusiasm when the Monarchs went out in front and stayed there. And no one could blame them. There were their own boys, playing on big league grounds, performing in big league style – yet these same players are denied the right to earn a good living at their profession."[29]

A separate story in the same issue of the *Defender*, headlined "Open Fight to Get Negroes in Major Leagues," reported on a meeting held in Chicago to start a campaign that would result in the majors allowing Black ballplayers. The newspaper's sports editor, Frank A. Young, included four Monarchs among the players he believed could easily hold their own in the majors: Willard Brown, Ted Strong, Satchel Paige, and Hilton Smith. Awareness of the "politics" involved was reflected in one sentence:

• 1942 Kansas City Monarchs Timeline •

"Knowing that Judge Landis would shift the blame on the club owners and the owners would put it on the managers, the committee decided to inform the judge that the time was here to stop playing everybody for children."[30]

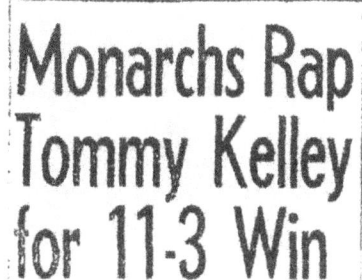

Daily Nonpareil, Council Bluffs, Iowa

May 26, 1942: Kansas City Monarchs 11, Council Bluffs All-Stars 3 (eight innings), at Legion Park, Council Bluffs, Iowa

The game drew only a small crowd of 400. A thoughtful article in the *Omaha World-Herald* offered some good perspective on the game. In days gone by, Robert Phipps wrote, there were touring teams such as the House of David team, Gilkerson's Union Giants, the Ethiopian Clowns, and the Canadian Clowns. "But the Monarchs set the par." He continued, "Those gypsy clubs vanished a sports age ago, but the Monarchs still travel in style. And if they don't come around as often to Omaha or Council Bluffs, it's because this metropolitan area no longer supports the game in the style to which the Monarchs have been accustomed."[31]

Phipps acknowledged that the team traveled "in a shiny new bus with good tires and lots of lettering on the sides. The team carried 18 players, including, at time, the celebrated Paige," and added, "No one has explained what kind of contract Satchel has, but apparently he draws his own schedule. A Super-attraction, he can write his own terms."

The Monarchs, he wrote, were "strictly business.... No one whooped or took off into gleeful high jinks."[32]

LaMarque started for the Monarchs and allowed a run in the bottom of the first on a walk, a sacrifice, and a single. Serrell doubled to open the Monarchs' third inning and scored on LaMarque's single. A fielder's choice, a walk, and a single by Strong (one of his three hits) gave Kansas City a 2-1 lead. Pitcher Tommy Kelley of Council Bluffs actually struck out the side in the fourth inning, but the third strike got away from the catcher and the Monarchs scored five runs on a double by Buck O'Neil, , a couple of singles, a couple of errors, a fielder's choice, and a wild pitch.

The All-Stars scored a couple of runs in their fourth, when catcher Eldred "Punk" Arch hit a "towering home run over the left field fence."[33] Their first baseman, Harwood McKain, had three of the team's five hits. Two days later he was to leave for Army service.

Connie Johnson relieved LaMarque in the fifth and pitched shutout ball. Phipps observed of the game, in which Kansas City scored five in the fourth and four more in the sixth, that the Monarchs "merely adjusted their sights for the first few innings, then waded in for the kill with a vengeance."[34]

May 27, 1942: Kansas City Monarchs vs. Legion Redbirds, at Stockyards Park, Sioux City, Iowa - postponed

A scheduled game in Sioux City between the Monarchs and the Legion Redbirds had just gotten underway when a sudden downpour washed out the game. There were two outs in the top of the first and the Monarchs had scored one run. The game was rescheduled for the following evening.[35]

May 28, 1942: Kansas City Monarchs 9, Legion Redbirds 0, at Stockyards Park, Sioux City, Iowa

LaMarque, Matchett, and McDaniel shared the pitching duties, allowing a total of four hits and shutting out the local Legion Redbirds. Joe Greene caught. The Monarchs scored twice in the first, twice in the second, twice in the fourth, and three times in the eighth. Willard Brown hit two home runs.[36]

May 30, 1942: Kansas City Monarchs 9, Chicago American Giants 4 (first game), at Ruppert Stadium

The Saturday afternoon doubleheader was dubbed "Ministers Day" and all ministers from Greater Kansas City were invited to attend. The first game was set for 2:00 P.M., preceded and followed during the intermission by the 44-piece band from Summer High School. The announced attendance was 3,560. Hilton Smith pitched the first game. The Monarchs scored one in the first, one in the fourth, and then seven runs in the seventh. Smith had a shutout going and a 9-0 lead heading into the top of the ninth "when his support went haywire at shortstop on a double-play ball hit by Canady with one away. Before the rally could be stopped, four runs had been counted."[37]

Jesse Williams committed two errors at shortstop but also scored twice in the seven-run seventh. The losing pitcher was left-hander Willie Ferrell.

May 30, 1942: Kansas City Monarchs 5, Chicago American Giants 4 (second game, 7 innings), at Ruppert Stadium

Matchett started the second game for Kansas City. The Monarchs got one run in the first on an error and a double by Ted Strong. The Giants took a 3-1 lead in the third. Strong tripled in the bottom of the third and scored on a wild throw home from Giants shortstop Ralph Wyatt. In the fifth, KC took a 4-3 lead when Strong walked and Willard Brown homered over the wall in left field. The Giants tied it in the sixth, then loaded the bases in the seventh, but could not score. The Monarchs won the game in the seventh on a double by Brown and an RBI single by Joe Greene.

Paige was not on hand. He was in Washington, "loaned" by J.L. Wilkinson to the Homestead Grays to pitch an 8-1 game against a team of White all-stars.[38]

BIRMINGHAM LOSES 2 TO KANSAS CITY

After 45 Minutes Of Rain, Monarchs Grab Double Header

Chicago Defender, June 6, 1942

May 31, 1942: Kansas City Monarchs 3, Birmingham Black Barons 1 (first game), at Ruppert Stadium

After nearly an hour's rain delay, the Monarchs and Black Barons were able to play both games of a Sunday doubleheader, with the Monarchs winning both games and elevating themselves into first place. Each team had eight base hits in the first game. The Monarchs hadn't scored for five innings, then added single runs in the sixth, seventh, and eighth. It's not clear how the runs were scored, but is noteworthy that Strong had three base hits and O'Neil had two. Gread McKinnis pitched seven innings for Birmingham.

Booker McDaniel pitched the first game for the Monarchs and held the Barons to the one lone run. He'd allowed just five hits for eight innings, but surrendered three consecutive singles with no outs in the top of the ninth. Matchett was called on in relief. A sacrifice fly scored one and then Matchett retired the next two batters.

May 31, 1942: Kansas City Monarchs 1, Birmingham Black Barons 0 (second game, 7 innings), at Ruppert Stadium

In the second game, a seven-inning contest, only one run was scored – by the Monarchs in the second. Pipkin held Kansas City to three hits (including doubles by Strong and McDaniel, neither of which featured in the scoring); Lefty Jim LaMarque held Birmingham to two singles, only one of them going to the outfield.[39] The Monarchs scored in the second inning on a grounder by O'Neil that was misplayed, followed by two productive infield outs. The Barons had runners on second and third with one out in the top of the final inning, but LaMarque struck out center fielder Davenport, and Willard Brown saved the game with a "circus catch of Lockett's long drive to center."[40]

While the Monarchs were taking two from the Black Barons, Satchel Paige was in Washington pitching for the Homestead Grays in an exhibition game against Dizzy Dean's All-Stars, winning 8-1 in front of 22,000 at Griffith Stadium.[41]

June 1, 1942: Kansas City Monarchs 4, Birmingham Black Barons 1, at Athletic Park, Muskogee, Oklahoma

The local Muskogee Reds were out of town, playing in Topeka. It's not at all bad routing to stop over in Muskogee en route from Kansas City to Oklahoma City, so a game in Muskogee worked out nicely for June 1, particularly when both the Black Barons and Monarchs were made welcome. The *Muskogee Daily Phoenix* explained that it was "in keeping with a policy of the Muskogee Athletic Association which has pledged to provide famous negro teams in action while the Western association locals are on the road."[42] The paper added that "the most famous negro player of all, the Monarchs' 'Satchel' Paige, whom most sports writers have termed the greatest negro baseball star of all time, will be here also."

Whether Paige pitched or not, or for how much of the game, is unclear, but the June 2 *Muskogee Times Democrat* said the game was played before a "record

-breaking crowd" of unspecified number, and was "one of the most thrilling Negro American league games ever played here."[43] The Monarchs prevailed, 4-1, scoring once in the second inning, once in the seventh, and twice in the eighth, while Birmingham was kept scoreless until the ninth inning. The Black Barons outhit the Monarchs, five hits to four, but all the Monarchs hits were for extra bases – a double, a triple, and two home runs. Kansas City made three errors, while Birmingham played error-free ball. Eight Monarchs struck out, but the team did come out on top.

Kevin Johnson reports that Athletic Park had a reported capacity of 3,500. Dimensions were 300-385-334 with only 25 feet to the backstop. He adds, "Between 1942 and 1948 the Monarchs stopped in Muskogee at least 12 times. If we include the playoff game of 1939, the Monarchs were 13-0 in Muskogee lifetime. Memphis played 7 games in Muskogee between 1943 and 1948. Four of those were against the Monarchs."[44]

Monarchs Win On Early Spree, 5-2

Daily Oklahoman, June 3, 1942

June 2, 1942: Kansas City Monarchs 5, Birmingham Black Barons 2, at Holland Field, Oklahoma City, Oklahoma

The Monarchs singled five times in the bottom of the first inning – Cyrus (Souell), Simms, Strong, Willard Brown, and Newt Allen all singled off Barons right-hander Johnny Markham. The Monarchs added another run in the third and, after Birmingham got its first run in the top of the seventh, added another run in the bottom of the seventh. For the Barons, Double Duty Radcliffe caught Markham and had three base hits – two singles and a double. Matchett started and shared the pitching duties with Hilton Smith.[45]

June 3, 1942: Birmingham Black Barons 6, Kansas City Monarchs 2, at Rebel Stadium, Dallas

Both the *Kansas City Star* and the *Fort Worth Star-Telegram* carried brief notes about the game, but provided little in the way of details. The Fort Worth paper said, "The winners' four-run margin was all scored in the eighth, breaking a 2-all deadlock."[46] Neither paper provided any more information. The *Dallas Morning News* announced 3,846 paid admissions and said the "Monarchs grabbed a 1-to-0 lead in the first inning and the score was tied twice before the Birmingham Negroes won in the eighth."[47] Frank Bradley was the starting pitcher for the Monarchs, and bore the loss. LaMarque relieved him.

June 4, 1942: A Kansas City Monarchs vs. Birmingham Black Barons game was scheduled for 8:00 P.M. at Bringhurst Field in Alexandria, Louisiana. "A section will be reserved for white fans. A large crowd is expected to see the colored diamond stars."[48] Once again, efforts by SABR researchers, and reaching out to local Alexandria historical societies have turned up no information regarding this possible game.

A game scheduled this week against the Birmingham Black Barons, at Port Arthur, Texas, canceled because of a "dimout." (Such events were common in wartime to conserve power or, in coastal cities like Port Arthur, to mitigate the possible threat from enemy ships and submarines.)

June 7, 1942: Birmingham Black Barons 12, Kansas City Monarchs 2 (first game), at Rickwood Field, Birmingham

Hilton Smith went the distance, hammered for 17 hits and an even dozen runs, scoring in every inning but the second, sixth, and eighth, while Barons left-hander Diamond Pipkins held the Monarchs to seven hits, three of them by Newt Allen and two by Jesse Williams.

June 7, 1942: Kansas City Monarchs 5, Birmingham Black Barons 4 (second game, 7 innings), at Rickwood Field, Birmingham

In the first inning, Matchett hit a batter, then gave up a single and a double. Buck O'Neil hit a solo home run in the top of the second. Fielding Tommy Sampson's bunt in the third, Matchett threw the ball wildly into right field, allowing Lloyd Davenport, who had been on first, to come around and score, as did Sampson when the return throw got away from catcher Joe Greene. It was 4-1, Barons. The Monarchs tied it with three in the top of the sixth. Brown singled, O'Neil missed a homer by inches, settling for a double, Greene dropped a single into left, and Jesse Williams tripled in the two runners. With two outs in the top of the seventh, Ted Strong homered into the right-field pavilion.[49]

Satchel Paige, McDaniels Allow Frigidaire No Hits

3,200 Fans See Negro Stars Fan 16 Batters; 2 Balls Hit Out Of Infield

Journal Herald, Dayton, Ohio, June 10, 1942

June 9, 1942: Kansas City Monarch 4, Frigidaires 0, at Ducks Park, Dayton, Ohio

A no-hitter. Satchel Paige pitched four innings, striking out eight of the team from Frigidaire's local Industrial League. Booker McDaniel pitched the final five innings, also striking out eight. Neither one allowed a base hit. Each saw one opponent reach base – Paige walked the opposing pitcher in the third inning and McDaniel saw one reach on an error by Williams in the seventh. Only two balls were hit out of the infield by the Frigidaires, both to Willard Brown in center field off McDaniel later in the game. The Monarchs collected 11 base hits, but only Cyrus (Souell) had an extra-base hit, a double as one of his three hits. O'Neil drove in two of the runs and Souell another. A packed house of 3,200 saw the no-hitter.[50]

There had apparently been another game scheduled this same day (June 9), against Jess Elster's Colored Athletics, at Grand Rapids, Michigan. That game was reported to have been canceled due to rain.[51]

June 10, 1942: There was to have been a game against the Cincinnati-Cleveland Buckeyes – at Flint, Michigan – but nothing has been found to indicate whether or not the game was played.

June 12, 1942: A planned exhibition game in Toledo dubbed as a "Satchel Paige exhibition … had to be postponed because of wet grounds. The Monarchs will make a Toledo appearance later in the season."[52]

Sports editor Sam McKibben wrote in the *Call* that baseball teams should present themselves wearing clean uniforms, and that the Monarchs were one of the cleanest, Negro teams in baseball, if not the cleanest, "thanks to four men: J.L. Wilkinson, T.Y. Baird, Dizzy Dismukes, and Frank Duncan."[53]

June 14, 1942: Cincinnati-Cleveland Buckeyes 2, Kansas City Monarchs 1 (first game), at League Park II, Cleveland

The two teams swapped low-scoring games in Cleveland in front of "3,000 shivering fans."[54] Paige and Matchett pitched the first game, with Paige giving up two first-inning runs on three base hits – Billy Horne and Duke Cleveland sandwiched around a double by Sam Jethroe. The Monarchs got one back in the top of the second, and so ended the scoring. Buckeyes righty Eugene Brewer gave up two of the Monarchs' five hits in the ninth, to Cyrus (Souell) and Williams, but closed out the inning (and game) without permitting a run.

June 14, 1942: Kansas City Monarchs 2, Cincinnati-Cleveland Buckeyes 0 (second game, 7 innings), at League Park II, Cleveland

Booker McDaniel pitched to Johnnie Dawson in the second game and shut out the Buckeyes, allowing just two hits. The Monarchs scored one run in the sixth and another in the seventh when Sam Jethroe overran a groundball. The hard-luck loser was Smokey Owens.[55] The *Plain Dealer* of Cleveland showed the Monarchs scoring two runs in the eighth, and thus winning 3-0. Its box score showed three hits allowed by McDaniel.[56] It also said the two teams would be playing in Youngstown, Ohio, on June 15 and Meadville, Pennsylvania, on the 16th.

June 15, 1942: Kansas City Monarchs 6, Cincinnati-Cleveland Buckeyes 4 (10 innings), at Idora Park, Youngstown, Ohio

Facing LaMarque, the Buckeyes scored once in the bottom of the first and once in the bottom of the third. Right-hander Willie Jefferson seemed to have the game in hand for the Buckeyes; the score was 2-0, Buckeyes, through the first eight innings. The Buckeyes crumbled in the top of the ninth, though, the team committing three errors and the Monarchs collecting three base hits (one of them a home run by second baseman Serrell). Kansas City took a 4-2 lead. Hilton Smith pitched the ninth for the Monarchs and gave up two runs, sending the game to the 10th inning. A two-run rally built on a walk and three hits gave the Monarchs another two-run lead, this time one that Smith didn't squander. Center fielder Emmett Wilson homered for the Buckeyes. Catcher Raymond Taylor was assessed three of the Buckeyes' four errors.[57]

June 16, 1942: Kansas City Monarchs 6, Cincinnati-Cleveland Buckeyes 3, at Athletic Park, Meadville, Pennsylvania

This time the "shivering fans" numbered 700.[58] Ted Strong's three-run fifth-inning home run provided the margin of difference, enabling the Monarchs to hold on as the Buckeyes scored one run each in the sixth, eighth, and ninth. Lefty Robinson pitched for the Buckeyes and Connie Johnson for the Monarchs.

June 17, 1942: Kansas City Monarchs 6, Baltimore Elite Giants 1, at Bugle Field, Baltimore

Jack Matchett was on his way to a complete game, having allowed five singles and one sixth-inning run over eight innings, but was then "waved to the dugout after a prolonged argument with Umpire Frank McCrary over a called strike."[59] Booker McDaniel took over and closed out the game. The run the Elites scored was due to a temporary spate of lost control on Matchett's part. With one out, Bill Harvey singled. Another out followed but so did another single. He walked the next two batters, forcing in a run. Matchett struck out six, but walked five.

The Monarchs scored one in the second inning, but then bunched five of their 11 hits in the sixth inning, with three runners crossing the plate. The biggest hit was Joe Greene's "booming triple." Strong doubled twice; O'Neil also doubled.

June 18, 1942: Homestead Grays 2, Kansas City Monarchs 1 (10 innings), at Griffith Stadium, Washington

In one of several stories leading up to the game, the June 12 *Washington Post* said the game would be the first between the two reigning champs of the two Negro leagues in 10 years. The Grays had been Negro National League champs for 1940 and 1941 and the Monarchs had reigned over the Negro American League for three years. The 9:00 P.M. game played under the lights of Griffith Stadium drew 28,000 and showcased superb baseball.[60] Pitchers Roy Partlow and Satchel Paige both allowed three hits over the first five innings. Paige gave way to Hilton Smith, but Partlow stayed on – and it was good for the Grays that he did.

The Monarchs had almost gotten one in the top of the first. Simms led off with a triple. Newt Allen hit a fly ball to Jerry Benjamin in center field. It looked like a run, for sure. and Simms jogged in from third as "Josh Gibson stood near home plate with both hands down at his sides. … But as (Simms) neared the plate, Gibson tagged him out standing up. Benjamin had made one of the greatest and most perfect throws ever seen in a ball game."[61]

After nine full innings, neither team had scored.

Leading off the top of the 10th, Jim Greene walked. Buck O'Neil laid down a sacrifice bunt, and reached safely when three Grays fielders all went for the ball and Buck Leonard's throw to second base was late. A fly ball and a popup followed. Hilton Smith singled up the middle to give the Monarchs a 1-0 lead. Simms flied out. In the bottom of the 10th, the Grays pitcher also drove in a run. Sam Bankhead walked, but was erased on a fielder's choice. Pinch-hitter Jud Wilson dropped in a Texas Leaguer to tie the game, 1-1. That brought up Roy Partlow, who tripled over Simms' head into the left-field corner. Partlow was carried off the field by excited Grays fans who celebrated for a full half-hour after the game.[62]

June 21, 1942: Kansas City Monarchs 6, Memphis Red Sox 5, at Ruppert Stadium

The Monarchs returned to Kansas City after three weeks on the road. It was Elks Day at Ruppert Stadium, with about 3,500 "Negro Elks" attending from an eight-state Midwest Association region meeting: Missouri, Kansas, Colorado, Iowa, Minnesota, Nebraska, Oklahoma, and Wyoming. Findley Wilson of Washington, grand exalted ruler, threw out the first pitch for the 3:00 P.M. start. Then Booker McDaniel took over the pitching. He had allowed a total of two base hits in his prior 14 innings. He allowed five hits and four runs, watching Memphis overcome the 4-0 lead the Monarchs had taken with two runs in the first and two in the second. The Red Sox got two in the fourth and three in the fifth. It was 5-4 through 8½. Connie Johnson had taken over after 4⅔ innings, surrendering the fifth of Memphis's five runs. Heading into the bottom of the ninth, catcher Jim Greene hit the first pitch he saw for a home run over the center-field scoreboard.[63] Game tied. O'Neil singled over second base, and moved to second base and then third on back-to-back infield outs. Johnson was due up, but manager Frank Duncan had another pitcher – Hilton Smith – pinch-hit for him. On a 2-and-2 count, Smith singled to right field.

Mathis bore the complete-game loss. Total attendance was around 5,000.

There had been an unfortunate incident in the game when umpire Hurley McNair, a former Monarch, had called out Serrell at third base on what would have been a triple, provoking a "mild riot of bottle throwing." Serrell was ejected. Sam McKibben wrote that, although McNair had waited "much too long" to make the call, there was no room for "poor sportsmanship and unwarranted attacks on officials."[64]

June 22, 1942: Kansas City Monarchs 14, Memphis Red Sox 3, at Belleville, Illinois

Hilton Smith held Memphis in a way the Red Sox pitchers were unable to match. Jelly Taylor collected a triple and two singles off Smith, but the Red Sox offense was otherwise pretty well held in check. Simms made a great throw from deep in the outfield to erase McDaniel at home plate when he tried to tag and score on Mathis's fly ball. Willard Brown was 3-for-5 for the Monarchs. The biggest blow was a grand slam by Joe Greene.[65]

Democrat and Chronicle, Rochester, New York

June 24, 1942: Kansas City Monarchs 6, Eber-Seagrams 1, at Red Wing Stadium, Rochester, New York

Satchel Paige was the drawing card for the 8:30 P.M. game and attracted 4,500 who saw him throw one-hit ball, walking only two in his five innings. Veteran left-hander Ted Kleinhans was "imported from Syracuse for the occasion," to pitch for Eber-Seagram.[66] The team was the three-time Western New York semipro champions.[67] Kleinhans struck out 11 Monarchs, two more than Paige, though Paige got to him for a double and a run batted in. In the fifth and sixth, though, three errors (one committed by Kleinhans) and a wild pitch helped the Monarchs add five runs. O'Neil tripled, Paige singled him in, Serrell singled, Kleinhans threw away the ball on a bunt he fielded, and a sacrifice fly accounted for the Monarchs' last three runs. Connie Johnson pitched the last four innings, allowing just one hit.

June 25, 1942: Kansas City Monarchs 5, Birmingham Black Barons 4, at Offermann Stadium, Buffalo, New York

There was a considerable buildup for this game in the Buffalo newspapers, touting Satchel Paige, Dan Bankhead, described as "the next Satchel Paige," and the fact that the two teams were at the top of the first-half standings in the NAL, Birmingham holding a slight edge.[68] The *Birmingham News* reported: "Lefty McKinnis pitched good ball all the way, giving up only eight hits, while his mates collected 12, but an eighth-inning home run gave the Monarchs the decision."[69]

The Buffalo newspapers provided more detail. Paige started and worked the first three innings, "in lackadaisical fashion."[70] The Barons scored once in the first. The Monarchs took a 2-1 lead in the first inning when Newt Allen singled and Ted Strong homered. Birmingham then scored one more in the top of the second. There were a reported 4,000 fans, some arriving late despite the 8:30 P.M. start time. There was general "disappointment" that Paige left after three innings, shown by "scattered hissing."[71]

Jack Matchett took over and pitched well. The Monarchs scored another run in the fourth and Joe Greene hit a solo home run in the sixth, giving the Monarchs a 4-2 lead, but the Barons came back with two runs in top of the eighth. Greene put the Monarchs in the lead again with another solo home run in the bottom of the eighth, leading the *Buffalo Evening News* to headline its brief game account, "Green's [sic] 2 Homers Steal Show from Paige in Stadium."[72]

June 26, 1942: Birmingham Black Barons 3, Kansas City Monarchs 1, at Halloran Park, Lima, Ohio

A 7:00 P.M. twilight game played in a crisp 1:29 saw three Barons pitchers each work three innings: Alvin Gibson, Diamond Pipkins, and Johnny Markham. McDaniel pitched all nine innings for the Monarchs. The Monarchs' only run came in the

• 1942 Kansas City Monarchs Timeline •

first inning when Souell and Strong doubled. From that point on, nary a Monarch advanced farther than second base. The Monarchs had just three more hits, two of them (including a two-base hit) by Newt Allen. Pipkins' three innings were hitless; he walked two. The Barons got on the board with a solo home run over the right-field fence by Lloyd Davenport in the top of the sixth, then took a 2-1 lead on a double by the next batter, Leroy Morney, and a single by a player named Bennett, the right fielder. An error and a sacrifice set up another run in the seventh, driven home by Tommy Sampson's single.[73]

SABR member Mike Lackey explains why this game enjoyed a solid buildup: "Lima had minor-league teams about half the time between the late 1880s and the early 1950s, but Black baseball was about the only game in town in 1942. The Class-D Ohio State League, where Lima had competed from 1939 through 1941, suspended operations in 1942. That summer, touring Black teams played here almost every week. There was another official league game that featured the Philadelphia Stars and the Homestead Grays in August. Two factors made Lima an attractive stop, I believe: the absence of professional baseball after the fans had come accustomed to having it, and an increase in the city's African American population as workers were recruited in the South to fill jobs in Lima's wartime industries, including the Ohio Steel foundry and the Lima Locomotive Works, which was converted to produce Sherman battle tanks for the military."[74]

June 27, 1942: Kansas City Monarchs 2, East Chicago Giants 1, at Block Stadium, East Chicago, Indiana

In a 6:00 P.M. twilight game, Giants pitcher McCarthy held the Monarchs to just four hits, one of which was a double by Strong. Phillips and someone named "Natches" pitched for Kansas City.[75]

June 28, 1942: Kansas City Monarchs 9, Chicago American Giants 7 (13 innings), at Borchert Field, Milwaukee

Hilton Smith took over for Paige after Satchel had given up three runs in the fifth. He saw four runs score, three of them when ball hit by Art Pennington bounded away from Ted Strong in right field, and rolled to the flagpole, giving Pennington a three-run inside-the-park home run. That gave the Giants a 7-5 lead. Smith gave up only four hits over the next eight innings of relief. Likewise, Sam Thompson relieved starter Lefty Shields in the fourth, and generally pitched stellar ball until the 13th, save for a couple of runs that tied the game in the sixth inning.

In the top of the 13th, Thompson faltered. Willard Brown led off with his fourth single of the game, but was forced at second on Greene's grounder. Buck O'Neil doubled and Serrell singled him in. Serrell somehow got to third base and scored on a force play. The two-run lead held and the Monarchs won.[76]

June 29, 1942: Chicago American Giants 6, Kansas City Monarchs 4, at Canton, Illinois

Before more than 1,000 fans, the Chicago team beat the Monarchs under the arc lights. Connie Johnson, described as "Cliff Johnson, a 20-year old Atlanta, Ga. Rookie," was said to have "steadied after a wobbly start and, despite the costly error of his batterymate, pitched good ball, striking out three men in the first inning, and a total on nine, three of them in a row in the third frame."[77]

The Monarchs had actually scored first, with two runs in the first inning, but the Giants came back and scored three runs in their half of the first (despite Johnson recording all three outs by strikeout) on two walks, a single, and a passed ball. The Canton newspaper account ascribed at least two of the runs to a "misplay" by Monarchs catcher Johnnie Dawson, "who let a throw from the outfield get away from him." They scored three more runs in the fourth, in part due to shortstop Jesse Williams's error fielding Double Duty Radcliffe's roller.

The Monarchs were said to have scored a third run in the fifth and another in the sixth. The game account raises a question about its veracity, however, when it went on to say that the Monarchs also scored "another in the ninth before a fast double play crashed what looked like a certain chance to at least knot the count." Those keeping track will note that this would add up to five Monarchs runs, but both the lead paragraph of the story and the box score agree that the final score was 6-4. There was no line score provided.

Willard Brown was 2-for-4, with two runs scored.

July 2, 1942: Kansas City Monarchs 7, Chicago American Giants 6 (first game, 7 innings), at Ruppert Stadium

The Monarchs took two by identical scores of 7-6 in a twi-night twin bill with a scheduled 7:00 P.M. start, each game planned to be seven innings.

Matchett and McDaniel each gave up three runs in the first game, McDaniel getting the win as the pitcher of record when Kansas City scored in the bottom of the seventh. Each team had scored in four different innings and the game also featured five triples. There was unfortunately no explanation in the *Kansas City Star* on how the winning run scored.

July 2, 1942: Kansas City Monarchs 7, Chicago American Giants 6 (second game, 7 innings), at Ruppert Stadium

Both teams scored once in the first. The Monarchs scored once in the second. Both teams scored twice in the third. The Monarchs scored two more in the fourth, then the Giants tied it 6-6 in the top of the sixth. The Giants committed five errors in the game. The Monarchs scored a seventh run in the bottom of the sixth, then held on. Phillips, LaMar, and Johnson pitched, with Johnson getting the win. There was one home run in the game, by the Monarchs' "Bob Strong."[78]

July 4, 1942: Memphis Red Sox 7, Kansas City Monarchs 6 (first game, 10 innings), at Martin's Park, Memphis

The Red Sox had won 15 games in a row and were putting on a very strong push to upset the Monarchs for the league lead in the first half of the NAL season. The Monarchs were leading by a few percentage points.

Submariner Porter Moss threw a complete-game 10-inning game. His shortstop, T.J. Brown, gave him a 1-0 lead in the first, scoring from second on a daring sprint while catcher Greene fielded a slow roller down the first-base line and threw to first. Brown homered for K.C. and Simms tripled, but Moss himself was 3-for-5 and singled in the winning run in the bottom of the 10th after Hilton Smith – who'd gone the distance as well – had intentionally walked catcher Bob Smith. with two outs, to get to Moss.

July 4, 1942: Kansas City Monarchs 9, Memphis Red Sox 3 (second game, 7 innings), at Martin's Park, Memphis

The Monarchs turned the tables in the second game, and promptly, scoring six runs in the top of the second off starter Verdell Mathis and reliever Felix Evans. Connie Johnson pitched all seven innings for the Monarchs.

July 5, 1942: Kansas City Monarchs 11, Birmingham Black Barons 5 (first game), at Rickwood Field, Birmingham

Oddly, both Birmingham's Gread McKinnis and Kansas City's Jack Matchett started both games of the July 5 doubleheader in Birmingham. McKinnis didn't last long at all; he gave up four runs to the Monarchs in the first inning and never recorded an out. Alvin Gibson took his place and worked six innings, giving up six runs. An 11th run scored in the top of the ninth off Specs Ellis, the third pitcher of the game for the Barons. The Monarchs held an 8-0 lead before the first Barons run scored. Matchett threw the first 2⅓ innings in game one before turning the game over to Booker McDaniel, who finished it out.

The Monarchs offense included two home runs by Bonnie Serrell. Strong hit one, too, as did both Lloyd Davenport and Leroy Morney for the Black Barons.

July 5, 1942: Birmingham Black Barons 2, Kansas City Monarchs 1 (second game, 7 innings), at Rickwood Field, Birmingham

The game was a good pitcher's battle between left-hander McKinnis and the Monarchs' Matchett, who started the second game, too, and pitched all six innings of the seven-inning game. He hadn't had to pitch the bottom of the seventh because Tommy Sampson's two-run homer in the bottom of the sixth inning was enough to overcome the 1-0 lead the Monarchs had held since the fourth, and to deal Matchett a defeat when Kansas city failed to score in the top of the seventh.

Frank Duncan caught both games for the Monarchs.

July 7, 1942: Memphis Red Sox 1, Kansas City Monarchs 0 (10 innings), at Pelican Stadium, New Orleans

The July 5 *Daily Oklahoman* announced a game between the Monarchs and the Memphis Red Sox, saying that Memphis had won 15 consecutive games and was just a few points behind the Monarchs.[79]

Verdell Mathis of Memphis and Satchel Paige squared off for a Tuesday night game at Pelican Stadium. Mathis came out on top, throwing 10 innings of four-hit ball and shutting out Kansas City. Paige worked the first five innings, allowing three hits but no runs, and was relieved by Connie Johnson. Johnson also worked five innings and gave up only one hit, but it was a hit that produced a run and a win for the Red Sox. The Monarchs had had two good chances to score. They loaded the bases in the sixth inning with two singles and a hit batter, but were unable to get a run across.

With the teams scoreless through nine, Bonnie Serrell tripled for the Monarchs in the top of the 10th, but was left stranded.

Fred McDaniel was hit by a Johnson pitch in the bottom of the 10th. He moved up to second base on a grounder by Jelly Taylor. Then Johnson gave up his first hit, a single by Fred Bankhead that drove in McDaniel.[80]

July 9, 1942: Memphis Red Sox 4, Kansas City Monarchs 2, at Waco, Texas

Booker McDaniel held Memphis to four runs, but right-hander Willie Hutchinson pitched better, holding the Monarchs to just two.[81] Neither SABR researchers nor the Waco Historical Foundation were able to get more information about this game.

Kansas City Monarchs Win Negro Baseball Tilt

Wichita Falls Record News, July 11, 1942

July 10, 1942: Kansas City Monarchs 11, Memphis Red Sox 5, at Spudder Field, Wichita Falls, Texas

The Memphis Red Sox gave pitcher Felix Evans a 4-0 lead, scoring once in the first and three more times in the third inning. Lefty LaMarque pitched the full game for Kansas City. The Monarchs tied it up by scoring four times in the bottom of the third, only to see Memphis take a one-run lead in the top of the fourth. In the bottom of the sixth, the Monarchs scored another four runs. They added a ninth and 10th run in the seventh, and an 11th in the bottom of the eighth.[82]

July 11, 1942: Kansas City Monarchs 5, Memphis Red Sox 0 (first game), at Dallas, Texas

July 11, 1942: Kansas City Monarchs 7, Memphis Red Sox 0 (second game), at Dallas, Texas

The above scores came from the *Commercial Appeal* of July 13, the Monday newspaper. It said that the Monarchs had won both games of the doubleheader in Dallas by the above-reported scores, but said the games were on Sunday. There were two games between the two teams at Dallas on Sunday, as reported in more detail below. This leads us to believe that these two games were played on Saturday. No more details could be found.

July 12, 1942: Kansas City Monarchs 11, Memphis Red Sox 0 (first game, 7 innings), at Rebel Stadium, Dallas

Memphis was shut out twice and outscored 17-0 in the July 12 doubleheader. Satchel Paige pitched a complete seven-inning game, allowing five hits, striking out nine, and going 3-for-4, with a double and two singles.[83] Duncan caught Paige. The Monarchs scored two runs in the first and third innings, with one run scored in the second, then poured it on with six runs in the fifth inning.

July 12, 1942: Kansas City Monarchs 6, Memphis Red Sox 0 (second game, 7 innings), at Rebel Stadium, Dallas

The second game was also a seven-inning game, Jack Matchett going the distance, pitching to Dawson for a shutout. He allowed four hits, while the Monarchs scored six runs off Moss, one in the fourth, one in the fifth, and four in the sixth inning.

A confounding story appeared in the Tuesday, July 14, issue of the *Rock Island* (Illinois) *Argus,* declaring, "The House of David really has a ball club, as evidenced last Sunday at Kansas City, where the team defeated Satchel Paige and the Kansas City Monarchs, 16-5."[84] Yet the prior Sundays had been July 12, when the Monarchs played two against the Memphis Red Sox in Dallas, and July 5, when they played a doubleheader in Birmingham against the Black Barons. Going back even one more Sunday, we find the Monarchs were in Milwaukee on June 28.

July 13, 1942: Kansas City Monarchs against the Memphis Red Sox, at Muskogee, Oklahoma

A game between these two teams was announced for July 13, but whether or not it occurred is something we have been unable to determine, even after a search of Muskogee, Memphis, and other newspapers.

July 14, 1942: Kansas City Monarchs 5, Memphis Red Sox 0, at Holland Field, Oklahoma City

Norris Phillips shut out the Red Sox in an 8:30 P.M. game, allowing just four hits, as the Monarchs beat Memphis, 5-0. There were two home runs in the game. The first two runs came in the bottom of the second when Willard Brown doubled and "John O'Neill (Buck O'Neil) hit a ball to right field. Memphis's Cowan "Bubba" Hyde tried for a shoestring catch but the ball got by him and just kept rolling. In the fourth inning, "Home Run" Brown lined a solo homer over the left-field fence. In the fifth, three singles (Simms, Allen, and Williams) and a double steal gave the Monarchs two more runs.[85]

July 15, 1942: Memphis Red Sox 6, Kansas City Monarchs 0, at Owl Park, Topeka, Kansas

An 8:15 P.M. game, at "regular Western Association prices," pitted two visiting Negro American League teams against each other and the Memphis Red Sox came out on top. In fact, Verdell Mathis ("a southpaw with everything") shut out the Monarchs, 6-0.[86] It wasn't as though the Monarchs couldn't put the bat on the ball – they collected 11 hits off him. Four of them were made by Joe Greene – three singles and a double. Willard Brown hit three singles. And Connie Johnson pinch-hit in the bottom of the ninth and tripled. There were two outs at the time. Another Monarchs pitcher, LaMarque, pinch-hit after Johnson, but he grounded out to end the game. In both the sixth and eighth, the Monarchs had gotten two runners on base, but Mathis and his teammates rose to the occasion and escaped harm. One newspaper credited the Red Sox for two double plays and said "scoring chances were erased by sensational fielding by the Memphis club."[87]

Starting for Kansas City was McDaniel, who went four innings; Matchett pitched the rest of the game. The first Red Sox run was produced by Cowan Hyde, who hit the first pitch of the third inning over the fence in right field. They added another run in the fourth, two more in the fifth, a fifth run in the sixth, and a final run in the top of the ninth. The game drew an audience of 1,222.

July 16, 1942: Kansas City Monarchs 4, Memphis Red Sox 3, at City Stadium, St. Joseph, Missouri

It was the biggest crowd of the year in St. Joseph, with 1,900 coming to City Stadium to see the Monarchs "pull an American Negro League game out of the fire" and beat Memphis, 4-3.[88] It was thought to have been the biggest grossing gate in the history of the facility, come out to see the "classy negro clubs."[89] Lefty LaMarque started for Kansas City and allowed only four hits but a walk, a triple by Neil Robinson, and a single gave the Red Sox a 2-0 lead in the fourth inning. In the seventh he walked Bubba Hyde, who stole second, took third on an infield hit, and scored when Jelly Taylor singled to left. Connie Johnson came in to relieve a tiring LaMarque. It was Johnson who became the hero of the game.

The Monarchs scored once in the sixth off Felix "Chin" Evans. Newt Allen singled, and Cyrus (Souell) doubled him home. In the bottom of the seventh, Kansas City tied it. As with Memphis, the first batter (LaMarque) walked and stole second. He went to third base on a passed ball, and came home easily when Allen tripled to left field. Cyrus then singled, and Allen scored. Both Cyrus and Allen had three-hit games.

In the eighth, Jesse Williams reached first base on an error. Johnson then slugged a ball some 400 feet to center field. Williams scored the go-ahead run. Johnson was out at the plate on a perfect relay, trying to add an insurance ran and get himself an inside-the-park home run. Johnson held back Memphis in the top of the ninth and got the win.

Clark Griffith was reported to have said, "The Monarchs play a keen brand of heads up ball and have several players in their lineup who could make the majors if negroes were allowed to play in the majors. It's a real treat to watch this team perform."[90]

July 17, 1942: Kansas City Monarchs 6, Jefferson Barracks 0, at Ruppert Stadium

This benefit game, advanced with a great deal of coverage in local newspapers over the preceding two weeks, featured the Monarchs against a White team of soldiers recruited from professional and college ballplayers, billed as Johnny Sturm's Jefferson Barracks. Sturm was a native of St. Louis who had played for the American Association's Kansas City Blues (a New York Yankees farm club) in 1939 and 1940 and then in 124 games as first baseman for the Yankees in 1941. After Pearl Harbor, he enlisted in the Army Air Force.

The proceeds from the 8:45 P.M. game were split

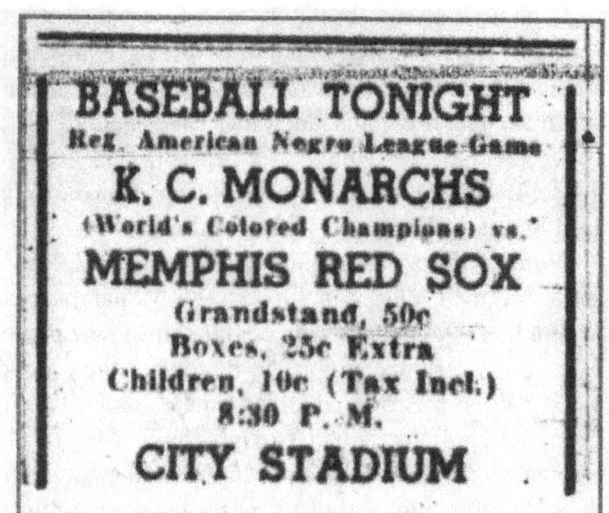

St. Joseph Gazette, July 16, 1942

• 1942 Kansas City Monarchs Timeline •

50-50 between the Army Relief Fund and the Salvation Army's Penny Ice Fund. The game was the idea of Monarchs owners J.L. Wilkinson and Tom Baird, who covered all the Monarchs' expenses. The Yankees covered all the expenses of the ballpark.[91]

Competing against "major and top minor league teams," Sturm's team had a record of 23-8 coming into the game, and had recently battled the Chicago Cubs for 11 innings before losing, but the April 17 morning edition of the *Kansas City Times* suggested that the Monarchs would be favored, since they were "conceded to be the strongest Negro club in the nation and good enough to hold their own with any of the major league clubs."[92]

The game drew early 6,000 and the Monarchs dominated, in a one-hitter thrown by Satchel Paige and Hilton Smith. The one hit came with two outs in the first inning, a single by Johnny Sturm. Paige pitched three innings and Smith pitched the remaining six. The Monarchs scored three in the first inning on back-to-back singles by Willie Simms and third baseman "Cyrus," a run-producing groundout by Strong, and then a two-run homer over the left-center-field scoreboard by Willard Brown. Leading off the eighth inning, Brown hit another home run, an inside-the-park one to the fence in right-center.[93]

The *Star* reported that the majority of the fans were "followers of the hustling Monarchs." When the Blues played at Ruppert, seating was segregated. When the Monarchs played this game, it was not – a fact that had been announced in advance. Sam McKibben of the *Call* wrote, "There was no discrimination, nor segregation" and said that the game saw "Whites seated next to Negroes without incident," with some of the White patrons asking, "Why don't they allow the Blues to play the Monarchs?" and "Why are Negroes kept out of the majors and minors?"[94]

A couple of weeks later, McKibben noted that while seating at this game was not segregated, later games saw Negroes kept out of the box seats and otherwise discriminated against, including insults and slurs from ballpark attendants. He said that patrons should stay away from Ruppert Stadium until management adopted more democratic ways.[95]

Note: A two-sentence article in the *Commercial Appeal* of Memphis adds confusion. It said that the Memphis Red Sox "trampled" the Monarchs, 12-1 at Springfield, Illinois on Friday night, July 17, and that Submarine Moss of the Memphians had hit a home run.[96]

July 19, 1942: Kansas City Monarchs 11, Chicago American Giants 5 (first game), at Comiskey Park, Chicago

The doubleheader was a benefit for the South Side Boys Club and for the Joe Louis Chapter of the Women Defense Corps of America. Marva Trotter Barrow, wife of Joe Louis, was the Corps president. An estimated 8,000 fans came to watch the games. The Monarchs won both games, with 17 base hits in the first game and seven in the latter. Connie Johnson and Booker McDaniel worked the first game, and between them gave up 13 hits, four of them by Ralph Wyatt (one of those a triple). Very unusually, all five of the Giants' runs were scored by shortstop Wyatt; he kept crossing the plate but no other Giants did. The Monarchs' Joe Greene homered twice.

July 19, 1942: Kansas City Monarchs 5, Chicago American Giants 4 (second game), at Comiskey Park, Chicago

The Monarchs used four pitchers in the second game, which ran a full nine innings. Paige pitched the first three innings, relieved in turn by McDaniel, LaMarque, and Phillips. The Monarchs used two catchers, too – Duncan and Greene. Chicago held a 4-2 lead after seven innings. Lefty Shields pitched the whole game for Chicago. In the top of the eighth, he walked Newt Allen and Strong singled. There were two outs and Willard Brown at the plate. He homered into the right-field grandstand.

July 21, 1942: Homestead Grays 5, Kansas City Monarchs 4 (11 innings), at Forbes Field, Pittsburgh

The 11,000 spectators at Forbes Field were reported by the *Pittsburgh Sun-Telegraph* as the largest crowd to ever watch at Grays game at the ballpark. They saw a thriller. Satchel Paige went the distance and Roy Partlow of the Grays pitched into the 10th, but hurt his leg and had to leave in favor of Ray Brown – who wound up scoring the winning run.

The Monarchs built up a 4-0 lead, with Paige himself driving in the first two runs. In the top of the third, Bonnie Serrell tripled. Paige's infield hit scored him. In the fifth inning, another triple – this time by Jess Williams – set up a possible run; he scored on an infield out off Paige's bat. Serrell hit an inside-the-park two-run homer in the seventh for the other two Monarchs runs.

Greene had to leave the game due to a split finger in the eighth.

Grays manager Vic Harris made a "sensational, leaping, one-handed catch of Catcher Frank Duncan's long drive to the scoreboard in the tenth inning." Harris had driven in Sam Bankhead with the fourth and tying run back in the eighth inning, the four-run rally that kept the Grays in the game. In the 11th, Brown singled with one out, was sacrificed to second base, and then scored when Homestead center fielder Jerry Benjamin struck his third hit of the game.

July 22, 1942: Kansas City Monarchs 4, Jaycees 1 – at Fremont, Ohio

The Friday, July 24, *Fremont News-Messenger* had one sentence: "The game between Gallion and Fremont was postponed with the Jaycees playing the Kansas City Monarchs and losing, 4 to 1, while Tiffin was idle." It's unclear when this game might have been played, or whether the Jaycees were from Fremont, but that would appear to be the case.

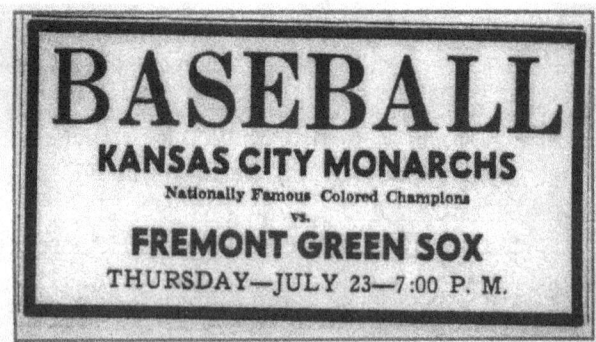

News-Messenger of Fremont, Ohio, July 22, 1942

July 23, 1942: Kansas City Monarchs 7, Fremont Green Sox 5 (eight innings), at Anderson Field, Fremont, Ohio

The Fremont Green Sox had come from behind, overcoming a 3-0 deficit with one run in the fourth two in the sixth, and one in the seventh to take a 4-3 lead. The 700 area residents were no doubt "envisioning a great victory when one miscue changed the entire complexion of the game."[97] It was the top of the eighth, which was planned to be the final inning. There were two outs and a runner on third base. Second baseman Johnny Adams simply bobbled a fairly routine groundball, and Ted Strong was safe on first, with a run scoring. Rather than game over, it was now 4-4. Willard Brown hit a two-run homer – a "long, low drive over the left field fence." That gave the Monarchs a 6-4 lead. Buck O'Neil doubled. In came a reliever. Newt Allen singled, O'Neil advancing to third. The Monarchs then pulled off a double steal, and scored a seventh run, the fourth of the inning.

The Monarchs used four pitchers before the game was over. Hilton Smith started, then moved to play left field after three innings, LaMarque coming in for 2⅔ (the Fremont paper had him as "Lamar.") "Matich – presumably Jack Matchett – worked a couple of innings. And "Jones" worked the final third. Might this have been Connie Johnson?

July 25, 1942: Kansas City Monarchs 17, East Chicago Giants 4, at Block Stadium, East Chicago, Indiana

The game was perhaps mercifully only a seven-inning game. It was one of the more lopsided ones. Ted Strong hit two home runs over the right-field fence at Block Stadium, the first two balls ever hit over the fence.[98] The Monarchs scored in every inning but the second, including half a dozen runs in the third and six more runs in the sixth. Every player in the lineup had exactly two base hits save for Allen and Serrell who had one each. LaMarque went the distance. Jack Matchett played left field in the game.

July 26, 1942: Memphis Red Sox 10, Kansas City Monarchs 4 (first game), at Wrigley Field, Chicago

It was "Satchel Paige Day" at Wrigley Field and he was honored between games. He was presented with a huge array of flowers, an Elgin watch, a suit, a gold trophy, a radio, and a traveling bag. Then he went out and won the day's second game.

The Memphis Red Sox won the first game, solving Hilton Smith in taking a 7-1 lead through the first 4½ innings. McDaniel relieved and gave up three more runs. Neil Robinson homered in the game, wining himself a pair of street shoes. Jelly Taylor got a necktie for hitting the first two-bagger. The Monarchs' Willard Brown tripled, for which he was presented a sport shirt. Memphis won, 10-4. *(Also see story on page 214.)*

July 26, 1942: Kansas City Monarchs 4, Memphis Red Sox 2 (second game, 7 innings), at Wrigley Field, Chicago

After the ceremonies, Paige pitched the second game, retiring the first six batters in order. The Monarchs built up a 4-2 lead, so when Paige allowed a pair of runs to score in top of the seventh (in part due to an error), that was sufficient to beat Verdell Mathis and the Red Sox, 4-2. Paige had scored the first Kansas City run, when he singled to right in the third inning. Simms sacrificed him to second. He took third when Allen singled and scored on Strong's sacrifice fly. Singles by Williams and Serrell and a sacrifice fly by Duncan brought in another run, in the fourth. They added two more in the fifth when both Allen and Strong walked and Brown singled to center.

July 27, 1942: Kansas City Monarchs 7, Chicago Brown Bombers 5, at Indianapolis, Indiana

The two teams traded leads four times. The Monarchs led 1-0 after the first inning. The Bombers tied it in the second and then took a 2-1 lead in the fourth. Back came Kansas City with two in the fifth, to take a 3-2 lead. The Bombers scored twice in the sixth, and went on top, 4-3. But in the bottom of the seventh, the Monarchs put a "4" on the scoreboard. That the Bombers got one in the eighth mattered not in terms of the final score. Matchett started, relieved by Phillips during the sixth-inning rally, taking over with two outs. Ted Strong was 4-for-4, with a home run, a double, and two singles.[99]

July 28, 1942: Kansas City Monarchs 12, Altes Lagers 0, at Swayne Field, Toledo, Ohio

The Altes Lagers team of Detroit was "composed of a number of minor league players," explained the *Toledo Blade*, "most of whom have given up baseball to take jobs in defense jobs for the duration of the war. The Lagers defeated the Homestead Grays in Swayne Field a few years ago and are said to be an even more formidable outfit this season."[100] The game against the Monarchs proved to be pretty one-sided, with a final score of 12-0. Hilton Smith allowed just two singles and struck out 15. The Monarchs scored four runs in the second, three in the sixth, and five in the seventh, two of the seventh-inning runs on a triple to center field by Willard Brown.[101]

July 30, 1942: Kansas City Monarchs 5, Bob Feller's All-Stars 1, at MacArthur Stadium, Syracuse, New York

It's difficult to know what really may have occurred with regard to this game. Was it really "Bob Feller's All-Stars"? Researchers in the Syracuse area have been unable to find any trace of the game in area newspapers, though the *Fayetteville Eagle Bulletin* of July 31 mentions the "Kansas City Monarks" [*sic*] as coming to play "next Thursday, July 30" in an 8:30 P.M. game against "a team of college all-stars recruited from Syracuse, Colgate and Cornell ranks, under the lights at MacArthur Stadium."[102] The *Kansas City Call* listed the game in its August 14 issue as one of several on the road trip, referring to the opposition as College All Stars. One of the students was Charles J. McPhail, who died in 2006 at age 87. He was a four-year member of the Syracuse University baseball, football, and hockey teams, and captain of the baseball team his senior years. He graduated in 1942, and his obituary said that "He was honored to participate in an exhibition game against Satchel Paige and the Kansas City Monarchs at MacArthur Stadium and was thrilled to have hit an inside-the-park home run."[103]

On July 30, Boston's *Christian Science Monitor* reported that Pittsburgh Pirates President William E. Benswanger had said he would hold tryouts for "Negro players." Commissioner Kenesaw M. Landis, the paper wrote, had said there was no ruling against the use of Negroes in Organized Baseball. Monarchs President J.L. Wilkinson told the Associated Press, "I think it would be a fine thing for the game, even though we would lose some of our stars." Though he held a two-year contract with Satchel Paige, he said he had told Paige, "We certainly won't stand in your way if you have a chance to play." Wilkinson said he believed there were at least 25 Negro Leagues players who could play in the majors.[104]

July 31, 1942: Kansas City Monarchs 7, Philadelphia Stars 4, at Scranton-Dunmore Stadium, Scranton, Pennsylvania

It was Satchel Paige who drew the crowds. He was billed as "positive to pitch four innings" – but did not. He pitched the last two – the eighth and the ninth. He allowed only one hit, but the Scranton newspaper said the 2,361 fans who were expecting to see Satch were "thoroughly disappointed" – they "hooted" and gave him a "raucous reception." The newspaper also blasted the Monarchs: "Their defensive play was sloppy as four errors prove and aside from a fair amount of power lacked the semblance of a championship troupe."[105]

It was Connie Johnson who started, and got the win. The Monarchs got a pair of insurance runs in the top of the ninth, a two-run 380-foot home run to right field by Ted Strong (Allen was on base at the time), described as "the only big-league touch to the party."

• When the Monarchs Reigned •

August 2, 1942: Kansas City Monarchs 9, New York Cubans 0 (7 innings), at Yankee Stadium, New York

Once again (see July 17), Satchel Paige and Hilton Smith combined on a one-hitter. Paige pitched the first four innings, allowing only a fourth-inning double by Dave Thomas. Cubans pitcher Dave "Impo" Barnhill lasted only an inning and a third, blasted for seven hits and six runs before being replaced by Bill Anderson. Jesse Williams homered in the game, Ted Strong doubled twice, and Bonnie Serrell tripled.

Some 30,000 attended the game. The *Kansas City Times* added an interesting bit of information: "Major league scouts made notes on the Monarch and Cuban players."[106]

August 3, 1942: Kansas City Monarchs 3, Baltimore Elite Giants 0, at Bugle Field, Baltimore

In a game against the 1941 Negro National League champion Baltimore Elite Giants, the Monarchs recorded another shutout, this time thanks to the three-hit pitching of Big Jack Matchett.

August 4, 1942: game postponed

There had been a game planned against the Philadelphia Stars at Island Park, Harrisburg, but on August 3, it was postponed and rescheduled for August 12. "Injuries to members of the Monarchs team was given as the reason for the postponement," reported the *Harrisburg Evening News*.[107] The Monarchs did manage to shut out Baltimore on the 3rd, as we see above. As it transpired, they did not play on August 12. Weather prevented that one.

August 5, 1942: Kansas City Monarchs 12, Capital District All-Stars 0, at Hawkins Stadium, Albany, New York

Satchel Paige worked three innings helping pitch the Monarchs to a 5-0 shutout win over a White team in Albany before a crowd of 2,000. The postgame coverage in a local newspaper focused more on remarks he was said to have made in which he said he was "not interested in a major league career and believes the mixing of Negro and white players would be a mistake." The *Knickerbocker News* asserted that his substantial earnings "account for his lack of interest in a major league career." Paige said that players from different races would have problems training in the South, and would not be able to stay at the same hotels, even in other parts of the country. He suggested an unlikely scenario: "I'd rather see an entire Negro team represent some city in the league."[108]

August 6, 1942: Kansas City Monarchs 10, Philadelphia Stars 2, at Penmar Park, Philadelphia [park called Bolden's Bowl, in *KC Star*] Center fielder Willard "Sonny" Brown had a big day at the plate, going 5-for-5 with two RBIs and two runs scored. The pitching was the tandem of Paige (for three innings) and Hilton Smith (for the final six), and they held the Stars to two runs, one in the fifth and one in the seventh. The Monarchs had piled up five runs before the Stars scored and added five more as the game progressed, getting to both Barney Brown and Fireball Fillmore.[109]

August 7, 1942: Kansas City Monarchs 3, All-Worcesters 0 (seven innings), at Fitton Field, Worcester, Massachusetts

Satchel Paige and the Monarchs played a game before 2,000 at Fitton Field, with proceeds from the game to benefit the Disabled American Veterans Buddies Club. Worcester Mayor William A. Bennett threw out the first pitch. Connie Johnson worked the first four innings, giving up four hits. Paige worked the fifth and sixth, walking one and giving up a hit on a successful bunt toward third base. Jack Matchett finished the game. Sixteen-year major-league veteran Bump Hadley, winner of 161 big-league games (and a native of Lynn, Massachusetts), pitched for the All-Worcesters, giving up just four hits and two runs (one earned) over six innings. Shortstop Jesse Williams opened the third inning with a triple to right field, and came in on substitute catcher Frazier Robinson's single. A two-out single to left by Bill Simms set up a run; he scored all the way from first when Herb Souell's infield single led to a wild throw. In the sixth, Paige singled, saw the next two batters reach base, then scored when pitcher Joe Lango hit Ted Strong with a pitch.[110]

August 10, 1942: Kansas City Monarchs 2, Savitt Gems 0 (first game), at Bulkeley Stadium, Hartford, Connecticut

The Monarchs were to play the Savitt Gems in a benefit game at Hartford's Bulkeley Stadium on August 9 but the game was rained out. Tom Baird of the Monarchs arranged to have the team stay over another day in hopes of getting in the planned doubleheader. The fans sure got their money's worth, seeing 22 innings of well-played baseball in two low-scoring games.

Paige himself told the *Hartford Courant* he was the number-2 pitcher on the Monarchs: "The No. 1 pitcher is Hilton Smith."[111]

Paige pitched very well indeed, though, in game one of this twin bill in Hartford against a leading area semipro team. The first game ran seven innings; Paige gave up four hits in his five innings – two of them to a center fielder named Ray Curry, who must have retained bragging rights for years. Curry got another hit later in the game off McDaniel. The Monarchs got their two runs in the first inning, but were shut down for the rest of the game.

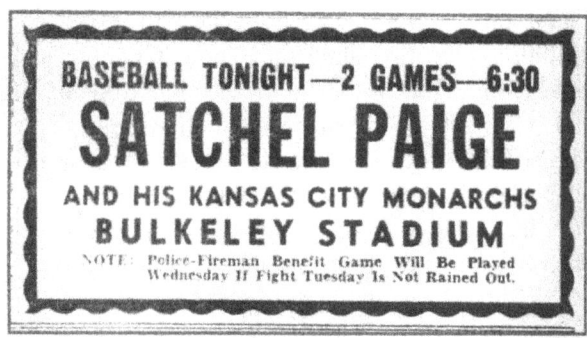

Hartford Courant, August 10, 1942

August 10, 1942: Kansas City Monarchs 2, Savitt Gems 1 (second game, 13 innings), at Bulkeley Stadium, Hartford, Connecticut

The second game lasted more than twice as long as the first – 3:20 as opposed to 1:20. LaMarque worked 3⅓ innings and Matchett pitched the final 9⅔. The Gems scored one in the first inning; the Monarchs scored one in the eighth on Strong's triple and a single by Brown. The game went to the 13th when Serrell reached on an infield hit. Catcher Frazier Robinson reached on an error by the shortstop, Matchett walked to fill the bases, and Simms hit a sacrifice fly.[112]

Frazier "Slow" Robinson had joined the Monarchs in the first part of August. When the team visited Baltimore on August 3, he'd gone to see them. He'd been under contract to the Monarchs back in 1940, but had not reported in 1941 – playing instead for the Sparrows Point Giants and, later, the Baltimore Elite Giants. Some of the Monarchs spotted him in the stands so he went to say hello after that game. "I'm sure they didn't know I'd jumped the Monarchs contract," he later wrote. "Dizzy Dismukes, the old submarine pitcher who had moved to the Monarchs front office, was sitting next to the bus driver and spotted me. He got out of the bus, walked up behind me, tapped me on the shoulder and asked, how long would it take you to get your clothes and everything and get ready to be with the team when it leaves here tonight?'" Since Joe Greene hurt his finger, they had only Frank Duncan to catch and wanted Robinson. He joined the team.[113]

August 11, 1942: The Kingston Recs (of Kingston, New York) were to play this night, with Hilton Smith starting. Paige "has worked almost every day in the past few weeks," wrote the Poughkeepsie paper, but "may be seen in a relief role if the Recs blast Smith from the box."[114]

While the Monarchs were on the road, more than 4,100 turned out at Ruppert Stadium on August 9 to see the Birmingham Black Barons take two from the Ethiopian Clowns, 3-0 and 2-1.

August 13, 1942: Homestead Grays 3, Kansas City Monarchs 2 (12 innings), at Griffith Stadium, Washington

Paige pitched 12 innings against the Homestead Grays at Washington's Griffith Stadium before 26,000 spectators. The Monarchs scored once in the first, then saw the game get tied in the fourth. They took a 2-1 lead when Willard Brown homered to right field in the top of the sixth, but Buck Leonard of the Grays tied it in the bottom of the ninth. Paige faced a bases-loaded situation but escaped.

The Monarchs had eight hits; the Grays had seven. Right fielder David Whatley had three of the hits for the Grays, including the single in the bottom of the 12th that drove in Vic Harris with the winning run.[115]

August 16, 1942: The East-West Game was played in Chicago's Comiskey Park. The East beat the West (and Satchel Paige), 5-2. *(Also see East-West story on page 217.)*

August 16, 1942: Kansas City Monarchs 6, House of David 2, at Lakeside Park, Canton, Ohio.

While five of the Monarchs were in Chicago playing at the East-West Game, the rest of the Monarchs took on the House of David. Willard Brown, Joe Greene, Buck O'Neil, Satchel Paige, Hilton Smith, and Ted Strong were all at the East-West Game. Two Monarchs – Paige and Smith – were the two top vote-getters in fan balloting for the East-West Game.

Connie Johnson pitched the Monarchs game, allowing the House of David team one run (without a base hit) in the top of the first and one in the sixth, on a triple and double – the only two hits he allowed all night. The Monarchs quickly matched the opposition's first-inning run with one of their own. The game was tied after 5½ innings but the Monarchs then scored twice in the bottom of the sixth, and added one run each in the seventh and eighth.

Johnson also had two base hits in the game, as did Serrell, both of them singling and doubling. Robinson caught Johnson. Jack Matchett played right field. Frank Duncan played first base.[116]

> **MONARCHS TAKE 4-3 GAME IN 10TH INNING**
>
> *Repository*, Canton, Ohio, August 18, 1942

August 17, 1942: Kansas City Monarchs 4, House of David 3 (10 innings), at Lakeside Park, Canton, Ohio

Booker McDaniel pitched all 10 innings of the game at Canton, with two of his fellow pitchers behind him on the field. LaMarque played first base and Matchett was in right field again. There was a lot of hitting in the game, the Davids collecting 14 base hits and the Monarchs 15. Kansas City struck first, scoring once in the bottom of the first. The lead held until the fifth, when the House of David team tied it. In the sixth inning, the "bewhiskered" House of David team took a 3-1 lead. The Monarchs got one back in the seventh and tied the game in the eighth. Neither team scored in the ninth. A walk, an error, and a single (apparently by Matchett) won the game in the bottom of the 10th.[117]

August 21, 1942: Kansas City Monarchs 5, Cincinnati Ethiopian Clowns 1, at Crosley Field, Cincinnati

Heavy rains before the game depressed the crowd size but 5,000 were seated nonetheless. Three Kansas City pitchers each worked three innings: Smith, Johnson, and Paige. Three consecutive one-out singles in the bottom of the first gave Cincinnati its one run. Simms walked and stole second base in the Monarchs' first inning. Strong sacrificed him and Allen (who had drawn a base on balls), and Simms scored on Brown's long fly ball to center field. Brown singled in the fourth, an infield hit played by the catcher. Greene tripled him in and O'Neil singled to score Greene. They got two more runs in the fifth. Paige doubled to lead off. Sims walked and Allen singled, but Frank Duncan held Paige at third base. Strong popped up to the catcher, and it looked as though a double play would end the threat, but the shortstop's throw to first went wild and two runs scored. The game was enlivened when the Clowns pulled off the hidden-ball trick, catching Willard Brown off second.[118]

August 23, 1942: Kansas City Monarchs 4, Chicago American Giants 3 (first game, 14 innings), at Ruppert Stadium

The battle for the second half NAL championship was heating up with the Chicago American Giants starting to win a few games. Heavyweight boxing champion Joe Louis threw out the first pitch. Norris Phillips started the game for Kansas City, but had to leave with a foot injury after he singled in the third and then got into a rundown at first base. Booker McDaniel worked the rest of the game, which turned out to be an 11-inning relief stint. McDaniel allowed only three hits in those 11 innings. The Giants scored one run each in the first, second, and fifth innings. The Monarchs got one in the third and two in the sixth (on Ted Strong's two-run homer). Willie Ferrell went the distance for Chicago. It was pitcher McDaniel who got to him in the bottom of the 14th, driving a ball to the flagpole for a triple. Newt Allen came in to run for McDaniel and scored when Simms hit a drive that glanced off the shortstop's glove. Second baseman Bonnie Serrell had a three-hit game.

August 23, 1942: Kansas City Monarchs 6, Chicago American Giants 1 (second game, 7 innings), at Ruppert Stadium

The Giants got to Jack Matchett for one run in the top of the first, but that was the only run they managed all game, as Matchett threw a three-hitter. The Monarchs scored all six of their runs in the bottom of the third inning on a walk and six hits – all singles. They had eight hits in the game, including two apiece by O'Neil and Matchett.[119]

Plans were for the two teams to play a league game on August 24 in St. Joseph, and then return to Ruppert for a fifth game on the 25th.

August 24, 1942: Kansas City Monarchs 10, Chicago Giants 4, at City Stadium, St. Joseph, Missouri

The game was said to be the third game in a regularly-scheduled series of four, with the final game

• 1942 Kansas City Monarchs Timeline •

to be played back in Kansas City on August 25. This Monday night game produced the third win in a row for the Monarchs, all won by comfortable margins and this one by more than the prior two. About 2,500 fans came to the ballpark. The next day's St. Joseph newspaper said, "Kansas City had just too much power and finesse last night for Candy Taylors's Chicago entry. Cliff Johnson [Connie Johnson], the young Monarch speedballer, scattered nine hits and fanned 11 men, but was seldom called to bear down with his high, hard one."[120] Johnson pitched a complete game. Strong had a pair of doubles. Serrell hit a homer.

August 25, 1942: There was to have been a game with the Giants on August 25 in KC, but apparently weather prevented the game from being played.

August 27, 1942: Kansas City Monarchs 1, Ethiopian Clowns 0 (10 innings), at Swayne Field, Toledo

The 8:30 P.M. game was scoreless through a full nine innings, with more than 3,500 fans looking on. They'd seen Peanuts (Nyasses) Davis and Satchel Paige each pitch three innings, with Gread McKinnis and Jim LaMarque taking over from the fourth inning on. Paige had not allowed a hit; LaMarque allowed only three over the seven innings he worked. The *Toledo Times* explained how the winning run scored: "Jesse Williams opened the final frame with a double to the bleachers, but LaMarque and Simms fanned. Allen then delivered his hit [a single] down the right field line to send Williams across."[121]

August 28, 1942: Kansas City Monarchs 2, Fort Niagara Soldiers 1, at Offermann Stadium, Buffalo, New York

"Can Uncle Sam's soldiers beat the mighty Paige?" So asked a poster promoting the Friday night 8:30 P.M. game. Sgt. Jim Moody of Fort Niagara had been pitching extremely well, having won 22 consecutive games before a recent defeat; the soldier/pitcher's season record so far was 25-5. The game was a benefit for the Army Emergency Relief Fund. Servicemen were to be admitted free of charge. Satchel Paige – the "Joe Louis of Negro baseball" – was expected to pitch for the Monarchs.[122]

Before the game, Paige said, "There are more than enough Negro players in this country to make up an all-Negro big league baseball team. I offer this as a solution [to what he had called "a social problem"]: Give them a franchise in either major league and let them play as a team. I believe such a team would strengthen either league and be a big asset."[123]

The game drew 3,000. McDaniel pitched the first six innings for the Monarchs. He gave up one run in the bottom of the third when Moody led off with a single to left field, the ball falling in between two outfielders. He moved to second on a sacrifice, took third on an infield out, then scored on a single. In the top of the seventh, Joe Greene homered over the left-field wall to give the Monarchs a 2-1 lead. It was one of only three hits allowed by Moody, but it was the hit that won the game. The Fort Niagara Soldiers had seven hits. Paige pitched the final three innings, working his way out of a jam in the bottom of the ninth.[124]

August 30, 1942: Kansas City Monarchs 10, Philadelphia Stars 5, at Comiskey Park, Chicago

Some 10,000 fans flocked to Comiskey Park and saw Roy Partlow of the Homestead Grays throw a seven-inning no-hitter against the Chicago American Giants, winning 3-0 in the day's second game. The first game was never really in doubt. The Monarchs collected single runs in the first and third, and had four-

Old Fort Niagara

run innings in the fifth and seventh. Willard Brown and Ted Strong both homered. Brown's third-inning homer went into the upper deck of the left-center grandstand, reckoned at 480 feet. Strong's also went to left field, a two-run shot that went into the upper deck in left and was said to have gone 360 feet.

Matchett was the starting pitcher, giving way to Connie Johnson. The Stars scored one run in the sixth and four in the eighth, all the runs charged to Johnson, who pitched the sixth through the ninth. It was dubbed a "slow game which took two hours and 45 minutes to play."[125]

September 1, 1942: Kansas City Monarchs 10, Cincinnati Ethiopian Clowns 2, at Crosley Field, Cincinnati

The game was scoreless through the first four innings, with Peanuts (Nyasses) Davis pitching for the Clowns and Satchel Paige for the Monarchs. The Monarchs scored five times in the fifth and when they added a sixth run in the sixth, finally drove Nyasses from the game. He was replaced by Henry – possibly pitcher Preacher Henry. Paige wrapped up his work after the fifth inning "and was accorded a big ovation" by the 8,500 fans at Crosley Field before being replaced by LaMarque.[126] Frazier Robinson caught for the Monarchs.[127] Kansas City added three runs in the seventh and a 10th run in the eighth. The Clowns got two runs in the bottom of the ninth, thus avoiding being shut out.

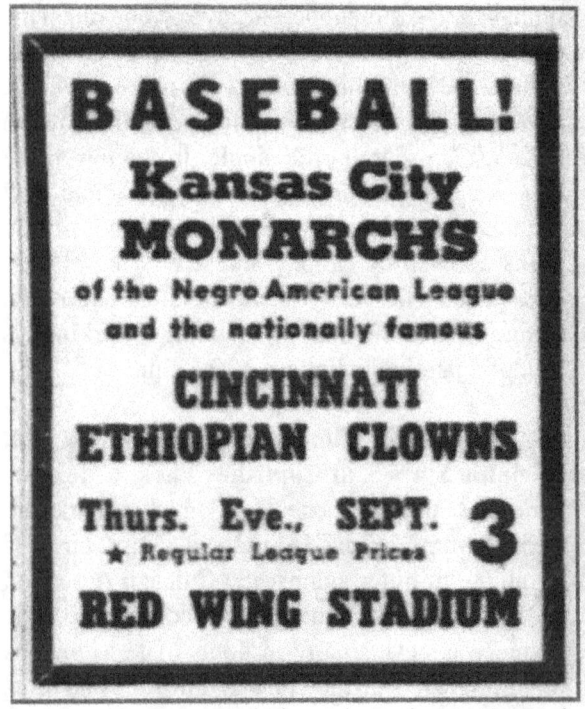

Democrat and Chronicle, Rochester, New York

September 2, 1942: Cincinnati Ethiopian Clowns 3, Kansas City Monarchs 2, at League Park, Akron, Ohio

The last time the Monarchs had lost a game was on August 13, nearly three weeks earlier. But they lost this 6 P.M. game before a "large crowd" in Akron. Connie Johnson pitched for the Monarchs. The *Cincinnati Enquirer* offered some game details: "The seven-hit hurling of Al (Kankol) Saylor and two home runs by Dave (Wahoo) Hoskins, the last one coming in the ninth to break a 2-all tie, featured the Clowns' play."[128] His first homer was over the left-field wall in the second inning; the other one went out to right field. Serrell had two doubles for the Monarchs.[129]

September 3, 1942: The Clowns/Monarchs game scheduled at Red Wing Stadium, Rochester, was canceled to weather.

September 4, 1942: There was a Clowns/Monarchs game scheduled in Flint, Michigan, on September 4, but nothing can be found to indicate whether the game was played.

September 6, 1942: Kansas City Monarchs 4, Cincinnati Ethiopian Clowns 3, at Wrigley Field, Chicago

Both games of a four-team doubleheader were suspenseful to the end. The first game saw the Birmingham Black Barons beat the Memphis Red Sox, 7-4, in 10 innings, the game won in the top of the 10th when, with two outs and the bases loaded, relief pitcher Ted Radcliffe singled to left, driving in two runs, with a third scoring when the ball was poorly fielded.

The Monarchs and Clowns game was resolved in the bottom of the ninth. The Clowns had scored single runs in the first, fourth, and sixth. The Monarchs had scored one in the second and two in the sixth. McDaniel pitched a complete game for Kansas City. Peanuts Nyasses had started for the Clowns; McKinnis (who had pitched for the Black Barons earlier in the year) took over in the seventh. In the ninth, Greene walked. He stole second and reached third on a bad throw from the catcher. O"Neil was intentionally walked, and then Serrell was, too. They were clearly hoping for anything but what they got – Jesse Williams hit a long fly ball into foul territory near the right-field seats. Instead of just letting the ball land foul and moving on to the next pitch, right fielder Khora (Fred Wilson) caught the ball and threw home but the relay had no chance and the winning run scored easily. The games were played before 7,000 fans.[130]

WORLD SERIES

Also see story on page 211, The 1942 Negro League World Series by Rich Puerzer for more complete details on each game.

The two teams – the Monarchs and Grays – were very evenly matched. They had split a preseason doubleheader on April 26, with the Monarchs winning the first game, 6-5 in 10 innings, and then losing the second, 10-7. They faced each other three times throughout the 1942 season and each one of the three games had gone into extra innings, with the Grays winning all three games:

June 18: Grays 2, Monarchs 1 (10 innings)
July 21: Grays 5, Monarch 4 (10 innings)
August 13: Grays 3, Monarchs 2 (12 innings)

September 8, 1942: Kansas City Monarchs 8, Homestead Grays 0, at Griffith Stadium (World Series Game One)

Paige (five innings) and Matchett (the final four innings) held the Grays to just two hits (both off Paige in the fourth inning) in Game One of the best-of-seven Negro World Series in front of 25,000 fans.

September 10, 1942: Kansas City Monarchs 8, Homestead Grays 4, at Forbes Field (World Series Game Two)

Each team had 11 hits, but all four extra-base hits were made by the Monarchs. Hilton Smith started, relieved by Paige after five with the Monarchs ahead, 2-0. Paige was hit for four runs in the bottom of the eighth but the Monarchs had scored three in the top of the eighth and so still held a 5-4 lead. They added three more in the top of the ninth to salt it away.

September 13, 1942: Kansas City Monarchs 9, Homestead Grays 3 (first game of day), at Yankee Stadium (World Series Game Three)

A large crowd of 25,000 saw Mayor Fiorello LaGuardia throw out the first pitch. The Grays got to Paige for two runs in the first inning. After a Simms grand slam in the top of the third gave the Monarchs the edge, Jack Matchett took over and allowed just one run while Kansas City added two runs in the fourth (Ted Strong homered) and three more in the fifth. Matchett had now allowed one run and four hits in 12 innings of relief.

September 13, 1942: Kansas City Monarchs 5, Homestead Grays 0 (second game of day), at Yankee Stadium

After Game Three was over, the two teams played a seven-inning exhibition game "which had no bearing on the Series."[131] The Monarchs won, 5-0.

EXHIBITION GAMES

The World Series paused to squeeze in a few exhibition games. The Grays traveled to Hartford, Connecticut, for a doubleheader on September 14 with the Newark Eagles, losing both games, 5-1 and 2-1.

On the 15th, they played the Philadelphia Stars, in Philadelphia, to a 5-5 12-inning tie.

And on September 16, they went to Bugle Field and played the Baltimore Elite Giants, losing 2-1. For this the game, they signed a few players from Newark (Leon Day, Lennie Pearson, and Ed Stone); they also added two of the Philadelphia Stars to their roster, Bus Clarkson and Edsall Walker.

[Exhibition game] September 15, 1942: Fort Niagara Soldiers 3, Kansas City Monarchs 1, at Offermann Stadium, Buffalo, New York

The rematch of the August 28 game drew a larger crowd, some 5,000 or so. John P. Walsh described the action: "Satchel Paige pitched the first three scoreless innings for the Monarchs, striking out six of the nine batters he faced. On the mound for the soldiers was Corporal Steve Peek. Peek, who pitched the entire game for the Fort, limited the Monarchs to four hits, striking out 10 batters along the way.

"The pitcher who replaced Paige on the mound for the Monarchs gave up two hits in the fourth inning. That along with two Monarch errors and a pair of wild pitches gave the soldiers a three-run lead. Peek gave up a solo home run in the seventh inning making the final score Fort Niagara 3 Kansas City 1."[132]

[Exhibition game] September 18, 1942: Kansas City Monarchs 2, Cincinnati Clowns 1 (13 innings), at Parkway Field, Louisville, Kentucky

While the Grays played these four exhibition games, without winning one, and bolstered their roster, the only game we know the Monarchs to have played in their six days off was in Louisville, where they played a Friday night exhibition game against the Cincinnati Clowns at Parkway Field. Lefty LaMarque went the distance – 13 innings – before the Monarchs won, 1-0. Slow Robinson was his batterymate.[133]

The Grays and Monarchs moved on to Kansas City to re-engage for the World Series.

September 20, 1942: Homestead Grays 4, Kansas City Monarchs 1, at Ruppert Stadium, Kansas City (World Series game, thrown out for use of ineligible players)

The Grays appeared to redeem themselves in front of 8,542, in what would have been Game Four – but the game was played under protest because of the Grays' use of four ineligible players, one of whom was starting pitcher (and future Hall of Famer) Leon Day. The other three "ringers" were Lennie Pearson (who scored two runs), Bus Clarkson at shortstop, and Ed Stone, who drove in two of the runs.[134] Cum Posey of the Homestead Grays told said co-owner Tom Baird of the Monarchs had agreed to allow them the replacement players since two players (Carlisle and Whatley) had been taken into the Army, Bankhead had broken his arm, and Partlow was suffering a case of boils under his pitching arm.[135]

After the game, William Dismukes said, "We didn't play the Homestead Grays. We lost to the National League All-Stars."[136] Kansas City's protest was upheld in a meeting the following days and the game did not count.

[Exhibition game] September 22, 1942: Birmingham Black Barons 5, Kansas City Monarchs 0 (seven innings), at City Stadium, St. Joseph, Missouri

Hilton Smith and Jack Matchett worked three innings apiece, each giving up one run. Connie Johnson, on furlough from the Army, pitched the seventh inning and was tagged for three runs. Since the Monarchs scored not once off Birmingham's Robert Keyes, the loss went to Smith.

[Exhibition game] September 24, 1942: Kansas City Monarchs 8, Central Missouri All-Stars 1, at Washington Park, Jefferson City, Missouri

No more information has yet been found about this "all negro baseball game" held on the night of the 24th.[137]

September 29, 1942: Kansas City Monarchs 9, Homestead Grays 5, at Shibe Park, Philadelphia (World Series Game Four)

The game planned for Wrigley Field in Chicago on the 27th was postponed one hour before game time due to cold weather and wet grounds, and rescheduled

Daily Times, Chicago, September 24, 1942

for the 29th in Philadelphia. Satchel Paige arrived just at game time; driving to the game from Pittsburgh, he had been arrested in Lancaster, Pennsylvania, and had to pay a fine.[138] Jack Matchett started but wasn't as strong in the unexpected start as he had been in relief; he was hit for three runs in the first and two more in the third, while the Monarchs scored just once in each of the same innings. Once Paige took the mound in the fourth, he pitched no-hit ball in 5⅓ innings while Monarchs batters banged in seven runs to win the game and the 1942 Negro World Series.

POSTSEASON GAMES

The two teams squared off in a pair of postseason games, misleadingly advertised in advance as "3 Official Negro World Series Games."[139] There were supposed to have been three, but the October 5 game in Newport News was rained out. Satchel Paige was the starting pitcher in both games that were played.

October 2, 1942: Homestead Grays 8, Kansas City Monarchs 5, at Tar Park, Norfolk, Virginia

The Monarchs were set to close out their season with a series of three games against the Homestead Grays in the Tidewater region of Virginia. The first game of the series was an 8:00 P.M. game in Norfolk. Satchel Paige pitched the first three innings, allowing one run. When he left, the score was 1-1. Connie Johnson came in and gave up three runs before getting an out, and was quickly yanked in favor of Jim LaMarque. The Grays scored one more off LaMarque in the fourth, added a pair in the first and an eighth run in the eighth. Ray Brown pitched for the Grays. The Monarchs scored their second run in the fifth and three more in their eighth, two of them on Joe Greene's home run over the left-field barrier.

• 1942 Kansas City Monarchs Timeline •

Norfolk, October 3, 1942 Display Ad

October 4, 1942: Kansas City Monarchs 12, Homestead Grays 2, at City Stadium, Portsmouth, Virginia

In a Sunday afternoon game at Portsmouth, Paige pitched again, this time facing Roy Partlow. The Grays took a 1-0 lead in the second, then saw the Monarchs edge ahead, 2-1, in the fourth. Paige turned the ball over to Hilton Smith after the inning, and Smith held the Grays to just one more run over the next five frames. Each team scored once in the sixth. It was 3-2 through seven but then Partlow weakened "and the clever Monarch batters began to reach him with a sensational flurry of hitting power." They scored five runs in the eighth inning, and four more runs in the top of the ninth, despite relief work by Ernie Carter. The Monarchs collected 17 hits to the Grays' five. Joe Greene and Willard Brown each had three hits.

There was to have been a game on the evening of Monday, October 5, in Newport News but rain began to fall at Builder's Stadium at around 5:30 and the game was canceled.[140]

...

Sam McKibben's November 13 column in the *Call* reported that Frank Duncan had passed his Army physical at Fort Leavenworth and was classified 1-A. A number of Kansas City businessmen gathered at a sporting-goods store and presented him a military "call-all" kit with his name engraved on it. It's too bad, he wrote, that the city couldn't have mounted a more fitting tribute "to a man who guided his team, the Monarchs, to the highest pinnacle in the Negro baseball world, the National championship. 'Tis bad because we might not have baseball next year, and for a few next years."[141]

Sources

Thanks to Gary Ashwill, Bill Ballou, Rick Bush, Bob Ellis, Brian M. Frank, Jan Johnson, Kevin Johnson, Ted Knorr, Cathy LaGrande, Jim Leeke, Doug Lehman, Larry Lester, Andrew Noe, David W. Pugh, Eric Robinson, Jason Scheller, Pete Stevens, Dave Wilkie, and Bill Young for assistance in proving information and locating newspaper accounts. Thanks as well to I.C. Murrell of the *Port Arthur News*; Linda Smith of the Portsmouth Public Library in Virginia; Troy Valos of the Sargeant Memorial Collection, Norfolk Public Library; Michael M. (no last name provided) of the New York State Library, Albany; and Kimberly Bunner, Parlin-Ingersoll Public Library, Canton, Illinois.

Notes

1 "K.C. Monarchs Will Prep at Monroe, La., for 1942 Race," *Pittsburgh Courier*, March 21, 1942: 16.

2 "Newt Allen Quits Kaycee," *Pittsburgh Courier*, April 4, 1942: 17.

3 R.S. Simmons, "Speaking of Baseball in General," *Weekly Review* (Birmingham, Alabama), April 17, 1942: 7. "Oneal" is, of course, Hall of Famer Buck O'Neil.

4 Fay Young, "The Stuff Is Here," *Chicago Defender*, January 3, 1942: 23. The following page had a lengthier article along with photographs of league officials. See "Bar League Clubs from Playing Clowns," *Chicago Defender*, January 3, 1942: 24.

5 "Monarchs and Barons, Here Friday, Two of Leading Colored Clubs," *Lima* (Ohio) *News*, June 25, 1942: 18.

• When the Monarchs Reigned •

6 "Remains with Kansas City," *Chicago Defender*, April 25, 1942: 20.

7 "Kansas City Allen Quits as Manager," *Chicago Defender*, April 4, 1942: 19.

8 "Kansas City Negroes Beat Cleveland, 11-1," *Houston Chronicle*, April 13, 1942: 8.

9 "Monarchs Win, 13-1," *Kansas City Call*, April 24, 1942.

10 "Bears Beaten by Monarchs," *Port Arthur* (Texas) *News*, April 15, 1942: 8.

11 "Monarchs Nip Bears by 10-9," *Port Arthur News*, April 16, 1942: 10.

12 "Monarchs in 19-9 Victory," *Port Arthur News*, April 17, 1942: 5.

13 "Negro Diamond Tilt Here Is Postponed," *Anniston* (Alabama) *Star*, April 19, 1942: 12.

14 "Kansas City Splits Even with Grays," *Chicago Defender*, May 9, 1942: 21.

15 "Monarchs, Grays All Even Before Overflow Crowd," *New Orleans Times-Picayune*, April 27, 1942: 14. See also "Monarchs Break Even," *Kansas City Times*, April 27, 1942: 11. The New Orleans paper says Paige had given up three runs; the Kansas City paper said he had given up one run through five innings.

16 "K.C. Club Fined $25 When Paige Refuses to Hurl," *Delta Democrat-Times* (Greenville, Mississippi), May 7, 1942: 6.

17 Romney Wheeler, "Sports Huddle," *Advocate* (Baton Rouge, Louisiana), May 14, 1942: 17.

18 "Monarchs Open Today," *Kansas City Star*, May 10, 1942: 19.

19 "American Giants Open Today Against Kansas City," *Chicago Tribune*, May 10, 1942: B4.

20 "Monarchs Take Doubleheader from Chicago in the American League Opener Sunday, 7-4; 6-0," *Kansas City Call*, May 15, 1942.

21 "Monarchs Take Doubleheader from Chicago in the American League Opener Sunday, 7-4, 6-0," *Kansas City Call*, May 15, 1942. See the April 12 game where a similar situation was reported.

22 "Memphis at Kansas City for Opener," *Chicago Defender*, May 16, 1942: 19.

23 "Monarchs Boosters Plan Biggest Opening Game Ceremony Ever," *Kansas City Call*, May 15, 1942.

24 William A. Young, *J.L. Wilkinson and the Kansas City Monarchs* (Jefferson, North Carolina: McFarland & Co., Inc., 2016), 125.

25 "Only 2 Monarch Hits," *Kansas City Star*, May 18, 1942: 9.

26 The attendance was about 10,000 more than the 19,198 at Comiskey Park to see a doubleheader between the major-league White Sox and the St. Louis Browns.

27 "Monarchs, Plus Paige, Beat Stars, Minus Feller, 3 to 1," *Chicago Tribune*, May 25, 1942: 19.

28 R.S. Simmons, "Satchel Paige, Monarchs Whip White Big Leaguers Before 30,000 in Chicago, 3 to 1," *Atlanta Daily World*, May 27, 1942: 5.

29 "Paige and Smith Tame Dizzy Dean's All-Stars," *Chicago Defender*, May 30, 1942: 19.

30 "Open Fight to Get Negroes in Major Leagues," *Chicago Defender*, May 30, 1942: 20.

31 Robert Phipps, "Alas, Good Old Days of Colorful Shows by Monarchs Are Gone," *Omaha World-Herald*, May 27, 1942: 21.

32 Phipps.

33 "Monarchs Rap Tommy Kelley for 11-3 Win," *Daily Nonpareil* (Council Bluffs, Iowa), May 27, 1942: 16.

34 Phipps.

35 "Redbirds' Game Halted by Rain; To Play Tonight," *Sioux City* (Iowa) *Journal*, May 28, 1942: 19.

36 "Monarchs Shut Out Redbirds," *Sioux City Journal*, May 28, 1942: 15.

37 "Two for the Monarchs," *Kansas City Star*, May 31, 1942: 15.

38 William A. Young, *J L. Wilkinson and the Kansas City Monarchs*, 126.

39 "Birmingham Barons Lose Doubleheader," *Kansas City Call*, June 5, 1942; "Birmingham Loses 2 to Kansas City," *Chicago Defender*, June 1, 1942: 20.

40 "Monarchs Go to Top," *Kansas City Times*, June 1, 1942: 12.

41 "22,000 See Satchel Paige Pitch in Washington," *Chicago Defender*, June 6, 1942: 20.

42 "Negro Nines Are Here for Game Monday," *Muskogee* (Oklahoma) *Daily Phoenix*, May 31, 1942.

43 "Monarchs Defeat Barons in Athletic Park Thriller," *Muskogee Times Democrat*, June 2, 1942: 8.

44 Kevin Johnson, email to author on April 6, 2021.

45 "Monarchs Win on Early Spree, 5-2," *Daily Oklahoman* (Oklahoma City), June 3, 1942: 16.

46 "Black Barons Win," *Fort Worth Star-Telegram*, June 4, 1942: 20.

47 "Black Barons Spill Monarch Nine, 6 to 2," *Dallas Morning News*, June 4, 1942: 14.

48 "Two Negro Teams Clash Tonight," *Town Talk* (Alexandria, Louisiana), June 4, 1942: 12.

49 "Kansas City and Birmingham Split," *Pittsburgh Courier*, June 13, 1942: 17.

50 "Satchel Paige, McDaniels Allow Frigidaire No Hits," *Journal Herald* (Dayton, Ohio), June 10, 1942: 9. See also, "'Satch' Paige and McDaniels in No-Hitter," *Dayton Daily News*, June 10, 1942.

51 "Elster's Nine to Play Custer Team; Paige Scheduled," *Grand Rapids Press*, June 11, 1942: 16.

52 "Sox vs. Barons," *Toledo Blade*, June 13, 1942.

53 Sam McKibben, "Sports Potpourri," *Kansas City Call*, June 12, 1942.

54 "Buckeyes in Split with Kansas City," *Chicago Defender*, June 20, 1942: 19.

55 "Cincy Buckeyes Split with Kay Cee Monarchs," *Pittsburgh Courier*, June 20, 1942: 17.

56 See "Satchel Paige Is Edged Here, 2-1," *Plain Dealer* (Cleveland), June 15, 1942: 18.

57 "Kansas City Winner, 6-4," *Youngstown* (Ohio) *Vindicator*, June 16, 1942: 11.

58 "Monarchs Win Again," *Atlanta Daily World*, June 20, 1942: 5.

59 "Giants Bow 6-1 to NAL Champions," *Afro-American* (Baltimore), June 20, 1942.

60 Eddie Gant, writing in the *Chicago Defender*, said that White major-league games had been unable to draw more than 10,000 for their games. See Eddie Gant, "I Cover the Eastern Front," *Chicago Defender*, June 27, 1942: 21. Cum Posey wrote that 4,000 fans had been turned away. Cum Posey, "Posey's Points," *Pittsburgh Courier*, June 27, 1942: 17.

61 "Two Runs in Tenth Wins for Grays as Paige, Partlow Star," *Pittsburgh Courier*, June 27, 1942: 16.

62 "28,000 Watch Grays Upset Monarchs, 2-1," *Washington Post*, June 19, 1942: 24. See also, "Grays Beat Monarchs and Paige in Tenth," *Chicago Defender*, June 27, 1942: 21.

63 "Game to Monarchs in 9th," *Kansas City Times*, June 23, 1942: 12.

64 Sam McKibben, "Sports Potpourri," *Kansas City Call*, June 26, 1942.

65 "K.C. Tops Memphis," *Chicago Defender*, July 4, 1942: 21.

66 Paul Pinckney, "Paige Yields 1 Hit in 5 Frames; Kay Cees Win," *Chicago Defender*, July 4, 1942: 21.

• 1942 Kansas City Monarchs Timeline •

67 This per an advertisement for the game on page 17 of the June 20 *Democrat and Chronicle* (Rochester). The same advertisement declared of Satchel Paige that "Countless expert and big league players rate him and [sic] the greatest pitcher of all time."

68 See, for instance, "Satchel Paige Here Tomorrow," *Buffalo Courier-Express*, June 24, 1942: 16.

69 "Black Barons Return Home, Play Memphis Double Bill Sunday," *Birmingham News*, June 27, 1942: 6.

70 "Kansas City Beats Barons in Negro Tilt," *Buffalo Courier-Express*, June 26, 1942: 21.

71 "Kansas City Beats Barons in Negro Tilt."

72 "Green's [sic] 2 Homers Steal Show from Paige in Stadium," *Buffalo Evening News*, June 26, 1942: 36.

73 "Barons Defeat Monarchs," *Lima News*, June 27, 1942: 6.

74 Letter to author from Mike Lackey, July 2, 2020.

75 "Kansas City Trims East Chicago, 2-1," *Chicago Defender*, July 4, 1942: 21.

76 "Kansas City Nips Chicago in Thirteenth," *Chicago Defender*, July 4, 1942: 20. The *Call* reported that the game had drawn 12,000.

77 "American Giants Defeat Kansas City Monarchs," *Canton* (Illinois) *Daily Ledger*, June 30, 1942: 7.

78 "Twin Monarch Triumph," *Kansas City Star*, July 3, 1942: 13.

79 "Monarchs to Play Memphis Negroes Here," *Daily Oklahoman*, July 5, 1942: 30.

80 "Memphis Red Sox Defeat Monarchs in Tenth Inning," *New Orleans Times-Picayune*, July 8, 1942: 14.

81 "Red Sox Prevail," *Memphis Commercial Appeal*, July 10, 1942: 15.

82 "Kansas City Monarchs Win Negro Tilt," *Wichita Falls* (Texas) *Record News*, July 11, 1942: 3.

83 "Opponents Blanked By Negro Pitcher," *Dallas Morning News*, July 13, 1942: 7.

84 "Ethiopian Clowns and House of David Clubs Rematched," *Rock Island* (Illinois) *Argus*, July 14, 1942: 10.

85 "Monarchs' Homers Jolt Memphis, 5-0," *Daily Oklahoman*, July 15, 1942: 34.

86 "Mathis Blanks Monarchs as Memphis Red Sox Take Game Here, 6 to 0," *Topeka Daily Capital*, July 16, 1942: 9.

87 "Monarchs Shut Out by Memphis," *Topeka State Journal*, July 16, 1942: 6.

88 "Johnson Bangs Long Wallop to Decide Contest," *St. Joseph* (Missouri) *Gazette*, July 17, 1942: 13.

89 The "classy" phrase comes from an advance story: "Monarchs Play Here Thursday," *St. Joseph Gazette*, July 15, 1942: 5.

90 "Monarchs Play Here Thursday."

91 C.E. McBride, "Sporting Comment," *Kansas City Star*, July 21, 1942: 10.

92 "An Ice Fund Game," *Kansas City Times*, July 17, 1942: 13.

93 See the game accounts: "Soldiers in Loss," *Kansas City Times*, July 18, 1942: 16, and "Close to No-Hit Game," *Kansas City Star*, July 18, 1942: 7. Cyrus was Herb Souell, who was the team's third baseman and also went by the name Herb Cyrus. See, for instance, his listing on Seamheads: http://www.seamheads.com/NegroLgs/player.php?playerID=souel01her

94 Sam McKibben, *Kansas City Call*, July 24 and 31, 1942.

95 Sam McKibben, *Kansas City Call*, July 31, 1942.

96 "Red Sox Prevail," *Memphis Commercial Appeal*, July 18, 1942: 10.

97 All the information regarding this game comes from one of the more detailed accounts of a 1942 Monarchs game, though the spellings of many names is confusing. See "Hose Leading When Error Costs 4 Runs," *News-Messenger* (Fremont, Ohio), July 24, 1942: 9.

98 "Giants Beaten 17 to 4; Meet Gary This Eve," *Times* (Munster, Indiana), July 26, 1942: 13. Someone named Evans was listed in the box score as playing third base.

99 "Kansas City Monarchs Conquer Chicago club," *Indianapolis Star*, July 28, 1942: 15.

100 "Monarchs to Play at Swayne Field," *Toledo Blade*, July 28, 1942.

101 "Monarchs Gain Easy 12-0 Win in Exhibition," *Toledo Times*, July 29, 1942.

102 "Syracuse Sports for Victory Council Will Share In Baseball Receipts," *Fayetteville* (New York) *Eagle Bulletin*, July 31, 1942: 11.

103 "Charles J. McPhail," *Syracuse Post Standard*, January 17, 2006.

104 Associated Press, "Many Negro Stars Ready for Majors," *Christian Science Monitor*, July 30, 1942: 9. See also Associated Negro Press, "White Owner of Kansas City Monarchs Is Eager to Eliminate Baseball Jim-Crow," *Atlanta Daily World*, August 2, 1942: 8. A number of major-league owners and players are quoted as well, including Larry MacPhail and Clark Griffith, neither of whose statements seemed welcoming. MacPhail had expressed that some Negro League club owners believed it would hurt them financially if major-league teams were to "raid their clubs for talent." See ANP, "Owner of Monarchs Okeys Big League Tryout," *Plaindealer* (Kansas City, Kansas), August 7, 1942: 34. During the World Series between the Monarchs and Homestead Grays, Dan Burley wrote a piece that concluded with several paragraphs suggesting that Benswanger's comments (and others by Gerry Nugent of the Phillies) had been trial balloons and that it was really MacPhail whose voice would count most. Dan Burley, "Negro World Series a Revelation," *New York Amsterdam Star-News*, September 19, 1942: 14. MacPhail clearly stated that there was no need to hold tryouts for Negro Leagues players. "They're ready and willing to go into the majors. Negroes should have the opportunity not only to play in the big leagues but should have a lot of other opportunities in employment, housing and other things." See "Monarchs vs. Brooklyn if 'Bums' Lose Pennant," *Chicago Defender*, September 26, 1942: 3. Burley also said the Brooklyn Dodgers would play the Kansas City Monarchs at Ebbets Field if the Dodgers failed to win the National League pennant. They did, in fact, fall short, but the promised matchup did not occur.

105 "Indifferent Paige Hooted by 2,316 Irked Stadium Guests for Brief, Late Appearance," *Scranton Tribune*, August 1, 1942: 11.

106 "Shoutouts for Monarchs," *Kansas City Times*, August 6, 1942: 13.

107 "Postpone Game Listed for Negro Teams Here," *Harrisburg Evening News*, August 3, 1942: 6.

108 "Paige Scorns Big League Career," *Albany Knickerbocker News*, August 6, 1982.

109 "Monarchs Win Easy One," *Kansas City Star*, August 7, 1942: 18.

110 John F. Houlihan, "2000 See Paige's Team Blank Locals, 3-2," *Worcester Telegram*, August 8, 1942: 10.

111 Bill Lee, "With Malice Toward None," *Hartford Courant*, August 8, 1942: 9.

112 William Newell, "Paige Hurls Five Frames as Monarchs Win Twice," *Hartford Courant*, August 11, 1942: 11.

113 Frazier "Slow" Robinson, *Catching Dreams* (Syracuse, New York: Syracuse University Press, 1999), 80, 83.

114 "Paige Heads Negro Club Against Recs at Kingston," *Eagle-News* (Poughkeepsie, New York), August 10, 1942: 8. SABR member Bill Hoynes searched both the *Poughkeepsie Journal* and the *Kingston Daily Freeman* but found no indication the game was played.

115 Ed Lawson, "20,000 See 'Satch's' Team Lose in 12th," *Washington Post*, August 14, 1942: 22.

116 "Monarchs Win Over House of David 6-2," *Canton* (Ohio) *Repository*, August 17, 1942: 10.

117 "Monarchs Take 4-3 Game in 10th Inning," *Canton Repository*, August 18, 1942: 17.

118 "Kansas City Wins 5 to 1 from Clowns," *Chicago Defender*, August 29, 1942: 21.

119 "To Monarchs in 14th," *Kansas City Times*, August 24, 1942: 9.

120 "Monarchs Beat Giants Before Record Crowd," *St. Joseph (Missouri) News-Press/Gazette*, August 25, 1942: 5.

121 "Monarchs Beat Clowns, 1 to 0," *Toledo Times*, August 28, 1942.

122 "Paige's Name Makes Baseball Turnstiles Click," *Buffalo Evening News*, August 27, 1942: 28.

123 "All Negro Team for Majors Suggested by Satchel Paige," *Buffalo Evening News*, August 28, 1942: 35.

124 "Monarchs Beat Fort Niagara by 2-1 Margin," *Buffalo Courier-Express*, August 29, 1942: 18.

125 "Kansas City Monarchs Down Philadelphia Stars," *Chicago Defender*, September 5, 1942: 22, 24.

126 "Clowns Downed, 10-2," *Cincinnati Enquirer*, September 2, 1942: 20.

127 Frazier "Slow" Robinson was a backup catcher to Joe Greene. Buck O'Neil said of Robinson's time on the 1942 Monarchs, "'Slow' had good, quick hands and a strong, accurate arm as a catcher. A quick compact swing with average power as a hitter. Joe Greene was our starting catcher, and I felt that 'Slow' had too much to offer as second string. Therefore, I was very pleased when he went to the Elites." Buck O'Neil, in Frazier "Slow" Robinson, *Catching Dreams*, xi.

128 "Clowns Beat Monarchs," *Cincinnati Enquirer*, September 3, 1942: 17.

129 "Wahoo's Homers Upset Monarchs," *Akron Beacon Journal*, September 3, 1942.

130 "Birmingham Beats Memphis in Tenth, 7 to 3," *Chicago Defender*, September 12, 1942: 23.

131 "Monarchs Make It Three," *Kansas City Times*, September 14, 1942: 11. See also, "25,000 See Monarchs Defeat Grays, 9 to 3," *New York Times*, September 14, 1942: 21.

132 John P. Walsh, "Fort Niagara Baseball and Satchel Paige," *Old Fort Niagara*, April 2021. https://www.oldfortniagara.org/featured-article. Accessed May 10, 2021.

133 "Clowns in Midst of Long Playing Tour," *Jackson* (Mississippi) *Advocate,* October 3, 1942: 6.

134 The words "borrowed help" and "ringers" were both used in "Monarchs Lose Here," *Kansas City Times*, September 21, 1942: 8. Owner J.L. Wilkinson of the Monarchs offered the Grays a choice between calling off the Series or playing a fourth game, without the "borrowed" players. Representing the Grays, manager Vic Harris opted to play on. Because the final Game Four was played at Shibe Park, fans in Kansas City who might have exulted in seeing their team sweep the Grays at home were reduced to reading the final results in the newspaper. (There was, of course, no television at the time.)

135 "Grays Win, 4 to 1; Monarchs Protest," *Pittsburgh Courier*, September 26, 1942: 16.

136 "K.C. Monarchs Win Protest," *The Sporting News*, October 1, 1942: 8.

137 "Monarchs Win," *Daily Capital News* (Jefferson City, Missouri), September 25, 1942: 11.

138 Paige details the story in Leroy (Satchel) Paige, *Maybe I'll Pitch Forever* (Lincoln: University of Nebraska Press, 1993), 146-8.

139 See advertisement in *Journal and Guide* (Norfolk, Virginia), October 3, 1942: A14.

140 Details of the two postseason games come from "Grays, Monarchs Split Two Games in Tidewater," *Norfolk Journal and Guide*, October 10, 1942: 14.

141 Sam McKibben, "Sports Potpourri," *Kansas City Call*, November 13, 1942.

Monarchs vs. Dizzy Dean All-Stars

May 24, 1942: Kansas City Monarchs 3, Dizzy Dean All-Stars 1, at Wrigley Field, Chicago

By Tony S. Oliver

On this crisp afternoon, the sky was a vivid blue, the grass and ivy were a radiant green, and the infield dirt was a golden brown. One color, though, was making its debut at Wrigley Field. For the first time, a Black baseball team would play in the famous ballpark, a hallmark of racially segregated north Chicago. Its southern cousin, Comiskey Park, venue for the Chicago American Giants, had previously hosted the Negro League East-West All-Star games and other Black-White contests.

With many big leaguers swapping their wool uniforms for Army fatigues, White owners felt exhibition games would draw a big crowd, regardless of the race. Against this backdrop, 29,775 souls packed box seats, grandstands, and bleachers to see two living legends, Satchel Paige and Dizzy Dean. The nation had been at war for only half a year but any opportunity to disconnect from the event, if only for a few hours, was a welcome respite for its citizens.

Modern fans regard exhibition games as anachronisms. We are privy to spring training, where teams try new players and get their expected starters into playing shape. They are not meaningless but rather necessary exercises, like a cardio session before serious weight-lifting. The Harlem Globetrotters and their hapless rivals, the Washington Generals, typically play in front of sparse modern crowds as the present-day NBA, with its interminable playoff contests, captures the attention of the basketball fans. But back in the pre-television era, Dean and Paige traveled south, west, or any other direction where the weather was hospitable enough to don their uniforms, entertain crowds, and fatten their pockets.

The two had first locked horns on October 16, 1933, with phenomenal success at the ticket office to ensure various sequels. Others followed, with a 1934 dress rehearsal, not in the Midwest but rather in the facsimile Wrigley Field of Hollywood, California, pitting the two aces as part of the Dizzy and Daffy Dean Barnstorming Tour. Dizzy's arm injury ended the partnership, which was then transferred to Bob Feller. On May 23, 1942, the *New York Times* failed to note the history, with the fifth and last sentence of its story meekly noting that the Dean All-Stars would face the Monarchs.[1]

Fans expecting to see Feller – arguably the best hurler in the majors at the time – were disappointed when the Army canceled his previously granted leave. While the military decision was final, many wondered whether a dislike for such Black-White competition from Commissioner Kenesaw Mountain Landis was to blame. A major leaguer by age 17, an All-Star at 19, a 20-game winner by 20, and possessing 100 career victories by 22, Feller was among the first professional athletes to enlist in the armed forces after the attack on Pearl Harbor. His promise to donate his appearance fee for this game to the Navy Relief Fund had earned accolades; his willingness to appear against Paige ensured that the integrated crowd would be treated to a spectacle.

Playing as the visitors, the Monarchs rode not just Paige's strong arm but also his experience. He did not seek to mow down every opponent but instead sought to "pitch to the batter's weakness."[2] Across the diamond, Dean pitched one flawless inning before yielding to Johnny Grodzicki, who had debuted with the Cardinals in 1941 and compiled a 1.35 ERA in five games. While stationed at Fort Knox for training, Grodzicki participated in various exhibition games before being deployed to Europe. Wounded in Germany in 1945, he won a Purple Heart for his service and returned to the majors a year later.[3]

After retiring the big leaguers with ease in the first two frames, Paige allowed an unearned run in the third. A slow roller by former Yankee, Dodger, and St. Louis Brown Joe Gallagher yielded the first baserunner; he advanced to third on Grodzicki's bunt when Buck O'Neil uncharacteristically did not cover the base on time. Emmett "Heinie" Mueller knocked in Gallagher with a groundball to put the All-Stars on top. Both Gallagher, who was drafted into service in 1941, and Mueller, who joined in 1942 served in Jefferson Barracks, Missouri.[4] Neither one would return to the big leagues after the war.

SATCHEL PAIGE, MONARCHS WHIP WHITE BIG LEAGUERS BEFORE 30,000 IN CHICAGO, 3-1

Atlanta Daily World, May 27, 1942

In the fourth, Herb Cyrus (aka Herb Souell and Baldy), a capable third baseman who appeared in several Negro League All-Star games by the decade's end, was driven in by slugger Willard Brown. Brown, a multiple all-star in the Negro Leagues and future record-holder of many Puerto Rican Winter League records (where he is still known as "ese hombre" or "that man"), also served in the European Theater prior to the war's end.[5] His brief, unsuccessful major-league career did not taint his overall credentials, and he was belatedly inducted into Cooperstown in 2006.

No further excitement ensued until the Monarchs' James Joe Greene (a.k.a. Pea, Pig, and Green) doubled with two outs in the sixth. Greene, a power-hitting catcher through most of the 1940s, served in Italy; his regiment was tasked with procuring the body of fallen Italian ruler Benito Mussolini after the despot's execution by partisans.[6] Paige, having given his team – and more importantly, the paying public – six strong innings, was lifted for Hilton Smith. Smith, a right-handed hurler, often relieved Paige in such exhibitions, but was himself a commanding presence on the mound, earning induction into the National Baseball Hall of Fame in 2001.

Al Piechota, the third pitcher for the All-Stars, allowed a single to speedster Willie "Bill" Simms, who reached third after a bunt and a fly ball. Piechota played in the majors in 1940 and 1941 before serving in the military while stationed at Michigan and Indiana bases. With two outs, Brown walked and stole second before Greene drove in both runners with a line-drive double, adding both the winning and insurance runs.

While the African American press front pages lauded the Monarchs' victory, crafting detailed columns on the game's play and atmosphere, the White newspapers provided the bare minimum. If history is written by the winners, no one bothered to tell the mainstream media.

The *New York Times* mentioned the attendance and named a dozen of Dean's teammates; from the Monarchs, only Paige was noted.[7] *The Sporting News* literally buried the story, giving it one-sixteenth of a page, including the box score.[8] The weekly was far from impartial, as its opposition to integration was well-known. In 1945 it gave Yankees President Larry MacPhail the opportunity to discuss his stance, as requested by New York City Mayor Fiorello LaGuardia. In a half-page op-ed, McPhail fulminated, "there is not a single Negro player with major league possibilities in 1946."[9] Echoing the decades-old unwritten rule, he concluded, "I have no consistency in saying the Yankees have no intention of signing Negro" by arguing that "the Negro Leagues cannot exist without good players."[10] Roughly two weeks later, under a condescending editorial, it observed that "(Jackie) Robinson, at 26, is reported to possess baseball abilities which, were he white, would make him eligible for a trial with, let us say, the Brooklyn Dodgers' Class B farm at Newport News, if he were six years younger." Despite being the nation's undisputed sports journal, it had somehow failed to notice Robinson's torrid performance with the Kansas City Monarchs, given his .414 batting average in 63 plate appearances. His .349 mark with Montreal of the International League in his sole minor-league campaign would further demonstrate the absurdity of the statement.[11]

Perhaps it was consolation to see the dark ink printed on the pale newspaper stock, symbolizing the superiority of the Monarchs.

The weekly *Baltimore Afro-American* published an in-depth account of the game, saying it was "one of the most exciting contests held at the Clubs' [sic] park for some time," and adding, "People came from far and near, including Atlanta, to watch the contest."[12] The newspaper was also eager to publicize the repeat engagement, scheduled for May 31, pitting the Dean All-Stars against the Homestead Grays in Washington, DC.

Despite consistent efforts by the Black press to cajole the big leagues to integrate, the commissioner, team owners, civic leaders, and even prominent players managed to stifle progress. Baseball fans eager to see the best athletes on the field, regardless of race, were left with barnstorming competitions to quench their thirst until 1947. Instead, such events whetted their appetite by expanding the "what ifs" into reality. The *Chicago Defender's* account sought to further the argument, stating, "[T]he crowd was there to see Paige tame the major leaguers … and that's what happened … and no one could blame them. There were their own boys, playing on big league grounds, performing in big league style – yet these same players are denied the right to earn a good living at their profession."[13]

Opinion writer Fay Young juxtaposed the quality of the product, acerbically writing that "the White Sox were taking a 14 to 0 licking in one game of the double header at Comiskey Park" and "brown American fans are baseball hungry but are sick of paying their hard-earned money to see second rate performers." [14]

After the game, Dean returned to the broadcast booth, covering games for both St. Louis franchises before appearing in one final big-league contest on September 28, 1947. After stating that he could pitch better than the Browns' sorry staff, he backed up his claim by tossing four innings without allowing a run. Feller earned eight battle stars for his military service before returning to the majors in late 1945. Paige eventually made it to the big leagues, joining Feller on the 1948 World Series champion Cleveland Indians. All three were selected to the National Baseball Hall of Fame.

Acknowledgment

Josh Mabe, newspaper librarian for the Harold Washington Library, Chicago, for providing the *Chicago Defender* articles.

Notes

1 "Dizzy Dean Pitches Today," *New York Times*, May 24, 1942: S3.

2 "Paige and Smith Tame Dizzy Dean's All-Stars," *Chicago Defender*, May 30, 1942: 19.

3 Gary Bedingfield, "Baseball's Greatest Sacrifice," baseballsgreatestsacrifice.com/wounded_in_combat/grodzicki-johnny.html.

4 "Baseball's Greatest Sacrifice," baseballinwartime.com/player_biographies/gallagher_joe.htm; baseballsgreatestsacrifice.com/wounded_in_combat/mueller-heinie.html.

5 "Baseball's Greatest Sacrifice," baseballinwartime.com/player_biographies/brown_willard.htm.

6 James A. Riley, *The Biographical Encyclopedia of the Negro Baseball Leagues* (New York: Carroll and Graf Publishers, 1984), 337-8; Gary Bedingfield, "Baseball's Greatest Sacrifice," baseballinwartime.com/negro.htm.

7 "Paige's Team Tops Dean's All-Stars," *New York Times*, May 25, 1942: 19.

8 "Dean's Service Team Loses," *The Sporting News*, May 28, 1942: 15.

9 Larry MacPhail, "MacPhail for Sound Plan to Qualify Negroes in O.B.," *The Sporting News*, October 4, 1945: 14.

10 "MacPhail for Sound Plan to Qualify Negroes in O.B."

11 "Montreal Puts Negro Player on Spot," *The Sporting News*, November 1, 1945: 12.

12 R.S. Simons, "Satchel Allows All-Stars Only 2 Hits in 6 Innings," *Baltimore AfroAmerican*, May 30, 1942: 27.

13 "Paige and Smith Tame Dizzy Dean's All-Stars."

14 Fay Young, "Through the Years," *The Chicago Defender*, May 30, 1942: 19.

Paige Garners Victory on Day in his Honor

July 26, 1942: Kansas City Monarchs 4, Memphis Red Sox 2, second (seven-inning) game of a doubleheader, at Wrigley Field, Chicago

By Frederick C. Bush

Negro League historian James A. Riley wrote about Satchel Paige, "A mixture of fact and embellishment, Satchel's stories are legion and form a rich array of often-repeated folklore."[1] There is truth in the assertion that a lot of myth-making has been involved in constructing Paige's life story; however, as Riley also noted, "The stories are endless. But the facts are also impressive."[2] Such was the case on the occasion of Satchel Paige Day at Chicago's Wrigley Field on Sunday, July 26, 1942. Kansas City Monarchs co-owner J.L. Wilkinson, ace promoter Abe Saperstein of Harlem Globetrotters fame, and the *Chicago Defender* set a propaganda machine in motion to promote the first-ever day to be held in Paige's honor.[3]

By 1942 Paige was already a living legend among Negro League players and fans. The *Defender* noted that Paige had long "been coming to Chicago thrilling the fans with his hurling feats. He has pitched in charity games benefitting hospitals, boys' clubs and other fine causes."[4] Thus, as the newspaper asserted, "his admirers ... feel it is about time that he be the recipient of a day in his honor."[5] Wilkinson and Saperstein considered Wrigley Field to be the ideal venue, and they scheduled the Memphis Red Sox, the Monarchs' Negro American League rivals, as the opponent for the day's doubleheader. In addition to the accolades and gifts to be showered upon Paige between games, the nightcap was to be a "revenge game" between Paige and Memphis hurler Verdell "Lefty" Mathis.[6]

Mathis was having a breakout season and had prevailed against Paige twice already in the 1942 season. On May 17 he had triumphed, 4-1, in the second game of a doubleheader on Opening Day at Kansas City's Ruppert Stadium. Mathis had held the Monarchs to two hits in the seven-inning game, while the *Defender* had described the contest as "a nightmare for Satchel Paige," who surrendered 10 hits and six walks.[7] Then, on July 7, at Pelican Stadium in New Orleans, Mathis again won, 1-0, in 10 innings.[8] There was a caveat to this second game, however, in that Paige pitched only the first five innings for Kansas City, allowing three hits. Connie Johnson pitched the final five frames for the Monarchs and was the losing pitcher. Nevertheless, most newspaper articles invariably stated that Mathis had defeated Paige twice. Thus, the idea of a grudge rematch had been conceived.

As it turned out, Paige and Mathis opposed each other again just five days later at Rebel Stadium in Dallas, Texas. In the first game of a July 12 doubleheader which – for reasons unknown – was also shortened to seven innings, Paige showed his mettle. He went the distance in an 11-0 shutout, and "proved he could do more than just pitch by banging out a double and two singles in four times at bat."[9]

Paige's dominance in Dallas almost scuttled Wilkinson and Saperstein's "revenge" hype machine, but the *Defender* conveniently ignored that game as it helped to promote the Wrigley Field matchup for all it was worth. In its July 25 edition, the *Defender* ran a preview article for the next day's doubleheader that contained quotes from both pitchers. Mathis had idolized Paige as a young boy, so it is unlikely that he truly held any rancor toward the Monarchs' hurler, but he dutifully played along by stating, "I beat him before and I'll beat him again ... and I'll beat him Sunday."[10] Paige, who was never shy about boasting, replied, "Bring on Mathis. ... I've beaten better pitchers than he is and I'll be ready for him Sunday."[11]

When the big day finally arrived, 20,000 fans were in attendance at Wrigley Field. It is a certainty that none of them were there out of great interest in the first game, in which Memphis pitcher Porter "Ankleball" Moss earned the win as the Red Sox clipped the Monarchs and future Hall of Famer Hilton Smith, 10-4.[12] One event that had attracted so many spectators took place between games as Paige was feted by the *Defender*. Standing at home plate, Paige received a huge ovation and was presented with a basket of flowers and an Elgin gold watch from the newspaper in addition to a radio, clothing, and other items that

• Paige Garners Victory on Day in his Honor •

Chicago Tribune, July 20, 1942

were given by various businesses and organizations. Mathis, the other half of the day's feature attraction, received a traveling bag from his team.[13]

Paige received his second ovation of the day when he took the mound in the top of the first inning of the nightcap, which was the game most fans had come to see.[14] The cliché that "it's not bragging if you can back it up" can undoubtedly be applied to Paige, and his fourth matchup against Mathis provided another instance in which he demonstrated his knack for rising to the top on a major occasion.

Paige set the Red Sox batters down in order in the first two innings. Memphis had traffic on the basepaths in the third inning but to no avail. Paige walked leadoff batter Tom "T.J." Brown, but catcher Frank Duncan gunned him down as he attempted to steal second. After that, Memphis catcher Larry Brown reached first safely on Newt Allen's error at third base, but Paige picked him off first and then struck out Mathis to retire the side.

Mathis kept pace with Paige for the first two innings, though he was aided greatly by third baseman Marlin Carter's unassisted double play that got him out of a second-inning jam in which he had runners on second and third with only one out. Paige's determination to win on his day came to the fore when he singled to lead off the bottom of the third. He advanced to second on Willie Simms's sacrifice, made it to third on a single by Allen, and crossed home plate on Ted Strong's fly to center. Mathis induced a grounder from Willard Brown to end the inning, but he now trailed Paige and the Monarchs.

While Paige continued to cruise, the Monarchs added to their lead in the next two innings. In the bottom of the fourth, Jesse Williams hit a one-out single, advanced to third on Bonnie Serrell's base hit to right field, and scored on a sacrifice fly by Duncan. Then, in the sixth, Mathis walked the first two batters, Allen and Strong, and surrendered consecutive singles to Brown and Buck O'Neil that resulted in a 4-0 deficit.

For six innings, Paige had allowed the Red Sox only three hits and had kept them off the scoreboard. However, Memphis mounted a late challenge that caused the *Atlanta Daily World* to lament that Paige "would probably have had a shutout had there not been an error behind him in the seventh."[15] Carter singled to lead off the inning, and the next batter, Olan "Jelly" Taylor, was safe when Allen airmailed his throw from third base on Taylor's grounder. Allen's throw was so wild that Carter scored and Taylor got to third. Subby Byas pinch-hit for Tom Brown and grounded out to O'Neil at first, but Taylor scored as O'Neil opted not to try for a play at home plate. After that last bit of excitement, Paige got the final out to preserve a 4-2 triumph.

Although Memphis had been able to throw a minor scare into the Monarchs at the end of the game, it had seemed a foregone conclusion that there was no way

Paige was going to lose a game on a day held in his honor. Whether it involved winning a championship for a foreign dictator, calling in the outfield while he struck out the side, or walking the bases loaded so that he could face Josh Gibson – the most-feared batter in the Negro Leagues – and then strike him out, the lanky Paige always came out on top when the spotlight shined brightest on him.

Sources

The play-by-play account of the game was adapted from the following article:

"Chicago Fans Honor Satchel Paige Who Wins 4-2," *Chicago Defender*, August 1, 1942: 19.

Notes

1 James A. Riley, *The Biographical Encyclopedia of the Negro Baseball Leagues* (New York: Carroll & Graf Publishers, Inc., 1994), 598.

2 Riley, 598.

3 Mark Ribowsky, *Don't Look Back: Satchel Paige in the Shadows of Baseball* (New York: Simon & Schuster, 1994), 209.

4 "Chicago to Honor Satchel Paige Sunday/Paige Will Face Lefty Mathis and Memphis at Wrigley Field July 26," *Chicago Defender*, July 25, 1942: 19.

5 "Chicago to Honor Satchel Paige Sunday."

6 "Paige Faces Mathis in Revenge Game at Cub's [sic] Park, Sunday, July 26," *Chicago Defender*, July 18, 1942: 20.

7 "Kansas City Splits Even with Memphis," *Chicago Defender*, May 23, 1942: 20.

8 "Memphis Red Sox Defeat Monarchs in Tenth Inning," *New Orleans Times-Picayune*, July 8, 1942: 14.

9 "Opponents Blanked by Negro Pitcher," *Dallas Morning News*, July 13, 1942: 7. Although this game took place two weeks before the Paige-Mathis duel at Wrigley Field, it was reported only in the local press; not only the *Defender*, but all other newspapers failed to mention the game in preview articles about the Satchel Paige Day matchup between the two hurlers. However, Mathis still recalled it decades later, saying, "I remember in Dallas one Sunday it was awful hot. Satchel beat me down there." See John B. Holway, *Black Diamonds: Life in the Negro Leagues from the Men Who Lived It* (New York: Stadium Books, 1991), 148.

10 "Chicago to Honor Satchel Paige Sunday."

11 "Chicago to Honor Satchel Paige Sunday."

12 The *Chicago Defender* gave the attendance as 18,000 in its August 1 article about Satchel Paige Day, but all other newspapers, including the *Chicago Tribune* (July 27), *Chicago Times* (July 27), and *Atlanta Daily World* (August 1), reported the attendance as 20,000.

13 "Chicago Fans Honor Satchel Paige Who Wins 4-2," *Chicago Defender*, August 1, 1942: 19; "Kansas City and Memphis Divide Paige Day Games," *Chicago Tribune*, July 27, 1942: 17.

14 The game was scheduled to go seven innings, as was the case with the second games of all Negro League doubleheaders.

15 "Satchel Paige Thrills Crowd in Chicago Tilt," *Atlanta Daily World*, August 1, 1942: 5.

East Team Sweeps Comiskey Classic and Cleveland Benefit Games

By Frederick C. Bush

August 16, 1942: East 5, West 2, at Comiskey Park, Chicago

As the 10th annual East-West All-Star Game at Chicago's Comiskey Park approached, the Black press was abuzz with the expectation that Negro League players might finally have the opportunity to break into the major leagues. This hope stemmed from Commissioner Kenesaw Mountain Landis's July statement in which he had declared, "There is no rule in organized baseball prohibiting [Blacks'] participation and never has been to my knowledge."[1] Soon after, the *Chicago Defender* reported a rumor that second baseman Sammy Hughes, catcher Roy Campanella, and pitcher Dave "Impo" Barnhill were to have a tryout with the Pittsburgh Pirates on August 4. The *Defender* also claimed, "[S]everal big league scouts will be on hand Sunday, August 16, to take a good look at our boys in action."[2]

The Pittsburgh tryouts never came to pass, which revealed the disingenuousness of Landis's statement as well as the true sentiments of Organized Baseball's owners. White baseball's color line had reared its ugly head again, and the Black press made no mention of any scouts attending Comiskey Park in postgame articles either.

Nonetheless, the Chicago game had become the highlight of every Negro League season, and upward of 50,000 fans were expected to attend in 1942.[3] What those fans, who came from all over the country, did not know was that the eagerly anticipated game almost did not come to pass. The *Pittsburgh Courier* later reported that on the eve of the game, "The money question was the bugaboo that sent the western squad into a huddle from which emanated the ultimatum that unless their ante was raised[,] they refused to play the game."[4] The East team was also unhappy, but manager Vic Harris caught wind of his players' clandestine grievance session and stepped into the proceedings. According to the *Courier*, "After Vic had belched his little woof[,] the easterners rescinded their plot of revolt, and the westerners agreed to a compromise."[5]

There were additional snags on game day. Although a crowd of 48,179 (45,179 paid) filed into Comiskey, that number fell short of the previous year's record of 50,256.[6] Attendance might have been greater had it not been for the fact that "in some mix-up not enough [tickets] were printed. Consequently, over 5,000 fans milled in 35th Street on Shields Avenue and on 34th Street trying vainly to buy their way in."[7] The excess throng resulted in "traffic outside the park [being] so heavy that Satchel Paige was unable to get to the dressing room until the game was well on its way."[8] Paige had been scheduled to start for the West opposite Leon Day for the East, but the traffic delay resulted in both hurlers being saved until the seventh inning.

On top of the chaos outside the ballpark, there was one last issue to be settled inside as "[p]regame matters among the umpires for the game also went awry. Three of the four arbiters came equipped to work behind the plate, each evidently intent on being the head-man of the extravaganza."[9] This problem, too, was solved and it was time to play ball.

Hilton Smith stepped into the host West team's starting slot in place of Paige while Jonas Gaines took the mound first for the East. Both hurlers put up zeros on the scoreboard in the first two innings before each surrendered a run in the third. The East got to Smith when Dan Wilson of the New York Black Yankees "dropped a Texas leaguer into left center that was good for two bases" and Sam Bankhead followed with an RBI double.[10]

The West scored its tally in the bottom of the third primarily because of two uncharacteristic errors by the East's third baseman, Andrew "Pat" Patterson. Smith hit an easy one-out grounder to third, but Patterson's wild throw to first allowed him to take second; Fred Bankhead (Sam's brother) ran for Smith. James "Cool Papa" Bell hit a grounder that East shortstop Willie Wells fielded and threw to Patterson to cut down Bankhead at third; however, Patterson dropped the ball, Bankhead hustled back to second, and the West had two men on with one out. Parnell Woods hit a potential double-play grounder to Sam Bankhead at second, but he was unable to throw out Woods at first and Fred Bankhead scored for a 1-1 tie. Gaines escaped further trouble and the affair remained knotted through the fourth.

In the top of the fifth, Wilson drew a leadoff walk from Porter Moss and stole second. After a fly out by Wells, slugger Josh Gibson laced a single through the hole at shortstop that drove in Wilson for the second East run of the day. The West came back in the bottom of the sixth. Woods started things off with a triple and scored three batters later via Joe Greene's slow-rolling fielder's-choice grounder to Sam Bankhead.

In the top of the seventh, the player everyone wanted to see – Leroy "Satchel" Paige – finally strode to the mound for the West. Newark's Len Pearson lofted a fly that fell for a double when right fielder Ted Strong lost the ball in the sun. Wilson, making a case as the game's unofficial MVP, beat out a bunt for a hit and advanced Pearson to third. Sam Bankhead's fly ball plated Pearson for a 3-2 East lead. Wells singled and pulled off a double steal with Wilson, after which Paige intentionally walked his old batterymate Gibson. The gamble paid off when Bill Wright grounded into an inning-ending double play.

Southpaw Barney Brown took the mound for the East in the bottom of the seventh but was pulled when he allowed two-out singles to Paige and Bell. Day entered the game and quelled the nascent West uprising by retiring pinch-hitter Marlin Carter, who was batting for Woods. After a scoreless eighth inning, the East's man of the hour again found himself in the middle of the action.

Wilson led off the ninth a slow roller in Buck O'Neil's direction, and the Monarchs first sacker overthrew Paige, who was covering the base, which allowed Wilson to advance to second. Sam Bankhead bunted and was safe at first when second baseman Tommy Sampson, the next player to cover first, dropped O'Neil's throw. For the second time, Paige

New York Black Yankees outfielder Dan Wilson was the star of the August 16 East-West Game at Comiskey Park as he batted 2-for-4 with one walk, scored three runs, and stole two bases. (Courtesy Noir-Tech Research, Inc.)

issued a free pass to Gibson to load the bases. This time the strategy backfired as Wright singled to drive in Wilson and Bankhead with the final two runs of the game. In the bottom of the frame, Day struck out the side to seal the East's 5-2 victory.

After the Comiskey Park game, the same two All-Star squads traveled to Cleveland to stage a second game for the Eastern crowd at Municipal Stadium. It was only the second time in the 10-year history of the East-West Game that an Eastern tilt took place, the first having occurred in 1939. This time around, the second game was not played to fill owners' and promoters' pockets but to benefit the Army and Navy Emergency Relief Fund.

August 18, 1942: East 9, West 2, at Municipal Stadium, Cleveland

The August 18 East-West Game marked the first of its kind in Cleveland – the 1939 Eastern game had been played at Yankee Stadium – and the *Chicago Defender* averred, "The city is all agog over this great game and no efforts are being spared to make this attraction one of the greatest in the history of Cleveland."[11] The *Defender's* assertion was not entirely true and a debate ensued over the lighting to be used for the night game that delayed play by 25 minutes. Under the terms of the contract for the event, the game was to be played under the lights used for football; however, the crowd began to clamor for the floodlights used during Indians games at the ballpark. The players left the field until the issue was resolved when "Dick Kroesen, chairman of the Army and Navy Relief Fund of Cuyahoga County, arranged to have the brighter lights turned on and guaranteed to pay the added expense for their usage."[12]

Once the added lighting was on, the players and the 10,794 spectators, who constituted the "largest [crowd] ever to see a Negro game in the stadium," were satisfied.[13] After Cleveland's mayor, Frank J.

• East Team Sweeps Comiskey Classic and Cleveland Benefit Games •

Hall of Famer Leon Day of the Newark Eagles pitched the final 2 1/3 innings of the August 16 East-West Classic, striking out five batters and earning the win in the East's 5-2 triumph. (Courtesy Noir-Tech Research, Inc.)

Lausche, threw the ceremonial first pitch to the Negro American League president, Dr. J.B. Martin, the game began at last.

Although the event was held for a good cause, the press treated the game itself as an afterthought to the annual Comiskey Park classic and barely covered the on-field action.[14] Cincinnati Buckeyes pitcher Eugene Bremer started for the West – Paige was out with a sore arm – and was tagged for five runs in the top of the third inning. The West recouped two runs in the bottom of the frame, but those marked their only scores in a 9-2 defeat that gave the East squad a sweep of the two games. Newark's Willie Wells led the East's hitters as he went 3-for-4 at the plate with three RBIs and one run scored. While the media neglected to cover the game in any detail, it did note that the crowd "contributed $9,499.04, the largest amount raised by an individual Negro organization" for the Relief Fund.[15]

Taken together, the two East-West games, in the opinion of one *Atlanta Daily World* columnist, also had helped to accomplish more than to highlight the best players in the Negro Leagues and to raise money for the Army and Navy Relief Fund. Columnist Lucius "Melancholy" Jones wrote:

"Whether or not Negro players get their rightful and deserved chance at performing in major league baseball next season ... I note four significant gains, all of which may be attributed to the effort of those leading the Negro baseball integration fight. They are as follows:

1. An improved attitude generally toward Negro professional baseball as an institution;
2. Increased white attendance at Negro games;
3. Increased pride on the part of Negroes generally in their own stars; and
4. The fight has become a fine vehicle for integrating the efforts of Negroes in all other lines of endeavor."[16]

The annual East-West All-Star Game continued to provide a venue that featured the best players in the Negro Leagues. It took another five years, but Organized Baseball finally relented and former Kansas City Monarch Jackie Robinson made his debut as the first twentieth-century Black player in the major leagues on April 15, 1947, when he started at first base for the Brooklyn Dodgers.

Sources

The descriptions of the scoring plays from the August 16 game at Comiskey Park were adapted from the following article:

Day, John C. "Play by Play," *Chicago Defender*, August 22, 1942: 19.

Notes

1 David Pietrusza, *Judge and Jury: The Life and Times of Judge Kenesaw Mountain Landis* (South Bend, Indiana: Diamond Communications, 1998), 417.

2 "Big League Scouts to Watch East-West Game: Campanella Leads Gibson for Backstop/Paige and Barnhill to Pitch in Classic on August 16," *Chicago Defender*, August 1, 1942: 20.

3 "Expect 50,000 at East-West Game: East-West Classic Will Draw 50,000/Pick Paige and Day to Start Game Sunday at Comiskey Park," *Chicago Defender*, August 15, 1942: 1.

4 Randy Dixon, "The Sports Bugle," *Pittsburgh Courier*, September 5, 1942: 16.

5 Dixon.

6 Dan Burley, "East Wins First Game in Four Years; Brains, Wilson Did It," *New York Amsterdam News*, August 22, 1942: 1. The *Amsterdam News*' headline was in error as the East had won, 11-0, in 1940 and by

an 8-3 score in 1941. There was also a minor discrepancy over the exact attendance as the *Amsterdam News* reported a total of 48,179 while the *Chicago Defender* gave a total attendance of 48,400; both papers listed the paid attendance as 45,179. See also: Frank A. Young, "48,000 See East All-Stars Beat Paige and West," *Chicago Defender*, August 22, 1942: 19.

7   Burley.

8   "48,000 See Paige Lose: Negro All-Star Nine of East Is Victor over West by 5-2," *New York Times*, August 17, 1942: 21.

9   Dixon.

10   John C. Day, "Play by Play," *Chicago Defender*, August 22, 1942: 19.

11   G.L. Porter, "Same Teams Play Benefit Game in Cleveland, Aug. 18," *Chicago Defender*, August 15, 1942: 19.

12   "East's All-Stars Whip West, 9-2/Controversy over Lights Delays Negro Benefit Game," *Cleveland Plain Dealer*, August 19, 1942: 18.

13   "East's All-Stars Whip West, 9-2."

14   In addition to the 1939 and 1942 seasons, two East-West games were played in 1946, 1947, and 1948. Attendance at the Eastern games normally paled in comparison to the turnout for the annual Western game at Comiskey Park. Only once, in 1947 at New York's Polo Grounds, did Eastern attendance come anywhere close to the crowd at Comiskey; that year 38,402 spectators attended the Eastern game, which was still considerably fewer than the 48,112 who attended the Chicago game.

15   "East Bumps West Again: Army and Navy Relief Funds Get $9,499," *Chicago Defender*, August 29, 1942: 19.

16   Lucius (Melancholy) Jones, "Sports Slants," *Atlanta Daily World*, August 16, 1942: 8.

The 1942 Negro League World Series

By Richard J. Puerzer

The 1942 Negro League World Series was the first championship series since 1927 that pitted teams from two separate Black baseball leagues. The Homestead Grays, champions of the Negro National League, faced the Kansas City Monarchs, winners of the Negro American League pennant. The Series featured great teams and players, controversy, and perhaps the most iconic pitcher-batter matchup in the history of baseball, Satchel Paige of the Monarchs and Josh Gibson of the Grays, who were both at the height of their powers.

The Homestead Grays dominated the NNL in 1942, winning 47 games and posting a .712 winning percentage in the league, and an overall record of 64-23-3. Vic Harris managed the team while playing as the starting left fielder. Josh Gibson was among the best hitters in the league, leading the league in walks and on-base percentage, finishing second in home runs and runs batted in, and sporting a .327/.447/.580 slash line for the season. The Kansas City Monarchs were crowned the champions of the Negro American League, finishing with a record of 27-12 in the league and a 35-17 overall record for the season. Frank Duncan managed the team and occasionally played as a backup catcher throughout the season. Switch-hitting right fielder Ted Strong was the leading hitter on the team, with a slash line of .364/.425/.561. The team had an excellent offense, but the pitching staff, led by future Hall of Famers Satchel Paige and Hilton Smith, was its strongest component.

In 1942 the Grays and Monarchs faced each other in five games before the World Series, with the Grays winning four of the five, including all four games started by Satchel Paige. The Monarchs and Grays split a preseason exhibition doubleheader in New Orleans on April 26.[1] On June 18, before a crowd of 28,000 fans at Washington's Griffith Stadium, the Grays won 2-1 in 10 innings.[2] On July 21, in the first Negro League night game in Forbes Field and Satchel Paige's first appearance in Pittsburgh since 1936, the Grays beat the Monarchs and Paige, 5-4 in 11 innings.[3] On August 13 at Griffith Stadium, the Grays defeated the Monarchs 3-2 in 12 innings before a crowd of 20,000.[4] Paige and the Monarchs were ready for revenge in the best-of-seven World Series.

Game One

Tuesday, September 8, 1942: Kansas City Monarchs 8, Homestead Grays 0, at Griffith Stadium, Washington

Game One of the World Series was played at Griffith Stadium in Washington on the evening of Tuesday, September 8, before a crowd of approximately 24,000. In 1942 the Grays played home games in both Washington and Pittsburgh, and were the home team in the game. Starting pitchers Satchel Paige of the Monarchs and lefty Roy Welmaker of the Grays faced off against each other and both started the game strong. Then the Grays posed a threat in the fourth inning. With one out, Sam Bankhead and Tom Easterling singled. But Paige was able to get Josh Gibson to fly out to deep center field and Buck Leonard to foul out to the catcher to end the threat. Paige pitched another scoreless inning in the fifth before being relieved by Jack Matchett. The side-arm-slinging Matchett pitched the remainder of the game, and did not allow a Gray to reach base.

Welmaker also pitched five shutout innings before he and the Grays ran into trouble in the sixth. With one out, Monarchs third baseman Newt Allen singled and moved to second on Ted Strong's base hit. Willard Brown then grounded to Grays second baseman Matt Carlisle, who tossed the ball to shortstop Sam Bankhead to get the runner at second, but Bankhead dropped the ball. With the ball loose, Allen broke for home and scored the game's first run when Gibson dropped the throw to the plate. The Grays held the Monarchs to one run in the sixth inning, but Kansas City broke the game open in the seventh by scoring three runs, including one by Jesse Williams on a double steal. The Monarchs scored twice more in the eighth inning and added two in the ninth, including an RBI triple by Willard Brown hit to deepest center field of cavernous Griffith Stadium, for a commanding 8-0 victory.

Paige earned the win, having allowed just two hits and a walk while striking out five in his five innings of work.[5] Welmaker struck out seven Monarchs, but allowed 13 hits and one walk, and took the loss in his complete-game effort. The Grays were guilty of sloppy play behind him as the team's defense committed six errors in the game.[6]

Game One Line Score

Monarchs	0	0	0	0	0	1	3	2	2	8	13	0
Grays	0	0	0	0	0	0	0	0	0	0	2	6

Monarchs: Paige 5 IP, Matchett 4 IP; Grays: Welmaker 9 IP

Game Two

Thursday, September 10, 1942: Kansas City Monarchs 8, Homestead Grays 4, at Forbes Field, Pittsburgh

Game Two of the Series was played on the night of Thursday, September 10, at Forbes Field in Pittsburgh, the Grays' other home field. A crowd of only 5,219 was in attendance on the rainy evening. Hard-throwing lefty Roy Partlow started the game for the Grays and Hilton Smith started for the Monarchs.

In the top of the first, the Monarchs tallied the first run of the game on a single by catcher Joe Greene that drove in Ted Strong. In the fourth, the Monarchs scored on a double steal for the second time in the Series, with Greene crossing the plate standing up. Smith scattered five hits, two walks, and a hit batsman and did not allow a run in his five innings on the mound before he was relieved by Paige.

In the bottom of the seventh inning, the Grays, down 2-0, put together a rally. Roy Partlow, Vic Harris, and Tom Easterling all singled to load the bases. Josh Gibson now stepped to the plate to face Paige. This matchup between the Negro Leagues' two biggest stars was a defining event in the game, and over the years the at-bat took on mythic proportions. Paige embellished the story, claiming that he walked the three batters ahead of Gibson to face Gibson with the bases loaded and the game on the line. Paige also claimed that he taunted Gibson during the at-bat, announcing that he was going to fire fastballs by him, and that Gibson did not swing at a pitch.[7] Regardless of any later exaggeration, the at-bat with Gibson at the plate, Paige on the mound, the bases loaded with two outs, and the Grays down by two runs late in the game was a dramatic moment in baseball history. As contemporaneous news stories reported, Paige did not deliberately load the bases to face Gibson, and there was no report of Gibson being goaded into a strikeout. The fact remains, however, that Paige prevailed as Gibson fouled off the first two pitches and then swung and missed at the third offering to end the inning.

In the top of the eighth inning the Monarchs loaded the bases for second baseman Bonnie Serrell, who knocked in all three runners but was himself thrown out at the plate as he attempted to tally an inside-the-park grand slam. This outbreak chased Partlow from the game and extended the Monarchs' lead to 5-0. However, the Grays answered in the bottom of the inning as Buck Leonard led off with a single and Sam Bankhead followed with another base hit. Ray Brown then hit a fly ball to left that Bill Simms dropped, allowing Leonard to score. Forty-six-year-old Jud Wilson pinch-hit for Chester Williams and tripled to right-center, bringing in Bankhead and Brown. David Whatley, batting for pitcher John Wright, grounded out on a dribbler in front of the plate. Wilson then scored the fourth Grays run on Jerry Benjamin's fielder's choice grounder. The Grays were now down by only one run, 5-4.

In the top of the ninth, the Monarchs extended their lead. Roy Welmaker entered the game to pitch for the Grays, but was ineffective, allowing the Monarchs to load the bases with two out. Spoon Carter relieved Welmaker to try to get the final out, but Buck O'Neil singled, scoring Simms and Brown, with Green scoring as well on an error by Vic Harris. Paige finished the game with an uneventful bottom of the ninth, giving the Monarchs the victory and a two-games-to-none lead in the Series as Smith earned the win and Partlow took the loss.[8]

Game Two Line Score

Monarchs	1	0	0	1	0	0	0	3	3	8	11	1
Grays	0	0	0	0	0	0	0	4	0	4	11	4

Monarchs: Smith 5 IP, Paige 4 IP; Grays: Partlow 7⅔ IP, Wright ⅓ IP, Welmaker ⅔ IP, Carter ⅓ IP

Game Three

Sunday, September 13, 1942: Kansas City Monarchs 9, Homestead Grays 3, at Yankee Stadium, New York

The Series moved on to Yankee Stadium for Game Three, which was played on the afternoon of Sunday, September 13, with the Grays as the home team. The teams actually played a doubleheader, with the agreement that only the first game would count toward the Series. A crowd of over 25,000 was in attendance, and New York City Mayor Fiorello LaGuardia threw out the first ball. Satchel Paige started the game for the Monarchs and faced Grays ace Ray Brown.

This time the Grays struck first when, with two out in the bottom of the first, Howard Easterling homered over the right-field wall. Josh Gibson then walked, stole second, and scored on a single by Buck Leonard, giving the Grays a 2-0 lead. After pitching a scoreless second inning and batting in the top of the third, Paige left the game, ostensibly due to a stomach ailment, and was relieved by Jack Matchett.

In the top of the third, the Monarchs' Ted Strong slugged a three-run homer to right field, scoring Bill Simms and Herb Cyrus. Willard Brown followed with another home run to give the Monarchs a 4-2 lead. Kansas City continued to rough up Grays starter Ray Brown, scoring two runs in the fourth inning and three more in the fifth inning to take a 9-2 lead.

Meanwhile, just as he had done in Game One, Matchett pitched masterfully. The Grays could muster only one more run in the game, when Chester Williams singled, advanced to second on a groundout, and scored on Ray Brown's ground-rule double. Otherwise Matchett quelled the Grays' bats as the Monarchs cruised to the victory, taking a three-games-to-none lead in the Series.

Brown struck out seven, but he gave up two walks and 16 hits in taking the complete-game loss. Matchett gave up five hits and four walks in his seven innings of work and earned the win.

The two teams played the second game of the doubleheader, which was limited to seven innings, as an exhibition game. The Grays started Roy Welmaker while the Monarchs countered with Gread McKinnis, who had pitched for the Birmingham Black Barons during the regular season. For good measure, the Monarchs also won this game, 5-0. McKinnis allowed only three hits in his shutout performance, and the highlight of the Monarchs' offense was an inside-the-park home run by catcher Joe Greene.[9]

Game Three Line Score

Monarchs	0	0	4	2	3	0	0	0	0	9	16	3
Grays	2	0	0	0	0	1	0	0	0	3	7	4

Monarchs: Paige 2 IP, Matchett 7 IP; Grays: Brown 9 IP

It was agreed that Game Four of the Series would be played at Ruppert Stadium in Kansas City at 2 P.M. on Sunday, September 20. This left both teams with a week before the next game in the Series. Before making their way to Kansas City, the Grays played several exhibition games. They first played a doubleheader against the Newark Eagles on Monday, September 14, in New Haven, Connecticut, losing both games, 5-1 and 2-1. The next day they played the Philadelphia Stars to a 5-5 tie in a 12-inning game in Philadelphia. They then traveled to Baltimore to play a game on September 16 against the Baltimore Elite Giants at Bugle Field, which they lost 2-1. After the game, they bolstered their roster by adding Leon Day, Lennie Pearson, and Ed Stone from the Newark Eagles and Bus Clarkson and Edsall Walker from the Elite Giants; all five of these players joined the team in traveling to Kansas City.

The Monarchs also played an exhibition game during the break in the Series. They took on the Cincinnati Clowns at Parkway Field in Louisville, Kentucky, on Friday, September 18, and won 2-1 in 13 innings.

Game Four (later disallowed)
Sunday, September 20, 1942: Homestead Grays 4, Kansas City Monarchs 1, at Ruppert Stadium, Kansas City

When the Grays took the field at Ruppert Stadium in Kansas City on the afternoon of September 20, they had four new players in their lineup. Ed Stone was in right field, Bus Clarkson was at shortstop, Lennie Pearson was at second base, and toeing the pitching rubber was Leon Day. Cumberland Posey, business manager of the Grays, later claimed that Homestead had the agreement of Tom Baird, Monarchs general manager, to add the additional players to their lineup due to the number of players that they had lost to injury or other circumstances in recent weeks.[10] The tipping point for the Grays in seeking new players came when they lost shortstop Sam Bankhead with a broken arm suffered before Game Three at Yankee Stadium. In addition to losing Bankhead, Matt Carlisle and Dave Whatley had been required to report to the Army, and pitcher Wilmer Fields had returned to college at Virginia State a few weeks earlier. Additionally, the Grays sought to justify the addition of the new players by claiming that Roy Partlow had lost much of his pitching effectiveness due to boils under his pitching arm and because Jud Wilson was nursing an injured heel.[11] The game was played with the additions to the Grays' lineup, but the Monarchs were not happy as they took the field.

A crowd of 8,542 was in attendance for the Sunday afternoon matchup of future Hall of Fame pitchers Satchel Paige and Leon Day. The game was scoreless until the top of the fifth, when Grays player-manager Vic Harris singled and scored on Jerry Benjamin's triple. Benjamin then scored on a double by Ed Stone. The Grays added a third run in the seventh inning when Lennie Pearson doubled and scored on Harris's smash that was mishandled by Monarchs second baseman Bonnie Serrell.

The Monarchs scored their lone run of the game in the eighth when Buck O'Neil singled, advanced to third on Serrell's single, and scored on an infield out. The Grays notched their fourth and final tally in the ninth inning when Pearson doubled for the second time in the game, took third on a wild pitch, and scored on a groundout. Paige struck out seven and walked one, taking the complete-game loss. Day earned the win with a dazzling performance, giving up just five hits and one walk while striking out 12 Monarchs. However, it was also reported that in addition to protesting the Grays' expanded roster, the Monarchs were complaining that Day was cutting the ball and that 13 balls were removed from the game by the umpires.

After the game and given the stellar performance of the newly signed players, the Monarchs lodged a protest. Monarchs team secretary Dizzy Dismukes was quoted as saying, "We didn't play the Homestead Grays, we lost to the National League All-Stars."[12] The next day Cum Posey, Rufus Jackson, and Vic Harris, the business manager, owner, and manager respectively of the Grays, and Monarchs owner J.L. Wilkinson, general manager Tom Baird, and Dismukes met with Fay Young, the secretary of the Negro American League and sports editor of the *Chicago Defender*, to discuss the situation. The Monarchs' protest was upheld, and it was ruled that the Grays' victory would not count due to the "ringers" they had played. The next game in the Series was scheduled for Sunday, September 27, at Wrigley Field in Chicago.[13]

Disallowed Game Four Line Score

Monarchs	0	0	0	0	2	0	1	0	1	4	9	0
Grays	0	0	0	0	0	0	0	1	0	1	5	1

Grays: Day 9 IP; Monarchs: Paige 9 IP

Kansas City Call, September 11, 1942

The game scheduled for September 27 in Wrigley Field was canceled just one hour before game time because of rainy and cold conditions. It was reported that the Series would now resume in Philadelphia, where it would be played to completion.[14]

Game Four (official)

Tuesday, September 29, 1942: Kansas City Monarchs 9, Homestead Grays 5, at Shibe Park, Philadelphia

The replayed fourth game of the Series was played on the chilly night of Tuesday, September 29, at Shibe Park in Philadelphia, with the Grays as the home team. Sixteen days had passed since Game Three (nine days since the original, disallowed Game Four), and both teams were eager to resume the Series. Satchel Paige was to start the game for the Monarchs, but he was not in the ballpark at the start of the game. Instead, Jack Matchett made the start for the Monarchs while Roy Partlow took the mound for the Grays. The Grays' lineup no longer had any replacement players, and Chester Williams started at shortstop for the injured Sam Bankhead.

The Monarchs struck quickly in the top of the first as Bill Simms slugged a leadoff triple and scored on Newt Allen's single. The Grays answered with three runs in the bottom of the first. With two outs, Howard

Easterling drew a walk. Josh Gibson hit a popup that catcher Jim Greene muffed, putting runners on first and second. Buck Leonard followed with a single that drove in Easterling. Ray Brown then doubled, scoring Gibson and Leonard, to give the Grays a 3-1 lead.

In the second inning, Partlow left the game with two on and one out. Johnny Wright took the mound for the Grays and maneuvered out of the inning unscathed. However, in the top of the third, the Monarchs plated a run. Willard Brown reached on an error and advanced to second on Greene's single. Buck O'Neil sacrificed, advancing both runners. Brown then scored on a groundout to first. In the bottom of the third, the Grays added two runs as Easterling, Leonard, and Brown reached base, then Williams singled to drive in Easterling and Leonard.

The Grays now led, 5-2, and seemed to be on their way to their first win in the Series. However, the Monarchs scored two more runs in the top of the fourth on Greene's home run, closing the gap to 5-4. Paige finally arrived at the game in the bottom of the fourth and immediately relieved Matchett, getting the final out of the inning with two inherited runners on base. After the game Paige said he was late because as he drove to Philadelphia from Pittsburgh, he was detained for speeding in Lancaster, Pennsylvania. After paying a fine of $20, he was allowed to go on his way.

Kansas City's offense came to life again in the seventh, when the Monarchs scored twice to take a 6-5 lead, and in the eighth inning, when they scored three more times. O'Neil scored twice and Strong, Brown, and Greene each scored once in the two scoring barrages. Meanwhile, despite his late arrival, Paige pitched brilliantly after replacing Matchett in the fourth. He allowed no hits and two walks while striking out seven in the 5⅓ innings he pitched to complete the game. Paige garnered his second win of the Series while Johnny Wright took the loss for the Grays.

With the 9-5 victory, the Monarchs completed the four-game sweep of the Grays in the Series.[15]

Official Game Four Line Score

Monarchs	1	0	1	2	0	0	2	3	0	9	13	2
Grays	3	0	2	0	0	0	0	0	0	5	7	1

Monarchs: Matchett 3⅔ IP, Paige 5⅓ IP; Grays: Partlow 1⅓ IP, Wright 6⅔ IP, Welmaker 1 IP

World Series Postscript

Joe Greene was the offensive star for the Monarchs in the Series, slugging eight hits, including a home run, and working three walks in 19 plate appearances. Jesse Williams also impressed by stealing five bases in the four games. The Monarchs used only three pitchers in the Series: Satchel Paige, Jack Matchett, and Hilton Smith. Collectively they had an ERA of 2.00 and a WHIP of 1.08 in the Series. Paige pitched in all four games, getting the win in two, and struck out 18 Grays in 16⅓ innings.

The Grays suffered from a surprisingly anemic offense in the Series, hitting .196 and slugging .239. Josh Gibson had a particularly poor Series offensively, getting only one hit in 13 at-bats. There is no question that the Grays were a depleted team at the time of the Series, and the loss of Carlisle and Whatley to the military and Bankhead to injury during the Series made things worse. Pitchers Ray Brown and Roy Partlow both played significant time in right field in the Series because Homestead was so shorthanded. However, it would have been difficult for any team to beat the Monarchs' magnificent pitching triumvirate of Paige, Smith, and Matchett.

The two teams played twice more soon after the completion of the World Series. On Friday evening, October 2, they played at High Rock Park in Norfolk, Virginia. Satchel Paige started the game for the Monarchs and gave up one run in three innings before giving way to Jack Matchett. Ray Brown started for the Grays and went the distance. The Grays won the game, 8-5. They played one last game on Sunday, October 4, at City Stadium in Portsmouth, Virginia. Paige again started the game for the Monarchs opposite Roy Partlow for the Grays. The Monarchs prevailed by a score of 12-2.[16]

Sources

In addition to the sources cited in the Notes, the author also consulted: Seamheads.com

Clark, Dick, and Larry Lester, eds. *The Negro Leagues Book* (Cleveland: Society for American Baseball Research, 1994).

Riley, James A. *The Biographical Encyclopedia of the Negro Baseball Leagues* (New York: Carroll and Graf, 1994).

Snyder, Brad. *Beyond the Shadow of the Senators* (New York: McGraw-Hill, 2003).

Thanks to Todd Peterson for providing many of the references used.

• When the Monarchs Reigned •

Notes

1 "Kansas City Splits Even with Grays," *Chicago Defender*, May 9, 1942: 21; "Monarchs, Grays All Even Before Overflow Crowd," *New Orleans Times-Picayune*, April 27, 1942: 14; "Monarchs Break Even," *Kansas City Times*, April 27, 1942: 11.

2 "Two Runs in Tenth Wins for Grays as Paige, Partlow Star," *Pittsburgh Courier*, June 27, 1942: 16; "28,000 Watch Grays Upset Monarchs, 2-1," *Washington Post*, June 19, 1942: 24; "Grays Beat Monarchs and Paige in Tenth," *Chicago Defender*, June 27, 1942: 21.

3 "Satchel Beaten in 5-4 Game," *Afro-American*, July 25, 1942: 27.

4 "20,000 See Grays Beat 'Satch' in D.C.," *Pittsburgh Courier*, August 22, 1942: 16.

5 It should be noted that the *Pittsburgh Courier* awarded the win to Jack Matchett, while the *Washington Post* awarded the win to Satchel Paige, as does www.seamheads.com. In this case, and in any other case where there is a discrepancy in the reporting of statistics, the information provided at the seamheads website is used.

6 For Game One the following references were used: "24,000 See Grays Beaten by Monarchs," *Washington Post*, September 9, 1942: 11; "Kansas City Takes First from Grays," *Chicago Defender*, September 19, 1942: 23; Wendell Smith, "Third Straight Loss Dooms Grays Hopes," *Pittsburgh Courier*, September 19, 1942: 17. (This article covers Games One, Two, and Three.)

7 Paige, Leroy (Satchel), as told to Hal Lebovitz, *Pitchin' Man: Satchel Paige's Own Story* (Cleveland: Cleveland News, 1948), 48-50; Paige, LeRoy (Satchel) as told to David Lipman, *Maybe I'll Pitch Forever* (Garden City, NewYork: Doubleday & Company, 1962), 152-153. Others would tell the embellished story as well, including Buck O'Neil in the *Ken Burns Baseball* documentary series.

8 For Game Two the following references were used: "Grays Laced by Monarchs," *Pittsburgh Press*, September 11, 1942: 38; "Kansas City Whips Grays Second Time," *Chicago Defender*, September 19, 1942: 23; Wendell Smith, "Third Straight Loss Dooms Grays Hopes," *Pittsburgh Courier*, September 19, 1942: 17.

9 For Game Three and the exhibition game the following references were used: Wendell Smith, "Third Straight Loss Dooms Grays Hopes," *Pittsburgh Courier*, September 19, 1942: 17; Frank Forbes, "Monarchs Take Third World Series Games [sic] in a Row from Easterners." *Chicago Defender*, September 19, 1942: 23; Buster Miller, "K.C. Monarchs Lead by Three Games in World Series; Take Doubleheader at the Stadium," *New York Age*, September 19, 1942: 11; "Weren't Foolin'," *Pittsburgh Courier*, September 19, 1942: 17.

10 "Grays Win, 4-1; Monarchs Protest," *Pittsburgh Courier*, September 26, 1942: 16.

11 Art Carter, "From the Bench," *Afro American*, October 10, 1942: 23.

12 "K.C. Monarchs Win Protest," *The Sporting News*, October 1, 1942: 8.

13 For this game, the following references were used: "Monarchs Lose Here," *Kansas City Times*, September 21, 1942: np; "Ringers Help Grays Win 4-1," *Chicago Defender*, October 3, 1942: 22; "Protested Game Kicked Out," *Chicago Defender*, October 3, 1942: 22; "Grays Win, 4-1; Monarchs Protest," *Pittsburgh Courier*, September 26, 1942: 16.

14 "Rain and Cold Prevent World Series Game," *Chicago Defender*, October 3, 1942: 22.

15 For Game Four the following references were used: "Kansas City Monarchs Win World Championship," *Chicago Defender*, October 10, 1942: 23; William Scheffer, "15,000 See Grays Lose to Kansas," *Philadelphia Inquirer*, September 30, 1942: 35.

16 "Grays, Monarchs Split Two Games in Tidewater," *Norfolk Journal and Guide*, October 10, 1942: 14.

Ruppert Stadium, Kansas City

By Bill Lamberty

Satchel Paige left the mound in Kansas City's Municipal Stadium to enormous ovations many times in his pitching career, barely noticing the fuss of adoring crowds and some of baseball's brightest stars. However, September 25, 1965, was different.[1]

Long removed from his prime as a Negro Leagues legend, or even as the White major leagues' oldest player when he debuted for the Cleveland Indians in 1948, the man estimated to have pitched to more batters in more ballparks than anyone else in history left his final big-league game as a 59-year-old (his most-accepted age) future Hall of Famer on a night that began as a stunt but ended adding to his amazing legend. He used 28 pitches to twirl three scoreless innings for the hometown Kansas City A's against Boston, with Carl Yastrzemski's first-inning double the only hit allowed.[2]

Signed by Athletics owner Charlie Finley for the "princely sum of $3,500"[3] to pitch one last time, Paige famously occupied a wooden rocking chair in the bullpen before the game and in the dugout between innings. A hired nurse rubbed liniment on his pitching arm, and a personal waterboy brought him beverages. Negro Leagues legends Buck O'Neil, Cool Papa Bell, Hilton Smith, and Bullet Rogan returned to their former stamping grounds for a luncheon and brief exhibition game before Kansas City's game against the Red Sox. Future major leaguers Rick Sutcliffe and Frank White joined the nearly 10,000 fans in attendance, a remarkable jump from the 690 fans who had watched the A's two days earlier.[4]

Paige's career intersected with Kansas City's longest-lasting ballpark (until the Royals begin their 1973 season at Royals Stadium, which was renamed Kauffman Stadium in 1993) for much of its lifespan, and that stadium also links the community's rise "from rowdy frontier backwater to major league city."[5]

The Municipal Stadium in which Paige pitched in 1965 was a ballpark known by several names over the course of its lifetime. *(See Editor's note at the end of this article for a chronology of stadium names.)*

Its construction in 1923 as Muehlebach Field provided a permanent home for the minor-league Blues and the Negro National League Monarchs, by then three years into their existence as a charter member of that loop, and Paige likely pitched there beginning in the late 1920s with the Birmingham Black Barons.[6] Before its construction on what was once a swimming hole, frog pond, and ash heap, the city's various ballclubs played in Athletic Park (the 1884 home of Kansas City's Union Association team), Association Park (1886-88, home of the Kansas City Cowboys of the National League and American Association), Exposition Park (1888-89, home of the Double-A Cowboys), and Gordon and Koppel Field (1914-15, Federal League Packers).[7]

The ballpark built by brewer and hotelier George Muehlebach for his Blues opened on July 3, 1923, with home plate resting near the intersection of 22nd Street and Brooklyn Avenue. From 1920 to 1922 the Blues and Monarchs had played in Association Park, a single-deck wooden structure owned by George Tebeau, not far from the city's 18th and Vine District. When he and Muehlebach fell into a dispute in 1922, members of the local Black press "hoped that if a fight between the two were to force Muehlebach to build a new stadium, the Monarchs could continue their lease with Tebeau for the park at Nineteenth and Olive and thus have a park of their own."[8] Monarchs owner J.L. Wilkinson could not afford Tebeau's lease terms and, not long after, "a railroad exercised an option to run tracks through the property" to end its time as a ballpark.[9]

In its original incarnation, Muehlebach's dimensions favored pitching. From home plate to center field was a 450-foot stretch; the foul poles each stood 350 feet distant.[10] The ballpark rested a mile and a half southeast of downtown in a primarily Black neighborhood, across the street from a high school and within walking distance of legendary barbecue restaurants like Arthur Bryant's and Gates BBQ.

The intersection of 18th and Vine Streets, just three-quarters of a mile from the ballpark and only one block

• When the Monarchs Reigned •

Ruppert Stadium, the home of the Monarchs. The stadium was first known as Muehlebach Field (1923), then Ruppert Stadium (1937), and later Blues Stadium (1943). It was completely rebuilt and renamed Municipal Stadium in 1955. (Courtesy Noir-Tech Research, Inc.)

from the Paseo YMCA, which hosted the meeting that formed the Negro National League in 1920, formed the heart of Kansas City's Black community for much of the twentieth century. "The epicenter of the African American community was located around 18th Street between Vine and The Paseo," historian Japheth Knopp wrote in the Spring 2016 *Baseball Research Journal*. "Businesses of all types, from barber and shoe repair shops to doctors' and lawyers' offices were found in this neighborhood. This section of town was perhaps known best for its night life, with patrons packing clubs with colorful names such as the Cherry Blossom, the Chez Paree, Lucille's Paradise, and the Ol' Kentuck' Bar-B-Q."[11]

Monarchs players, as well as Negro League opponents, patronized the nearby Street Hotel, called by longtime Monarchs player and manager Buck O'Neil "the best black hotel in Kansas City at the time."[12] Post-World War II economic expansion kept the boundaries of Kansas City's Black neighborhood fluid, but through much of the ballpark's existence, the boundaries formed by "Ninth street south to Twenty-eighth and from Troost east to Indiana Street" allowed "Kansas City's Blacks to create) a network of businesses, social organizations, fraternal groups, and churches." Yet, the city's rigid segregation forced substandard living conditions upon an area that resonated with pride. "The wards in which blacks lived had the highest percentage of rental housing and the lowest of resident-owned housing in the city. The illiteracy rate was ten times higher; the death rate was twice as high as for white Kansas Citians."[13]

Still, the area encompassing the ballpark and the 18th and Vine District pulsated with joy. Milton

• Ruppert Stadium, Kansas City •

Morris, a neighborhood saloonkeeper, told author and historian Janet Bruce, "Kansas City was swinging. Nobody slept – they were afraid they'd miss something." Musicians considered the 18th and Vine district as a venue for a continual "jam session."[14]

Particularly in relation to the Monarchs, baseball was deeply rooted in the neighborhood. Longtime Monarchs second baseman Newt Allen helped with the large canvas tarp that covered the infield during rainy times and as an "ice boy at the American Association Park when the Monarchs organized in 1920. He practiced with the team, pulled the canvas (tarp) over the field, and in return received two or three baseballs from the groundskeeper."[15] Frank Duncan toiled as a batboy for the view that work afforded, and "Chet Brewer remembered having sat up in a tree outside the left-field grandstand at Muehlebach Stadium watching Bullet Joe Rogan pitch" as a youngster, dreaming of the day he might toe that same rubber.[16]

The players who did not take in-season residence at the Street Hotel often lived in the neighborhood near the ballpark. "We were kind of special in the neighborhood," O'Neil recalled, "And as far as I recall we were a bit more special than" Kansas City Royals players in later years, when that team moved to distant Royals Stadium, "because of the fact that it was all black and we mingled with all black (people)."[17]

During the time when the Blues and Monarchs shared the ballpark, it provided as many stars as the jazz district, among them Al Rosen, Mickey Mantle, and Phil Rizzuto, along with Blues manager and Kansas City native Casey Stengel. Among the Negro Leagues greats who called the ballpark home were Paige, Ernie Banks, Jackie Robinson, Bullet Rogan, Hilton Smith, and Turkey Stearnes. All earned induction into the National Baseball Hall of Fame; other notables included Buck O'Neil, John Donaldson, and Elston Howard. Jazz stars made regular stops in Kansas City, including Count Basie, Dizzy Gillespie, and Louis Armstrong.

While both the American Association Blues and the NAL Monarchs called the ballpark home until the Athletics arrived in 1955, the organizations had vastly different relationships with it. The Blues played a standard American Association schedule and commonly drew an average of around 2,000 fans to the 80 or so home games per season. The Blues played in four Junior or Little World Series from 1923 to 1954, their lifetime playing home games at 22nd and Brooklyn. The Blues beat Baltimore five games to four in 1923 and beat Rochester by the same tally in 1929. The team lost to Rochester (4-3 in 1952) and Montreal (4-1 in 1953) in best-of-seven series near the end of Kansas City's time as a minor-league city.[18]

The Monarchs, on the other hand, often found the road a more profitable venture, writes author and Negro Leagues historian Phil S. Dixon. "Starting in 1931, the Monarchs had become a barnstorming team. They were continuously on the road, a vast difference compared to their pennant run in 1923, when they played a record 57 games in Kansas City. In 1934, the number of Monarchs home games dipped to three – and one of these games was played across the Missouri River in Kansas City, Kansas."[19]

While barnstorming took the Monarchs on the road, crisscrossing the near South and Midwest, it also gave the team opportunities to host other clubs on similar tours. The season before the ballpark opened, any possibility of the Blues and Monarchs deciding city superiority ended with the Negro Leagues entry avenging a city series loss of one year earlier with a five-games-to-one best-of-nine series win against the Blues. Muehlebach swore his team would never again play the Monarchs, a vow he kept, and Commissioner Kenesaw Mountain Landis clamped down on major-league players barnstorming against Negro League teams in the offseason. The Monarchs' doubleheader wins over a club featuring Yankees stars Babe Ruth and Bob Meusel in Association Park (October 6, 1922) figured into that decision.[20] Ruth never bowed to race-relations norms of the time, and Kansas City offered a stage. In addition to his appearance against the Monarchs in 1922, Ruth barnstormed against teams featuring Negro Leagues players throughout his career. In 1927 he appeared in a Kansas City fundraising event at the Guardian Angels Home for Negro Children and four years later was in town to play a night game against the Monarchs, which was rained out and not rescheduled.[21]

In 1934, with America struggling through the Great Depression and the St. Louis Cardinals holding the imagination of Middle America captive with the antics of the Gas House Gang teams, Redbirds pitchers Dizzy Dean, his brother Paul, and other major-league stars commenced a tour that featured the Monarchs and three Negro Leagues teams – the New York Black Yankees, Philadelphia Stars, and Pittsburgh Crawfords – which has been chronicled brilliantly by Dixon in *The Dizzy and Daffy Dean Barnstorming Tour – Race, Media, and America's National Pastime*.

• When the Monarchs Reigned •

Muehlebach Field and the Monarchs hosted the Dean All-Stars on October 6, 1934, with 14,000 fans on hand. T.J. Young tripled off Paul Dean in the second inning, scoring the only run the Monarchs needed in a 7-0 win. Andy Cooper anchored a brilliant pitching performance for a Kansas City team that scored off both Dean brothers and future big leaguer Mort Cooper. Young expressed gratitude for the opportunity to perform against the game's best-known pitchers – "All my life it's been one of my ambitions to hit the best hurlers in the majors" – and Dizzy Dean praised the Monarchs hitters.[22]

In 1930 the Monarchs and Muehlebach Field played a role in altering baseball history by hosting night baseball games. Monarchs owner J.L. Wilkinson, in an effort to fight fiscal losses brought on in part by the Great Depression, conjured up the idea of a portable lighting system that could be used at home and could also be taken on the team's tours. The Giant Manufacturing Company of Omaha, Nebraska, built a system of telescoping poles supporting six four-foot-wide floodlights that rose 45 to 50 feet above the playing surface. The poles attached to truck beds, with the vehicles stationed down each foul line and at advantageous points around the field. The system cost between $50,000 and $100,000, and while the crashing economy forced ticket prices from 65 cents per ticket down to a low of 25 cents, Wilkinson credited the lighting system with keeping his ballclub afloat during the difficult times.[23]

The environment in the ballpark mirrored the good-time culture of the neighborhood, and its role as a cultural cauldron. Bruce wrote, "The crowds at Negro-league baseball were loud and lively in support of the home team. The ball-park behavior of many of the newly arrived southerners, however, sometimes offended the sensibilities of middle-class blacks. They saw this boisterous 'rowdyism' (including everything from drinking and gambling to harassing the umpires, throwing seat cushions, and fighting) as an embarrassment for the race."[24] Still, Dixon called Kansas City a "really jumping" and "robust Midwestern city" in the late 1930s, "the prairies' capital for ethnic sports, entertainment, music and religious activities. Sunday was the big day for baseball, the day when African-American fans came out to support their Monarch team at Ruppert Stadium, and most came directly from church."[25] That tradition resonates to this day, with the Royals hosting an annual "Dressed to the Nines Day" and encouraging fans to arrive for a selected Sunday game honoring the Negro Leagues dressed in a manner befitting the glory days of Ruppert Stadium.

Buck O'Neil praised Ruppert Stadium in Phil S. Dixon's *John "Buck" O'Neil – The Rookie, The Man, The Legacy,* calling it "an outstanding park, always had good groundskeepers, the grounds were always good, and you're playing at home. And when you say 'playing at home,' in Kansas City it meant quite a bit to you cause you always had a lot of people there, and these same people, after you got through playing ball you were going to meet them at the Blue Room or (at) the Subway (club), it was just a great feeling. All of the ballplayers that played all over the country wanted to come to Kansas City. [They] liked the park and they liked the city."[26] O'Neil added that in most Negro Leagues ballparks the visiting team dressed either before arriving at the ballpark or in the same space the home team used, while Ruppert Stadium offered a full visiting clubhouse.[27]

The ballpark also offered a glimpse into the city's strong but ever-shifting segregation, with ownership regimes setting their own standards. While George Tebeau forced all Black fans into segregated seating sections for all games, even when Negro League teams played, Muehlebach relaxed those standards when he built the ballpark at 22nd and Brooklyn. Seating was segregated for Blues games, but those signs were removed when the Monarchs played. When former Cubs star Johnny Kling purchased the Blues and the ballpark in the mid-1930s, he desegregated it for all games, but under Ruppert's management fans at Blues games again became separate by race.[28] As was the case in Kansas City, college and professional sports across the nation stood as local negotiation grounds for race relations during the first three-quarters of the twentieth century.

In the years after World War II, baseball again took center stage in the sporting consciousness, and cities across the nation began dreaming of attaining major-league status. Kansas City was among the communities hoping to become a "major-league city," but no American or National League franchise had moved since 1903. In 1953, though, the Boston Braves moved to Milwaukee. One year later the St. Louis Browns relocated to Baltimore. Suddenly franchise relocation became reality, and the Athletics emerged as a target due to the Mack family's struggle to keep the team financially viable in the two-team Philadelphia market.[29]

Ruppert Stadium, Kansas City

By 1953, Chicago businessman Arnold Johnson owned both Yankee Stadium and Ruppert Stadium in an arrangement that benefited both the New York American League club and Johnson financially. That served as Johnson's entry into the process of pursuing a major-league franchise, and through the summer and fall of 1954 in a series of meetings, negotiations with A's owner Connie Mack and his family, and occasional interventions by baseball power brokers, he pursued Philadelphia's American League entry in a very public way. Finally, on November 12, Johnson beat a group of local investors to Mack's Germantown apartment and acquired the elder statesman's stock in the A's to gain controlling interest. That helped pave the road to relocation to Kansas City.[30]

One of the elements that made Kansas City an attractive location was the idea that Ruppert Stadium could be rebuilt quickly into a major-league ballpark because the subterranean footings had been designed three decades earlier with that in mind. However, exposing the structure's underpinnings showed that that was not the case, and a rebuild could have been considered unsafe for what was there. The site was excavated in December 1954, and, in the first month of 1955, city officials formed a plan with representatives of the Webb-Winn-Senter corporation that had consolidated to build a big-league ballpark in three months to "make a civic occasion out of the first pouring of the concrete for the new footings."[31]

Construction progressed rapidly and echoed a past project. In 1900 Kansas City had been forced to rebuild its convention center in three months to host the Democratic National Convention, and 55 years later a similar race against the clock began. All parties made public mention that, in such a public-private partnership, "rarely had there been such harmony displayed."[32] With cars regularly slowing on Brooklyn Avenue so occupants could gaze at the construction, up to 400 men worked long hours to complete the task. Creation of the Kansas City Stadium Association allowed city and business leaders to circumvent "rules made to protect city voters." As construction progressed into February, even Yankees manager Casey Stengel expressed admiration.[33]

Legal and financial maneuvering continued almost until the day the players arrived from spring training. More than 100,000 fans welcomed the squad with a parade, and on April 12, 1955, the team opened Kansas City's era as a major-league community with a 6-2 win over the Detroit Tigers. The 32,147 fans gathered at Municipal Stadium comprised the city's largest crowd ever for a sporting event.[34]

During the Athletics' stay as the ballpark's home team, the franchise enjoyed little on-field success. The Athletics' sixth-place finish in 1955, its first season in Kansas City, was its highest ever there. After the team drew more than 1 million fans in each of its first two seasons, attendance steadily declined before spiking in 1966 and 1967, when owner Charles O. Finley began advocating for another move (which came in 1968, to Oakland). Despite the abysmal on-field performance, the A's era brought considerable whimsy to the ballpark. The phenomena of the era included a zoo in the embankment beyond right field featuring "Charlie O. the Mule, sheep, China golden pheasants, Capuchin monkeys, German checker rabbits, peafowl, and a German shorthaired pointer dog named Old Drum," with the animals fed by "fresh food from the K.C. Farmers Market."[35] Detroit players were alleged to have got the monkeys drunk with vodka-soaked oranges one night, and for a time a mechanical rabbit named Harvey sprang from the earth near home plate to provide the umpire with clean baseballs. After Finley became convinced that one of the Yankees' keys to success was Yankee Stadium's short right-field porch, the A's owner created a 296-foot porch in right field before the 1965 season. After Commissioner Ford Frick ordered the wall moved back, Finley created a flimsy half-pennant porch that jutted in before returning to regulation distance. The home-plate umpire ordered that removed before the game began on Opening Day 1965, thus ending that episode.[36]

The Athletics moved to Oakland after the 1967 season, and the American League granted Kansas City an expansion franchise to begin play in 1969. Contrasting Finley's flamboyance (and the Arnold Johnson era, when promising young players were regularly shuttled to the Yankees), local businessman and entrepreneur Ewing Kauffman ran the Royals with relative dignity and professionalism. The Royals joined the Chiefs, formerly the AFL Dallas Texans, who moved to Kansas City in 1963 and eventually joined the NFL when the leagues merged, as the ballpark's last act. The Chiefs of the 1960s brought thrills and glory to Municipal Stadium, winning the 1966 AFL championship and the Super Bowl after the 1969 season and serving as the home team for nine future Pro Football Hall of Fame players or coaches.

• When the Monarchs Reigned •

It also precipitated the ballpark's demise, when the NFL passed minimum capacity requirements of 50,000 beginning with the 1971 season that Municipal Stadium could not meet.

Municipal Stadium served as home ground for many brilliant major-league baseball players, although the best seasons of most stars occurred elsewhere. Vic Power moved from Philadelphia to Kansas City with the team, but his best years came in Cleveland. Bob Cerv and Roger Maris had good years with the A's but starred on World Series winners with the Yankees, while future stars like Sal Bando, Bert Campaneris, and Reggie Jackson cut their teeth in Municipal Stadium before starring for Oakland's dynasty teams of the early 1970s. Several of the Royals' all-time greatest players also roamed Municipal Stadium – John Mayberry, Freddie Patek, Amos Otis, Cookie Rojas, and Paul Splittorff – but rose to stardom in the later Royals Stadium. One of the finest Royals to call 22nd and Brooklyn home, 1969 American League Rookie of the Year Lou Piniella, starred for the Yankees in the late 1970s but found true stardom as a World Series-winning manager with the Cincinnati Reds in 1990. In that way, he joined the list of future managerial stars to call Municipal Stadium their home as players that includes Hank Bauer, Doc Edwards, Whitey Herzog, Dick Howser, Rene Lachemann, Tony LaRussa, Tommy Lasorda, and Billy Martin.

Ruppert Stadium provided the setting for baseball legend Lou Gehrig's final stanza. After 10 Yankees games in 1939 Gehrig famously pulled himself from the lineup before a game at Detroit. He never played in a major-league game again, but as a team captain continued to travel with the team. A 13-game road trip in early June took the team to the American League's western-most cities, Chicago and St. Louis, and after sweeping a doubleheader against the Browns on June 11 New York traveled to Kansas City for an exhibition against its top minor league team.[37] Two days before the exhibition Gehrig disclosed his late-June appointment at the Mayo Clinic to attempt to diagnose his "sluggishness," so his status as an active player remained in limbo when the Yankees arrived in Kansas City. On the day that the Baseball Hall of Fame officially opened in Cooperstown, New York, 23,864 fans crowded into Ruppert Stadium, more than 6,000 more than its listed capacity, filling every corner of the property and even sitting on the stadium's roof. As a tribute to the fans, Gehrig opted to play in that contest, grounding out in his only plate appearance and handling four chances at first base in his three innings. It marked his final appearance on a baseball diamond.[38]

As Satchel Paige's career ended in Ruppert Stadium's twilight, in many ways it began there, too. By his estimation he pitched in 2,500 ballparks during his career, but Paige experienced his strongest feelings for a home ballpark when he joined the Monarchs in 1941. Paige found a kindred spirit in Wilkinson, "an unlikely mentor to the Negro League icon" who "did whatever it took for his players and teams, choreographing games, recruiting promising rookies, providing grubstakes along with counsel, and maneuvering around Jim Crow wherever the Monarchs went."[39] Similarly, Paige fell in love with Kansas City, buying his first home and enjoying the cultural opportunities of a thriving African American community that "orchestrated the jazz, belted out the blues, seared the barbecue, and supplied much of the sweat that fed the economic boom."[40]

Kansas City's Ruppert Stadium began as a minor-league ballpark that also hosted a legendary Negro Leagues squad, underwent a rebuild, then served as home for a big-league team in 13 of its final 15 seasons. In this way, it fits into a category of ballparks that allowed major-league baseball to expand relatively quickly, usually to the west, with communities generally making rapid upgrades to smaller existing facilities. Beginning with the St. Louis Browns' move to Baltimore in 1954 – which transitioned a 52-year old multi-use facility into Memorial Stadium – and including similar moves to Milwaukee, Minneapolis, Oakland, and Arlington (Texas), Kansas City's arrival as a major-league squad was largely due to possession of a suitable stadium, or at least one that could be rebuilt into one. These multi-use structures, which also housed pro football teams and other community events, reshaped the professional sports landscape in America in the years after World War II. Under whatever name was in use at the time, Kansas City's Ruppert Stadium was at the vanguard of that movement.

However, as is often the case, all good things must come to an end. The ballpark was torn down in 1976, and a community garden currently stands on the site.[41]

Editor's Note

The ballpark at 22nd and Brooklyn in Kansas City was known as Muehlebach Field from 1923 to 1937, named for owner George E. Muehlebach of the minor-league Kansas City Blues, who built the original structure. When the New York Yankees owned the franchise and ballpark (1938-42), it was renamed Ruppert Stadium for Yankees owner Jacob Ruppert, but when Ruppert died it was renamed Blues Stadium (1943-54). When the Athletics relocated to Kansas City in 1955, and for the remainder of its existence, the building was named Municipal Stadium because of the heavy amount of public financing.

Because the 1942 Monarchs played in Ruppert Stadium, that is how it is identified in this article. The Monarchs played in the ballpark from 1923 through 1961. Negro League World Series games were played there in 1924 (Games Five through Seven), 1925 (Games One through Four), 1942 (Game Four), and 1946 (Games Three and Four).[42]

The architectural firm that oversaw construction of the park was Osborn Engineering.

Notes

1 Sam Mellinger, "Fifty Years Ago, Satchel Paige Pitched His Last Big-League Game in KC … at Age 59," *Kansas City Star*, September 18, 2015. https://www.kansascity.com/sports/spt-columns-blogs/sam-mellinger/article35763006.html.

2 Mellinger.

3 Rob Neyer, "Satchel Paige's Last Stand," SBNation.com, September 25, 2013. http://sbnation.com/2013/9/25/4767976/satchel-paige-kansas-city-athletics-1965-oldest-mlb-pitcher.

4 Mellinger.

5 Brian Burnes, "Dreaming of Fields: A Brief History of Kansas City Ballparks," KCFlatland.org, December 19, 2019. https://www.flatlandkc.org/news-issues/dreaming-of-fields-a-brief-history-of-kansas-city-ballparks/ Accessed May 13, 2021.

6 Larry Tye, *Satchel – The Life and Times of an American Legend* (New York: Random House Trade Paperbacks, 2009), 42-44.

7 Philip Lowry, ed., *Green Cathedrals*, fifth edition (Phoenix: Society for American Baseball Research, 2019), 159-161.

8 Janet Bruce, *The Kansas City Monarchs – Champions of Black Baseball* (Lawrence: University Press of Kansas, 1982), 51-52.

9 Brian Burnes, "Dreaming of Fields."

10 Lowry, 159-161.

11 Japheth Knopp, "Negro League Baseball, Black Community, and The Socio-Economic Impact of Integration," *Baseball Research Journal*, Spring 2016: 67, 68.

12 Jack Etkin, *Innings Ago – Recollections by Kansas City Ballplayers of Their Days in the Game* (Kansas City, Missouri: Normandy Square Publications, 1987), 10.

13 Bruce, 38-39.

14 Bruce, 38.

15 Bruce, 24-25.

16 Bruce, 24-25.

17 Etkin, 10.

18 "Kansas City Blues Franchise History (1888-1954)," Statscrew.com/minorbaseball/t-kb12304. Accessed May 9, 2021.

19 Phil S. Dixon, *The Dizzy and Daffy Dean Barnstorming Tour – Race, Media, and America's National Pastime* (Lanham, Maryland: Rowman & Littlefield, 2019), 55.

20 Flatlandkc.org; Jason Roe, "Kings of the City," https://kchistory.org/week-kansas-city-history/kings-city. Accessed May 13, 2021.

21 Bill Jenkinson, "Babe Ruth and the Issue of Race," BabeRuthCentral.com, 2009, updated 2016. Baberuthcentral.com/babe-ruth-and-the-issue-of-race-bill-jenkinson. Accessed May 13, 2021.

22 Dixon, *The Dizzy and Daffy Dean Barnstorming Tour*, 55.

23 Bruce, 70-71. According to uni-watch.com, the concept of baseball under portable lighting was tested in a game between the Monarchs and Phillips University in Enid, Oklahoma, played under the portable lights in front of 3,000 fans. https://uni-watch.com/2019/04/20/let-there-be-lights/.

24 Bruce, 50-51.

25 Phil S. Dixon, *John "Buck" O'Neil – The Rookie, The Man, The Legacy, 1938* (Bloomington, Indiana: AuthorHouse, 2009), 23.

26 Dixon, *John "Buck" O'Neil*, 36.

27 Dixon, *John "Buck" O'Neil*, 66.

28 Bruce, 51-52.

29 Lowry, 53-55, 103-105.

30 Ernest Mehl, *The Kansas City Athletics* (Henry Holt: New York, 1956), 57-121.

31 Mehl, 139-140.

32 Mehl, 142.

33 Mehl, 146-148.

34 Mehl, 179-180.

35 Lowry, 165-166.

36 Lowry, 165-166.

37 https://www.baseball-reference.com/teams/NYY/1939-schedule-scores.shtml

38 Bill Francis, "Hall of Fame Opened the Day of Lou Gehrig's Final Game," baseballhall.org. https://baseballhall.org/discover/gehrig-played-final-game-on-day-hall-of-fame-opened Accessed June 4, 2021.

39 Tye, 136-137.

40 Tye, 136-137.

41 *Green Cathedrals*, 162.

42 *Green Cathedrals*, 161.

Willa Bea Harmon, *Kansas City Call* Sportswriter

By Donna L. Halper

During the 1942 baseball season, many of the articles about the Kansas City Monarchs were written by Sam McKibben, the *Kansas City Call*'s sports editor. McKibben not only covered sports but was sometimes also asked to cover a breaking news story. And for the Black press, one of the biggest stories in early 1942 was the lynching of a Black man named Cleo Wright by a White mob in Sikeston, Missouri, about six hours from Kansas City. In addition to McKibben,[1] among the other Black reporters who made the trip to cover that story was a young woman who had only recently graduated from college. Her name was Willie Bea Harmon, and she was working for the *St. Louis Argus*.[2] However, her goal was to work in her hometown of Kansas City, preferably for the *Call*.

The 1941 City Directory for Kansas City already listed Harmon as an employee of the *Call*, but there is little evidence that she worked full-time for the newspaper until late in 1942. On the other hand, she had been hanging around the *Call*'s newsroom since she was in high school. As she told sportswriter Dan Burley in a 1944 interview, she first became interested in working there when a guest speaker, Frank "Fay" Young, the "Dean of the Black Sportswriters," came to talk to her news writing class at Lincoln High School. While Young was best known for his work with the *Chicago Defender*, he spent several years working as the managing editor of the *Call*, and young Willie Bea was so inspired by him that she decided she wanted a job.[3] She began as a "gofer," but gradually she was given a chance to do some copyediting and then some occasional reporting. After high school, she went off to college to study journalism, and once she graduated, she went to work for the *Argus* until the *Call* had an opening. But it wasn't for a news reporter – the *Call* needed an entertainment writer. By December 1942, she was writing a bylined column called the "Gossipel Truth."

She was also experimenting with her name, alternately writing as Bea Harmon, W. Bea Harmon or Willie Bea Harmon. It seems to have been Dan Burley who began referring to her as Willa Bea Harmon, circa 1944; gradually, she started using "Willa" in her byline. As for her entertainment column, it was a blend of movie and concert reviews, as well as the latest information about local and national artists coming to town. It often ventured into social commentary, as she lamented how nearly every venue in Kansas City was segregated or remarked upon how White businesses were happy to take the money of Black patrons yet felt no obligation to treat those Black patrons with respect.

During 1942, Harmon was not covering sports at the *Argus*, nor did that seem to be a goal for her. She had been trained as a news reporter, and her focus was on current issues. Of course, given that her entire family was from Kansas City, she was undoubtedly aware of how well the Monarchs were doing; in addition, the *Argus* had a sports page, and the Monarchs were frequently covered, along with some of the other Negro League teams.[4] When Harmon returned to Kansas City sometime in late 1942, she did get an opportunity to cover some hard news: Her duties included reporting on the courts and the police, in addition to working as the entertainment columnist.

Within a short time, everything changed. Throughout 1942 and 1943, a growing number of men were getting drafted and sent overseas to fight in World War II. Other men supported the war effort by working in the defense industry, and that is what Sam McKibben decided to do. He left the *Call* to work at a defense plant, and he didn't return; in fact, he subsequently left journalism to dedicate his life to being a Baptist minister.[5] Suddenly, in early 1943, there was an opening for a sports editor, and Harmon offered to give it a try.

She had always enjoyed participating in sports – mainly swimming and tennis – but by her own admission she was not very knowledgeable about professional baseball, and covering the Monarchs was a large part of being the sports editor. Fortunately, she had two excellent mentors, who taught her what she needed to know: the Monarchs' business manager (and former pitching star), Dizzy Dismukes, and the team's co-owner, Tom Baird.[6] She learned quickly,

• Willa Bea Harmon Kansas City Call Sportswriter •

The Kansas City Call's *Willa Bea Harmon, who worked her way from sports reporter to a position as the second Black female sports editor in America (after the* Baltimore Afro-American's *Nell Dodson). (St. Louis Star and Times, March 11, 1942)*

and by the start of the 1943 season, she was covering the Monarchs as well as reporting on college track and field, boxing, and other local sports. By April, she was bylined as the *Call*'s sports editor.[7] (Harmon was not the first Black female sports editor. Nell Dodson, later Nell Dodson Russell, held that position at the *Baltimore Afro-American* in the late 1930s. By most accounts, these two women were unique for their era. When Harmon left the *Call* in late 1945, she was described by reporters as "the only woman sports editor in the country."[8])

In early 1943, a controversy arose that affected the Negro Leagues: the US Office of Defense Transportation, whose mission was to encourage Americans to conserve transportation resources (including gasoline and tires) by reducing unnecessary travel,[9] decided to ban the use of privately owned buses by the 12 Negro Leagues teams that relied upon them.[10] The *Call* noted that the owners had pleaded with ODT Director Joseph B. Eastman to reconsider, but Eastman refused to make an exception, thus putting Negro Leagues players in a nearly impossible situation.[11] Harmon wrote about this issue on several occasions. For example, in her April 2, 1943, sports column, she took Eastman to task, accusing him of being willfully ignorant of the unique problems Black athletes faced in a segregated country. She dismissed his suggestion that the trains would be an acceptable alternative, and she invited him to see for himself why traveling through the Deep South by train would work much better for him and other White people than it would for Black people. She also criticized the Negro Leagues owners for having no real plan of their own and simply hoping for a miracle (which thus far had not arrived).[12] Meanwhile, in her entertainment columns, she continued to speak out about racism, chastising Hollywood for stereotyping Black actors and actresses,[13] and criticizing Kansas City theater and club owners for their patronizing treatment of Black customers – including her. Even though she was the theater critic for a widely-read newspaper, most White-owned venues refused to let her use the same door as the White reporters.[14]

Throughout the 1943 season, Harmon kept the *Call*'s readers informed about the latest Monarchs news. For someone who had never been a baseball reporter, she proved to have good instincts, and adapted well to her new duties. Known for being a talented writer, she was able to put those skills to use when reporting on the Monarchs' games. One good example was her report from the East-West "Dream Classic" in Chicago. It was a game witnessed by more than 50,000 fans and featured a masterful performance by Satchel Paige.[15] She not only noted the exciting plays; her thorough descriptions made readers feel as if they were there. Harmon also gained a reputation for truthfulness. She had learned from "Fay" Young that, even when covering the hometown team, it was important to be fair and factual. That year, due to a combination of injuries and the loss of key players to the military, the Monarchs did not get to the World Series. Harmon was sympathetic, but she was also accurate when describing how the team played throughout the season. When they played well, she praised them; but when they didn't, she avoided making excuses.

In addition, she offered readers deeper insights into what the players were like as people. For example, when Monarchs first baseman Buck O'Neil joined the Navy, she explained that he was more than just another skillful athlete. O'Neil, she said, was the kind of person who kept his teammates motivated, win or lose, and who played hard every game and never gave up. Of course, such a man was a major asset to the armed forces but, unfortunately for the Monarchs, it was a big loss for the team.[16]

From early 1943 until late 1945, Willa Bea Harmon earned the respect of her peers for her work on the baseball beat. When she decided to pursue a master's degree in journalism, many of her colleagues, and many of her readers, expressed their disappointment that she was leaving. They all hoped she would return to the *Call* one day, but she never did. After getting her degree, she wrote for the Associated Negro Press and for Black magazines like *Ebony* before marrying and moving to the West Coast. It is unfortunate that, thus far, the newspapers for which she wrote have not been digitized, limiting the number of people who can read her work. Whether writing about the entertainment industry or covering the world of sports, Harmon was unique – in a country that was segregated, and where women's opportunities in journalism were often limited, she did not let anything stop her. She was a true pioneer in sports reporting.

Notes

1 Sam McKibben, "Negroes Would Name Leaders if Given Protection," *Pittsburgh Courier*, March 7, 1942: 3.

2 Bea Harmon, "My Trip to Sikeston," *St. Louis Argus*, February 6, 1942: 1.

3 Dan Burley, "Confidentially Yours," *Amsterdam News*, November 25, 1944: 6B.

4 See for example, "Cincy Beats Paige and K.C. Monarchs," *St. Louis Argus*, June 19, 1942: 11, or "Satchel to Pitch Against Clowns," *St. Louis Argus*, August 21, 1942: 10.

5 "Marion Jackson's Sports News Reel," *Alabama Tribune* (Montgomery), December 19, 1947: 4.

6 Dan Burley, "Confidentially Yours," *Amsterdam News*, November 25, 1944: 6B.

7 W. Bea Harmon, "Sportorial ... by the Call's Sports Editor," *Kansas City Call*, April 9, 1943: 11.

8 "Swan Song," *Kansas City* (Kansas) *Plaindealer*, September 14, 1945: 8.

9 Bradley Flamm, "Putting the Brakes on 'Non-Essential' Travel: 1940s Wartime Mobility, Prosperity, and the US Office of Defense," *The Journal of Transport History* (vol. 27: 2006), 72-73.

10 William A. Young, *J.L. Wilkinson and the Kansas City Monarchs* (Jefferson, North Carolina: McFarland, 2016), 129-130.

11 "Start Fight for Negro Baseball," *Kansas City Call*, April 2, 1943: 1.

12 W. Bea Harmon, "Sportorial ... by the Call's Sports Editor," *Kansas City Call*, April 9, 1943: 11.

13 Willie Bea Harmon, "The Gossipel Truth," *Kansas City Call*, May 7, 1943: 15.

14 W. Bea Harmon, "The Gossipel Truth," *Kansas City Call*, August 27, 1943: 10.

15 Willie Bea Harmon, "West Topples East 2-1," *Kansas City Call*, August 6, 1943: 10.

16 Willie Bea Harmon, "Sportorial," *Kansas City Call*, August 20, 1943: 10.

The *Kansas City Call* and the Kansas City Monarchs

By William A. Young

Were it not for the *Chicago Defender, New York Amsterdam News, Pittsburgh Courier, Baltimore Afro-American*, and other African American newspapers, there would have been scant coverage of Black professional baseball. White-owned and -run dailies like the *Chicago Tribune, New York Times, Pittsburgh Post-Gazette,* and *Washington Post* published few informative articles on the African American baseball teams in their cities. In Kansas City, Missouri, the *Kansas City Star* included periodic articles on the city's main African American team, the Kansas City Monarchs, but the Black-owned and -operated weekly *Kansas City Call* covered the team much more thoroughly. Without a doubt, the *Call* provided the most complete record of the Monarchs, one of the best teams in the history not only of Black baseball, but all of baseball.

Serendipitously, the *Call* was founded in May 1919, a year before the formation of the first successful professional Black league, the Negro National League, and the organization of the Kansas City Monarchs. The *Call's* founder was Chester Arthur "C.A." Franklin (1880-1955). Franklin was born in Denison, Texas, to a barber and a teacher at a time when African Americans were leaving Texas and other Southern states in search of better educational opportunities for their children. In 1887 the Franklin family moved to Omaha, Nebraska, where C.A.'s father established a newspaper, the *Omaha Enterprise*. C.A. attended the University of Nebraska for two years, but because of his father's ill health had to leave school to take over as editor of the *Enterprise*. To improve his father's health, the family moved to Colorado in 1898 and bought another paper, eventually called the *Star*.

In 1913 C.A. Franklin moved to Kansas City, where six years later he began publishing the *Call*. The paper started as a four-page sheet with a weekly run of 2,000. Its circulation grew rapidly, soon reaching 18,000. Before long nearly every African American home in Kansas City was receiving a copy from a carrier. At the same time, mail circulation throughout Missouri and the states to the southwest expanded. The *Call* was on its way to becoming one of the largest, most successful Black businesses in the region. By the 1950s the *Call* had expanded to 32 pages with 40,000 copies sold each week.[1]

As soon became obvious in his first weekly editorials, C.A. Franklin was a strong advocate of Black self-reliance, endorsing the philosophy of W.E.B. Du Bois. For example, in the January 14, 1922, edition of the *Call*, under the headline "The Manhood of Kansas City Negroes Is Challenged," Franklin decried the manipulation of Blacks in Kansas City politics, concluding "[we] are not underlings because other men say we are, we are masters of our fate. Strong men, just men of every race, will applaud the day when we cease to be measured by the scorn of our contemners, and offer our own proved merit."

During its first decades the *Call* covered fully the campaign to expand the right to vote for African Americans and for equal opportunities for Blacks in employment, education, and housing. One of the *Call's* first victories was breaking the ban in Kansas City that prohibited African Americans from serving on juries.

Nor did the *Call* shy away from addressing the most highly charged national issues facing African Americans. The paper strongly endorsed the struggle against segregation in the armed forces and the fight for nondiscriminatory hiring in government agencies. It also ran front-page stories on the scourge of lynching and kept track of the numbers of lynching victims state by state.

Some of the *Call's* first subscribers were members of the Paseo YMCA volleyball team, on which Franklin played. Whether at the YMCA, where in 1920 the meeting to organize the NNL was held, or another venue, Franklin met and became good friends with J.L. Wilkinson (1878-1964), founder and principal owner of the Kansas City Monarchs. For the nearly three decades Wilkinson owned the Monarchs, he and Franklin worked closely together, and the paper was an enthusiastic supporter of the team and Black baseball in general. In its coverage of the organizational meeting of the NNL, the *Call* enthused in its February 27, 1920, edition that "[i]t was the first time in the history of a baseball meeting that there was exhibited so much harmony and good spirit."

Known for his acumen as a promoter, Wilkinson quickly recognized the importance of a good relationship with Franklin and the *Call*. He assigned the Monarchs business manager, Q.J. Gilmore, the responsibility of providing the *Call* with a steady stream of positive articles about the Monarchs. The *Call* reciprocated with frequent endorsements of the team. When Wilkinson decided to name the team the Monarchs (upon the recommendation of one of his players, John Donaldson), the *Call* later proclaimed that the team had proven in its first years of play, in the words of eighteenth-century poet William Cowper, that they were "MONARCHS OF ALL THEY SURVEY."[2]

C.A. Franklin recognized the role that Wilkinson and the Monarchs were playing in improving racial harmony in Kansas City. In its October 22, 1922, edition the *Call* noted that "[f]rom a sociological point of view, the Monarchs have done more than any other single agent to break the damnable outrage of prejudice that exists in this city. White fans, the thinking class at least, cannot have watched the orderly crowds at Association Park ... and not concede that we are humans at least, and worthy of consideration as such." When the team began playing games in Association Park, Wilkinson had insisted that the signs marking "colored section" be taken down and that patrons, regardless of race, be allowed to sit anywhere in the stands.

When the Monarchs moved to Muehlebach Field in 1923, Wilkinson's agreement with the stadium's owner, brewer George Muehlebach, allowed Black spectators to sit throughout the stands. In reporting on the agreement, the *Call* noted that "[f]ans from both races will continue to be able to sit side by side, and, after a while, the same relation may be carried to the workshop" (November 3, 1922). The *Call* had long recognized that Wilkinson expected clean play on the field, noting his slogan for how the Monarchs players were expected to deal with an opponent was "treat him right, but get him out."[3]

In the July 20, 1923, edition of the *Call,* sports editor Charles A. Sparks claimed that the Monarchs and other Black teams were showing that the racist attitude of "the superiority of the whites and the inferiority of the Blacks" is dead. The Monarchs were proving that "Negroes play the game with much more thought and snap than the average white player." The public is beginning to question, Starks maintained, the results of a World Series championship played between two white teams "when perhaps there are one of several colored teams in the country better than the contenders."

When necessary, the *Call* also could be critical of the Monarchs and Black baseball, as in a scathing December 16, 1927, editorial by sports editor A.D. Williams that laid out the concerns he claimed needed to be addressed in the Negro leagues. Williams also chastised African American fans in Kansas City for lack of support of the team. At the end of the 1929 season Williams wrote, "If there ever was a club deserving the support of a city – it is [the Monarchs]. Their brand of baseball is second to none in the country. [J.L. Wilkinson has] always placed a real ball club on the field. ... I wonder where that old Monarch loyalty is."[4]

When Wilkinson introduced portable lights in 1930 to make night games possible, Williams and the *Call* were among the first to endorse the scheme that other journalists and baseball executives were rejecting as foolish and unworkable. In its January 10 and 24, 1930, editions the *Call* explained Wilkinson's rationale for the experiment and Williams declared that the Monarchs owner had tested the lights sufficiently to go ahead. "Believe it or not," Williams concluded, "there's method in the supposed madness of friend Wilkinson. There's one thing about him – he knows baseball ... and the highway to the dollars." After the lighting scheme had proved successful, the *Call* asserted that Wilkinson had risked everything financially and kept the Monarchs afloat "for the sake of the men who played for him. ..."[5]

After six years (1931-36) spent exclusively barnstorming with his portable lighting system, as far north as Canada and south into Mexico, Wilkinson decided it was time to return the Monarchs to league play. He had a key role in the formation of the Negro American League in 1937 and was elected the new league's treasurer.

In 1942 the *Call's* reporting began with a January 2 article on the annual meeting of the NAL. The key issue at the meeting was the decision to join with the NNL in banning all clubs from playing the Ethiopian Clowns. Tom Wilson, president of the NNL, who was present at the NAL meeting, said that "the Eastern owners had long been of the opinion that the painting of faces by the Clowns players, their antics on the diamond and their style of play was a detriment to Negro league baseball."

For Wilkinson and the Monarchs, not playing the Clowns represented a change in policy. The *Call* reported on Monarchs and Clowns preseason exhibition games and tours in 1940, playing in towns as far north as Winnipeg, Canada, and in 1941. For scheduling games with the Clowns, the Monarchs had drawn the ire of Cum Posey, owner of the Homestead Grays, and other Negro Leagues magnates, who claimed that the Clowns were playing to White stereotypes of Black baseball. However, Wilkinson maintained that the Monarchs played the Clowns not only because their showmanship drew crowds but because they played excellent baseball.

The 1942 Monarchs trained in Monroe, Louisiana, beginning their exhibition season on Easter Sunday, April 5, with a game against the Cincinnati Tigers. On April 24 the *Call* reported to the delight of Monarchs fans that Satchel Paige would be with the team for the 1942 season. On April 26 an overflow crowd of 15,000 at Pelican Stadium in New Orleans watched Paige pitch five innings against 1941's top team, the Homestead Grays. It was the second game of a doubleheader, won by the Grays 10-7. The Monarchs took the first contest, 6-5, with Hilton Smith and Connie Johnson on the mound.

The 1942 Monarchs were considered by many, including Buck O'Neil, to be the best team in the franchise's history, and games when Paige pitched drew large crowds; however, as the season got underway overall attendance began to decline. The *Call's* new sports editor, Sam McKibben, questioned why African Americans were supporting the [White] Kansas City Blues instead of their own Monarchs. At Blues games, Blacks were still forced to sit in the bleachers, exposed to the sun and rain. "Apparently," McKibben wrote sarcastically, "rank discrimination doesn't spin their enjoyment of the game." By contrast, at the Monarchs home opener, McKibben observed, "whites and Negroes sat together, cheered together, slapped each other on the back."[6]

The Monarchs opened the 1942 regular season in Chicago on May 10, taking both games of a doubleheader with the Chicago American Giants, 7-4 and 6-0. Paige earned the shutout victory in the second game, and, according to the *Call* of May 15, "Old Satchel" showed "some of the smartest pitching of his brilliant career."

The home opener at Ruppert Stadium on May 17 against the Memphis Red Sox featured a patriotic theme, with War Bonds on sale and soldiers in uniform admitted free (as they were throughout World War II). The Monarchs and Red Sox split a doubleheader as Paige took the loss in the second game.

On May 24, 1942, the Monarchs and Satchel Paige faced off at Wrigley Field in Chicago against a white team composed of major and minor leaguers led by Dizzy Dean. The game drew nearly 30,000 fans. The *Call* noted in its promotional article for the game (May 22, 1942) that Dean was still smarting at the losses he had suffered to Paige several years earlier. Indians ace Bob Feller was scheduled to play but had to withdraw when he was called back to active service in the Navy; he donated his fee to a Navy relief fund. The Monarchs won the game, 3-1, with both Dean and Paige taking the mound. As he would often do, after Paige pitched the first innings (in this game, six), Hilton Smith finished the contest. According to the *Call's* game report (May 29, 1942), several of the big leaguers on Dean's team "were loud and sincere in their praise of the Monarchs[,]" saying the several Monarchs could play in the white majors. However, the game drew the attention of Commissioner Kenesaw Mountain Landis. The *Call* reported on July 3, 1942, that Landis was about to rule that games between teams led by Paige and Dean would not be allowed to be played in white parks.

On June 5, 1942, the *Call* reported that Frank Duncan, who had been sharing managerial duties with Dizzy Dismukes, was named permanent skipper. According to the *Call*, with the departure of J.L. Wilkinson's brother Lee from team duties, Dismukes resumed the role of business manager and traveling secretary. The ban on NAL teams playing games against the Ethiopian Clowns did not stop the *Call* from publishing a picture of Clowns pitcher Peanuts Nyassas, "who performs antics that keep fans in an uproar." On June 26 the *Call* noted that the Clowns were playing throughout the Midwest, drawing an average of 5,000 per game.

The lure of a big payday proved too great. Skirting the ban on games by NAL and NNL teams against the Clowns, "by special arrangement with KC Monarchs management[,]" a game between the Ethiopian Clowns and Birmingham Black Barons was played at Ruppert Stadium in Kansas City on August 9, 1942. In a promotional article on August 7, the *Call* noted that "all the Clowns' stunts will be on display." For example, Pepper Bassett would catch the game seated in a rocking chair, the *Call* reported. The Clowns were currently barnstorming before huge crowds through the Dakotas, Iowa, Ohio, Minnesota, and Illinois. More than 600,000 fans had paid to see them, the *Call* added. They had played to crowds as large as 25,000. In his "Sports Potpourri" column, Sam McKibben wrote that the Ethiopian Clowns would present their "baseball tomfoolery" … "Incredible feats will be accomplished before the final ball is thrown." The game was a "must" for baseball fans, he dutifully wrote. They will "clown their way into the hearts of the Heart of America." The Clowns lost both ends of the doubleheader before 4,000 fans.

NAL owners decided at their February 1943 meeting not only to allow teams to play the Ethiopian (now Cincinnati and later Indianapolis) Clowns but also to allow the Clowns to join the league.[7] The Clowns played their home games at Crosley Field in Cincinnati. In August 1943 the Monarchs played a profitable series against the Clowns.

In 1942 the *Call* was also lending its voice to the campaign to break the through the color barrier in major-league baseball. On June 12 the paper published the full text of a resolution adopted by the 2,000 members of the National Maritime Union calling for Negro players to be allowed in the major leagues. Another union, the United Retail, Wholesale, and Department Store employees, had already passed a similar resolution. A copy was sent to Commissioner Landis.

In addition to its NAL schedule, the 1942 Monarchs were continuing to barnstorm. The *Call* reported on a June tour through Michigan, Ohio, and Pennsylvania, including a no-hitter hurled by Paige and Booker McDaniel against the Frigidaire Icemen at Ducks Park in Dayton, Ohio, on June 16.[8]

During the 1942 campaign Wilkinson made the turnstiles spin by booking games for the Paige All-Stars. The Original House of David team continued to be a popular rival, as on July 5 in Louisville, Kentucky. The *Call* enthused that "there is little doubt about the magnetic quality of Paige's box office appeal." In 1942 he was, according to the *Call*, having one of his best seasons, noting that "his fast hopper is jumping."[9]

On Friday, July 17, 1942, the Monarchs met an Army team, Johnny Sturm's Jefferson Barracks All-Stars, which featured several former major leaguers. The game took place at Ruppert Stadium, and the *Call* made clear in its July 24 issue that there would be integrated seating. The game was the brainchild of J.L. Wilkinson and Monarchs co-owner Tom Baird. They covered all the Monarchs' expenses and the New York Yankees, for whom Sturm had played, and who owned the white Kansas City Blues, covered the ballpark expenses. The proceeds were to go to charity. The Monarchs staged a rendition of the popular pepper game before the first pitch and then shut out the All-Stars, 6-0.

In its July 24, 1942, edition the *Call's* Sam McKibben noted that on July 17 "death claimed Segregation, Discrimination and Jim Crow, father, son and grandson, all pioneer residents of Ruppert Stadium. … There were no mourners, just 6,000 enjoying a baseball drama. The ushers, who are usually rude to Negro patrons, were bubbling with friendliness. That's democracy at work. Whites seated next to Negroes without incident and asked, 'Why don't they allow the [white Kansas City] Blues to play the Monarchs?' and 'Why are Negroes kept out of the majors and minors?' There was no trouble-making, no vile language, no fights. The Ruppert management had contended that white patrons would object to sitting next to Negroes at ball games. Oh well, if it never happens again, it happened Friday night. There was no segregation nor discrimination. Whites will benefit more than Negroes as a result of the charity proceeds, but Negro fans came out in huge numbers in support of the game." McKibben went on to write that Commissioner Landis has let it be known he had not laid down a law saying Negroes cannot play in the majors, that it is up to club owners. There were some White owners willing to sign Negroes. "Let Negro league teams like the Monarchs play leading major league teams and owners could tell how Negro and white players compare in ability," McKibben concluded.

The next week the *Call* printed the full statement of Commissioner Landis. In part, Landis proclaimed: "If [Leo] Durocher, or any other manager, or all of them want to sign one or 25 Negro players it is all right with me. That is the business of the manager and the club owners." The statement was provoked by comment from Durocher that "he would hire Negro players if he were permitted." The *Call* also included a response to Landis by civil-rights leader A. Philip Randolph that "the door was now open for Negro players, but it will not remain open. It is up to Negroes themselves with the support of their white friends to keep it open and open it wider. With so many players going into the military, the demand is now greater than the supply. If Negro players do not break in during the war, it is not likely they will after the war. We do not want Negroes to enter the majors as Negro teams we want them integrated into every baseball club in the country."[10]

The July 31 edition of the *Call* returned to the July 17 game in an editorial by McKibben headlined "Modern Version: Dr. Jekel [*sic*] – Mr. Hyde." He again contrasted the courtesy of the white ushers at the Monarchs-Jefferson Barracks game with the attitude toward Black fans attending games between the Kansas City Blues and other white teams. At a Blues-Toledo Mud Hens game, attendants insulted Black fans with racial slurs. Two Negro men responded to the ushers, saying, "[w]e are American citizens and entitled to the rights of Americans." Before long Negro players, McKibben asserted, will be in the majors, and "the jim-crow practice will be drowning in its own sweat." McKibben had guessed three weeks earlier that "some cellar-dwelling big-league team would buy some Negro players. [Josh] Gibson, [Buck] O'Neil, [Joe] Greene, [Satchel] Paige, [Hilton] Smith, [Willard] Brown, and [Ted] Strong, to name a few, are "on the threshold of a new day."

On August 7, 1942, under the headline "The Monarchs Owner Is Elated," the *Call* published an Associated Negro Press wire story. According to the release, "J.L. Wilkinson, co-owner of the Kansas City Monarchs, champions of the Negro American League, gave approbation this week to the plan of William E. Benswanger, owner of the Pittsburgh Pirates, to give Negro baseball players a tryout with his team. Moghuls [*sic*] of major league teams expressed themselves pro and con on the issue. 'I think it would be a fine [day] for the game,' said Wilkinson, 'although we would lose some of our stars.' Wilkinson is a former minor league pitcher who has been [involved with] Negro ball teams with his partner, Tom Board [*sic*], since [1920]." Wilkinson said he had talked "with Leroy 'Satchel' Paige, the pitching great" recently "and said he advised the right hand speed-ball [artist], 'we certainly won't stand in your way if you have a chance to play.' Paige is under a two-year contract with the Kansas City club. ... Wilkinson said he believed Josh Gibson, catcher for the Washington Homestead Grays, would attract the most attention next to Paige. ... 'There are at least a score of players who could make any major league team,' added the Monarchs owner."

Sam McKibben conducted an interview with Satchel Paige at the 1942 Negro Leagues East-West All-Star Game played on August 16 before 45,179 at Comiskey Field in Chicago. It was published in the August 21 edition of the *Call* under the headline "Paige Says Abolish Jim Crow and He Will Be Ready for His Major League Debut but Not Before at Any Price." It clearly showed that Paige had given careful consideration to the prospect of his signing with a major-league team. McKibben wrote, "Satchel Paige doesn't want a major league tryout, nor to play major league ball ... unless two things come to pass: the complete abolition of JIM CROW on a NATIONAL scale ... and he is given a contract identical to that tendered a white player getting a tryout. The white papers have been saying Paige is through. When Paige told a reporter that he wouldn't sign a $10,000 contract with a big-league team, and refused to reveal his current salary, it was written that he was receiving $40,000 a year. Satchel is an enthusiastic talker and I just let him talk," McKibben commented. "'Imagine,' he says, 'me living at a Negro hotel although I play with a white team. Record my feelings when dishes, out of which I eat, are broken up in my presence. How could I pitch a decent game with insulting jeers coming from spectators and even some of the players? ... Just convince me that agitation can be halted and I'll push fast balls by Joe DiMaggio.' 'Why,' he says, 'if the President hasn't made southern DEFENSE plants hire, and use Negro labor in government plants, how can Judge Landis, Connie Mack or anyone make the southern white folk accept the Negro as a ball player. His training camp life in the South would be miserable ... and the camps won't be moved for one or two Negroes. ... What about the tryouts allegedly scheduled by the Pittsburgh Pirates. Who will 'bell the cat' (meaning end jim crow)? Will the white trainers work on a Negro to say nothing to take care of him. Indeed not. I've never been able to get any service out of one. ... Tell the reading public,' says Satch, 'not to believe half of what it reads that I say in the [white] daily papers. I say to others what I am saying to you, but my statements are twisted. Negroes will never get into the major leagues because of jim crow. It's a wonderful dream but will never come true. With the nation at war not one is going to try to abolish jim crow .... and even in peace time, jim crowism will flourish. Me, I am going to stick with Wilkie, J.L. Wilkinson, Monarchs owner, and whoever says I am afraid I can't make the grade ... is just plain nuts. I experience enough prejudice now, why court more?'"

In the same edition, in his "Sports Potpourri" feature, McKibben opined that "Negro soldiers are being killed in the South while in uniform for 'mixing' with whites. What will happen to Negro ballplayers training in the South?" He said that as a native Southerner, he believed "Jim Crowism will keep Negroes out of major league baseball. ... Jim Crow must be destroyed but who will accomplish it? Truthfully, I am 100 per cent for Negroes in the majors – but too young to attempt self-disillusionment when overwhelming odds are stacking against it. ... [I]t will take two years to properly season and infiltrate Negroes into major league ball." "It's time we sport writers cease sugar-coating. ..."

The next week the *Call* noted reports of "[Ku Klux] Klan activity in a plot to stir up race hatred in the war industry" and "destroy national unity behind the administration's win-the-war program."[11]

In its September 4 edition the *Call* began its coverage of the 1942 Colored World Series between the Monarchs and the Homestead Grays, with the prediction that 32,000 would strain the capacity of Griffith Stadium in Washington when the Grays crossed bats with the Monarchs in the opening game of the 1942 Colored World Series on September 8. The *Call* noted that "the great Satchel Paige will be on the mound with power hitting Josh Gibson in the box. In two previous meetings this season in Washington, the Grays have edged out the Monarchs in extra-inning games."

Since the *Call* was published weekly, fans would already have learned the outcomes and likely seen the box scores of the Series games, so the rest of the *Call's* reporting on the Series (in the September 18 and 25 editions) focused not on individual games but on Satchel Paige's famed confrontation with Josh Gibson in the second game, played in Pittsburgh on September 10, and a controversy that threatened to derail the Series. The former clash has become part of Negro Leagues baseball lore, but the latter event has received lesser attention.

In the September 25 *Call*, McKibben wrote an article headlined "Grays Employ Outside Talent to Beat Monarchs, 4-1" in which he gave a straightforward description of what the Grays had done. "With the aid of the Newark Eagles' ace pitcher, Leon Day, who is reputed to be one of the classiest performers in baseball today, and who was aided and abided [*sic*] by more of his Newark Eagles' teammates, Pearson and Stone, and Buster Clarkson of the Philly Stars," McKibben wrote, "the Homestead Grays *et al.* defeated the Kansas City Monarchs 4 to 1, Sunday afternoon [September 24], at Ruppert Stadium. If the Monarchs had won[,] it would have ended the series. If won by the Grays[,] the series would have been extended from 4 of 7 to 5 of 9. ... The facts make known the desperation of the Homestead Grays and explained why the 'ringers' were brought in to stem the tide." The game was interrupted several times because someone was using emery to scuff the ball, but the offender was not discovered.

McKibben noted that the game was nullified at a meeting of NAL moguls called by Wilkinson and Baird. That left the Monarchs with a 3-0 lead in the series. Additionally, the use of emery boards and "other infractions of sportsmanlike ethics were ironed out to the satisfaction of all parties concerned." The game was replayed in Philadelphia on September 29 and the Monarchs prevailed for a 4-0 Series win.

During the 1942-43 offseason the Office of Defense Transportation ruled that, effective March 15, 1943, the use of all privately owned buses by baseball teams would be forbidden. The order drew a quick reaction from NAL and NNL owners. They pointed out that Negro League teams appeared in several different parks each week and would not be able to play enough games to have financial stability without travel in private buses. In addition, since Black ballplayers were denied hotel accommodations in some cities, the buses were essential as sleeping quarters. The owners also emphasized that Negro League games provided much-needed entertainment for Black war workers in 11 metropolitan areas as well as competition for military teams.

Unmoved, the ODT refused to grant Black baseball an exemption to the ban. Wilkinson and *Call* editor C.A. Franklin joined forces in mounting a campaign to overturn the ruling. The *Call* published a series of articles condemning the ban and printed a "Save Negro Baseball" petition.[12] It took until midway through the 1943 season for the campaign to convince the ODT to reverse its decision and to allow teams to use private buses.

The Monarchs continued to draw decent crowds through the 1945 season and peaked when Wilkinson and Baird signed Jackie Robinson. The turning point for the Monarchs and other Negro Leagues clubs was, of course, Branch Rickey's acquisition of Robinson's contract in August 1945, followed by Robinson's joining the Brooklyn Dodgers in April 1947.

The Monarchs fielded teams in various manifestations into the 1960s and the *Call* continued its coverage, although more sporadically. In the final years of the Monarchs, the greatest attention in the

Call's sports section was devoted to Monarchs whose contracts were sold to major-league teams, more than from any other Negro League teams. The list includes Hall of Famers Paige, Willard Brown, Andy Cooper, and Ernie Banks, and the first African American to play for the New York Yankees, Elston Howard.

Sources

In addition to the articles in the *Kansas City Call* cited, other Kansas City Monarchs game reports are drawn from a timeline for the 1942 season compiled by Bill Nowlin: *see story on page 182*.

Portions of this essay are drawn from William A. Young, *J.L. Wilkinson and the Kansas City Monarchs: Trailblazers in Black Baseball* (Jefferson, North Carolina: McFarland & Company, 2016).

Notes

1 William H. Young and Nathan B. Young Jr., "The Story of the Kansas City Monarchs," *Your Kansas City and Mine* (Kansas City: Midwest Afro-American Genealogy Interest Coalition, 1950), 137-38, 142.

2 *Kansas City Call,* July 27, 1928.

3 *Kansas City Call,* June 17, 1922.

4 *Kansas City Call,* August 30, 1929.

5 *Kansas City Call,* January 26, 1934.

6 *Kansas City Call,* May 15 and 22, 1942.

7 *Kansas City Call,* February 26, 1943.

8 *Kansas City Call,* June 19, 1942.

9 *Kansas City Call,* July 3, 1942.

10 *Kansas City Call,* July 31, 1942.

11 *Kansas City Call,* August 28, 1942.

12 *Kansas City Call,* April 9 and 16, 1943.

J.L. Wilkinson and the Rebirth of Satchel Paige

By William A. Young

By the fall of 1938 Kansas City Monarchs owner J.L. Wilkinson was well aware of the marketing potential of Leroy "Satchel" Paige. The Monarchs had seen the talented pitcher on opposing teams over the years, and Wilkie (as Wilkinson was known to his players) had often taken advantage of Paige's practice of assuring that he could be rented out to clubs other than the one he was playing for. Now Wilkinson was about to take full advantage of Satchel's star power.

In 1934 Paige pitched for the Monarchs in a game against an all-star team put together around the St. Louis Cardinals Gas House Gang's ace pitching duo, Dizzy and Paul Dean. The Monarchs hired Paige again the next year for another series against the Dean All-Stars. Dizzy told Paige as they were saying goodbye after the tour, "You're a better pitcher'n I ever hope to be, Satch."[1] On another occasion, Dizzy said, "If Satch and I was pitching on the same team, we'd cinch the pennant by July Fourth and go fishin' until World Series time."[2]

During portions of two seasons (1933 and 1935) Paige pitched for car dealer Neil Churchill's integrated team in Bismarck, North Dakota. The ethnically diverse team also had a Cuban, a Jew, a Lithuanian, an Italian, an Irishman, a Swede, and a German, much like J.L. Wilkinson's famed All Nations club. Paige pitched in more than 60 games in three months for the Churchills, won 30 of 32 decisions, and averaged nearly 15 strikeouts per game. More than once Wilkinson's Monarchs played the Churchills while they were barnstorming. For example, in June 1935, Paige hurled a 2-0 shutout against the Monarchs' Chet Brewer.

While playing for Bismarck in the summer of 1935, Paige said he was given some snake oil by Sioux Indians he met. They told him it was "hot stuff" and not to put it on anything but snake bites. Figuring it might be good for him in the cold North Dakota air, Paige put some on his arm after pitching and it loosened him up. He began using it after every game and kept some on hand in a jar.[3]

With the help of stars like Quincy Trouppe, Hilton Smith, and Ted "Double Duty" Radcliffe, the Bismarck team won the 1935 National Baseball Congress Tournament in Wichita, Kansas. After the tournament, the Churchills barnstormed their way to Kansas City, where, on September 15, Paige (with Radcliffe as his batterymate) took the mound against the Monarchs. Satchel told Churchill the umpire's tight strike zone was causing him "unwarranted pain and suffering" and he wanted to leave the game. Churchill appealed, saying it was his last game as manager, and offered Satchel an extra $750 if they beat the Monarchs. Satchel relented, struck out 15, and pocketed the cash after an 8-4 victory.

In the spring of 1936, Paige rejoined Gus Greenlee's Pittsburgh Crawfords, where he had played earlier in the 1930s. In 1937 Satchel left the Crawfords to play for a month in the Dominican Republic, for the Dragons, a team sponsored by dictator Rafael Trujillo. He was 8-2 and won the championship game.

When Paige and the other players who had jumped to the Dominican Republic returned to the States, they formed an all-star team that outdrew Negro League clubs. Greenlee offered him $450 a week to return to the Crawfords, but Satchel told him, "I wouldn't throw ice cubes for that kind of money."[4] Greenlee then sold Paige's contract to the Newark Eagles for $5,000, but the "travelin' man," as Satchel called himself, went to Mexico instead, where he signed for $2,000 a month. Enraged, Greenlee led the charge that resulted in Negro League owners voting to ban Paige for life.[5]

In Mexico, Paige's arm hurt so much he could barely throw. He was hit hard by virtually every batter he faced. At times Satchel said that the spicy Mexican food was to blame for his arm trouble.[6] On other occasions he said he had run out of the special oil the Sioux Indians had given him. In fact, years of pitching so many games had caught up with Satchel. Some speculate he had suffered a rotator cuff injury. Infielder Newt Allen said Satchel's arm had gotten so bad he couldn't rub the back of his neck.

Looking back, a decade later, the *Kansas City Call* suggested alliteratively, "[t]he great one owned a wing

• J.L. Wilkinson and the Rebirth of Satchel Paige •

that was as dead as a new bride's biscuit. … It was at that time that J.L. Wilkerson [*sic*], owner of the Monarchs, toyed with the idea of employing Satch, who was nursing the once-poisonous paw in pathetic pity."[7] Indeed, almost everyone in the baseball world, except Wilkinson, thought Paige was washed up. He called Paige, and Satchel remembered the conversation well:

> "Satch, this is J.L. Wilkinson. I own the Kansas City Monarchs. Remember me?"
>
> Paige said, "I remembered good. I'd put in some time for Mr. Wilkinson. … 'Yes, sir, Mr. Wilkinson,' I said."
>
> "Satchel, Tom Baird, my partner, and I just got your contract from Newark. When can you report to Kansas City?"
>
> "I can be there tomorrow."
>
> "Make it next week and meet me there."

Satchel said he felt "I'd been dead. Now I was alive again. I didn't have an arm, but I didn't even think of that. I had me a piece of work."[8]

Wilkinson's signing of Paige turned out to be transformative for the Monarchs as well. As John Holway has described the moment: "[T]he decision Wilkinson made, while they talked, represented the second great achievement that would help bring the Monarchs a new dynasty [the first being night baseball]. It was an achievement born of baseball acumen, of wisdom about muscle and bone, skill and sporting spirit. Wilkinson decided to give Satchel Paige a second chance." As it turned out, "Wilkinson saved Satchel Paige's career. And Paige rejuvenated the Monarchs."[9]

When Paige met Wilkinson and Baird, he explained that he couldn't throw. Wilkinson responded that the plan was for him to play first base. Then Satchel asked when he could join the Monarchs. Wilkinson was quiet for a moment, then said, "[Y]ou're not going to play with the Monarchs. We've got a Monarchs traveling team, a barnstorming team. We planned to send you up North on a tour with them. You couldn't pitch with that arm of yours, and you haven't played first enough to hold it down in the Negro Leagues."

Paige said, "that good feeling I'd had just sort of floated away." However, he said to Wilkinson, "I guess that's how it will be."

Then Paige asked why Wilkinson was giving him a job, if he wasn't good enough for the Monarchs:

> "We think you're still big enough to pull the fans," Wilkie said.
>
> "My name," Paige responded, "ain't gonna lure that many fans."
>
> Wilkinson was quiet again for a moment, then said, "It'll lure enough. Anyway, I thought you needed a hand."

In a 1971 interview, Bill "Plunk" Drake said "Wilkerson," [sic] whom Drake called an "awful good man," even took Satchel to Chicago for treatment of his stomach trouble.[10]

Wilkinson and Paige may have been pleased that Satchel would be playing again, but Effa Manley, co-owner with her husband, Abe, of the Newark Eagles, and the only woman inducted (with Wilkinson in 2006) into the National Baseball Hall of Fame, was furious. She believed that the Monarchs owner should have sided with her when Satchel jumped his contract with the Eagles to play in Mexico. She accused Wilkinson of being no different than other White booking agents or ballpark owners, interested only in making money, and threatened to sign players from the Monarchs in retaliation.[11] Wilkinson responded to Mrs. Manley's outrage calmly, telling her that "no one had offered Paige a contract, so I picked him up."[14] Technically, Wilkinson was right. The deal in which the Crawfords had sold Paige's contract to the Eagles was contingent on Satchel showing up, and he hadn't.

In the end, Paige was allowed to remain with the Monarchs, and the Eagles were permitted to keep two Negro American League players they had signed in violation of interleague rules.

According to Monarchs pitcher Chet Brewer, the first thing the Monarchs owner did after signing Paige in 1938 was to take Satchel to a dentist and get him a new set of teeth. Wilkinson just had a way, Brewer said, of knowing what a player needed.[12] As J.L.'s son, Dick, said, "Satchel had a 'whalebone arm,' all bone, not much muscle. Dad could tell by looking at a ball player whether he could play ball or had potential. They talked, and Dad gave him another chance."[13] Buck O'Neil remembered that "J.L. Wilkinson saw the potential there [in Paige, after he hurt his arm], knew that he was a great drawing card."[14]

Wilkinson sent Satchel, with Newt Joseph, to play in the West, all the way to Canada, on a team sometimes called the "Second Monarchs," "Junior Monarchs," or "Kansas City Travelers." The players often called the team the "Baby Monarchs." During one stretch, the Shreveport Acme Giants journeyed with the Travelers and played against them, O'Neil recalled.

• When the Monarchs Reigned •

With the Monarchs traveling squad, before a game, Satchel would often perform a "pepper show," doing tricks with the ball, like rolling it across his arm and chest to the other arm and hand, and some shadowball playing, slow-motion throws, and gags. When the game started, he would sometimes take the pitcher's mound and soft-toss his way through a few innings with what he called his "Alley Oops and Bloopers." Then he would play first or occupy the first-base coaching box, to the delight of the fans in the small towns where they played.[15]

As Satchel remembered, on the traveling team the other players at first treated him like he "was dead and buried." About the only one not like that was Newt Joseph, an old-timer who was the traveling club's secretary, who told him "maybe we can work that arm of yours out." At least, Paige said, he was making spending money.[16]

Before long, the Monarchs "B" squad was outdrawing and earning more than the main team, because of the "Paige effect." Wilkinson wisely began advertising the Travelers as "Satchel Paige's All-Stars." They played games against "community teams, post office teams, industrial league teams, church squads, Sunday-school teams, railroad-sponsored teams, pharmacy-sponsored teams, and any local nine that came together with enough cash to sponsor the contest, cover travel expenses, and guarantee a reasonable gate."[17] For many semipro teams, the entire year's budget was based on booking Paige. He kept many clubs solvent just by appearing.

The Monarchs traveling team included young talent but also older players such as Newt Joseph as well as George Giles and Cool Papa Bell. Paige respected Wilkinson for giving jobs to older players like him, whom others ridiculed as being past their prime. He quoted Wilkinson as saying, "[t]hey can still do some good. And they've done a lot for the Negro Leagues and made us all some money, so I'm just trying to pay them back a little." Wilkinson also realized that their well-known names would still be draws at the box office. The Paige All-Stars toured the Northwest and played in the California Winter League as well as barnstorming in the Midwest. Backed by Wilkinson, Paige refused to play in towns where they could not eat or sleep. Wilkinson also made "Jew Baby" Floyd the pitcher's personal trainer.[18]

One of the most successful matchups was between Paige's All-Stars and the Ethiopian Clowns. On June 11, 1939, 4,000 turned out in Peoria, Illinois, to see the two teams split a doubleheader. According to the June 16 *Call*, the Clowns "captured the crowd's fancy in both games with their whirlwind fielding practice speed and their determined efforts." Their "remarkable shadow ball exhibition took the crowd by storm." The two teams met again in Milwaukee.

During the 1939 barnstorming season, while the traveling squad was in Canada, Satchel's arm and overpowering fastball miraculously returned. Some say it was on a warm Sunday, as he pitched against one of the House of David teams, that Satchel's arm strength and fastballs returned. O'Neil recalled: "'Jew Baby' Floyd went out to rub Satchel's arm, and … his arm came back, the batters didn't hold back [as they had at first been instructed to do by Wilkinson], and he struck out seventeen in one night."[19] Floyd's remedies were "massages, ointments (including one he called 'Yellow Juice,' so potent it scared away mosquitoes), a combination of scalding and ice-cold baths for his arm, and warm and cold wraps."[20]

Newt Joseph "called Wilkinson, [and] said '[Satchel's] ready to come back,' so he came back to the Monarchs. He was a natural showman. He was just a natural."[21] Satchel's control was once again excellent. "He could throw the ball right by your knees all day," said Cool Papa. However, Wilkie "told Paige to take it easy and to stay with the traveling squad through the end of the season." Wilkinson had not yet received league approval to reinstate Paige, but he was sure he would because of the hurler's box-office appeal.[22]

Without Paige the Monarchs won the first-half 1939 NAL pennant race and met the winners of the second half, the St. Louis Stars, in a playoff for the league championship. Kansas City won the series, taking four of the five games played. During the playoffs, Satchel Paige's All-Stars were guests of the Monarchs management. Receipts of one of the games played went to a rescue mission.

The Monarchs ended the 1939 season with two "dream games" against Satchel Paige's All-Stars (who, the *Call* pointed out, were under Monarchs management) the last week in September at Ward Field in Kansas City, Kansas. The Monarchs won them both, 11-0 and 1-0. Paige pitched four innings in the first game and gave up seven runs. Hilton Smith hurled for the Kaysees, scattering four hits.[23]

The dispute over rights to Paige festered on, finally coming to a head when, on June 27, 1940, the Negro National League and the NAL came to an agreement that both leagues had a justified claim on

• J.L. Wilkinson and the Rebirth of Satchel Paige •

After Satchel Paige's dead arm recovered while he pitched for J. L. Wilkinson's traveling Monarchs B-team, his career literally took off again. (Courtesy of William A. Young)

Paige. However, Paige indicated he wanted to stay with the Monarchs. Almost 30 years before Curt Flood challenged the reserve clause in the White major leagues, Paige contended that slavery was over and he could play for whomever he pleased. "The leagues' owners tried to strong-arm Paige to leave the Monarchs for the Eagles and told him that unless he did, 'there will be a war between the two leagues.'"[24] However, as historian Donald Spivey has noted, "Paige and Wilkinson ignored the threats. Paige was declared ineligible for the 1940 East-West All Star Game in Chicago, but he just continued barnstorming and going south to the Caribbean islands."[25]

In late September 1940, after Paige had completed two years on the Monarchs traveling team, Wilkinson decided the time was right for the pitcher to rejoin the main Monarchs club. He signed Satchel to a new contract for the 1941 season and sweetened the deal with something he knew Paige would love – a new car. To test him out, Wilkie put Paige to work before the 1940 season ended. Satchel's first start in Chicago, against the American Giants, drew 10,000; the next game in Detroit brought out 12,000 fans.

Having showcased Paige's box-office appeal, Wilkie next sent Satchel to the Puerto Rican winter league, where he was named the league's most valuable player.[26] According to Paige biographer Larry Tye, J.L. Wilkinson "was savvy enough to know that Satchel's two years of toiling in the wilderness with the traveling team had kept him out of sight and mind of Negro sportswriters and their hundreds of thousands of readers. So he enlisted New York playwrights Moss Hart and George S. Kaufman to help script the pitcher's return."[27] They agreed that the only proper platform to reintroduce Paige was New York City, so Wilkinson booked him to pitch the 1941 season opener for the New York Black Yankees on May 15. Mayor Fiorello La Guardia threw out the first pitch before a record crowd for an opening-day Negro League game: 20,000. Paige pitched all nine innings, struck out eight, and won the game over Philadelphia, 5-3. The game was covered not only by the Black press but also by the *New York Times. Life* magazine ran an article on Paige in its June 2, 1941, issue. Effa Manley objected, but promoter Eddie Gottlieb pointed out to her that having Paige pitch was helping the Black Yankees get out of debt.

A week later Paige pitched the Monarchs home opener and let it be known that his habit of jumping teams was over. With his fastball reduced, as Paige put it, from "blinding' speed" to "just blazin' speed," he relied more on a curve, a knuckleball Cool Papa Bell had taught him, and a slow sinker. Drawing on the still strong buzz surrounding Paige's traveling team, in June 1941 Wilkinson reassembled the Paige All-Stars for a doubleheader against the Ethiopian Clowns at Crosley Field in Cincinnati.[28]

By midseason in 1941 Paige's rehabilitation with Negro League owners was complete. Wilkinson and Baird were willing to lend Paige to any NNL team for exhibition games ... at a price. Eddie Gottlieb promptly booked another doubleheader in Yankee Stadium for July 20, featuring Paige's Monarchs and three NNL teams. Philadelphia and other NNL clubs also booked the Monarchs on the Kansas City team's Eastern swing. A large crowd showed up at Parkside Field in Philadelphia on July 17, 1941, in response to advance publicity that promised Paige "will definitely hurl part of the game."[29]

Paige received 276,418 fan votes for the 1941 East-West All-Star Game, 100,000 more than the next pitcher, the Monarchs' Hilton Smith. Satchel was cleared to play by the owners and pitched two innings in the July 27 game in Chicago. It didn't matter that Paige's West team lost, 8-3. The fans had seen Satchel pitch.[30]

Wilkinson surely understood that the Kansas City Monarchs were well on their way to morphing into the Paige All-Stars. After Paige joined the team, in addition to their games in Kansas City and in the Midwest, they were playing to huge crowds throughout the East, with the stipulation that Wilkinson's team get a higher percentage of the gate for the privilege of having Paige on the field.[31]

According to his Monarchs teammate Chet Brewer, who had also played with Paige on the Bismarck, North Dakota, team, Wilkinson would "hire [Paige]" out on Sunday and take 15 percent off the top of the gate receipts, right after the government got their money."[32] In particular, whenever a team was in financial trouble, Wilkinson's willingness to "lend" Paige helped the team boost gate receipts. Of course, the deal would also put money in Paige's and Wilkie's pockets.

Because Paige was perpetually late to games, Wilkinson had Brewer sometimes ride with him. After one harrowing trip, Brewer told J.L., "I don't want to ride with Satchel anymore. He's going to get us both killed." Satchel would pitch a game at Yankee Stadium on a Sunday, then take off in his big Cadillac and not show up until the next Sunday. "The Monarchs put up with it," Brewer said, "because they were making money off him. J.L. got rich on him."[33]

At the same time as Wilkinson was treating Satchel with dignity and respect (and cashing in on his fan appeal), the White media, now well aware of the public's interest in the lanky Monarch hurler, portrayed him stereotypically. In its June 30, 1940, edition, *Time* featured Paige in a condescending article, calling him "Satchelfoots." A month later the *Saturday Evening Post's* Ted Shane wrote an article on Paige. It was titled "The Chocolate Rube Waddell," and described Black baseball as "much more showman like than white baseball. ... Their baseball is to white baseball as the Harlem stomp is to the sedate ballroom waltz. ... They play faster, seem to enjoy it more than white players." According to Shane, Paige had "apelike arms" and a "Stepinfetchit accent in his speech," but "behind his sleepy eyes was a shrewd brain."[34]

Frazier "Slow" Robinson played with and became a good friend of Paige when both were on the Monarchs in 1942. Robinson believed that "J.L. Wilkinson knew what made Satchel tick." He "knew that as long as Satchel lived out of a suitcase" he was liable to vanish at any time. So Wilkie took Paige under his wing, as he did his own children. He helped Satchel buy a home in Kansas City. It was the first time Satchel had any home to go back to. According to Robinson, "Wilkinson let him know the value of making money while you were able to make it. Especially playing baseball." Wilkinson was showing him that "if he wanted to make something of himself, he'd have to change his way of living." Satchel "never did jump anymore," Robinson pointed out.[35]

There must have been some confusion as to Satchel's status with the Monarchs at the outset of the 1942 season, as the *Kansas City Call* felt it necessary on April 24 to assure fans Paige would be back with the team for the season.

Before the 1942 regular season started, Paige

was already drawing fans to exhibition games. An overflow crowd of 15,000 saw the Monarchs split a doubleheader with the Homestead Grays at Pelican Stadium in New Orleans on Sunday, April 26. Paige pitched five innings in the nightcap.[36]

Paige was on the mound in the second game of a doubleheader with the Memphis Red Sox on May 3 at Martin's Park in Memphis. He pitched the first four innings, giving up three runs, before Hilton Smith took over. Smith held the Memphis bats in check for a 4-3 victory. Paige was scheduled to pitch on May 6 in another game with the Red Sox, but he refused and was fined $25.

Paige's first appearance in the 1942 regular season was in a doubleheader with the Chicago American Giants on May 10 in Chicago. The May 15 *Call* reported that "Old Satchel" showed "some of the smartest pitching of his brilliant career," going five innings in a 6-0 victory.

In the Monarchs' 1942 home opener on May 17, Paige took the loss (4-1) in the second game of a twin bill against the Memphis Red Sox. According to the May 22 *Call*, Paige's "jump ball" was hopping but his change proved to be his undoing.

On May 24 the Monarchs took on Dizzy Dean and his major-league all-star team at Wrigley Field in Chicago. Most of the nearly 30,000 in attendance were Black. According to the May 29 *Call*, Dean hadn't been able to heal the wound left when Paige outpitched him several years earlier. The Monarchs beat Dean's All Stars, 3-1. Smith took over for Paige in the seventh and allowed one run and two hits. *Call* sports editor Sam McKibben noted that the big leaguers were "loud and sincere in their praise of the Monarchs." They said several of the Monarchs could play in the White majors.[37]

In his July 3 "Sports Potpourri" column, McKibben wrote that Paige's "pinning back the ears of Dizzy Dean's All-Stars has incurred the wrath of [Commissioner] Judge Landis. Word is out that he is ruling out all future games between Paige and Dean by making white parks off limits for such games. If so, it will kill the scheduled game in July at Indianapolis. There is only one Negro park, in Memphis. The clamor for Negroes in the major leagues may have something to do with it." "Can't have the Negro ball players showing up the whites y'know."

Paige was not on hand for a May 30 game against the American Giants at Ruppert Stadium in Newark. Wilkinson had "loaned" him to the Homestead Grays for a game against a White all-star team at Griffith Stadium in Washington. The Grays won, 8-1, before a largely Black crowd of 22,000.

On June 14 at Cleveland, the Monarchs split a doubleheader with the Buckeyes before 2,000. The Buckeyes plated two runs off Satchel Paige in the first inning, and they held up for a 2-1 win in the initial matchup. On June 16, at Dayton's Duck Park, Paige and Booker McDaniels teamed up to toss a 4-0 no-hitter against the Frigidaire Icemen. Paige worked the first four innings.[38]

Paige pitched the first five scoreless innings of a game against the Homestead Grays in Washington on June 18, 1942, before 28,000. It was the first time the Monarchs had met the Grays in 10 years. Satchel gave way to Hilton Smith, who took the 2-1, 10-inning loss.

At an exhibition matchup with the Eber-Seagrams in Rochester, New York, on June 24, Paige threw one-hit ball through five innings and contributed with his bat in a 6-1 Monarchs victory. It took 13 innings, but the Monarchs defeated the Chicago American Giants, 9-7, in Milwaukee at Borchert Field before 12,000 enthusiastic fans on June 28. Paige started and gave up seven hits and four runs before being relieved by Smith, who was credited with the win.

A promotional article in the July 3 *Call* announced that Paige would bring his all-stars to Louisville for a game against the House of David on July 5. "There is little doubt about the magnetic quality of Paige's box office appeal. … And he is having one of his best seasons. … His fast hopper is jumping." The game may not have been played as there was no further mention of it in the *Call*.

Paige and the Monarchs suffered a 1-0, 10-inning loss to the Memphis Red Sox at Pelican Stadium in New Orleans on July 7. The Monarchs shut out the Red Sox in both games of a doubleheader played at Rebel Stadium in Dallas on July 12 before 5,000 (11-0 and 6-0). Paige, "the magnet of the crowd," pitched all seven innings in the first game, striking out 10, and was 3-for-4 at the plate.[39]

On July 17, 1942, the Monarchs met the Jefferson Barracks All Stars, who featured some former major leaguers, at Ruppert Stadium. The Army-Navy Relief Fund received 50 percent of the gate while the other 50 percent went to the Salvation Army Penny Ice Fund. The Monarchs won, 6-0. Paige started and went five, relieved by Hilton Smith. Both struck out seven. The two each allowed only one hit, and each had a hit.

An August 7 Associated Negro Press article printed

in the *Call* cited J.L. Wilkinson's support for Negro players in the major leagues. The Monarchs owner said he had talked with Leroy "Satchel" Paige, the pitching great of Negro baseball, about the situation in Chicago recently and said he advised the right-handed speedball artist, "[W]e certainly won't stand in your way if you have a chance to play." The ANP article noted that Paige was under a two-year contract with the Kansas City club and that he held decisions over Dizzy Dean, Schoolboy Rowe, and Bob Feller. It further observed that the pitching star had received as high as $2,000 for working one game and is reputed to have earned as much as $200,000 in a single year.

On August 13 Paige pitched all 12 innings at Griffith Stadium in a 3-2 loss to the Homestead Grays before a boisterous crowd of 26,000.

Paige took the loss in the first of two 1942 East-West All-Star Games, played before 45,179 at Comiskey Park in Chicago on August 16. He took the mound in the seventh with the score knotted 2-2 and surrendered the winning run. The August 21 *Call* blamed loose play behind him. While Satchel and four other Monarchs were at the All-Star Game the rest of the team was in Canton, Ohio, to play the House of David, winning 6-2.

On August 21 heavy rain in Cincinnati held the crowd to 5,000, but the soaked fans were treated to a 5-1 Monarchs win over the Ethiopian (now Cincinnati) Clowns. Paige pitched three innings. The two teams met again on September 1, also at Crosley Field in Cincinnati. Satchel pitched the first five innings in a 10-2 Monarchs mauling of the Clowns.

For the August 21, 1942, edition of the *Call,* Sam McKibben penned an article headlined "Paige Says Abolish Jim Crow and He Will Be Ready for His Major League Debut but Not Before at Any Price." "Satchel Paige," McKibben wrote, "doesn't want a major league tryout, nor to play major league ball ... unless two things come to pass: the complete abolition of JIM CROW on a NATIONAL scale ... and he is given a contract identical to that tendered a white player getting a tryout. The white papers have been saying Paige is through. When Paige told a reporter that he wouldn't sign a $10,000 contract with a big-league team and refused to reveal his current salary, it was written that he was receiving $40,000 a year. Satchel is an enthusiastic talker," McKibben noted, "and I just let him talk. 'Imagine,' he says, 'me living at a Negro hotel although I play with a white team. Record my feelings when dishes, out of which I eat, are broken up in my presence. How could I pitch a decent game with insulting jeers coming from spectators and even some of the players. ... Just convince me that agitation can be halted and I'll push fast balls by Joe DiMaggio. 'Why,' he says, 'if the President hasn't made southern DEFENSE plants hire, and use Negro labor in government plants, how can Judge Landis, Connie Mack or anyone make the southern white folk accept the Negro as a ball player. His training camp life in the South would be miserable ... and the camps won't be moved for one or two Negroes. What about the tryouts allegedly scheduled by the Pittsburgh Pirates. Who will 'bell the cat' [meaning end Jim Crow]? Will the white trainers work on a Negro to say nothing to take care of him. Indeed not. I've never been able to get any service out of one. Tell the reading public,' says Satch, 'not to believe half of what it reads that I say in the daily papers. I say to others what I am saying to you, but my statements are twisted. Negroes will never get into the major leagues because of jim crow. It's a wonderful dream but will never come true. With the nation at war not one is going to try to abolish jim crow ... and even in peace time, jim crowism will flourish. Me, I am going to stick with Wilkie, J.L. Wilkinson, Monarchs' owner, and whoever says I am afraid I can't make the grade ... is just plain nuts. I experience enough prejudice now, why court more.'"[40] The interview was conducted before the East-West game at Comiskey Park in Chicago.

Paige appeared in all four games that counted in the 1942 Colored World Series against the Homestead Grays. He was credited with a victory in the fourth game and a save in the second game. He did not figure in the decisions in the first and third games.

If the second game of the 1942 Series, played on a stormy September 10 night in Pittsburgh, had been in a White World Series, it would go down with Babe Ruth's "called shot" in the third game of the 1932 World Series, historian John Holway has contended, as "a transcendental moment of baseball lore."[41] There are various versions of the game's highlight: a confrontation between two of baseball's most storied players, Josh Gibson and Satchel Paige. According to one, Paige entered the game in the seventh inning with the Monarchs leading 2-0. Two were out, and there was a Gray on first base. Satchel called first baseman Buck O'Neil to the mound and told Buck he was going to walk the next two hitters to get to Josh Gibson.

O'Neil said he told Paige, "Aw, man you gotta be crazy!"

• J.L. Wilkinson and the Rebirth of Satchel Paige •

Then Monarchs manager Frank Duncan, joined by J.L. Wilkinson (in at least one version of the story), came onto the field "waving their arms wildly." Unable to change Paige's mind, they shrugged, "It's your funeral."

With Gibson already in the batter's box, Satchel called for the Monarchs trainer, "Jew Baby" Floyd, to bring him a foaming glass of bicarbonate of soda, which he drank and then let out a big belch.

"The bases was drunk," Paige later recalled. To Gibson he said, "I heard all about how good you hit me. Now I fixed it for you. Let's see how good you can hit me now."

"I'm ready," Josh replied testily. "Throw it."

Satchel remembered saying to Gibson, "Now I'm gonna throw you a fast ball, but I'm not going to trick you." Then "I wound up and stuck my foot in the air. It hid the ball and almost hid me. Then I fired." Side-arm, knee-high. Josh, thinking curve, took it for strike one. He didn't lift the bat from his shoulder.

"Now I'm gonna throw you another fast ball, only it's gonna be a little faster than the other one," said Satchel. "It was so tense you could feel everything jingling," Paige remembered.

The last pitch was a three-quarter side-arm curveball. Satchel recalled that Josh "got back on his heels; he was looking for a fastball." However, it was knee-high on the outside corner – strike three. "Josh threw that bat of his 4,000 feet."

Paige said he could not remember Gibson ever paying the $5 he owed him. The Grays' Buck Leonard always said he had no recollection of Paige walking two to get Gibson to the plate.[42]

The 1942 postseason saw a repeat of the Series in a pair of games in the Tidewater region of Virginia. On October 2 Paige hurled the first three innings, allowing one run, in the game played in Norfolk, Virginia. The Grays' bats came alive when Connie Johnson took the mound for the Monarchs, and Homestead won 8-5. Satchel also started the second game, played in Portsmouth, Virginia, on October 4, going four innings before giving way to Hilton Smith. Paige and Smith allowed only one run each. The Monarchs blasted Grays pitching for 12 runs.

What stood out for Satchel Paige during his years with the Monarchs was his relationship with J.L. Wilkinson. "Working for Mr. Wilkinson was something no man'd forget," Paige recalled. "He was as good a boss as you could ask for. And he was a real promoter." With Wilkie's portable lights, Paige remembered pitching in as many as three games in one day. In one three-game stretch in the East, Paige said, he drew 105,000 fans, pitching between three and six innings each game. His speed was back, and people were talking about him more than any other pitcher – White or Black.[43]

Paige biographer Larry Tye called J.L. Wilkinson "the father figure that Gus Greenlee, Alex Herman, and John Page [other owners for whom Paige played] had tried and failed to be." Paige "felt a loyalty that he had never known before to an owner, team, and city."[44] "A lover of ribs, riffs, and reporters, he found Kansas City irresistible."[45] Satchel said, "The folks in Kansas City treated me like a king and you never saw a king of the walk if you didn't see O' Satch around Eighteenth and Vine in those days, rubber-necking all the girls walking by."[46]

According to Tye, "It was a love instantly requited. For if Satchel adored Kansas City, Kansas City loved him right back. ..."[47] "Wilkinson pushed Paige to buy real estate in Kansas City, the only way he ever was able to save," Tye has observed. Satchel was 35 when he bought his first home in Kansas City – on Twelfth Street, high on a terrace, with 14 rooms, and plenty of space for his cars, guns, and antiques as well as "a backyard big enough for hundreds of chickens, a dozen dogs, and a cow."

Tye concluded that "[h]ome ownership had precisely the effect on Satchel that Wilkinson had hoped: It settled him down. He would remain a devoted Monarch for as long as he remained in the Negro Leagues and a devotee of J.L. Wilkinson as long as he lived." As Satchel told the *Pittsburgh Courier* in 1943, his contract-jumping days were over. "I am going to play with the Kansas City Monarchs as long as the owner and manager will have me."[48]

Satchel filled his house "with Chippendale chairs and roomfuls of trophies and guns." Not surprisingly, it was Wilkinson, whose wife, Bessie, had owned an antiques store in Kansas City since 1931, who led Paige into the world of collecting, and Satchel took to it with the same gusto he had for hunting and fishing. Someone told him that in his first couple of years what he had collected was worth $20,000.[49]

Paige benefited from Wilkie's promotional acumen, but, as he always had been, Satchel continued to be his own best publicist. In a July 24, 1943, *Chicago Defender* column, Frank "Fay" Young described a conversation he had had with Paige. Satchel was recalling that he had beaten Bob Feller in two of three games, winning the rubber game 6-3. He said Dizzy Dean had quit trying to outpitch him, as Satchel had won all but one of the games in which they had met.[50]

By 1945 others were noting the effect Wilkinson was having on Paige. In a May 16, 1945, *Philadelphia Tribune* column, Dr. W. Rollo Wilson observed that Satchel had changed his prima donna lifestyle since recovering from his arm problems and playing with the Monarchs. "He retained the on-duty color and slugged off the off-duty trimmings," Wilson wrote. "Now, he travels with his fellows, in uniform every day and is on the field for all pre-game activities. The snob is now a regular fellow."[51]

Intent on getting his moneymaker to as many appearances as possible, in June 1946, J.L. Wilkinson leased a two-seat, single-engine Cessna. The pilot was his son, Dick, who had been captain of a B-24 Liberator bomber on multiple missions during World War II. "Satchel Paige" was stenciled on the side of the Cessna. The day after the plane was delivered, Dick flew Paige from Kansas City to Madison, Wisconsin, without any problems. On the return flight, however, they encountered a storm system and bounced up and down all the way to Kansas City. "You trying to kill me! Get me out of here!" Paige yelled at Dick. Although he said he would never fly again, Paige relented (after Dick told him he would lose $500) and flew to Oklahoma. Again, the first leg of the flight was fine, but mechanical trouble made for a hectic return to Kansas City. After only two flights, the Cessna was returned to its owner when Paige let it be known in no uncertain terms that he would not fly in it again. According to Satchel, that was the last time he flew in a little plane. Wilkie didn't force the issue.[52]

According to Paige, after J.L. Wilkinson "decided to kind of retire" and Tom Baird was his boss, Satchel took a sizable pay cut from the Monarchs for the 1948 season. As attendance dropped, so did his income, since he was getting a percentage of the gate on top of his salary. Even though he was almost 42 years old he still thought he was "too young to take any cut in pay."[53]

During the summer of 1948 Paige was on a barnstorming tour in Iowa with his All-Stars when Dick Wilkinson, who was traveling with the team, said he got a phone call from J.L. in Kansas City. Dick recalled years later: "Dad called me on the phone and said, 'The majors want Satch to report to Cleveland.' I walked over to Satchel and said, 'You're going to the majors. Dad says get home.' He looked at me with a big grin and said, 'Oh boy!' He jumped into his Cadillac and took off. That's the last time I saw Satchel."[54]

According to Paige, the first indication that he would be signed by the Cleveland Indians came in a letter from promoter Abe Saperstein, owner of the Harlem Globetrotters basketball team, who told him that Bill Veeck was looking for pitching help. Saperstein recommended Satchel and Veeck brought him to Cleveland for a tryout on July 7, Paige's 42nd birthday. Manager Lou Boudreau caught Satchel as Paige hit the strike zone on 46 of 50 throws.

Veeck signed Paige the same day and gave the former Monarch a $10,000 signing bonus and $5,000 a month – a total of $25,000 for the season. After Satchel told Veeck that he thought Mr. Wilkinson and Mr. Baird should get something for taking him on when his arm went dead, the Indians owner agreed to give them $5,000 (according to Paige, or $15,000 in other sources) for his contract. Veeck also gave Abe Saperstein $15,000 as a finder's fee ($10,000 according to some sources).[55]

In its overview of Paige's career, the National Baseball Hall of Fame describes Satchel's start in the majors: "At the age of 42, Paige made his big league debut when Bill Veeck signed him to a contract with the Indians on July 7, 1948. Two days later, he made his debut for a Cleveland club involved in one of the tightest pennant races in American League history. That summer and fall, Paige went 6-1 with three complete games and a save and a 2.48 earned-run average. Cleveland won the AL pennant in a one-game playoff against [the] Boston [Red Sox], then captured the World Series title in six games against the [Boston] Braves. Paige became the first African-American pitcher to pitch in the World Series when he worked two-thirds of an inning in Game 5."[56] Most importantly for the Indians and Paige, the turnstiles were twirling. More than 200,000 showed up to see Paige's first three major-league starts, and the crowds continued.[57]

Bob Feller said of his Indians teammate, "He could throw the ball through a keyhole and did. ..."[58] However, the aging Paige could not sustain that high level of performance. After a disappointing 4-7 record for the Indians in 1949 (which Satchel attributed to a return of his stomach trouble) and the sale of the team by Bill Veeck, Paige was offered a contract for the 1950 season of $19,000 by Hank Greenberg, the new controlling owner of the Cleveland club. It was $6,000 less than his 1949 contract.

• J.L. Wilkinson and the Rebirth of Satchel Paige •

Satchel asked his wife, Lahoma, what he should do, and she said, "Maybe we'd better see Mr. Wilkinson. He'll know. Maybe he can tell us what to do."

Paige contacted Wilkinson at home where the retired Monarchs owner was spending most of his time since he'd sold his share of the team. When Satchel went to see him, Wilkie said, "[Y]ou'd better accept. Negro baseball and barnstorming aren't what they used to be, not with the major leagues open now. You'd be better off with that steady job. Maybe you'd make more barnstorming, but maybe you wouldn't."

"I'll sign the contract, then," Satchel said.

"Call them up and let them know," Wilkinson advised him. "You've had that contract a couple of weeks now without letting them know anything. It might be better to call."

Paige called Hank Greenberg. It seemed settled, but Greenberg called back and told Paige that manager Boudreau had told him that he couldn't use Satchel. In late January 1950, Greenberg announced the release of Paige, saying, "[o]lder players will have to make way for rookies."[59] Satchel was officially let go from the team on February 17, 1950:

Paige called Wilkinson and asked, "Can you get me some work? I ought to be worth something barnstorming after those two years in the major leagues."

"Do you want to hook up with a team?" Wilkinson asked him.

"No," Paige responded, "I don't want'a get tied down. I want to stay loose so those big boys can call me if they want me."

"I'll see what I can do about booking you independent, then," Wilkinson told him. Wilkie contacted Eddie Gottlieb and Abe Saperstein, whom Paige considered "pretty fair promoters and real sharp." Pitching offers started coming in fast.

"It looks like you have some good jobs coming up, Satchel," Wilkinson told him.

"When do I start?" Paige asked.

In a couple of days. I've gotten a hold of a reporter and he wants to come around to talk to you. It'll help us get more bookings. You going to be home?" Paige told him he was home, babysitting his two girls until Lahoma returned. Wilkinson and the reporter arrived about an hour later.[60]

When Bill Veeck purchased the St. Louis Browns in 1951, he made good on his promise to give Paige a job if he was able to acquire a new team. Satchel's record for the year was 3-4. When it was rumored that Paige was being offered a salary of $22,000 for the 1952 season, he retorted that he had "made lots more in 1950 barnstorming for J.L. Wilkinson, my manager, and Eddie Gottlieb."[61] However, Paige would continue to pitch with the Browns through 1953 and was selected to play in two All-Star Games (1952 and 1953).

Satchel went back on the road and, by 1961, according to his own estimate, he had pitched in more than 2,500 games, winning about 2,000. He claimed he had pitched as many as 153 games a year. On September 25, 1965, at the age of 58, Paige appeared one last time in a major-league game, appropriately for the Kansas City Athletics, pitching the first three innings. In 1967 he toured for the Indianapolis Clowns for $1,000 a month. The next year illness kept him home. Satchel worked briefly as a sheriff's deputy in Kansas City, and ran unsuccessfully for the Missouri legislature, before, in 1968, the Atlanta Braves took him on as a coach so he could qualify for a major-league pension. He died in Kansas City on June 8, 1982, a month before his 76th birthday.

Satchel Paige was, as a *Collier's* writer put it, "one of the last surviving totally unregimented souls." To paraphrase Paige himself, he did as he did. According to two of the greatest hitters of all time, Joe DiMaggio and Ted Williams, Satchel was the best pitcher they'd ever seen.[62]

Satchel was in a class by himself in terms of what he was paid, as he was in so many other respects. During the best years of Black ball, he regularly made $30,000 to $40,000 a year. Far behind was the next highest player – Josh Gibson – who made about $1,000 a month during his peak period in the early 1940s. The secret, of course, was Satchel's drawing power as the best pitcher of his time, as well as a master showman. He negotiated bonuses and special deals because the mere announcement that he would appear at a game meant an additional 5,000-10,000 tickets sold in the bigger parks.[63]

Though he was schooled in a reformatory, Paige bought a typewriter and wrote drafts of his autobiography, a 96-page version in 1948 (*Pitchin' Man*) and a 300-page 1962 version (*Maybe I'll Pitch Forever*). He did collaborate with Hal Lebovitz in the writing of the first and David Lipman in the second, but the two works reflect Satchel's voice and perspective. "Unlettered yes, but not unlearned," his biographer Larry Tye has suggested.[64]

In another well-researched biography of Paige, historian Donald Spivey linked J.L. Wilkinson, Abe Saperstein, Bill Veeck, and Satchel Paige as "the four [who] together wrote in bold and bright ink for future generations the how-to book of promoting professional team sports and marquee athletes. ..." They also showed that "black and whites could work together for mutual self-interests in professional athletics. ..."[65]

Buck O'Neil said, "Satchel was a comedian. Satchel was a preacher. Satchel was just about everything. We had a good baseball team, but when Satchel pitched, a *great* baseball team. The amazing part about it was that he brought the best out in the opposition, too."[66] O'Neil had more stories to tell about Paige than any of the countless other ballplayers, Black and White, he had known. One is particularly moving. When the Monarchs were on the road in Charleston, South Carolina, Satchel said to O'Neil, "Nancy [the nickname Satchel had given Buck, but that's another story], c'mon with me. We're gonna take a little trip." They went to Drum Island, where slaves had once been auctioned off, and there was a big tree with a plaque on it, marking where the slave market was. Buck and Satchel stood there in silence, for about 10 minutes. Finally, Satchel said, "Seems like I been here before." And O'Neil said, "Me too, Satchel." Buck wanted it known that Paige was "a little bit deeper than most people thought."[67]

Robert Leroy "Satchel" Paige was elected to the National Baseball Hall of Fame in 1971 as the first selection of the Committee on Negro Baseball Leagues. When word filtered out that the Hall of Fame planned to put Paige's plaque and those of any future Negro Leagues inductees in a special exhibit rather than the hall where the plaques of White major-league Hall of Famers were displayed, Paige retorted, "[B]aseball has turned [me] from a second-class citizen into a second-class immortal."[68] The public outcry was so great that the decision was reversed and Paige's Hall of Fame plaque and those of subsequent Negro Leaguers selected for the Hall were placed in the same room as those honoring Christy Mathewson, Babe Ruth, and Jackie Robinson.

Sources

An earlier version of this essay appeared in William A. Young, *J.L. Wilkinson and the Kansas City Monarchs: Trailblazers in Black Baseball* (Jefferson, North Carolina: McFarland & Company, 2016).

In addition to the articles cited from the *Kansas City Call*, other Kansas City Monarchs game reports are drawn from a timeline for the 1942 season compiled by Bill Nowlin: *see story on page 182.*

Notes

1　Leroy "Satchel" Paige, as told to David L. Lipman, *Maybe I'll Pitch Forever; A Great Baseball Player Tells the Hilarious Story Behind the Legend* (Lincoln: University of Nebraska Press, 1993), 92.

2　Roger Kahn, *Rickey and Robinson: The True, Untold Story of the Integration of Baseball* (New York: Rodale, 2014), 59.

3　Paige, 97.

4　Buck O'Neil with Steve Wolf and Daniel Conrads, *I Was Right on Time* (New York: Simon & Schuster, 1996), 105.

5　Neil Lanctot, *Negro League Baseball: The Rise and Ruin of a Black Institution* (Philadelphia: University of Pennsylvania Press, 2004), 73.

6　Janet Bruce, *The Kansas City Monarchs: Champions of Black Baseball* (Lawrence: University of Kansas Press, 1985), 93.

7　*Kansas City Call*, March 11, 1949.

8　Paige, 130-131.

9　John B. Holway, *Voices from the Great Black Baseball Leagues* (New York: Dover, 2010 [originally published 1975]), 87; John B. Holway, *Black Ball Stars, Negro League Pioneers* (Westport, Connecticut: Meckler, 1988), 339-40.

10　Interview with Bill "Plunk" Drake conducted by Dr. Charles Korr and Dr. Steven Hause (December 8, 1971), Negro Baseball League Project, https://shsmo.org/stlouis/manuscripts/%20transcripts/s0829/t0067.pdf.

11　Larry Tye, *Satchel: The Life and Times of an American Legend* (New York: Random House, 2009), 144.

12　John B. Holway, *Black Diamonds: Life in the Negro Leagues from the Men Who Lived It* (Westport, Connecticut: Meckler Books, 1989), 21.

13　Holway, 1988, 339.

14　Fay Vincent, *The Only Game in Town: Baseball Stars of the 1930s and 1940s Talk About the Game They Loved* (New York: Simon & Schuster, 2006), 88.

15　Tye, 123.

16　Paige, 132.

17　Donald Spivey, *"If You Were Only White": The Life of Leroy "Satchel" Paige* (Columbia: University of Missouri Press, 2012), 168-69.

18　Bruce, 93-94.

19　Vincent, 88-89.

20　Tye, 126.

21　Vincent, 88-89.

22　Spivey, 169.

23　*Kansas City Call,* September 29, 1939.

24　Spivey, 176.

25　Spivey, 176.

26　Mark Ribowsky, *A Complete History of the Negro Leagues* (New York: Birch Lane Press, 1995), 231-32; Tye, 145.

27　Tye, 146.

28　Charles C. Alexander, *Breaking the Slump: Baseball in the Depression Era* (New York: Columbia University Press, 2002), 235.

29　Lanctot, 105-06.

30　Larry Lester, *Black Baseball's National Showcase* (Lincoln: University of Nebraska Press, 2001), 153-71.

31 Ribowsky, 237.

32 Holway, 1989, 21.

33 Holway, 1989, 22.

34 *Time*, June 30, 1940: 44; *Saturday Evening Post*, July 27, 1940: 79-81. Cited in Alexander, 233-34, and Lanctot, 227.

35 Frazier "Slow" Robinson, with Paul Bauer, *Catching Dreams: My Life in the Negro Baseball Leagues* (Syracuse: Syracuse University Press, 1999), 37-38.

36 *Kansas City Call*, May 1, 1942.

37 *Kansas City Call*, May 29, 1942.

38 *Kansas City Call*, June 19, 1942.

39 *Kansas City Call*, July 17, 1942.

40 Sam McKibben, "Paige Says Abolish Jim Crow and He Will Be Ready for His Major League Debut but Not Before at Any Price.," *Kansas City Call*, August 21, 1942.

41 John B. Holway, *The Complete Book of Baseball's Negro Leagues: The Other Half of Baseball History* (Fern Park, Florida: Hastings House, 2001), 398-99.

42 Sources for the 1942 Colored World Series: *Kansas City Call*, September 18 and 25; Holway, 2001, 398-99; Ribowsky, 258-62; Robinson, 93, 95; Bruce, 103-04; Luke, 91-92; Paige, 146-47, 152; O'Neil, 126-38; James A. Riley, *Of Monarchs and Black Barons: Essays on Baseball's Negro* Leagues (Jefferson, North Carolina: McFarland, 2012), 153.

43 Paige, 138-139.

44 Tye, 137.

45 Tye, 137.

46 Tye, 142.

47 Tye, 137.

48 Cited by Tye, 166.

49 Tye, 136-38, 165-66. See also Robinson, 50; Paige 1993: 142, 168-69; Larry Lester and Sammy Miller, *Black Baseball in Kansas City* (Charleston, South Charleston: Arcadia, 2000), 103; Interview with Richard "Dick" Wilkinson conducted by Janet Bruce (October 1, 1979). Kansas City Monarchs Oral History Collection (K0047), Tape No. A0016-17. State Historical Society of Missouri Research Center-Kansas City.

50 Frank "Fay" Young, *Chicago Defender*, July 24, 1943.

51 Jim Reisler, *Black Writers, Black Baseball: An Anthology of Articles from Black Sportswriters Who Covered the Negro Leagues*, revised edition. (Jefferson, North Carolina: McFarland, 2007), 128.

52 *Kansas City Call*, July 5, 1946; Spivey, 199, 209-11; Paige, 75-78; Thomas Fredrick, "KC Connection Began Baseball's Globalization," *Kansas City Star*, October 16, 2004: C6 (J.L. Wilkinson File, National Baseball Hall of Fame, Cooperstown, New York).

53 Paige, 195.

54 Tye, 205.

55 Paige, 196-98. See also Tye, 217-18; Lanctot 335-36.

56 baseballhall.org/hof/paige-satchel.

57 For Paige's vivid description of his Indians debut, see Paige, 200-205.

58 Interview with Bob Feller conducted by Fay Vincent; Vincent, 51.

59 Spivey, 246; Tye, 264.

60 Paige, 234-35.

61 Spivey, 250.

62 Dunkel, 277.

63 Robert Peterson, *Only the Ball Was White* (New York: Oxford University Press), 120-21.

64 Tye, 288-89.

65 Spivey, xix-xx.

66 Dunkel, 70.

67 O'Neil, 100-101.

68 O'Neil, 222.

World War II and the Kansas City Monarchs

By Dr. Milbert O. Brown Jr.

The year 1941 marked the beginning of an unforgettable period in American history. While some US soldiers basked in the comfortable confines of a Hawaiian breeze, half a world away the bulk of the United States citizenry had begun to rebuild their lives after digging out of the rubble from America's Great Depression years. The country was emerging from the valley that once had birthed unforeseen challenges. The daybreak of a promising new decade presented hopeful fruits for American growth in commerce and industry. Race relations were thought to have improved; after all, the heavyweight boxing crown was worn by a fellow called the Brown Bomber: Joe Louis. The Negro Leagues' East-West All-Star Game in Chicago drew a crowd of just over 50,000 people. But Jim Crow still smothered the hopes and dreams of Black people. The lynching of Black men remained a custom practiced in small Southern hamlets and large Northern towns. The excitement of seeing a little white baseball dance through the air still could not replace the hurt that families felt when they heard how their loved ones died at the hands of a racist mob. One such individual, Felix Hall, 19, had volunteered to train with an all-Black Army unit but was later found hanging from a tree with a rope around his neck on the Army base at Fort Benning, Georgia.[1]

In December 1941, the world saw the smoldering fire that charred the iron guns and, even from a distance, they could smell the burned human fresh; and the pillaring smoke opened America's nostrils during a time filled with disarray. After an early-morning surprise attack by Japan on Pearl Harbor, just west of Honolulu, on December 7, much of the United States Navy's Pacific fleet lay damaged and destroyed. Resting in the cool waters was the broken steel of the *USS Arizona*. The warship's hull was now surrounded by oil-contaminated waves, which served as a fluid coffin for over 1,000 sailors' bodies committed to a watery grave. On the day when the United States was attacked, Negroes were still considered second-class citizens due to America's insidious apartheid system known as Jim Crow. Negro soldiers and sailors had limited possibilities while serving in the military, but that all changed after that surprise December morning: "From the moment the embers began to burn at Pearl Harbor, Black society, in general, vowed that it would not be shut out of the American war effort and its palpable unifying effects at home."[2]

As the Japanese pilots swooped down and targeted bombs into the belly of the *USS West Virginia*, Dorie Miller, a Black cook from Waco, Texas, who lacked any combat training operated an antiaircraft gun and began firing at the swirling enemy planes. Only a few hours earlier, Miller had just finished serving breakfast and was simply gathering laundry. Like society, the Navy had the perception that Blacks had low mental aptitudes and that they should be relegated to menial chores like laundry duty, serving as cooks, and shining white officers' shoes. Dorie Miller turned that perception upside down and his act of bravery at Pearl Harbor earned him the Navy Cross. The Black press, the National Association for the Advancement of Colored People (NAACP), and Black leaders publicized Miller as a symbol of Black achievement in the military.[3]

Miller, the grandson of slaves, had worked on his family's farm but could not find work elsewhere, so he joined the Navy in 1939. The little Texas town he was from supported strong racist attitudes against Black people; in one instance, a 17-year-old boy was burned alive at the town's square a few years before Dorie's birth in 1919.[4] Miller carried a 6-foot-3 frame, and with over 200 pounds of weight behind his punches, he was crowned as his ship's heavyweight boxing champion. Back in Texas, he had been the school's fullback, and he could have played baseball well, but Dorie Miller's destiny involved more than just hitting a ball across the field. His courageous act of heroism helped changed the military's evaluation of Black men in uniform. It also helped to pave the way for Negro League players to be accepted as professional baseball players.

Approximately 120 Negro League baseball players participated in World War II by serving in the Army,

World War II and the Kansas City Monarchs

Army Air Corps, Navy, and Marines. The Kansas City Monarchs had over 13 players who served during the war years. Henry "Hank" Thompson, a second baseman, fought in the Battle of the Bulge in the Army's 1695th Combat Engineers unit.[5] Monarchs catcher Joe Greene was part of a well-decorated unit, the 92nd Infantry. Greene's company removed the body of disgraced Italian dictator Benito Mussolini after his execution during the liberation of Milan, Italy.[6] The Monarchs' Willard Brown of the Army Quartermaster Corps fought on France's Normandy beaches. Brown, a great outfielder, was a seven-time Negro League home-run champion and was enshrined in the National Baseball Hall of Fame in 2006.[7]

In 1942 the Kansas City Monarchs won the Negro World Series over the Homestead Grays. That same year, the team had a father and son drafted into the Army. Frank Duncan Jr., a catcher for the team, and his son, pitcher Frank III, created professional baseball's first known father-son battery before their military service.[8] According to Negro League historian James Riley, Frank Jr. was considered one of the top catchers in Negro League baseball. One of Frank Duncan's epic stories was that Dizzy Dean, a major-league pitching great, needed a good catcher to play an exhibition game against the Monarchs. It was said that Dean pulled Duncan out of a poolroom and had him catch the game.[9] In the beginning of his career, the senior Duncan was acquired by Kansas City in a three-player trade in 1921. From 1923 to 1925, he helped the Monarchs win three Negro National League pennants.[10]

During his career with the Monarchs, Duncan left and returned to the team four times. At the age of 42, he was drafted into the Army, serving in the 371st Infantry Regiment of the 92nd Division. Although he served in the Army for only six months, Duncan set a marksmanship record and was promoted to sergeant.[11] Wartime service affected the careers of many baseball players and teams. After Frank Duncan III was discharged from the service, he started pitching for the Baltimore Elite Giants and played in the Mexican League but was not as productive as he had been during his time with the Monarchs.

Just as Frank Duncan Jr. arrived back to the Monarchs in 1943, other Kansas City teammates were shipping out. Outfielder Ted Strong joined the Navy while Connie Johnson and James "Pea" Greene committed to the Army. Buck O'Neil, the team's solid first baseman, was drafted and attached to a Navy Construction Battalion.

American society began to change as the Second World War progressed. More women began to work outside the home, and with the loss of many White baseball players to the armed services, the talk of Negro players integrating into the major leagues increased. A *Pittsburgh Courier* reporter asked the new commissioner, Happy Chandler, what his thoughts were on the integration of Negro players. Chandler said, "If they can fight and die in Okinawa, Guadalcanal, and in the South Pacific, they can play baseball in America."[12] Unlike Judge Kenesaw Mountain Landis, Chandler's predecessor, Chandler, a U.S. senator from Kentucky, was more commonly known as a player-friendly baseball executive. For years, Landis had a negative racial attitude toward baseball integration and "publicly maintained there was no discrimination in baseball, and privately worked against any effort to end discrimination."[13]

One of Senator Chandler's promises was to support the continuance of baseball during World War II. The new commissioner was also responsible for ushering in Jackie Robinson's opportunity to break the color line and bringing fair treatment for Black players. After Robinson entered the league, he met with several incidents of blatant racial taunting. Chandler threatened to suspend the Philadelphia Phillies' manager, Ben Chapman, for hostile racial insults directed at Robinson.[14] Buck O'Neil later commented that integration for Black people still moved at a turtle's pace. While in the Navy, O'Neil got letters that informed him about how the Monarchs team was making out. One letter mentioned that the Monarchs had just signed a "colored" Army officer to play shortstop. The letter stated that this Army officer was a football and track standout named Jackie Robinson. The University of California, Los Angeles, star was an electrifying player who could hit and steal bases.[15]

While in the Army, Lieutenant Jack Roosevelt Robinson had been waiting for his physical to clear so that he could join the 761st Tank Battalion, a segregated combat unit at Fort Hood, Texas.[16] One day, Robinson, a handsome, gentlemanly young man dressed in his distinguished Army uniform, flanked with officer's insignia, boarded an Army bus and set off an incident that greatly impacted his Army career. After boarding the bus, Robinson was told to move to the back of the segregated Army bus. He refused and was later court-martialed. Robinson was found not guilty and, after he completed his service commitment, he was honorably discharged.[17]

Kansas City Monarchs pitcher Hilton Smith had seen Robinson playing baseball for an all-Black Army team against a White service team during a 1942 exhibition game. As Robinson waited for his Army discharge papers, he heard that the Monarchs needed players, so he wrote the team and was granted a tryout.[18]

After enduring two seasons without some of the Kansas City Monarchs' stars, who were missing due to the war, owner J.L. Wilkinson signed two players who became household names within the Negro Leagues: Jackie Robinson and Ted "Double Duty" Radcliffe.[19] Robinson played only one season for the Monarchs, but he significantly impacted baseball history for a lifetime. Radcliffe played only 12 games with Monarchs after being hurt in a home-plate collision.[20] He was referred to as "Double Duty" because he sometimes pitched one game of a doubleheader and then caught the other. He was a six-time Negro League All-Star, selected three times as a pitcher and three times as a catcher. Radcliffe played for a few other teams before becoming a manager. Talent-wise, Radcliffe was equal to or greater than his younger roommate Robinson during their time with Kansas City. During their short time together, the two men had a special bond. As Radcliffe put it, "I roomed with Jackie the two months before he was called up to Montreal. I don't think I've met a guy with more class in my life."[21]

In 1947 Robinson was the first of five Negro League players who was admitted into the White major leagues; Larry Doby, Dan Bankhead, Willard Brown, and Hank Thompson were the others who soon followed. All five of the players were World War II veterans, which demonstrated that White society was more accepting of Black players who had served in the military during the war years. After the color barrier was broken, the Monarchs and other Negro Leagues teams began a rapid decline, as White minor- and major-league teams signed away all of the best Black talent. The once-powerful Monarchs lasted until 1965; they were an independent team for the final three years of their existence as the Negro American League had finally folded after the 1962 season; the Negro National League already had disbanded after the 1948 season. Monarchs owner J.L. Wilkinson never received any benefit from Robinson's signing by the Brooklyn Dodgers. As Hilton Smith recalled at Wilkinson's 1964 funeral, "[T]hey just took Jackie, made all that money off him, and Wilkinson was the man that was responsible for him playing, and he didn't get a dime out of it."[22]

On the other hand, one of the Monarchs players who enjoyed the fruits of Wilkinson's grace was Satchel Paige. One of the greatest pitchers, Black or White, Paige spent the majority of his career in the Negro Leagues. He was later inducted into the Hall of Fame in 1971. Paige's reputation allowed him to demand, and to receive, a cut of the gate, and Wilkinson provided him the use of his airplane to ferry Paige to games across the country.[23]

Although many Monarchs players left to serve in the military during the war years, Paige remained behind and made a sizable name and income through self-promotion and by barnstorming with several teams. Paige's glorious return to the Monarchs signaled the team's "Second Dynasty" and the Negro World Series Championship in 1942. They also won six Negro American League pennants in 10 years from 1937 to 1947. The 1942 Negro World Series featured two of the league giants, Satchel Paige pitching for Kansas City Monarchs and Josh Gibson catching for the Homestead Grays.

In 1939 Wilkinson had introduced a portable lighting system that enabled the Monarchs to play night games, thus allowing them to attract larger crowds.[24] Between NAL games, barnstorming tours, and the advent of night baseball for some teams, many Negro League franchises had become profitable organizations. At the height of the World War II in 1944, the Monarchs franchise was one of the most popular of all Negro League organizations and a top money-maker as well, with $100,000 in gate receipts and a profit of $56,281.[25] The popularity of the Monarchs and their Negro League peers during wartime helped to set the stage for the integration of White baseball in the years that followed.

Notes

1   Alexa Mills, "The Story of the Only Known Lynching on a U.S. Military Base in American History," *Washington Post*, September 2, 2016: 1.

2   Mark Ribowsky, *A Complete History of the Negro Leagues, 1884 to 1955* (New York: Carol Publishing Group, 1995), 245.

3   Robert K. Chester, "'Negroes' Number One Hero': Doris Miller, Pearl Harbor, and Retroactive Multiculturalism in World War II," *American Quarterly*, March 2013: 31, 61.

4   Thomas W. Cutrer and T. Michael Parrish, "How Dorie Miller's Bravery Helped Fight Navy racism," *World War II* magazine, October 31, 2019.

• World War II and the Kansas City Monarchs •

"A Red Rose On The Grave Of LINCOLN"...

It was occasion of the writers' banquet in early 1942—honoring Joe Louis who, fresh from giving the entire net, $170,000, from two defenses of his title to the Army and Navy Relief Funds, had been asked to stand by Jimmy Walker, former New York mayor and main speaker for this event, who, beaming at Louis' then new GI uniform, declared:

"Joe Louis, you have ennobled the highest ideals of American patriotism, achievement and sportsmanship—not only are you king of Fistiana, you are a gentleman and a great American. YOU HAVE LAID A RED ROSE ON THE GRAVE OF LINCOLN."

The Louis era has earmarked an upsurge of colored champions in many fields — all influenced by his lofty ideals. LICHTMAN THEATRES, in accord with the times, have for four years sponsored the famous world pro basketball champions— the Lichtman Bears. During that time, in the true Louis spirit, this team has been responsible for raising approximately $40,000 for charity.

To the hundreds of active professional colored ball players, we say: a bright future lies ahead for you. A future that will be brighter still if you prepare yourself for it. You have a new tradition; you can place thousands of red roses on the grave of Lincoln if you only will. Carry on!

Lichtman Theatres

WASHINGTON RICHMOND NORFOLK PORTSMOUTH
NEWPORT NEWS PETERSBURG LYNCHBURG ROANOKE

World War II-era advertisement exhorting Black ballplayers and athletes in every sport to support America's war effort. (Courtesy of Frederick C. Bush)

5   Davis Barr, "Negro Leagues Players Played Major Role in World War II," MLBlogs, November 10, 2017. https://nlbm.mlblogs.com/negro-leagues-players-played-major-role-in-world-war-ii-97421eb0130a. Retrieved February 7, 2021.

6   Bill Swank, "They Also Served with Valor," in Todd Anton and Bill Nowlin, editors., *When Baseball Went to War* (Chicago: Triumph Books, 2008), 174.

7   Swank, 173-174.

8   James A. Riley, *The Biographical Encyclopedia of the Negro Baseball Leagues* (New York: Carroll & Graf Publishers, Inc., 1994), 256.

9   Riley, 254.

10 Riley, 255.

11 Riley, 255.

12 Buck O'Neil and Steve Wulf, *I Was Right on Time* (New York: Simon & Schuster, 1996), 166.

13 O'Neil, 166.

14 John Paul Hill, "Commissioner A.B. 'Happy' Chandler and the Integration of Major League Baseball: A Reassessment," *NINE: A Journal of Baseball History and Culture*, Fall 2010: 40.

15 O'Neil, 163.

16 Swank, 172.

17 Swank, 172.

18 William A. Young, *J.L. Wilkinson and the Kansas City Monarchs* (Jefferson, North Carolina: McFarland & Co., Inc., 2016), 142.

19 Young, 137.

20 Young, 137.

21 Patricia McKissack and Fredrick McKissack Jr., *Black Diamond: The Story of the Negro Baseball Leagues* (New York: Scholastic, Inc., 1994), 134.

22 Young, 148-149.

23 Ribowsky, 248.

24 Ribowsky, 144.

25 Young, 135.

Contributors

Richard Bogovich is the author of *Kid Nichols: A Biography of the Hall of Fame Pitcher* and *The Who: A Who's Who*, both published by McFarland & Co. He has contributed to such SABR books as *Pride of Smoketown: The 1935 Pittsburgh Crawfords* and *Bittersweet Goodbye: The Black Barons, the Grays, and the 1948 Negro League World Series*. He works for the Wendland Utz law firm in Rochester, Minnesota.

Dr. Milbert O. Brown Jr., is a remarkable storyteller. Brown's work has captured the historical and cultural tapestry of the Black community using his gifts as an artist, photojournalist, and writer. Dr. Brown's interest in the Negro Leagues began in the 1990s when he began interviewing and photographing his favorite Negro League player, Ted "Double Duty" Radcliffe. His journalism career includes work at the *Boston Globe* and the *Chicago Tribune*. While at the *Tribune*, Brown shared journalism's highest honor – the Pulitzer Prize in Journalism for Explanatory Reporting as a contributing staff member in 2001. The Indiana native was educated at Morgan State, Ohio, and Ball State Universities.

Frederick C. (Rick) Bush has written articles for more than two dozen SABR books as well as for the Biography and Games Project websites. This volume is the fourth SABR Negro Leagues book that he has co-edited with Bill Nowlin; previous titles include *Bittersweet Goodbye* (1948 Birmingham Black Barons and Homestead Grays); *The Newark Eagles Take Flight* (1946 Newark team); and *Pride of Smoketown* (1935 Pittsburgh Crawfords). Rick and Bill are currently collaborating on the next book in the series (for 2022), which will feature the 1920 Chicago American Giants. Rick lives with his wife, Michelle, their three sons – Michael, Andrew, and Daniel – and their border collie mix, Bailey, in Cypress, Texas, northwest of Houston. Rick has been an educator for over 25 years and, in the fall of 2021, will embark upon his 18th year of teaching English at Wharton County Junior College's satellite campus in Sugar Land, Texas.

Alan Cohen has been a SABR member since 2010. He serves as vice president-treasurer of the Connecticut Smoky Joe Wood Chapter, is datacaster (MiLB First Pitch stringer) for the Hartford Yard Goats, the Double-A affiliate of the Colorado Rockies, and has been head of SABR's fact-checking committee since December 13, 2020. His biographies, game stories, and essays have appeared in more than 50 SABR publications. His research into Negro League players began with the 1948 Homestead Grays and he recently had a story on Josh Gibson published in the *Baseball Research Journal*. Since his first *BRJ* article appeared in 2013, Alan has continued to expand his research into the Hearst Sandlot Classic (1946-1965), from which 88 players advanced to the major leagues. Alan has four children and eight grandchildren and resides in Connecticut with wife Frances, their cats Morty, Ava, and Zoe, and their dog Buddy.

Rory Costello has an interest in Negro Leaguers that started with learning about their play in Latin American winter leagues. He lives in Brooklyn, New York, with his wife, Noriko, and son, Kai.

Charles F. Faber was a retired public high-school and university teacher and administrator who lived in Lexington, Kentucky. He was a frequent contributor to SABR and edited the SABR book *The 1934 St. Louis Cardinals: The World Champion Gas House Gang*. Among his publications are dozens of professional journal articles, encyclopedia entries, and research reports in fields such as school administration, education law, and country music. In addition to textbooks, he wrote 10 books (mostly on baseball) published by McFarland.

Steven Greenes is a corporate and real estate attorney who received his J.D. from NYU Law School. He is a longtime SABR member specializing in study of the Negro Leagues. Greenes is the author of *Negro Leaguers and the Hall of Fame: The Case for Inducting 24 Overlooked Ballplayers* (2020). His articles on vintage Negro League collectibles have appeared in *Old Cardboard* and *SMR* magazines. He also served as research assistant on Philip Garry's *Negro League Baseball Collectibles Guide*, the first comprehensive guide to Negro League memorabilia. He resides in Florida and New York.

Margaret M. "Peggy" Gripshover is a professor of geography at Western Kentucky University. She earned her Ph.D. in Geography at the University of Tennessee and her M.S. and B.S. degrees in Geography from Marshall University. She has been a SABR member since 2006 and combines her love of baseball with her geographic research on race, ethnicity, urbanization, horse racing, and cultural landscapes. Peggy has published articles in the *Baseball Research Journal*, and contributed a chapter to *Northsiders: Essays on the History and Culture of the Chicago Cubs*, edited by Gerald R. Wood and Andy Hazucha (McFarland, 2008). She also wrote chapters for *Bittersweet Goodbye: The Black Barons, the Grays, and the 1948 Negro League World Series* (SABR 2017); *The Newark Eagles Take Flight: The Story of the 1946 Negro League Champions* (SABR 2019); and *Pride of Smoketown: The 1935 Pittsburgh Crawfords* (SABR 2020), all edited by Frederick C. Bush and Bill Nowlin. She is a native of Cincinnati and a lifelong Reds fan. She lives in Bowling Green, Kentucky, with her husband, Thomas L. Bell, and their Australian shepherd, Bella.

Tim Hagerty is the broadcaster for the Triple-A El Paso Chihuahuas and has called professional baseball games since 2004. He has broadcast two major-league games and has been heard nationally covering various sports for Fox Sports Radio and Westwood One. He's the author of one baseball book and of freelance articles for *The Sporting News*, *The Hardball Times*, and other publications. He resides in El Paso, Texas, with his wife, Heather, and son, Carson.

Donna L. Halper, Ph.D. is a professor of media studies at Lesley University in Cambridge, Massachusetts. A former broadcaster, she is the author of six books and numerous articles and chapters, including "Murphy Before the Mets" in *The New York Mets in Popular Culture*, edited by David Krell, McFarland & Co. (2020); and "Written Out of History: Women Baseball Writers, 1905-1945," in *The Cooperstown Symposium on Baseball and American Culture, 2017-2018*, edited by William Simons. McFarland & Co. (2019). She is also a contributor to SABR's BioProject: among her entries are baseball writers Frank "Fay" Young and Russell J. Cowans, and sportscaster Sherman "Jocko" Maxwell.

Leslie Heaphy is an associate professor of history at Kent State University at Stark, Ohio. She is the author and/or editor of a number of books, book chapters, and articles on the Negro Leagues, women's baseball, and the New York Mets. She is currently serving as the vice president of SABR and is an executive board member for the International Women's Baseball Center.

Chris Hicks began watching baseball with his grandfather as a child, which led to a lifelong passion for the game and his local Kansas City Royals. A wheelchair user since childhood, Chris became interested in the history of the game and the baseball card collecting hobby. His uncle brought him to a Monarchs reunion in the early 1990s. This began years of learning independently about the history of the game. He joined SABR in 2020.

Jay Hurd is a longtime member of SABR and is particularly interested in the Negro Leagues, women in baseball, and nineteenth-century baseball. A librarian and museum educator, he is a Red Sox fan who moved from Medford, Massachusetts, to Bristol, Rhode Island in 2016. He studies baseball history in Rhode Island and has presented on the state's connection with the Negro Leagues and women in baseball. Although disappointed that the Triple-A Pawtucket (Rhode Island) Red Sox have relocated to Worcester, Massachusetts, he will attend games played by the Worcester Red Sox (aka WooSox).

Kirk C. Jenkins practices appellate and constitutional law in San Francisco. A dedicated childhood fan of the Cincinnati Reds, he switched his allegiance in 1994 to the San Francisco Giants. He developed an absorbing interest in Negro League baseball history while researching a novel.

William H. Johnson is the author of *Hal Trosky: A Baseball Life* (McFarland, 2017), along with more than 30 essays for the SABR BioProject. He is currently an adjunct assistant professor at Embry-Riddle Aeronautical University, teaching unmanned system control.

Contributors

Thomas E. Kern was born and raised in Southwest Pennsylvania. Listening to the mellifluous voices of Bob Prince and Jim Woods, how could one not become a lifelong Pirates fan? Tom has been a SABR member dating back to the mid-1980s. He now lives in Washington, DC, and sees the Nationals and Orioles as often as possible. With a love and appreciation for Negro League baseball, Tom wrote a SABR biography of Leon Day after having met him at a baseball card show in the early 1990s. He has since written a number of Negro League bios for SABR's BioProject. Tom's day job is in the field of transportation technology.

Bill Lamberty grew up in Fremont, Nebraska, just down the road from where Sam Crawford worked as a barber before finding success as a ballplayer. He graduated from the University of Wyoming with a journalism degree in 1986, and has worked as assistant athletic director for communications at Montana State University (where he earned his MA in history) since 1990. His son, Nate, played baseball at Whitworth University in Spokane, Washington, where his daughter, Ellie, worked as that program's official scorekeeper, and along with his wife, Lynn, the four continue to spend as much time as ballparks as possible.

Bob LeMoine is a librarian and adjunct professor in New Hampshire. A lifelong Red Sox fan, Bob has contributed to several SABR projects and was co-editor of two SABR books: *Boston's First Nine: The 1871-75 Boston Red Stockings* and *The Glorious Beaneaters of the 1890s*.

Larry Lester is co-founder of the Negro Leagues Baseball Museum and serves as chairman of SABR's Negro League Research Committee. Since 1998, he has chaired the annual Jerry Malloy Negro League Conference, the only scholarly symposium devoted exclusively to Black baseball. Lester is the recipient of SABR's Bob Davids (2017) and Henry Chadwick (2016) Awards. He is a listed contributor to more than 215 books on sports history. Lester has authored or edited 12 books. They are available on Amazon at https://tinyurl.com/ycbv67n3. Lester lives in Raytown, Missouri.

Len Levin is a longtime newspaper editor in New England, now retired. He lives in Providence with his wife, Linda, and an overachieving orange cat. He now (Len, not the cat) is the grammarian for the Rhode Island Supreme Court and edits its decisions. He also copyedits many SABR books, including this one. He is just down the interstate from Fenway Park, where he has spent many happy hours.

Bill Nowlin lives in Cambridge, Massachusetts, and has followed the Boston Red Sox for more than a few years. With Rick Bush, he has co-edited a series of books on great Negro League teams, and edited or co-edited a number of other books for SABR since the SABR Digital Library was begun in December 2011.

Tony S. Oliver is a native of Puerto Rico currently living in Sacramento, California, with his wife and daughter. While he works as a Six Sigma professional, his true love is baseball and he cheers for both the Red Sox and whoever happens to be playing the Yankees. He is fascinated by baseball cards and is currently researching the evolution of baseball tickets. He believes there is no prettier color than the vibrant green of freshly mown grass on a baseball field.

Richard J. Puerzer is an associate professor and chairperson of the Department of Engineering at Hofstra University. He has contributed to several SABR Books, including *Bittersweet Goodbye: The Black Barons, The Grays, and the 1948 Negro League World Series* (2017), *The Newark Eagles Take Flight: The Story of the 1946 Negro League Champions* (2019), and *Pride of Smoketown: The 1935 Pittsburgh Crawfords* (2020). His writings on baseball have also appeared in *Nine: A Journal of Baseball History and Culture, Black Ball, The National Pastime, The Cooperstown Symposium on Baseball and American Culture* proceedings, *Zisk*, and *Spitball*.

Carl Riechers retired from United Parcel Service in 2012 after 35 years of service. With more free time, he became a SABR member that same year. Born and raised in the suburbs of St. Louis, he became a big fan of the Cardinals. He and his wife, Janet, have three children and he is the proud grandpa of two.

Glen Sparks has contributed to several SABR books and is writing a full-length biography of Hall of Fame shortstop Pee Wee Reese. A native of Santa Monica, California, and a lifelong Dodgers fan, Sparks lives deep in the heart of Cardinal country with his wife, Pam, and their two cats, Teddy and Lucy.

• When the Monarchs Reigned •

A fan of the Negro League baseball ever since he read *Only the Ball Was White* by Robert Peterson, **Mark S. Sternman** also contributed to the SABR books on the 1935 Pittsburgh Crawfords and the 1946 Newark Eagles.

Jeb Stewart is a lawyer in Birmingham, Alabama, who enjoys taking his sons, Nolan and Ryan, and his wife, Stephanie, to the Rickwood Classic each year. He has been a SABR member since 2012 and is co-president of the Rickwood Field SABR Chapter. He is an executive committee member on the Board of the Friends of Rickwood Field and is a regular contributor to the *Rickwood Times*. He also edits the Friends' quarterly newsletter, "Rickwood Tales." He has written several biographies for SABR's Baseball Biography Project.

Tim Tassler is chair of SABR's Kekionga Chapter of Fort Wayne. He has spent 10 years researching Black baseball in Fort Wayne, and also serves on the board of the Northeast Indiana Baseball Hall of Fame.

Larry Tye is a *New York Times* best-selling author whose latest book, a biography of Senator Joe McCarthy, was released on July 7, 2020, from Houghton Mifflin Harcourt. He has also written bios of PR pioneer Edward L. Bernays, the Pullman porters who helped kick-start the civil rights revolution, Superman, former attorney general and presidential candidate Robert F. Kennedy, and *Satchel: The Life and Times of an American Legend*). Tye runs the Boston-based Health Coverage Fellowship, which helps the media do a better job reporting on critical issues like public health, mental health, and high-tech medicine. From 1986 to 2001, Tye was an award-winning reporter at *the Boston Globe*, where his primary beat was medicine. Before that, he was the environmental reporter at the *Courier-Journal* in Louisville, and he covered government and business at *the Anniston Star* in Alabama. Tye, who graduated from Brown University, was a Nieman Fellow at Harvard University in 1993-94. He is currently writing a book entitled *The Jazzmen: How Duke Ellington, Satchmo Armstrong, and Count Basie Transformed America.*

Bob Webster grew up in northwest Indiana and has been a Cubs fan since 1963. After relocating to Portland, Oregon, in 1980, Bob spends his time working on baseball research and writing, and is a contributor to quite a few SABR projects. He worked as a stats stringer on the MLB Gameday app for three years. He is a member of the Pacific Northwest Chapter of SABR and is on the board of directors of the Old-Timers Baseball Association of Portland.

Dave Wilkie is a teacher at the Montessori School of the Mahoning Valley in Youngstown, Ohio. He grew up in Western Canada idolizing Willie McCovey and the San Francisco Giants. His obsession with Negro League baseball can be traced to a 1983 mail-order purchase of the book *The All-Time All-Stars of Black Baseball* by SABR member James A. Riley. He has written SABR biographies on Negro League greats Sam Bankhead, Johnny Davis, Chester Williams, Cool Papa Bell, and Frank Duncan. He plans to continue writing biographies on these forgotten legends with the hopes of someday publishing his own book.

William A. Young is professor emeritus of religious studies at Westminster College, Fulton, Missouri. He is the author of *J.L. Wilkinson and the Kansas City Monarchs: Trailblazers in Black Baseball* (McFarland, 2016), for which he received a SABR Research Award (2018). Young has also written *John Tortes "Chief" Meyers: A Baseball Biography* (McFarland, 2012), and several books on the world's religions. He is a member of SABR and resides with his wife, Sue, in Columbia, Missouri.

1940s era advertisment (Courtesy of Frederick C Bush collection.)

SABR Books on the Negro Leagues and Black Baseball

From Rube to Robinson: SABR's Best Articles on Black Baseball

From Rube to Robinson brings together the best Negro League baseball scholarship that the Society of American Baseball Research (SABR) has ever produced, culled from its journals, Biography Project, and award-winning essays. The book includes a star-studded list of scholars and historians, from the late Jerry Malloy and Jules Tygiel, to award winners Larry Lester, Geri Strecker, and Jeremy Beer, and a host of other talented writers. The essays cover topics ranging over nearly a century, from 1866 and the earliest known Black baseball championship, to 1962 and the end of the Negro American League.

Edited by John Graf; Associate Editors Duke Goldman and Larry Lester
$24.95 paperback (ISBN 978-1-970159-41-7)
$9.99 ebook (ISBN 978-1-970159-40-0)
8.5"X11", 220 pages

Pride of Smoketown: The 1935 Pittsburgh Crawfords

The 1935 Pittsburgh Crawfords team, one of the dominant teams in Negro League history, is often compared to the legendary 1927 "Murderer's Row" New York Yankees. The squad from "Smoketown"—a nickname that the *Pittsburgh Courier* often applied to the metropolis better-known as "Steel City"—boasted four Hall-of-Fame players in outfielder James "Cool Papa" Bell, first baseman/manager Oscar Charleston, catcher Josh Gibson, and third baseman William "Judy" Johnson. This volume contains exhaustively-researched articles about the players, front office personnel, Greenlee Field, and the exciting games and history of the team that were written and edited by 25 SABR members. The inclusion of historical photos about every subject in the book helps to shine a spotlight on the 1935 Pittsburgh Crawfords, who truly were the Pride of Smoketown.

Edited by Frederick C. Bush and Bill Nowlin
$29.95 paperback (ISBN 978-1-970159-25-7)
$9.99 ebook (ISBN 978-1-970159-24-0)
8.5"X11", 340 pages, over 60 photos

The Newark Eagles Take Flight: The Story of the 1946 Negro League Champions

The Newark Eagles won only one Negro National League pennant during the franchise's 15-year tenure in the Garden State, but the 1946 squad that ran away with the NNL and then triumphed over the Kansas City Monarchs in a seven-game World Series was a team for the ages. The returning WWII veterans composed a veritable "Who's Who in the Negro Leagues" and included Leon Day, Larry Doby, Monte Irvin, and Max Manning, as well as numerous role players. Four of the Eagles' stars—Day, Doby, Irvin, and player/manager Raleigh "Biz" Mackey, as well as co-owner Effa Manley—have been enshrined in the National Baseball Hall of Fame in Cooperstown. In addition to biographies of the players, co-owners, and P.A. announcer, there are also articles about Newark's Ruppert Stadium, Leon Day's Opening Day no-hitter, a sensational midseason game, the season's two East-West All-Star Games, and the 1946 Negro League World Series between the Eagles and the renowned Kansas City Monarchs.

Edited by Frederick C. Bush and Bill Nowlin
$24.95 paperback (ISBN 978-1-970159-07-3)
$9.99 ebook (ISBN 978-1-970159-06-6)
8.5"X11", 228 pages, over 60 photos

Bittersweet Goodbye: The Black Barons, The Grays, and the 1948 Negro League World Series

This book was inspired by the last Negro League World Series ever played and presents biographies of the players on the two contending teams in 1948—the Birmingham Black Barons and the Homestead Grays—as well as the managers, the owners, and articles on the ballparks the teams called home. Also included are articles that recap the season's two East-West All-Star Games, the Negro National League and Negro American League playoff series, and the World Series itself. Additional context is provided in essays about the effects of baseball's integration on the Negro Leagues, the exodus of Negro League players to Canada, and the signing away of top Negro League players, specifically Willie Mays. Many of the players' lives and careers have been presented to a much greater extent than previously possible.

Edited by Frederick C. Bush and Bill Nowlin
$21.95 paperback (ISBN 978-1-943816-55-2)
$9.99 ebook (ISBN 978-1-943816-54-5)
8.5"X11", 442 pages, over 100 photos and images

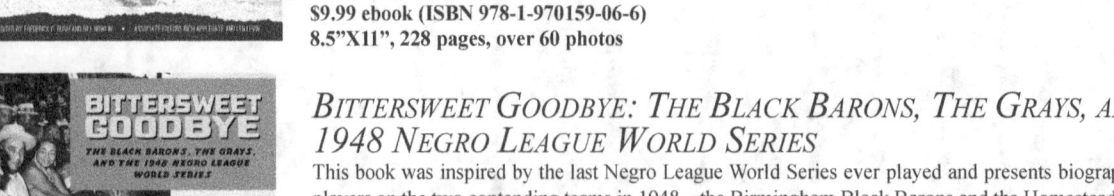

www.ingramcontent.com/pod-product-compliance
Lightning Source LLC
Chambersburg PA
CBHW081305070526
44578CB00006B/809